STUDY GUIDE

STUDY GUIDE

Richard O. Straub
University of Michigan, Dearborn

with
**Focus on Vocabulary and Language
by *Cornelius Rea***
Douglas College, British Columbia

to accompany

David G. Myers
Psychology
Sixth Edition

WORTH PUBLISHERS

Study Guide
by Richard O. Straub
to accompany
Myers: **Psychology**, Sixth Edition

Printed in the United States of America

ISBN: 1-57259-958-8

Printing: 5 4 3 2

Year: 04 03 02 01

Cover art by John Collier

Worth Publishers
41 Madison Avenue
New York, New York 10010
www.worthpublishers.com

Contents

Preface

This Study Guide is designed for use with *Psychology*, Sixth Edition, by David G. Myers. It is intended to help you to learn material in the textbook, to evaluate your understanding of that material, and then to review any problem areas. Beginning on page ix, "How to Manage Your Time Efficiently and Study More Effectively" provides detailed instructions on how to use the textbook and this Study Guide for maximum benefit. It also offers additional study suggestions based on principles of time management, effective notetaking, evaluation of exam performance, and an effective program for improving your comprehension while studying from textbooks.

The sixth edition of this Study Guide offers many useful features. Each chapter includes three review tests: In addition to the two Progress Tests that focus on facts and definitions, there is a Thinking Critically Test that evaluates your understanding of the text chapter's broader conceptual material and its application to real-world situations. This test contains at least 20 multiple-choice questions and an essay question. For all three review tests, the correct answers are given, followed by textbook page references (so you can easily go back and reread the material). In addition, complete explanations are given not only of why the answer is correct but also of why the other choices are incorrect.

The chapter review is organized by major text section. Each section includes a Section Preview—the objectives for that section—and Stepping Through the Section—detailed questions about the topics covered. The detailed guidelines provided for the objectives are useful for a section-by-section review of each textbook chapter and as a source of additional essay questions. As appropriate, chapters may include a section called *Web Sighting*, which is a brief Internet activity in which students are directed to one or more web sites to extend their exploration of concepts and issues discussed in the chapter. Some chapters also include a Cross-Check, which provides an engaging crossword puzzle review of chapter terms and concepts. Other chapters include fill-in-the-blank flow charts, which promote a deeper understanding of the conceptual relationships among chapter issues. In addition, each chapter includes Focus on Vocabulary and Language, written by Cornelius Rea of Douglas College, British Columbia. This section provides brief, clear explanations of some of the idioms and expressions used by David Myers that may be unfamiliar to some students. They are first listed in the relevant section of the Guided Study, then explained at the back of the chapter.

General Internet Resources

In addition to the specific web exercises provided throughout this Study Guide, you might want to consult some web sites that provide general information about psychology-related topics. David Mahony's Psychology Internet Resource List (PIRL) is an effort to compile all psychology-related material, including mailing lists, discussion groups, World Wide Web (WWW) sites, File Transfer Protocol (FTP) sites for downloading files from other machines, and Gopher sites for locating items on the Internet through a series of nested menus. The PIRL, now in its third edition, is available at the following WWW site: http://www.gasou.edu/psychweb/psychweb.html.

Deborah Kelley-Milburn and Michael A. Milburn's "Cyberspace: Resources for Psychologists on the Internet" (*Psychological Science*, [1995, July], Volume 6, pp. 203–211) provides another excellent resource. This feature review provides helpful information on Listservs, Usenet groups, electronic journals and newsletters, databases, grant and job information, and library catalogues.

Psych Web with host Russ Dewey, which opened April 15, 1995, also provides a good source of information. Currently available at this location are Web-accessible psychology resources sorted by topic, a separate list of psychology self-help resources on the Internet, and a stereogram gallery containing public images that you can print out. The location is as follows:

http://www.gasou.edu/psychweb/psychweb.htm

Both the American Psychological Association (APA) and the American Psychological Society (APS) have Internet services. These services provide not only information about their organizations but also selected articles from their main journals, information about current research in the discipline, and links to other science-related sites on the Internet. Their locations are as follows:

APA: http://www.apa.org/ and APS: http://psychologicalscience.org

Finally, and perhaps most important, is Psychtalk, a list for students interested in discussion topics and controversies related to psychology. Topics that have been discussed over the past few years include child abuse, the nature-nurture issue, homosexuality, and pornography. To subscribe, send a message to:

psychtalk-request@fre.fsu.umd.edu

The message should read "subscribe psychtalk (your name)."

Acknowledgments

I would like to thank all the students and instructors who used this Study Guide in its previous editions and provided such insightful and useful suggestions. Special thanks are also due to Betty Shapiro Probert for her extraordinary editorial contributions. Most important, I want to thank Jeremy, Rebecca, Melissa, and Pam for their enduring love and patience.

Richard O. Straub
June 2000

How to Manage Your Time Efficiently and Study More Effectively

How effectively do you study? Good study habits make the job of being a college student much easier. Many students, who *could* succeed in college, fail or drop out because they have never learned to manage their time efficiently. Even the best students can usually benefit from an in-depth evaluation of their current study habits.

There are many ways to achieve academic success, of course, but your approach may not be the most effective or efficient. Are you sacrificing your social life or your physical or mental health in order to get A's on your exams? Good study habits result in better grades *and* more time for other activities.

Evaluate Your Current Study Habits

To improve your study habits, you must first have an accurate picture of how you currently spend your time. Begin by putting together a profile of your present living and studying habits. Answer the following questions by writing *yes* or *no* on each line.

_____ 1. Do you usually set up a schedule to budget your time for studying, recreation, and other activities?

_____ 2. Do you often put off studying until time pressures force you to cram?

_____ 3. Do other students seem to study less than you do, but get better grades?

_____ 4. Do you usually spend hours at a time studying one subject, rather than dividing that time between several subjects?

_____ 5. Do you often have trouble remembering what you have just read in a textbook?

_____ 6. Before reading a chapter in a textbook, do you skim through it and read the section headings?

_____ 7. Do you try to predict exam questions from your lecture notes and reading?

_____ 8. Do you usually attempt to paraphrase or summarize what you have just finished reading?

_____ 9. Do you find it difficult to concentrate very long when you study?

_____ 10. Do you often feel that you studied the wrong material for an exam?

Thousands of college students have participated in similar surveys. Students who are fully realizing their academic potential usually respond as follows: (1) yes, (2) no, (3) no, (4) no, (5) no, (6) yes, (7) yes, (8) yes, (9) no, (10) no.

Compare your responses to those of successful students. The greater the discrepancy, the more you could benefit from a program to improve your study habits. The questions are designed to identify areas of weakness. Once you have identified your weaknesses, you will be able to set specific goals for improvement and implement a program for reaching them.

Manage Your Time

Do you often feel frustrated because there isn't enough time to do all the things you must and want to do? Take heart. Even the most productive and successful people feel this way at times. But they establish priorities for their activities and they learn to budget time for each of them. There's much in the saying "If you want something done, ask a busy person to do it." A busy person knows how to get things done.

If you don't now have a system for budgeting your time, develop one. Not only will your academic accomplishments increase, but you will actually find more time in your schedule for other activities. And you won't have to feel guilty about "taking time off," because all your obligations will be covered.

Establish a Baseline

As a first step in preparing to budget your time, keep a diary for a few days to establish a summary, or baseline, of the time you spend in studying, socializing, working, and so on. If you are like many students, much of your "study" time is nonproductive; you may sit at your desk and leaf through a book, but the time is actually wasted. Or you may procrastinate. You are always getting ready to study, but you rarely do.

Besides revealing where you waste time, your diary will give you a realistic picture of how much time you need to allot for meals, commuting, and other fixed activities. In addition, careful records should indicate the times of the day when you are consistently most productive. A sample time-management diary is shown in Table 1.

Plan the Term

Having established and evaluated your baseline, you are ready to devise a more efficient schedule. Buy a calendar that covers the entire school term and has ample space for each day. Using the course outlines provided by your instructors, enter the dates of all exams, term paper deadlines, and other important academic obligations. If you have any long-range personal plans (concerts, weekend trips, etc.), enter the dates on the calendar as well. Keep your calendar up to date and refer to it often. I recommend carrying it with you at all times.

Develop a Weekly Calendar

Now that you have a general picture of the school term, develop a weekly schedule that includes all of your activities. Aim for a schedule that you can live with for the entire school term. A sample weekly schedule, incorporating the following guidelines, is shown in Table 2.

1. Enter your class times, work hours, and any other fixed obligations first. *Be thorough.* Using information from your time-management diary, allow plenty of time for such things as commuting, meals, laundry, and the like.

Table 1   Sample Time-Management Diary

Behavior	Time Completed	Duration Hours: Minutes
Sleep	7:00	7:30
Dressing	7:25	:25
Breakfast	7:45	:20
Commute	8:20	:35
Coffee	9:00	:40
French	10:00	1:00
Socialize	10:15	:15
Video game	10:35	:20
Coffee	11:00	:25
Psychology	12:00	1:00
Lunch	12:25	:25
Study Lab	1:00	:35
Psych. Lab	4:00	3:00
Work	5:30	1:30
Commute	6:10	:40
Dinner	6:45	:35
TV	7:30	:45
Study Psych.	10:00	2:30
Socialize	11:30	1:30
Sleep		

Prepare a similar chart for each day of the week. When you finish an activity, note it on the chart and write down the time it was completed. Then determine its duration by subtracting the time the previous activity was finished from the newly entered time.

2. Set up a study schedule for each of your courses. The study habits survey and your time-management diary will help direct you. The following guidelines should also be useful.

(a) Establish regular study times for each course. The 4 hours needed to study one subject, for example, are most profitable when divided into shorter periods spaced over several days. If you cram your studying into one 4-hour block, what you attempt to learn in the third or fourth hour will interfere with what you studied in the first 2 hours. Newly acquired knowledge is like wet cement. It needs some time to "harden" to become memory.

(b) Alternate subjects. The type of interference just mentioned is greatest between similar topics. Set up a schedule in which you spend time on several *different* courses during each study session. Besides reducing the potential for interference, alternating subjects will help to prevent mental fatigue with one topic.

(c) Set weekly goals to determine the amount of study time you need to do well in each course. This will depend on, among other things, the difficulty of your courses and the effectiveness of your methods. Many

Table 2   Sample Weekly Schedule

Time	Mon.	Tues.	Wed.	Thurs.	Fri.	Sat.
7–8	Dress Eat	Dress Eat	Dress Eat	Dress Eat	Dress Eat	
8–9	Psych.	Study Psych.	Psych.	Study Psych.	Psych.	Dress Eat
9–10	Eng.	Study Eng.	Eng.	Study Eng.	Eng.	Study Eng.
10–11	Study French	Free	Study French	Open Study	Study French	Study Stats.
11–12	French	Study Psych. Lab	French	Open Study	French	Study Stats.
12–1	Lunch	Lunch	Lunch	Lunch	Lunch	Lunch
1–2	Stats.	Psych. Lab	Stats.	Study or Free	Stats.	Free
2–3	Bio.	Psych. Lab	Bio.	Free	Bio.	Free
3–4	Free	Psych.	Free	Free	Free	Free
4–5	Job	Job	Job	Job	Job	Free
5–6	Job	Job	Job	Job	Job	Free
6–7	Dinner	Dinner	Dinner	Dinner	Dinner	Dinner
7–8	Study Bio.	Study Bio.	Study Bio.	Study Bio.	Free	Free
8–9	Study Eng.	Study Stats.	Study Psych.	Open Study	Open Study	Free
9–10	Open Study	Open Study	Open Study	Open Study	Free	Free

This is a sample schedule for a student with a 16-credit load and a 10-hour-per-week part-time job. Using this chart as an illustration, make up a weekly schedule, following the guidelines outlined here.

professors recommend studying at least 1 to 2 hours for each hour in class. If your time-management diary indicates that you presently study less time than that, do not plan to jump immediately to a much higher level. Increase study time from your baseline by setting weekly goals [see (4)] that will gradually bring you up to the desired level. As an initial schedule, for example, you might set aside an amount of study time for each course that matches class time.

(d) Schedule for maximum effectiveness. Tailor your schedule to meet the demands of each course. For the course that emphasizes lecture notes, schedule time for a daily review soon after the class. This will give you a chance to revise your notes and clean up any hard-to-decipher shorthand while the material is still fresh in your mind. If you are evaluated for class participation (for example, in a language course), allow time for a review just *before* the class meets. Schedule study time for your most difficult (or least motivating) courses during hours when you are the most alert and distractions are fewest.

(e) Schedule open study time. Emergencies, additional obligations, and the like could throw off your

schedule. And you may simply need some extra time periodically for a project or for review in one of your courses. Schedule several hours each week for such purposes.

3. After you have budgeted time for studying, fill in slots for recreation, hobbies, relaxation, household errands, and the like.

4. Set specific goals. Before each study session, make a list of specific goals. The simple note "7–8 PM: study psychology" is too broad to ensure the most effective use of the time. Formulate your daily goals according to what you know you must accomplish during the term. If you have course outlines with advance assignments, set systematic daily goals that will allow you, for example, to cover fifteen chapters before the exam. And be realistic: Can you actually expect to cover a 78-page chapter in one session? Divide large tasks into smaller units; stop at the most logical resting points. When you complete a specific goal, take a 5- or 10-minute break before tackling the next goal.

5. Evaluate how successful or unsuccessful your studying has been on a daily or weekly basis. Did you

reach most of your goals? If so, reward yourself immediately. You might even make a list of five to ten rewards to choose from. If you have trouble studying regularly, you may be able to motivate yourself by making such rewards contingent on completing specific goals.

6. Finally, until you have lived with your schedule for several weeks, don't hesitate to revise it. You may need to allow more time for chemistry, for example, and less for some other course. If you are trying to study regularly for the first time and are feeling burned out, you probably have set your initial goals too high. Don't let failure cause you to despair and abandon the program. Accept your limitations and revise your schedule so that you are studying only 15 to 20 minutes more each evening than you are used to. The point is to *identify a regular schedule with which you can achieve some success.* Time management, like any skill, must be practiced to become effective.

Techniques for Effective Study

Knowing how to put study time to best use is, of course, as important as finding a place for it in your schedule. Here are some suggestions that should enable you to increase your reading comprehension and improve your notetaking. A few study tips are included as well.

Using PRTR to Increase Reading Comprehension

How do you study from a textbook? If you are like many students, you simply read and reread in a *passive* manner. Studies have shown, however, that most students who simply read a textbook cannot remember more than half the material ten minutes after they have finished. Often, what is retained is the unessential material rather than the important points upon which exam questions will be based.

This *Study Guide* employs a program known as PRTR (Preview, Read, Think actively and critically, and Review) to facilitate, and allow you to assess, your comprehension of the important facts and concepts in *Psychology*, sixth Edition, by David G. Myers.

Research has shown that students using PRTR achieve significantly greater comprehension of textbooks than students reading in the more traditional passive manner. Once you have learned this program, you can improve your comprehension of any textbook.

Preview Before you read a text chapter, determine whether the text or the study guide has an outline or list of objectives. Read this material and the summary at the end of the chapter. Next, read the textbook

chapter fairly quickly, paying special attention to the major headings and subheadings. This survey will give you an idea of the chapter's contents and organization. You will then be able to divide the chapter into logical sections in order to formulate specific goals for a more careful reading of the chapter.

In this Study Guide, the *Chapter Overview* summarizes the major topics of the textbook chapter. This section also provides a few suggestions for approaching topics you may find difficult.

You will retain material longer when you have a use for it. If you look up a word's definition in order to solve a crossword puzzle, for example, you will remember it longer than if you merely fill in the letters as a result of putting other words in. Previewing the chapter will allow you to generate important questions that the chapter will proceed to answer. These questions correspond to "mental files" into which knowledge will be sorted for easy access.

As you survey, jot down several questions for each chapter section. One simple technique is to generate questions by rephrasing a section heading. For example, the "Preoperational Thought" head could be turned into "What is preoperational thought?" Good questions will allow you to focus on the important points in the text. Examples of good questions are those that begin as follows: "List two examples of . . . ." "What is the function of . . .?" "What is the significance of . . .?" Such questions give a purpose to your reading. Similarly, you can formulate questions based on the chapter outline.

The *Section Previews* of this Study Guide provide the types of questions you might formulate while surveying each chapter. This section is a detailed set of objectives covering the points made in the text. Guidelines for answers to these objectives are provided at the end of each chapter.

Read When you have established "files" for each section of the chapter, review your first question, begin reading, and continue until you have discovered its answer. If you come to material that seems to answer an important question you don't have a file for, stop and write down the question.

Using this Study Guide, read the chapter one section at a time. First, preview the section by skimming it, noting headings and boldface items. Next, study the appropriate section objectives in the *Section Preview.* Then, as you read the chapter section, search for the answer to each objective.

Be sure to read everything. Don't skip photo or art captions, graphs, or marginal notes. In some cases, what may seem vague in reading will be made clear by a simple graph. Keep in mind that test questions are sometimes drawn from illustrations and charts.

Think When you have found the answer to a question, close your eyes and mentally recite the question and its answer. Then *write* the answer next to the question. It is important that you recite an answer in your own words rather than the author's. Don't rely on your short-term memory to repeat the author's words verbatim.

In responding to the objectives, pay close attention to what is called for. If you are asked to identify or list, do just that. If asked to compare, contrast, or do both, you should focus on the similarities (compare) and differences (contrast) between the concepts or theories. Answering the objectives carefully not only will help you to focus your attention on the important concepts of the text but also will provide excellent practice for essay exams.

Rehearsal is an extremely effective study technique, recommended by many learning experts. In addition to increasing reading comprehension, it is useful for review. Trying to explain something in your own words clarifies your knowledge, often by revealing aspects of your answer that are vague or incomplete. If you repeatedly rely upon "I know" in recitation, you really *may not know.*

Rehearsal has the additional advantage of simulating an exam, especially an essay exam; the same skills are required in both cases. Too often students study without ever putting the book and notes aside, which makes it easy for them to develop false confidence in their knowledge. When the material is in front of you, you may be able to *recognize* an answer, but will you be able to *recall* it later, when you take an exam that does not provide these retrieval cues?

After you have recited and written your answer, continue with your next question. Read, recite, and so on.

Review When you have answered the last question on the material you have designated as a study goal, go back and review. Read over each question and your written answer to it. Your review might also include a brief written summary that integrates all of your questions and answers. This review need not take longer than a few minutes, but it is important. It will help you retain the material longer and will greatly facilitate a final review of each chapter before the exam.

In this Study Guide, *Stepping Through the Section* contains fill-in and brief essay questions for you to complete after you have finished reading the section and have written answers to the objectives. The correct answers are given at the end of the chapter. Gen-

erally, your answer to a fill-in question should match exactly (as in the case of important terms, theories, or people). In some cases, the answer is not a term or name, so a word close in meaning will suffice. You should answer these questions several times before taking an exam, so it is a good idea to mentally fill in the answers until you are ready for a final pretest review. Textbook page references are provided with each section title, in case you need to reread any of the material.

Also provided to facilitate your review are two *Progress Tests* that include multiple-choice questions and, where appropriate, matching or true–false questions. These tests are *not* to be taken until you have read the chapter, written answers to the objectives, and completed the *Chapter Review.* Correct answers, along with explanations of why each alternative is correct or incorrect, are provided at the end of the chapter. The relevant text page numbers for each question are also given. If you miss a question, read these explanations and, if necessary, review the text pages to further understand why. The *Progress Tests* do not test every aspect of a concept, so you should treat an incorrect answer as an indication that you need to review the concept.

Following the two *Progress Tests* is a *Thinking Critically Test*, which should be taken just prior to an exam. It includes questions that test your ability to analyze, integrate, and apply the concepts in the chapter. Each *Thinking Critically Test* includes an essay question dealing with a major concept covered in the chapter. As with the *Progress Tests*, answers for the *Thinking Critically Test* are provided at the end of each chapter, along with relevant page numbers.

In most cases, the core of the chapter concludes with *Key Terms.* For chapters that contain many new technical terms, this section includes not only a list of key terms but also a crossword puzzle. *Writing Definitions* requires that you write definitions of all key terms on a separate piece of paper. *Cross-Check* reverses the process, asking you to complete a crossword puzzle by filling in the terms that apply to the definitions provided. As with the *Section Preview* objectives, it is important that these answers be written from memory, and in your own words. The *Answers* section at the end of the chapter gives a definition of each term, sometimes along with an example of its usage and/or a tip to help you remember its meaning. It also includes answers to the crossword puzzle.

Where appropriate, *Key Terms* is followed by *Summing Up*, one or two fill-in-the-blank flow charts. These charts are designed to help you integrate and apply major concepts described in the chapter.

Following the answers is a list of potentially unfamiliar idioms, words, and expressions (*Focus on Vocabulary and Language*), ordered by text page number and accompanied by definitions and examples.

This Study Guide also contains an additional section called *Web Sighting*, which describes web resources related to concepts discussed in the text chapter. In addition to serving as refreshing study break from the other sections of the Study Guide, the *Web Sighting* will enhance your understanding of the text material by helping you to apply it to new information. Integrating text material with this new information is an excellent way for you to learn by actively participating, rather than by merely repeating information from the text.

One final suggestion: Incorporate PRTR into your time-management calendar. Set specific goals for completing PRTR with each assigned chapter. Keep a record of chapters completed, and reward yourself for being conscientious. Initially, it takes more time and effort to "read" using PRTR, but with practice, the steps will become automatic. More important, you will comprehend significantly more material and retain what you have learned longer than passive readers do.

Taking Lecture Notes

Are your class notes as useful as they might be? One way to determine their worth is to compare them with those taken by other good students. Are yours as thorough? Do they provide you with a comprehensible outline of each lecture? If not, then the following suggestions might increase the effectiveness of your notetaking.

   1. Keep a separate notebook for each course. Use $8\frac{1}{2} \times 11$-inch pages. Consider using a ring binder, which would allow you to revise and insert notes while still preserving lecture order.

   2. Take notes in the format of a lecture outline. Use roman numerals for major points, letters for supporting arguments, and so on. Some instructors will make this easy by delivering organized lectures and, in some cases, by outlining their lectures on the board. If a lecture is disorganized, you will probably want to reorganize your notes soon after the class.

   3. As you take notes in class, leave a wide margin on one side of each page. After the lecture, expand or clarify any shorthand notes while the material is fresh in your mind. Use this time to write important questions in the margin next to notes that answer them.

This will facilitate later review and will allow you to anticipate similar exam questions.

Evaluate Your Exam Performance

How often have you received a grade on an exam that did not do justice to the effort you spent preparing for the exam? This is a common experience that can leave one feeling bewildered and abused. "What do I have to do to get an A?" "The test was unfair!" "I studied the wrong material!"

The chances of this happening are greatly reduced if you have an effective time-management schedule and use the study techniques described here. But it can happen to the best-prepared student and is most likely to occur on your first exam with a new professor.

Remember that there are two main reasons for studying. One is to learn for your own general academic development. Many people believe that such knowledge is all that really matters. Of course, it is possible, though unlikely, to be an expert on a topic without achieving commensurate grades, just as one can, occasionally, earn an excellent grade without truly mastering the course material. During a job interview or in the workplace, however, your A in Cobol won't mean much if you can't actually program a computer.

In order to keep career options open after you graduate, you must know the material and maintain competitive grades. In the short run, this means performing well on exams, which is the second main objective in studying.

Probably the single best piece of advice to keep in mind when studying for exams is to *try to predict exam questions.* This means ignoring the trivia and focusing on the important questions and their answers (with your instructor's emphasis in mind).

A second point is obvious. How well you do on exams is determined by your mastery of *both* lecture and textbook material. Many students (partly because of poor time management) concentrate too much on one at the expense of the other.

To evaluate how well you are learning lecture and textbook material, analyze the questions you missed on the first exam. If your instructor does not review exams during class, you can easily do it yourself. Divide the questions into two categories: those drawn primarily from lectures and those drawn primarily from the textbook. Determine the percentage of questions you missed in each category. If your errors are evenly distributed and you are satisfied with your grade, you have no problem. If you are weaker in one area, you will need to set future goals for increasing and/or improving your study of that area.

Similarly, note the percentage of test questions drawn from each category. Although exams in most courses cover *both* lecture notes and the textbook, the relative emphasis of each may vary from instructor to instructor. While your instructors may not be entirely consistent in making up future exams, you may be able to tailor your studying for each course by placing *additional* emphasis on the appropriate area.

Exam evaluation will also point out the types of questions your instructor prefers. Does the exam consist primarily of multiple-choice, true–false, or essay questions? You may also discover that an instructor is fond of wording questions in certain ways. For example, an instructor may rely heavily on questions that require you to draw an analogy between a theory or concept and a real-world example. Evaluate both your instructor's style and how well you do with each format. Use this information to guide your future exam preparation.

Important aids, not only in studying for exams but also in determining how well prepared you are, are the *Progress* and *Thinking Critically Tests* provided in this Study Guide. If these tests don't include all of the types of questions your instructor typically writes, make up your own practice exam questions. Spend extra time testing yourself with question formats that are most difficult for you. There is no better way to evaluate your preparation for an upcoming exam than by testing yourself under the conditions most likely to be in effect during the actual test.

A Few Practical Tips

Even the best intentions for studying sometimes fail. Some of these failures occur because students attempt to work under conditions that are simply not conducive to concentrated study. To help ensure the success of your time-management program, here are a few suggestions that should assist you in reducing the possibility of procrastination or distraction.

1. If you have set up a schedule for studying, make your roommate, family, and friends aware of this commitment, and ask them to honor your quiet study time. Close your door and post a "Do Not Disturb" sign.

2. Set up a place to study that minimizes potential distractions. Use a desk or table, not your bed or an extremely comfortable chair. Keep your desk and the walls around it free from clutter. If you need a place other than your room, find one that meets as many of the above requirements as possible—for example, in the library stacks.

3. Do nothing but study in this place. It should become associated with studying so that it "triggers" this activity, just as a mouth-watering aroma elicits an appetite.

4. Never study with the television on or with other distracting noises present. If you must have music in the background in order to mask outside noise, for example, play soft instrumental music. Don't pick vocal selections; your mind will be drawn to the lyrics.

5. Study by yourself. Other students can be distracting or can break the pace at which *your* learning is most efficient. In addition, there is always the possibility that group studying will become a social gathering. Reserve that for its own place in your schedule.

If you continue to have difficulty concentrating for very long, try the following suggestions.

6. Study your most difficult or most challenging subjects first, when you are most alert.

7. Start with relatively short periods of concentrated study, with breaks in between. If your attention starts to wander, get up immediately and take a break. It is better to study effectively for 15 minutes and then take a break than to fritter away 45 minutes out of an hour. Gradually increase the length of study periods, using your attention span as an indicator of successful pacing.

Some Closing Thoughts

I hope that these suggestions help make you more successful academically, and that they enhance the quality of your college life in general. Having the necessary skills makes any job a lot easier and more pleasant. Let me repeat my warning not to attempt to make too drastic a change in your life-style immediately. Good habits require time and self-discipline to develop. Once established, they can last a lifetime.

Introduction

Chapter Overview

Psychology's historical development and current activities lead us to define the field as the science of behavior and mental processes. This Introduction discusses the development of psychology and the range of behaviors and mental processes being investigated by psychologists in each of the various specialty areas. In addition, it describes the seven major perspectives from which psychologists work. This is followed by an overview of the diverse subfields in which psychologists conduct research and provide professional services.

The Introduction concludes by explaining how to get your study of psychology off on the right foot by learning (and pledging to follow!) the PRTR study method. This study method is also discussed in the essay at the beginning of this Study Guide.

NOTE: Answer guidelines for all Introduction questions begin on page 9.

Psychology's Roots (pp. 2–4)

> David Myers at times uses idioms that are unfamiliar to some readers. If you do not know the meaning of any of the following words, phrases, or expressions in the context in which they appear in the text, refer to pages 14–15 for an explanation: *peekaboo; grist for psychology's mill; Magellans of the mind; unpack this definition; sift opinions or ideas; hunches; smorgasbord . . . fare.*

Section Preview

First, skim this section, noting headings and boldface items. Then read the following objectives and, as you read the section, search for the information that will enable you to meet each objective. Answer guidelines are provided on page 9.

1. Define *psychology.*

2. Trace the historical development of psychology.

Stepping Through the Section

After you have read the section, complete the sentences and answer the questions. As you proceed, evaluate your performance by consulting the answers on page 10. Do not continue with the next section until you understand each answer. If you need to, review or reread the section in the textbook before continuing.

1. The Greek naturalist and philosopher _____ theorized about learning, memory, and other psychological phenomena.

2. The first psychological laboratory was founded in 1879 by Wilhelm _____ .

3. The historical roots of psychology include the fields of _____ and _____ .

4. Some early psychologists included Ivan Pavlov, who pioneered the study of _____ ; the personality theorist _____ ; Jean Piaget, who studied _____ ; and _____ , the author of an important 1890 psychology textbook.

5. In its earliest years, psychology was defined as the science of _____ life. From the 1920s into the 1960s, psychology in America was redefined as the science of _____ behavior. The author of your text defines psychology as the science of _____ and _____ processes.

6. In this definition, "behavior" refers to any action that we can _____ and _____ , and "mental processes" refers to the internal _____ _____ we can _____ from behavior.

7. As a science, psychology is less a set of findings than a way of _____ _____ .

Psychology's Big Issues (pp. 4–6)

> If you do not know the meaning of any of the following words, phrases, or expressions in the context in which they appear in the text, refer to page 15 for an explanation: *wrestled with some issues; outstrip the smartest computers; rules of thumb; shoehorn reality; longstanding; rekindled the debate; weaves a thread; nature-nurture tension dissolve.*

Section Preview

Answer guidelines are provided on page 10.

1. Identify and explain three major issues that cut across psychology.

2. Discuss Charles Darwin's role in supporting or refuting the views of Locke and Descartes on the nature-nurture debate.

Stepping Through the Section

Answers are provided on page 10.

1. Whether an individual's traits persist or change throughout life is referred to as the _____-_____ issue.

2. The extent to which our thoughts and actions are logical and efficient and the extent to which they are prone to inaccuracy is the _____-_____ issue.

3. The controversy over the relative contributions of biology and experience on behavior is called the

_____-_____

issue.

4. The Greek philosopher who assumed that character and intelligence are inherited is

_____ . The Greek philosopher who argued that all knowledge comes from sensory experience is _____ .

5. In the 1600s, the views of the Greek philosophers were revived by _____ , who believed that most knowledge comes in through the senses, and _____ , who believed that some ideas are innate.

6. In 1859, naturalist _____ explained species variation by proposing the process of _____ , which works through the principle of _____

_____ .

Psychology's Perspectives and Psychology's Subfields (pp. 6–9)

> If you do not know the meaning of any of the following words, phrases, or expressions in the context in which they appear in the text, refer to pages 15–16 for an explanation: *red in the face"; "hot under the collar"; nature's building blocks; But there is a payoff.*

Section Preview

Answer guidelines are provided on page 10.

1. Identify and briefly describe the different perspectives of psychology.

2. Explain how psychology's different perspectives contribute to a complete view of human behavior.

3. Identify the major subfields of psychology.

Stepping Through the Section

Answers are provided on page 10.

1. (Table 1) Psychologists who study how the body and brain create emotions, memories, and sensory experiences are working within the _____ perspective.

2. (Table 1) Psychologists who study how natural selection influences behavior tendencies are working within the _____ perspective, whereas those concerned with the relative influences of genes and environment on individual differences are working within the

_____ _____

perspective.

3. (Table 1) Psychologists who believe that behavior springs from unconscious drives and conflicts are working from the _____ perspective.

4. (Table 1) Psychologists who study the mechanisms by which observable responses are acquired and changed are working within the _____ perspective.

5. (Table 1) The _____ perspective explores how our minds process, store, and retrieve information.

6. (Table 1) Psychologists who study how thinking and behavior vary in different situations are working within the _____-_____ perspective.

7. The different perspectives on the big issues _____ (contradict/complement) one another.

8. Psychologists may be involved in conducting _____ _____, which builds psychology's knowledge base, or _____ _____, which seeks solutions to practical problems.

9. Psychologists who study, assess, and treat troubled people are called _____ psychologists.

10. Medical doctors who provide psychotherapy and treat physical causes of psychological disorders are called _____.

11. Worldwide, the number of psychologists has _____ (increased/decreased) since 1980. The number of women earning degrees in psychology is _____ (increasing/decreasing).

12. The first woman president of the American Psychological Association was _____.

Studying Psychology (pp. 10–11)

> If you do not know the meaning of the following expression in the context in which it appears in the text, refer to page 16 for an explanation: *spaced practice*.

Section Preview

Answer guidelines are provided on page 11.

1. Explain the PRTR study method.

Stepping Through the Section

Answers are provided on page 11.

1. In order to master any subject, you must _____ process it.

2. The _____ study method incorporates four steps: **a.** _____ , **b.** _____ , **c.** _____ _____ , and **d.** _____ .

List four additional study tips identified in the text.

a. _____

b. _____

c. _____

d. _____

Web Sighting

Preparing for a career in psychology usually requires a graduate degree. To earn a doctorate in psychology (Ph.D. or Psy.D.), students complete a four- to six-year program, at the end of which they must design and conduct an original research project. Although a doctorate is required for many jobs in psychology—indeed, more than 60 percent of all psychologists hold this degree—the degree of Master of Arts (M.A.) is sufficient for others, such as teaching at some community colleges or being a school psychologist. The M.A. degree program typically requires one or two years of training beyond the undergraduate curriculum. A bachelor's degree does not prepare students to work as psychologists any more than it prepares them to work as physicians or attorneys.

An excellent, up-to-date source of information on careers in psychology (as well as psychological information of interest to the general public) is the web site maintained by the American Psychological Association (www.apa.org). Another is the web site of the American Psychological Society (www.psychological science. org). Consult these sites to find answers to the following questions:

- What is the difference between a Psy.D. and a Ph.D. degree?

- What are the requirements for licensing as a psychologist?

- What can I do with a master's degree? with a doctoral degree?

- How much, on average, do psychologists earn each year?

- What is the best graduate program for a certain subfield of psychology or a particular region?
- Which subfields of psychology currently lead to the best opportunities for employment?

Progress Test 1

Multiple-Choice Questions

Circle your answers to the following questions and check them with the answers on page 11. If your answer is incorrect, read the explanation for why it is incorrect and then consult the appropriate pages of the text (in parentheses following the correct answer).

1. In its earliest days, psychology was defined as the:
   a. science of mental life.
   b. study of conscious and unconscious activity.
   c. science of observable behavior.
   d. science of behavior and mental processes.

2. Who would be most likely to agree with the statement, "Psychology should investigate only behaviors that can be observed"?
   a. Wilhelm Wundt
   b. Sigmund Freud
   c. an American psychologist in the 1950s
   d. William James

3. Today, psychology is defined as the:
   a. study of mental phenomena.
   b. study of conscious and unconscious activity.
   c. study of behavior.
   d. science of behavior and mental processes.

4. Wilhelm Wundt, the founder of the first psychology laboratory, was initially a:
   a. physiologist.
   b. philosopher.
   c. physiologist and philosopher.
   d. historian.

5. Who wrote an important 1890 psychology textbook?
   a. Wilhelm Wundt   d. William James
   b. Ivan Pavlov   e. Sigmund Freud
   c. Jean Piaget

6. Psychologists who study the degree to which genes influence our personality are working within the _____ perspective.
   a. behavioral   d. neuroscience
   b. evolutionary   e. cognitive
   c. behavior genetics

7. Which of the following exemplifies the issue of the relative importance of nature and nurture on our behavior?
   a. the issue of the relative influence of biology and experience on behavior
   b. the issue of the relative influence of rewards and punishments on behavior
   c. the debate as to the relative importance of heredity and instinct in determining behavior
   d. the debate as to whether mental processes are a legitimate area of scientific study

8. The seventeenth-century philosopher who believed that the mind is blank at birth and that most knowledge comes through sensory experience is:
   a. Plato.
   b. Aristotle.
   c. Descartes.
   d. Locke.

9. Which seventeenth-century philosopher believed that some ideas are innate?
   a. Aristotle
   b. Plato
   c. Descartes
   d. Locke

10. Which psychological perspective emphasizes the interaction of the brain and body in behavior?
    a. neuroscience perspective
    b. cognitive perspective
    c. behavioral perspective
    d. behavior genetics perspective
    e. evolutionary perspective

11. A psychologist who explores how Asian and North American definitions of attractiveness differ is working within the _____ perspective.
    a. behavioral   c. cognitive
    b. evolutionary   d. social-cultural

12. A psychologist who conducts experiments solely intended to build psychology's knowledge base is engaged in:
    a. basic research.
    b. applied research.
    c. industrial/organizational research.
    d. clinical research.

13. Psychologists who study, assess, and treat troubled people are called:
    a. basic researchers.
    b. applied psychologists.
    c. clinical psychologists.
    d. psychiatrists.

14. Today, psychology is a discipline that:
    a. connects with a diversity of other fields.
    b. is largely independent of other disciplines.
    c. is focused primarily on basic research.
    d. is focused primarily on applied research.

15. In order, the sequence of steps in the PRTR method is:
    a. preview, review, think critically, read.
    b. plan, read, take notes, review.
    c. preview, read, think critically, review.
    d. plan, review, take notes, read.

Matching Items

Match each psychological perspective and subfield with its definition or description.

Terms

_____ 1. neuroscience perspective
_____ 2. social-cultural perspective
_____ 3. psychiatry
_____ 4. clinical psychology
_____ 5. behavior genetics perspective
_____ 6. behavioral perspective
_____ 7. industrial/organizational psychology
_____ 8. cognitive perspective
_____ 9. basic research
_____ 10. applied research
_____ 11. evolutionary perspective
_____ 12. psychodynamic perspective

Definitions or Descriptions

a. behavior in the workplace

b. how people differ as products of different environments

c. the study of practical problems

d. how much genes and environment contribute to individual differences

e. the mechanism by which observable responses are acquired and changed

f. how the body and brain create emotions, memories, and sensations

g. how the mind processes, stores, and retrieves information

h. adds to psychology's knowledge base

i. how natural selection favors traits that promote the perpetuation of one's genes

j. the study, assessment, and treatment of troubled people

k. the medical treatment of psychological disorders

l. the disguised effects of unfulfilled wishes and childhood traumas

Progress Test 2

Progress Test 2 should be completed during a final chapter review. Answer the following questions after you thoroughly understand the correct answers for the section reviews and Progress Test 1.

Multiple-Choice Questions

1. The first psychology laboratory was established by _____ in the year _____ .
    a. Wundt; 1879   c. Freud; 1900
    b. James; 1890   d. Watson; 1913

2. Who would be most likely to agree with the statement, "Psychology is the science of mental life"?
    a. Wilhelm Wundt
    b. John Watson
    c. Ivan Pavlov
    d. virtually any American psychologist during the 1960s

3. In psychology, "behavior" is best defined as:
    a. anything a person says, does, or feels.
    b. any action we can observe and record.
    c. any action, whether observable or not.
    d. anything we can infer from a person's actions.

4. Which of the following is *not* a major issue in psychology?
   a. stability versus change
   b. rationality versus irrationality
   c. top-down versus bottom-up processing
   d. nature versus nurture

5. In defining psychology, the text notes that psychology is most accurately described as a:
   a. way of asking and answering questions.
   b. field engaged in solving applied problems.
   c. set of findings related to behavior and mental processes.
   d. nonscientific approach to the study of mental disorders.

6. Two historical roots of psychology are the disciplines of:
   a. philosophy and chemistry.
   b. physiology and chemistry.
   c. philosophy and biology.
   d. philosophy and physics.

7. The Greek philosopher who believed that intelligence was inherited was:
   a. Aristotle.   c. Descartes.
   b. Plato.   d. Simonides.

8. The way the mind processes, stores, and retrieves information is the primary concern of the _____ perspective.
   a. neuroscience   d. behavioral
   b. evolutionary   e. cognitive
   c. social-cultural

9. Which of the following individuals is also a physician?
   a. clinical psychologist
   b. experimental psychologist
   c. psychiatrist
   d. biological psychologist

10. Dr. Jones's research centers on the relationship between changes in our thinking over the life span and changes in moral reasoning. Dr. Jones is most likely a:
    a. clinical psychologist.
    b. personality psychologist.
    c. psychiatrist.
    d. developmental psychologist.

11. Which subfield is most directly concerned with studying human behavior in the workplace?
    a. clinical psychology
    b. personality psychology
    c. industrial/organizational psychology
    d. psychiatry

12. Dr. Ernst explains behavior in terms of different situations. Dr. Ernst is working within the _____ perspective.
    a. behavioral   c. social-cultural
    b. evolutionary   d. cognitive

13. Which perspective emphasizes the learning of observable responses?
    a. behavioral   c. neuroscience
    b. social-cultural   d. cognitive

14. A psychologist who studies how worker productivity might be increased by changing office layout is engaged in _____ research.
    a. applied   c. clinical
    b. basic   d. developmental

15. A major principle underlying the PRTR study method is that:
    a. people learn and remember material best when they actively process it.
    b. many students overestimate their mastery of text and lecture material.
    c. study time should be spaced over time rather than crammed into one session.
    d. "overlearning" disrupts efficient retention.

True-False Items

Place a T or an F in the blank next to each statement.

_____   1. In recent years, psychology has flourished more in North America than in countries such as China.
_____   2. The primary research tool of the first psychologists was the experiment.
_____   3. The subject matter of psychology has changed over the history of the field.
_____   4. Every psychological event is simultaneously a biological event.
_____   5. Today, most psychologists work within the behavioral perspective.
_____   6. The major perspectives in psychology contradict one another.
_____   7. Most psychotherapists are psychiatrists.
_____   8. "Spaced practice" promotes better retention than "massed practice."
_____   9. "Overlearning" hinders retention.

_____ **10.** A major goal of psychology is to teach us how to ask important questions and to think critically as we evaluate competing ideas.

Thinking Critically About the Introduction

Answer these questions the day before an exam as a final check on your understanding of the chapter's terms and concepts.

Multiple-Choice Questions

1. Psychology is defined as the "science of behavior and mental processes." Wilhelm Wundt would have omitted which of the following words from this definition?
   a. science
   b. behavior and
   c. and mental processes
   d. Wundt would have agreed with the definition as stated.

2. Jawan believes that psychologists should go back to using introspection as a research tool. This technique is based upon:
   a. survey methodology.
   b. experimentation.
   c. self-examination of mental processes.
   d. the study of observable behavior.

3. Dharma's term paper on the history of American psychology notes that:
   a. psychology began as the science of mental life.
   b. from the 1920s into the 1960s, psychology was defined as the science of observable behavior.
   c. contemporary psychologists study both overt behavior and covert thoughts.
   d. all of the above are true.

4. Sensations, dreams, beliefs, and feelings are:
   a. examples of behavior.
   b. examples of subjective experiences.
   c. not considered appropriate subject matter for psychology today.
   d. b. and c.

5. Dr. Ramirez is studying whether emotionally reactive infants tend to become emotionally reactive adults. Dr. Ramirez's research illustrates the _____ issue in psychology.
   a. stability versus change
   b. rationality versus irrationality
   c. nature-nurture
   d. internal-external

6. The philosophical views of John Locke are to those of René Descartes as _____ is to _____.
   a. nature; nurture
   b. nurture; nature
   c. rationality; irrationality
   d. irrationality; rationality

7. To say that "psychology is a science" means that:
   a. psychologists study only observable behaviors.
   b. psychologists approach the study of thoughts and actions with careful observation and rigorous analysis.
   c. psychological research should be free of value judgments.
   d. all of the above are true.

8. In concluding her report on the "nature-nurture debate in contemporary psychology," Karen notes that:
   a. most psychologists believe that nature is a more important influence on the development of most human traits.
   b. most psychologists believe that nurture is more influential.
   c. the issue is more heatedly debated than ever before.
   d. nurture works on what nature endows.

9. Dr. Waung investigates how a person's interpretation of a situation affects his or her reaction. Evidently, Dr. Waung is working within the _____ perspective.
   a. neuroscience   c. cognitive
   b. behavioral   d. social-cultural

10. Dr. Aswad is studying people's enduring inner traits. Dr. Aswad is most likely a(n):
    a. clinical psychologist.
    b. psychiatrist.
    c. personality psychologist.
    d. industrial/organizational psychologist.

11. The psychological perspective that places the *most* emphasis on how observable responses are learned is the _____ perspective.
    a. behavioral   c. behavior genetics
    b. cognitive   d. evolutionary

12. During a dinner conversation, a friend says that the cognitive and behavioral perspectives are quite similar. You disagree and point out that the cognitive perspective emphasizes_____ , whereas the behavioral perspective emphasizes

_____ .

   a. conscious processes; observable responses
   b. unconscious processes; conscious processes
   c. overt behaviors; covert behaviors
   d. introspection; experimentation

13. Concerning the major psychological perspectives on behavior, the text author suggests that:

   a. researchers should work within the framework of only one of the perspectives.
   b. only those perspectives that emphasize objective measurement of behavior are useful.
   c. the different perspectives often complement one another; together, they provide a fuller understanding of behavior than provided by any single perspective.
   d. psychologists should avoid all of these traditional perspectives.

14. Your roommate announces that her schedule permits her to devote three hours to studying for an upcoming quiz. You advise her to:

   a. spend most of her time reading and rereading the text material.
   b. focus primarily on her lecture notes.
   c. space study time over several short sessions.
   d. cram for three hours just before the quiz.

15. A fraternity brother rationalizes the fact that he spends very little time studying by saying that he "doesn't want to peak too soon and have the test material become stale." You tell him that:

   a. he is probably overestimating his knowledge of the material.
   b. if he devotes extra time to studying, his retention of the material will be improved.
   c. the more often students review material, the better their exam scores.
   d. all of the above are true.

Essay Question

Explain how researchers working from each of psychology's major perspectives might investigate an emotion such as love. (Use the space below to list the points you want to make, and organize them. Then write the essay on a separate piece of paper.)

Key Terms

Writing Definitions

Using your own words, on a separate piece of paper write a brief definition or explanation of each of the following.

1. psychology
2. nature-nurture issue
3. natural selection
4. basic research
5. applied research
6. clinical psychology
7. psychiatry

Answers

Psychology's Roots

Section Preview

1. Psychology is the science of behavior and mental processes. It began as the science of mental life, with Wilhelm Wundt's focus on inner sensations, feelings, and thoughts. From the 1920s into the 1960s, psychology in the United States was most influenced by John Watson and others who redefined it as the "science of observable behavior." In the 1960s, psychology began to recapture its interest in mental processes so that today psychology encompasses the scientific study of both overt behavior and covert thoughts and feelings.

2. Psychology's ancestors date back to the world's earliest writings. The Greek naturalist and philosopher Aristotle theorized about many contemporary psychological phenomena, including learning, memory, motivation, emotion, perception, and personality. The young science of psychology evolved from philosophy and biology. Wilhelm Wundt, who founded the first psychology laboratory in 1879, was a philosopher and a physiologist. Charles Darwin, who introduced the idea of evolutionary psychology, was a naturalist. Ivan Pavlov, who pioneered the study of learning, was a Russian physiologist. Jean Piaget, the most influential observer of children, was a Swiss biologist, and William James was a philosopher.

Stepping Through the Section

1. Aristotle

2. Wundt

3. biology; philosophy

4. learning; Sigmund Freud; children; William James

5. mental; observable; behavior; mental

6. observe; record; subjective experiences; infer

7. asking and answering questions

Psychology's Big Issues

Section Preview

1. The first issue, "stability versus change," has to do with whether the individual's traits persist or change throughout life. The second issue, "rationality-versus irrationality," concerns the extent to which our thoughts and actions are logical and efficient, and the extent to which they are prone to inaccuracy. The nature-nurture issue is concerned with the relative contributions of genes (nature) and experience (nurture).

2. The nature-nurture debate has its roots in ancient Greek philosophy. Plato believed that much of human character and intelligence was inherited, whereas Aristotle believed that experience accounts for the contents of the mind. In the 1600s, John Locke and René Descartes revived the controversy, with Locke arguing that knowledge depends on experience and Descartes maintaining that some knowledge is inborn. Two hundred years later, Descartes' views gained support from Charles Darwin, who argued that through chance variations in organisms, nature selects those that contribute to survival and reproduction.

Stepping Through the Section

1. stability-instability

2. rationality-irrationality

3. nature-nurture

4. Plato; Aristotle

5. Locke; Descartes

6. Charles Darwin; evolution; natural selection

Psychology's Perspectives and Psychology's Subfields

1. Psychologists who work from a neuroscience perspective study how the body and brain create behavior and mental processes. Psychologists who work from an evolutionary perspective study how natural selection favors traits that promote the perpetuation of one's genes. Behavior geneticists study how genes and environment contribute to individual differences. The behavioral perspective emphasizes how observable behaviors are learned. Psychologists who work from a psychodynamic perspective believe that behavior springs from unconscious drives and conflicts. The cognitive perspective explores how people process, store, and retrieve information. The social-cultural perspective calls attention to the importance of each person's social and cultural environment in shaping his or her thoughts, emotions, and behaviors.

2. Psychology's different perspectives need not contradict one another. In fact, they usually complement one another. Each perspective has its questions and its limits. Together, they provide a complete picture.

3. Some psychologists conduct basic research that builds psychology's knowledge base. Biological psychologists explore the links between brain and mind, developmental psychologists study our changing abilities, and personality psychologists investigate our inner traits. Others conduct applied research to solve practical problems. Industrial/organizational psychologists, for example, study and advise on behavior in the workplace. Still others provide professional services. Clinical psychologists study, assess, and treat troubled people. Psychiatrists are physicians who treat the physical causes of psychological disorders.

Stepping Through the Section

1. neuroscience

2. evolutionary; behavior genetics

3. psychodynamic

4. behavioral

5. cognitive

6. social-cultural

7. complement

8. basic research; applied research

9. clinical

10. psychiatrists

11. increased; increasing

12. Mary Whiton Calkins

Studying Psychology

Section Preview

1. The PRTR study method incorporates the idea that mastery of a subject requires active processing of it. PRTR stands for the four steps of the method: *Preview*, *Read*, *Think Critically*, and *Review*. The text and this study guide are organized to facilitate use of the PRTR method.

Stepping Through the Section

1. actively

2. PRTR; **a.** preview; **b.** read; **c.** think actively and critically; **d.** review
   a. Distribute study time.
   b. Listen actively in class.
   c. Overlearn material.
   d. Be a smart test-taker.

Progress Test 1

Multiple-Choice Questions

1. **a.** is the answer. (p. 4)
   b. Psychology has never been defined in terms of conscious and unconscious activity.
   c. From the 1920s into the 1960s, psychology was defined as the science of observable behavior.
   d. Psychology today is defined as the science of behavior and mental processes. In its earliest days, however, psychology focused exclusively on mental phenomena.

2. **c.** is the answer. (p. 4)
   a. Wilhelm Wundt, the founder of the first psychology laboratory, used the method of introspection to study mental phenomena.
   b. Sigmund Freud developed an influential theory of personality that focused on unconscious processes.
   d. William James, author of a psychology text-

book in 1890, was a philosopher and was more interested in mental phenomena than observable behavior.

3. **d.** is the answer. (p. 4)
   a. In its earliest days psychology was defined as the science of mental phenomena.
   b. Psychology has never been defined in terms of conscious and unconscious activity.
   c. From the 1920s into the 1960s, psychology was defined as the science of behavior.

4. **c.** is the answer. (p. 2)

5. **d.** is the answer (p. 2)
   a. Wilhelm Wundt founded the first psychology laboratory.
   b. Ivan Pavlov pioneered the study of learning.
   c. Jean Piaget was this century's most influential observer of children.
   e. Sigmund Freud wrote *The Interpretation of Dreams* in 1900.

6. **c.** is the answer. (p. 6)

7. **a.** is the answer. Biology and experience are internal and external influences, respectively. (p. 5)
   b. Rewards and punishments are both external influences on behavior.
   c. Heredity and instinct are both internal influences on behavior.
   d. The legitimacy of the study of mental processes does not relate to the internal/external issue.

8. **d.** is the answer. For Locke, the mind at birth was a blank tablet. (p. 5)
   a. Plato assumed that much of intelligence is inherited and therefore present at birth. Moreover, he was a philosopher of ancient Greece.
   b. Aristotle held essentially the same viewpoint as Locke, but he lived in the fourth century B.C.
   c. Descartes believed that knowledge does not depend on experience.

9. **c.** is the answer. (p. 5)
   a. Although he would have agreed with Locke, Aristotle was a philosopher in ancient Greece.
   b. Plato assumed that character and intelligence are inherited.
   d. Locke believed that the mind is a blank slate at birth.

10. **a.** is the answer. (p. 6)
    b. The cognitive perspective is concerned with how we process, store, and retrieve information.
    c. The behavioral perspective studies the mechanisms by which observable responses are acquired and changed.

d. The behavior genetics perspective focuses on the relative contributions of genes and environment to individual differences.

e. The evolutionary perspective studies how natural selection favors traits that promote the perpetuation of one's genes.

11. **d.** is the answer. (p. 6)

    a. Behavioral psychologists investigate how learned behaviors are acquired. They generally do not focus on subjective opinions, such as attractiveness.

    b. The evolutionary perspective studies how natural selection favors traits that promote the perpetuation of one's genes.

    c. Cognitive psychologists study the mechanisms of thinking and memory, and generally do not investigate attitudes. Also, because the question specifies that the psychologist is interested in comparing two cultures, d. is the best answer.

12. **a.** is the answer. (p. 8)

    b. & c. Applied and industrial/organizational psychologists tackle practical problems.

    d. Clinical psychologists (and researchers) focus on treating troubled people.

13. **c.** is the answer. (p. 8)

    d. Psychiatrists are medical doctors rather than psychologists.

14. **a.** is the answer. (p. 8)

    c. & d. Psychologists are widely involved in both basic and applied research.

15. **c.** is the answer. (p. 10)

Matching Items

1. f (p. 6)	**5.** d (p. 6)	**9.** h (p. 8)
2. b (p. 6)	**6.** e (p. 6)	**10.** c (p. 8)
3. k (p. 8)	**7.** a (p. 8)	**11.** i (p. 6)
4. j (p. 8)	**8.** g (p. 6)	**12.** l (p. 6)

Progress Test 2

Multiple-Choice Questions

1. **a.** is the answer. (p. 2)

2. **a.** is the answer. (p. 2)

    b. & d. John Watson, like many American psychologists at this time, believed that psychology should focus on the study of observable behavior.

    c. Because he pioneered the study of learning, Pavlov focused on observable behavior and would certainly have *disagreed* with this statement.

3. **b.** is the answer. (p. 4)

4. **c.** is the answer. (pp. 4–5)

5. **a.** is the answer. (p. 4)

    b. Psychology is equally involved in basic research.

    c. Psychology's knowledge base is constantly expanding.

    d. Psychology is the *science* of behavior and mental processes.

6. **c.** is the answer. (p. 2)

7. **b.** is the answer. (p. 5)

    a. Aristotle believed that all knowledge originates with sensory experience.

    c. Descartes was a philosopher of the seventeenth century.

    d. Simonides was a well-known Greek orator.

8. **e.** is the answer. (p. 6)

    a. The neuroscience perspective studies the biological bases for a range of psychological phenomena.

    b. The evolutionary perspective studies how natural selection favors traits that promote the perpetuation of one's genes.

    c. The social-cultural perspective is concerned with variations in behavior across situations and cultures.

    d. The behavioral perspective studies the mechanisms by which observable responses are acquired and modified in particular environments.

9. **c.** is the answer. After earning their M.D. degrees, psychiatrists specialize in the diagnosis and treatment of mental health disorders. (p. 8)

    a., b., & d. These psychologists generally earn a Ph.D. rather than an M.D.

10. **d.** is the answer. The emphasis on change during the life span indicates that Dr. Jones is most likely a developmental psychologist. (p. 8)

    a. Clinical psychologists study, assess, and treat people who are psychologically troubled.

    b. Personality psychologists study our inner traits.

    c. Psychiatrists are medical doctors.

11. **c.** is the answer. (p. 8)

    a. Clinical psychologists study, assess, and treat people with psychological disorders.

    b. & d. Personality psychologists and psychiatrists do not usually study people in work situations.

12. **c.** is the answer. (p. 6)

    a. Psychologists who follow the behavioral perspective emphasize observable, external influences on behavior.

b. The evolutionary perspective focuses on how natural selection favors traits that promote the perpetuation of one's genes.

d. The cognitive perspective places emphasis on conscious, rather than unconscious, processes.

13. **a.** is the answer. (p. 6)

14. **a.** is the answer. The research is addressing a practical issue. (p. 8)
    b. Basic research is aimed at contributing to the base of knowledge in a given field, not at resolving particular practical problems.
    c. & d. Clinical and developmental research would focus on issues relating to psychological disorders and life-span changes, respectively.

15. **a.** is the answer. (p. 10)
    b. & c. Although each of these is true, PRTR is based on the more *general* principle of active learning.
    d. In fact, just the opposite is true.

True–False Items

1. T (p. 9)
2. F (p. 4) The first psychologists used the method of introspection.
3. T (p. 2)
4. T (p. 6)
5. F (p. 6) The behavioral perspective is one of *several* major contemporary perspectives.
6. F (p. 6) The major perspectives *complement*, rather than contradict, one another.
7. F (p. 9) There are many more psychologists than psychiatrists.
8. T (p. 10)
9. F (p. 11) Overlearning improves retention.
10. T (p. 10)

Thinking Critically About the Introduction

Multiple-Choice Questions

1. **b.** is the answer. (p. 4)
   a. As the founder of the first psychology laboratory, Wundt certainly based his research on the scientific method.
   c. The earliest psychologists, including Wilhelm Wundt, were concerned with the self-examination of covert thoughts, feelings, and other mental processes.

2. **c.** is the answer. (p. 4)

3. **d.** is the answer. (p. 4)

4. **b.** is the answer. (p. 4)
   a., c., & d. Psychologists today study both overt *and* covert behavior.

5. **a.** is the answer. (p. 4)
   b. This issue concerns the degree to which our thinking is logical, and at times, illogical.
   c. This issue concerns the relative contributions of biology (nature) and experience (nurture) to the development of psychological traits and behaviors.
   d. This is a restatement of the nature-nurture issue.

6. **b.** is the answer. Locke believed that all knowledge comes from experience (nurture). Descartes believed that some ideas are innate (nature). (p. 5)
   c. & d. The text does not discuss the views of these philosophers regarding this issue.

7. **b.** is the answer. (p. 4)
   a. Psychologists study both overt (observable) behaviors and covert thoughts and feelings.
   c. Psychologists' values definitely *do* influence their research.

8. **d.** is the answer. Because both nature and nurture influence most traits and behaviors, the tension surrounding this issue has dissolved. (p. 6)

9. **c.** is the answer. (p. 6)
   a. This perspective emphasizes the influences of physiology on behavior.
   b. This perspective emphasizes environmental influences on observable behavior.
   d. This perspective emphasizes how behavior and thinking vary across situations and cultures.

10. **c.** is the answer. (p. 8)
    a. Clinical psychology is concerned with the study and treatment of psychological disorders.
    b. Psychiatry is the branch of medicine concerned with the physical diagnosis and treatment of psychological disorders.
    d. Industrial/organizational psychologists study behavior in the workplace.

11. **a.** is the answer. (p. 6)

12. **a.** is the answer. (p. 6)
    b. Neither perspective places any special emphasis on conscious or unconscious processes.
    c. Neither perspective emphasizes covert behaviors.
    d. Introspection was a research method used by the earliest psychologists, not those working from the cognitive perspective.

13. **c.** is the answer. (p. 7)

a. The text suggests just the opposite: By studying behavior from several perspectives, psychologists gain a fuller understanding.

b. & d. Each perspective is useful in that it calls researchers' attention to different aspects of behavior. This is equally true of those perspectives that do not emphasize objective measurement.

14. **c.** is the answer. (p. 10)
    a. To be effective, study must be *active* rather than passive in nature.
    b. Most exams are based on lecture *and* textbook material.
    d. Cramming hinders retention.

15. **d.** is the answer. (p. 10)

Essay Question

A psychologist working from the neuroscience perspective might study the brain circuits and body chemistry that trigger attraction and sexual arousal. A psychologist working from the evolutionary perspective might analyze how love has facilitated the survival of our species. A psychologist working from the behavior genetics perspective might attempt to compare the extent to which the emotion is attributable to our genes and the extent to which it is attributable to our environment. A psychologist working from the psychodynamic perspective might search for evidence that a person's particular emotional feelings are disguised effects of unfulfilled wishes. A psychologist working from the behavioral perspective might study the external stimuli, such as body language, that elicit and reward approach behaviors toward another person. A psychologist working from a cognitive perspective might study how our thought processes, attitudes, and beliefs foster attachment to loved ones, and a psychologist working from a social-cultural perspective might explore situational influences on attraction and how the development and expression of love varies across cultural groups.

Key Terms

1. **Psychology** is the science of behavior and mental processes. (p. 4)
2. The **nature-nurture issue** is the controversy over the relative contributions that genes (nature) and experience (nurture) make to the development of psychological traits and behaviors. (p. 5)
3. **Natural selection** is the principle that those traits of a species that contribute to reproduction and survival are most likely to be passed on to succeeding generations. (p. 5)
4. **Basic research** is pure science that aims to increase psychology's scientific knowledge base rather than to solve practical problems. (p. 8)
5. **Applied research** is scientific study that aims to solve practical problems. (p. 8)
6. **Clinical psychology** is the branch of psychology concerned with the study, assessment, and treatment of people with psychological disorders. (p. 8)
7. **Psychiatry** is the branch of medicine concerned with the physical diagnosis and treatment of psychological disorders. (p. 8)

FOCUS ON VOCABULARY AND LANGUAGE

Page 1: Have you ever played *peekaboo* with a 6-month-old infant . . . ? Peekaboo is a game played in most cultures where a person hides or pretends to hide from a child and then reappears saying "PEEK-ABOO!" The important question for psychologists is why do infants all over the world react similarly to this game; what are they actually feeling, perceiving, and thinking?

Page 1: Such questions provide *grist for psychology's mill* . . . . The expression "*provide grist for the mill*" derives from the practice in the past where farmers brought their grain (*grist*) to the *mill* (a building with machinery for grinding grain into flour). Today the expression means that a greater volume of work (*grist*) does not present a problem; in fact, it is welcomed. The amount of grain (*grist*) is analogous to the variety of questions asked, and the research conducted to answer them is like the *mill* producing flour from the grist. Thus, psychology is a science that thrives on attempting to answer a variety of questions about how we think, feel, and act through scientific methodology (research).

Psychology's Roots

Page 2: This list of pioneering psychologists . . . "*Magellans of the mind*" . . . . Ferdinand Magellan

(1489–1521) was a famous Portuguese navigator who made many discoveries and explored areas of the world previously unknown to his fellow Europeans. Because early psychologists made exciting discoveries and explored unknown frontiers, they are "*Magellans of the mind.*"

Page 4: Let's *unpack* this definition. *Unpack* here means to take apart or disassemble. So psychology, defined as the science of behavior and mental processes, is broken down into overt behavior (i.e., observable events) and covert processes (i.e., events hidden within, such as thoughts, feelings, perceptions, beliefs, and so on) and is studied using the scientific or empirical method.

Page 4: . . . psychology attempts to *sift* opinions and evaluate ideas . . . . Literally, *sift* means to separate the finer particles from the coarser ones by passing material through a sieve. Myers uses the word *sift* to explain how psychology examines or evaluates ideas, opinions, facts, and concepts and separates those that are useful and worthwhile from those that are not. (Be sure you understand the word *sift*, because Myers uses it quite often.)

Page 4: . . . psychological science welcomes *hunches* and plausible-sounding theories. In popular usage a *hunch* is an intuitive feeling about a situation or event. Psychology can use subjective ideas to help formulate hypotheses or predictions which can then be tested empirically or scientifically.

Page 4: Its scientific sifting of ideas has produced a *smorgasbord* of concepts and findings, from which we can only sample the *fare*. A *smorgasbord* is a buffet meal at which a great variety of foods (*fare*) is offered. Myers is suggesting that psychology's examination and evaluation (*testing*) of ideas has produced a great variety of concepts and findings for us to sample or look at.

Psychology's Big Issues

Page 4: . . . psychology has *wrestled* with some issues . . . . Psychology has struggled (*wrestled*) with a number of issues, particularly those of stability/change, rationality/irrationality, and nature/nurture, and these issues may be perceived differently by the various perspectives in the discipline (i.e., several issues *cut across* psychology). Myers points out that these different views may be complementary or compatible rather than antagonistic or opposite.

Page 5: . . . we *outstrip* the smartest computers. *Outstrip* means to outperform or do much better than. The point being made is that humans are superior at doing many tasks such as pattern recognition, dealing with everyday language, and processing abstract concepts than are the most sophisticated modern computers.

Page 5: Indeed, using certain *rules of thumb*, we make snap judgments with amazing efficiency and sufficient rationality. *Rule of thumb:* a simple guide or principle that is true in general. Myers is pointing out that we make quick (*snap*) decisions very easily but we often make mistakes using these general principles (*rules of thumb*).

Page 5: We sometimes *shoehorn* reality into our preconceptions. A *shoehorn* is a flat, curved lever used to help force or shove our feet into our shoes. Myers suggests that we humans, in a psychological rather than a physical way, force reality to fit into our preconceived ideas of what is true or false; we are prone to making errors when we do this but are often unaware of our own lack of critical thinking (*irrationality*).

Page 5: . . . *longstanding:* going on for an extended period of time. The nature-nurture issue has been debated for thousands of years (*longstanding*), from Greek times to the present.

Page 5: In the 1600s, philosophers *rekindled* the debate (nature-nurture). *Rekindled* means to restart as in to restart a fire (*rekindle*). John Locke in the 1600s repeated what Aristotle had said 2000 years before—that humans are born without any knowledge (i.e., that we are blank slates, or blank paper, at birth) and that all knowledge comes from experience (*nurture*). Plato and, later, René Descartes argued that we are born with some innate knowledge (*nature*).

Page 5: The nature-nurture debate *weaves a thread* from the distant past to our time. This simply means that the issue has been of concern to scholars and others from the time of the Greek philosophers right up to modern times. The debate connects the past to the present (*weaves a thread* between the two).

Page 6: Yet over and over again we will see the nature-nurture *tension dissolve*. The main point is that both sides of the debate have something to offer: Each contributes to the search for the truth. Thus, the tension gets less (*dissolves*).

Psychology's Perspectives

Page 6: "*Red in the face*" and "*hot under the collar*" refer to the physical changes that often accompany emotional arousal (e.g., anger). A person's face may become red due to blood rushing to it (blushing), and he or she may feel hot and perspire (*hot under the collar*). Different perspectives (neuroscience, evolutionary, behavior genetics, psychodynamic, behavioral, cognitive, and social-cultural) view the same event (emotional change) from different points of view (see Table 1, p. 6). Myers points out that these different perspectives are not necessarily in opposition to each other but, rather, are complementary; that is, each helps to complete the puzzle of why the event occurs by supplying answers from different points of view (perspectives).

Page 7: The basic sciences investigate nature's *building blocks . . . . Building blocks* are the basic or fundamental parts that make up a structure (building). Basic science investigates how nature (life in general) is constructed or put together. These investigations are on a continuum from subjective at one end to objective at the other. Psychology is in the middle, using scientific methods (objective) in order to explore behavior, thoughts, and feelings (subjective states).

Psychology's Subfields

Page 8: But there is a *payoff:* Psychology is a *meeting ground* for different disciplines, and is thus a *perfect home* for those with *wide-ranging* interests. Myers points out that there is much diversity in the discipline of psychology (i.e., it lacks unity), but this is beneficial (a *payoff*) because it is a nice place (area) to work in (a *perfect home*) for those who have broad or diverse (*wide-ranging*) interests. Thus, psychology is the ideal meeting place or *meeting ground* for different disciplines.

Studying Psychology

Page 10: One of psychology's oldest findings is that *spaced practice* promotes better retention than *massed practice*. *Spaced practice* refers to studying over a longer period of time, say 2 hours a day over 5 days rather than 10 hours on one day (*massed practice* or cramming). Distributing your study time is much better for learning and retention than one long study period (a *blitz*).

Thinking Critically With Psychological Science

Chapter Overview

Chapter 1 explains the limits of intuition and common sense in reasoning about behavior and mental processes. To counteract our human tendency toward faulty reasoning, psychologists adopt a scientific attitude that is based on healthy skepticism, open-minded humility, and critical thinking. Chapter 1 also explains how psychologists, using the scientific method, employ the research strategies of description, correlation, and experimentation in order to objectively describe, predict, and explain behavior.

The next section discusses how statistical reasoning is used to help psychologists describe data and to generalize from instances. To describe data, psychologists often rely on measures of central tendency such as the mean, median, and mode, as well as variation measures such as the range and standard deviation. Statistical reasoning also helps psychologists determine when it is safe to generalize from a sample to the larger population.

Chapter 1 concludes with a discussion of several questions people often ask about psychology, including why animal research is relevant, whether laboratory experiments are ethical, whether behavior varies with culture and gender, and whether psychology's principles don't have the potential for misuse.

Chapter 1 introduces a number of concepts and issues that will play an important role in later chapters. Pay particular attention to the strengths and weaknesses of descriptive and correlational research. In addition, make sure that you understand the method of experimentation, especially the importance of control conditions and the difference between independent and dependent variables. Finally, you should be able to discuss three important principles concerning populations and samples, as well as the concept of significance in testing difference.

NOTE: Answer guidelines for all Chapter 1 questions begin on page 32.

The Need for Psychological Science
(pp. 13–20)

> David Myers at times uses idioms that are unfamiliar to some readers. If you do not know the meaning of any of the following words, phrases, or expressions in the context in which they appear in the introduction to this chapter and in this section, refer to pages 40–42 for an explanation: *to remedy their woes; winnow sense from nonsense; dresses it in jargon; after-the-fact pundits; out of sight, out of mind; absence makes the heart grow fonder; familiarity breeds contempt; drop a course; drop out; hard-headed curiosity; leap of faith; the proof is in the pudding; auras; crazy-sounding ideas; arena of competing ideas; so much the worse for our ideas; the rat is always right; the spectacles of our preconceived ideas; gut feelings; debunked; "play the tape"; we outsmart the smartest computers; sift reality from illusion.*

Section Preview

First, skim this section, noting headings and boldface items. Then read the following objectives and, as you read the section, search for the information that will enable you to meet each objective. Answer guidelines are provided on page 32.

1. Identify two pitfalls in thinking that make intuition and common sense untrustworthy.

2. Discuss the attitudes that characterize scientific inquiry and explain the nature of critical thinking.

3. Explain the importance of theories, hypotheses, operational definitions, and replication in psychology.

4. Reasoning that examines assumptions, discerns hidden values, evaluates evidence, and assesses conclusions is called _____ _____ .

5. An explanation using an integrated set of principles that organizes and predicts observable behaviors or events is a _____ . Testable predictions that allow a scientist to evaluate a theory are called _____ .

6. In order to prevent theoretical biases from influencing scientific observations, research must be reported precisely—using clear _____ _____ of all concepts—so that others can _____ the findings.

7. The three basic research strategies in psychology are _____ , _____ , and _____ methods.

Description (pp. 20–24)

> If you do not know the meaning of any of the following words, phrases, or expressions in the context in which they appear in the text, refer to page 42 for an explanation: *handful of case studies; numbers are numbing; anecdotes are alarming; bludgeoned to death; a thimbleful; target group; snapshot of the opinions; having affairs.*

Stepping Through the Section

After you have read the section, complete the sentences and answer the questions. As you proceed, evaluate your performance by consulting the answers on page 32. Do not continue with the next section until you understand each answer. If you need to, review or reread the section in the textbook before continuing.

1. The tendency to perceive an outcome that has occurred as being obvious and predictable is called the _____ _____ .

2. Our everyday thinking is also limited by _____ in what we think we know.

3. The scientific approach is characterized by the attitudes of curious _____ and open-minded _____ .

Section Preview

Answer guidelines are provided on page 32.

1. Discuss the descriptive research strategies.

2. Discuss the limitations and possible pitfalls of descriptive research.

Stepping Through the Section

Answers are provided on page 32.

1. The research strategy in which one or more individuals is studied in depth in order to reveal universal principles of behavior is the

   _____ _____ .

   A potential problem with this method is that any given individual may be _____ .

2. The method in which a group of people is questioned about their attitudes or behavior is the _____ method.

3. An important factor in the validity of survey research is the _____ of questions.

4. The tendency to overestimate others' agreement with us is the _____

   _____ _____ .

5. Surveys try to obtain a _____ sample, one that will be representative of the _____ being studied. In such a sample, every person _____ (does/does not) have a chance of being included.

6. Large, representative samples _____ (are/are not) better than small ones.

7. We are more likely to overgeneralize from select samples that are especially _____ .

8. The research strategy in which people or animals are directly observed in their natural environments is called _____

   _____ .

9. Case studies, surveys, and naturalistic observation do not explain behavior; they simply

   _____ it.

10. Using naturalistic observation of walking speed and the accuracy of public clocks, researchers have concluded that the pace of life

    _____ (varies/does not vary)

    from one culture to another.

Correlation (pp. 24–30)

> If you do not know the meaning of any of the following words, phrases, or expressions in the context in which they appear in the text, refer to pages 42–43 for an explanation: *naked eye; laypeople; flipped a coin; hot and cold streaks.*

Section Preview

Answer guidelines are provided on page 32.

1. Describe the types of correlation, and discuss why correlation enables prediction but not explanation.

2. Explain the nature and significance of illusory correlations.

Stepping Through the Section

Answers are provided on page 33.

1. When changes in one factor are accompanied by changes in another, the two factors are said to be _____ , and one is thus able to _____ the other. If the factors increase or decrease together, they are

   _____ _____ .

   If, however, one decreases as the other increases, they are _____ _____ .

2. Graphs called _____ are often used to depict the relationship between two sets of scores.

3. A negative correlation between two variables does not indicate the _____ or _____ of the relationship. Nor does correlation prove _____ ; rather, it merely indicates the possibility of a

   _____ - _____

   relationship.

4. A perceived correlation that does not really exist is an _____

   _____ . This error in thinking helps explain many _____ beliefs.

If your level of test anxiety goes down as your time spent studying for the exam goes up, would you say these events are positively or negatively correlated? Explain your reasoning.

5. Another common tendency is to perceive order in

   _____ _____ .

6. (Thinking Critically) Basketball players and fans mistakenly believe that players are _____ (no more likely/more likely) to score after having just made the last two or three shots.

Experimentation (pp. 31–34)

If you do not know the meaning of the following word in the context in which it appears in the text, refer to page 43 for an explanation: *recap*.

Section Preview

Answer guidelines are provided on page 33.

1. Describe the nature and advantages of experimentation.

2. Discuss the importance of random assignment and control techniques in research.

Stepping Through the Section

Answers are provided on page 33.

1. To study cause-effect relationships, psychologists conduct _____ . Using this method, a researcher _____ the

factor of interest, while _____

_____ other factors.

2. Researchers sometimes give certain subjects a pseudotreatment, called a _____ , and compare their behavior with that of subjects who receive the actual treatment. When merely thinking that one is receiving a treatment produces results, a _____

_____ is said to occur.

3. When neither the subjects nor the person collecting the data knows which condition a subject is in, the researcher is making use of the

_____-_____

_____ .

4. An experiment must involve at least two conditions: the _____ condition, in which the experimental treatment is absent, and the _____ condition, in which it is present.

5. Experimenters rely on the _____

_____ of individuals to experimental and control groups.

6. The factor that is being manipulated in an experiment is called the _____ variable. The measurable factor that may change as a result of these manipulations is called the

_____ variable.

Explain at least one advantage of the experiment as a research strategy.

Statistical Reasoning (pp. 34–38)

> If you do not know the meaning of any of the following words, phrases, or expressions in the context in which they appear in the text, refer to page 43 for an explanation: *Off the top-of-the-head estimates; national income cake; gauges; data are "noisy."*

Section Preview

Answer guidelines are provided on page 33.

1. Define the three measures of central tendency, and explain how they describe data differently.

2. Describe two measures of variation.

3. Discuss three important principles in making generalizations about populations on the basis of samples.

4. Describe how psychologists make statistical inferences about differences between groups.

Stepping Through the Section

Answers are provided on page 33.

1. The three measures of central tendency are the _____ , the _____ , and the _____ .

2. The most frequently occurring score in a distribution is called the _____ .

3. The mean is computed as the _____ _____ of all the scores divided by the _____ of scores.

4. The median is the score at the _____ percentile.

5. When a distribution is lopsided, or _____ , the _____ (mean/median/mode) can be biased by a few extreme scores.

6. Averages derived from scores with _____ (high/low) variability are more reliable than those with _____ (high/low) variability.

7. The measures of variation include the _____ and the _____ _____ .

8. The range is computed as the _____ _____ .

9. The range provides a(n) _____ (crude/accurate) estimate of variation because it _____ (is/is not) influenced by extreme scores.

10. The standard deviation is a _____ (more accurate/less accurate) measure of variation than the range. Unlike the range, the stan-

dard deviation _____ (takes/does not take) into consideration information from each score in the distribution.

11. It is safer to generalize from a _____ sample than from a _____ sample.

12. Averages are more reliable when they are based on scores with _____ (high/low) variability.

13. Small samples provide a _____ (more/less) reliable basis for generalizing than large samples.

14. Tests of statistical _____ are used to estimate whether observed differences are real—that is, to make sure that they are not simply the result of _____ variation. The differences are probably real if the sample averages are _____ and the difference between them is _____ .

Frequently Asked Questions About Psychology (pp. 39–44)

> If you do not know the meaning of any of the following words, phrases, or expressions in the context in which they appear in the text, refer to pages 43–44 for an explanation: *plunge in; To understand how a combustion engine works . . . .; idle curiosity; screen; color "the facts."*

Section Preview

Answer guidelines are provided on page 34.

1. Discuss questions regarding the artificiality of experimentation and whether psychological principles are culture- or gender-free.

2. Explain why psychologists study animals and discuss the ethics of experimentation.

3. Describe how psychologists' values influence their work, and discuss whether psychology is potentially dangerous.

Stepping Through the Section

Answers are provided on page 34.

1. Laboratory experiments in psychology are sometimes criticized as being _____ . However, psychologists' concern is not with the specific behaviors but with the underlying theoretical _____ .

2. Culture refers to shared _____ , _____ , _____ , and _____ that one generation passes on to the next.

3. Although specific attitudes and behaviors vary across cultures, the underlying _____ are the same. Likewise, similarities between the _____ far outweigh differences.

4. Some people question whether experiments with animals are _____ . They wonder whether it is right to place the _____ of humans over those of animals.

Describe the goals of the ethical guidelines for psychological research.

5. Psychologists' values _____ (do/do not) influence their theories, observations, and professional advice.

6. (Thinking Critically) The viewpoint called _____ questions scientific objectivity, arguing that most scientific concepts are merely _____ constructs. Psychological scientists _____ (agree/disagree) on whether there is, in fact, a "real world" of psychological principles that science can reveal.

7. (Thinking Critically) Most Americans _____ (favor/oppose) capital punishment but not for people with _____ _____ . Attitudes toward capital punishment _____ (vary/do not vary) from one nation to another.

8. (Thinking Critically) States with a death penalty _____ (have/do not have) lower homicide rates.

Progress Test 1

Multiple-Choice Questions

Circle your answers to the following questions and check them with the answers on page 34. If your answer is incorrect, read the explanation for why it is incorrect and then consult the appropriate pages of the text (in parentheses following the correct answer).

1. After detailed study of a gunshot wound victim, a psychologist concludes that the brain region destroyed is likely to be important for memory functions. Which research strategy did the psychologist use to deduce this?
   a. the case study
   b. a survey
   c. correlation
   d. experimentation

2. In an experiment to determine the effects of exercise on motivation, exercise is the:
   a. control condition.
   b. intervening variable.
   c. independent variable.
   d. dependent variable.

3. In order to determine the effects of a new drug on memory, one group of subjects is given a pill that contains the drug. A second group is given a sugar pill that does not contain the drug. This second group constitutes the:
   a. random sample.
   b. experimental group.
   c. control group.
   d. test group.

4. Theories are defined as:
   a. testable propositions.
   b. factors that may change in response to manipulation.
   c. statistical indexes.
   d. principles that help to organize, predict, and explain facts.

5. A psychologist studies the play behavior of third-grade children by watching groups during recess at school. Which research strategy is being used?
   a. correlation
   b. case study
   c. experimentation
   d. naturalistic observation

6. To ensure that other researchers can repeat their work, psychologists use:
   a. control groups.
   b. random assignment.
   c. double-blind procedures.
   d. operational definitions.

7. The scientific attitude of skepticism is based on the belief that:
   a. people are rarely candid in revealing their thoughts.
   b. mental processes can't be studied objectively.
   c. the scientist's intuition about behavior is usually correct.
   d. ideas need to be tested against observable evidence.

8. Which of the following is *not* a basic research strategy used by psychologists?
   a. description
   b. replication
   c. experimentation
   d. correlation

9. Psychologists' personal values:
   a. have little influence on how their experiments are conducted.
   b. do not influence the interpretation of experimental results because of the use of statistical techniques that guard against subjective bias.
   c. can bias both scientific observation and interpretation of data.
   d. have little influence on investigative methods but a significant effect on interpretation.

10. If shoe size and IQ are negatively correlated, which of the following is true?
    a. People with large feet tend to have high IQs.
    b. People with small feet tend to have high IQs.
    c. People with small feet tend to have low IQs.
    d. IQ is unpredictable based on a person's shoe size.

11. Which of the following research strategies would be best for determining whether alcohol impairs memory?
    a. case study
    b. naturalistic observation
    c. survey
    d. experiment

12. Well-done surveys measure attitudes in a representative subset, or _____ , of an entire group, or _____ .
    a. population; random sample
    b. control group; experimental group
    c. experimental group; control group
    d. random sample; population

13. What is the mean of the following distribution of scores: 2, 3, 7, 6, 1, 4, 9, 5, 8, 2?
    a. 5
    b. 4
    c. 4.7
    d. 3.7

14. What is the median of the following distribution of scores: 1, 3, 7, 7, 2, 8, 4?
    a. 1   c. 3
    b. 2   d. 4

15. What is the mode of the following distribution: 8, 2, 1, 1, 3, 7, 6, 2, 0, 2?
    a. 1   c. 3
    b. 2   d. 7

16. In generalizing from a sample to the population, it is important that:
    a. the sample is representative of the population.
    b. the sample is large.
    c. the scores in the sample have low variability.
    d. all of the above are observed.

17. When a difference between two groups is "statistically significant," this means that:
    a. the difference is statistically real but of little practical significance.
    b. the difference is probably the result of sampling variation.

    c. the difference is not likely to be due to chance variation.
    d. all of the above are true.

18. A lopsided set of scores that includes a number of extreme or unusual values is said to be:
    a. symmetrical.   c. skewed.
    b. normal.   d. dispersed.

19. Juwan eagerly opened an online trading account, believing that his market savvy would allow him to pick stocks that would make him a rich day trader. This belief best illustrates:
    a. the false consensus effect.
    b. illusory correlation.
    c. hindsight bias.
    d. overconfidence.

20. Which of the following is the measure of central tendency that would be most affected by a few extreme scores?
    a. mean   c. median
    b. range   d. mode

Matching Items

Match each term and concept with its definition or description.

Terms

_____   1. culture
_____   2. median
_____   3. placebo
_____   4. hindsight bias
_____   5. mode
_____   6. range
_____   7. standard deviation
_____   8. scatterplot
_____   9. mean
_____ 10. measures of central tendency
_____ 11. measures of variation
_____ 12. false consensus effect
_____ 13. critical thinking
_____ 14. illusory correlation

Definitions or Descriptions

a. the mean, median, and mode
b. the difference between the highest and lowest scores
c. the arithmetic average of a set of scores
d. the range and standard deviation
e. the most frequently occurring score
f. the middle score in a distribution
g. a graphed cluster of dots depicting the values of two variables
h. a measure of variation based on every score
i. shared ideas and behaviors passed from one generation to the next
j. "I-knew-it-all-along" phenomenon
k. reasoning that does not blindly accept arguments
l. chemically inert substance
m. overestimating others' agreement with us
n. false perception of a relationship between two variables

Progress Test 2

Progress Test 2 should be completed during a final chapter review. Answer the following questions after you thoroughly understand the correct answers for the section reviews and Progress Test 1.

Multiple-Choice Questions

1. Which of the following research methods does *not* belong with the others?
   a. case study
   b. survey
   c. naturalistic observation
   d. experiment

2. In the experiment on subliminal perception, students listened for five weeks to tapes they thought would enhance their memory or self-esteem. At the end of the experiment:
   a. students who thought they had a memory tape believed their memories had improved; but, in fact, there was no improvement.
   b. self-esteem, but not memory, improved.
   c. memory, but not self-esteem, improved.
   d. both self-esteem and memory improved over the course of the experiment.

3. Which statement about the ethics of experimentation with people and animals is *false*?
   a. Only a small percentage of animal experiments use shock.
   b. Allegations that psychologists routinely subject animals to pain, starvation, and other inhumane conditions have been proven untrue.
   c. The American Psychological Association and the British Psychological Society have set strict guidelines for the care and treatment of human and animal subjects.
   d. Animals are used as subjects in almost 25 percent of all psychology experiments.

4. In an experiment to determine the effects of attention on memory, memory is the:
   a. control condition.
   b. intervening variable.
   c. independent variable.
   d. dependent variable.

5. One reason researchers base their findings on representative samples is to avoid the false consensus effect, which refers to our tendency to:
   a. overestimate the extent to which others share our belief.
   b. falsely perceive a relationship between two events when none exists.
   c. underestimate errors in our judgment.
   d. make all of the above reasoning errors.

6. Which of the following *best* describes the hindsight bias?
   a. Events seem more predictable before they have occurred.
   b. Events seem more predictable after they have occurred.
   c. A person's intuition is usually correct.
   d. A person's intuition is usually not correct.

7. The procedure designed to ensure that the experimental and control groups do not differ in any way that might affect the experiment's results is called:
   a. variable controlling.
   b. random assignment.
   c. representative sampling.
   d. stratification.

8. Illusory correlation refers to:
   a. the perception that two negatively correlated variables are positively correlated.
   b. the perception of a correlation between two unrelated variables.
   c. an insignificant correlation.
   d. a correlation that equals −1.0.

9. In generalizing from a sample to the population, it is important that:
   a. the sample be representative.
   b. the sample be nonrandom.
   c. the sample not be too large.
   d. all of the above be true.

10. The strength of the relationship between two vivid events will most likely be:
    a. significant.
    b. positive.
    c. negative.
    d. overestimated.

11. Which of the following is true, according to the text?
    a. Because laboratory experiments are artificial, any principles discovered cannot be applied to everyday behaviors.
    b. No psychological theory can be considered true until tested.
    c. Psychology's theories reflect common sense.
    d. Psychology has few ties to other disciplines.

12. Which type of research strategy would allow you to determine whether students' college grades accurately predict later income?
    a. case study
    b. naturalistic observation
    c. experimentation
    d. correlation

13. In a test of the effects of air pollution, groups of students performed a reaction-time task in a polluted or an unpolluted room. To what condition were students in the unpolluted room exposed?
    a. experimental
    b. control
    c. randomly assigned
    d. dependent

14. In order to study the effects of lighting on mood, Dr. Cooper had students fill out questionnaires in brightly lit or dimly lit rooms. In this study, the independent variable consisted of:
    a. the number of subjects assigned to each group.
    b. the students' responses to the questionnaire.
    c. the room lighting.
    d. the subject matter of the questions asked.

15. What is the mode of the following distribution of scores: 2, 2, 4, 4, 4, 14?
    a. 2
    b. 4
    c. 5
    d. 6

16. What is the mean of the following distribution of scores: 2, 5, 8, 10, 11, 4, 6, 9, 1, 4?
    a. 2
    b. 10
    c. 6
    d. 15

17. What is the median of the following distribution: 10, 7, 5, 11, 8, 6, 9?
    a. 6
    b. 7
    c. 8
    d. 9

18. Which of the following is the measure of variation that is most affected by extreme scores?
    a. mean
    b. standard deviation
    c. mode
    d. range

19. The set of scores that would likely be most representative of the population from which it was drawn would be a sample with a relatively:
    a. large standard deviation.
    b. small standard deviation.
    c. large range.
    d. small range.

20. If a difference between two samples is not statistically significant, which of the following can be concluded?
    a. The difference is probably not a true one.
    b. The difference is probably not reliable.
    c. The difference could be due to sampling variation.
    d. All of the above can be concluded.

Matching Items

Match each term with its definition or description.

Terms

_____ 1. hypothesis
_____ 2. theory
_____ 3. independent variable
_____ 4. dependent variable
_____ 5. experimental condition
_____ 6. control condition
_____ 7. case study
_____ 8. survey
_____ 9. replication
_____ 10. random assignment
_____ 11. experiment
_____ 12. double-blind

Definitions or Descriptions

a. an in-depth observational study of one person
b. the variable being manipulated in an experiment
c. the variable being measured in an experiment
d. the "treatment-absent" condition in an experiment
e. testable proposition
f. repeating an experiment to see whether the same results are obtained
g. the process in which subjects are selected by chance for different groups in an experiment
h. an explanation using an integrated set of principles that organizes and predicts observations
i. the research strategy in which the effects of one or more variables on behavior are tested
j. the "treatment-present" condition in an experiment
k. the research strategy in which a representative sample of individuals is questioned
l. experimental procedure in which neither the subject nor the experimenter knows which condition the subject is in

Thinking Critically About Chapter 1

Answer these questions the day before an exam as a final check on your understanding of the chapter's terms and concepts.

Multiple-Choice Questions

1. You decide to test your belief that men drink more soft drinks than women by finding out whether more soft drinks are consumed per day in the men's dorm than in the women's dorm. Your belief is a(n) _____ , and your research prediction is a(n) _____ .
    a. hypothesis; theory
    b. theory; hypothesis
    c. independent variable; dependent variable
    d. dependent variable; independent variable

2. Your roommate is conducting a survey to learn how many hours the typical college student studies each day. She plans to pass out her questionnaire to the members of her sorority. You point out that her findings will be flawed because:
    a. she has not specified an independent variable.
    b. she has not specified a dependent variable.
    c. the sample will probably not be representative of the population of interest.
    d. of all the above reasons.

3. The concept of control is important in psychological research because:
    a. without control over independent and dependent variables, researchers cannot describe, predict, or explain behavior.
    b. experimental control allows researchers to study the influence of one or two independent variables on a dependent variable while holding other potential influences constant.
    c. without experimental control, results cannot be generalized from a sample to a population.
    d. of all the above reasons.

4. Martina believes that high doses of caffeine slow a person's reaction time. In order to test this belief, she has five friends each drink three 8-ounce cups of coffee and then measures their reaction time on a learning task. What is wrong with Martina's research strategy?
    a. No independent variable is specified.
    b. No dependent variable is specified.
    c. There is no control condition.
    d. There is no provision for replication of the findings.

5. A researcher was interested in determining whether her students' test performance could be predicted from their proximity to the front of the classroom. So she matched her students' scores on a math test with their seating position. This study is an example of:
    a. experimentation.
    b. correlational research.
    c. a survey.
    d. naturalistic observation.

6. Your best friend criticizes psychological research for being artificial and having no relevance to behavior in real life. In defense of psychology's use of laboratory experiments you point out that:
    a. psychologists make every attempt to avoid artificiality by setting up experiments that closely simulate real-world environments.
    b. psychologists who conduct basic research are not concerned with the applicability of their findings to the real world.
    c. most psychological research is not conducted in a laboratory environment.
    d. psychologists intentionally study behavior in simplified environments in order to gain greater control over variables and to test general principles that help to explain many behaviors.

7. A professor constructs a questionnaire to determine how students at the university feel about nuclear disarmament. Which of the following techniques should be used in order to survey a random sample of the student body?
    a. Every student should be sent the questionnaire.
    b. Only students majoring in psychology should be asked to complete the questionnaire.
    c. Only students living on campus should be asked to complete the questionnaire.
    d. From an alphabetical listing of all students, every tenth (or fifteenth, e.g.) student should be asked to complete the questionnaire.

8. If eating saturated fat and the likelihood of contracting cancer are positively correlated, which of the following is true?
    a. Saturated fat causes cancer.
    b. People who are prone to develop cancer prefer foods containing saturated fat.
    c. A separate factor links the consumption of saturated fat to cancer.
    d. None of the above is necessarily true.

9. To say that "psychology is a science" means that:
   a. psychologists study only observable behaviors.
   b. psychologists study thoughts and actions with an attitude of skepticism and derive their conclusions from direct observations.
   c. psychological research should be free of value judgments.
   d. all of the above are true.

10. Rashad, who is participating in a psychology experiment on the effects of alcohol on perception, is truthfully told by the experimenter that he has been assigned to the "high-dose condition." What is wrong with this experiment?
   a. There is no control condition.
   b. Rashad's expectations concerning the effects of "high doses" of alcohol on perception may influence his performance.
   c. Knowing that Rashad is in the "high-dose" condition may influence the experimenter's interpretations of Rashad's results.
   d. Both b. and c. are correct.

11. A friend majoring in anthropology is critical of psychological research because it often ignores the influence of culture on thoughts and actions. You point out that:
   a. there is very little evidence that cultural diversity has a significant effect on specific behaviors and attitudes.
   b. most researchers assign subjects to experimental and control conditions in such a way as to fairly represent the cultural diversity of the population under study.
   c. it is impossible for psychologists to control for every possible variable that might influence research participants.
   d. even when specific thoughts and actions vary across cultures, as they often do, the underlying processes are much the same.

12. The scientific attitude of humility is based on the idea that:
   a. researchers must evaluate new ideas and theories objectively rather than accept them blindly.
   b. scientific theories must be testable.
   c. simple explanations of behavior make better theories than do complex explanations.
   d. researchers must be prepared to reject their own ideas in the face of conflicting evidence.

13. Which of the following procedures is an example of the use of a placebo?
   a. In a test of the effects of a drug on memory, a subject is led to believe that a harmless pill actually contains an active drug.
   b. A subject in an experiment is led to believe that a pill, which actually contains an active drug, is harmless.
   c. Subjects in an experiment are not told which treatment condition is in effect.
   d. Neither the subjects nor the experimenter know which treatment condition is in effect.

14. If height and body weight are positively correlated, which of the following is true?
   a. There is a cause-effect relationship between height and weight.
   b. As height increases, weight decreases.
   c. Knowing a person's height, one can predict his or her weight.
   d. All of the above are true.

15. The football team's punter wants to determine how consistent his punting distances have been during the past season. He should compute the:
   a. mean.   c. mode.
   b. median.   c standard deviation.

16. Joe believes that his basketball game is always best when he wears his old gray athletic socks. Joe is a victim of the phenomenon called:
   a. statistical significance.
   b. overconfidence.
   c. illusory correlation.
   c. hindsight bias.

17. Esteban refuses to be persuaded by an advertiser's claim that people using their brand of gasoline average 50 miles per gallon. His decision probably is based on:
   a. the possibility that the average is the mean, which could be artificially inflated by a few extreme scores.
   b. the absence of information about the size of the sample studied.
   c. the absence of information about the variation in sample scores.
   d. all of the above.

18. Bob scored 43 out of 70 points on his psychology exam. He was worried until he discovered that most of the class earned the same score. Bob's score was equal to the:
   a. mean.   c. mode.
   b. median.   d. range.

19. The four families on your block all have annual household incomes of $25,000. If a new family with an annual income of $75,000 moved in, which measure of central tendency would be most affected?

a. mean   c. mode
b. median   d. standard deviation

20. Dr. Salazar recently completed an experiment in which she compared reasoning ability in a sample of females and a sample of males. The means of the female and male samples equaled 21 and 19, respectively, on a 25-point scale. A statistical test revealed that her results were not statistically significant. What can Dr. Salazar conclude?

a. Females have superior reasoning ability.
b. The difference in the means of the two samples is probably due to chance variation.
c. The difference in the means of the two samples is reliable.
d. None of the above is true.

Essay Question

Elio has a theory that regular exercise can improve thinking. Help him design an experiment evaluating this theory by answering questions (a) through (d). (Use the space below to list the points you want to make, and organize them. Then write the essay on a separate piece of paper.)

a. How would you restate Elio's theory as a testable hypothesis?

b. What are the independent and dependent variables and how could they be manipulated, or measured?

c. Do you need a control group? If so, why, and what should they do?

d. How should subjects be selected and assigned to the various conditions of the experiment?

Key Terms

Writing Definitions

Using your own words, on a separate piece of paper write a brief definition or explanation of each of the following.

1. hindsight bias
2. critical thinking
3. theory
4. hypothesis
5. operational definition
6. replication
7. case study
8. survey
9. false consensus effect
10. population
11. random sample
12. naturalistic observation
13. correlation
14. scatterplot
15. illusory correlation
16. experiment
17. placebo
18. double-blind procedure
19. placebo effect
20. experimental condition
21. control condition
22. random assignment
23. independent variable
24. dependent variable
25. mode
26. mean
27. median
28. range
29. standard deviation
30. statistical significance
31. culture

Cross-Check

As you learned in the Introduction, reviewing and overlearning of material are important to the learning process. After you have written the definitions of the key terms in this chapter, you should complete the crossword puzzle to ensure that you can reverse the process—recognize the term, given the definition.

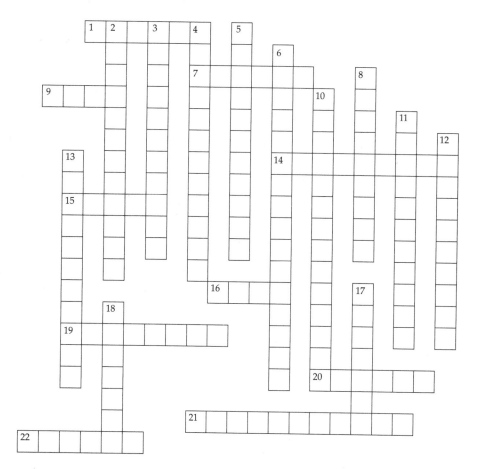

ACROSS

1. Score that falls at the 50th percentile, cutting a distribution in half.
7. Integrated set of principles that organizes and predicts observations.
9. Most frequently occurring score in a distribution.
14. Descriptive research strategy in which one person is studied in great depth.
15. Measure of variation computed as the difference between the highest and lowest scores in a distribution.
16. Measure of central tendency computed by adding the scores in a distribution and dividing by the number of scores.
19. False perception of a correlation between two events when none exists.
20. Descriptive research strategy in which a representative, random sample of people are questioned about their attitudes or behaviors.
21. Depiction of the relationship between two sets of scores by means of a graphed cluster of dots.
22. Sample in which every member of the population has an equal chance of being included.

DOWN

2. Experimental condition in which subjects are exposed to the independent variable being studied.
3. In an experiment, the variable being manipulated and tested by the investigator.
4. Research strategy in which behavior is observed and recorded in naturally occurring situations without any manipulation or control.
5. A precise statement of the procedures used to define a variable.

6. Careful reasoning that examines assumptions, discerns hidden values, evaluates evidence, and assesses conclusions.
8. The bias in which we believe, after learning an outcome, that we could have foreseen it.
10. Our tendency to overestimate the extent to which others share our beliefs and behaviors.
11. Control procedure in which neither the experimenter nor the research subjects are aware of which condition is in effect.
12. Testable prediction, often implied by a theory.
13. Statistical measure that indicates the extent to which one factor predicts another factor.
17. Experimental condition in which the treatment of interest is withheld.
18. Inert substance or condition that is administered as a test of whether the experimental subject, who mistakenly thinks the treatment is in effect, behaves in the same way as he or she would if the treatment were actually present.

Answers

The Need for Psychological Science

Section Preview

1. Two reliable phenomena—hindsight bias and overconfidence—make intuition and common sense untrustworthy. Hindsight bias is the tendency to perceive an outcome that has already occurred as being obvious and predictable. Overconfidence is the tendency to think we know more about an issue than we actually do and to overestimate the accuracy of that knowledge.

2. As scientists, psychologists attempt to study thoughts and actions with an attitude of open-minded, curious skepticism. Scientists must also possess an attitude of humility, because they may have to reject their ideas in the light of new evidence. Whether applied to reading news reports or listening to a lecture, critical thinking examines assumptions, discerns hidden values, evaluates evidence, and assesses conclusions.

3. Scientists rely on theories to explain, organize, and predict the behaviors or events under study. Good theories give direction to research by generating testable predictions, called hypotheses. Operational definitions specify the procedures used to define and measure research variables. Such definitions prevent ambiguity by providing an exactness of meaning that allows other scientists to replicate (repeat) the study.

Stepping Through the Section

1. hindsight bias
2. overconfidence
3. skepticism; humility
4. critical thinking
5. theory; hypotheses
6. operational definitions; replicate
7. description; correlation; experimentation

Description

Section Preview

1. The simplest research strategy is description; examples include case studies, surveys, and naturalistic observation. In the case study one or more individuals is studied in great depth in the hope of revealing general principles underlying the behavior of all people. Surveys measure the self-reported attitudes or behaviors of a randomly selected representative sample of an entire group, or population. Naturalistic observation seeks to observe and record the behavior of organisms (including humans) in their natural environments.

2. Although descriptive research can suggest hypotheses for further study, it is limited to describing behavior and cannot reveal predictive, or cause-effect, relationships. One possible pitfall of case studies is that any given individual may be atypical, making the case misleading. Survey results may be misleading because even subtle changes in the order or wording of questions can influence responses. And the samples on which surveys are based may not be representative of the populations from which they are drawn.

Stepping Through the Section

1. case study; atypical
2. survey
3. wording
4. false consensus effect
5. random; population; does
6. are
7. vivid
8. naturalistic observation
9. describe
10. varies

Correlation

Section Preview

1. A correlation is a statistical measure of relationship, revealing how accurately one event predicts another. Correlations are often graphically represented as scatterplots. A positive correlation indicates a *direct* relationship in which two things increase or decrease together. A negative correlation indicates an *inverse* relationship in which one thing increases as the other decreases. A zero correlation means no relationship exists. A correlation between two events or behaviors means only that one event can be predicted from the other. Because two events may both be caused by some other event, a correlation between the two events does not mean that one caused the other. Correlation thus does not enable explanation.

2. A perceived correlation that does not really exist is an illusory correlation. Illusory correlations help explain superstitious beliefs; they arise from our eagerness to perceive order in events, even those that are random.

Stepping Through the Section

1. correlated; predict; positively correlated; negatively correlated

2. scatterplots

3. strength; weakness; causation; cause-effect

4. illusory correlation; superstitious

This is an example of a negative correlation. As one factor (time spent studying) increases, the other factor (anxiety level) decreases.

5. random events

6. more likely

Experimentation

Section Preview

1. Conducting experiments allows psychologists to explain behaviors in terms of cause-and-effect relationships. This is because experiments allow researchers to manipulate one or more experimental factors (the independent variables) while holding all other potential independent variables constant. If a subject's behavior (the dependent variable) changes, the change can be attributed to the influence of the independent variable under study. In the typical experiment, subjects are randomly assigned to either a control condition, in which the experimental treatment is absent, or an experimental condition, in which the treatment of interest is present.

2. Researchers randomly assign research subjects to the experimental and control conditions of experiments in order to minimize any pre-existing differences between the groups. Two other control techniques involve use of a placebo and the double-blind procedure. These help ensure that any changes in the dependent variable that occur are due to the independent variable rather than to researchers' or subjects' expectations.

Stepping Through the Section

1. experiments; manipulates; holding constant

2. placebo; placebo effect

3. double-blind procedure

4. control; experimental

5. random assignment

6. independent; dependent

Experimentation has the advantage of increasing the investigator's control of both relevant and irrelevant variables that might influence behavior. Experiments also permit the investigator to go beyond observation and description to uncover cause-and-effect relationships in behavior.

Statistical Reasoning

Section Preview

1. The mode is the most frequently occurring score in a distribution. The mean, or arithmetic average, is the sum of the scores divided by the number of scores. Although the mean is the most commonly reported measure of central tendency, it is extremely sensitive to unusual scores and therefore is potentially misleading as a representation of the average of a distribution that is skewed. The median is the score that falls at the 50th percentile.

2. The simplest measure of variation is the range— the difference between the lowest and highest scores in a distribution. As a measure of variation, the range is rather crude because it is based on only the two extreme scores in a distribution. A better gauge of variation is the standard deviation, which measures how much scores deviate from one another.

3. Although it is tempting to overgeneralize from highly select samples, the most reliable inferences about a population are based on a representative sample. A second important principle is that averages derived from samples with low variability are more reliable than those based on samples with high variability. A third is that averages based on more cases are more reliable than averages based on only a few cases. Generalizing to the population from a small sample with high variability is therefore inadvisable and potentially misleading.

4. When psychologists compare two samples to determine if their difference is statistically significant, they want to know whether the difference is real and not due to chance variation between the samples. When sample averages are reliable, and the difference between the averages for two samples is large, researchers can say that the difference has statistical significance.

Stepping Through the Section

1. mode; median; mean

2. mode

3. total sum; number

4. 50th

5. skewed; mean

6. low; high
7. range; standard deviation
8. gap between the lowest and highest scores
9. crude; is
10. more accurate; takes
11. representative; biased
12. low
13. less
14. significance; chance; reliable; relatively large

Frequently Asked Questions About Psychology

Section Preview

1. Psychologists intentionally conduct experiments on simplified behaviors in an artificial laboratory environment in order to gain control over the numerous independent and dependent variables present in more complex behaviors and the "real world." By studying simplified behaviors under controlled circumstances psychologists are able to test general principles of behavior that also operate in the real world.

   For similar reasons, psychologists often apply their findings from psychological studies of people from one culture to people in general. Although attitudes and behaviors vary greatly from culture to culture, the underlying principles are much the same. Furthermore, although males and females are different in many ways, psychologically and biologically they are also overwhelmingly alike.

2. Some psychologists study animals simply to understand animal behavior. For the same reasons that psychologists investigate human behavior in simplified laboratory environments before attempting to understand more complex everyday behaviors, other psychologists attempt to learn more about human behavior by studying simpler, yet similar, behaviors in animals.

   Although animals in psychological research rarely experience pain, opposition to animal experimentation raises two important issues: (1) whether it is morally right to place the well-being of humans above that of animals, and (2) what safeguards should protect the well-being of animals.

   Ethical standards developed by the American Psychological Association and the British Psychological Society provide strict guidelines regarding the treatment of people and animals in psychology experiments.

3. No science, including psychology, is value-free.

Psychologists' values influence their choice of research topics, their observations, and their interpretations of research findings. Psychological knowledge is a power that, like all powers, can be used for good or evil. Many psychologists conduct research aimed at solving some of the world's most serious problems, including war, prejudice, overpopulation, and crime.

Stepping Through the Section

1. artificial; principles
2. ideas; behaviors; attitudes; traditions
3. principles or processes; genders
4. ethical; well-being

Ethical guidelines require investigators to (1) obtain informed consent from potential subjects, (2) protect them from harm and discomfort, (3) treat information obtained from subjects confidentially, and (4) fully explain the research afterward.

5. do
6. postmodernism; social; agree
7. favor; mental retardation; vary
8. do not have

Progress Test 1

Multiple-Choice Questions

1. a. is the answer. In a case study one subject is studied in depth. (p. 20)
   b. In survey research a group of people are interviewed.
   c. Correlations identify whether two factors are related.
   d. In an experiment an investigator manipulates one variable to observe its effect on another.

2. c. is the answer. Exercise is the variable being manipulated in the experiment. (p. 32)
   a. A control condition for this experiment would be a group of people not permitted to exercise.
   b. An intervening variable is a variable other than those being manipulated that may influence behavior.
   d. The dependent variable is the behavior measured by the experimenter—in this case, the effects of exercise.

3. c. is the answer. The control condition is that for which the experimental treatment (the new drug) is absent. (p. 32)
   a. A random sample is a subset of a population in which every person has an equal chance of being selected.

b. The experimental condition is the group for which the experimental treatment (the new drug) is present.

d. "Test group" is an ambiguous term; both the experimental and control group are tested.

4. **d.** is the answer. (p. 18)

   a. Hypotheses are testable propositions.

   b. Dependent variables are factors that may change in response to manipulated independent variables.

   c. Statistical indexes may be used to test specific hypotheses (and therefore as indirect tests of theories), but they are merely mathematical tools, no general principles, as are theories.

5. **d.** is the answer. In this case, the children are being observed in their normal environment rather than in a laboratory. (p. 23)

   a. Correlational research measures relationships between two factors. The psychologist may later want to determine whether there are correlations between the variables studied under natural conditions.

   b. In a case study, one subject is studied in depth.

   c. This is not an experiment because the psychologist is not directly controlling the variables being studied.

6. **d.** is the answer. (p. 19)

7. **d.** is the answer. (p. 17)

8. **b.** is the answer. Replication is the repetition of an experiment in order to determine whether its findings are reliable. It is not a research strategy. (p. 33).

9. **c.** is the answer. (p. 43)

   a., b., & d. Psychologists' personal values can influence all of these.

10. **b.** is the answer. (p. 24)

    a. & c. These answers would have been correct had the question stated that there is a *positive* correlation between shoe size and IQ. Actually, there is probably no correlation at all!

11. **d.** is the answer. In an experiment, it would be possible to manipulate alcohol consumption and observe the effects, if any, on memory. (p. 31)

    a., b., & c. These answers are incorrect because only by directly controlling the variables of interest can a researcher uncover cause-and-effect relationships.

12. **d.** is the answer. (p. 22)

    a. A sample is a subset of a population.

    b. & c. Control and experimental groups are used in experimentation, not in survey research.

13. **c.** is the answer. The mean is the sum of scores divided by the number of scores. $[(2 + 3 + 7 + 6 + 1 + 4 + 9 + 5 + 8 + 2)/10 = 4.7.]$ (p. 35)

14. **d.** is the answer. When the scores are put in order (1, 2, 3, 4, 7, 7, 8), 4 is at the 50th percentile, splitting the distribution in half. (p. 35)

15. **b.** is the answer. The mode is the most frequently occurring score. Since there are more "twos" than any other number in the distribution, 2 is the mode. (p. 35)

16. **d.** is the answer. (p. 37)

17. **c.** is the answer. (p. 37)

    a. A statistically significant difference may or may not be of practical importance.

    b. This is often the case when a difference is not statistically significant.

18. **c.** is the answer. (p. 36)

19. **d.** is the answer. (p. 15)

    a. This is the tendency to overestimate the extent to which others share our beliefs.

    b. This is the false perception of a relationship between two events.

    c. This is the tendency to believe, after learning an outcome, that one could have foreseen it.

20. **a.** is the answer. As an average, calculated by adding all scores and dividing by the number of scores, the mean could easily be affected by the inclusion of a few extreme scores. (p. 36)

    b. The range is not a measure of central tendency.

    c. & d. The median and mode give equal weight to all scores; each counts only once and its numerical value is unimportant.

Matching Items

1. i (p. 37)	6. b (p. 36)	11. d (p. 36)
2. f (p. 35)	7. h (p. 36)	12. m (p. 22)
3. l (p. 32)	8. g (p. 24)	13. k (p. 17)
4. j (p. 14)	9. c (p. 35)	14. n (p. 27)
5. e (p. 35)	10. a (p. 35)	

Progress Test 2

Multiple-Choice Questions

1. **d.** is the answer. Only experiments can reveal cause-and-effect relationships; the other methods can only *describe* relationships. (p. 31)

2. **a.** is the answer. (p. 33)

   b., c., & d. There was no actual improvement in memory or self-esteem in this experiment.

3. **d.** is the answer. Only about 7 percent of all psychological experiments involve animals. (p. 41)

4. **d.** is the answer. (p. 32)

   a. The control condition is the comparison group, in which the experimental treatment (the treatment of interest) is absent.

b. Memory is a directly observed and measured dependent variable in this experiment.

c. Attention is the independent variable, which is being manipulated.

5. **a.** is the answer. (p. 22)
   b. This refers to illusory correlation.
   c. This refers to overconfidence.

6. **b.** is the answer. (p. 14)
   a. The phenomenon is related to hindsight rather than foresight.
   c. & d. The phenomenon doesn't involve whether or not the intuitions are correct but rather people's attitude that they had the correct intuition.

7. **b.** is the answer. If enough subjects are used in an experiment and they are randomly assigned to the two groups, any differences that emerge between the groups should stem from the experiment itself. (p. 32)
   a., c., & d. None of these terms describes precautions taken in setting up groups for experiments.

8. **b.** is the answer. (p. 27)

9. **a.** is the answer. (p. 22)
   b. & c. Large, random samples are more likely to be representative of the populations from which they are drawn.

10. **d.** is the answer. Because we are sensitive to dramatic or unusual events, we are especially likely to perceive a relationship between them. (p. 27)
    a., b., & c. The relationship between vivid events is no more likely to be significant, positive, or negative than that between less dramatic events.

11. **b.** is the answer. (pp. 18–19)
    a. In fact, the artificiality of experiments is part of an intentional attempt to create a controlled environment in which to test theoretical principles that are applicable to all behaviors.
    c. Some psychological theories go against what we consider common sense; furthermore, on many issues that psychology addresses, it's far from clear what the "common sense" position is.
    d. Psychology has always had ties to other disciplines, and in recent times, these ties have been increasing.

12. **d.** is the answer. Correlations show how well one factor can be predicted from another. (p. 26)
    a. Because a case study focuses in great detail on the behavior of an individual, it's unlikely to be useful in showing whether predictions are possible.
    b. Naturalistic observation is a method of describing, rather than predicting, behavior.

c. In experimental research the effects of manipulated independent variables on dependent variables are measured. It is not clear how an experiment could help determine whether IQ tests predict academic success.

13. **b.** is the answer. The control condition is the one in which the treatment—in this case, pollution—is absent. (p. 32)
    a. Students in the polluted room would be in the experimental condition.
    c. Presumably, all students in both conditions were randomly assigned to their groups. Random assignment is a method for establishing groups, rather than a condition.
    d. The word *dependent* refers to a kind of variable in experiments; conditions are either experimental or control.

14. **c.** is the answer. The lighting is the factor being manipulated. (p. 32)
    a. & d. These answers are incorrect because they involve aspects of the experiment other than the variables.
    b. This answer is the dependent, not the independent, variable.

15. **b.** is the answer. (p. 35)

16. **c.** is the answer. The mean is the sum of the scores divided by the number of scores. (60/10 = 6.) (p. 35)

17. **c.** is the answer. When the scores are put in order (5, 6, 7, 8, 9, 10, 11), 8 is at the 50th percentile, splitting the distribution in half. (p. 35)

18. **d.** is the answer. Since the range is the difference between the highest and lowest scores, it is by definition affected by extreme scores. (p. 36)
    a. & c. The mean and mode are measures of central tendency, not of variation.
    b. The standard deviation is less affected than the range because, when it is calculated, the deviation of every score from the mean is computed.

19. **b.** is the answer. Averages derived from scores with low variability tend to be more reliable estimates of the populations from which they are drawn. Thus, a. and c. are incorrect. Because the standard deviation is a more accurate estimate of variability than the range, d. is incorrect. (p. 36)

20. **d.** is the answer. A difference that is statistically significant is a true difference, rather than an apparent difference due to factors such as sampling variation, and it is reliable. (p. 37)

Matching Items
1. e (p. 19)   5. j (p. 32)   9. f (p. 19)
2. h (p. 18)   6. d (p. 32)   10. g (p. 32)
3. b (p. 32)   7. a (p. 20)   11. i (p. 31)
4. c (p. 32)   8. k (p. 21)   12. l (p. 32)

Thinking Critically About Chapter 1

Multiple-Choice Questions

1. **b.** is the answer. A general belief such as this one is a theory; it helps organize, explain, and generate testable predictions (called hypotheses) such as "men drink more soft drinks than women." (pp. 18–19)
   c. & d. Independent and dependent variables are experimental treatments and behaviors, respectively. Beliefs and predictions may involve such variables, but are not themselves those variables.

2. **c.** is the answer. The members of one sorority are likely to share more interests, traits, and attitudes than will the members of a random sample of college students. (p. 22)
   a. & b. Unlike experiments, surveys do not specify or directly manipulate independent and dependent variables. In a sense, survey questions are independent variables, and the answers, dependent variables.

3. **b.** is the answer. (p. 32)
   a. Although case studies, surveys, naturalistic observation, and correlational research do not involve control of variables, they nevertheless enable researchers to describe and predict behavior.
   c. Whether or not a sample is representative of a population, rather than control over variables, determines whether results can be generalized from a sample to a population.

4. **c.** is the answer. In order to determine the effects of caffeine on reaction time, Martina needs to measure reaction time in a control, or comparison, group that does not receive caffeine. (p. 32)
   a. Caffeine is the independent variable.
   b. Reaction time is the dependent variable.
   d. Whether or not Martina's experiment can be replicated is determined by the precision with which she reports her procedures, which is not an aspect of research strategy.

5. **b.** is the answer. (p. 24)
   a. This is not an experiment because the researcher is not manipulating the independent variable (seating position); she is merely measuring whether variation in this factor predicts test performance.

   c. If the study were based entirely on students' self-reported responses, this would be a survey.
   d. This study goes beyond naturalistic observation, which merely describes behavior as it occurs, to determine if test scores can be predicted from students' seating position.

6. **d.** is the answer. (p. 39)

7. **d.** is the answer. Selecting every tenth person would probably result in a representative sample of the entire population of students at the university. (p. 22)
   a. It would be difficult, if not impossible, to survey every student on campus.
   b. Psychology students are not representative of the entire student population.
   c. This answer is incorrect for the same reason as b. This would constitute a biased sample.

8. **d.** is the answer. (p. 24)
   a. Correlation does not imply causality.
   b. Again, a positive correlation simply means that two factors tend to increase or decrease together; further relationships are not implied.
   c. A separate factor may or may not be involved. That the two factors are correlated does not imply a separate factor. There may, for example, be a direct causal relationship between the two factors themselves.

9. **b.** is the answer. Psychology is a science because psychologists use the scientific method and approach the study of behavior and mental processes with attitudes of open-minded skepticism and humility. (p. 17)
   a. Psychologists study both overt (observable) behaviors and covert thoughts and feelings.
   c. Psychologists' values definitely do influence their research.

10. **d.** is the answer. (p. 32)
    a. The low-dose comparison group is the control group.

11. **d.** is the answer. (p. 40)
    a. In fact, just the opposite is true.
    b. Actually, psychological experiments tend to use the most readily available subjects, often white North American college students.
    c. Although this may be true, psychological experiments remain important because they help explain underlying processes of human behavior everywhere. Therefore, d. is a much better response than c.

12. **d.** is the answer. (p. 17)
    a. This follows from the attitude of open-minded skepticism, rather than humility.

b. & c. Although both of these are true of the scientific method, neither has anything to do with humility.

13. **a.** is the answer. (p. 32)
    b. Use of a placebo tests whether the behavior of an experimental subject, who mistakenly believes that a treatment (such as a drug) is in effect, is the same as it would be if the treatment were actually present.
    c. & d. These are examples of "blind" and "double-blind" control procedures.

14. **c.** is the answer. If height and weight are positively correlated, increased height is associated with increased weight. Thus, one can predict a person's weight from his or her height. (p. 24)
    a. Correlation does not imply causality.
    b. This situation depicts a negative correlation between height and weight.

15. **d.** is the answer. A small or large standard deviation indicates whether a distribution is homogeneous or variable. (p. 36)
    a., b., & c. These statistics would not give any information regarding the consistency of performance.

16. **c.** is the answer. A correlation that is perceived but doesn't actually exist, as in the example, is known as an illusory correlation. (p. 27)
    a. Statistical significance is a statement of how likely it is that an obtained result occurred by chance.
    b. Overconfidence is the tendency to think we are more right than we actually are.
    d. Hindsight bias is the tendency to believe, after learning an outcome, that one would have foreseen it.

17. **d.** is the answer. (pp. 35, 36, & 37)

18. **c.** is the answer. (p. 35)
    a. The mean is computed as the sum of the scores divided by the number of scores.
    b. The median is the midmost score in a distribution.
    d. The range is the difference between the highest and lowest scores in a distribution.

19. **a.** is the answer. The mean is strongly influenced by extreme scores. In this example, the mean would change from $25,000 to (75,000 + 25,000 + 25,000 + 25,000 + 25,000)/5 = $35,000. (p. 35)
    b. & c. Both the median and the mode would remain $25,000, even with the addition of the fifth family's income.
    d. The standard deviation is a measure of variation, not central tendency.

20. **b.** is the answer. (pp. 37–38)

a. If the difference between the sample means is not significant, then the groups probably do not differ in the measured ability.
c. When a result is not significant it means that the observed difference is unreliable.

Essay Question

a. Sample hypothesis: Daily aerobic exercise for one month will improve memory.

b. Exercise is the independent variable. The dependent variable is memory. Exercise could be manipulated by having people in an experimental group jog for 30 minutes each day. Memory could be measured by comparing the number of words subjects recall from a test list studied before the exercise experiment begins, and again afterward.

c. A control group that does not exercise *is* needed so that any improvement in the experimental group's memory can be attributed to exercise, and not to some other factor, such as the passage of one month's time or familiarity with the memory test. The control group should engage in some nonexercise activity for the same amount of time each day that the experimental group exercises.

d. The subjects should be randomly selected from the population at large, and then randomly assigned to the experimental and control groups.

Key Terms

Writing Definitions

1. **Hindsight bias** refers to the tendency to believe, after learning an outcome—including a psychological research finding—that one would have foreseen it. (p. 14)

2. **Critical thinking** is careful reasoning that examines assumptions, discerns hidden values, evaluates evidence, and assesses conclusions. (p. 17)

3. A **theory** is an explanation using an integrated set of principles that organizes and predicts observations. (p. 18)

4. A **hypothesis** is a testable prediction, often implied by a theory; testing the hypothesis helps scientists to test the theory. (p. 19)

   Example: In order to test his theory of why people conform, Solomon Asch formulated the testable **hypothesis** that an individual would be more likely to go along with the majority opinion of a large group than with that of a smaller group.

5. **Operational definitions** are precise statements of the procedures (operations) used to define independent and dependent variables. (p. 19)

6. **Replication** is the process of repeating an experiment, often with different subjects and in different situations, to see whether the basic finding generalizes to other subjects and circumstances. (p. 19)

7. The **case study** is a descriptive research strategy in which one person is studied in great depth, often with the intention of revealing universal principles. (p. 20)

8. The **survey** is a descriptive research strategy in which a representative, random sample of people are questioned about their attitudes or behavior. (p. 21)

9. The **false consensus effect** is the tendency to overestimate the extent to which others share our beliefs and behaviors. (p. 22)

10. A **population** consists of all the members of a group being studied. (p. 22)

11. A **random sample** is one that is representative because every member of the population has an equal chance of being included. (p. 22)

12. **Naturalistic observation** involves observing and recording behavior in naturally occurring situations without trying to manipulate or control the situation. (p. 23)

13. **Correlation** is a statistical measure that indicates the extent to which two factors vary together and thus how well one factor can be predicted from the other. Correlations can be positive or negative. (p. 24)

    Example: If there is a **positive correlation** between air temperature and ice cream sales, the warmer (higher) it is, the more ice cream is sold. If there is a **negative correlation** between air temperature and sales of cocoa, the cooler (lower) it is, the more cocoa is sold.

14. A **scatterplot** is a depiction of the relationship between two variables by means of a graphed cluster of dots. (p. 24)

15. **Illusory correlation** is the false perception of a relationship between two events when none exists. (p. 27)

16. An **experiment** is a research strategy in which a researcher directly manipulates one or more factors (independent variables) in order to observe their effect on some behavior or mental process (the dependent variable); experiments therefore make it possible to establish cause-and-effect relationships. (p. 31)

17. A **placebo** is an inert substance or condition that is administered as a test of whether an experimental subject, who mistakenly thinks a treatment is in effect, behaves the same as he or she would if the treatment were actually present. (p. 32)

18. A **double-blind procedure** is a control procedure in which neither the experimenter nor the research subjects are aware of which condition is in effect. It is used to prevent experimenters' and subjects' expectations from influencing the results of an experiment. (p. 32)

19. The **placebo effect** is any effect on behavior caused by a placebo. (p. 32)

20. The **experimental condition** of an experiment is one in which subjects are exposed to the independent variable being studied. (p. 32)

    Example: In the study of the effects of a new drug on reaction time, subjects in the **experimental condition** would actually receive the drug being tested.

21. The **control condition** of an experiment is one in which the treatment of interest, or independent variable, is withheld so that comparison to the experimental condition can be made. (p. 32)

    Example: The **control condition** for an experiment testing the effects of a new drug on reaction time would be a group of subjects given a placebo (inactive drug or sugar pill) instead of the drug being tested.

22. **Random assignment** is the procedure of assigning subjects to the experimental and control conditions by chance in order to minimize preexisting differences between the groups. (p. 32)

23. The **independent variable** of an experiment is the factor being manipulated and tested by the investigator. (p. 32)

    Example: In the study of the effects of a new drug on reaction time, the drug is the **independent variable**.

24. The **dependent variable** of an experiment is the factor being measured by the investigator. (p. 32)

    Example: In the study of the effects of a new drug on reaction time, the subjects' reaction time is the **dependent variable**.

25. The **mode** is the most frequently occurring score in a distribution; it is the simplest measure of central tendency to determine. (p. 35)

26. The **mean** is the arithmetic average, the measure of central tendency computed by adding the scores in a distribution and dividing by the number of scores. (p. 35)

27. The **median**, another measure of central tendency, is the score that falls at the 50th percentile, cutting a distribution in half. (p. 35)

    Example: When the mean of a distribution is affected by a few extreme scores, the median is the more appropriate measure of central tendency.

28. The **range** is a measure of variation computed as the difference between the highest and lowest scores in a distribution. (p. 36)

29. The **standard deviation** is the average amount by which the scores in a distribution deviate around the mean. Because it is based on every score in the distribution, it is a more precise measure of variation than the range. (p. 36)

30. **Statistical significance** means that an obtained result, such as the difference between the averages for two samples, very likely reflects a real difference rather than sampling variation or chance factors. Tests of statistical significance help researchers decide when they can justifiably generalize from an observed instance. (p. 37)

31. **Culture** is the enduring behaviors, ideas, attitudes, and traditions shared by a large group of people and transmitted from one generation to the next. (p. 37)

Cross-Check

ACROSS	DOWN
1. median	2. experimental
7. theory	3. independent
9. mode	4. naturalistic
14. case study	5. operational
15. range	6. critical thinking
16. mean	8. hindsight
19. illusory	10. false consensus
20. survey	11. double-blind
21. scatterplot	12. hypothesis
22. random	13. correlation
	17. control
	18. placebo

FOCUS ON VOCABULARY AND LANGUAGE

Page 13: . . . to remedy their woes, millions of people turn to "psychology." In order to alleviate or fix (*remedy*) their misery, anxiety, grief, pain, and suffering (*woes*), people seek help from "psychology." (Psychology is in quotes because Myers wants to point out that not everything you think of as "psychology" is part of scientific psychology.)

The Need for Psychological Science

Page 13: . . . helps *winnow* sense from nonsense. *Winnow* means to separate out and was originally used to describe the separation of chaff (dust, etc.) from the grains of wheat. The scientific method helps sort out, or separate (*winnow*), good ideas from bad ones.

Page 13: Some say psychology merely *documents* what people already know and *dresses it in jargon.* Some people criticize psychology, saying that it simply reports (*documents*) common sense, or what's obvious to everyone. Instead of stating something plainly, the critics suggest, psychology translates the information into the specialized and obscure vocabulary of the discipline (*dresses it up in jargon*). Myers makes it very clear with some good examples (pp. 14, 15) that this criticism is not justified and points out that our intuitions about reality can often be very mistaken.

Page 14: We're all *after-the-fact pundits.* A pundit is a very knowledgeable person. After the outcome of an event is known, anyone familiar with the result can claim to have foreseen it (an *after-the-fact pundit*). Myers refers to this tendency as the "I-knew-it-all-along" phenomenon or "hindsight bias."

Page 14: How easy it is to seem *astute* when *drawing the bull's eye after the arrow has struck.* In the sport of archery the task is to shoot the arrow at the red circle in the center of the target (the *bull's eye*). If we first shoot an arrow, then draw the target so that the arrow is in the center (in the *bull's eye*), we can appear to be very accurate. Myers uses this analogy to illustrate how the hindsight bias can lead us to believe that we are shrewd (*astute*) and would have been able to predict outcomes that we have learned after-the-fact.

Page 14: "Out of sight, out of mind" and *"Absence makes the heart grow fonder."* These two sayings, or expressions, about romantic love have opposite meanings. The first one suggests that when couples are apart (*out of sight*) they are less likely to think about each other (*out of mind*) than when they are together. The second saying makes the point that being separated (*absence*) increases the feelings of love the couple shares (*makes the heart grow fonder*). People who are told that the results of a study support the first expression (*out of sight, out of mind*) see this as mere common sense. People told that the results support the second expression (*absence makes the heart grow fonder*) also say this is obviously true. There is clearly a problem here; relying on common sense can lead to opposite conclusions.

Page 15: . . . our intuition may tell us that familiarity breeds contempt. . . . This expression (and others) are based on many casual observations but are often wrong. For example, is it true that the better you know someone (*familiarity*), the more likely it is that you will dislike the person (have *contempt*)? In fact, research shows that the opposite is probably true. (Your text, again and again, will emphasize the fact that our common sense and intuition do not always provide us with reliable evidence.)

Page 16: . . . drop a course . . . This means to stop going to class and to have your name removed from the class list.

Page 16: . . . drop out. . . . This means to stop going to school either permanently or temporarily. (A person who drops out of college or university is called a drop-out.) Research shows that students are frequently overconfident about their own predictions that they will not cancel (*drop*) any courses and that they will obtain their college degrees within five years (i.e., they won't become *drop-outs*).

Page 16: Underlying all science is a *hard-headed curiosity*. *Hard-headed* here means to be practical, uncompromising, realistic, or unswayed by sentiment. All science, including psychology, is guided by this realistic desire to know (*curiosity*) about nature and life.

Page 16: . . . leap of faith. This is a belief in something in the absence of demonstrated proof. Some questions—about the existence of God or life after death, for example—cannot be answered by science and cannot be scientifically proved or disproved; if a person believes, then it is on the basis of trust and confidence alone (*leap of faith*).

Page 16: . . . the proof is in the pudding. This comes from the expression "*the proof of the pudding is in the eating.*" A *pudding* is a sweet dessert. We can test (or prove) the quality of the dessert (*pudding*) by trying it (*eating*). Likewise, many questions, even if they appear to make little sense (*crazy-sounding ideas*—p. 17), can be tested using the scientific method.

Page 17: . . . auras . . . An *aura* is a bright glow surrounding a figure or an object. Some believe that humans have auras which only certain people can see. The magician James Randi proposed a simple test of this claim, but nobody who is alleged to have this magical power (*aura-seer*) has taken the test.

Page 17: More often, it relegates *crazy-sounding ideas* to the *mountain* of forgotten claims. . . . The use of scientific inquiry can get rid of or dispose of (*relegate*) non-sensible concepts (*crazy-sounding ideas*) to the large stack or pile (*mountain*) of ridiculous ideas now forgotten.

Page 17: In the *arena* of competing ideas . . . An *arena* is an area where games, sports, and competitions take place. Myers is suggesting that in an area (*arena*) where there is a contest between ideas (*competing ideas*), skeptical testing can help discover the truth.

Page 17: . . . then so much the worse for our ideas. This means that we have to give up, or get rid of, our ideas if they are shown to be wrong (*so much the worse for them*). We have to be humble (i.e., have humility).

Page 17: "The rat is always right." This early *motto* (a phrase used as a maxim or guiding principle) comes from the fact that for most of the first half of this century psychology used animals in its research (especially in the study of learning). The *rat* became a symbol of this research, and its behavior or performance in experiments demonstrated the truth. If the truth, as shown by the rat, is contrary to the prediction or hypothesis, then one has to be humble about it and try another way.

Page 17: We all view nature through the *spectacles* of our *preconceived ideas*. This means that what we already believe (*our preconceived ideas*) influences, and to some extent determines, what we look for and actually see or discover in nature. It's as though the type of eyeglasses (*spectacles*) we wear limits what we can see.

Page 18: . . . gut feelings . . . This refers to basic intuitive reactions or responses. Critical thinking requires determining whether a conclusion is based simply on a subjective opinion (*gut feeling*) or anecdote (a story someone tells) or on reliable scientific evidence.

Page 18: . . . debunked . . . This means to remove glamor or credibility from established ideas, persons, and traditions. Myers points out that scientific evidence and critical inquiry have indeed discredited (*debunked*) many popular presumptions.

Page 18: . . . one cannot simply *"play the tape"* and relive long-buried or *repressed* memories. . . . This is an example of a discredited (*debunked*) idea that hidden (*repressed*) memories can be accurately and reliably retrieved (*brought back*) intact and complete in the same way that *playing a tape* on a VCR allows us to watch exactly the same show over and over again.

Page 20: Although in some ways we *outsmart* the smartest computers, our *intuition* often goes *awry*. The main point is that humans are in many ways superior to computers (*we outsmart them*), but our beliefs, feelings, and perceptions (*intuition*) can often lead us astray (*awry*) or away from the truth. To be human means we can, and do, make mistakes (*to err is human*).

Page 20: . . . a scientific approach helps us *sift* reality from illusion, taking us beyond the limits of our intuition and common sense. A scientific (*or empirical*) attitude can separate (*sift*) what's real from what is not and take us beyond the limits of our vision and experience.

Description

Page 20: Sigmund Freud constructed his theory of personality from *a handful of case studies*. A *handful* means a very small number. Freud published only about twelve (*a handful of*) in-depth investigations of individuals (*case studies*).

Page 21: Numbers are numbing . . . and *Anecdotes can be alarming. . . .* Myers is playing with words here, using *alliteration* (repeating the same initial letter in a group of words). We are often overwhelmed and our senses deadened (*numbed*) by the sometimes inappropriate use of statistics and numbers. We are also startled or frightened (*alarmed*) by the strange stories people tell (*anecdotes*).

Page 21: . . . *bludgeoned to death* . . . To *bludgeon* means to hit repeatedly with a blunt object such as a stick or baseball bat. The true case of a 2-year-old child who was abducted or taken by force (*kidnapped*) and beaten and killed (*bludgeoned to death*) caused children and parents all over the country to become very alarmed (*scared*), even though this was an extremely rare and isolated incident.

Page 21: As psychologist Gordon Allport said, "Given a *thimbleful* of [dramatic] facts we rush to make *generalizations as large as a tub*." A *thimble* is a small metal container which fits over the top of the thumb or finger and is used while sewing to push the needle through the material, and a *tub* is a very large container (e.g., a *bathtub*). Allport is saying that given a *small* amount of information (a *thimbleful*),

we tend to make very *big* assumptions (*generalizations as large as a tub*).

Page 22: Most surveys sample a *target group*. The group of interest (*target group*) can be any group the researcher wants to talk about (*generalize to*), such as all people who smoke, or all college students, or all single mothers. It would be impossible to question or interview all the people in the group (*the population*), so a representative sample is chosen at random.

Page 23: . . . 1500 randomly sampled people, drawn from all areas of a country, provide a remarkably accurate *snapshot* of the opinions of a nation. A *snapshot* is a picture taken with a camera, and it captures what people are doing at a given moment in time. A good survey (*1500 randomly selected representative people*) gives an accurate picture (*snapshot*) of the opinions of the whole population of interest (the *target group*).

Page 23: . . . *having affairs* . . . Myers points out that the results of a large, nonrandom, nonrepresentative sample of married women which suggested that a large percentage (70 percent) were having sexual relations with someone other than their spouse (*having affairs or love affairs*) were not valid or reliable. A better study, using a smaller but a more representative and random sample, showed that the figure was actually closer to 10 percent. (Note: The word *affair* has other meanings. For example, in the phrase *"applying science to human affairs,"* the word *affairs* refers to human concerns or business.)

Correlation

Page 24: Statistics can help us see what the *naked eye* sometimes misses. When looking at an array of data consisting of different measures (e.g., height and temperament) for many subjects, it is very difficult to discern what, if any, relationships exist. Statistical tools, such as the correlation coefficient and the scatterplot, can help us see clearly what the unaided (*naked*) eye might not see. As Myers notes, we sometimes need statistical illumination to see what is in front of us.

Page 26: . . . *laypeople* . . . refers to people who do not belong to a particular profession. Both professionals and nonprofessionals (*laypeople*) mistakenly assume that correlation proves causation. It does not. Correlation means that one variable goes along with (predicts) another variable. For growing children, shoe size goes along with cognitive ability, but obviously one variable does not *cause* the other.

Page 28: If someone *flipped a coin* six times, would one of the following sequences of heads (H) or tails (T) be most likely: HHHTTT or HTTHTH or HHH-HHH? *Flipping a coin* means throwing or tossing the coin into the air and observing which side is facing up when it lands. (The side of the coin that usually has the imprint of the face of a famous person on it—e.g., the president or the queen—is called *heads* (*H*) and the other side is called *tails* (*T*). By the way, all of the above sequences are equally likely, but most people pick HTTHTH. Likewise, any series of 5 playing cards (e.g., a bridge or poker hand in a game of cards) is just as likely as any other hand.

Page 30: Thinking critically: *Hot and cold streaks.* Players who have *"hot hands"* can't seem to miss. Those who have *"cold"* ones can't find the center of the hoop. In this context, *hot* and *cold* do not refer to temperature. Here, being *hot* means doing well, and doing well consistently is *having a hot streak.* Having a run of poor luck is a *cold streak.* The crucial point, however, is that our intuition about sequences of events (*streaks*) often deceives us. Random sequences often are not what we think they should be, so when we think we're doing well (*hot*), we're not.

Experimentation

Page 32: Recap is an abbreviation of *recapitulate,* which means to repeat or go over briefly, to summarize. Myers summarizes (*recaps*) the important points in each section of the chapter.

Statistical Reasoning

Page 34: Off the top-of-the head estimates often misread reality and mislead the public. Without knowing actual data and numbers (statistics), people may guess at the figures (*top-of-the-head estimates*), which does not reflect the facts (*misreads reality*) and can deceive (*mislead*) the public. The figures generated in this manner are often easy to articulate, such as 10 percent or 50 percent (*big round numbers*) and, when repeated (*echoed*) by others, may eventually be believed to be true by most people (*they become public misinformation*).

Page 36: Because the bottom *half* of British income earners receive only a *quarter* of the *national income cake,* most British people, like most people everywhere, make less than the mean. Incomes are not normally distributed (they do not follow a bell-shaped curve when plotted as a data distribution), so a better measure of central tendency than the mean (arithmetic average) is either the median (the

score in the middle) or the mode (the most frequently occurring score). In Myers' example, half the people account for 25 percent of all the money earned in the country (*national income cake*); in this uneven (*skewed*) distribution, therefore, most people earn below-average wages.

Page 36: It [**standard deviation**] better *gauges* whether scores are packed together or dispersed, because it uses information from each score. The most commonly used statistic for measuring (*gauging*) how much scores differ from one another (their variation) is the standard deviation (SD). Using this formula, each score is compared to the mean; the result is an index of how spread out (*dispersed*) the scores are. A relatively small SD indicates that most of the scores are close to the average; a relatively large SD indicates that they are much more variable.

Page 36: Data are *"noisy."* Differences between groups may simply be due to random (*chance*) variations (*fluctuations*) in those particular samples. When data have a great deal of variability, they are said to be *"noisy,"* which may limit our ability to generalize them to the larger population. In order to determine if differences are reliable, we should be sure that (a) samples are random and representative, (b) scores in the sample are similar to each other (have low variability), and (c) a large number of subjects or observations are included. If these principles are followed, we can confidently make inferences about the differences between groups.

Frequently Asked Questions About Psychology

Page 39: . . . plunge in. In this context, *plunge in* means to move ahead quickly with the discussion. (Similarly, when you dive into a swimming pool [*plunge in*], you do so quickly.) Before going on with the discussion of psychology (*plunging in*), Myers addresses some important issues and questions.

Page 41: To understand how a combustion engine works, you would do better to study *a lawn mower's engine than that of a Mercedes.* A *Mercedes* is a very complex luxury car, and a *lawn mower* (a machine for cutting grass in the garden) has a very simple engine. To understand the principles underlying both machines, it is easier to study the simpler one. Likewise, when trying to understand the nervous system, it is better to study a simple one (e.g., sea slugs) than a complex one (humans).

Page 41: . . . idle curiosity. Curiosity means an eagerness to know, and *idle curiosity* means an eagerness to know for no particular reason. The critics of animal research claim that animals are made to suffer for no worthwhile reason (*out of idle curiosity*). Myers points out that these claims are unfounded.

Page 43: . . . most universities today screen research proposals through an *ethics committee. . . . Ethics committees* (groups of people concerned with moral behavior and acceptable standards of conduct) sub-ject research proposals to rigorous tests (*screen them*) to ensure that they are fair and reasonable and that they do not harm the participants' well-being.

Page 43: Values can also *color* "the facts." Our values (what we believe is right and true) can influence (*color*) our observations, interpretations, and conclusions ("the facts").

2:

Neuroscience and Behavior

Chapter Overview

Chapter 2 is concerned with the functions of the brain and its component neural systems, which provide the basis for all human behavior. Under the direction of the brain, the nervous and endocrine systems coordinate a variety of voluntary and involuntary behaviors and serve as the body's mechanisms for communication with the external environment.

The brain consists of the brainstem, the thalamus, the cerebellum, the limbic system, and the cerebral cortex. Knowledge of the workings of the brain has increased with advances in neuroscientific methods. Studies of split-brain patients have also given researchers a great deal of information about the specialized functions of the brain's right and left hemispheres.

Many students find the technical material in this chapter difficult to master. Not only are there many terms for you to remember, but you must also know the organization and function of the various divisions of the nervous system. Learning this material will require a great deal of rehearsal. Working the chapter review several times, drawing and labeling brain diagrams, and mentally reciting terms are all useful techniques for rehearsing this type of material.

NOTE: Answer guidelines for all Chapter 2 questions begin on page 63.

Introduction Preview

First, skim the introduction. Then read the following objective and, as you read, search for the information that will enable you to meet each objective. Answer guidelines are provided on page 63.

1. Explain why psychologists are concerned with human biology.

Stepping Through the Introduction

After you have read this material, complete the sentences and answer the questions. As you proceed, evaluate your performance by consulting the answers on page 63. Do not continue with the next section until you understand each answer. If you need to, review or reread the text material before continuing.

1. In the most basic sense, every idea, mood, memory, and behavior that an individual has ever experienced is a _____ phenomenon.

2. The theory that linked our mental abilities to bumps on the skull was _____ .

3. Researchers who study the links between biology and behavior are called _____

    _____ .

Neural Communication (pp. 48–54)

> David Myers at times uses idioms that are unfamiliar to some readers. If you do not know the meaning of any of the following words, phrases, or expressions in the context in which they appear in the text, refer to pages 74–75 for an explanation: *an ill-fated theory; a wrong-headed theory; fortunate fact of nature; building blocks; a sluggish 2 miles per hour to . . . a breakneck 200 or more miles; like a line of dominoes falling; somewhat like pushing a neuron's accelerator . . . rather like pushing its brake; How do we distinguish a gentle touch from a big hug; "protoplasmic kisses"; Roughly speaking, the neuron is democratic; runner's high; They trigger unpleasant, lingering aftereffects; Agonists excite by mimicking a particular neurotransmitter; some chemicals don't have the right shape to slither through this barrier.*

Section Preview

Answer guidelines are provided on page 63.

1. Explain why, at every level, our existence is both part of a larger system and a combination of smaller systems.

2. Describe the structure of a neuron and the process by which an action potential is triggered.

3. Describe how nerve cells communicate, and discuss the importance of neurotransmitters for human behavior.

4. Discuss the significance of endorphins, and explain how drugs influence neurotransmitters.

Stepping Through the Section

Answers are provided on page 64.

1. We are each a _____ , composed of _____ that are parts of larger _____ . Our body's neural system is built from billions of nerve cells, or _____ .

2. The extensions of a neuron that receive messages from other neurons are the _____ .

3. The extensions of a neuron that transmit information to other neurons are the _____ ; some of these extensions are insulated by a layer of fatty cells called the _____ _____ , which helps speed the neuron's impulses.

4. Identify the major parts of the neuron diagrammed below:

   a. _____ c. _____
   b. _____ d. _____

5. The neural impulse, or _____
   _____ , is a brief electrical charge
   that travels down a(n) _____ .

6. The fluid interior of a resting axon carries mostly
   _____ (positively/negatively)
   charged ions, while the fluid outside has mostly
   _____ (positively/negatively)
   charged ions. This polarization, called the
   _____ _____ , occurs
   because the cell membrane is selectively
   _____ .

7. An action potential occurs when the first part of
   the axon opens its gates and _____
   (positively/negatively) charged ions rush in,
   causing that part of the neuron to become
   _____ .

8. During the resting pause following an action
   potential, called the _____
   _____ , the neuron pumps
   _____ (positively/negatively)
   charged ions outside the cell.

9. In order to trigger a neural impulse,
   _____ signals minus
   _____ signals must exceed a certain
   intensity, called the _____ .
   Increasing a stimulus above this level
   _____ (will/will not) increase the
   neural impulse's intensity. This phenomenon is
   called an _____ -
   _____ -_____
   response.

Outline the sequence of reactions that occur when a
neural impulse is generated and transmitted from one
neuron to another.

10. The strength of a stimulus _____
    (does/does not) affect the speed of a neural
    impulse.

11. The junction between two neurons is called a
    _____ , and the gap is called the
    _____ _____ .

12. The chemical messengers that convey information across the gaps between neurons are called
    _____ . These chemicals unlock tiny
    channels on receptor sites, allowing electrically
    charged _____ (ions) to enter the
    neuron.

13. Neurotransmitters influence neurons either by
    _____ or _____ their
    readiness to fire. Excess neurotransmitters are
    reabsorbed by the sending neuron in a process
    called _____ .

14. Among the neurotransmitters that researchers
    have pinpointed are _____ , which
    influences movement, learning, attention, and
    emotion; _____ , which affects
    mood, hunger, sleep, and arousal;
    _____ , which helps control alertness and arousal; and _____ ,
    which is an inhibitory neurotransmitter implicated in eating and sleep disorders.

15. A neurotransmitter that is important in muscle contraction is _____ . The poison _____ produces paralysis by blocking the activity of this neurotransmitter.

16. Naturally occurring opiatelike neurotransmitters that are present in the brain are called _____ . When the brain is flooded with drugs such as _____ or _____ , it may stop producing these neurotransmitters.

17. Drugs that produce their effects by mimicking neurotransmitters are called _____ . Drugs that block the effects of neurotransmitters by occupying their _____ _____ are called _____ .

18. The molecular shape of some drugs prevents them from passing through the _____-_____ _____ by which the brain fences out unwanted chemicals.

19. The tremors of _____ disease are due to the death of neurons that produce the neurotransmitter _____ . People with this condition can be helped to regain control over their muscles by taking _____ .

The Nervous System (pp. 54–57)

> If you do not know the meaning of any of the following words, phrases, or expressions in the context in which they appear in the text, refer to pages 75–76 for an explanation: *Like an automatic pilot, it may be consciously overridden; yield an ever-changing wiring diagram that dwarfs a powerful computer; information highway; The knee-jerk response, for example; a headless warm body could do it.*

Section Preview

Answer guidelines are provided on page 64.

1. Identify the major divisions of the nervous system and their primary functions, and describe the neurons that carry information throughout the system.

2. Describe the operation of reflexes in the spinal cord and neural networks in the brain.

Stepping Through the Section

Answers are provided on page 64.

1. Taken altogether, the neurons of the body form the _____ _____ .

2. The brain and spinal cord comprise the _____ nervous system. The neurons that link the brain and spinal cord to the body's sense receptors, muscles, and glands form the _____ nervous system.

3. Sensory and motor axons are bundled into electrical cables called _____ .

4. Information arriving in the central nervous system from the body travels in _____ neurons. The neurons that enable internal communication within the central nervous system are called _____ .

5. The central nervous system sends instructions to the body's tissues by means of _____ neurons.

6. The division of the peripheral nervous system that transmits sensory input to the central nervous system and directs the movements of the skeletal muscles is the _____ nervous system.

7. Involuntary, self-regulating responses—those of the glands and muscles of internal organs—are controlled by the _____ nervous system.

8. The body is made ready for action by the _____ division of the autonomic nervous system.

9. The _____ division of the autonomic nervous system produces relaxation.

Describe and explain the sequence of physical reactions that occur in the body as an emergency is confronted and then passes.

10. Automatic responses to stimuli, called _____ , illustrate the work of the _____ _____ . Simple pathways such as these are involved in the _____-_____ response and in the _____ reflex.

Beginning with the sensory receptors in the skin, trace the course of a spinal reflex as a person reflexively jerks his or her hand away from an unexpectedly hot burner on a stove.

11. To perform complex computations, neurons in the brain cluster into work groups called _____ _____ .

The Brain (pp. 58–80)

If you do not know the meaning of any of the following words, phrases, or expressions in the context in which they appear in the text, refer to pages 76–78 for an explanation: *neural cartographers; we live in our heads; snoop on the messages . . . and on the mass action of billions; the right side of the body is wired to . . .; Other new windows into the brain . . . Supermanlike; snapshots of the brain's mind-making activity provide . . . divides its labor; exceptions to the rule of thumb; This peculiar cross-wiring is but one of many surprises the brain has to offer; . . . what London is to England's trains; a doughnut-shaped neural system; psychosurgery reduced fits of rage; magnificent mistake; wrinkled organ, shaped somewhat like the meat of an oversized walnut; eyes in the back of our head; most widespread falsehoods; What you experience as . . . the visible tip of the information-processing iceberg; hard-wired; one patient even managed to quip that he had a "splitting headache"; When the "two minds" are at odds; look alike to the naked eye . . . harmony of the whole; pretzel-shaped findings . . . breadstick-shaped story.*

Section Preview

Answer guidelines are provided on page 65.

1. Identify and explain the methods used in studying the brain.

2. Describe the functions of structures within the brainstem, as well as those of the thalamus and the cerebellum.

3. Describe the functions of the structures in the limbic system.

4. Describe the structure and functions of the cerebral cortex.

5. Discuss how damage to one of several different cortical areas can impair language functioning, and outline the process by which the brain directs reading aloud.

6. Discuss brain plasticity and what it reveals about brain reorganization.

7. Describe research on divided and undivided brains, and discuss what it reveals regarding normal brain functioning.

8. Discuss the brain organization of left-handed people and why left-handedness seems to diminish with age.

Stepping Through the Section

Answers are provided on page 66.

1. Researchers sometimes study brain function by producing _____ or by selectively destroying brain cells. The oldest technique for studying the brain involves _____ _____ of patients with brain injuries or diseases.

2. The _____ is a recording of the electrical activity of the whole brain.

3. A computer-generated image of a slice of the brain based on a series of x-ray photographs taken from different angles is called a

_____ _____ .

4. The technique depicting the level of activity of brain areas by measuring the brain's consumption of glucose is called the

_____ _____ .

Briefly explain the purpose of the PET scan.

5. A technique that produces clearer images of the brain by using magnetic fields and radio waves is known as _____ . By taking pictures less than a second apart, the

_____ _____

detects blood rushing to the part of the cortex thought to control the bodily activity being studied.

6. The oldest and innermost region of the brain is the _____ .

7. At the base of the brainstem, where the spinal cord enters the skull, lies the

_____ , which controls

_____ and _____ .

8. Nerves from each side of the brain cross over to connect with the body's opposite side in the

_____ .

9. The _____ _____ is contained inside the brainstem and helps control _____ . Electrically stimulating this area will produce an _____ animal. Lesioning this area will cause an animal to lapse into a _____ .

10. At the top of the brainstem sits the

_____ , which serves as the brain's sensory switchboard.

11. At the rear of the brainstem lies the

_____ . It influences one type of

_____ _____ and memory, but its major function is coordination of voluntary movement and _____ control.

12. The lower brain functions occur without

_____ effort, indicating that our brains process most information _____ (inside/outside) of our awareness.

13. Between the brainstem and cerebral hemispheres is the _____ system. One component of this system that processes memory is the

_____ .

14. Rage or fear will result from stimulation of different regions of the _____ .

15. Amygdala lesions, produced by _____ techniques, have been used to treat violent humans. This treatment is controversial and _____ (widely/seldom) used today.

16. Below the thalamus is the _____ , which regulates bodily maintenance behaviors such as _____ ,

_____ , and _____ . The hypothalamus also regulates behavior chemically through its influence on the _____ gland. Olds and Milner discovered that this region also contains _____ centers, which animals will work hard to have stimulated.

17. Some researchers believe that alcoholism, drug abuse, food binging, and other

_____ disorders, may stem from a genetic _____

_____ _____

in the pleasure systems of the brain.

18. The most complex functions of human behavior are linked to the most developed part of the brain, the _____ _____ .

19. The non-neural cells that support, protect, and nourish cortical neurons are called

_____ _____ .

20. Compared to the cortexes of lower mammals, the human cortex has a _____ (smoother/more wrinkled) surface. This _____ (increases/decreases) the overall surface area of our brains.

21. List the four lobes of the brain.

    a. _____ c. _____

    b. _____ d. _____

22. Electrical stimulation of one side of the _____ cortex, an arch-shaped region at the back of the _____ lobe, will produce movement on the opposite side of the body.

23. At the front of the parietal lobe lies the _____ cortex, which, when stimulated, elicits a sensation of _____ .

24. The more sensitive a body region, the greater the area of _____ _____ devoted to it.

25. Visual information is received in the _____ lobes, whereas auditory information is received in the _____ lobes.

26. Areas of the brain that don't receive sensory information or direct movement but, rather, integrate and interpret information received by other regions are known as _____ _____ . Approximately _____ of the human cortex is of this type. Such areas in the _____ lobe are involved in recognizing faces, making judgments, and carrying out plans, and in some aspects of personality.

27. Brain injuries may produce an impairment in language use called _____ . Studies of people with such impairments have shown that _____ _____ is involved in producing speech, _____ _____ is involved in understanding speech, and the _____ _____ is involved in recoding printed words into auditory form.

28. Although the mind's subsystems are localized in particular brain regions, the brain acts as a _____ _____ .

29. The quality of the brain that makes it possible for undamaged brain areas to take over the functions of damaged regions is known as _____ .

30. Although most severed neurons _____ (will/will not) regenerate, neural tissue can _____ in response to damage. New evidence also reveals the existence of master _____ cells in the developing fetal brain that can develop into any type of brain cell.

31. Because damage to it will impair language and understanding, the _____ hemisphere came to be known as the _____ hemisphere.

32. In treating several patients with severe epilepsy, Vogel and Bogen separated the two hemispheres of the brain by cutting the _____ _____ . When this structure is severed, the result is referred to as a _____ _____ .

33. In a split-brain patient, only the _____ hemisphere will be aware of an unseen object held in the left hand. In this case, the person would not be able to _____ the object. When different words are shown in the left and right visual fields, if the patient fixates on a point on the center line between the fields, the patient will be able to say only the word shown on the _____ .

Explain why a split-brain patient would be able to read aloud the word *pencil* flashed to his or her right visual field, but would be unable to identify a pencil by touch using only the left hand.

34. Researchers studying undivided brains

_____ (have/have not) found evidence of hemispheric specialization. For example, pictures are recognized more rapidly when they are flashed to the _____ (right/left) hemisphere, whereas words are recognized faster and more accurately when flashed to the _____ (right/left) hemisphere.

35. In all cultures of the world, most of the human population is _____ (right/left)-handed. With age, the percentage of left-handers _____ (increases/decreases). One controversial explanation of this difference is that _____ (right/left)-handers die at a younger age than their counterparts.

Identify several health risks that left-handers are more likely to have experienced.

The Endocrine System (pp. 80–81)

> If you do not know the meaning of any of the following words, phrases, or expressions in the context in which they appear in the text, refer to page 78 for an explanation: _kindred systems; Conducting and coordinating this whole electrochemical orchestra is that maestro we call the brain._

Section Preview

Answer guidelines are provided on page 67.

1. Discuss the functioning of the endocrine system.

2. Identify two important endocrine glands, and specify their functions.

Stepping Through the Section

Answers are provided on page 67.

1. The body's chemical communication network is called the _____ _____ . This system transmits information through chemical messengers called _____ at a much _____ (faster/slower) rate than the nervous system.

2. In a moment of danger, the _____ glands release _____ and

_____ .

3. The most influential gland is the _____ , which, under the control of the brain area called the _____ , helps regulate _____ and the release of hormones by other endocrine glands.

Write a paragraph describing the feedback system that links the nervous and endocrine systems.

Web Sighting

The Franklin Institute (**http://www.fi.edu/**) maintains an excellent web site, which provides a variety of online multimedia activities related to neuroscience. Check out the virtual tours of the nervous system. Compare the brains of different animal species. Read the latest brain research news and participate in interactive experiments that shed light on how the brain works. Travel through time and review the history of brain science. To get started, see if you can find the answers to the following questions.

1. Follow the link to *Brain Poke* and imagine that you are a brain surgeon standing over the exposed brain of a patient. How does the patient respond as you stimulate different areas?

2. How many neurons are in the average human brain? How big would the surface of the cerebral cortex be if it were spread out on a table and all its folds were ironed out?

3. Check out *Jay's Brain* and participate in an interactive experiment to find out which area of the brain seems to control laughter.

4. How much does the average elephant brain weigh?

5. How did the myth about people "using only ten percent of their brains" get started? Why is it so widespread?

6. What is a day in the life of a neuroscientist like? What are five major challenges faced by neuroscientists in the future?

Progress Test 1

Multiple-Choice Questions

Circle your answers to the following questions and check them with the answers on page 67. If your answer is incorrect, read the explanation for why it is incorrect and then consult the appropriate pages of the text (in parentheses following the correct answer).

1. The axons of certain neurons are covered by a layer of fatty tissue that helps speed neural transmission. This tissue is:
   a. the glia.
   b. the myelin sheath.
   c. acetylcholine.
   d. an endorphin.

2. Heartbeat, digestion, and other self-regulating bodily functions are governed by the:
   a. voluntary nervous system.
   b. autonomic nervous system.
   c. sympathetic division of the autonomic nervous system.
   d. somatic nervous system.
   e. central nervous system.

3. A strong stimulus can increase the:
   a. speed of the impulse the neuron fires.
   b. intensity of the impulse the neuron fires.
   c. number of times the neuron fires.
   d. threshold that must be reached before the neuron fires.

4. The pain of heroin withdrawal may be attributable to the fact that:
   a. under the influence of heroin the brain ceases production of endorphins.
   b. under the influence of heroin the brain ceases production of all neurotransmitters.
   c. during withdrawal the brain's production of all neurotransmitters is greatly increased.
   d. heroin destroys endorphin receptors in the brain.

5. The brain research technique that involves monitoring the brain's usage of glucose is called (in abbreviated form) the:
   a. PET scan.   c. EEG.
   b. CT scan.   d. MRI.

6. In a resting state, the axon is:
   a. depolarized, with mostly negatively charged ions outside and positively charged ions inside.
   b. depolarized, with mostly positively charged ions outside and negatively charged ions inside.
   c. polarized, with mostly negatively charged ions outside and positively charged ions inside.
   d. polarized, with mostly positively charged ions outside and negatively charged ions inside.

7. Though there is no single "control center" for emotions, their regulation is primarily attributed to the brain region known as the:
   a. limbic system.   c. brainstem.
   b. reticular formation. d. cerebral cortex.

8. Which is the correct sequence in the transmission of a simple reflex?
   a. sensory neuron → interneuron → sensory neuron
   b. interneuron → motor neuron → sensory neuron
   c. sensory neuron → interneuron → motor neuron
   d. interneuron → sensory neuron → motor neuron

9. Damage to _____ will usually cause a person to lose the ability to comprehend language.
   a. the angular gyrus
   b. Broca's area
   c. Wernicke's area
   d. frontal lobe association areas

10. Which of the following is typically controlled by the right hemisphere?
    a. language
    b. learned voluntary movements
    c. arithmetic reasoning
    d. perceptual tasks

11. Dr. Hernandez is studying neurotransmitter abnormalities in depressed patients. She would most likely describe herself as a:
    a. psychiatrist.
    b. clinical psychologist.
    c. psychoanalyst.
    d. biological psychologist.

12. As the brain evolved, the increasing complexity of animals' behavior was accompanied by a(n):
    a. increase in the size of the brainstem.
    b. decrease in the ratio of brain to body weight.
    c. increase in the size of the frontal lobes.
    d. increase in the amount of association area.

13. Voluntary movements, such as writing with a pencil, are directed by the:
    a. sympathetic nervous system.
    b. somatic nervous system.
    c. parasympathetic nervous system.
    d. autonomic nervous system.

14. A neuron will generate action potentials more often when it:
    a. remains below its threshold.
    b. receives an excitatory input.
    c. receives more excitatory than inhibitory inputs.
    d. is stimulated by a neurotransmitter.
    e. is stimulated by a hormone.

15. Which is the correct sequence in the transmission of a neural impulse?
    a. axon → dendrite → cell body → synapse
    b. dendrite → axon → cell body → synapse
    c. synapse → axon → dendrite → cell body
    d. axon → synapse → cell body → dendrite
    e. dendrite → cell body → axon → synapse

16. Chemical messengers produced by endocrine glands are called:
    a. agonists.
    b. neurotransmitters.
    c. hormones.
    d. enzymes.

17. Following a head injury, a person has ongoing difficulties staying awake. Most likely, the damage occurred to the:
    a. thalamus.
    b. corpus callosum.
    c. reticular formation.
    d. cerebellum.

18. Based on research, which of the following seems true about the specialized functions of the right and left hemispheres?
    a. They are more clear-cut in men than in women.
    b. They are more clear-cut in women than in men.
    c. Most complex tasks emerge from the activity of one or the other hemisphere.
    d. Most complex activities emerge from the integrated activity of both hemispheres.

19. Cortical areas that are not primarily concerned with sensory, motor, or language functions are:
    a. called projection areas.
    b. called association areas.
    c. located mostly in the parietal lobe.
    d. located mostly in the temporal lobe.

20. In the brain, learning occurs as experience strengthens certain connections in cell work groups called:
    a. action potentials.
    b. neural networks.
    c. endocrine systems.
    d. dendrites.
    e. synaptic gaps.

Matching Items

Match each structure with its corresponding function or description.

Structures

_____ 1. hypothalamus
_____ 2. lesion
_____ 3. EEG
_____ 4. CT scan
_____ 5. reticular formation
_____ 6. MRI
_____ 7. thalamus
_____ 8. corpus callosum
_____ 9. cerebellum
_____ 10. amygdala
_____ 11. medulla

Functions or Descriptions

a. amplified recording of brain waves
b. technique that uses radio waves and magnetic fields to image the brain
c. serves as sensory switchboard
d. contains reward centers
e. tissue destruction
f. a technique that uses x-rays to image the brain
g. helps control arousal
h. links the cerebral hemispheres
i. influences rage and fear
j. regulates breathing and heartbeat
k. enables coordinated movement

Progress Test 2

Progress Test 2 should be completed during a final chapter review. Answer the following questions after you thoroughly understand the correct answers for the section reviews and Progress Test 1.

Multiple-Choice Questions

1. The visual cortex is located in the:
   a. occipital lobe.
   b. temporal lobe.
   c. frontal lobe.
   d. parietal lobe.

2. Which of the following is typically controlled by the left hemisphere?
   a. spatial reasoning
   b. arithmetic reasoning
   c. the left side of the body
   d. perceptual skills

3. When Sandy scalded her toe in a tub of hot water, the pain message was carried to her spinal cord by the _____ nervous system.
   a. somatic
   b. sympathetic
   c. parasympathetic
   d. central

4. Which of the following are governed by the simplest neural pathways?
   a. emotions
   b. physiological drives, such as hunger
   c. reflexes
   d. movements, such as walking
   e. balance

5. Melissa has just completed running a marathon. She is so elated that she feels little fatigue or discomfort. Her lack of pain is probably the result of the release of:
   a. ACh.
   b. endorphins.
   c. dopamine.
   d. norepinephrine.
   e. acetylcholine.

6. Parkinson's disease involves:
   a. the death of nerve cells that produce a vital neurotransmitter.
   b. impaired function in the right hemisphere only.
   c. impaired function in the left hemisphere only.
   d. excess production of the neurotransmitters dopamine and acetylcholine.

7. The technique that uses magnetic fields and radio waves to produce computer images of structures within the brain is called:
   a. the EEG.
   b. a CT scan.
   c. a PET scan.
   d. MRI.

8. The myelin sheath that is on some neurons:
   a. increases the speed of neural transmission.
   b. slows neural transmission.
   c. regulates the release of neurotransmitters.
   d. does a. and c.
   e. does b. and c.

9. During an action potential, the electrical state of the axon becomes:
   a. polarized, as positively charged atoms are admitted.
   b. polarized, as negatively charged atoms are admitted.
   c. depolarized, as positively charged atoms are admitted.
   d. depolarized, as negatively charged atoms are admitted.

10. The neurotransmitter acetylcholine (ACh) is most likely to be found:
    a. at the junction between sensory neurons and muscle fibers.
    b. at the junction between motor neurons and muscle fibers.
    c. at junctions between interneurons.
    d. in all of the above locations.

11. The gland that regulates body growth is the:
    a. adrenal.   d. pituitary.
    b. thyroid.   e. hyperthyroid.
    c. hypothalamus.

12. Epinephrine and norepinephrine are _____ that are released by the _____ gland.
    a. neurotransmitters; pituitary
    b. hormones; pituitary
    c. neurotransmitters; adrenal
    d. hormones; adrenal
    e. hormones; thyroid

13. Jessica experienced difficulty keeping her balance after receiving a blow to the back of her head. It is likely that she injured her:
    a. medulla.   d. cerebellum.
    b. thalamus.   e. cerebrum.
    c. hypothalamus.

14. Moruzzi and Magoun caused a cat to lapse into a coma by severing neural connections between the cortex and the:
    a. reticular formation.   d. cerebellum.
    b. hypothalamus.   e. medulla.
    c. thalamus.

15. Research has found that the amount of representation in the motor cortex reflects the:
    a. size of the body parts.
    b. degree of precise control required by each of the parts.
    c. sensitivity of the body region.
    d. area of the occipital lobe being stimulated by the environment.

16. The effect of a drug that is an agonist is to:
    a. cause the brain to stop producing certain neurotransmitters.
    b. mimic a particular neurotransmitter.
    c. block a particular neurotransmitter.
    d. disrupt a neuron's all-or-none firing pattern.

17. The nerve fibers that enable communication between the right and left cerebral hemispheres and that have been severed in split-brain patients form a structure called the:
    a. reticular formation.   d. parietal lobes.
    b. association areas.   e. limbic system.
    c. corpus callosum.

18. Beginning at the front of the brain and working backward then down and around, which of the following is the correct order of the cortical regions?
    a. occipital lobe; temporal lobe; parietal lobe; frontal lobe
    b. temporal lobe; frontal lobe; parietal lobe; occipital lobe
    c. frontal lobe; occipital lobe; temporal lobe; parietal lobe
    d. frontal lobe; parietal lobe; occipital lobe; temporal lobe
    e. occipital lobe; parietal lobe; temporal lobe; frontal lobe

19. Following a gunshot wound to his head, Jack became more uninhibited, irritable, and profane. It is likely that his personality change was the result of injury to his:
    a. parietal lobe.   d. frontal lobe.
    b. temporal lobe.   e. endocrine system.
    c. occipital lobe.

20. Three-year-old Marco suffered damage to the speech area of the brain's left hemisphere when he fell from a swing. Research suggests that:
    a. he will never speak again.
    b. his motor abilities will improve so that he can easily use sign language.
    c. his right hemisphere will take over much of the language function.
    d. his earlier experience with speech will enable him to continue speaking.

Matching Items

Match each structure or term with its corresponding function or description.

Structures or Terms

_____ **1.** right hemisphere
_____ **2.** brainstem
_____ **3.** CT scan
_____ **4.** aphasia
_____ **5.** EEG
_____ **6.** Broca's area
_____ **7.** Wernicke's area
_____ **8.** limbic system
_____ **9.** association areas
_____ **10.** left hemisphere
_____ **11.** angular gyrus

Functions or Descriptions

a. controls speech production
b. specializes in rationalizing reactions
c. translates writing into speech
d. specializes in spatial relations
e. a series of x-ray photographs of the brain taken from different angles
f. language disorder
g. oldest part of the brain
h. regulates emotion
i. recording of brain waves
j. responsible for language comprehension
k. brain areas involved in higher mental functions

In the diagrams to the right, the numbers refer to brain locations that have been damaged. Match each location with its probable effect on behavior.

Location

_____ **1.**
_____ **2.**
_____ **3.**
_____ **4.**
_____ **5.**
_____ **6.**
_____ **7.**
_____ **8.**
_____ **9.**

Behavioral Effect

a. vision disorder
b. insensitivity to touch
c. motor paralysis
d. hearing problem
e. lack of coordination
f. abnormal hunger
g. split brain
h. sleep/arousal disorder
i. loss of smell
j. loss of taste
k. altered personality

Thinking Critically About Chapter 2

Answer these questions the day before an exam as a final check on your understanding of the chapter's terms and concepts.

Multiple-Choice Questions

1. A biological psychologist would be *more* likely to study:
   a. how you learn to express emotions.
   b. how to help people overcome emotional disorders.
   c. life-span changes in the expression of emotion.
   d. the chemical changes that accompany emotions.

2. The part of the human brain that is most like that of a fish is the:
   a. cortex.
   b. limbic system.
   c. brainstem.
   d. right hemisphere.
   e. corpus callosum.

3. You are able to pull your hand quickly away from hot water before pain is felt because:
   a. movement of the hand is a reflex that involves intervention of the spinal cord only.
   b. movement of the hand does not require intervention by the central nervous system.
   c. the brain reacts quickly to prevent severe injury.
   d. the autonomic division of the peripheral nervous system intervenes to speed contraction of the muscles of the hand.

4. In order to pinpoint the location of a tumor, a neurosurgeon electrically stimulated parts of the patient's sensory cortex. If the patient was conscious during the procedure, which of the following was probably experienced?
   a. "hearing" faint sounds
   b. "seeing" random visual patterns
   c. movement of the arms or legs
   d. a sense of having the skin touched

5. If Dr. Rogers wishes to conduct an experiment on the effects of stimulating the reward centers of a rat's brain, he should insert an electrode into the:
   a. thalamus.
   b. sensory cortex.
   c. hypothalamus.
   d. corpus callosum.

6. A split-brain patient has a picture of a knife flashed to her left hemisphere and that of a fork to her right hemisphere. She will be able to:
   a. identify the fork using her left hand.
   b. identify a knife using her left hand.
   c. identify a knife using either hand.
   d. identify a fork using either hand.

7. Which of the following is *not* a correct description of a brain research technique?
   a. using a PET scan to examine the brain's structure
   b. using the EEG to record the brain's electrical activity
   c. using MRI to examine the brain's structure
   d. using a CT scan to examine the brain's structure

8. Following Jayshree's near-fatal car accident, her physician noticed that the pupillary reflex of her eyes was abnormal. This *may* indicate that Jayshree's _____ was damaged in the accident.
   a. occipital cortex
   b. autonomic nervous system
   c. left temporal lobe
   d. cerebellum
   e. brainstem

9. Anton is applying for a technician's job with a neurosurgeon. In trying to impress his potential employer with his knowledge of the brain, he says, "After my father's stroke I knew immediately that the blood clot had affected his left cerebral hemisphere because he no longer recognized a picture of his friend." Should Anton be hired?
   a. Yes. Anton obviously understands brain structure and function.
   b. No. The right hemisphere, not the left, specializes in picture recognition.
   c. Yes. Although blood clots never form in the left hemisphere, Anton should be rewarded for recognizing the left hemisphere's role in picture recognition.
   d. No. Blood clots never form in the left hemisphere, and the right hemisphere is more involved than the left in recognizing pictures.

10. Which of the following is *not* true regarding brain organization and handedness?
    a. If a person has a left-handed identical twin, odds are that he or she will also be left-handed.
    b. Right-handedness is far more common than left-handedness throughout the world.
    c. On average, right-handers live longer than left-handers.
    d. Left-handers are more common than usual among people with reading disabilities.
    e. With age, the percentage of left-handers declines dramatically.

11. Dr. Johnson briefly flashed a picture of a key in the right visual field of a split-brain patient. The patient could probably:
    a. verbally report that a key was seen.
    b. write the word *key* using the left hand.
    c. draw a picture of a key using the left hand.
    d. do none of the above.

12. In primitive vertebrate animals, the brain primarily regulates _____ ; in lower mammals, the brain enables _____ .
    a. emotion; memory
    b. memory; emotion
    c. survival functions; emotion
    d. reproduction; emotion
    e. reproduction; memory

13. Since Malcolm has been taking a drug prescribed by his doctor, he no longer enjoys the little pleasures of life, such as eating and drinking. His doctor explains that this is because the drug:
    a. triggers release of dopamine.
    b. inhibits release of dopamine.
    c. triggers release of ACh.
    d. inhibits release of ACh.

14. A scientist from another planet wishes to study the simplest brain mechanisms underlying emotion and memory. You recommend that the scientist study the:
    a. brainstem of a frog.
    b. limbic system of a dog.
    c. cortex of a monkey.
    d. cortex of a human.
    e. brainstem of a dog.

15. Which of the following was a major problem with phrenology?
    a. It was "ahead of its time" and no one believed it could be true.
    b. The brain is not neatly organized into structures that correspond to our categories of behavior.
    c. The brains of humans and animals are much less similar than the theory implied.
    d. All of the above were problems with phrenology.

16. I am a relatively slow-acting (but long-lasting) chemical messenger carried throughout the body by the bloodstream. What am I?
    a. a hormone
    b. a neurotransmitter
    c. acetylcholine
    d. dopamine

17. Your brother has been taking prescription medicine and experiencing a number of unpleasant side effects, including unusually rapid heartbeat and excessive perspiration. It is likely that the medicine is exaggerating activity in the:
    a. reticular formation.
    b. sympathetic nervous system.
    c. parasympathetic nervous system.
    d. amygdala.

18. Dr. Frankenstein made a mistake during neurosurgery on his monster. After the operation, the monster "saw" with his ears and "heard" with his eyes. It is likely that Dr. Frankenstein "rewired" neural connections in the monster's:
    a. hypothalamus.
    b. cerebellum.
    c. amygdala.
    d. thalamus.
    e. hippocampus.

19. A bodybuilder friend suddenly seems to have grown several inches in height. You suspect that your friend's growth spurt has occurred because he has been using drugs that affect the:
    a. pituitary gland.
    b. thalamus.
    c. adrenal glands.
    d. medulla.
    e. cerebellum.

20. Raccoons have much more precise control of their paws than dogs. You would expect that raccoons have more cortical space dedicated to "paw control" in the _____ of their brains.

   a. frontal lobes   **c.** temporal lobes

   b. parietal lobes   **d.** occipital lobes

Essay Question

Discuss how the brainstem, limbic system, and cerebral cortex are each involved when a person plays a musical instrument. (Use the space below to list the points you want to make and organize them. Then write the essay on a separate sheet of paper.)

Key Terms

Writing Definitions

Using your own words, on a piece of paper write a brief definition or explanation of each of the following terms.

1. biological psychology
2. neuron
3. dendrites
4. axon
5. myelin sheath
6. action potential
7. threshold
8. synapse
9. neurotransmitters
10. acetylcholine (ACh)
11. endorphins
12. nervous system
13. central nervous system (CNS)
14. peripheral nervous system (PNS)
15. nerves
16. sensory neurons
17. interneurons
18. motor neurons
19. somatic nervous system
20. autonomic nervous system
21. sympathetic nervous system
22. parasympathetic nervous system
23. reflex
24. neural networks
25. lesion
26. electroencephalogram (EEG)
27. CT (computed tomography) scan
28. PET (positron emission tomography) scan
29. MRI (magnetic resonance imaging)
30. brainstem
31. medulla
32. reticular formation
33. thalamus
34. cerebellum
35. limbic system
36. amygdala
37. hypothalamus
38. cerebral cortex
39. glial cells
40. frontal lobes
41. parietal lobes
42. occipital lobes
43. temporal lobes
44. motor cortex
45. sensory cortex
46. association areas
47. aphasia
48. Broca's area
49. Wernicke's area
50. plasticity
51. corpus callosum
52. split brain
53. endocrine system
54. hormones
55. adrenal glands
56. pituitary gland

Cross-Check

As you learned in the Introduction, reviewing and overlearning of material are important to the learning process. After you have written the definitions of the key terms in this chapter, you should complete the crossword puzzle to ensure that you can reverse the process—recognize the term, given the definition.

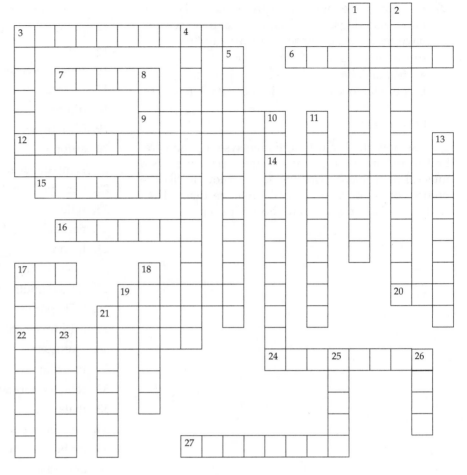

ACROSS

3. The division of the nervous system that connects the brain and spinal cord to the body's sense receptors, muscles, and glands.
6. Located on the sides of the brain, these lobes contain the auditory areas, which receive information from the ears.
7. Located at the back of the frontal lobe, the part of the cortex that controls voluntary movement.
9. Located just behind the forehead, these lobes are involved in speaking and muscle movements and in making plans and judgments.
12. Glands that produce the hormones epinephrine and norepinephrine.
14. Located in the brainstem, this structure controls breathing and heartbeat.
15. The thin outer covering of the cerebral hemispheres.
16. Junction between the axon tip of the sending neuron and the dendrite or cell body of the receiving neuron.
17. Amplified recording of the waves of electrical activity of the brain.
19. Destruction of tissue.
20. Technique that uses magnetic fields and radio waves to produce computer-generated images of brain structures.
22. Located at the back and base of the brain, these lobes contain the visual cortex, which receives information from the eyes.
24. The part of the limbic system involved in regulation of the emotions of fear and rage.
27. Situated between the frontal and occipital lobes, these lobes contain the sensory cortex.

DOWN

1. Limbic system structure that regulates hunger, thirst, and body temperature and contains the so-called reward centers of the brain.
2. Large band of neural fibers that links the right and left hemispheres.
3. Technique that measures the levels of activity of different areas of the brain by tracing their consumption of a radioactive form of glucose.
4. Neural impulse generated by the movement of positively charged atoms in and out of channels in the axon's membrane.
5. Neurotransmitter that triggers muscle contractions.
8. Simple, automatic, inborn response to a sensory stimulus.
10. Doughnut-shaped neural system that plays an important role in the regulation of emotions and basic physiological drives.
11. Natural opiatelike neurotransmitters linked to pain control and to pleasure.
13. Division of the peripheral nervous system that controls the glands and the muscles of internal organs.

17. The body's slower chemical communication system, consisting of glands that secrete hormones into the bloodstream.
18. The brain and spinal cord, collectively.
21. An impairment of language as a result of damage to any of several cortical areas.
23. A series of x-ray photographs of the brain taken from different positions and analyzed by computer, creating an image that represents a slice through the brain.
25. More numerous than cortical neurons, these cells of the brain guide neural connections and provide nutrients and insulating myelin.
26. Extension of a neuron that sends impulses to other nerve cells or to muscles or glands.

Answers

Introduction

Introduction Preview

1. Biological processes underlie every aspect of our behavior and mental processes. By studying the links between biology and psychology, biological psychologists achieve a greater understanding of such behaviors as sleep, hunger, sex, stress and disease, depression, and other human conditions.

Stepping Through the Introduction

1. biological
2. phrenology
3. biological psychologists

Neural Communication

Section Preview

1. Body organs such as the stomach, heart, and brain, which are composed of smaller systems (cells), form larger systems for digestion, circulation, and information processing, which are part of an even larger system—the individual as a person, who in turn forms a part of a family, a community, and a culture. We are bio-psycho-social systems.
2. Each neuron consists of a cell body, branching fibers called dendrites that receive information from other neurons, and an extension fiber called an axon through which the neuron passes information to other neurons or to muscles or glands. Some axons are insulated with a myelin sheath, which helps speed neural impulses.

A neural impulse, or action potential, occurs if the excitatory signals minus the inhibitory signals received by the neuron on its dendrites or cell body exceeds the neuron's threshold. Then, the gates in the axon open, allowing positively charged atoms to rush inside. This depolarizes that part of the axon, which causes the axon's next channel to open and leads to the electrical chain reaction by which electrically charged atoms (ions) travel down the axon into junctions with other neurons and with the muscles and glands of the body.

3. When an action potential reaches the end of the axon, chemical messengers called neurotransmitters are released into the synaptic gap between the sending and receiving neuron. This junction is called a synapse. Neurotransmitter molecules bind to receptor sites on the receiving neuron and have either an excitatory or inhibitory influence on that neuron's tendency to generate its own action potential. If the receiving neuron receives more excitatory than inhibitory inputs, more neural impulses are generated.

A particular neural pathway may use only one or two neurotransmitters, each of which may have a specific effect on behavior. Acetylcholine, for example, is the neurotransmitter at every synapse between a motor neuron and a skeletal muscle. Other known neurotransmitters include dopamine, which influences movement, learning, attention, and emotion; serotonin, which affects mood, hunger, sleep, and arousal; norepinephrine, which helps control alertness and arousal; and gamma-aminobutyric acid (GABA), which is an inhibitory neurotransmitter implicated in eating and sleep disorders.

4. Endorphins are morphinelike neurotransmitters found in the brain that are released in response to pain and vigorous exercise. The existence of endorphins may help explain good feelings such as the "runner's high," the pain-killing effects of acupuncture, and the indifference to pain in some injured people.

Drugs have a number of different effects on neurotransmitters. Some (agonists) mimic a particular neurotransmitter; others (antagonists) block a particular neurotransmitter. Still others interfere with the breakdown or reabsorption of the neurotransmitter. Opiate drugs, for example, may cause the brain to stop producing endorphins.

Stepping Through the Section

1. system; subsystems; systems; neurons
2. dendrites
3. axons; myelin sheath
4. **a.** dendrites
   b. cell body
   c. axon
   d. myelin sheath
5. action potential; axon
6. negatively; positively; resting potential; permeable
7. positively; depolarized
8. refractory period; negatively
9. excitatory; inhibitory; threshold; will not; all-or-none

A neural impulse is generated by excitatory signals minus inhibitory signals exceeding a certain threshold. The stimuli are received through the dendrites, combined in the cell body, and electrically transmitted in an all-or-none fashion down the length of the axon. When the combined signal reaches the end of the axon, chemical messengers called neurotransmitters are released into the synaptic cleft, or gap, between two neurons. Neurotransmitter molecules bind to receptor sites on the dendrites of neighboring neurons and have either an excitatory or inhibitory influence on that neuron's tendency to generate its own neural impulse.

10. does not
11. synapse; synaptic cleft (gap)
12. neurotransmitters; atoms
13. exciting; inhibiting; reuptake
14. dopamine; serotonin; norepinephrine; gamma-aminobutyric acid (GABA)
15. acetylcholine (ACh); curare
16. endorphins; heroin; morphine
17. agonists; receptor sites; antagonists
18. blood-brain barrier
19. Parkinson's; dopamine; L-dopa

The Nervous System

Section Preview

1. The central nervous system includes all the neurons in the brain and spinal cord. The peripheral nervous system, which links the central nervous system with the body's sense receptors, muscles, and glands, has two divisions: somatic and autonomic. The somatic nervous system controls the voluntary movements of the skeletal muscles.

The autonomic nervous system, which influences the glands and muscles of our internal organs, also is a dual system. The sympathetic nervous system arouses the body during emergencies by accelerating heartbeat, slowing digestion, raising blood sugar, dilating arteries, and creating perspiration. When the emergency has passed, the parasympathetic nervous system relaxes the body by producing the opposite effects.

Sensory neurons relay information from the body's tissues and sensory organs to the brain and spinal cord. Interneurons of the brain and spinal cord (the central nervous system) are involved in processing this information from the sensory neurons. The central nervous system then sends instructions to the body's tissues by means of the motor neurons.

2. Reflexes, which are automatic responses to stimuli, are governed by the simplest neural connections. In response to a painful stimulus to the fingertips, for example, a sensory neuron conveys the message to an interneuron in the spinal cord. The interneuron triggers an action potential in motor neurons that cause muscles of your arm to jerk your hand away.

   To enable complex operations, the neurons in the brain cluster into work groups called neural networks. Each cell in a given layer of the network connects with various cells in the next layer.

Stepping Through the Section

1. nervous system
2. central; peripheral
3. nerves
4. sensory; interneurons
5. motor
6. somatic
7. autonomic
8. sympathetic
9. parasympathetic

The sympathetic division of the autonomic nervous system becomes aroused in response to an emergency. The physiological changes that occur include accelerated heartbeat, elevated blood sugar, dilation of arteries, slowing of digestion, and increased perspiration to cool the body. When the emergency is over, the parasympathetic nervous system produces the opposite physical reactions.

10. reflexes; spinal cord; knee-jerk; pain

From sensory receptors in the skin the message travels via sensory neurons to an interneuron in the spinal cord, which in turn activates a motor neuron.

This motor neuron causes the muscles in the hand to contract, and the person jerks his or her hand away from the heat.

11. neural networks

The Brain

Section Preview

1. The oldest method of studying the brain is by observing the effects of brain disease and injuries. More recently, electrical, chemical, or magnetic stimulation in humans and surgical lesions of brain tissue in animals have been used to study the brain. The electroencephalogram (EEG) is a recording of the brain's electrical activity from electrodes placed on its surface. Scientists also examine the brain with CT (computed tomography) scans, PET (positron emission tomography) scans, and magnetic resonance imaging (an MRI or a functional MRI). Although the text discusses the use of scanning and imaging on the brain only, these techniques are also used to diagnose problems elsewhere in the body.

2. The brainstem is the oldest and innermost region of the brain. It begins where the spinal cord enters the skull and contains the medulla and reticular formation. The medulla controls breathing and heartbeat and is the point where nerves to and from each side of the brain cross over to connect with the opposite side of the body. The reticular formation helps control arousal. The thalamus serves as the brain's sensory switchboard, routing information from sensory neurons to higher brain regions dealing with seeing, hearing, tasting, and touching. The cerebellum enables one type of nonverbal learning and memory; its most obvious function is coordinating voluntary movement.

3. In the limbic system, the hippocampus processes memory. The amygdala influences aggression and fear. When this region is surgically lesioned, aggressive behavior in animals is diminished. When one region of the amygdala is electrically stimulated, a normally placid domestic animal will behave aggressively; when another area is stimulated, the animal will display signs of fear.

   The hypothalamus contains neurons that regulate hunger, thirst, body temperature, and sexual behavior; it also contains the so-called reward centers. The hypothalamus also secretes hormones that control the pituitary gland, which influences hormone release by other glands, which the hypothalamus monitors.

4. The cerebral cortex is a thin surface layer of nerve cells supported by even more glial cells. It covers the left and right cerebral hemispheres. Each hemisphere is divided into four regions called lobes: frontal, parietal, temporal, and occipital. The frontal lobes control movement through the motor cortex and contain association areas that are involved in making plans and judgments. When specific parts of the motor cortex in the left and right hemispheres are electrically stimulated, movement is triggered in specific body parts on the opposite side of the body.

   The parietal lobes house the sensory cortex which, when electrically stimulated, triggers a sense of a particular body part having been touched. The more sensitive a body region, the greater the area of sensory cortex devoted to it.

   The temporal lobes receive auditory information primarily from the opposite ear, and the occipital lobes similarly receive input from the eyes.

   Approximately three-fourths of the cortex consists of uncommitted association areas that communicate with one another and with neurons of the sensory and motor areas. Association areas influence personality, recognition of faces, and many other "higher" mental abilities.

5. Damage to any one of several areas of the cortex can cause aphasia, an impaired use of language. Damage to Broca's area in the left frontal lobe disrupts speaking. Damage to Wernicke's area in the left temporal lobe disrupts language comprehension and leaves people able to speak words but in a meaningless way. Damage to the angular gyrus will disrupt the ability to read aloud.

   When you read aloud, words are registered in the visual area of the cortex and then relayed to the angular gyrus, which transforms the words into an auditory code. This code is comprehended by Wernicke's area and then sent to Broca's area, which directs the motor cortex to produce speech.

6. When a particular area of the brain is damaged, such as occurs following a stroke, other areas may in time reorganize and assume its functions (plasticity). Neurons that are near damaged ones compensate for the damage by making new neural connections to replace the damaged ones. The brains of young children, in which functions are not yet regionally fixed, exhibit the greatest plasticity. New evidence reveals that adult humans can generate new brain cells.

7. In order to control severe epileptic seizures, surgeons sometimes sever the wide band of fibers

(the corpus callosum) that connects the two hemispheres of the brain.

Sperry and Gazzaniga studied such split-brain patients, revealing that the left and right hemispheres each have special functions. In a person with an intact brain, information in the left or right side of our field of vision of both eyes projects directly to the opposite hemisphere of the brain and is quickly passed to the other hemisphere through the corpus callosum. In the split-brain patient, however, a briefly flashed image on the subject's right, for example, will be perceived only in the left hemisphere. By flashing images in this way, researchers are able to send information to either the left or right hemisphere and thereby determine its capabilities.

Using the latest tools for studying the brain, researchers have also found evidence of hemispheric specialization in the *intact* (undivided) brain. These experiments demonstrate that the right hemisphere is superior to the left at recognizing pictures, perceiving differences, and expressing emotions. The left hemisphere is more logical and verbal. Despite these specialized functions, the two hemispheres work together in an integrated manner during most activities.

8. Approximately 95 percent of right-handers process speech primarily in the left hemisphere. In contrast, left-handers are more diverse in their processing of language. About half process speech in the left hemisphere, one-quarter in the right hemisphere, and one-quarter in both hemispheres equally. Throughout the world, right-handedness is far more common than left-handedness. Furthermore, the percentage of left-handers declines dramatically with age, perhaps because, according to Coren and Halpern, left-handers live, on average, about three years less than right-handers. This difference in life span may be due to the fact that left-handers are more likely to have experienced birth stress, have more accidents, use more tobacco and alcohol, and suffer more immune system problems.

Stepping Through the Section

1. lesions; clinical observation

2. electroencephalogram (EEG)

3. CT scan

4. PET scan

By depicting the brain's consumption of radioactively labeled glucose, the PET scan allows researchers to see which brain areas are most active as a person performs various tasks. This provides additional information on the specialized functions of various regions of the brain.

5. MRI (magnetic resonance imaging); functional MRI

6. brainstem

7. medulla; breathing; heartbeat

8. brainstem

9. reticular formation; arousal; alert (awake); coma

10. thalamus

11. cerebellum; nonverbal learning; balance

12. conscious; outside

13. limbic; hippocampus

14. amygdala

15. psychosurgery; seldom

16. hypothalamus; hunger, thirst, body temperature (or sex); pituitary; reward

17. addictive; reward deficiency syndrome

18. cerebral cortex

19. glial cells

20. more wrinkled; increases

21. a. frontal lobe
    b. parietal lobe
    c. occipital lobe
    d. temporal lobe

22. motor; frontal

23. sensory; touch

24. sensory cortex

25. occipital; temporal

26. association areas; three-fourths; frontal

27. aphasia; Broca's area; Wernicke's area; angular gyrus

28. unified whole

29. plasticity

30. will not; reorganize; stem

31. left; dominant (major)

32. corpus callosum; split brain

33. right; name; right

The word *pencil* when flashed to a split-brain patient's right visual field would project only to the opposite, or left, hemisphere of the patient's brain. Because the left hemisphere contains the language control centers of the brain, the patient would be able to read the word aloud. The left hand is controlled by the right hemisphere of the brain. Because the right hemisphere would not be aware of the word, it would not be able to guide the left hand in identifying a pencil by touch.

34. have; right; left

35. right; decreases; left

Left-handers are more likely to have experienced premature or stressful births. They also have more headaches and accidents, use more tobacco and alcohol, and suffer more immune system problems.

The Endocrine System

Section Preview

1. The endocrine system is a relatively slow-acting chemical communication system of glands that secrete hormones influencing growth, reproduction, metabolism, mood, and reactions to stress.

2. The adrenal glands release epinephrine (adrenaline) and norepinephrine (noradrenaline) during emergencies. These hormones provide a source of energy by increasing heart rate, blood pressure, and blood sugar. The pituitary gland, located in the base of the brain, releases hormones that influence growth and the release of hormones by other glands. It forms an elaborate feedback system with the brain (the hypothalamus) in its influence on behavior.

Stepping Through the Section

1. endocrine system; hormones; slower
2. adrenal; epinephrine; norepinephrine
3. pituitary; hypothalamus; growth

The hypothalamus in the brain influences secretions by the pituitary. The pituitary regulates other endocrine glands, which release hormones that influence behavior. The hypothalamus monitors these changes in blood chemistry and thereby adjusts its inputs to the pituitary.

Progress Test 1

Multiple-Choice Questions

1. **b.** is the answer. (p. 48)
   a. Glial cells support and nourish nerve cells.
   c. Acetylcholine is a neurotransmitter that triggers muscle contraction.
   d. Endorphins are opiatelike neurotransmitters linked to pain control and to pleasure.

2. **b.** is the answer. The autonomic nervous system controls internal functioning, including heartbeat, digestion, and glandular activity. (p. 55)
   a. The functions mentioned are all automatic, not voluntary, so this answer cannot be correct.

c. This answer is incorrect because most organs are affected by both divisions of the autonomic nervous system.
d. The skeletal nervous system transmits sensory input to the central nervous system and directs the movements of skeletal muscles.
e. The central nervous system need not be involved in automatic activities.

3. **c.** is the answer. Stimulus strength can affect only the number of times a neuron fires or the number of neurons that fire. (p. 50)
   a., b., & d. These answers are incorrect because firing is an all-or-none response, so intensity remains the same regardless of stimulus strength. Nor can stimulus strength change the neuronal threshold or the impulse speed.

4. **a.** is the answer. Endorphins are neurotransmitters that function as natural painkillers. When the body has a supply of artificial painkillers such as heroin, endorphin production stops. (pp. 52–53)
   b. The production of neurotransmitters other than endorphins does not cease.
   c. Neurotransmitter production does not increase during withdrawal.
   d. Heroin makes use of the same receptor sites as endorphins.

5. **a.** is the answer. The PET scan measures glucose consumption in different areas of the brain to determine their levels of activity. (p. 59)
   b. The CT scan is a series of x-rays taken from different angles and then analyzed by a computer to create an image representing a slice through the brain.
   c. The EEG is a measure of electrical activity in the brain.
   d. MRI uses magnetic fields and radio waves to produce computer-generated images of soft tissues of the body.

6. **d.** is the answer. (p. 49)

7. **a.** is the answer. (p. 62)
   b. The reticular formation is linked to arousal.
   c. The brainstem governs the mechanisms of basic survival—heartbeat and breathing, for example—and has many other roles.
   d. The cerebral cortex governs the "higher" functions of the brain.

8. **c.** is the answer. In a simple reflex, a sensory neuron carries the message that a sensory receptor has been stimulated to an interneuron in the spinal cord. The interneuron responds by activating motor neurons that will enable the appropriate response. (p. 56)

9. **c.** is the answer. Wernicke's area is involved in comprehension, and aphasics with damage to Wernicke's area are unable to understand what is said to them. (p. 69)

a. The angular gyrus translates printed words into speech sounds; damage would result in the inability to read aloud.

b. Broca's area is involved in the physical production of speech; damage would result in the inability to speak fluently.

d. The cortex's association areas are involved, among other things, in processing language; damage to these areas wouldn't specifically affect comprehension.

10. **d.** is the answer. (p. 74)

a. In most persons, language is primarily a left hemisphere function.

b. Learned movements are unrelated to hemispheric specialization.

c. Arithmetic reasoning is generally a left hemisphere function.

11. **d.** is the answer. Biological psychologists study the links between biology (in this case, neurotransmitters) and psychology (depression, in this example). (p. 48)

a., b., & c. These mental health professionals are more involved in the *treatment* of troubled behavior than in research.

12. **d.** is the answer. As animals increase in complexity, there is an increase in the amount of association areas. (p. 68)

a. The brainstem controls basic survival functions and is not related to the complexity of an animal's behavior.

b. The ratio of body and brain weight is a poor predictor of behavior complexity.

c. The frontal lobe is concerned with personality, planning, and other mental functions, but its size is unrelated to intelligence or the complexity of behavior.

13. **b.** is the answer. (p. 55)

a., c., & d. The autonomic nervous system, which is divided into the sympathetic and parasympathetic divisions, is concerned with regulating basic bodily maintenance functions.

14. **c.** is the answer. (p. 50)

a. An action potential will occur only when the neuron's threshold is *exceeded*.

b. An excitatory input that does not reach the neuron's threshold will not trigger an action potential.

d. This answer is incorrect because some neurotransmitters inhibit a neuron's readiness to fire.

e. Hormones are produced by the glands of the endocrine system.

15. **e.** is the answer. A neuron receives incoming stimuli on its dendrites and cell body. These electrochemical signals are combined in the cell body, generating an impulse that travels down the axon, causing the release of neurotransmitter substances into the synaptic cleft or gap. (pp. 48–50)

16. **c.** is the answer. (p. 80)

a. Agonists are drugs that excite neural firing by mimicking a particular neurotransmitter.

b. Neurotransmitters are the chemicals involved in synaptic transmission in the nervous system.

d. Enzymes are chemicals that facilitate various chemical reactions throughout the body but are not involved in communication within the endocrine system.

17. **c.** is the answer. The reticular formation plays an important role in arousal. (p. 61)

a. The thalamus relays sensory input.

b. The corpus callosum links the two cerebral hemispheres.

d. The cerebellum is involved in coordination of voluntary movement.

18. **d.** is the answer. (p. 75)

19. **b.** is the answer. Association areas interpret, integrate, and act on information from other areas of the cortex. (p. 68)

20. **b.** is the answer. (p. 57)

a. Action potentials are neural impulses that occur in all forms of communication in the nervous system.

c. The endocrine system is the body's glandular system of chemical communication.

d. Dendrites are the branching extensions of neurons that receive messages from other nerve cells.

e. Synaptic gaps are the spaces between neurons.

Matching Items

1. d (p. 63)   5. g (p. 61)   9. k (p. 62)
2. e (p. 58)   6. b (p. 59)   10. i (p. 62)
3. a (p. 59)   7. c (p. 62)   11. j (p. 61)
4. f (p. 59)   8. h (p. 72)

Progress Test 2

Multiple-Choice Questions

1. **a.** is the answer. The visual cortex is located at the very back of the brain. (p. 65)

2. **b.** is the answer. (pp. 74–75)

a., c., & d. Spatial reasoning, perceptual skills, and the left side of the body are primarily influenced by the right hemisphere.

3. **a.** is the answer. Sensory neurons in the somatic nervous system relay such messages. (p. 56)

b. & c. These divisions of the autonomic nervous system are concerned with the regulation of bodily maintenance functions such as heartbeat, digestion, and glandular activity.

d. The spinal cord itself is part of the central nervous system, but the message is carried to the spinal cord by the skeletal division of the peripheral nervous system.

4. **c.** is the answer. As automatic responses to stimuli, reflexes are the simplest complete units of behavior and require only simple neural pathways. (p. 56)

a., b., & d. Emotions, drives, and voluntary movements are all behaviors that are much more complex than reflexes and therefore involve much more complicated neural pathways.

e. Balance is regulated by the cerebellum.

5. **b.** is the answer. Endorphins are neurotransmitters that function as natural painkillers and are evidently involved in the "runner's high" and other situations in which discomfort or fatigue are expected but not experienced. (p. 52)

a. ACh is a neurotransmitter involved in muscular control.

c. Dopamine is a neurotransmitter involved in, among other things, motor control.

d. Norepinephrine is an adrenal hormone released to help us respond in moments of danger.

e. Acetylcholine is the complete name of ACh.

6. **a.** is the answer. Parkinson's disease causes the death of brain tissue that produces dopamine. (p. 54)

b. & c. This disease affects both hemispheres of the cortex.

d. This disease causes insufficient production of the neurotransmitters.

7. **d.** is the answer. (p. 59)

a. The EEG is an amplified recording of the brain's electrical activity.

b. The CT scan involves x-ray photographs of the brain.

c. The PET scan is a visual display of brain activity that detects the movement of a radioactive form of glucose as the brain performs a task.

8. **a.** is the answer. (p. 48)

c., d., & e. Myelin sheaths are not involved in regulating the release of neurotransmitters.

9. **c.** is the answer. (p. 49)

10. **b.** is the answer. ACh is a neurotransmitter that causes the contraction of muscle fibers when stimulated by motor neurons. This function explains its location. (p. 52)

a. & c. Sensory neurons and interneurons do not directly stimulate muscle fibers.

11. **d.** is the answer. The pituitary regulates body growth, and some of its secretions regulate the release of hormones from other glands. (p. 81)

a. The adrenal glands are stimulated by the autonomic nervous system to release epinephrine and norepinephrine.

b. The thyroid gland produces a hormone that controls the rates of various chemical reactions in the body.

c. The hypothalamus regulates the pituitary but does not itself directly regulate growth.

e. There is no such gland. Hyperthyroidism is a *condition* in which the thyroid gland is overactive.

12. **d.** is the answer. Also known as adrenaline and noradrenaline, epinephrine and norepinephrine are hormones released by the adrenal glands. (p. 81)

13. **d.** is the answer. The cerebellum is involved in the coordination of voluntary muscular movements. (p. 62)

a. The medulla regulates breathing and heartbeat.

b. The thalamus relays sensory inputs to the appropriate higher centers of the brain.

c. The hypothalamus is concerned with the regulation of basic drives and emotions.

e. The cerebrum is the center of all complex activities.

14. **a.** is the answer. The reticular formation controls arousal via its connections to the cortex. Thus, separating the two produces a coma. (p. 61)

b., c., d., & e. None of these structures controls arousal. The hypothalamus regulates hunger, thirst, sexual behavior, and other basic drives; the thalamus is a sensory relay station; the cerebellum is involved in the coordination of voluntary movement; and the medulla controls heartbeat and breathing.

15. **b.** is the answer. (p. 67)

c. & d. These refer to the sensory cortex.

16. **b.** is the answer. (p. 53)

a. Abuse of certain drugs, such as heroin, may have this effect.

c. This describes the effect of an antagonist.

d. Drugs do not have this effect on neurons.

17. **c.** is the answer. The corpus callosum is a large band of neural fibers linking the right and left cerebral hemispheres. To sever the corpus callosum is in effect to split the brain. (p. 72)

18. **d.** is the answer. The frontal lobe is in the front of the brain. Just behind is the parietal lobe. The occipital lobe is located at the very back of the

head and just below the parietal lobe. Next to the occipital lobe and toward the front of the head is the temporal lobe. (p. 65)

19. **d.** is the answer. As demonstrated in the case of Phineas Gage, injury to the frontal lobe may produce such changes in personality. (p. 69)
a. Damage to the parietal lobe might disrupt functions involving the sensory cortex.
b. Damage to the temporal lobe might impair hearing.
c. Occipital damage might impair vision.
e. The endocrine system is the body's slower chemical communication system that transmits hormones through the bloodstream from tissue to tissue.

20. **c.** is the answer. (p. 71)

Matching Items

1. d (p. 75)	**5.** i (p. 59)	**9.** k (p. 68)
2. g (p. 61)	**6.** a (p. 69)	**10.** b (p. 74)
3. e (p. 59)	**7.** j (p. 69)	**11.** c (p. 69)
4. f (p. 69)	**8.** h (p. 62)	

Brain Damage Diagram (pp. 58–70)

1. a	**4.** d	**7.** f
2. h	**5.** e	**8.** g
3. c	**6.** b	**9.** k

Thinking Critically About Chapter 2

Multiple-Choice Questions

1. **d.** is the answer. Biological psychologists study the links between biology (chemical changes in this example) and behavior (emotions in this example). (p. 48)
a., b., & c. Developmental, experimental, and clinical psychologists would be more concerned with the learning of emotional expressions, the treatment of emotional disorders, and life-span changes in emotions, respectively.

2. **c.** is the answer. The brainstem is the oldest and most primitive region of the brain. It is found in lower vertebrates, such as fish, as well as in humans and other mammals. The structures mentioned in the other choices are associated with stages of brain evolution beyond that seen in the fish. (p. 61)

3. **a.** is the answer. Since this reflex is an automatic response and involves only the spinal cord, the hand is jerked away before the brain has even received the information that causes the sensation of pain. (p. 56)
b. The spinal cord, which organizes simple reflex-es such as this one, is part of the central nervous system.
c. The brain is not involved in directing spinal reflexes.
d. The autonomic nervous system controls the glands and the muscles of the internal organs; it does not influence the skeletal muscles controlling the hand.

4. **d.** is the answer. Stimulation of the sensory cortex elicits a sense of touch, as the experiments of Penfield demonstrated. (p. 67)
a., b., & c. Hearing, seeing, or movement might be expected if the temporal, occipital, and motor regions of the cortex, respectively, were stimulated.

5. **c.** is the answer. As Olds and Milner discovered, electrical stimulation of the hypothalamus is a highly reinforcing event, because it is the location of the animal's reward centers. The other brain regions mentioned are not associated with reward centers. (p. 64)

6. **a.** is the answer. The left hand, controlled by the right hemisphere, would be able to identify the fork, the picture of which is flashed to the right hemisphere. (pp. 73)

7. **a.** is the answer. The PET scan, which traces the brain's use of a radioactive form of glucose, measures brain *activity* in various regions. It does not reveal anything about structure. (p. 59)
b., c., & d. Each of these techniques is utilized to study the structure or activity of the brain.

8. **b.** is the answer. Simple reflexes, such as this one, are governed by activity in the autonomic nervous system. (p. 55)
a. The occipital lobes process sensory messages from the eyes; they play no role in the reflexive response of the pupils to light.
c. The left temporal lobe specializes in processing language.
d. The cerebellum specializes in coordinating movement.
e. The brainstem is the oldest and innermost region of the brain.

9. **b.** is the answer. (p. 74)
a., c., & d. The left hemisphere does not specialize in facial recognition. And blood clots can form anywhere in the brain.

10. **a.** is the answer. In fact, handedness is one of only a few traits that identical twins are not especially likely to share. (p. 75)

11. **a.** is the answer. The right visual field projects directly to the verbal left hemisphere. (p. 73)

b. & c. The left hand is controlled by the right hemisphere, which, in this situation, would be unaware of the word since the picture has been flashed to the left hemisphere.

12. **c.** is the answer. (p. 60)
d. & e. Reproduction is only one of the basic survival functions the brain regulates.

13. **b.** is the answer. (p. 51)
a. By triggering release of dopamine, such a drug would probably *enhance* Malcolm's enjoyment of the pleasures of life.
c. & d. ACh is the neurotransmitter at synapses between motor neurons and muscle fibers.

14. **b.** is the answer. The hippocampus of the limbic system is involved in processing memory. The amygdala of the limbic system influences fear and anger. (p. 62)
a. & e. The brainstem controls vital functions such as breathing and heartbeat; it is not directly involved in either emotion or memory.
c. & d. These answers are incorrect because the limbic system is an older brain structure than the cortex. Its involvement in emotions and memory is therefore more basic than that of the cortex.

15. **b.** is the answer. (p. 47)
a. "Ahead of its time" implies the theory had merit, which later research clearly showed it did not. Moreover, phrenology *was* accepted as an accurate theory of brain organization by many scientists.
c. Phrenology said nothing about the similarities of human and animal brains.

16. **a.** is the answer. (p. 80)
b., c., & d. Acetylcholine and dopamine are fast-acting neurotransmitters released at synapses, not in the bloodstream.

17. **b.** is the answer. Sympathetic arousal produces several effects, including accelerated heartbeat and excessive perspiration. (p. 55)
a. Stimulation of the reticular formation increases alertness, but would not necessarily accelerate heartbeat or cause excessive perspiration.
c. Arousal of the parasympathetic nervous system would have effects opposite to those stated.
d. If the medication were affecting his amygdala, your brother might experience emotions such as anger or fear at illogical times.

18. **d.** is the answer. The thalamus relays sensory messages from the eyes, ears, and other receptors to the appropriate projection areas of the cortex. "Rewiring" the thalamus, theoretically, could have the effects stated in this question. (p. 62)
a., b., c., & e. These brain structures are not directly involved in brain processes related to sensation or perception.

19. **a.** is the answer. Hormones of the pituitary gland regulate body growth. (p. 81)
b., d., & e. Because they are not endocrine glands, the thalamus, medulla, and cerebellum are not influenced by hormones.
c. The adrenal glands produce hormones that provide energy during emergencies; they are not involved in regulating body growth.

20. **a.** is the answer. The motor cortex, which determines the precision with which various parts of the body can be moved, is located in the frontal lobes. (p. 66)
b. The parietal lobes contain the sensory cortex, which controls sensitivity to touch.
c. The temporal lobes contain the primary projection areas for hearing and, on the left side, are also involved in language use.
d. The occipital lobes contain the primary projection areas for vision.

Essay Question

The brainstem contains the medulla, which controls heartbeat, breathing, and other vital life functions that keep the musician alive. It is also the crossover point, where nerves to and from each side of the brain mostly connect with the opposite side of the the body.

Atop the brainstem sits the thalamus, which routes sensory information from the musician's eyes, ears, and fingertips to the higher brain regions concerned with seeing, hearing, and touching. Through the thalamus the musician's brain receives the necessary sensory information to enable decision making regarding all aspects of playing the instrument. The thalamus also routes some of the higher brain responses to the cerebellum, which helps coordinate movements involved in playing the instrument.

Within the brainstem the reticular formation receives inputs from the thalamus and the cerebral cortex that help maintain the musician's arousal, which is important in performing before a group.

The limbic system's involvement in emotion, motivation, and memory will influence many aspects of a musical performance. The hippocampus will be involved in the formation of memories of how to play the musical instrument, as well as memories of the notes and lyrics for each song. The pleasure centers of the hypothalamus comprise the brain's reward system and will help maintain the musician's motivation for learning and playing the instrument.

The cerebral cortex will oversee all aspects of the musician's behavior. Sensory projection areas in the occipital, temporal, and parietal lobes will process messages from the musician's eyes, ears, and fingertips. The motor cortex of the frontal lobes will organize the necessary body movements. Finally, association areas in the frontal lobes and other parts of the brain will be involved in the planning and decision making inherent in playing the musical instrument.

Key Terms

Writing Definitions

1. **Biological psychology** is the study of the links between biology and behavior. (p. 48)

2. The **neuron**, or nerve cell, is the basic building block of the nervous system. (p. 48)

3. The **dendrites** of a neuron are the bushy, branching extensions that receive messages from other nerve cells and conduct impulses toward the cell body. (p. 48)

4. The **axon** of a neuron is the extension that sends impulses to other nerve cells or to muscles or glands. (p. 48)

5. The **myelin sheath** is a layer of fatty tissue that covers many axons and helps speed neural impulses. (p. 48)

6. An **action potential** is a neural impulse generated by the movement of positively charged atoms in and out of channels in the axon's membrane. (p. 49)

7. A neuron's **threshold** is the level of stimulation that must be exceeded in order for the neuron to fire, or generate an electrical impulse. (p. 50)

8. A **synapse** is the junction between the axon tip of the sending neuron and the dendrite or cell body of the receiving neuron. The tiny gap at this junction is called the synaptic cleft or gap. (p. 50)

9. **Neurotransmitters** are chemicals that are released into synaptic gaps and so *transmit neural messages* from neuron to neuron. (p. 50)

10. **Acetylcholine (ACh)** is a neurotransmitter that triggers muscle contractions. (p. 52)

11. **Endorphins** are natural, opiatelike neurotransmitters linked to pain control and to pleasure. (p. 52)

    Memory aid: <u>End</u>orphins *end* pain.

12. The **nervous system** is the speedy, electrochemical communication system, consisting of all the nerve cells in the peripheral and central nervous systems. (p. 54)

13. The **central nervous system** consists of the brain and spinal cord; it is located at the *center*, or internal core, of the body. (p. 54)

14. The **peripheral nervous system** connects the central nervous system to the body's sense receptors, muscles, and glands; it is at the *periphery* of the body relative to the brain and spinal cord. (p. 54)

15. **Nerves** are bundles of neural axons that connect the central nervous system with muscles, glands, and sense organs. (p. 54)

16. **Sensory neurons** carry information from the sense receptors to the central nervous system for processing. (p. 54)

17. **Interneurons** are the neurons of the central nervous system that link the sensory and motor neurons in the transmission of sensory inputs and motor outputs. (p. 54)

18. **Motor neurons** carry information and instructions for action from the central nervous system to muscles and glands. (p. 54)

19. The **somatic nervous system** is the division of the peripheral nervous system that controls voluntary movements of the skeletal muscles. (p. 55)

20. The **autonomic nervous system** is the division of the peripheral nervous system that controls the glands and the muscles of internal organs and thereby controls internal functioning; it regulates the *automatic* behaviors necessary for survival. (p. 55)

21. The **sympathetic nervous system** is the division of the autonomic nervous system that arouses the body, mobilizing its energy in stressful situations. (p. 55)

22. The **parasympathetic nervous system** is the division of the autonomic nervous system that calms the body, conserving its energy. (p. 55)

23. A **reflex** is a simple, automatic, inborn response to a sensory stimulus; it is governed by a very simple neural pathway. (p. 56)

24. **Neural networks** are interconnected neural cells, the specific connections of which are strengthened as learning occurs. (p. 57)

25. A **lesion** is destruction of tissue; studying the consequences of lesions in different regions of the brain—both surgically produced in animals and naturally occurring—helps researchers to determine the normal functions of these regions. (p. 58)

26. An **electroencephalogram (EEG)** is an amplified recording of the waves of electrical activity of the

brain. *Encephalo* comes from a Greek word meaning "related to the brain." (p. 59)

27. The **CT (computed tomography) scan** is a series of x-ray photographs of the brain taken from different positions and analyzed by computer, creating an image that represents a slice through the brain. (p. 59)

28. The **PET (positron emission tomography) scan** measures the levels of activity of different areas of the brain by tracing their consumption of a radioactive form of glucose, the brain's fuel. (p. 59)

29. **MRI (magnetic resonance imaging)** uses magnetic fields and radio waves to produce computer-generated images that show brain structures more clearly. (p. 59)

30. The **brainstem**, the oldest and innermost region of the brain, is an extension of the spinal cord and is the central core of the brain; its structures direct automatic survival functions. (p. 61)

31. Located in the brainstem, the **medulla** controls breathing and heartbeat. (p. 61)

32. Also part of the brainstem, the **reticular formation** is a nerve network that plays an important role in controlling arousal. (p. 61)

33. Located atop the brainstem, the **thalamus** routes incoming messages to the appropriate cortical centers and transmits replies to the medulla and cerebellum. (p. 62)

34. The **cerebellum** assists in balance and the coordination of voluntary movement. (p. 62)

35. A doughnut-shaped neural system, the **limbic system** plays an important role in the regulation of emotions and basic physiological drives. (p. 62)
Memory aid: Its name comes from the Latin word *limbus*, meaning "border"; the **limbic system** is at the border of the brainstem and cerebral hemispheres.

36. The **amygdala** is part of the limbic system and is involved in regulation of the emotions of fear and rage. (p. 62)

37. Also part of the limbic system, the **hypothalamus** regulates hunger, thirst, and body temperature and contains the so-called reward centers of the brain. (p. 63)

38. The **cerebral cortex** is the thin outer covering of the cerebral hemispheres. The seat of information processing, the cortex is responsible for those complex functions that make us distinctively human. (p. 64)
Memory aid: Cortex in Latin means "bark." As

bark covers a tree, the **cerebral cortex** is the "bark of the brain."

39. More numerous than cortical neurons, the **glial cells** of the brain guide neural connections, provide nutrients and insulating myelin, and help remove excess ions and neurotransmitters. (p. 65)

40. Located at the front of the brain, just behind the forehead, the **frontal lobes** are involved in speaking and muscle movements and in making plans and judgments. (p. 65)

41. Situated between the frontal and occipital lobes, the **parietal lobes** contain the sensory cortex. (p. 65)

42. Located at the back and base of the brain, the **occipital lobes** contain the visual cortex, which receives information from the eyes. (p. 65)

43. Located on the sides of the brain, the **temporal lobes** contain the auditory areas, which receive information from the ears. (p. 65)
Memory aid: The **temporal lobes** are located near the *temples.*

44. Located at the back of the frontal lobe, the **motor cortex** controls voluntary movement. (p. 66)

45. The **sensory cortex** is located at the front of the parietal lobes, just behind the motor cortex. It registers and processes body sensations. (p. 67)

46. Located throughout the cortex, **association areas** of the brain are involved in higher mental functions, such as learning, remembering, and abstract thinking. (p. 68)
Memory aid: Among their other functions, **association areas** of the cortex are involved in integrating, or *associating*, information from different areas of the brain.

47. **Aphasia** is an impairment of language as a result of damage to any of several cortical areas, including Broca's area and Wernicke's area. (p. 69)

48. **Broca's area**, located in the left frontal lobe, is involved in controlling the motor ability to produce speech. (p. 69)

49. **Wernicke's area,** located in the left temporal lobe, is involved in language comprehension. (p. 69)

50. **Plasticity** is the brain's capacity for modification, as evidenced by brain reorganization following damage (especially in children). (p. 71)

51. The **corpus callosum** is a large band of neural fibers that links the right and left cerebral hemispheres. Without this band of nerve fibers, the two hemispheres could not interact. (p. 72)

52. **Split brain** is a condition in which the major connections between the two cerebral hemispheres (the corpus callosum) are severed, literally resulting in a split brain. (p. 72)

53. The **endocrine system**, the body's "slower" chemical communication system, consists of glands that secrete hormones into the bloodstream. (p. 80)

54. **Hormones** are chemical messengers, mostly those manufactured by the endocrine system, that are produced in one tissue and circulate through the bloodstream to their target tissues, on which they have specific effects. (p. 80)

55. The **adrenal glands** produce epinephrine and norepinephrine, hormones that prepare the body to deal with emergencies or stress. (p. 81)

56. The **pituitary gland**, under the influence of the hypothalamus, regulates growth and controls other endocrine glands; sometimes called the "master gland." (p. 81)

Cross-Check

ACROSS

3. peripheral
6. temporal
7. motor
9. frontal
12. adrenal
14. medulla
15. cortex
16. synapse
17. EEG
19. lesion
20. MRI
22. occipital
24. amygdala
27. parietal

DOWN

1. hypothalamus
2. corpus callosum
3. PET scan
4. action potential
5. acetylcholine
8. reflex
10. limbic system
11. endorphins
13. autonomic
17. endocrine
18. central
21. aphasia
23. CT scan
25. glial
26. axon

FOCUS ON VOCABULARY AND LANGUAGE

Page 47: . . . an ill-fated theory. . . . Myers is referring to the theory that bumps or lumps on the skull could reveal our personality (*phrenology*). It was a theory destined for failure (*ill-fated*), despite its popularity during the early 1800s.

Page 48: A wrong-headed theory . . . Even though phrenology was without any scientific merit (*wrong-headed*), it did suggest the idea that different parts of the brain influence a variety of functions and behaviors.

Neural Communication

Page 48: For scientists, it is a *fortunate fact of nature* that the information systems of humans and other animals operate similarly. The structure and function of neurons are very similar in humans and other animals (e.g., squids and sea slugs) and this is fortunate (*a happy fact of nature*) for those researching the nervous system. Myers makes the important point about this similarity, noting that it would not be possible to tell the difference between a small piece of your brain tissue and that of a monkey.

Page 48: Its *building blocks* are **neurons,** or nerve cells. Building blocks are the basic or fundamental parts (e.g., bricks) that make up a structure (e.g., a house). The structure of our nervous system, or neural information system, is made up of neurons (*its building blocks*) .

Page 48: . . . the neural impulse travels at speeds ranging from a *sluggish* 2 miles per hour to, in some myelinated fibers, a *breakneck* 200 or more miles per hour. The speed of the neural impulse ranges from extremely slow (*sluggish*) to very fast (a *breakneck* speed). Compared to the speed of electricity or sophisticated electronics systems your neural impulses travel at a relatively slow pace.

Page 49: . . . the **action potential**, is a brief electrical charge that travels down the axon, *rather like a line of dominoes falling, each one tripping the next.* Dominoes are the flat pieces used in the game of dominoes. If they are stacked side by side on end (like a shelf of books) and one end is pushed, all the rest fall over one by one. The impulse travels down the axon in much the same way, in a series of electrochemical events.

Page 50: Some of these signals are *excitatory, somewhat like pushing a neuron's accelerator.* Other signals are *inhibitory, more like pushing its brake.* Myers is making a comparison between the effect of a neuron firing and the effect of speeding up a car when accelerating (*excitatory effect*) or slowing it down by applying the brake (*inhibitory effect*).

Page 50: How do we distinguish a gentle touch from a big hug? This question is concerned with how we become aware of the magnitude of a stimulus, from a soft stroke or pat (*gentle touch*) to a strong embrace (*firm hug*). The answer is that the intensity of the stimulus is a function of the number and frequency of neurons firing. A strong stimulus (*firm hug*) does not initiate (*trigger*) a more powerful or faster impulse than a weak stimulus (*gentle touch*); rather, it triggers more neurons to fire, and to fire more often.

Page 50: . . . these near-unions of neurons—"protoplasmic kisses". . . were another of nature's marvels. The reference here is to the fact that the axon terminal of one neuron is separated from the receiving neuron by a tiny space called the synaptic gap. Protoplasm is the material that constitutes all living cells, and the communication between cells is likened to a kiss between cells. The transmission between sender and receiver is via chemicals called neurotransmitters. The cells don't actually touch but send messages across the synaptic gap.

Page 50: Roughly speaking, the neuron is democratic. . . . What this means is that, in general (*roughly speaking*), the neuron will fire depending on whether or not there are more excitatory than inhibitory messages, just as one candidate may get elected over another depending on how many votes he or she gets in a democratic election.

Page 52: . . . "runner's high" . . . This refers to the feeling of emotional well-being or euphoria (*high*) following vigorous exercise such as running or jogging and is the result of the release of opiatelike substances called endorphins.

Page 53: They trigger unpleasant, lingering aftereffects. For suppressing the body's own neurotransmitter production, *nature charges a price.* Mood-altering drugs, such as alcohol, nicotine, heroin, and morphine, all initiate (*trigger*) disagreeable changes that persist for a long period of time (*lingering aftereffects*). When flooded with these opiates, the brain stops producing its own endorphins (i.e., they suppress production), and for the addict who stops taking the drugs the cost may be a great deal of pain and agony (*nature charges a price*).

Page 53: Agonists excite by mimicking a particular neurotransmitter or by blocking its reuptake. Antagonists inhibit by blocking neurotransmitters or by diminishing their release. An *agonist* drug molecule is enough like the neurotransmitter to imitate (*mimic*) its effects (for example, by producing a temporary euphoric feeling—a "high"). An *antagonist* drug molecule is enough like the neurotransmitter

to stop (*block*) its effects but not similar enough to stimulate the receptor (for example, some toxins may cause muscle paralysis by blocking acetylcholine receptors).

Page 54: . . . some chemicals don't have the right shape to slither through this [blood-brain] barrier . . . Some neurotransmitter substances (*chemicals*) such as dopamine do not work when given to patients because they can't slide or slip smoothly (*slither*) through the *blood-brain barrier* since they are the wrong shape. The *blood-brain barrier* is a system that blocks or obstructs unwanted chemicals circulating in the blood from getting into the brain (the brain *fences them out*).

The Nervous System

Page 55: Like an automatic pilot, it may sometimes be consciously overridden. The autonomic nervous system automatically takes care of the operation of our internal organs much as a plane can be flown by the automatic (*or mechanical/computerized*) pilot. The system can, however, be consciously taken over (*overridden*) in the same way that the real pilot can take over flying the plane.

Page 56: Tens of billions of neurons, each in communication with thousands of other neurons, yield an ever-changing wiring diagram that dwarfs a powerful computer. The complexity of the central nervous system, which allows or makes possible (*enables*) our thinking, feeling, and behavior, is similar to the electronic circuitry (*wiring diagrams*) of the best computer, except, by comparison, the computer would appear to be extremely tiny or small (*dwarfed by*) and the brain's wiring would seem to be constantly modifying or altering itself (*ever-changing*).

Page 56: . . . information highway. . . . The spinal cord is similar to the freeway (*highway*), but instead of cars moving up and down, sensory and motor messages (*information*) travel between the peripheral nervous system and the brain. This information moves either up (*ascending*) or down (*descending*) bundles of nerve fibers (*tracts*).

Page 56: The knee-jerk response, for example, involves one such simple pathway; a headless warm body could do it. When the patellar tendon of a bent knee is struck, the whole leg reflexively straightens out (*the knee-jerk response*). This automatic reaction is a function of a simple spinal reflex pathway so it does not require mediation by the brain (*a headless warm [live] body could do it*).

Page 57: Being human takes a lot of nerve. Myers is using humor to make a point here. The expression "it takes a lot of nerve" means to be very brave or courageous. Since the expression follows the discussion of the number of nerve cells and connections in the human cortex, it takes on a very different meaning (i.e., humans are made up of many nerves).

Page 57: Neurons cluster into *work groups* called neural networks. Myers points out that the brain works much like a computer making many simultaneous computations. This is accomplished by neural networks which are clusters of interconnected neurons (*work groups*). Neurons work with nearby neurons for much the same reason people live in cities—it is easier for brief, quick interactions.

The Brain

Page 58: The known universe's most amazing organ is being probed and mapped by a new generation of neural cartographers. A cartographer is someone who prepares or makes maps. Myers is suggesting that the brain (*the known universe's most amazing organ*) is going to be graphically depicted (*mapped*) by a new younger group of neuroscientists (a new generation of neural *cartographers*).

Page 58: . . . we live in our heads. What this means is that you subjectively feel that the essence of your being, your mind, resides in your brain, which is inside your head. The brain in our head allows us to function psychologically as well as physically: *the mind is what the brain does.*

Page 58: We can *snoop on* the messages of individual neurons and on the *mass action* of billions. With today's technological tools it is possible to pry or spy on (*snoop on*) single nerve cells (neurons) as well as graphically depict the collective behavior (*mass action*) of millions and millions of cells.

Pages 58–59: . . . the right side of the body is *wired* to the brain's left side, and *vice versa.* This means that the functions of one side of the body are controlled by (*wired to*) the opposite side of the brain. The right side of the body is controlled by the left hemisphere, and the other way is also true (*vice versa*): the left side of the body is controlled by the brain's right side.

Page 59: Other *new windows into the brain* give us a *Supermanlike* ability to see inside the brain without *lesioning it.* Modern technological means of viewing the brain (*new windows into the brain*), such as the CT and the PET scans, provide us with a greater than normal (*Supermanlike*) ability to look inside the cortex without destroying tissue (*lesioning it*). (*Note:*

Superman is a comic-book, TV, and movie character with x-ray vision which allows him to see through solid matter.)

Page 60: Such *snapshots* of the brain's *activity* provide new insights into how and where the brain *divides its labor.* The MRI technique allows pictures (*snapshots*) to be taken of different brain areas at work (the brain *divides its labor*) while a person is carrying out various mental tasks.

Page 60: So there are *exceptions* to the *rule of thumb* that the ratio of brain to body weight provides a clue to a species' intelligence. A *rule of thumb* is a general principle which is usually true, but there are some occasions (*exceptions*) when the maxim or guide (*rule of thumb*) is incorrect. Myers suggests that a more practical and productive approach than the brain-body weight ratio is the study of the various structures of the brain.

Page 61: This peculiar cross-wiring is but one of many surprises the brain has to offer. In the brainstem most nerves from the left side of the body connect to the right side of the brain and those from the right connect to the left side of the brain. This strange (*peculiar*) traverse of nerves from one side to the other (*cross-wiring*) is one of the many marvels or astonishing findings (*surprises*) about the brain.

Page 62: Think of the thalamus as being to sensory input what *London is to England's trains.* London is the relay center for trains going to all parts of the country just as Chicago is the hub or relay center for many airlines flying to different parts of the United States. Myers uses this as an analogy for the thalamus, which receives messages from sensory neurons and sends them on, or relays them to higher brain areas.

Page 62: . . . a *doughnut-shaped* neural system, the **limbic system**. This system is in the shape of a ring (*doughnut-shaped*) and has three components: the **hippocampus,** which is involved in forming (*laying down*) new memories; the **amygdala,** which influences aggression and fear; and the **hypothalamus,** which regulates hunger, thirst, body temperature, and sexuality.

Page 63: In a few cases involving patients who suffered brain abnormalities, it ["*psychosurgery*"] *reduced fits of rage,* though sometimes with devastating side effects on the patient's everyday functioning. *Psychosurgery* refers to destruction (lesioning) of healthy brain tissue to achieve some psychological change in a patient, such as making a violent patient calm and relaxed (*reducing fits of rage*). Because there were also other severe changes (*side effects*), this drastic procedure is almost never used today.

Page 64: . . . they made *a magnificent mistake*. Olds and Milner accidentally discovered (*stumbled upon*) a brain area that provides a pleasurable reward and then went on to find other similar areas which they called "*pleasure centers.*" Myers calls this a splendid and spectacular error (*a magnificent mistake*). When rats are allowed to stimulate these areas by pressing a bar (*pedal*) they seem to prefer this to any other activity and will continue at a very rapid rate (*feverish pace*) until they are too tired to go on (*until they drop from exhaustion*).

Page 65: If you opened a human skull, exposing the brain, you would see a *wrinkled* organ, shaped somewhat like the *meat of an oversized walnut*. The human brain has a convoluted (*wrinkled*) surface, and the cerebral cortex is divided into two halves or hemispheres just like the two lobes of the edible portion (*the meat or seed*) in the shell of a very large (*oversized*) walnut.

Page 67: In a sense, we *do* have *eyes in the back of our head!* The reference here is to the visual cortex (or occipital lobes) which processes visual information and is located at the rear of the brain. So, in a way seeing is not just done with the eyes but also involves specialized areas at the back of the brain.

Page 68: . . . one of pop psychology's most widespread *falsehoods:* that we ordinarily *use only 10 percent of our brains*. Research into the association areas of the brain showed that they don't have specific functions but rather are involved in many different operations such as interpreting, integrating, and acting on information processed by the sensory areas. The incorrect notion (*falsehood*) that *we use only 10 percent of our brains* may have arisen because early researchers were unsure about the function of the association areas. Remember, we use all of our brain, all the time. Damage to the frontal lobes (association areas) would result in very serious deficits.

Page 70: *What you experience as a continuous, indivisible stream of perception is actually but the visible tip of the information-processing iceberg, most of which lies beneath the surface of your conscious awareness.* Myers is making an analogy here. Most of the important functions that allow you to see the world as a whole are not part of conscious experience, but like most of the mass of an iceberg, are below the surface and out of awareness.

Page 71: Thus, the brain may not be as "*hard-wired*" as once thought. Myers is noting a comparison that

used to be made between the brain's neural networks and the fixed circuits of computer hardware. We now know that the brain is much more flexible—it is not "*hard-wired.*" Myers uses the term *plastic* or *brain plasticity* to describe this malleability or adaptability.

Page 72: Waking from the surgery, one patient even managed to *quip* that he had a "*splitting headache*" . . . . People have had their corpus callosum severed or cut in order to control epileptic seizures. Despite such a major operation this patient managed to joke (*quip*) that he had a very bad headache (*a splitting headache*). Personality and intellectual functioning were not affected by this procedure, and you would not be able to detect anything unusual if you were having a casual conversation with a split-brain patient.

Page 74: When the "two minds" are at odds, the left hemisphere seems to act as *the brain's press agent*, doing *mental gymnastics* to *rationalize* reactions it does not understand. In split-brain patients, if information or commands are delivered to the right hemisphere (which does not have language), then the left hemisphere, which can talk, would not be aware of what was requested. So if the patient carried out the command to do something (e.g., "walk" or "clap"), the left hemisphere will go through all kinds of contortions (*mental gymnastics*) to make up some plausible story (*rationalize*); in this way it acts to make sense of and explain behavior, much as *press agents* do for the company or person they represent.

Page 75: From simply looking at the two hemispheres, which *look alike* to the *naked eye*, who would suppose that they contribute so uniquely to *the harmony of the whole*? Myers points out that research with split-brain people and normal people shows that we have unified brains with different parts that have specialized functions. Thus, if we observe the two hemispheres without optical aids (*with the naked eye*), they may appear to be the same (*look alike*); however, their differential functioning combines to produce an integrated unit (*the harmony of the whole*).

Page 79: When at their worst, they distort *pretzel-shaped findings* into a *breadstick-shaped story*: Some people are left-brained, others right-brained. . . . A *pretzel* is a snack food, a piece of thinly rolled bread dough shaped like an open knot. A unique and unusual set of findings (*pretzel-shaped*) gets transformed through the process of oversimplification and distortion into something totally different (*a breadstick-shaped* [very straight] *story*). Thus, public myths, such as *"some people are left-brained, others right brained,"* develop and get more attention than the scientific facts.

The Endocrine System

Page 80: The endocrine system and nervous system are therefore *kindred* systems. These two systems are very similar and have a close relationship (*kindred systems*). The hormones of the endocrine system are chemically equivalent to neurotransmitters, but operate at a much slower speed (i.e., the endocrine messages use *the slow lane* while the nervous system *zips* [or speeds] messages from eyes to brain in a fraction of a second).

Page 81: Conducting and coordinating this whole *electrochemical orchestra* is that *maestro* we call the brain. Myers is comparing the functioning of the neurotransmitters and hormones to a large group of musicians (*electrochemical orchestra*) whose movements and actions are directed by the conductor or master (*maestro*), the brain.

Page 82: Yet what is unknown still *dwarfs* what is known. This means that all that has been discovered so far is very, very small (*dwarfed*) compared to what yet remains to be discovered.

3:

The Nature and Nurture of Behavior

Chapter Overview

Chapter 3 is concerned with the ways in which our biological heritage, or nature, interacts with our individual experiences, or nurture, to shape who we are. After a brief explanation of basic terminology, the chapter discusses psychology's use of evolutionary principles to answer universal questions about human behavior. The next section explores the fields of behavior genetics, which studies twins and adopted children to weigh genetic and environmental influences on behaviors, and molecular genetics, which focuses on the specific genes that influence behavior.

The third section of the chapter shifts the spotlight to focus on environmental influences on behavior. The impact of parents, the prenatal environment, early experience, peers, and culture on the development of the brain and behavior are each discussed in depth. The final section of the chapter explores how genes and environment interact to shape both the biological and social aspects of our gender. In the end, the message is clear: our genes and our experience together form who we are.

NOTE: Answer guidelines for all Chapter 3 questions begin on page 93.

Genes: Our Biological Blueprint (pp. 86–87)

> David Myers at times uses idioms that are unfamiliar to some readers. If you do not know the meaning of the following word in the context in which it appears in the text, refer to page 100 for an explanation: *blueprint.*

Section Preview

First, skim this section, noting headings and boldface items. Then read the following objectives and, as you read the section, search for the information that will enable you to meet each objective. Answer guidelines are provided on page 93.

1. Identify the mechanisms of heredity.

2. Explain why geneticists and psychologists are interested in the commonalities and variations in our genetic makeup.

Stepping Through the Section

After you have read the section, complete the sentences and answer the questions. As you proceed, evaluate your performance by consulting the answers on page 93. Do not continue with the next section until you understand each answer. If you need to, review or reread the section in the textbook before continuing.

1. A fundamental question in psychology deals with the extent to which we are shaped by our heredity, called our _____ , and by our life history, called our _____ .

2. The master plans for development are stored in the _____ . In number, each person inherits _____ of these structures, _____ from each parent. Each is composed of a coiled chain of a molecule called

_____ .

3. If chromosomes are the "books" of heredity, the "words" that make each of us a distinctive human being are called _____ .
These, in turn, are defined by pairings of four biochemical "letters" called _____ .
The sequence of these letters is _____ (very different/virtually the same) from person to person.

4. The complete instructions for making an organism are referred to as the human

_____ .

Evolutionary Psychology: Explaining Universal Behaviors (pp. 87–93)

If you do not know the meaning of any of the following words, phrases, or expressions in the context in which they appear in the text, refer to page 100 for an explanation: *tight genetic leash; Casual hit-and-run sex; sexual come-on; In our ancestral history, females sent their genes into the future by pairing wisely, men by pairing widely; potential dads over likely cads; mobile gene machines.*

Section Preview

Answer guidelines are provided on page 93.

1. Explain the scope of the new field of evolutionary psychology, focusing on the importance of the concept of natural selection.

2. Discuss gender differences in sexuality, and outline the evolutionary explanation for these differences.

3. Identify several criticisms of evolutionary explanations of gender differences in sexuality.

Stepping Through the Section

Answers are provided on page 93.

1. According to the principle of _____ _____ , traits that contribute to reproduction and survival will be most likely to be passed on to succeeding generations.

2. Genetic _____ are random errors in genetic replication that are the source of all genetic _____ .

3. Genetic constraints on human behavior are generally _____ (tighter/looser) than those on animal behavior.

4. Researchers who study natural selection and the adaptive nature of human behavior are called _____ _____ . The principles of natural selection favor behaviors that spread one's _____ .

5. Compared to females, males are _____ (equally/more/less) likely to engage in casual hit-and-run sex, and they are _____ (equally/more/ less) likely to initiate sexual activity. This is an example of a _____ difference.

6. Men have a _____ (higher/lower) threshold for perceiving a woman's friendliness as a sexual come-on. This helps explain men's greater sexual _____ .

7. The _____ explanation of gender differences in attitudes toward sex is based on differences in the optimal strategy by which women and men pass on their _____ . According to this view, because _____ (eggs/sperm) are much more prevalent than _____ (eggs/sperm), males and females are selected for different patterns of sexuality.

8. Cross-cultural research reveals that men judge women as more attractive if they have a _____ appearance, whereas women judge men who appear _____ , _____ , and _____ as more attractive.

9. Critics of the evolutionary explanation of the gender sexuality difference argue that it often works _____ (forward/backward) to propose a _____ explanation. Critics also contend that evolutionary reasoning about sex often reinforces gender _____ . A third critique is that gender differences in sexuality vary with _____ expectations and social and family structures. Gender differences in mate preferences are largest in cultures characterized by greater gender _____ (equality/inequality).

Behavior Genetics: Explaining Individual Differences (pp. 93–101)

> If you do not know the meaning of any of the following words, phrases, or expressions in the context in which they appear in the text, refer to pages 100–101 for an explanation: *To disentangle the threads of heredity and environment, behavior geneticists often use two sets of tweezers; startling twin similarity stories; Genes-R-Us; "uptight" or "easygoing"; the area of a field is more the result of its length or width; sleuth; two-edged sword.*

Section Preview

Answer guidelines are provided on page 93.

1. Describe the focus of behavior genetics, and explain why researchers use twin and adoption studies to study individual differences.

2. Discuss the origins of temperament, and explain the concept of heritability.

3. Discuss the scope of the new frontier of molecular genetics.

Stepping Through the Section

Answers are provided on page 94.

1. Researchers who specifically study the effects of genes on behavior are called _____ _____ . As used by these researchers, the term *environment* refers to every _____ influence.

2. To study the power and limits of genetic influences on behavior, researchers use _____ and _____ studies.

3. Twins who developed from a single egg are genetically _____. Twins who developed from different fertilized eggs are no more genetically alike than siblings and are called _____ twins. In terms of the personality traits of extraversion and neuroticism, identical twins are _____ (more/no more) alike than are fraternal twins.

4. Divorce rates are _____ (more/no more) similar among identical twins than among fraternal twins.

5. Through research on identical twins raised apart, psychologists are able to study the influence of the _____ .

6. Studies tend to show that the personalities of adopted children _____ (do/do not) closely resemble those of their adoptive parents. Still, adoption studies show that parenting _____ (does/does not) matter. For example, adoptive children often score _____ (higher/lower) than their biological parents on intelligence tests.

7. The term that refers to the inborn rudiments of an infant's personality, especially the child's emotional excitability, is _____ , which _____ (does/does not) endure over time.

8. Faced with a new or strange situation, high-strung infants become _____ (more/less) physiologically aroused than less excitable infants.

9. Genetic influences may also help explain why infants of _____ (Asian/European) descent may be calmer than those of _____ (Asian/European) descent.

10. The proportion of variation in a trait within a group that is attributable to genes is called its _____ . As environments become more similar, heredity as a source of differences becomes _____ (more/less) important.

11. Heritable individual differences _____ (imply/need not imply) heritable group differences.

12. For _____ traits, human differences are nearly always the result of both _____ and _____ influences.

13. Although genetic influences help explain individual differences in _____ _____ and criminal and _____ tendencies, _____ also plays a role.

14. Throughout life, we are the product of the _____ of our _____ predispositions and our surrounding _____ .

15. The new subfield of biology that investigates the specific genes that influence behavior is _____ _____ . One result of their research, genetic screening, allows expectant parents to ascertain, and even choose, the _____ of their offspring. Prenatal screening, however, raises many _____ issues.

Environmental Influence (pp. 102–110)

> If you do not know the meaning of any of the following words, phrases, or expressions in the context in which they appear in the text, refer to pages 101–102 for an explanation: *as a potter molds clay; while the excess connections are still on call; pathways through a forest; wiring of Eric Clapton's brain; cerebral hard drive . . . cultural software; norms grease the social machinery; cultures collide; distilling data; bodes well.*

Section Preview

Answer guidelines are provided on page 94.

1. Discuss the effect of parental behavior and the prenatal environment on person-to-person differences in children's personalities.

2. Describe the role of experience on brain development and the socializing influence of peers on children and youth.

3. Discuss the effect of culture on behavior and child-rearing practices.

Stepping Through the Section

Answers are provided on page 95.

1. Genetic influences explain about _____ percent of individual variations in many personality traits.

2. Children's shared environmental influences—including the same home influences—typically account for less than _____ percent of their personality differences.

3. Environmental influences begin during the period of _____ development. Even identical twins may differ in this respect, because they may or may not share the same

   _____ .

4. Rosenzweig and Krech discovered that rats raised from a young age in enriched environments had _____ (thicker/thinner) cortexes than animals raised in isolation.

Describe the effects of sensory stimulation on neural development.

5. Experiences with _____ have a powerful effect on how children develop, partly as a result of a "_____ effect" by which kids seek out others with similar attitudes and interests.

6. The enduring behaviors, ideas, attitudes, and traditions of a group of people and transmitted from one generation to the next defines the group's

   _____ .

7. All cultural groups evolve their own rules for expected behavior, called _____ .
   For example, one such rule involves the buffer zone that people maintain around their bodies, called _____ _____ .

Identify several cultural differences in personal space, expressiveness, and pace of life.

8. Cultures may change so rapidly that evolutionary psychologists have coined a term, _____ , to refer to the self-replicating ideas, fashions, and innovations passed from person to person.

9. Whereas most Western parents place more emphasis on _____ (emotional closeness/independence) in their children, many Asian and African parents focus on cultivating _____ (emotional closeness/independence).

10. In general, differences between groups are _____ (smaller/larger) than person-to-person differences within groups.

Gender and Postscript: Reflections on Nature and Nurture (pp. 110–116)

> If you do not know the meaning of any of the following words, phrases, or expressions in the context in which they appear in the text, refer to page 102 for an explanation: *throws a master switch; "tomboyish"; initiate dates . . . pick up the check; With the flick of an apron.*

Section Preview

Answer guidelines are provided on page 95.

1. Explain how nature defines our gender.

2. Explain how gender is also socially constructed.

3. Summarize the results and implications of research on the nature-nurture issue.

Stepping Through the Section

Answers are provided on page 95.

1. The twenty-third pair of chromosomes determines the developing person's _____ . The mother always contributes a(n) _____ chromosome. When the father contributes a(n) _____ chromosome, the testes begin producing the hormone _____ . In about the _____ (what week?), this hormone initiates the development of external male sex organs.

2. Genetically female infants who were exposed to excess testosterone during prenatal development develop _____-appearing genitals. Behaviorally, until adolescence, they tend to act in more aggressive "_____ " ways than do most girls.

3. Our expectations about the way men and women behave define our culture's _____ _____ .

4. Gender roles _____ (are/are not) rigidly fixed by evolution, as evidenced by the fact that they vary across _____ and over _____ .

5. Our individual sense of being male or female is called our _____ _____ . The degree to which we exhibit traditionally male or female traits and interests is called _____-_____ .

6. According to _____ _____ theory, children learn gender-linked behaviors by observing others and being rewarded or punished.

7. When their families discourage traditional gender-typing, children _____ (do/do not) organize themselves into "boy worlds" and "girl worlds."

8. According to _____ _____ theory, children learn from their _____ what it means to be male or female and adjust their behavior accordingly.

Progress Test 1

Multiple-Choice Questions

Circle your answers to the following questions and check them with the answers on page 95. If your answer is incorrect, read the explanation for why it is incorrect and then consult the appropriate pages of the text (in parentheses following the correct answer).

1. Dr. Ross believes that principles of natural selection help explain why infants come to fear strangers about the time they become mobile. Dr. Ross is most likely a(n):
    a. behavior geneticist.
    b. molecular geneticist.
    c. evolutionary psychologist.
    d. molecular biologist.

2. A pair of adopted children or identical twins reared in the same home are most likely to have similar:
    a. temperaments.
    b. personalities.
    c. religious beliefs.
    d. emotional reactivity.

3. The sequence of the four nucleotide letters:
    a. is virtually the same in all humans.
    b. is virtually the same throughout the animal kingdom.
    c. varies from race to race.
    d. is more similar among females than among males.

4. If a fraternal twin becomes schizophrenic, the likelihood of the other twin developing serious mental illness is much lower than with identical twins. This suggests that:
    a. schizophrenia is caused by genes.
    b. schizophrenia is influenced by genes.
    c. environment is unimportant in the development of schizophrenia.
    d. identical twins are especially vulnerable to mental disorders.

5. Of the following, the best way to separate the effects of genes and environment in research is to study:
    a. fraternal twins.
    b. identical twins.
    c. adopted children and their adoptive parents.
    d. identical twins raised in different environments.

6. Through natural selection, the traits that are most likely to be passed on to succeeding generations are those that contribute to:
    a. reproduction.   d. a. and b.
    b. survival.   e. a., b., and c.
    c. aggressiveness.

7. Which of the following is *not* true regarding gender and sexuality?
    a. Men more often than women attribute a woman's friendliness to sexual interest.
    b. Women are more likely than men to cite affection as a reason for first intercourse.
    c. Men are more likely than females to initiate sexual activity.
    d. Gender differences in sexuality are noticeably absent among gay men and lesbian women.

8. Evolutionary psychologists attribute gender differences in sexuality to the fact that women have:
    a. greater reproductive potential than do men.
    b. lower reproductive potential than do men.
    c. weaker sex drives than men.
    d. stronger sex drives than men.

9. According to evolutionary psychology, men are drawn sexually to women who seem _____ , while women are also attracted to men who seem _____ .
    a. nurturing; youthful
    b. youthful and fertile; mature and affluent
    c. slender; muscular
    d. exciting; dominant

10. Unlike _____ twins, who develop from a single fertilized egg, _____ twins develop from separate fertilized eggs.
    a. fraternal; identical
    b. identical; fraternal
    c. placental; nonplacental
    d. nonplacental; placental

11. Temperament refers to a person's characteristic:
    a. emotional reactivity and intensity.
    b. attitudes.
    c. behaviors.
    d. role-related traits.

12. Compared to infants of European descent, infants of Asian descent tend to be:
    a. more spontaneous.
    b. fearless and uninhibited.
    c. more strongly attached to their caregivers.
    d. calmer and less reactive.

13. In a hypothetical world where all schools are of uniform quality, all families equally loving, and all neighborhoods equally healthy, the heritability of person-to-person differences would be:
    a. large.
    b. small.
    c. zero.
    d. unpredictable.

14. The subfield that studies the specific genes that influence behavior is:
    a. behavior genetics.
    b. molecular genetics.
    c. evolutionary psychology.
    d. memes analysis.

15. Which of the following most accurately expresses the extent of parental influence on personality?
    a. It is more extensive than most people believe.
    b. It is weaker today than in the past.
    c. It is more limited than popular psychology supposes.
    d. It is almost completely unpredictable.

16. Gender refers to:
    a. the biological and social definition of male and female.
    b. the biological definition of male and female.
    c. one's sense of being male or female.
    d. the extent to which one exhibits traditionally male or female traits.

17. The fertilized egg will develop into a boy if, at conception:
    a. the sperm contributes an X chromosome.
    b. the sperm contributes a Y chromosome.
    c. the egg contributes an X chromosome.
    d. the egg contributes a Y chromosome.

18. Which theory states that gender becomes a lens through which children view their experiences?
    a. social learning theory
    b. Vygotsky's sociocultural theory
    c. Piaget's theory
    d. gender schema theory

19. The hormone testosterone:
    a. is found only in females.
    b. determines the sex of the developing person.
    c. stimulates growth of the female sex organs.
    d. stimulates growth of the male sex organs.

20. Research studies have found that when infant rats and premature human babies are regularly touched or massaged, they:
    a. gain weight more rapidly.
    b. develop faster neurologically.
    c. have more agreeable temperaments.
    d. do a. and b.
    e. do a., b., and c.

Matching Items

Match each term with its corresponding definition or description.

Terms

_____ 1. X chromosome
_____ 2. heritability
_____ 3. fraternal
_____ 4. genes
_____ 5. DNA
_____ 6. identical
_____ 7. Y chromosome
_____ 8. gender role
_____ 9. gender identity
_____ 10. gender-typing
_____ 11. memes

Functions or Descriptions

a. the biochemical units of heredity
b. twins that develop from a single egg
c. one's personal sense of being female or male
d. a set of expected behaviors for males and females
e. twins that develop from separate eggs
f. variation among individuals due to genes
g. self-replicating ideas passed from person to person
h. the sex chromosome found in both women and men
i. the acquisition of a traditional gender role
j. a complex molecule containing the genetic information that makes up the chromosomes
k. the sex chromosome found only in men

Progress Test 2

Progress Test 2 should be completed during a final chapter review. Answer the following questions after you thoroughly understand the correct answers for the section reviews and Progress Test 1.

Multiple-Choice Questions

1. Each cell of the human body has a total of:
   a. 23 chromosomes.
   b. 23 genes.
   c. 46 chromosomes.
   d. 46 genes.

2. Genes direct our physical development by synthesizing:
   a. nucleotides.
   b. proteins.
   c. DNA.
   d. chromosomes.

3. The human genome is best defined as:
   a. a complex molecule containing genetic information that makes up the chromosomes.
   b. a segment of DNA.
   c. the complete instructions for making an organism.
   d. the four-letter genetic "alphabet."

4. Most human traits are:
   a. learned.
   b. determined by a single gene.
   c. influenced by many genes acting together.
   d. unpredictable.

5. Mutations are random errors in _____ replication that lead to a change in the sequence of _____ .
   a. gene; nucleotides
   b. chromosome; genes
   c. DNA; genes
   d. gene; DNA

6. Casual hit-and-run sex is most frequent among:
   a. males with high circulating levels of testosterone.
   b. males with traditional masculine attitudes.
   c. females and males who are weakly gender-typed.
   d. females and males who are strongly gender-typed.

7. Evolutionary explanations of gender differences in sexuality have been criticized for:
   a. being "after-the-fact" explanations.
   b. reinforcing male-female stereotypes.
   c. underestimating cultural influences on sexuality.
   d. all of the above reasons.

8. Several studies of long-separated identical twins have found that these twins:
   a. have little in common, due to the different environments in which they were raised.
   b. have many similarities, in everything from medical histories to personalities.
   c. have similar personalities, but very different likes, dislikes, and life-styles.
   d. are no more similar than are fraternal twins reared apart.

9. Adoption studies show that the personalities of adopted children:
   a. closely match those of their adoptive parents.
   b. bear more similarities to their biological parents than to their adoptive parents.
   c. closely match those of the biological children of their adoptive parents.
   d. closely match those of other children reared in the same home, whether or not they are biologically related.

10. Of the following, parents are most likely to influence their children's:
    a. temperament.
    b. personality.
    c. faith.
    d. emotional reactivity.

11. Chromosomes are composed of small segments of _____ called _____ .
    a. DNA; genes
    b. DNA; neurotransmitters
    c. genes; DNA
    d. DNA; enzymes

12. When the effect of one factor (such as environment) depends on another (such as heredity), we say there is a(n) _____ between the two factors.
    a. norm
    b. positive correlation
    c. negative correlation
    d. interaction

13. Compared to children raised in Western societies, those raised in communal societies, such as Japan or China:
    a. grow up with a stronger integration of the sense of family into their self-concepts.
    b. exhibit greater shyness toward strangers.
    c. exhibit greater concern for loyalty and social harmony.
    d. have all of the above characteristics.
    e. have none of the above characteristics.

14. The "selection effect" in peer influence refers to the tendency of children and youth to:
    a. naturally separate into same-sex playgroups.
    b. establish large, fluid circles of friends.
    c. seek out friends with similar interests and attitudes.
    d. do all of the above.

15. Which of the following is *not* true regarding cultural diversity?
    a. Culture influences emotional expressiveness.
    b. Culture influences personal space.
    c. Culture does not have a strong influence on how strictly social roles are defined.
    d. All cultures evolve their own norms.

16. Women and men are most likely to be attracted to strongly gender-typed mates in cultures characterized by:
    a. gender inequality.
    b. gender equality.
    c. flexible gender roles.
    d. few norms.

17. An evolutionary psychologist would be most interested in studying:
    a. why most parents are so passionately devoted to their children.
    b. hereditary influences on skin color.
    c. why certain diseases are more common among certain age groups.
    d. genetic differences in personality.

18. Children who are raised by parents who discourage traditional gender-typing:
    a. are less likely to display gender-typed behaviors themselves.
    b. often become confused and develop an ambiguous gender identity.
    c. nevertheless organize themselves into "girl worlds" and "boy worlds."
    d. display excessively masculine and feminine traits as adults.

19. Genetically female children often play in "masculine" ways if they were exposed to excess _____ during prenatal development.
    a. estrogen
    b. DNA
    c. testosterone
    d. nucleotides

20. Providing a child with a stimulating educational environment during early childhood is likely to:

   a. ensure the formation of a strong attachment with parents.

   b. foster the development of a calm, easygoing temperament.

   c. prevent neural connections from degenerating.

   d. do all of the above.

True–False Items

Indicate whether each statement is true or false by placing *T* or *F* in the blank next to the item.

_____ **1.** Gender differences in mate preferences vary widely from one culture to another.

_____ **2.** The most emotionally reactive newborns tend to be the most restrained 9-month-olds.

_____ **3.** Infants of European descent are generally calmer than infants of Asian descent.

_____ **4.** As environments become less similar, heredity as a source of differences becomes more important.

_____ **5.** Compared to identical twins reared in different families, fraternal twins recall their early family life more differently.

_____ **6.** Parents have a stronger influence than do peers on whether a youth starts smoking.

_____ **7.** Nature selects behavior tendencies that increase the likelihood of sending one's genes into the future.

_____ **8.** Genetic influences explain roughly 40 to 50 percent of our individual variations in many personality traits.

_____ **9.** Parental influence on personality is more limited than popular psychology supposes.

_____ **10.** North Americans prefer more personal space than do Latin Americans.

_____ **11.** Lacking any exposure to language before adolescence, a person will never master any language.

Thinking Critically About Chapter 3

Answer these questions the day before an exam as a final check on your understanding of the chapter's terms and concepts.

Multiple-Choice Questions

1. If chromosomes are the "books" of heredity, the "words" are the _____ and the "letters" are the _____ .

   a. genes; nucleotides

   b. nucleotides; genes

   c. genes; DNA

   d. DNA; genes

2. To say that the heritability of a trait is approximately 50 percent means that:

   a. genes are responsible for 50 percent of the trait in an individual, and the environment is responsible for the rest.

   b. the trait's appearance in a person will reflect approximately equal genetic contributions from both parents.

   c. of the variation in the trait within a group of people, 50 percent can be attributed to genes.

   d. all of the above are correct.

3. After comparing divorce rates among identical and fraternal twins, Dr. Alexander has concluded that genes do play a role. Dr. Alexander is most likely a(n):

   a. evolutionary psychologist.

   b. behavior geneticist.

   c. molecular geneticist.

   d. divorcee.

4. Despite growing up in the same home environment, Karen and her brother John have personalities as different from each other as two people selected randomly from the population. Why is this so?

   a. Personality is inherited. Because Karen and John are not identical twins, it is not surprising they have very different personalities.

   b. Gender is the most important factor in personality. If Karen had a sister, the two of them would probably be much more alike.

   c. The interaction of their individual genes and nonshared experiences accounts for the common finding that children in the same family are usually very different.

   d. Their case is unusual; children in the same family usually have similar personalities.

5. I am a rat whose cortex is lighter and thinner than my litter mates. What happened to me?
   a. You were born prematurely.
   b. You suffer from fetal alcohol syndrome.
   c. You were raised in an enriched environment.
   d. You were raised in a deprived environment.
   e. You did not imprint during the critical period.

6. Chad, who grew up in the United States, is more likely to encourage _____ in his future children than Asian-born Hidiyaki, who is more likely to encourage _____ in his future children.
   a. obedience; independence
   b. independence; emotional closeness
   c. emotional closeness; obedience
   d. loyalty; emotional closeness

7. One of the best ways to distinguish how much genetic and environmental factors affect behavior is to compare children who have:
   a. the same genes and environments.
   b. different genes and environments.
   c. similar genes and environments.
   d. similar genes and similar families.
   e. the same genes but different environments.

8. My sibling and I developed from a single fertilized egg. Who are we?
   a. opposite sex identical twins.
   b. same-sex identical twins.
   c. opposite sex fraternal twins.
   d. same-sex fraternal twins.

9. A psychologist working from the evolutionary perspective is likely to suggest that people are biologically predisposed to:
   a. protect their offspring.
   b. fear extreme heights.
   c. be attracted to fertile-appearing members of the opposite sex.
   d. do all of the above.

10. The heritability of a trait will be largest among genetically _____ individuals who grew up in _____ environments.
    a. dissimilar; dissimilar
    b. dissimilar; similar
    c. similar; similar
    d. similar; dissimilar

11. I am part of an "alphabet" that consists of only four letters, the sequence of which is nearly identical in all humans. What am I?
    a. A molecule of DNA
    b. A gene
    c. A chromosome
    d. A nucleotide

12. Of the relatively few genetic differences among humans _____ are differences among races.
    a. less than 1 percent
    b. less than 10 percent
    c. approximately 25 percent
    d. approximately 40 to 50 percent

13. Responding to the argument that gender differences are often by-products of a culture's social and family structures, an evolutionary psychologist is most likely to point to:
    a. our great human capacity for learning.
    b. the tendency of cultural arguments to reinforce traditional gender stereotypes.
    c. the infallibility of "hindsight" explanations.
    d. all of the above.

14. A person whose twin has Alzheimer's disease has _____ risk of sharing the disease if they are identical twins than if they are fraternal twins.
    a. less
    b. about the same
    c. much greater
    d. It is unpredictable.

15. Which of the following is an example of an interaction?
    a. Swimmers swim fastest during competition against other swimmers.
    b. Swimmers with certain personality traits swim fastest during competition, while those with other personality traits swim fastest during solo time trials.
    c. As the average daily temperature increases, sales of ice cream decrease.
    d. As the average daily temperature increases, sales of lemonade increase.

16. Which of the following most accurately summarizes the findings of the 40-year fox-breeding study described in the text?
    a. Wild wolves cannot be domesticated.
    b. "Survival of the fittest" seems to operate only when animals live in their natural habitats.
    c. By mating aggressive and unaggressive foxes, the researchers created a mutant species.
    d. By selecting and mating the tamest males and females, the researchers have produced affectionate, unaggressive offspring.

17. Compared to men, women are more likely to:
    a. be concerned with their partner's physical attractiveness.
    b. initiate sexual activity.
    c. cite "liking one another" as a justification for having sex in a new relationship.
    d. be less accepting of casual sex.

18. When his son cries when another child takes his favorite toy, Brandon admonishes him by saying, "Big boys don't cry." Evidently, Brandon is an advocate of _____ in accounting for the development of gender-linked behaviors.
    a. gender schema theory
    b. gender identity theory
    c. gender-typing theory
    d. social learning theory

19. The fact that by age 3, language forces children to begin organizing their worlds on the basis of gender is most consistent with which theory of how gender-linked behaviors develop?
    a. gender schema theory
    b. gender identity theory
    c. gender-typing theory
    d. social learning theory

20. Three-year-old Jack is inhibited and shy. As an adult, Jack is likely to be:
    a. cautious and unassertive.
    b. spontaneous and fearless.
    c. socially assertive.
    d. Who knows? This aspect of personality is not very stable over the life span.

Essay Question

Lakia's new boyfriend has been pressuring her to become more sexually intimate than she wants to at this early stage in their relationship. Strongly gender-typed and "macho" in attitude, Jerome is becoming increasingly frustrated with Lakia's hesitation, while Lakia is starting to wonder if a long-term relationship with this type of man is what she really wants. In light of your understanding of the evolutionary explanation of gender differences in sexuality, explain why the tension between Lakia and Jerome would be considered understandable.

Key Terms

Writing Definitions

Using your own words, on a piece of paper write a brief definition or explanation of each of the following terms.

1. chromosomes
2. DNA
3. genes
4. genome
5. natural selection
6. mutation
7. evolutionary psychology
8. gender
9. behavior genetics
10. environment
11. identical twins
12. fraternal twins
13. temperament
14. heritability
15. interaction
16. molecular genetics
17. culture
18. norm
19. personal space
20. memes

21. X chromosome

22. Y chromosome

23. testosterone

24. role

25. gender role

26. gender identity

27. gender-typing

28. social learning theory

29. gender schema theory

Cross-Check

As you learned in the Introduction, reviewing and overlearning of material are important to the learning process. After you have written the definitions of the key terms in this chapter, you should complete the crossword puzzle to ensure that you can reverse the process—recognize the term, given the definition.

ACROSS

6. Parents whose personalities bear little relevance to their children's personalities.
7. Complex molecule containing the genetic information that makes up the chromosomes.
9. Set of expected behaviors for those who occupy a particular social position.
10. An understood rule for expected and accepted behavior.
11. The biological and social characteristics by which people define male and female.
12. The enduring behaviors, ideas, attitudes, and traditions shared by a large group of people.
13. Environmental influences on behavior.
14. According to the evolutionary perspective, women are drawn to healthy-looking men who are also _____ .
15. Behavior geneticists often compare the traits of adopted children to those of their _____ parents.
16. Source of all genetic diversity.
19. The proportion of variation among individuals that can be attributed to genes.
20. Cultural mutations.
21. Threadlike structure made up largely of DNA molecules.

DOWN

1. The study of the relative power and limits of genetic and environmental influences on behavior.
2. Subfield of psychology that uses principles of natural selection to explore human traits and behaviors.
3. When the effect of one factor depends on another factor.
4. Any nongenetic influence.
5. A lens through which children organize their understanding of being male or female.
8. One's personal sense of being female or male.
17. Another word for heredity.
18. Segments of DNA capable of synthesizing proteins.

Answers

Genes: Our Biological Blueprint

Section Preview

1. When a mature egg is fertilized by a sperm, the 23 chromosomes carried in the egg pair up with the 23 chromosomes of the sperm. Each chromosome is composed of long threads of a molecule called DNA; DNA is made of thousands of genes that determine development by directing the manufacture of proteins. Our gene "words" are in turn defined by the sequencing of four biochemical "letters" called nucleotides: A, T, C, and G. The goal of the Human Genome project is to map the common nucleotide sequence that makes up human DNA.

2. Geneticists and psychologists are interested in our genetic commonalities and variations because they tell them why one person has a disease and another does not, why one person is short and another is tall. Knowing why, they may find ways to treat physical and psychological problems.

Stepping Through the Section

1. nature; nurture
2. chromosomes; 46; 23; DNA
3. genes; nucleotides; virtually the same
4. genome

Evolutionary Psychology: Explaining Universal Behaviors

Section Preview

1. Evolutionary psychologists study the adaptive nature of behavior using the principles of natural selection, which presumably favors those behaviors that contribute to the preservation of one's genes in future generations. Natural selection works on random errors in gene replication (mutations), that are the basis of genetic diversity.

2. Throughout the world, gender differences in sexuality are apparent. Men are more likely than females to initiate sexual activity, they are more accepting of casual sex, and they report masturbating much more often. Men also have a lower threshold for perceiving someone's warmth and friendliness as a sexual come-on. According to evolutionary psychologists, these differences may be grounded in biology. Because sperm are much more plentiful than eggs, natural selection may have favored different mating strategies and atti-

tudes toward sex in males and females. As support for this argument, they suggest that while men are drawn to healthy, fertile-appearing women, women also feel attracted to men who seem mature, dominant, and affluent.

3. Critics of evolutionary explanations of human behavior note that such explanations often start with an effect (such as the gender sexuality difference) and work backward to propose an explanation. Moreover, evolutionary explanations may reinforce male-female stereotypes. Critics also point to the fact that standards of attractiveness vary with time and place, indicating that cultural expectations also shape sexuality. Finally, gender differences in mate preferences are larger in cultures with gender inequality than in those characterized by gender equality.

Stepping Through the Section

1. natural selection
2. mutations; diversity
3. looser
4. evolutionary psychologists; genes
5. more; more; gender
6. lower; assertiveness
7. evolutionary; genes; sperm; eggs
8. youthful; mature; dominant; affluent
9. backward; hindsight; stereotypes; cultural; inequality

Behavior Genetics: Explaining Individual Differences

Section Preview

1. Behavior geneticists focus on our individual differences and the extent to which they are shaped by genetic and environmental influences. Because identical twins are genetically identical, the findings that they are more similar in a trait than fraternal twins or other siblings suggest that there is a substantial genetic influence on that trait. Studies of identical twins who were separated and raised by different families reinforce this point. In this way, twin studies provide psychologists with a greater understanding of the role of genes in our behaviors. Critics of twin studies contend that twin similarities may merely be coincidental rather than a reflection of heredity. Moreover, because adoption agencies tend to place separated twins in similar homes, critics argue that similarities in traits may reflect the impact of similar experiences rather than heredity alone.

Adoption studies enable psychologists to determine the relative influence of nature and nurture on development by asking whether adopted children are more like their biological parents, who contribute their genes, or their adoptive parents, who contribute a home environment. Such studies show that, although the personalities of adopted children do not much resemble their adoptive parents, parents do influence children's attitudes, values, manners, faith, and politics.

2. Temperament refers to a person's characteristic reactivity and intensity. Research studies with both humans and animals demonstrate that heredity seems to predispose differences in temperament. Anxious, high-strung infants become more physiologically aroused when facing new or strange situations. Moreover, identical twins are more likely to have similar temperaments.

Heritability refers to the extent to which variation in a trait among individuals is due to their differing genes. Because genes and experience interact in influencing development, it is incorrect to say that a certain trait is x percent due to genes and y percent due to experience. It is also incorrect to interpret heritable individual differences in specific traits as evidence of heritable group differences in those traits.

3. Molecular genetics is the new "bottom up" subfield of biology that studies the molecular structure and function of genes that influence specific traits such as obesity, reading ability, or shyness. In addition, molecular geneticists are also searching for genes that put people at risk for genetically influenced disorders such as bipolar disorder, depression, schizophrenia, and alcoholism. Although great advances have been made in prenatal screening of prospective parents, such tests raise significant ethical issues.

Stepping Through the Section

1. behavior geneticists; nongenetic
2. twin; adoption
3. identical; fraternal; more
4. more
5. environment
6. do not; does; higher
7. temperament; does
8. more
9. Asian; European
10. heritability; more
11. need not imply
12. psychological; genetic; environmental
13. eating disorders; aggressive; culture
14. interaction; genetic; environment
15. molecular genetics; sex; ethical

Environmental Influence

Section Preview

1. A widely held belief is that parental nurture is as important as genetic influences in shaping a child's personality. However, behavior geneticists have repeatedly found that shared environmental influences, including the home environment that siblings share, typically account for less than 10 percent of their personality differences. To some developmental psychologists, this implies that parents should be given less credit (and less blame) for the way their kids turn out.

Another early environmental influence that researchers are investigating is the prenatal environment. Because some twins have separate placentas, even those who are genetically identical may develop in environments that vary in nourishment and protection against viruses. These differences may partly explain later differences in their psychological traits.

2. Sights, smells, touches, and other experiences foster the development of neural connections within the brain. In a classic study, rats who were raised in an enriched environment developed heavier and thicker brain cortexes than did those raised in an impoverished environment. Other studies have found that premature infants and laboratory animals who receive extra handling and a variety of experiences develop faster neurologically than those raised in deprived environments.

Experiences with peers powerfully socialize children and youth, in part as a result of a "selection effect," in which kids seek out peers with similar attitudes and interests.

3. A culture is the enduring traditions, behaviors, ideas, and attitudes shared by a group of people and passed from one generation to the next. All cultural groups evolve their own norms for acceptable and expected behavior. Because of differing norms for personal space, expressiveness, and pace of life, for example, misunderstandings are commonplace. Cultural differences in child-rearing are another case in point. Unlike most Westerners, who now raise their children to be independent, many Asians and Africans live in communal cultures that focus on cultivating social harmony and emotional closeness.

Cultural norms change over time through self-replicating mutations called memes. Today, parents in Western societies place more emphasis on raising independent children than they did several generations earlier. Despite variations across culture and time, however, we must not lose sight of our human kinship. Compared with person-to-person differences within groups, the differences between groups are small.

Stepping Through the Section

1. 40 to 50 percent
2. 10
3. prenatal; placenta
4. thicker

Research has shown that human and animal infants given extra sensory stimulation develop faster neurologically. Throughout life, sensory stimulation activates and strengthens particular neural connections, while other connections weaken with disuse. In this way, our experiences shape the very structure of the neural pathways that process those experiences.

5. peers; selection
6. culture
7. norms; personal space

Most Americans, the British, and Scandinavians prefer more personal space than do Latin Americans, Arabs, and the French. Cultural differences in expressiveness and the pace of life often create misunderstandings. For example, people with northern European roots may perceive people from Mediterranean cultures as warm and charming but inefficient and time wasting, while Mediterraneans may see the northern Europeans as efficient but emotionally cold.

8. memes
9. independence; emotional closeness
10. smaller

Gender and Postscript: Reflections on Nature and Nurture

Section Preview

1. Our biological sex is determined by the twenty-third pair of chromosomes, the sex chromosomes, one of which comes from each parent. The mother always contributes an X chromosome. The father's sperm contributes an X or a Y chromosome; with an X chromosome, the developing person becomes a girl; with a Y chromosome, a boy develops. The Y chromosome contains a single gene that triggers the testes to develop and produce the principal male hormone, testosterone, which, in about the seventh week, starts the development of external male organs.

   Genetically female infants who were exposed to excess prenatal testosterone are born with masculine-appearing genitals, and tend to act in more aggressive "tomboyish" ways than other girls.

2. Gender is also socially constructed; gender identity is our personal sense of being male or female. Gender-typing, which refers to the acquisition of a traditional masculine or feminine role, has been alternatively explained by social learning theory and by gender schema theory. According to social learning theory, children acquire gender-linked behaviors by observing and imitating others and by being rewarded or punished. Gender schema theory assumes that the child's culture transmits a copy of what it means to be male or female. The child then adjusts his or her behavior to fit the concept.

3. While it is true that genes form us, it is also true that our experiences in families and social relationships teach us ways of thinking and acting. Moreover, differences initiated by our nature may be amplified by our nurture, as, for example, when cultural norms regarding masculinity and femininity encourage men and women to act differently. It is equally true that humans are an open system. Although genes and culture are pervasive influences, they are not immutable forces.

Stepping Through the Section

1. sex; X; Y; testosterone; seventh
2. male; tomboyish
3. gender roles
4. are not; cultures; time
5. gender identity; gender-typing
6. social learning
7. do
8. gender schema; schemas

Progress Test 1

Multiple-Choice Questions

1. **c.** is the answer. (p. 89)
   a., b., & c. Whereas evolutionary psychologists attempt to explain universal human tendencies, these researchers investigate genetic differences among individuals.

2. **c.** is the answer. Research has not shown a strong parental influence on personality, temperament, or emotional reactivity. (p. 96)

3. **a.** is the answer. (p. 87)
   b. Although more than 98 percent of our nucleotides match those of chimpanzees, the similarity with lower animals is much less.
   c. & d. More than 99.9 percent of our nucleotide sequences match those of all other humans, regardless of race and gender.

4. **b.** is the answer. (p. 93)
   a. & c. Although an identical twin is at increased risk, the relationship is far from perfect. Mental disorders, like all psychological traits, are influenced by *both* nature and nurture.
   d. This is not at all implied by the evidence from twin studies.

5. **d.** is the answer. (p. 94)
   a., b., & c. In order to pinpoint the influence of one of the two factors (genes and environment), it is necessary to hold one of the factors constant.

6. **d.** is the answer. (p. 89)
   c. Natural selection favors traits that send one's genes into the future, such as surviving longer and reproducing more often. Aggression does not necessarily promote either.

7. **d.** is the answer. Such gender differences characterize both heterosexual and homosexual people. (p. 90)

8. **b.** is the answer. Women produce fewer eggs than men do sperm. Moreover, women can incubate only one infant at a time. (p. 90)
   c. & d. The text does not suggest that there is a gender difference in the strength of the sex drive.

9. **b.** is the answer. (p. 91)
   a. According to this perspective, women prefer mates with the potential for long-term nurturing investment in their joint offspring.
   c. While men are drawn to women whose waists are roughly a third narrower than their hips, the text does not suggest that women equate muscularity with fertility.
   d. Excitement was not mentioned as a criterion for mating.

10. **b.** is the answer. (p. 93)
    c. & d. There are no such things as "placental" or "nonplacental"" twins. All twins have a placenta during prenatal development.

11. **a.** is the answer. (p. 97)

12. **d.** is the answer. (p. 98)

13. **a.** is the answer. (p. 98)
    b., c., & d. This hypothetical world is one in which there is no environmental variation. Therefore, any individual differences are predictably due to genes.

14. **b.** is the answer. (p. 100)
    a. Behavior geneticists use twin and adoption studies to explore the relative power and limits of nature and nurture on behavior.
    c. Evolutionary psychology is concerned with *universal* behavior tendencies.
    d. Although this sounds intriguing, there is no such field. Moreover, memes are cultural, rather than biological, phenomena.

15. **c.** is the answer. (p. 103)

16. **a.** is the answer. (p. 89)
    c. This defines gender identity.
    d. This defines gender-typing.

17. **b.** is the answer. (p. 111)
    a. In this case, a female would develop.
    c. & d. The egg can contribute only an X chromosome. Thus, the sex of the child is determined by which chromosome the sperm contributes.

18. **d.** is the answer. (p. 113)
    a. According to social learning theory, gender-typing evolves through imitation and reinforcement.
    b. & c. Neither theorist is discussed in this chapter. Moreover, neither proposed a theory of gender-typing.

19. **d.** is the answer. (p. 111)
    a. Although testosterone is the principal male hormone, it is present in both females and males.
    b. This is determined by the sex chromosomes.
    c. In the absence of testosterone, female sex organs will develop.

20. **d.** is the answer. (p. 104)

Matching Items

1. h (p. 111)	**5.** j (p. 86)	**9.** c (p. 113)
2. f (p. 98)	**6.** b (p. 93)	**10.** i (p. 113)
3. e (p. 93)	**7.** k (p. 111)	**11.** g (p. 108)
4. a (p. 86)	**8.** d (p. 111)	

Progress Test 2

Multiple-Choice Questions

1. **c.** is the answer. (p. 86)
   b. & d. Each cell of the human body contains hundreds of genes.

2. **b.** is the answer. (p. 86)
   a., c., & d. Nucleotides define DNA, segments of which comprise genes and chromosomes.

3. **c.** is the answer. (p. 87)
   a. This defines DNA.

b. This defines a gene.

d. This defines the four nucleotides.

4. **c.** is the answer. (p. 87)

5. **a.** is the answer. (p. 88)

6. **b.** is the answer. (p. 90)

a. Testosterone levels have not been linked to the frequency of casual sex.

c. & d. Males are far more accepting of casual sex than are females.

7. **d.** is the answer. (p. 92)

8. **b.** is the answer. (p. 95)

a., c., & d. Despite being raised in different environments, long-separated identical twins often have much in common, including likes, dislikes, and lifestyles. This indicates the significant heritability of many traits.

9. **b.** is the answer. (p. 96)

a., c., & d. The personalities of adopted children do not much resemble those of their adoptive parents (therefore, not a.) or other children reared in the same home (therefore, not c. or d.)

10. **c.** is the answer. (p. 96)

a. & d. Temperament, which refers to a person's emotional reactivity, is determined primarily by genes.

b. Genes limit parents' influence on their children's personalities.

11. **a.** is the answer (p. 86)

b. Neurotransmitters are the chemicals involved in synaptic transmission in the nervous system.

d. Enzymes are chemicals that facilitate various chemical reactions throughout the body but are not involved in heredity.

12. **d.** is the answer. (p. 100)

a. A norm is a culturally determined set of expected behaviors for a particular role, such as a gender role.

b. & c. When two factors are correlated, it means either that increases in one factor are accompanied by increases in the other (positive correlation), or that increases in one factor are accompanied by decreases in the other (negative correlation).

13. **d.** is the answer. (pp. 108–109)

14. **c.** is the answer. (p. 105)

15. **c.** is the answer. (pp. 106–107)

16. **a.** is the answer. (p. 112)

b. In such cultures gender differences in mate preferences tend to be much smaller.

c. Although flexibility in gender roles was not discussed per se, it is likely that greater flexibility would equate with greater equality in gender roles.

d. All cultures develop norms.

17. **a.** is the answer. This is an example of a universal trait that contributes to survival of the human species and the perpetuation of one's genes (p. 89)

b., c., & d. These traits and issues would likely be of greater interest to a behavior geneticist, since they concern the influence of specific genes on behavior.

18. **c.** is the answer. (p. 113)

b. & d. There is no evidence that being raised in a "gender neutral" home confuses children or fosters a backlash of excessive gender-typing.

19. **c.** is the answer. (p. 111)

20. **c.** is the answer. (p. 104)

a. Although early experiences are a factor in the development of attachment (discussed in a later chapter), educational stimulation is probably less important than warmth and nurturance.

b. Because temperament appears to be a strongly genetic trait, it is unlikely that early educational experiences would affect its nature.

True–False Items

1. False. Worldwide, men are drawn to healthy, fertile-appearing women, while women are also attracted to men who seem mature, dominant, and affluent. (p. 91)

2. False. Temperament remains quite stable over the entire life span. (p. 97)

3. False. In fact, just the opposite is true. (p. 98)

4. False. Heritability is highest when environments are more similar. (p. 98)

5. True. (p. 100)

6. False. Peer influence on behaviors such as smoking is generally much stronger than that of parents. (p. 105)

7. True. (p. 89)

8. True. (p. 102)

9. True. (p. 103)

10. True. (p. 107)

11. True. (p. 104)

Thinking Critically About Chapter 3

Multiple-Choice Questions

1. **a.** is the answer. (p. 86)

b. Genes are defined by sequences of nucleotides.

c. & d. Genes are segments of DNA.

2. **c.** is the answer. Heritability is a measure of the

extent to which a trait's variation within a group of people can be attributed to heredity. (p. 98)

a. & b. Heritability is not a measure of how much of an individual's behavior is inherited, nor of the relative contribution of genes from that person's mother and father. Furthermore, the heritability of any trait depends on the context, or environment, in which that trait is being studied.

3. **b.** is the answer. (p. 93)

a. Evolutionary psychologists seek to explain our universal behaviors.

c. Molecular geneticists search for the specific genes that influence behaviors. In his example, the researcher is merely comparing twins.

d. Who knows?

4. **c.** is the answer. (p. 103)

a. Although heredity does influence certain traits, such as outgoingness and emotional instability, it is the interaction of heredity and experience that ultimately molds personality.

b. There is no single "most important factor" in personality. Moreover, for the same reason two sisters or brothers often have dissimilar personalities, a sister and brother may be very much alike.

d. Karen and John's case is not at all unusual.

5. **d.** is the answer. (p. 104)

a. & b. Premature birth and fetal alcohol syndrome (discussed in a later chapter) usually do not have this effect on the developing brain.

c. If the question had stated "I have a heavier and thicker cortex," this answer would be correct.

e. Imprinting, which is discussed in the next chapter, has no effect on brain cells.

6. **b.** is the answer. Although parental values differ from one time and place to another, studies reveal that Western parents today want their children to think for themselves, while Asian and African parents place greater value on emotional closeness. (pp. 108–109)

d.   Both of these values are more typical of Asian than Western cultures.

7. **e.** is the answer. To separate the influences of heredity and experience on behavior, one of the two must be held constant. (pp. 94–95)

a., b., c., & d. These situations would not allow one to separate the contributions of heredity and environment.

8. **b.** is the answer. (p. 93)

a. Because they are genetically the same, identical twins are always of the same sex.

c. & d. Fraternal twins develop from two fertilized eggs.

9. **d.** is the answer. (pp. 88, 91)

10. **b.** is the answer. Because their environments are largely the same, differences in the traits of such individuals are likely to be due to genetic differences. (p. 98)

c. & d. If two individuals are genetically similar, any differences in their behaviors and traits are likely to be due to environmental factors.

11. **d.** is the answer. (p. 87)

12. **b.** is the answer. (p. 88)

13. **a.** is the answer. (p. 92)

b. & c. In fact, these are typical criticisms of evolutionary psychology.

14. **c.** is the answer. (p. 93)

15. **b.** is the answer. (p. 100)

a. An interaction requires at least two variables; in this example there is only one (competition).

c. This is an example of a negative correlation.

d. This is an example of a positive correlation.

16. **d.** is the answer. (p. 88)

17. **d.** is the answer. (p. 90)

a., b., & c. These are typical male attitudes and behaviors.

18. **d.** is the answer. Following social learning theory, Brandon is using verbal punishment to discourage what he believes to be an inappropriate gender-linked behavior in his son. (p. 113)

a. Gender schema theory maintains that children adjust their behaviors to match their cultural concept of gender. In this example, we have only the father's behavior on which to base our answer.

b. & c. No such theories were discussed.

19. **a.** is the answer. Many aspects of language, including masculine and feminine pronouns, provide children with schemas through which they begin organizing their worlds on the basis of gender. (pp. 113–114)

20. **a.** is the answer. (p. 97)

b., c., & d. Temperament is one of the most stable personality traits.

Essay Question

Evolutionary psychologists would not be surprised by the tension between Lakia and Jerome and would see it as a reflection of women's more relational and men's more recreational approach to sex. Since eggs are expensive, compared with sperm, women prefer mates with the potential for long-term investment in their joint offspring. According to this perspective, this may be why Lakia is not in a hurry to become sexually intimate with Jerome. Men, on the other hand, are selected for "pairing widely" but not necessarily wisely in order to maximize the spreading of their genes. This is especially true of men like Jerome, who have traditional masculine attitudes.

Key Terms

Writing Definitions

1. **Chromosomes** are threadlike structures made of DNA molecules, which contain the genes. In conception, the 23 chromosomes in the egg are paired with the 23 chromosomes in the sperm. (p. 86)

2. **DNA (deoxyribonucleic acid)** is a complex molecule containing the genetic information that makes up the chromosomes. (p. 86)

3. **Genes** are the biochemical units of heredity that make up the chromosomes; they are segments of the DNA molecules capable of synthesizing a protein. (p. 86)

4. A **genome** is the complete set of genetic instructions for making an organism. (p. 87)

5. **Natural selection** is the evolutionary principle that traits that contribute to reproduction and survival are the most likely to be passed on to succeeding generations. (p. 88)

6. **Mutations** are random errors in gene replication that are the source of genetic diversity within a species. (p. 88)

7. **Evolutionary psychology** is the study of the evolution of behavior using the principles of natural selection. (p. 89)

8. **Gender** refers to the biological and social characteristics by which people define male and female. (p. 89)

9. **Behavior genetics** is the study of genetic and environmental influences on specific behaviors. (p. 93)

10. In behavior genetics, **environment** refers to every nongenetic, or external, influence on our traits and behaviors. (p. 93)

11. **Identical twins** develop from a single fertilized egg that splits in two and therefore are genetically identical. (p. 93)

12. **Fraternal twins** develop from two separate eggs fertilized by different sperm and therefore are no more genetically similar than ordinary siblings. (p. 93)

13. **Temperament** refers to a person's characteristic emotional reactivity and intensity. (p. 97)

14. **Heritability** is the proportion of variation among individuals in a trait that is attributable to genetic factors. Current estimates place the heritability of intelligence at about 50 to 70 percent. (p. 98)

15. An **interaction** occurs when the effects of one factor (such as heredity) depends on another factor (such as environment). (p. 100)

Example: Because the way people react to us (an environmental factor) depends on our genetically influenced temperament (a genetic factor), there is an **interaction** between environment and heredity.

16. **Molecular genetics** is the subfield of biology that seeks to identify the specific genes that influence specific human traits and behaviors. (p. 100)

17. A **culture** is the enduring behaviors, ideas, attitudes, and traditions shared by a large group of people and transmitted from one generation to the next. (p. 106)

18. **Norms** are understood social prescriptions, or rules, for accepted and expected behavior. (p. 106)

19. **Personal space** refers to the buffer zone, or mobile territory, that people like to maintain around their bodies. (p. 107)

20. **Memes** are variations in ideas, fashions, and innovations passed from one person to another that cause rapid cultural mutations. (p. 108)

21. The **X chromosome** is the sex chromosome found in both men and women. Females inherit an X chromosome from each parent. (p. 111)

22. The **Y chromosome** is the sex chromosome found only in men. Males inherit an X chromosome from their mothers and a Y chromosome from their fathers. (p. 111)

23. **Testosterone** is the principal male sex hormone. During prenatal development, testosterone stimulates the development of the external male sex organs. (p. 111)

24. A **role** is a culturally prescribed set of behaviors expected of those who occupy a particular social position. (p. 111)

25. A **gender role** is a culturally prescribed set of behaviors for males and females. (p. 111)

26. **Gender identity** is one's personal sense of being male or female. (p. 113)

27. **Gender-typing** is the acquisition of a traditional feminine or masculine gender role. (p. 113)

28. According to **social learning theory**, people learn social behavior (such as gender roles) by observing and imitating and by being rewarded or punished. (p. 113)

29. According to **gender schema theory**, children acquire a cultural concept of what it means to be female or male and adjust their behavior accordingly. (p. 113)

Cross-Check

ACROSS	DOWN
6. adoptive	**1.** behavior genetics
7. DNA	**2.** evolutionary
9. role	**3.** interaction
10. norm	**4.** environment
11. gender	**5.** gender schema
12. culture	**8.** gender identity
13. nurture	**17.** nature
14. affluent	**18.** genes
15. biological	
16. mutation	

FOCUS ON VOCABULARY AND LANGUAGE

Genes: Our Biological Blueprint

Page 86: . . . *blueprint* . . . *Blueprint* is an architectural term for a copy of an original diagram or plan used as a working drawing for creating the building or structure. Myers notes that the 46 chromosomes in each body cell (23 from the egg and 23 from the sperm) contain the master plan (*blueprint*) in the form of genes that ultimately makes each of us a unique human being.

Evolutionary Psychology: Explaining Universal Behaviors

Page 88: Everyone agrees that the tight genetic *leash* . . . is looser on humans. Just as a dog is restrained or held in check by a strap or cord (*leash*), genes generally determine the behaviors of many animals. In humans, however, genes are less influential; thus, the usually strong genetic constraints (*tight genetic leash*) operate in a less determined way (*are looser*).

Page 90: Casual hit-and-run sex is most frequent among males with traditional masculine attitudes (Pleck & others, 1993). There are large gender differences in sexual values and attitudes, which are reflected in differences in male-female behaviors. Males (especially those with stereotyped views of females) tend to be nonchalant about and agreeable to having sex with someone they have just met and hardly know (*casual hit-and-run sex*).

Page 90: Men also have a lower threshold for perceiving warm responses as a *sexual come-on*. Males will typically misinterpret an affable, affectionate, friendly female's behavior (*her warmth*) as an invitation to have sex (*a sexual come-on*). Numerous studies have shown that men are more likely than women to attribute a woman's friendliness to sexual interest.

Page 90: In our *ancestral history*, females most often sent their genes into the future by *pairing wisely*, men by *pairing widely*. Evolutionary psychologists note that our normal desires (*natural yearnings*) help perpetuate our genes. In our evolutionary past (*ancestral history*) females accomplished this best by being selective in their choice of mate (*pairing wisely*) and men by more promiscuous behavior (*pairing widely*). Myers points out, however, that environmental factors, such as cultural expectations, can alter or shape how sexual behavior is expressed by both males and females (*can bend the genders*).

Page 91: They (women) prefer *potential dads over likely cads.* Women tend to prefer males who show the promise of becoming good fathers for their joint offspring (*potential dads*) rather than males who indicate little or no willingness to make such a co-parenting commitment (*likely cads*).

Page 91: As *mobile gene machines*, we are predisposed to prefer whatever worked for our ancestors. Evolutionary psychologists believe that behavioral tendencies that increase the probability of getting one's genes into the future have been selected for over the course of evolution. Humans who actively seek out mates and successfully procreate (*mobile gene machines*) are passing on inherited tendencies to behave in certain ways (*our natural yearnings*) because these behaviors were adaptive for our ancestors.

Behavior Genetics: Explaining Individual Differences

Page 93: To *disentangle the threads* of heredity and environment, behavior geneticists often use *two sets of tweezers*: twin studies and adoption studies. Myers is using an analogy here: To separate out (*disentangle*) two different strings (*threads*) that are tightly intertwined, you can use a small pincers (*tweezers*). Similarly, in an attempt to discover and separate out (*tease apart*) the differential effects of the environment and genes (*threads that are entangled*), behavior geneticists use two approaches (*two sets of tweezers*): twin studies and adoption studies.

Page 95: The *startling twin similarity stories* do not impress Bouchard's critics. Bouchard's investigation into the similarities between separated twins suggests that genes influence many behaviors, such as career choices, TV-watching habits, and food likes and dislikes (*startling stories*). The critics point out that any two strangers of the same sex and age would probably have many coincidental things in common if they were to spend hours comparing their behaviors and life histories.

Page 95: Genes-R-Us The name of a large retail chain, Toys-R-Us, is an abbreviated version of the idea that the company makes and sells only toys (*toys are us*). Myers is indicating something similar when he says *Genes-R-Us*; genes make and shape who we are.

Page 97: Researcher Stephen Suomi (1987) placed infant monkeys who were genetically predisposed to be *"uptight" or "easygoing" with foster mothers* who were themselves uptight or easygoing. The result? Heredity overrode rearing. This experiment demonstrated that innately fearful, anxious, and inhibited (genetically predisposed *"uptight"*) monkeys were not greatly affected by having relaxed, fearless, and sociable (*easygoing*) adoptive (*foster*) mothers. What they were born with (heredity) was not influenced by how they were treated by their mothers (reared).

Page 99: Thus, asking whether your intelligence or personality is more a product of your genes or environment is like asking whether *the area of a field is more the result of its length or width*. The area of a space, such as a soccer field or a football field, is determined by multiplying the length by the width. Obviously, you cannot find the area of the field without both length and width. Likewise, we do not become who we are without both nature and nurture. As Myers notes, for psychological characteristics, both genetic (*nature*) and environmental (*nurture*) factors are almost always involved.

Page 100 . . . sleuth . . . A *sleuth* is a detective. Just like detectives trying to catch the criminal and solve the crime, researchers throughout the world are currently trying to locate (*sleuth out*) the genes responsible for many disorders.

Page 101: But as always, progress is a *two-edged sword*, raising both hopeful possibilities and difficult problems. Myers is using the metaphor of a sword with two cutting edges (*two-edged sword*) to illustrate

the fact that progress has two aspects to it, one positive (hopeful possibilities) and one negative (new ethical issues and difficult problems).

Environmental Influence

Page 102: And society reinforces such parent-blaming: Believing that parents shape their children as a *potter molds clay*, people readily praise parents for their children's virtues and blame them for their children's vices. Myers suggests that, because some factors that affect development are under the parent's control and others are not, it is not appropriate to be judgmental. We should be slower to praise parents for their children's achievements and slower yet to be critical when the children do not perform up to our expectations. Children are not simply formed by their parents' child-rearing abilities (*as a potter molds clay*) but rather are influenced by many factors beyond their control.

Page 104: During early childhood—while the excess connections are *still on call*— . . . . To *be on call* means to be ready and available for use. Thus, during the early childhood years while there are many neural connections ready for use (*still on call*), an enriched and stimulating environment is extremely important for intellectual, perceptual, and social development. As Myers puts it, ". . . use it or lose it."

Page 105: Similar to *pathways* through a forest, less traveled paths gradually disappear, *popular paths* are broadened. This analogy suggests that brain development goes on throughout life. Neural connections (*pathways*) that are frequently used (*popular paths*) are widened and more clearly defined, while those connections that are seldom used (*in disuse*) become weakened and may eventually disappear.

Page 105: The *wiring of Eric Clapton's brain* reflects the thousands of hours he has spent playing the guitar. Repeated experience or practice will strengthen the neural pathways or connections (the *wiring*) in the brain. Eric Clapton is a very famous pop musician, and his expertise at playing the guitar is a function of many, many hours of practice and performing.

Page 106: We come equipped with a huge *cerebral hard drive ready to receive many gigabytes of cultural software.* Myers is comparing our capacity to learn and adapt through cultural transmission to that of a computer's operating system (*cerebral hard drive*) which, like a human, is capable of receiving very large amounts of information through programming (*gigabytes of cultural software*).

Page 107: Yet, norms *grease the social machinery.* Every society has its own rules and regulations about accepted and appropriate modes of conduct (social norms), and these standards differ from culture to culture. These proscriptions may sometimes seem unjust or senseless, but because they are known and practiced by most people, they serve the function of helping society run smoothly (*they grease the social machinery*).

Page 107: When cultures collide, their differing norms often *befuddle*. When people from different cultures meet, the interaction can be confusing (*befuddling*). Personal space (the distance we like to have between us and others) varies; someone who prefers more space may end up constantly retreating (*backpedaling*) from someone who needs to be close in order to have a comfortable conversation.

Page 109: Or so they [Rowe and others] concluded after *distilling data* from six major investigations of ethnic differences in behavior. These researchers analyzed (*distilled*) data from half a dozen prominent studies that found ethnic differences in behavior. They suggested that differences attributed to race may in fact result from other factors, which operate identically in all ethnic groups. In other words, there is a common underlying process in all groups despite some superficial differences in behavior patterns among various ethnic groups.

Page 110: But "it bodes well," say the researchers, "that developmental processes are alike in many subgroups of *Homo sapiens*." Psychologists note that although we differ from one another in many ways, it is a good thing (*it bodes well*) that there are common factors, both biological and psychological, that influence how human beings (*Homo sapiens*) change over time.

Gender

Page 111: The Y chromosome contains a single gene that *throws a master switch* triggering the testes to develop and produce the principal male hormone, testosterone. . . . We all get an X chromosome from our mothers and either an X (you'll be a girl) or a Y (you'll be a boy) from our fathers. Thus, the Y chromosome is crucial to making males, and a single gene is responsible for initiating the process (*it throws the switch*) that activates (*triggers*) the production of testosterone by the testes.

Page 111: . . . "tomboyish" . . . A tomboy is a girl who likes to play boys' sports and games. When a female embryo is exposed to too much testosterone (the male sex hormone), the developing child will act more aggressively and behave in ways more typical of boys (she will act in a *tomboyish* way).

Pages 111–112: Traditionally, men have *initiated dates*, driven the car, and *picked up the check*; women have decorated the house, bought and cared for children's clothes, and selected the wedding gifts. Gender roles are a culture's expectations for male and female behaviors, but these behaviors change over time and across cultures. Historically, males ask females to go out (*initiate dates*) and pay for the meal and entertainment (*pick up the check*) and women look after the domestic concerns.

Page 112: With the *flick of an apron*, the number of U.S. college women hoping to be full-time homemakers *plunged* during the late 1960s and early 1970s. Over time, gender roles have changed. Within a relatively brief period of time (*with the flick of an apron*), the number of women engaged in the traditional female role (full-time homemaker) declined rapidly (*plunged*) and the number of women in the work force increased substantially, especially in traditional male fields such as medicine, law, and engineering.

The Developing Person

Chapter Overview

Developmental psychologists study the life cycle, from conception to death, examining how we develop physically, mentally, and socially. Chapter 4 covers physical, cognitive, and social development over the life span and introduces three major issues in developmental psychology: (1) the relative impact of genes and experience on behavior, (2) whether development is best described as gradual and continuous or as a discontinuous sequence of stages, and (3) whether the individual's personality remains stable or changes over the life span.

Although there are not too many terms to learn in this chapter, there are a number of important research findings to remember. Pay particular attention to the stage theories of Piaget, Kohlberg, and Erikson, as well as to the discussion regarding intellectual stability during adulthood. Writing carefully prepared answers to the guided study items should be especially helpful in mastering the material in this chapter.

Note: Answer guidelines for all Chapter 4 questions begin on page 122.

Introducing the Developing Person
(p. 119)

> David Myers at times uses idioms that are unfamiliar to some readers. If you do not know the meaning of any of the following words, phrases, or expressions in the context in which they appear in the text, refer to page 134 for an explanation: . . . *journey through life from womb to tomb.*

Introduction Preview

First, skim the introduction. Then read the following objectives and, as you read the text, search for the information that will enable you to meet each objective. Answer guidelines are provided on page 122.

1. Briefly describe the work of developmental psychologists.

2. Identify and briefly describe three major issues that pervade developmental psychology.

Stepping Through the Introduction

After you have read the introduction, complete the sentences and answer the questions. As you proceed, evaluate your performance by consulting the answers on page 122. Do not continue with the next section until you understand each answer. If you need to, review or reread the section in the textbook before continuing.

1. Scientists who study physical, mental, and social changes throughout the life cycle are called

   _____ _____ .

2. One of the major issues in developmental psychology concerns the relative importance of genes and experience in determining behavior; this is called the _____ /

   _____ issue.

3. A second developmental issue,

   _____ / _____ ,

   concerns whether developmental changes are gradual or abrupt.

4. A third controversial issue concerns the consistency of personality and whether development is characterized more by _____ over time or by change.

Prenatal Development and the Newborn
(pp. 120–124)

Section Preview

Answer guidelines are provided on page 122.

1. Describe conception and outline the course of prenatal development.

2. Discuss the possible effects of teratogens on the developing embryo and fetus.

3. Describe the capacities of the newborn.

4. (Close-Up) Explain how psychologists are able to study infant thinking.

Stepping Through the Section

Answers are provided on page 122.

Describe the moment of conception and the beginning of prenatal development.

1. Fertilized human eggs are called

   _____ . During the first 2 weeks, the cells in this cluster begin to specialize in structure and function, that is, they begin to

   _____ . From about 2 until 8 weeks of age the developing human is called a(n)

   _____ . During the final stage of prenatal development, the developing human is called a(n) _____ .

2. Along with nutrients, a range of harmful substances known as _____ can pass through the placenta.

3. Moderate consumption of alcohol during pregnancy _____ (usually does not affect/can affect) the fetal brain. If a mother

drinks heavily, her baby is at risk for the birth defects and mental retardation that accompany _____

_____ _____ .

4. When an infant's cheek is touched, it will vigorously search for a nipple, a response known as the _____ _____ .

Give some evidence supporting the claim that a newborn's sensory equipment is biologically prewired to facilitate social responsiveness.

5. (Close-Up) To study infants' thinking, developmental researchers have focused on a simple form of learning called _____ , which involves a _____ in responding with repeated stimulation.

Infancy and Childhood (pp. 124–142)

> If you do not know the meaning of any of the following words, phrases, or expressions in the context in which they appear in the text, refer to pages 134–136 for an explanation: *toddler; wild growth spurt; formatted; sea of sensations; fruitless; double take; it gets high marks; cognitive milestones; concrete demonstrations . . . think for themselves; pit the drawing power; windows of opportunity; gosling; "Mere exposure"; mobile sperm banks; footprints on the brain; the scientific jury is still out; sneakily dabbed rouge; parenting styles . . . lax; heed this caution.*

Section Preview

Answer guidelines are provided on page 122.

1. Describe the brain development that occurs from infancy through childhood, including its impact on memory.

2. Describe the roles of nature and nurture in motor development through infancy and childhood.

3. Discuss Piaget's view of how the mind develops, and describe his cognitive stages.

4. Discuss current views of Piaget's theory of cognitive development.

5. Discuss the origins and effects of early attachment, and the roles of familiarity and parenting in the development of attachment.

6. Discuss how disruptions in attachment and day care affect child development.

7. Explain how children's behavior provides evidence of an emerging self-concept, and discuss the possible effects of different parenting styles on children.

Stepping Through the Section

Answers are provided on page 124.

1. At birth the human nervous system _____ (is/is not) fully mature.

2. Biological growth processes that enable orderly changes in behavior are called _____ .

3. The lack of neural connections helps explain why our earliest memories do not occur before age _____ .

4. Infants pass the milestones of _____ development at different rates, but the basic _____ of stages is fixed. Cultural differences in the age at which babies begin walking _____ (do/do not) exist. Until the necessary muscular and neural maturation is complete, experience has a _____

(large/small) effect on behavior.

5. The first researcher to show that the thought processes of adults and children are very different was _____ .

6. To organize his or her experiences, the developing child constructs cognitive concepts called _____ .

7. The interpretation of new experiences in terms of existing ideas is called _____ . The adaptation of existing ideas to fit new experiences is called _____ .

8. The term for all the mental activities associated with thinking, remembering, communicating, and knowing is _____ .

9. In Piaget's first stage of development, the _____ stage, children experience the world through their motor and sensory interactions with objects. This stage occurs between infancy and age _____ .

10. The awareness that things continue to exist even when they are removed from view is called _____ _____ . This awareness begins to develop at about _____ months of age.

11. Developmental researchers have found that Piaget and his followers _____ (overestimated/underestimated) young children's competence.

12. According to Piaget, during the preschool years and up to age _____ , children are in the _____ stage.

13. The principle that the quantity of a substance remains the same even when the shape of its container changes is called _____ . Piaget believed that preschoolers _____ (have/have not) developed this concept.

14. Preschoolers are often unable to perceive things from another person's point of view. This inability is called _____ .

15. The child's growing ability to take another's perspective is evidence that the child is acquiring a

_____ _____

_____ .

16. The childhood disorder marked by an impaired theory of mind is _____ .

17. In contrast to Piaget's findings, researchers have more recently discovered that the ability to perform mental _____ , to think _____ , and to take another's _____ develops _____ (abruptly/gradually) during the preschool years.

18. Soviet psychologist _____ _____ noted that by age _____ children stop thinking aloud and instead rely on _____ _____ .

19. Piaget believed that children acquire the mental abilities needed to comprehend mathematical transformations and conservation by about _____ years of age. At this time, they enter the _____ _____ stage.

20. In Piaget's final stage, the _____ _____ stage, reasoning expands from the purely concrete to encompass _____ thinking. Piaget believed most children begin to enter this stage by age _____ .

Explain briefly how contemporary researchers view Piaget's theory.

21. By about _____ months of age, soon after object permanence emerges, a new fear, called _____ _____ , emerges.

22. The development of a strong emotional bond between infant and parent is called _____ .

23. Harlow's studies of monkeys have shown that mother-infant attachment does not depend on the mother providing nourishment so much as it does on her providing the comfort of _____ _____ . Another key to attachment is _____ .

24. In some animals attachment will occur only during a restricted time called a _____ _____ . Konrad Lorenz discovered that young birds would follow almost any object if it were the first moving thing they observed. This phenomenon is called _____ .

25. Human infants _____ (do/do not) have a precise critical period for becoming attached.

26. Placed in a strange play situation, children show one of two patterns of attachment: _____ attachment or _____ attachment.

Contrast the responses of securely and insecurely attached infants to strange situations.

Discuss the impact of responsive parenting on infant attachment.

27. Separation anxiety peaks in infants around
    _____ months, then
    _____ (gradually declines/ remains
    constant for about a year). This is true of children
    _____ (in North America/through-
    out the world).

28. Infants who were securely attached at 12 to 18
    months typically show greater social
    _____ as toddlers than infants who
    were insecurely attached.

29. According to Erikson, securely attached infants
    approach life with a sense of
    _____ _____ .

30. Harlow found that when monkeys reared in so-
    cial isolation are placed with other monkeys, they
    reacted with either fear or _____ .

31. Most abused children _____
    (do/do not) later become abusive parents.

32. When placed in a more positive and stable envi-
    ronment, most infants _____
    (recover/do not recover) from disruptions in
    attachment.

33. Today, approximately _____ of
    mothers of preschoolers are employed. Maternal
    employment _____ (does/does not)
    seem to have a major impact on children's devel-
    opment. High-quality child care consists of
    warm, supportive interactions with adults in an
    environment that is _____ ,
    _____ , and _____ .

34. Some developmental psychologists, such as
    Belsky and Zigler, believe that infant day care
    may promote _____ attachment in
    children under age 2 and disobedience and
    _____ when children are older.

35. The primary social achievement of childhood is
    the development of a _____ , which
    occurs in most children by age _____ .

36. A child's self-image generally becomes stable
    between the ages of _____ and
    _____ , when children begin to describe
    themselves in terms of gender, group member-
    ships, and psychological _____ .

Identify several characteristics of children who have
formed a positive self-image.

37. Parents who impose rules and expect blind obe-
    dience are exhibiting a(n) _____
    style of parenting.

38. Setting and enforcing standards after discussion
    with their children is the approach taken by
    _____ parents.

39. Parents who make few demands of their children
    and tend to submit to their children's desires are
    identified as _____ parents.

40. Studies have shown that there tends to be a corre-
    lation between high self-esteem on the part of the
    child and the _____ style of parent-
    ing. This may be because this parenting style
    gives children the greatest sense of
    _____ over their lives.

Explain why the correlation between authoritative
parenting and social competence does not necessarily
reveal cause and effect.

Adolescence (pp. 142–153)

> If you do not know the meaning of any of the
> following words, phrases, or expressions in
> the context in which they appear in the text,
> refer to page 136 for an explanation: *out of
> sync; intellectual summit; character—the psycho-
> logical muscles for controlling impulses; moral lad-
> der; talk is cheap; slack; "psychosocial" task; forge
> their identity; surfaces early.*

Section Preview

Answer guidelines are provided on page 124.

1. Identify the major physical changes that occur in adolescence.

2. Describe developments in cognitive and moral reasoning during adolescence, focusing on Kohlberg's theory and its criticisms.

3. Describe how Erikson viewed adolescence and the nature of social relationships during adolescence, and explain adolescents' changing relationships with parents and peers.

Stepping Through the Section

Answers are provided on page 125.

1. Today, sexual maturity is beginning _____ (earlier/later), and adult independence _____ (earlier/later) than in the past.

2. The "storm and stress" view of adolescence is credited to _____ , one of the first American psychologists to describe adolescence.

3. Adolescence begins with the time of developing sexual maturity known as _____ . A 2-year growth spurt begins in girls at about the age of _____ and in boys at about the age of _____ . This growth spurt is marked by the development of the reproductive organs and external genitalia, or _____ _____ characteristics, as well as by the development of traits such as pubic hair and enlarged breasts in females and facial hair in males. These nonreproductive traits are known as _____ _____ characteristics.

4. The first menstrual period, called _____ , occurs by about age _____ . In boys, the first ejaculation occurs by about age _____ .

5. The _____ (timing/sequence) of pubertal changes is more predictable than their _____ (timing/sequence).

6. Boys who mature _____ (early/late) tend to be more popular, self-assured, and independent. For girls, _____ (early/late) maturation can be stressful, especially when their bodies are out of sync with their _____ .

7. During the early teen years, reasoning is often _____ , as adolescents often feel their experiences are unique.

8. Piaget's final stage of cognitive development is the stage of _____ _____ . The adolescent in this stage is capable of thinking logically about _____ as well as concrete propositions.

9. The theorist who proposed that moral thought progresses through stages is _____ . These stages are divided

into three basic levels: _____ ,
_____ , and _____ .

10. In the preconventional stages of morality, characteristic of children, the emphasis is on obeying rules in order to avoid _____ or gain _____ .

11. Conventional morality usually emerges by early _____ . The emphasis is on gaining social _____ or upholding the social _____ .

12. Individuals who base moral judgments on their own perceptions of basic ethical principles are said by Kohlberg to employ _____ morality.

Summarize the criticisms of Kohlberg's theory of moral development.

13. Because of _____ influences, moral _____ does not always match moral _____ . For example, the best predictor of whether a teenager smokes marijuana is _____ _____ .

14. Children who learn to delay _____ become more socially responsible, academically successful, and productive.

15. Moral ideas grow _____ (stronger/weaker) when acted on.

Complete the missing information in the following table of Erikson's stages of psychosocial development.

Group Age	Psychosocial Stage
Infancy	_____
_____	Autonomy vs. shame and doubt
Preschooler	_____
	Competence vs. inferiority
Adolescence	_____
_____	Intimacy vs. isolation
Middle Adulthood	_____
_____	Integrity vs. despair

16. According to Erikson, the task of adolescence is to develop a clear sense of self, or _____ . Erikson saw this development as a prerequisite for the development of _____ in young adulthood.

17. Between 13 and 23, the individual's self-concept usually becomes _____ (more/less) positive and more _____ .

18. Gilligan believes that females are _____ (more/less) concerned than males with establishing individualistic identities.

19. Girls play in _____ (smaller/larger) groups than boys. Girls' play also is less _____ than boys and more likely to imitate _____ .

Compare the genders in terms of social connectedness.

20. Adolescence is typically a time of increasing influence from one's _____ and decreasing influence from

_____ .

Adulthood (pp. 153–167)

> If you do not know the meaning of any of the following words, phrases, or expressions in the context in which they appear in the text, refer to pages 137–138 for an explanation: *explode misconceptions; stairs get steeper, the newsprint gets smaller, and people seem to mumble more; levies a tax; Use it or lose it; "You can't teach an old dog new tricks"; myth . . . laid to rest; "Pair-bonding is a trademark of the human animal"; test-driving life together; shower one another with affection; Highs become less high.*

Section Preview

Answer guidelines are provided on page 126.

1. Identify the major physical changes that occur in middle adulthood and later life.

2. Describe the major cognitive changes that occur in adulthood and old age.

3. Explain why stage theories of adult social development are controversial.

4. Discuss the importance of family and career commitments in adult development, and describe the sense of well-being across the life span.

Stepping Through the Section

Answers are provided on page 126.

1. During adulthood, age _____ (is/is not) a very good predictor of people's traits.

2. The mid-twenties are the peak years for

_____ _____ ,

_____ _____ ,

_____ _____ , and

_____ _____ . Because

they mature earlier, _____ (women/men) also peak earlier.

3. During early and middle adulthood, physical vigor has less to do with _____ than with a person's _____ and _____ habits.

4. The cessation of the menstrual cycle, known as _____ , occurs within a few years of _____ . This biological change results from lowered levels of the hormone _____ . A woman's experience during this time depends largely on her _____ and _____ .

5. Although men experience no equivalent to menopause, they do experience a more gradual decline in _____ count, level of the hormone _____ , and speed of erection and ejaculation during later life.

6. The fastest-growing age group is the _____-_____ population.

7. Worldwide, life expectancy at birth increased from 49 years in 1950 to _____ years in the more developed countries. Women outlive men by nearly _____ years worldwide and by nearly _____ years in Canada, the United States, and Australia.

8. According to one evolutionary theory, our bodies age and wear out because once we've completed our _____-_____ task by raising our young, there are no _____ _____ pressures against genes that cause degeneration in later life.

9. With age, the eye's pupil _____ (shrinks/enlarges) and its lens becomes _____ (more/less) transparent. As a result, the amount of light that reaches the retina is _____ (increased/reduced).

10. Although older adults are _____ (more/less) susceptible to life-threatening ailments, they suffer from short-term ailments such as flu _____ (more/less) often than younger adults.

11. Aging _____ (slows/speeds/ has no effect on) neural processing and causes a gradual loss of _____ _____ .

12. The mental erosion that results from progressive damage to the brain is called _____ .

13. The irreversible disorder that causes progressive brain deterioration is _____ disease. This disease has been linked to a deterioration of neurons that produce the neurotransmitter _____ .

14. Studies of developmental changes in learning and memory show that during adulthood there is a decline in the ability to _____ (recall/recognize) new information but not in the ability to _____ (recall/recognize) such information. One factor that influences memory in the elderly is the _____ of material.

15. Cognitive abilities among 70-year-olds are _____ (less/more) varied than among 20-year-olds.

16. A research study in which people of various ages are compared with one another is called a _____-_____ study. A research study in which the same people are retested over a period of years is called a _____ study. The first kind of study found evidence of intellectual _____ during adulthood; the second found evidence of intellectual _____ .

Explain why studies of intellectual decline and aging yielded conflicting results.

17. The accumulation of stored information that comes with education and experience is called _____ intelligence, which tends to _____ with age.

18. The ability to reason abstractly is referred to as _____ intelligence, which tends to _____ with age.

19. Contrary to popular opinion, job and marital dissatisfaction do not surge during the forties, thus suggesting that a midlife _____ need not occur.

20. The term used to refer to the culturally preferred timing for leaving home, getting a job, marrying, and so on is the _____ _____ . Today, the timing of such life events is becoming _____ (more/less) predictable. More important than age are _____ _____ .

21. According to Erikson, the two basic tasks of adulthood are achieving _____ and _____ . According to Freud, the healthy adult is one who can _____ and _____ .

22. Human societies have nearly always included a relatively _____ bond between men and women. Marriage bonds are usually lasting when couples marry after age _____ and are _____ .

23. Marriages today are _____ (half/twice) as likely to end in divorce as they were in 1960. Couples who live together before marrying have a _____ (higher/lower) divorce rate than those who do not. Of those who divorce, _____ percent eventually remarry. One reliable indicator of likely marital success is a large ratio of _____ to _____ interactions.

24. As children begin to absorb time and energy, satisfaction with the marriage itself _____ (increases/decreases). This is particularly true among _____ women, who shoulder most of the burden.

25. For most couples, the children's leaving home produces a(n) _____ (increase/decrease) in marital satisfaction.

26. Research studies of women who are or are not employed have found that a woman's satisfaction in life depends on the _____ of her experience in her life's role.

27. According to studies, older people _____ (do/do not) report as much happiness and satisfaction with life as younger people do.

28. Compared to younger adults, older adults prefer a _____ (larger/smaller) social network marked by _____ _____ relationships.

29. According to Erikson, the final task of adulthood is to achieve a sense of _____ .

30. Reactions to a loved one's death _____ (do/do not) vary according to cultural norms. Those who express the strongest grief immediately _____ (do/do not) purge their grief more quickly.

Reflections on the Major Developmental Issues (pp. 168–169)

> If you do not know the meaning of any of the following words, phrases, or expressions in the context in which they appear in the text, refer to page 138 for an explanation: *as a giant redwood differs from its seedling; goof-off.*

Section Preview

Answer guidelines are provided on page 127.

1. State current views of psychologists on the continuity versus stages issue.

2. State current views of psychologists on the stability versus change issue.

Stepping Through the Section

Answers are provided on page 127.

1. Stage theories that have been considered include the theory of cognitive development proposed by _____ , the theory of moral development proposed by _____ , and the theory of psychosocial development proposed by _____ .

2. Although research casts doubt on the idea that life proceeds through age-linked _____ , there are spurts of _____ growth during childhood and puberty that correspond roughly to the stages proposed by _____ .

3. The first 2 years of life _____ (do/do not) provide a good basis for predicting a person's eventual traits.

4. Research on the consistency of personality shows that some traits, such as those related to _____ , are more stable than others, such as social attitudes.

Progress Test 1

Circle your answers to the following questions and check them with the answers on page 127. If your answer is incorrect, read the explanation for why it is incorrect and then consult the appropriate pages of the text (in parentheses following the correct answer).

Multiple-Choice Questions

1. Dr. Joan Goodman is studying how memory changes as people get older. She is most likely a(n) _____ psychologist.

   a. social   c. developmental
   b. cognitive   d. experimental

2. In Piaget's stage of concrete operational intelligence, the child acquires an understanding of the principle of:

   a. conservation.   c. attachment.
   b. deduction.   d. object permanence.

3. Piaget held that egocentrism is characteristic of the:

   a. sensorimotor stage.
   b. preoperational stage.
   c. concrete operational stage.
   d. formal operational stage.

4. During which stage of cognitive development do children acquire object permanence?

   a. sensorimotor   c. concrete operational
   b. preoperational   d. formal operational

5. The rooting reflex occurs when a:

   a. newborn's foot is tickled.
   b. newborn's cheek is touched.
   c. newborn hears a loud noise.
   d. newborn makes eye contact with his or her caregiver.
   e. newborn hears his or her mother's voice.

6. Harlow's studies of attachment in monkeys showed that:

   a. provision of nourishment was the single most important factor motivating attachment.
   b. a cloth mother produced the greatest attachment response.
   c. whether a cloth or wire mother was present mattered less than the presence or absence of other infants.
   d. attachment in monkeys is based on imprinting.

7. When psychologists discuss maturation, they are referring to stages of growth that are *not* influenced by:

   a. conservation.   c. nurture.
   b. nature.   d. continuity.

8. The developmental theorist who suggested that securely attached children develop an attitude of basic trust is:

   a. Piaget.   d. Freud.
   b. Harlow.   e. Erikson.
   c. Vygotsky.

9. Research findings on infant motor development are consistent with the idea that:
   a. cognitive development lags significantly behind motor skills development.
   b. maturation of physical skills is relatively unaffected by experience.
   c. in the absence of relevant earlier learning experiences, the emergence of motor skills will be slowed.
   d. in humans, the process of maturation may be significantly altered by cultural factors.

10. According to Erikson, the central psychological challenges pertaining to adolescence, young adulthood, and middle age, respectively, are:
    a. identity formation; intimacy; generativity.
    b. intimacy; identity formation; generativity.
    c. generativity; intimacy; identity formation.
    d. intimacy; generativity; identity formation.
    e. identity formation; generativity; intimacy.

11. In preconventional morality, the person:
    a. obeys out of a sense of social duty.
    b. conforms to gain social approval.
    c. obeys to avoid punishment or to gain concrete rewards.
    d. follows the dictates of his or her conscience.

12. Which of the following is correct?
    a. Early maturation places both boys and girls at a distinct social advantage.
    b. Early maturing girls are more popular and self-assured than girls who mature late.
    c. Early maturation places both boys and girls at a distinct social disadvantage.
    d. Early maturing boys are more popular and self-assured than boys who mature late.

13. A person's general ability to think abstractly is called _____ intelligence. This ability generally _____ with age.
    a. fluid; increases
    b. fluid; decreases
    c. crystallized; decreases
    d. crystallized; increases

14. Among the hallmarks of growing up are a boy's first ejaculation and a girl's first menstrual period, which also is called:
    a. puberty.   c. menarche.
    b. menopause.   d. generativity.

15. An elderly person who can look back on life with satisfaction and reminisce with a sense of completion has attained Erikson's stage of:
    a. generativity.
    b. intimacy.
    c. isolation.
    d. acceptance.
    e. integrity.

16. According to Piaget, the ability to think logically about abstract propositions is indicative of the stage of:
    a. preoperational thought.
    b. concrete operations.
    c. formal operations.
    d. fluid intelligence.

17. The cognitive ability that has been shown to decline during adulthood is the ability to:
    a. recall new information.
    b. recognize new information.
    c. learn meaningful new material.
    d. use judgment in dealing with daily life problems.

18. Which of the following statements concerning the effects of aging is true?
    a. Aging almost inevitably leads to dementia if the individual lives long enough.
    b. Aging increases susceptibility to short-term ailments such as the flu.
    c. Significant increases in life satisfaction are associated with aging.
    d. The aging process can be significantly affected by the individual's activity patterns.

19. Longitudinal tests:
    a. compare people of different ages.
    b. study the same people at different times.
    c. usually involve a larger sample than do cross-sectional tests.
    d. usually involve a smaller sample than do cross-sectional tests.
    e. are less informative than cross-sectional tests.

20. The average age at which puberty begins is _____ in boys; in girls, it is _____ .
    a. 14; 13   c. 11; 10
    b. 13; 11   d. 10; 9

21. After puberty, the self-concept usually becomes:
    a. more positive in boys.
    b. more positive in girls.
    c. more positive in both boys and girls.
    d. more negative in both boys and girls.

22. Adolescence is marked by the onset of:
    a. an identity crisis.
    b. parent-child conflict.
    c. the concrete operational stage.
    d. puberty.

23. Of the following, which is a possible cause of dementia?
    a. stroke
    b. brain tumor
    c. alcoholism
    d. All of the above are possible causes.

24. The end of menstruation is called:
    a. menarche.
    b. menopause.
    c. the midlife crisis.
    d. generativity.

25. The popular idea that terminally ill and bereaved people go through predictable stages, such as denial, anger, and so forth:
    a. is widely supported by research.
    b. more accurately describes grieving in some cultures than others.
    c. is true of women but not men.
    d. is not supported by research studies.

True-False Items

Indicate whether each statement is true or false by placing *T* or *F* in the blank next to the item.

_____ 1. Most abused children later become abusive parents.

_____ 2. At birth, the brain and nervous system of a healthy child are fully developed.

_____ 3. The sequence in which children develop motor skills varies from one culture to another.

_____ 4. Recent research shows that young children are more capable and development is more continuous than Piaget believed.

_____ 5. The process of grieving is much the same throughout the world.

_____ 6. The impact of day care on child development remains controversial.

_____ 7. During adulthood, age only moderately correlates with people's traits.

_____ 8. Intelligence declines throughout adulthood.

_____ 9. By the age of 50, most adults have experienced a "midlife crisis."

_____ 10. Compared to those who are younger, elderly people are more susceptible to short-term ailments such as flu and cold viruses.

_____ 11. The symptoms of Alzheimer's disease are simply an intensified version of normal aging.

Progress Test 2

Progress Test 2 should be completed during a final chapter review. Answer the following questions after you thoroughly understand the correct answers for the section reviews and Progress Test 1.

1. Stranger anxiety develops at the same time as:
    a. the concept of conservation.
    b. egocentrism.
    c. a theory of mind.
    d. the concept of object permanence.

2. Before Piaget, people were more likely to believe that:
    a. the child's mind is a miniature model of the adult's.
    b. children think about the world in radically different ways from adults.
    c. the child's mind develops through a series of stages.
    d. children interpret their experiences in terms of their current understandings.

3. Which is the correct sequence of stages in Piaget's theory of cognitive development?
    a. sensorimotor, preoperational, concrete operational, formal operational
    b. sensorimotor, preoperational, formal operational, concrete operational
    c. preoperational, sensorimotor, concrete operational, formal operational
    d. preoperational, sensorimotor, formal operational, concrete operational
    e. sensorimotor, concrete operational, preoperational, formal operational

4. A child can be born a drug addict because:
    a. drugs used by the mother will pass into the child's bloodstream.
    b. addiction is an inherited personality trait.
    c. drugs used by the mother create genetic defects in her chromosomes.
    d. the fetus's blood has not yet developed a resistance to drugs.

5. A child whose mother drank heavily when she was pregnant is at heightened risk of:
   a. being emotionally excitable during childhood.
   b. becoming insecurely attached.
   c. being born with the physical and cognitive abnormalities of fetal alcohol syndrome.
   d. addiction to a range of drugs throughout life.

6. Which is the correct order of stages of prenatal development?
   a. zygote, fetus, embryo
   b. zygote, embryo, fetus
   c. embryo, zygote, fetus
   d. embryo, fetus, zygote
   e. fetus, embryo, zygote

7. The term *critical period* refers to:
   a. prenatal development.
   b. the initial 2 hours after a child's birth.
   c. the preoperational stage.
   d. a restricted time for learning.

8. Which of the following was *not* found by Harlow in socially deprived monkeys?
   a. They had difficulty mating.
   b. They showed extreme fear or aggression when first seeing other monkeys.
   c. They showed abnormal physical development.
   d. The females were abusive mothers.

9. Children who in infancy formed secure attachments to their parents are more likely than other children to:
   a. prefer the company of adults to that of other children.
   b. become permissive parents.
   c. show a great deal of social competence.
   d. be less achievement oriented.

10. Most people's earliest memories do not predate _____ of age.
    a. 6 months   d. 3 years
    b. 1 year   e. 4 years
    c. 2 years

11. Insecurely attached infants who are left by their mothers in an unfamiliar setting often will:
    a. hold fast to their mothers on their return.
    b. explore the new surroundings confidently.
    c. be indifferent toward their mothers on their return.
    d. display little emotion at any time.

12. Whose stage theory of moral development was based on how people reasoned about ethical dilemmas?
    a. Erikson   d. Kohlberg
    b. Piaget   e. Kübler-Ross
    c. Levinson

13. The cross-sectional method:
    a. compares people of different ages with one another.
    b. studies the same group of people at different times.
    c. tends to paint too favorable a picture of the effects of aging on intelligence.
    d. is more appropriate than the longitudinal method for studying intellectual change over the life span.

14. The social clock refers to:
    a. an individual or society's distribution of work and leisure time.
    b. adulthood responsibilities.
    c. typical ages for starting a career, marrying, and so on.
    d. age-related changes in one's circle of friends.

15. To which of Kohlberg's levels would moral reasoning based on the existence of fundamental human rights pertain?
    a. preconventional morality
    b. conventional morality
    c. postconventional morality
    d. generative morality

16. In Erikson's theory, individuals generally focus on developing _____ during adolescence and then _____ during young adulthood.
    a. identity; intimacy
    b. intimacy; identity
    c. basic trust; identity
    d. identity; basic trust

17. After menopause, most women:
    a. experience anxiety and a sense of worthlessness.
    b. lose interest in sex.
    c. secrete unusually high levels of estrogen.
    d. gain a lot of weight.
    e. feel a new sense of freedom.

18. Notable achievements in fields such as _____ are often made by younger adults in their late twenties or early thirties, when _____ intelligence is at its peak.
    a. mathematics; fluid
    b. philosophy; fluid
    c. science; crystallized
    d. literature; crystallized
    e. history; crystallized

19. After their grown children have left home, most couples experience:
    a. the distress of the "empty nest syndrome."
    b. increased strain in their marital relationship.
    c. both a. and b.
    d. greater happiness and enjoyment in their relationship.

20. Underlying Alzheimer's disease is a deterioration in neurons that produce:
    a. epinephrine.   d. acetylcholine.
    b. norepinephrine.   e. dopamine.
    c. serotonin.

21. Compared with men, women:
    a. use conversation to communicate solutions.
    b. emphasize freedom and self-reliance.
    c. talk more openly
    d. do all of the above.

22. A person's accumulation of stored information, called _____ intelligence, generally _____ with age.
    a. fluid; decreases
    b. fluid; increases
    c. crystallized; decreases
    d. crystallized; increases

23. In terms of incidence, susceptibility to short-term illnesses _____ with age and susceptibility to long-term ailments _____ with age.
    a. decreases; increases
    b. increases; decreases
    c. increases; increases
    d. decreases; decreases

24. One criticism of stage theories is that they fail to consider that development may be significantly affected by:
    a. variations in the social clock.
    b. each individual's experiences.
    c. each individual's historical and cultural setting.
    d. all of the above.

25. Research on the American family indicates that:
    a. fewer than 23 percent of unmarried adults, but nearly 40 percent of married adults, report being "very happy" with life.
    b. the divorce rate is now one-half the marriage rate.
    c. of those who divorce, 75 percent remarry.
    d. all of the above are true.

Thinking Critically About Chapter 4

Answer these questions the day before an exam as a final check on your understanding of the chapter's terms and concepts.

Multiple-Choice Questions

1. Compared to when he was younger, 4-year-old Antonio is better able to empathize with his friend's feelings. This growing ability to take another's perspective indicates that Antonio is acquiring a:
   a. self-concept.   c. temperament.
   b. schema.   d. theory of mind.

2. Calvin, who is trying to impress his psychology professor with his knowledge of infant motor development, asks why some infants learn to roll over before they lift their heads from a prone position, while others develop these skills in the opposite order. What should Calvin's professor conclude from this question?
   a. Calvin clearly understands that the sequence of motor development is not the same for all infants.
   b. Calvin doesn't know what he's talking about. Although some infants reach these developmental milestones ahead of others, the order is the same for all infants.
   c. Calvin needs to be reminded that rolling over is an inherited reflex, not a learned skill.
   d. Calvin understands an important principle: motor development is unpredictable.

3. Deborah is a mathematician and Willie is a philosopher. Considering their professions:
   a. Deborath will make her most significant career accomplishments at an earlier age than Willie will.
   b. Deborah will make her most significant career accomplishments at a later age than Willie will.

c. Deborah will make her most significant career accomplishments at about the same time as Willie.

d. there is still not enough information for predicting such accomplishments.

4. Based on the text discussion of maturation and popularity, who among the following is probably the most popular sixth grader?

a. Jessica, the most physically mature girl in the class

b. Roger, the most intellectually mature boy in the class

c. Rob, the tallest, most physically mature boy in the class

d. Cindy, who is average in physical development and is on the school debating team

5. As a child observes, liquid is transferred from a tall, thin tube into a short, wide jar. The child is asked if there is now less liquid in order to determine if she has mastered:

a. the schema for liquids.

b. the concept of object permanence.

c. the concept of conservation.

d. the ability to reason abstractly.

6. I am 14 months old and fearful of strangers. I am in Piaget's _____ stage of cognitive development.

a. sensorimotor   c. concrete operational
b. preoperational   d. formal operational

7. I am 3 years old, can use language, and have trouble taking another person's perspective. I am in Piaget's _____ stage of cognitive development.

a. sensorimotor   c. concrete operational
b. preoperational   d. formal operational

8. In Piaget's theory, conservation is to egocentrism as the _____ stage is to the _____ stage.

a. sensorimotor; formal operational
b. formal operational; sensorimotor
c. preoperational; sensorimotor
d. concrete operational; preoperational

9. Four-year-old Jamail has a younger sister. When asked if he has a sister, he is likely to answer _____ ; when asked if his sister has a brother, Jamail is likely to answer _____ .

a. yes; yes   c. yes; no
b. no; no   d. no; yes

10. In a 1998 movie, a young girl finds that a gaggle of geese follow her wherever she goes because she was the first "object" they saw after they were born. This is an example of:

a. conservation.   c. egocentrism.
b. imprinting.   d. basic trust.

11. Joshua and Ann Bishop have a 13-month-old boy. According to Erikson, the Bishops' sensitive, loving care of their child contributes to:

a. the child's sense of basic trust.
b. the child's secure attachment.
c. the child's sense of control.
d. a. and b. only.

12. Fourteen-year-old Cassandra feels freer and more open with her friends than with her family. Knowing this is the case, Cassandra's parents should:

a. be concerned, because deteriorating parent-adolescent relationships, such as this one, are often followed by a range of problem behaviors.

b. encourage Cassandra to find new friends.

c. seek family counseling.

d. not worry, since adolescence is typically a time of growing peer influence and diminishing parental influence.

e. ask *their* friends to suggest ways to communicate with Cassandra.

13. Thirteen-year-old Irene has no trouble defeating her 11-year-old brother at a detective game that requires following clues in order to deduce the perpetrator of a crime. How might Piaget explain Irene's superiority at the game?

a. Being older, Irene has had more years of schooling.

b. Girls develop intellectually at a faster rate than boys.

c. Being an adolescent, Irene is beginning to develop abstract reasoning skills.

d. Girls typically have more experience than boys at playing games.

14. Which of the following was *not* mentioned in the text as a criticism of Kohlberg's theory of moral development?

a. It does not account for the fact that the development of moral reasoning is culture-specific.

b. Postconventional morality appears mostly in educated, middle-class persons.

c. The theory is biased against the moral reasoning of people in communal societies such as China.

d. The theory is biased in favor of moral reasoning in men.

15. Compared with her teenage brother, 14-year-old Samantha is likely to play in groups that are:
    a. larger and less competitive.
    b. larger and more competitive.
    c. smaller and less competitive.
    d. smaller and more competitive.

16. Sixty-five-year-old Calvin cannot reason as well as he could when he was younger. More than likely, Calvin's _____ intelligence has declined.
    a. analytic   c. fluid
    b. crystallized   d. both b. and c.

17. Cross-sectional studies of intelligence are potentially misleading because:
    a. they are typically based on a very small and unrepresentative sample of people.
    b. retesting the same people over a period of years allows test performance to be influenced by practice.
    c. they compare people who are not only different in age, but of different eras, education levels, and affluence.
    d. of all the above reasons.

18. Which statement illustrates cognitive development during the course of adult life?
    a. Adults in their forties have better recognition memory than do adults in their seventies.
    b. Recall and recognition memory both remain strong throughout life.
    c. Recognition memory decreases sharply at midlife.
    d. Recall memory remains strong until very late in life.
    e. Adults in their forties have better recall memory than adults in their seventies.

19. Given the text discussion of life satisfaction patterns, which of the following people is likely to report the greatest life satisfaction?
    a. Billy, a 7-year-old second-grader
    b. Kathy, a 17-year-old high-school senior
    c. Alan, a 30-year-old accountant
    d. Mildred, a 70-year-old retired teacher
    e. too little information to tell

20. Which of the following statements is consistent with the current thinking of developmental psychologists?
    a. Development occurs in a series of sharply defined stages.
    b. The first two years are the most crucial in determining the individual's personality.

c. The consistency of personality in most people tends to increase over the life span.
d. Social and emotional style are among the characteristics that show the least stability over the life span.

21. Sam, a junior in high school, regularly attends church because his family and friends think he should. Which stage of moral reasoning is Sam in?
    a. preconventional
    b. conventional
    c. postconventional
    d. too little information to tell

22. Research on social relationships between parents and their adolescent children shows that:
    a. parental influence on children increases during adolescence.
    b. high school girls who have the most affectionate relationships with their mothers tend to enjoy the most intimate friendships with girlfriends.
    c. high school boys who have the most affectionate relationships with their fathers tend to enjoy the most intimate friendships with friends.
    d. most teens are strongly influenced by parents in matters of personal taste.
    e. parent-adolescent conflict is most common between mothers and daughters.

23. Most contemporary developmental psychologists believe that:
    a. personality is essentially formed by the end of infancy.
    b. personality continues to be formed until adolescence.
    c. the shaping of personality continues during adolescence and well beyond.
    d. adolescent development has very little impact on adult personality.

24. After a series of unfulfilling relationships, 30-year-old Carlos tells a friend that he doesn't want to marry because he is afraid of losing his freedom and independence. Erikson would say that Carlos is having difficulty with the psychosocial task of:
    a. trust versus mistrust.
    b. autonomy versus doubt.
    c. intimacy versus isolation.
    d. identity versus role confusion.
    e. generativity versus stagnation.

25. Research on the relationship between self-report-ed happiness and employment in American women has revealed that:

  a. women who work tend to be happier.

  b. women who do not work tend to be happier.

  c. women today are happier than in the past, whether they are working or not.

  d. the quality of a woman's experience in her various roles is more predictive of happiness than the presence or absence of a given role.

Essay Question

Sheryl is 12 years old and in the sixth grade. Describe the developmental changes she is likely to be experiencing according to Piaget, Kohlberg, and Erikson. (Use the space below to list the points you want to make and organize them. Then write the essay on a separate sheet of paper.)

Key Terms

Using your own words, on a piece of paper write a brief definition or explanation of each of the following terms.

1. developmental psychology

2. zygote

3. embryo

4. fetus

5. teratogens

6. fetal alcohol syndrome (FAS)

7. rooting reflex

8. habituation

9. maturation

10. schema

11. assimilation

12. accommodation

13. cognition

14. sensorimotor stage

15. object permanence

16. preoperational stage

17. conservation

18. egocentrism

19. theory of mind

20. concrete operational stage

21. formal operational stage

22. stranger anxiety

23. attachment

24. critical period

25. imprinting

26. basic trust

27. self-concept

28. adolescence

29. puberty

30. primary sex characteristics

31. secondary sex characteristics

32. menarche

33. identity

34. intimacy

35. menopause

36. Alzheimer's disease

37. cross-sectional study

38. longitudinal study

39. crystallized intelligence

40. fluid intelligence

41. social clock

Answers

Introduction Preview

1. Developmental psychologists study physical, mental, and social commonalities and changes throughout the human life cycle.

2. The nature/nurture issue is concerned with how much development is influenced by heredity and how much by experience. The continuity or stages issue concerns whether development is a gradual, continuous process or a sequence of separate stages. The stability or change issue asks whether individual traits persist over the life span or people become different persons as they age.

Stepping Through the Introduction

1. developmental psychologists
2. nature/nurture
3. continuity/stages
4. stability

Prenatal Development and the Newborn

Section Preview

1. A woman's ovary releases a mature egg. The few sperm from the man that reach the egg release digestive enzymes that eat away the egg's protective covering. As soon as one sperm penetrates the egg, the egg's surface blocks out all other sperm. The egg and sperm nuclei fuse and become one.

   Prenatal development is divided into three stages: zygote (from conception to 2 weeks); embryo (2 weeks through 8 weeks); and fetus (9 weeks to birth).

   During the period of the zygote, cell division is the primary task. Within two weeks of conception the increasingly numerous cells begin to differentiate—to specialize in structure and function. At this time the zygote's outer part attaches to the mother's uterine wall, becoming the placenta. During the period of the embryo, body organs begin to form and function. By the end of the sixth month the fetus's internal organs have become sufficiently functional to allow a premature fetus a chance of survival.

2. Teratogens are damaging agents such as drugs and viruses that pass from the mother's bloodstream through the placenta into the bloodstream of the embryo or fetus. Teratogens may result in a variety of physical and cognitive abnormalities in the developing child. For example, mothers who are heavy smokers often give birth to under-weight infants. Mothers addicted to drugs such as heroin give birth to addicted newborns. If a mother is a heavy alcohol drinker, her infant may suffer from fetal alcohol syndrome, which is characterized by small, misproportioned heads and brain abnormalities, which lead to mental retardation.

3. Newborns are born with a variety of reflexes that help ensure their survival. When touched on its cheek, for example, a baby will open its mouth and search for food (rooting reflex).

   The newborn's sensory capabilities facilitate social responsiveness. Newborns prefer human voices and drawings of human faces to artificial sounds and nonhuman visual patterns. Within days of birth, babies can distinguish their mother's odor and voice.

4. Psychologists use habituation, decreasing responsiveness with repeated stimulation, to study infant thinking. Infants respond to a novel stimulus with interest, but the more the stimulus is presented, the less the infant responds. If an infant responds when a new stimulus is presented, the researcher knows that the infant recognizes that the stimulus is different.

Stepping Through the Section

An egg has been released by the ovary; during intercourse, millions of sperm are deposited and travel toward the egg. At the moment of conception, those few sperm that reach the egg release digestive enzymes that eat away the egg's protective coating, allowing one sperm to penetrate. The fertilizing sperm is drawn into the egg, where the egg nucleus and sperm nucleus fuse.

1. zygotes; differentiate; embryo; fetus
2. teratogens
3. can affect; fetal alcohol syndrome
4. rooting reflex

Newborns reflexively turn their heads in the direction of human voices. They gaze longer at a drawing of a human face than at a bull's-eye pattern. They focus best on objects about 8 to 12 inches away, which is about the distance between a nursing infant's eyes and the mother's.

5. habituation; decrease

Infancy and Childhood

Section Preview

1. All the brain cells a person will ever have are present at birth. However, the neural connections that enable walking, talking, and memory are only beginning to form. This neural immaturity

may explain why we have no memories of events before 3 years of age. While lasting memories may not be formed before then, infants are capable of learning simple responses.

2. While nurture may play a role in motor development—Ugandan babies walk before age 10 months, as compared to babies with no experience—nature plays a major role. Before biological maturation creates a readiness to develop a particular skill, experience has a limited effect.

Although the age at which infants sit, stand, walk, and control bowel and bladder varies from child to child, the sequence in which babies develop these abilities is universal.

3. Piaget believed that children actively construct their understanding of the world in radically different ways from adults. He further believed that children's minds develop through a series of stages in which they form increasingly complex schemas that organize their past experiences and provide a framework for understanding future experiences.

In the sensorimotor stage, from birth to about 2 years, children experience their world through their senses and actions. During this stage, object permanence (and stranger anxiety) develop.

In the preoperational stage, from about 2 to 6 or 7 years, children are able to use language but lack logical reasoning. During this stage, egocentrism develops, along with the rudiments of a theory of mind.

In the concrete operational stage, from about 6 or 7 to 11 years, children are able to think logically about concrete events and perform mathematical operations. Conservation also develops during this stage.

The formal operational stage, from age 12 through adulthood, is characterized by abstract and systematic reasoning, as well as by the potential for mature moral reasoning.

4. Today's researchers see development as more continuous than did Piaget. For example, object permanence, conservation, and the abilities to take another's perspective and perform mental operations unfold gradually and are not utterly absent in one stage and then suddenly present. In fact, preschoolers acquire a "theory of mind" and come to realize that others may hold false beliefs.

Researchers also believe that Piaget underestimated young children's competence. They have found rudiments of various cognitive abilities at an earlier age than Piaget supposed.

In many ways, however, Piaget's theory continues to receive support. Despite variations in the rate at which children develop, research reveals that human cognition everywhere unfolds in the basic sequence he proposed.

5. Harlow's research with monkeys reveals that attachment usually grows from body contact with parents, rather than by association with feeding. In many animals, attachment is also based on familiarity and forms during a critical period shortly after hatching or birth (a process called imprinting). Although human infants prefer faces and objects with which they are familiar, they do not have a critical period for forming attachments.

Responsive parenting is also a factor. Sensitive, responsive mothers tend to have infants who become securely attached. Insensitive, unresponsive mothers often have insecurely attached infants. Securely attached infants are less anxious and more socially competent, and these differences persist through early childhood.

6. Erik Erikson believed that infants with sensitive, loving caregivers form a lifelong attitude of basic trust—a sense that the world is predictable and reliable. Children who suffer parental neglect or abuse may form lasting scars—nightmares, depression, a troubled adolescence, and a greater tendency to later abuse their own children.

Babies reared in institutions without nurturing care are often withdrawn, frightened, even speechless. Fortunately, most infants recover from disruptions of attachment if placed in a more positive and stable environment.

The impact of day care on children remains controversial. Many developmentalists believe that quality infant day care does not hinder secure attachment. In support of this belief, research has shown that children who had experienced quality day care during their first six months were more outgoing, popular, and academically successful than those who hadn't. However, some developmentalists believe that children placed in day care more than 20 hours per week in the first year of life are at heightened risk of insecure attachment and of being disobedient and aggressive at older ages.

7. Self-awareness emerges gradually over the first year, with the first sign being a child's self-recognition when staring into a mirror. By 15 to 18 months, children will wipe at a dab of rouge seen on their faces in a mirror's reflection. By school age, children begin to describe themselves in terms of gender, group memberships, and psychological traits.

Three parenting styles have been identified. Authoritarian parents impose rules and expect their children to be obedient. Authoritative parents are demanding, yet more responsive to their children. They set and enforce rules, but also are willing to explain and discuss the reasoning behind rules. Permissive parents make few demands of their children and submit to their wishes. Children with the highest self-esteem, self-reliance, and social competence usually have authoritative parents, perhaps because their parents provide them with the greatest sense of self-control.

Stepping Through the Section

1. is not

2. maturation

3. 3

4. motor; sequence; do; small

5. Piaget

6. schemas

7. assimilation; accommodation

8 cognition

9. sensorimotor; 2

10. object permanence; 8

11. underestimated

12. 6 or 7; preoperational

13. conservation; have not

14. egocentrism

15. theory of mind

16. autism

17. operations; symbolically; perspective; gradually

18. Lev Vygotsky; 7; inner speech

19. 6 or 7; concrete operational

20. formal operational; abstract; 12

Contemporary researchers see development as more continuous than did Piaget. By detecting the beginnings of each type of thinking at earlier ages, they have revealed conceptual abilities that Piaget missed. They also see formal logic as a smaller part of cognition than Piaget did. Despite these revisions to Piaget's theory, studies support the basic idea that cognitive development unfolds as a sequence of distinct stages.

21. 8; stranger anxiety

22. attachment

23. body contact; familiarity

24. critical period; imprinting

25. do not

26. secure; insecure

Placed in a strange situation, securely attached infants play comfortably, happily exploring their new environment. In contrast, insecurely attached infants are less likely to explore their surroundings and may even cling to their mothers. When separated from their mothers, insecurely attached infants are much more distressed than securely attached infants. When reunited with their mothers, insecurely attached infants may be indifferent.

Research studies conducted by Mary Ainsworth have revealed that sensitive, responsive mothers tend to have securely attached infants, whereas insensitive, unresponsive mothers often have insecurely attached infants. Other studies have found that temperamentally difficult infants whose mothers receive training in responsive parenting are more likely to become securely attached than are control infants.

27. 13; gradually declines; throughout the world

28. competence

29. basic trust

30. aggression

31. do not

32. recover

33. half; does not; safe; healthy; stimulating

34. insecure; aggression

35. self-concept; 12

36. 8; 10; traits

Children who have formed a positive self-concept tend to be more confident, independent, optimistic, assertive, and sociable.

37. authoritarian

38. authoritative

39. permissive

40. authoritative; control

There are at least three possible explanations of the correlation between authoritative parenting and social competence in children. (1) Parenting may foster children's competence. (2) Children's competence may promote authoritative parenting. (3) A third factor, such as heredity or parental education or socioeconomic status, may foster both authoritative parenting and child competence.

Adolescence

Section Preview

1. Adolescence begins with puberty, a two-year period of rapid development that begins in girls

at about age 11 and in boys at about age 13. During the growth spurt, sexual maturation occurs, as the primary sex characteristics (reproductive organs) and secondary sex characteristics (nonreproductive traits) develop dramatically.

The hallmarks of puberty are the first ejaculation in boys at about age 14 and the first menstrual period, called menarche, in girls at about age 13. As in earlier life stages, the sequence of physical changes is more predictable than their timing.

2. During the early teen years, reasoning tends to be self-focused. Eventually, however, most adolescents attain Piaget's stage of formal operations and become capable of abstract, logical thinking.

Kohlberg believed that moral reasoning builds on cognitive development and proceeds through as many as six stages. Before age 9, most children obey rules either to avoid punishment or to gain rewards (preconventional morality). By early adolescence, they develop the conventional morality of abiding by laws simply because "those are the rules." Postconventional morality, which is achieved by those who develop the abstract reasoning of formal operations, affirms people's agreed-upon rights or follows a personal code of ethics.

Critics contend that the postconventional level appears mostly in the educated middle class of countries that value individualism. Others contend that Kohlberg's stages reflect a male bias, and that for women, moral maturity is less a matter of abstract justice than it is an ethic of caring relationships. Critics also note that morality also lies in actions, which are influenced by factors beside moral reasoning. For example, because of social influences, people's willingness to cheat, to discriminate racially, and to smoke marijuana are not solely determined by their attitudes toward these behaviors.

3. According to Erikson, the primary task of adolescence is the formation of identity. Many adolescents try out different "selves" by playing different roles in various situations until their sense of identity becomes clearer.

Once adolescents have formed a sense of who they are, said Erikson, they focus on developing close relationships. Carol Gilligan believes that females are less concerned than males with developing a sense of identity as separate individuals *before* they strive to form close relationships.

This gender difference in connectedness carries into adulthood. Women emphasize caring more than men, and have closer, more intimate relationships.

Despite popular belief, only a very small percentage of teenagers report not getting along with their parents at all. However, adolescence is a time of growing peer influence and diminishing parental influence, especially on matters of personal taste and life-style.

Stepping Through the Section

1. earlier; later
2. G. Stanley Hall
3. puberty; 11; 13; primary sex; secondary sex
4. menarche; 13; 14
5. sequence; timing
6. early; early; emotional maturity
7. self-focused
8. formal operations; abstract
9. Kohlberg; preconventional; conventional; postconventional
10. punishment; rewards
11. adolescence; approval; order
12. postconventional

Critics of Kohlberg's theory argue that the perception of postconventional moral reasoning as the highest level of moral development reflects a Western middle-class bias. Others have argued that for women, morality is less a matter of abstract, impersonal justice and more an ethic of caring relationships.

13. social; action; reasoning; how many of the teen's friends smoke it
14. gratification
15. stronger

Erikson's stages of psychosocial development

Group Age	Psychosocial Stage
Infancy	**Trust vs. mistrust**
Toddler	Autonomy vs. shame and doubt
Preschooler	**Initiative vs. guilt**
Elementary School	Competence vs. inferiority
Adolescence	**Identity vs. role confusion**
Young Adulthood	Intimacy vs. isolation
Middle Adulthood	**Generativity vs. stagnation**
Late Adulthood	Integrity vs. despair

16. identity; intimacy
17. more; personalized
18. less

19. smaller; competitive; social relationships

Women provide most of the care to the very young and the very old. They also have closer, more intimate relationships, especially with other women.

20. peers; parents

Adulthood

Section Preview

1. Muscular strength, reaction time, sensory keenness, and cardiac output all peak by the mid-twenties and begin to decline thereafter. Health and exercise habits are important factors in the rate of physical decline.

   For women, menopause is the foremost biological change related to aging. Despite popular belief, menopause usually does not create psychological problems for women. Men experience a gradual decline in sperm count, testosterone level, and speed of erection and ejaculation as they get older.

   Decline in the functioning of the body's disease-fighting immune system makes the elderly more susceptible to life-threatening ailments such as cancer and pneumonia. Older people suffer short-term ailments, such as colds and the flu, less often, however.

   Aging also slows neural processes and results in a small, gradual loss of brain cells. Some adults experience the mental erosion of dementia that results from a series of strokes, a brain tumor, or alcoholism. A small percentage of older adults suffer Alzheimer's disease, in which acetyl-choline-producing neurons degenerate.

2. Individual variation in learning ability and memory throughout adulthood makes it difficult to generalize about age-related changes in cognition. Typically, however, the ability to recall (but not to recognize) new information, particularly material that is not meaningful to the individual, declines.

   Longitudinal studies of intelligence have laid to rest the myth that intelligence sharply declines with age. Whether intelligent performance on a task increases or decreases with age depends largely on the task. Tests of accumulated knowledge reveal that crystallized intelligence increases up to old age. Tests measuring one's ability to reason abstractly reveal that fluid intelligence decreases with age. These differences help explain why people in different professions produce their most notable work at different ages.

3. Some psychologists have suggested that the early forties are a time of emotional instability, when a "midlife transition," or crisis, is likely. Research has not found, however, that emotional distress of this kind peaks at any particular age.

   Researchers are skeptical of stage theories of adult social development for several reasons. For one, the settings of the *social clock* prescribing "proper" ages for various life events vary from culture to culture and from era to era. Even more important than one's age in defining new life stages are life events such as marriage, parenthood, job changes, divorce, and retirement. Increasingly, events such as these are occurring at unpredictable ages.

4. According to Erikson, the tasks of forming close relationships (intimacy) and being productive and supporting future generations (generativity) dominate adulthood. Freud expressed the same viewpoint in saying that the healthy adult is one who can love and work.

   Despite the rising divorce rate, most married Europeans and North Americans generally feel happier than those who are unmarried, especially those who are separated or divorced. Although having a child is for most people a happy event, as children begin to absorb time, money, and emotional energy, satisfaction with marriage often declines.

   Despite the popular belief that the departure of adult children usually causes parents to feel great distress and a loss of purpose, research reveals that those whose nest has emptied generally report greater happiness and enjoyment of their marriage.

   Studies of the relationship between happiness and having a career have compared employed and unemployed women. The results of these studies reveal that what matters is not which role(s) a woman occupies—as worker, wife, and/or mother—but the quality of her experience in each. People of all ages report similar feelings of happiness and satisfaction with life. As people age, however, emotions typically become less intense.

Stepping Through the Section

1. is not
2. muscular strength, reaction time, sensory keenness, cardiac output; women
3. age; health; exercise
4. menopause; 50; estrogen; expectations; attitude
5. sperm; testosterone
6. post-65
7. 75; 4; 7

8. gene-reproducing; natural selection

9. shrinks; less; reduced

10. more; less

11. slows; brain cells

12. dementia

13. Alzheimer's; acetylcholine

14. recall; recognize; meaningfulness

15. more

16. cross-sectional; longitudinal; decline; stability

Because cross-sectional studies compare people not only of different ages but also of different eras, education levels, family size, and affluence, it is not surprising that such studies reveal cognitive decline with age. In contrast, longitudinal studies test one group over a span of years. However, because those who survive to the end of longitudinal studies may be the brightest and healthiest, these studies may underestimate the average decline in intelligence. Research is also complicated by the fact that certain tests measure only one type of intelligence. Tests that measure fluid intelligence reveal decline with age; tests that measure crystallized intelligence reveal just the opposite.

17. crystallized; increase

18. fluid; decrease

19. crisis (transition)

20. social clock; less; life events

21. intimacy; generativity; love; work

22. monogamous; 20; well educated

23. twice; higher; 75; positive; negative

24. decreases; employed

25. increase

26. quality

27. do

28. smaller; emotionally meaningful

29. integrity

30. do; do not

Reflections on the Major Developmental Issues

Section Preview

1. Although research casts doubt on the idea that life proceeds through neatly defined, age-linked stages of cognitive, moral, and social development, the concept of stage remains useful. Stage theories show the order in which abilities develop and help focus awareness on how people of one age think and act differently when they arrive at a later age.

2. Recent research has revealed that there is a consistency to personality due to an underlying stability in basic social and emotional styles. Although the first 2 years of life provide a poor basis for predicting eventual traits, as people grow older dispositions become quite stable and attitudes much more predictable.

Stepping Through the Section

1. Piaget; Kohlberg; Erikson

2. stages; brain; Piaget

3. do not

4. temperament

Progress Test 1

Multiple-Choice Questions

1. **c.** is the answer. Developmental psychologists study physical, cognitive (memory, in this example), and social change throughout the life span. (p. 119)
   a. Social psychologists study how people influence and are influenced by others.
   b. Cognitive psychologists *do* study memory; because Dr. Goodman is interested in life-span *changes* in memory, she is more likely a developmental psychologist.
   d. Experimental psychologists study physiology, sensation, perception, learning, and other aspects of behavior. Only developmental psychologists focus on developmental changes in behavior and mental processes.

2. **a.** is the answer. (p. 130)
   b. Deduction, or deductive reasoning, is a formal operational ability.
   c. Piaget's theory is not concerned with attachment.
   d. Attaining object permanence is the hallmark of preoperational thought.

3. **b.** is the answer. The preoperational child sees the world from his or her own vantage point. (p. 130)
   a. As immature as egocentrism is, it represents a significant cognitive advance over the sensorimotor child, who knows the world only through senses and actions. Even simple self-awareness takes a while to develop.
   c. & d. As children attain the operational stages, they become more able to see the world through the eyes of others.

4. **a.** is the answer. Before object permanence is attained, "out of sight" is truly "out of mind." (pp. 128–129)
   b., c., & d. Developments during the preoperational, concrete operational, and formal operational stages include the use of language, conservation, and abstract reasoning, respectively.

5. **b.** is the answer. The infant turns its head and begins sucking when its cheek is stroked. (p. 122)

a., c., & d. These stimuli produce other reflexes in the newborn.

e. The mother's voice causes the newborn to turn toward the sound; no touch is involved.

6. **b.** is the answer. (pp. 134–135)

a. When given the choice between a wire mother with a bottle and a cloth mother without, the monkeys preferred the cloth mother.

c. The presence of other infants made no difference.

d. Imprinting plays no role in the attachment of higher primates.

7. **c.** is the answer. Through maturation—an orderly sequence of biological growth processes that are relatively unaffected by experience—all humans develop. (p. 124)

a. Conservation is the cognitive awareness that objects do not change with changes in shape.

b. The forces of nature *are* those that direct maturation.

d. The continuity/stages debate has to do with whether development is a gradual and continuous process or a discontinuous, stagelike process. Those who emphasize maturation see development as occurring in stages, not continuously.

8. **e.** is the answer. Erikson proposed that development occurs in a series of stages, in the first of which the child develops an attitude of either basic trust or mistrust. (p. 137)

a. Piaget's theory is concerned with cognitive development.

b. Harlow conducted research on attachment and deprivation.

c. Vygotsky focused on the influence of sociocultural factors on development.

d. Freud's theory is concerned with personality development.

9. **b.** is the answer. (p. 126)

10. **a.** is the answer. (pp. 149, 163)

11. **c.** is the answer. At the preconventional level, moral reasoning centers on self-interest, whether this means obtaining rewards or avoiding punishment. (p. 147)

a. & b. Moral reasoning based on a sense of social duty or a desire to gain social approval is associated with the conventional level of moral development.

d. Reasoning based on ethical principles is characteristic of the postconventional level of moral development.

12. **d.** is the answer. Boys who show early physical maturation are generally stronger and more athletic than boys who mature late; these qualities may lead to greater popularity and self-assurance. (p. 145)

a. & c. Early maturation tends to be socially advantageous for boys but not for girls.

b. Early-maturing girls often suffer embarrassment and are objects of teasing.

13. **b.** is the answer. (p. 162)

a. Fluid intelligence tends to decrease with age.

c. & d. Crystallized intelligence refers to the accumulation of facts and general knowledge that takes place during a person's life. Crystallized intelligence generally *increases* with age.

14. **c.** is the answer. (p. 145)

a. Puberty refers to the early adolescent period during which accelerated growth and sexual maturation occur, not to the first menstrual period.

b. Menopause is the cessation of menstruation, which typically occurs in the early fifties.

d. In Erikson's theory, generativity, or the sense of contributing and being productive, is the task of middle adulthood.

15. **e.** is the answer. (p. 167)

a. Generativity is associated with middle adulthood.

b. & c. Intimacy and isolation are associated with young adulthood.

d. The term *acceptance* is not associated with Erikson's theory.

16. **c.** is the answer. Once formal operational thought has been attained, thinking is no longer limited to concrete propositions. (p. 132)

a. & b. Preoperational thought and concrete operational thought emerge before, and do not include, the ability to think logically about abstract propositions.

d. Fluid intelligence refers to abstract reasoning abilities; however, it is unrelated to Piaget's theory and stages.

17. **a.** is the answer. (p. 162)

b., c., & d. These cognitive abilities remain essentially unchanged as the person ages.

18. **d.** is the answer. "Use it or lose it" seems to be the rule: Often, changes in activity patterns contribute significantly to problems regarded as being part of usual aging. (p. 158)

a. Most elderly people do not develop dementia; even among the very old, the risk of dementia is only 40 percent.

b. Although the elderly are more subject to long-term ailments than younger adults, they actually suffer fewer short-term ailments.

c. People of all ages report equal happiness or satisfaction with life.

19. **b.** is the answer. (p. 160)
    a. This answer describes cross-sectional research.
    c. & d. Sample size does not distinguish cross-sectional from longitudinal research.
    e. Just the opposite is true.

20. **b.** is the answer. (p. 144)

21. **c.** is the answer. Because the late teen years provide many new opportunities for trying out possible roles, adolescents' identities typically incorporate an increasingly positive self-concept. (p. 149)

22. **d.** is the answer. The physical changes of puberty mark the onset of adolescence. (p. 144)
    a. & b. An identity crisis or parent-child conflict may or may not occur during adolescence; neither of these formally marks its onset.
    c. Formal operational thought, rather than concrete reasoning, typically develops in adolescence.

23. **d** is the answer. (p. 158)

24. **b.** is the answer. (p. 154)
    a. Menarche refers to the onset of menstruation.
    c. When it does occur, the midlife crisis is a psychological, rather than biological, phenomenon.
    d. Generativity is Erikson's term for productivity during middle adulthood.

25. **d.** is the answer. (p. 167)

True-False Items

1. False. About 30 percent of those abused later abuse their own children. (p. 138)

2. False. Although you are born with essentially all the brain cells you will ever have, some brain processes—such as the formation of neural networks and myelination—continue to develop for many years. (p. 124)

3. False. Although the rate at which motor skills develop varies from child to child, the *sequence* is universal. (p. 126)

4. True. (p. 133)

5. False. Cultures differ widely in grieving norms. (p. 166)

6. True. (pp. 139–140)

7. True. (pp. 168–169)

8. False. It depends on how intelligence is defined. Fluid intelligence decreases slowly up to age 75, while crystallized intelligence increases up to old age. (p. 162)

9. False. This popular belief is a myth. (pp. 162–163)

10. False. In fact, just the opposite is true. (p. 157)

11. False. Alzheimer's symptoms reflect the existence of a disease, rather than normal aging processes. (p. 158)

Progress Test 2

1. **d.** is the answer. With object permanence, a child develops schemas for familiar objects, including faces, and may become upset by a stranger who does not fit any of these schemas. (p. 134)
    a. The concept of conservation develops during the concrete operational stage, whereas stranger anxiety develops during the sensorimotor stage.
    b. & c. Egocentrism and a theory of mind both develop during the preoperational stage. This follows the sensorimotor stage, during which stranger anxiety develops.

2. **a.** is the answer. (p. 127)
    b., c., & d. Each of these is an understanding developed by Piaget.

3. **a.** is the answer. (p. 128)

4. **a.** is the answer. Any drug taken by the mother passes through the placenta and enters the child's bloodstream. (p. 121)
    b. Addiction cannot be inherited; it requires exposure to an addictive drug.
    c. Drugs may disrupt the mechanisms of heredity, but there is no evidence that such changes promote addiction.
    d. This answer is incorrect because at no age does the blood "resist" drugs.

5. **c.** is the answer. (p. 121)
    a., b., & d. A child's emotional temperament, attachment, and addiction have not been linked to the mother's drinking while pregnant.

6. **b.** is the answer. (pp. 120–121)

7. **d.** is the answer. A critical period is a restricted time during which an organism must be exposed to certain influences or experiences for a particular kind of learning to occur. (p. 135)
    a. Critical periods refer to developmental periods after birth.
    b. Critical periods vary from behavior to behavior, but they are not confined to the hours following birth.
    c. Critical periods are not specifically associated with the preoperational period.

8. **c.** is the answer. Deprived monkeys were impaired in their social behaviors but not in their physical development. (p. 138)

a., b., & d. Each of these was found in socially deprived monkeys.

9. **c.** is the answer. Thus, for example, Sroufe found that children who were securely attached at 12 to 18 months of age were, as 2- to 3-year-olds, more outgoing than other children and more enthusiastic when working on challenging tasks. (p. 137)
a., b., & d. There is no indication that securely attached children prefer to be with adults, become permissive parents, or are less achievement oriented.

10. **d.** is the answer. This is because of a lack of neural connections before that age. (p. 125)

11. **c.** is the answer. (p. 136)
a. Insecurely attached infants often cling to their mothers when placed in a new situation; yet, when the mother returns after an absence, the infant's reaction tends to be one of indifference.
b. These behaviors are characteristic of securely attached infants.
d. Insecurely attached infants in unfamiliar surroundings will often exhibit a range of emotional behaviors.

12. **d.** is the answer. (p. 146)
a. Erikson is known for his theory of psychosocial development.
b. Piaget is known for his theory of cognitive development.
c. & e. These theorists were not discussed.

13. **a.** is the answer. (p. 160)
b. This answer describes the longitudinal research method.
c. & d. Cross-sectional studies have tended to exaggerate the negative effects of aging on intellectual functioning; for this reason they may not be the most appropriate method for studying lifespan development.

14. **c.** is the answer. Different societies and eras have somewhat different ideas about the age at which major life events should ideally occur. (p. 163)

15. **c.** is the answer. (p. 147)
a. Preconventional morality is based on avoiding punishment and obtaining rewards.
b. Conventional morality is based on gaining the approval of others and/or on following the law and social convention.
d. There is no such thing as generative morality.

16. **a.** is the answer. (pp. 149–150)
b. According to Erikson, identity develops before intimacy.
c. & d. The formation of basic trust is the task of infancy.

17. **e.** is the answer. (pp. 154–155)

a. Most women do not experience anxiety and distress following menopause; moreover, the woman's experience will depend largely on her expectations and attitude.
b. Sexual interest does not decline in post-menopausal women.
c. Menopause is caused by a *reduction* in estrogen.
d. This was not mentioned in the text.

18. **a.** is the answer. A mathematician's skills are likely to reflect abstract reasoning, or fluid intelligence, which declines with age. (p. 162)
b., d., & e. Philosophy, literature, and history are fields in which individuals often do their most notable work later in life, after more experiential knowledge (crystallized intelligence) has accumulated.
c. Scientific achievements generally reflect fluid, rather than crystallized, intelligence.

19. **d.** is the answer. (p. 165)
a., b., & c. Most couples do not feel a loss of purpose or marital strain following the departure of grown children.

20. **d.** is the answer. Significantly, drugs that block the activity of the neurotransmitter acetylcholine produce Alzheimer-like symptoms. (p. 158)
a. & b. Epinephrine and norepinephrine are hormones produced by glands of the endocrine system.
c. & e. Serotonin and dopamine are neurotransmitters, and hence produced by neurons, but they have not been implicated in Alzheimer's disease.

21. **c.** is the answer. (p. 150)
a & b. In fact, just the opposite is true.

22. **d.** is the answer. (p. 162)
a. & b. Fluid intelligence, which decreases with age, refers to the ability to reason abstractly.
c. Crystallized intelligence increases with age.

23. **a.** is the answer. (pp. 156–157)

24. **d.** is the answer. (pp. 162–163)

25. **d.** is the answer. (p. 164)

Thinking Critically About Chapter 4

Multiple-Choice Questions

1. **d.** is the answer. (p. 131)

2. **b.** is the answer. (p. 126)
a. & d. Although the rate of motor development varies from child to child, the basic sequence is universal and, therefore, predictable.
c. Rolling over and head lifting are both learned.

3. **a. is the answer.** Mathematical and philosophical reasoning involve fluid and crystallized intelli-

gence, respectively. Because fluid intelligence generally declines with age while crystallized intelligence increases, it is likely that significant mathematical accomplishments will occur at an earlier age than philosophical accomplishments. (p. 162)

4. **c.** is the answer. Early maturing boys tend to be more popular. (p. 145)
   a. Early maturing girls may temporarily suffer embarrassment and be the objects of teasing.
   b. & d. The social benefits of early or late maturation are based on physical development, not on cognitive skills.

5. **c.** is the answer. This test is designed to determine if the child understands that the quantity of liquid is conserved, despite the shift to a container that is different in shape. (p. 130)
   a. These are general processes related to concept building.
   b. Object permanence is the concept that an object continues to exist even when not perceived; in this case, the water is perceived throughout the experiment.
   d. This experiment does not require abstract reasoning, only the ability to reason logically about the concrete.

6. **a.** is the answer. This child's age and stranger anxiety clearly place him within Piaget's sensorimotor stage. (pp. 128, 134)

7. **b.** is the answer. This child's age, ability to use language, and egocentrism clearly place her within Piaget's preoperational stage. (p. 130)

8. **d.** is the answer. Conservation is a hallmark of the concrete operational stage; egocentrism is a hallmark of the preoperational stage. (pp. 130, 132)

9. **c.** is the answer. Being 4 years old, Jamail would be in Piaget's preoperational stage. Preoperational thinking is egocentric, which means Jamail would find it difficult to "put himself in his sister's shoes" and perceive that she has a brother. (p. 130)

10. **b.** is the answer. (p. 135)
    a. Conservation is the ability to realize that the amount of an object does not change even if its shape changes.
    c. Egocentrism is the inability to take another person's perspective.
    d. According to Erikson, basic trust is feeling that the world is safe as a result of sensitive, loving caregivers.

11. **a.** is the answer. Although loving parents will also produce securely attached children, Erikson's theory deals with trust or mistrust. (p. 137)

c. Control is not a factor in this stage of Erikson's theory.

12. **d.** is the answer. (pp. 151–152)
    a. This description of Cassandra's feelings does not suggest that her relationship with her parents is deteriorating. Like most adolescents, Cassandra's social development is coming under increasing peer influence and diminishing parental influence.
    b. & c. Because Cassandra's feelings are normal, there is no reason for her to change her circle of friends or for her parents to seek counseling.
    e. Her parents' friends are probably in the same situation.

13. **c.** is the answer. (p. 132)
    a., b., & d. Piaget did not link cognitive ability to amount of schooling, gender, or differences in how boys and girls are socialized.

14. **a.** is the answer. Children in various cultures do seem to progress through Kohlberg's preconventional and conventional levels, which indicates that some aspects of the development of moral reasoning are universal. (p. 148)

15. **c.** is the answer. (p. 150)

16. **c.** is the answer. Reasoning is based on fluid intelligence. (p. 162)
    a. There is no such thing as "analytic" intelligence.
    b. Crystallized intelligence increases up to old age.

17. **c.** is the answer. Because several variables (education, affluence, etc.) generally distinguish the various groups in a cross-sectional study, it is impossible to rule out that one or more of these, rather than aging, is the cause of the measured intellectual decrease. (p. 161)
    a. Small sample size and unrepresentativeness generally are not limitations of cross-sectional research.
    b. This refers to longitudinal research.

18. **e.** is the answer. (pp. 159–160)
    a. & c. In tests of recognition memory, the performance of older persons shows little decline.
    b. & d. The ability to recall material, especially meaningless material, declines with age.

19. **e.** is the answer. Research has not uncovered a tendency for people of any particular age group to report greater feelings of satisfaction or well-being. (p. 166)

20. **c.** is the answer. Although some researchers emphasize consistency and others emphasize potential for change, they all agree that consistency increases over the life span. (pp. 168–169)

a. One criticism of stage theories is that development does not occur in sharply defined stages.
b. Research has shown that individuals' adult personalities cannot be predicted from their first two years.
d. Social and emotional style are two of the most stable traits.

21. **b.** is the answer. Conventional morality is based in part on a desire to gain others' approval. (p. 147)
    a. Preconventional reasoning is based on external incentives such as gaining a reward or avoiding punishment.
    c. Postconventional morality reflects an affirmation of agreed-upon rights or universal ethical principles.
    d. Fear of others' disapproval is one of the bases of conventional moral reasoning.

22. **b.** is the answer. (p. 152)
    a. In fact, just the opposite is true: Parental influence on children *decreases* during adolescence.
    d. Teens reflect their parents' social, political, and religious views, but rely on peers for matters of personal taste.
    e. The text does not mention this.

23. **c.** is the answer. (p. 168)

24. **c.** is the answer. Carlos' age and struggle to form a close relationship place him squarely in this stage. (p. 150)
    a. Trust versus mistrust is the psychosocial task of infancy.
    b. Autonomy versus doubt is the psychosocial task of toddlerhood.
    d. Identity versus role confusion is the psychosocial task of adolescence.
    e. Generativity versus stagnation is the task of middle adulthood.

25. **d.** is the answer. (p. 165)

Essay Question

Sheryl's age would place her at the threshold of Piaget's stage of formal operations. Although her thinking is probably still somewhat self-focused, Sheryl is becoming capable of abstract, logical thought. This will increasingly allow her to reason hypothetically and deductively. Because her logical thinking also enables her to detect inconsistencies in others' reasoning and between their ideals and actions, Sheryl and her parents may be having some heated debates about now.

According to Kohlberg, Sheryl is probably at the threshold of postconventional morality. When she was younger, Sheryl probably abided by rules in order to gain social approval, or simply because "rules are rules" (conventional morality). Now that she is older, Sheryl's moral reasoning will increasingly be based on her own personal code of ethics and an affirmation of people's agreed-upon rights. Because she is a woman, her morality may be more concerned with caring about relationships.

According to Erikson, psychosocial development occurs in eight stages, each of which focuses on a particular task. As an adolescent, Sheryl's psychosocial task is to develop a sense of self by testing roles, then integrating them to form a single identity. Erikson called this stage "identity versus role confusion."

Key Terms

1. **Developmental psychology** is the branch of psychology concerned with physical, cognitive, and social change throughout the life span. (p. 119)

2. The **zygote** (a term derived from the Greek word for "joint") is the fertilized egg, that is, the cluster of cells formed during conception by the union of sperm and egg. (p. 120)

3. The **embryo** is the developing prenatal organism from about 2 weeks through 2 months after conception. (p. 120)

4. The **fetus** is the developing prenatal human from 9 weeks after conception to birth. (p. 121)

5. **Teratogens** (literally, poisons) are any drugs, viruses, or other substances that cross the mother's placenta and can harm the developing embryo or fetus. (p. 121)

6. The **fetal alcohol syndrome (FAS)** refers to the physical and cognitive abnormalities that heavy drinking by a pregnant woman may cause in the developing child. (p. 121)

7. The **rooting reflex** is the newborn's tendency, when his or her cheek is stroked, to orient toward the stimulus and begin sucking. (p. 122)

8. A simple form of learning used to study infant cognition, **habituation** is decreasing responsiveness to a stimulus that is repeatedly presented. (p. 123)

9. **Maturation** refers to the biological growth processes that enable orderly changes in behavior and are relatively uninfluenced by experience or other environmental factors. (p. 124)

   Example: The ability to walk depends on a certain level of neural and muscular **maturation**. For this reason, until the toddler's body is physically ready to walk, practice "walking" has little effect.

10. In Piaget's theory of cognitive development, **schemas** are mental concepts that organize and interpret information. (p. 127)

11. In Piaget's theory, **assimilation** refers to interpreting a new experience in terms of an existing schema. (p. 127)

12. In Piaget's theory, **accommodation** refers to changing an existing schema to incorporate new information that cannot be assimilated. (p. 127)

13. **Cognition** refers to the mental processes associated with thinking, knowing, remembering, and communicating. (p. 128)

14. In Piaget's theory of cognitive stages, the **sensorimotor stage** lasts from birth to about age 2. During this stage, infants gain knowledge of the world through their senses and their motor activities. (p. 128)

15. **Object permanence,** which develops during the sensorimotor stage, is the awareness that things do not cease to exist when not perceived. (pp. 128–129)

16. In Piaget's theory, the **preoperational stage** lasts from about 2 to 6 or 7 years of age. During this stage, language development is rapid, but the child is unable to understand the mental operations of concrete logic. (p. 130)

17. **Conservation** is the principle that properties such as number, volume, and mass remain constant despite changes in the forms of objects; it is acquired during the concrete operational stage. (p. 130)

18. In Piaget's theory, **egocentrism** refers to the difficulty that preoperational children have in considering another's viewpoint. "Ego" means "self," and "centrism" indicates "in the center"; the preoperational child is "self-centered." (p. 130)

19. Our ideas about our own and others' thoughts, feelings, and perceptions and the behaviors these might predict constitute our **theory of mind**. (p. 131)

20. During the **concrete operational stage,** lasting from about ages 6 or 7 to 11, children can think logically about concrete events and objects. (p. 132)

21. In Piaget's theory, the **formal operational stage** normally begins about age 12. During this stage people begin to think logically about abstract concepts. (p. 132)

Memory aid: To help differentiate Piaget's stages remember that "operations" are mental transformations. *Pre*operational children, who lack the ability to perform transformations, are "before"

this developmental milestone. Concrete operational children can operate on real, or concrete, objects. Formal operational children can perform logical transformations on abstract concepts.

22. **Stranger anxiety** is the fear of strangers that infants begin to display at about 8 months of age. (p. 134)

23. **Attachment** is an emotional tie with another person, shown in young children by their seeking closeness to a caregiver and showing distress on separation. (p. 134)

24. A **critical period** is a limited time shortly after birth during which an organism must be exposed to certain experiences or influences if it is to develop properly. (p. 135)

25. **Imprinting** is the process by which certain animals form attachments early in life, usually during a limited critical period. (p. 135)

26. According to Erikson, **basic trust** is a sense that the world is predictable and trustworthy—a concept that infants form if their needs are met by responsive caregiving. (p. 137)

27. **Self-concept** is a person's sense of identity and personal worth. (p. 140)

28. **Adolescence** refers to the life stage from puberty to independent adulthood, denoted physically by a growth spurt and maturation of primary and secondary sex characteristics, cognitively by the onset of formal operational thought, and socially by the formation of identity. (p. 143)

29. **Puberty** is the early adolescent period of sexual maturation, during which a person becomes capable of reproduction. (p. 144)

30. The **primary sex characteristics** are the body structures (ovaries, testes, and external genitalia) that enable reproduction. (p. 144)

31. The **secondary sex characteristics** are the nonreproductive sexual characteristics, for example, female breasts, male voice quality, and body hair. (p. 144)

32. **Menarche** is the first menstrual period. (p. 145)

33. In Erikson's theory, establishing an **identity**, or one's sense of self, is the primary task of adolescence. (p. 149)

34. In Erikson's theory, **intimacy**, or the ability to establish close, loving relationships, is the primary task of late adolescence and early adulthood. (p. 150)

35. **Menopause** is the cessation of menstruation and typically occurs in the early fifties. It also refers to the biological and psychological changes experi-

enced during a woman's years of declining ability to reproduce. (p. 154)

36. **Alzheimer's disease** is a progressive and irreversible brain disorder caused by deterioration of neurons that produce acetylcholine. It is characterized by a gradual loss of memory, reasoning, language, and, finally, physical functioning. (p. 158)

37. In a **cross-sectional study**, people of different ages are compared with one another. (p. 160)

38. In a **longitudinal study**, the same people are tested and retested over a period of years. (p. 160)

39. **Crystallized intelligence** refers to those aspects of intellectual ability, such as vocabulary and general knowledge, that reflect accumulated learning. Crystallized intelligence tends to increase with age. (p. 162)

40. **Fluid intelligence** refers to a person's ability to reason speedily and abstractly. Fluid intelligence tends to decline with age. (p. 162)

45. The **social clock** refers to the culturally preferred timing of social events, such as leaving home, marrying, having children, and retiring. (p. 163)

FOCUS ON VOCABULARY AND LANGUAGE

Page 119: As we *journey* through life from *womb to tomb*, when and how do we change? In the process of becoming who we are, and as we travel (*journey*) through life, from conception to death (*womb to tomb*) we change and develop physically, psychologically, and socially. (Another humorous expression describing the life span or life cycle is from "sperm to worm.")

Infancy and Childhood

Page 124: . . . toddler . . . This describes a child who is beginning to learn to walk, and who walks with short, uneven steps.

Page 124: After birth, the neural networks that enabled you to walk, talk, and remember had a *wild growth spurt.* Myers points out that when you were born, you had all the brain cells that you will ever have. But after birth there is a very rapid development (*a wild growth spurt*) in the number of connections between neurons.

Page 125: Trying to access such memories, note Elizabeth Loftus and Leah Kaufman (1992), *is like trying to read a document that was formatted by an earlier version of a computer operating system.* This reference is to the similarity between the brain and a computer. If computer software used for creating a document was programmed (*formatted*) on an earlier version of a computer, then it will not be easy to read the document on a newer version. Early preschool memories may not have been erased, but because they were programmed on a different, or earlier, system (*the child*), they are hard to access or retrieve later on a newer system (*the adult*).

Page 127: As a newborn, you confronted *a sea of sensations. . . .* When you came into the world (new-

born), you experienced an overwhelming amount of sensory stimulation (*a sea of sensations*); nevertheless, you were quickly and easily able to deal with and make sense of it all.

Page 127: . . . fruitless . . . This word means to be unproductive or useless (like a tree that does not produce fruit). It is pointless (*fruitless*), according to Piaget's theory, to try to teach a child who is in the preoperational stage of development how to use abstract logic to solve a complex problem (formal operational reasoning).

Page 129: When she lifted the screen, the infants sometimes *did a double take*, staring longer when shown a wrong number of objects. In this experiment with 5-month-old infants, Karen Wynn showed that these very young children were capable of conceptual thinking. She did this by measuring their reaction time to expected and unexpected outcomes. Shown an impossible outcome, infants stared longer (*they did a double take*).

Page 132: Piaget's stage theory is controversial. For some things it gets high marks. Piaget's theory has its supporters and its critics (*it is controversial*). Cross-cultural research supports the basic stages he proposed (*it gets high marks*), but most researchers believe that development is more continuous than Piaget thought. Children have more conceptual abilities at earlier periods than his theory suggested.

Page 133: . . . cognitive milestones . . . A milestone is an event of significance or importance. (Originally, a milestone was a large stone by the roadside on which was written the number of miles from nearby towns.) Myers notes that the age at which children usually succeed at important mental tasks (*cognitive milestones*) is of less relevance than the developmental order or sequence in which these abilities appear.

Page 133: Teachers would do better to *build on* what children already know, engaging them in *concrete demonstrations* and stimulating them to *think for themselves*. Preschool and elementary school children think differently from adults. In order for them to become independent thinkers (*think for themselves*), Piaget recommends that they be given specific, tangible examples (*concrete demonstrations*) that utilize (*build on*) their existing knowledge.

Page 134: To pit the drawing power of a food source against the contact comfort of the blanket, Harlow created two artificial mothers. Harlow's experiment was designed to test whether food or nourishment was more rewarding than the comfort of a soft terry cloth. Thus, when he tested the attraction (*pitted the drawing power*) of the artificial mother who supplied food against the soft comfort of the terry cloth mother (*contact comfort*), he was surprised that they preferred the cloth mother. They used "her" as a *secure base* from which to explore and a safe place (*safe haven*) to return to when frightened or anxious.

Page 135: . . . nature opens *windows of opportunity* for *wiring* the brain for vision or language, then slams them shut. In many animals there is an optimal time (*critical period*) for programming (*wiring*) the brain for vision or language, and for the formation of attachments. The organism will not develop properly if certain experiences do not occur during this limited timeframe (*window of opportunity*).

Page 135: The first moving object a *gosling, duckling, or chick* sees during the hours shortly after *hatching* is normally its mother. A *gosling* is a young goose, a *duckling* a young duck, and a *chick* is a young chicken. What all these young fowl have in common is a tendency to follow, or trail after, the first larger moving object they see shortly after they emerge (*hatch*) from the eggshell. This attachment process is called **imprinting**.

Page 136: "*Mere exposure*" to people and things fosters *fondness*. Children do not imprint in the same way that ducklings and other animals do; nevertheless, repeated encounters with (or *exposure to*) other humans and objects encourage or promote liking and attachment (*fondness*). As Myers puts it, "familiarity breeds content." (This is a twist on the old saying "familiarity breeds contempt.")

Page 137: But evidence increasingly indicates that fathers are more than just *mobile sperm banks*. A *sperm bank* is where donated sperm is stored until it is used for artificial insemination. More and more research shows that fathers are not simply sperm producers who can move around (*mobile sperm banks*) and get mothers pregnant. Rather, evidence suggests they are capable caregivers who may interact with their babies much as mothers do.

Page 138: Such experiences can leave *footprints* on the brain. Traumatic experiences that occur early in development can have an effect on brain functioning; metaphorically, they can leave impressions (*footprints*) on the brain. The production of neurotransmitters such as serotonin, which calms aggressive impulses, is slower (*sluggish*) in abused children who become aggressive teens and adults.

Page 139: But for infant day care *the scientific jury is still out.* The issue of infant day care is very complicated. Some suggest that day care, if high quality, can provide an environment just as safe and stimulating as at-home care. Others disagree. (*The scientific jury has not returned a verdict—it is still out.*) Myers makes the point that what all children need is a warm, consistent relationship with people who foster feelings of trust, regardless of whether the children are cared for at home or in a center.

Page 140: In a simple variation of the mirror procedure, researchers *sneakily dabbed rouge* on children's noses before placing them in front of the mirror. In order to find out at what point in development a child realizes that her mirror image is herself and not another child, researchers use a clever technique. Unobtrusively (*sneakily*) and without the child's awareness, they gently rubbed (*dabbed*) some red makeup (*rouge*) on the child's nose before allowing her to view herself in the mirror. If children have the concept of self, they will be surprised at the red spot and touch their noses. This actually happens around 15 to 18 months of age, and self-concept begins to grow from then on.

Page 141: Parenting styles vary. Some parents *spank*, some *reason*. Some parents are *strict* and some are *lax*. When it comes to child-rearing practices (*parenting styles*), there is much variability: (a) some parents use strict controls and physical punishment (*spanking*); (b) others talk and discuss problems and issues with their children (*reason with them*); and (c) still others allow the children to do what they want and make few demands of them (*they are lax*). Myers identifies these parenting styles as (a) *authoritarian*, (b) *authoritative*, and (c) *permissive*.

Page 141: Before jumping to conclusions about the results of different parenting styles, *heed this caution.*

Myers is suggesting that we must be careful (*heed a caution*) before quickly deciding (*jumping to conclusions*) about the merits of various parenting styles. He points out that the evidence is correlational and does not imply cause and effect. Thus, there may be other factors that are causally involved (e.g., some children may, because of their temperament, engender [elicit] greater trust and warmth from their parents).

Adolescence

Page 145: If a young girl's body is *out of sync* with her emotional maturity and with what her friends are experiencing, she may begin associating with older adolescents or may suffer teasing. *Sync* is an abbreviation of *synchronize*, which means to occur at the same time. So, if a girl's biological development is not proceeding at the same rate (*out of sync*) with her emotional and social development, she may start fraternizing (*associating*) with and imitating the behavior of older girls. Thus, early maturation can be a problem for girls, especially if the people around them react negatively to their physical development or make fun of them (*tease them*).

Page 146: Gradually, though, most achieve the *intellectual summit* that Piaget called *formal operations*. The *formal operational* stage is the highest level in Piaget's theory of cognitive development (*intellectual summit*). Most adolescents reach this stage and are capable of logical and abstract reasoning. For example, many think about (*ponder*) and discuss (*debate*) such issues as good and evil, truth and justice, and other abstract topics about human nature.

Page 146: A crucial task of childhood and adolescence is discerning right from wrong and developing *character—the psychological muscles for controlling impulses. Character* refers to the total qualities a person possesses, including attitudes, beliefs, interests, actions, and a philosophy of life. By developing *character*, adolescents learn to have the intellectual strength (*psychological muscles*) to refrain from acting immorally (*controlling impulses*). Kohlberg proposed a controversial stage theory of moral development which has three levels: preconventional, conventional, and postconventional.

Page 147: Kohlberg's controversial claim was that these levels form a *moral ladder*. In Kohlberg's view children have to go through each of the three stages (preconventional, conventional, and postconventional) in succession much as a person climbs a ladder, one rung at a time, from bottom to top. The lowest rung on this *moral ladder* involves self-interest

and avoidance of punishment; the highest rung, which often develops during and after adolescence, is concerned with personal ethical principles and universal justice. Critics contend that the theory is culturally biased.

Page 148: Our moral reasoning surely influences our moral talk. But sometimes *talk is cheap*. The expression *talk is cheap* means that it is easy to say you believe something or to say that you are going to do something; it costs you nothing just to speak about it (*talk is cheap*). However, action, or actually carrying out the correct behavior, is also involved in morality.

Page 148: Because of the *slack* between thinking and acting, effective moral education must focus on both. *Slack* means a lack of tension (e.g., a loose or slack rope), but in this context it is used to point out the gap or discrepancy (*slack*) between what we say, think, or believe and how we actually behave. Children can be taught about morals through discussion and by parents and teachers modeling appropriate behavior (i.e., practicing what they preach).

Page 148: . . . *"psychosocial"task* . . . According to Erikson, each stage of life involves a dilemma (*crisis*) that has to be resolved before we can move on to the next stage. These tasks involve interactions between ourselves, our surroundings, and other people; thus, they are *social* in nature. The psychosocial assignment (*psychosocial task*) of adolescence involves *role confusion vs. forming an identity.* (This is sometimes called an **identity crisis**).

Page 149: Erikson noticed that some adolescents *forge* their identity early, simply by taking on their parents' values and expectations. *Forge* literally means to form or shape by heating and hammering metal. Erikson observed that some young people form (*forge*) their identities early, while others never quite appear to acquire a strong feeling of who they are (i.e., they don't *find themselves*).

Page 150: These gender differences *surface early*, in children's play. Males and females differ in their feelings of belonging (*connectedness*), a disparity that is noticeable from a young age (*surfaces early*). When playing, boys tend to engage in competitive group activity without much close, confidential, or affectionate dialogue. Girls typically are more intimate with each other and play in smaller groups, frequently with one friend, and they are less competitive and more supportive and empathic.

Adulthood

Page 155: The above statements—all false—are among the *misconceptions* about aging *exploded* by recent research on the world's most rapidly growing population group. To "explode misconceptions" means to dispel or get rid of erroneous beliefs that have no foundation in fact. The false statements (*misconceptions*) listed on text page 155 have all been refuted by the results of new experiments and investigations.

Page 156: In later life, the stairs get steeper, the newsprint gets smaller, and people seem to *mumble* more. This is not meant to be taken literally. Myers is pointing out that as we become older, our sensory and perceptual abilities change so that our reaction time and our ability to see and hear decline. Thus, the stairs *appear* steeper, the newsprint *seems* smaller, and people do not appear to be speaking clearly (*they mumble*).

Page 157: Aging *levies a tax* on the brain by slowing our neural processing. Myers is pointing out that aging is accompanied by a decrease in some perceptual and cognitive abilities. Just as you have less money after taxes have been assessed (*levied*) on your income, there are some losses in the brain's ability to function optimally due to the aging process.

Page 158: We are more likely to *rust from disuse than to wear out from overuse*. "*Use it or lose it*" is sound advice. When adults remain active physically, sexually, and mentally (they "*use it*"), they are less likely to become inactive later in life ("*lose it*"). If we follow sedentary life-styles, we will be like unused pieces of metal that suffer from *rust*; on the other hand, if we keep active, we will benefit mentally and physically (we *won't wear out from overuse*).

Page 112: Does the common perception that elderly people are generally less sharp (Kite & Johnson, 1988), lend truth to the proverb "*You can't teach an old dog new tricks*"? Or does the evidence support another proverb: "*You're never too old to learn*"? A proverb is a brief, familiar saying or maxim based on folk wisdom. Unfortunately, in our search for the truth, proverbs are not very helpful: For almost every proverb there is another proverb that contradicts it, as in the above example. Empirical research shows that there is some truth to both maxims. You can continue to grow and develop (*learn new tricks*), but in doing some things older people may not be as

quick as younger people. As Myers notes later in the chapter, *age is sage*, meaning that wisdom (*sage*) accumulates as we grow older (*age*).

Page 161: According to this more optimistic view, the *myth* that intelligence sharply declines with age is *laid to rest*. The false idea (*myth*) that our intellectual abilities decrease as we get older has been destroyed or buried (*laid to rest*) by recent **longitudinal research**. This research tests the same group of people over many years and may give more accurate results than testing many groups of people (each group having a different age range) at one period in time (**cross-sectional research**). However, both research methods have their own problems (*pitfalls*).

Page 164: "*Pair-bonding is a trademark of the human animal,*" notes anthropologist Helen Fisher (1993). *Pair-bonding* refers to the monogamous attachment formed between one person and another, such as with a marriage partner, and this affiliation is characteristic (*a trademark*) of human beings.

Page 164: Might *test-driving life together* in a "trial marriage" minimize divorce risk? Does premarital cohabitation or a "trial marriage" (*test-driving life together*) separate out potentially unsuccessful marriages and reduce the risk of divorce? The research suggests it does not. Those who live together before marriage are more likely to get divorced than those who don't. (These findings are correlational and Myers warns against making causal inferences.)

Page 164: Some couples fight but also *shower* one another with affection afterward. Other couples never raise their voices yet also seldom praise or *nuzzle*. Myers notes that some couples have many open conflicts but also treat each other with warmth and care (*shower one another with affection*), while others who seldom argue (*raise their voices*) show little closeness or tenderness toward each other (*they seldom praise or nuzzle*). The best predictor, however, of likely marital success is a ratio of at least 5 to 1 of positive interactions (smiling, touching, complimenting, and laughing) to negative interactions (sarcasm, criticism, putdowns, and insults).

Page 166: As the years go by, *feelings mellow. . . . Highs become less high, lows less low.* Our feelings become less extreme (*they mellow*) as we age: The excitement and elation (*highs*) and the depression and gloom (*lows*) do not encompass such a broad range of feelings as they once did. Myers states it nicely when he says, "As we age, life becomes less an emotional roller coaster, and more like paddling a canoe."

Reflections on the Major Developmental Issues

Page 168: . . . do they differ as a giant redwood differs from its seedling . . . or . . . as a butterfly differs from a caterpillar . . . ? The giant redwood is a large coniferous tree that grows in a continuous, cumulative way from seedling to mature tree. On the other hand, the butterfly emerges as a different creature after passing through a stage as a caterpillar. The question developmental psychologists ask is: Are changes throughout the life span (from infant to adult) due to a slow, continuous shaping process (like the tree), or do we go through a series of genetically preprogrammed stages (like the butterfly)?

Page 169: Many a 20-year-old *goof-off* has matured into a 40-year-old business or cultural leader. To *goof off* means to avoid work and act in a lazy manner; a person who behaves this way is called a *goof-off*.

CHAPTER 5:

Sensation

Chapter Overview

Sensation refers to the process by which we detect physical energy from the environment and encode it as neural signals. This chapter describes the senses of vision, hearing, taste, touch, smell, kinesthesis, and the vestibular sense. It also presents research findings from studies of sensory restriction and subliminal stimulation.

In this chapter there are many terms to learn and several theories you must understand. Many of the terms are related to the structure of the eye, ear, and other sensory receptors. Doing the chapter review several times, labeling the diagrams, and rehearsing the material frequently will help you to memorize these structures and their functions. The theories discussed include the signal detection, Young-Helmholtz three-color and opponent-process theories of color vision, and the frequency and place theories of pitch. As you study these theories, concentrate on understanding the strengths and weaknesses (if any) of each.

NOTE: Answer guidelines for all Chapter 5 questions begin on page 155.

Introducing Sensation (p. 171)

David Myers at times uses idioms that are unfamiliar to some readers. If you do not know the meaning of any of the following words, phrases, or expressions in the context in which they appear in the text, refer to page 166 for an explanation: . . . *in the mirror she is again stumped.*

Introduction Preview

First, skim the introduction. Then read the following objectives and, as you read the text, search for the information that will enable you to meet each objective. Answer guidelines are provided on page 155.

1. Contrast the processes of sensation and perception.

Stepping Through the Introduction

After you have read the introduction, complete the sentences and answer the questions. As you proceed, evaluate your performance by consulting the answers on page 155. Do not continue with the next section until you understand each answer. If you need to, review or reread the section in the textbook before continuing.

1. The process by which we detect physical energy from the environment and encode it as neural signals is _____ . The process by which sensations are selected, organized, and interpreted is _____ .

2. Sensory analysis, which starts at the entry level and works up, is called _____-_____ _____.

    Perceptual analysis, which works from our experience and expectations, is called

    _____-_____

    _____ .

3. The perceptual disorder in which a person has lost the ability to recognize familiar faces is

    _____ .

Sensing the World: Some Basic Principles (pp. 172–177)

> If you do not know the meaning of any of the following words, phrases, or expressions in the context in which they appear in the text, refer to page 166 for an explanation: *A frog could starve to death knee-deep in motionless flies; The shades on our senses are open just a crack; the faintest whimper from the cradle; "satanic messages"; hucksters; price hike . . . to raise the eyebrows; everywhere that Mary looks the scene is sure to go.*

Section Preview

Answer guidelines are provided on page 155.

1. Distinguish between absolute and difference thresholds, and discuss research findings on signal detection.

2. Discuss whether subliminal stimuli are sensed, and whether they are persuasive.

3. Describe the phenomenon of sensory adaptation, and show how it focuses our attention on changing stimulation.

Stepping Through the Section

Answers are provided on page 155.

1. The study of relationships between the physical characteristics of stimuli and our psychological experience of them is _____ .

2. The _____ _____ refers to the minimum stimulation necessary for a stimulus to be detected _____ percent of the time.

3. The theory of _____ _____ led to the concept that absolute thresholds depend not only on the strength of the signal but also on a person's _____ state.

4. Some entrepreneurs claim that exposure to "below threshold," or _____ , stimuli can be persuasive, but their claims are probably unwarranted.

5. Some weak stimuli may trigger in our sense receptors a response that is processed by the brain, even though the response doesn't cross the threshold into _____ awareness.

6. The minimum difference required to distinguish two stimuli 50 percent of the time is called the
_____ _____ .
Another term for this value is the
_____ _____
_____ .

7. The principle that the difference threshold is not a constant amount, but a constant proportion, is known as _____
_____ . The proportion depends on the _____ .

8. After constant exposure to an unchanging stimulus, the receptor cells of our senses begin to fire less vigorously; this phenomenon is called
_____ _____ .

Explain why sensory adaptation is beneficial.

Vision (pp. 177–188)

> If you do not know the meaning of any of the following words, phrases, or expressions in the context in which they appear in the text, refer to pages 166–167 for an explanation: *This fact was baffling; blind spot; Rods have no such hotline to the brain; blindsight; Color, like all aspects of vision, . . . the theater of our brains.*

Section Preview

Answer guidelines are provided on page 155.

1. Explain the visual process, including the stimulus input, the structure of the eye, and the transduction of light energy.

2. Explain the cause of two common problems involving acuity.

3. Discuss how visual information is processed in parallel (through the eye's retina and the brain) and at increasingly abstract levels.

4. Discuss how both the Young-Helmholtz and the opponent-process theories contribute to our understanding of color vision.

5. Explain color constancy, and discuss its significance to our understanding of vision.

Stepping Through the Section

Answers are provided on page 156.

1. Stimulus energy is converted into _____ messages through the process of sensory _____ .

2. The visible spectrum of light is a small portion of the larger spectrum of _____ radiation.

3. The distance from one light wave peak to the next is called _____ . This value determines the wave's color, or _____ .

4. The amount of energy in light waves, or _____ , determined by a wave's _____ , or height, influences the _____ of a light.

5. Light enters the eye through the transparent _____ , then passes through a small opening called the _____ ; the size of this opening is controlled by the colored _____ .

6. By changing its curvature, the _____ can focus the image of an object onto the _____ , the light-sensitive inner surface of the eye.

7. The process by which the lens changes shape to focus light is called _____ . Clarity, or sharpness, of vision is called _____ .

8. In nearsightedness, light rays from _____ (nearby/distant) objects converge _____ (in front of/in back of) the retina, rather than on it, and _____ (nearby/distant) objects are seen more clearly than _____

(nearby/distant) objects. In farsightedness, light rays from _____ (nearby/distant) objects converge _____ (in front of/in back of) the retina, and _____ (nearby/distant) objects are seen more clearly than _____ (nearby/distant) objects.

9. The retina's receptor cells are the _____ and _____ .

10. The neural signals produced in the rods and cones activate the neighboring _____ cells, then activate a network of _____ cells. The axons of ganglion cells converge to form the _____ _____ , which carries the visual information to the _____ .

11. Where this nerve leaves the eye, there are no receptors; thus the area is called the _____ _____ .

12. Most cones are clustered around the retina's point of central focus, called the _____ , whereas the rods are concentrated in more _____ regions of the retina. Many cones have their own _____ cells to communicate with the visual cortex.

13. It is the_____ (rods/cones) of the eye that permit the perception of color.

14. Unlike cones, in dim light the rods are _____ (sensitive/insensitive). Adapting to a darkened room will take the retina approximately _____ minutes.

15. Hubel and Wiesel discovered that certain neurons in the_____ _____ of the brain respond only to specific features of what is viewed. They called these neurons _____ _____ .

16. Feature detectors in the visual cortex pass their information to higher-level brain cells in the _____ and _____ cortex, which respond to specific visual scenes. Research has shown that in monkey brains such cells specialize in responding to a specific _____ , _____

_____ , _____ , or _____ _____ .

Researchers have also identified nerve cells that may respond or not, depending on how the monkey _____ a given image.

17. The brain achieves its remarkable speed in visual perception by processing several subdivisions of a stimulus _____ (simultaneously/sequentially). This procedure, called _____ _____ , may explain why people who have suffered a stroke may lose just one aspect of vision. Other brain-damaged people may demonstrate _____ by responding to a stimulus that is not consciously perceived. Once the distributed parts of the brain have processed sensory stimuli, EEG recordings reveal a moment of neural _____ , lasting for about a fourth of a second and creating _____ waves.

18. An object appears to be red in color because it _____ the long wavelengths of red and because of our mental _____ of the color.

19. One out of every 50 people is color deficient; this is usually a male because the defect is genetically _____ -_____ .

20. According to the Young-Helmholtz trichromatic theory, the eyes have three types of color receptors: one reacts most strongly to _____ , one to _____ , and one to _____ .

21. After staring at a green square for a while, you will see the color red, its _____ color, as an _____ .

22. Hering's theory of color vision is called the _____ -_____ theory. According to this theory, after visual information leaves the receptors it is analyzed in terms of pairs of opposing colors: _____ versus _____ , _____ versus_____ , and _____ versus _____ .

Summarize the two stages of color processing.

3. Explain how sounds are located, and discuss the nature and causes of hearing loss.

23. The experience of color depends on the _____ in which an object is seen.

24. In an unvarying context, a familiar object will be perceived as having consistent color, even as the light changes. This phenomenon is called

_____ _____ .

Hearing (pp. 189–196)

> If you do not know the meaning of any of the following words, phrases, or expressions in the context in which they appear in the text, refer to pages 153–154 for an explanation: *sensitive to faint sounds; an obvious boon; A piccolo produces much shorter sound waves than does a tuba; earlids; If a car to the right honks. . . . ; ear-splitting noise or music are the culprits.*

Section Preview

Answer guidelines are provided on page 156.

1. Explain the auditory process, including the stimulus input and the structure and function of the ear.

2. Discuss how both the place and frequency theories contribute to our understanding of pitch perception.

Stepping Through the Section

Answers are provided on page 157.

1. The stimulus for hearing, or _____ , is sound waves, created by the compression and expansion of

_____ _____ .

2. The amplitude of a sound wave determines the sound's _____ .

3. The pitch of a sound is derived from the _____ of its wave.

4. Sound energy is measured in units called _____ . The absolute threshold for hearing is arbitrarily defined as _____ such units.

5. The ear is divided into three main parts: the _____ ear, the _____ ear, and the _____ ear.

6. The outer ear channels sound waves toward the _____ , a membrane that then vibrates.

7. The middle ear transmits the vibrations through a piston made of three small bones: the

_____ , _____ , and

_____ .

8. In the inner ear, a coiled tube called the _____ contains the receptor cells for hearing. The incoming vibrations cause the _____ _____ to vibrate the fluid that fills the tube, which causes ripples in the _____ _____ , which is lined with

_____ _____ , whose movement triggers impulses in adjacent nerve fibers that converge to form the auditory nerve. The brain interprets loudness from the _____ of hair cells a sound activates.

9. (Close-Up) On tasks requiring alert performance, people in noisy environments work _____ (more/less) efficiently. People who live in noisy environments suffer elevated rates of _____ -related disorders such as _____

   _____ _____ , _____ , and _____ _____ .

   Noise is especially stressful when it is _____ or _____ .

10. One theory of pitch perception proposes that different pitches activate different places on the cochlea's basilar membrane; this is the _____ theory. This theory has difficulty accounting for how we hear _____-pitched sounds, which do not have such localized effects.

11. A second theory proposes that neural impulses, sent to the brain at the same frequency as the sound wave, allow the perception of different pitches. This is the _____ theory. This theory fails to account for the perception of _____ -pitched sounds, because individual neurons cannot fire faster than _____ times per second.

12. For the higher pitches, cells may alternate their firing to match the sound's frequency, according to the _____ principle.

13. We locate a sound by sensing differences in the _____ and _____ with which it reaches our ears.

14. A sound that comes from directly ahead will be _____ (easier/harder) to locate than a sound that comes from off to one side.

15. Problems in the mechanical conduction of sound waves through the outer or middle ear may cause _____ _____ _____ .

16. Damage to the cochlea's hair cells or the auditory nerve can cause _____ hearing loss. It may be caused by disease, but more often it results from the biological changes linked with _____ and prolonged exposure to ear-splitting noise or music.

17. An electronic device that restores hearing among nerve-deafened people is a _____ _____ . Scientists have recently discovered ways of _____ stimulating hair cell regeneration.

18. Sign language _____ (is/is not) a complete language, _____ (with/without) its own grammar, syntax, and semantics. People who lose one channel of sensation (such as hearing) _____ (seem to/do not seem to) compensate with a slight enhancement in their other sensory abilities.

19. Hearing losses that develop with age are greatest in the _____ frequency ranges.

20. (Close-Up) Deaf children raised in a household where sign language is used express higher _____-_____ and feel more _____ .

The Other Senses (pp. 196–206)

If you do not know the meaning of any of the following words, phrases, or expressions in the context in which they appear in the text, refer to pages 167–168 for an explanation: *we yearn to touch—to kiss, to stroke, to snuggle; Rubbing the area around your stubbed toe; firewalking, . . . put his feet where his mouth was; A well-trained nurse may distract needle-shy patients by chatting with them; there is more to taste than meets the tongue; bathing your nostrils in a stream of scent-laden molecules; Words more readily portray the sound of coffee brewing than its aroma; biological gyroscopes; your sensory windows on the world snapped shut.*

Section Preview

Answer guidelines are provided on page 157.

1. Describe the sense of touch, focusing on pain and the gate-control theory of pain.

2. Describe taste, smell, kinesthesis, and the vestibular sense. Comment on the nature of sensory interaction.

3. Discuss the effects of sensory restriction.

Stepping Through the Section

Answers are provided on page 158.

1. The sense of touch is a mixture of at least four senses: _____ , _____ , _____ , and _____ . Other skin sensations, such as tickle, itch, hot, and wetness, are _____ of the basic ones.

2. Pain is a property of the _____ as well as of the _____ .

3. A sensation of pain in an amputated leg is referred to as a _____ _____ sensation.

4. The pain system _____ (is/is not) triggered by one specific type of physical energy. The body _____ (does/does not) have specialized receptor cells for pain.

5. Melzack and Wall have proposed a theory of pain called the _____- _____ theory, which proposes that there is a neurological _____ in the _____ _____ that blocks pain signals or lets them through. It may be opened by activation of _____ (small/large) nerve fibers and closed by activation of _____ (small/large) fibers or by information from the _____ .

6. Individual differences in perceiving are an example of _____ influences on pain. Such influences demonstrate that pain is not merely a _____ phenomenon, as proposed centuries ago by _____ . Rather, pain is created by the _____ .

List some pain control techniques used in the Lamaze method of prepared childbirth.

7. The four basic taste sensations are _____ , _____ , _____ , and _____ .

8. Taste, which is a _____ sense, is enabled by the 200 or more _____ _____ on the top and sides of the tongue. Each contains a _____ that catches food chemicals.

9. Taste receptors reproduce themselves every _____ .

10. When the sense of smell is blocked, as when we have a cold, foods do not taste the same; this illustrates the principle of _____ _____ .

11. Like taste, smell, or _____ , is a _____ sense. Unlike light, an odor _____ (can/cannot) be separated into more elemental odors.

12. The ability to identify scents peaks in _____ _____ and declines thereafter.

13. The system for sensing the position and movement of body parts is called _____ . The receptors for this sense are located in the _____ , _____ , and _____ of the body.

14. The sense that monitors the position and movement of the head (and thus the body) is the _____ _____ . The

receptors for this sense are located in the

_____ _____ and

_____ _____ of the

inner ear.

15. Sensory restriction may involve either

_____ of a sense or simply sensory

_____ .

Summarize the psychological effects of sensory restriction and suggest some potential applications.

Web Sighting

San Francisco's Exploratorium museum of science, art, and perception (**http://www.exploratorium. edu/**) maintains an excellent web site for extending your exploration of sensation (and perception for Chapter 6). Review the history of visual science. Check out the multimedia dissection of a cow's eye and see what an actual cornea, lens, and retina look like. Take an interactive animated tour of the eye. View the world from inside the eyes of a person with a cataract. Take a sensory tour of the environment with an artist who will change the way you perceive light, shadow, and image forever. And don't stop there! Use weblinks at this site as jumping off points to dozens of other internet resources for learning more about visual information processing. To focus your tour, see if you can find the answers to the following questions.

1. Where is the aqueous humor? The cilary body? What are the functions of these structures?

2. Why are the years 1610 and 1853 significant in the history of visual science? What is the most recent significant development in this field of research?

3. Just what is a tapetum anyway?

4. Where would you go if you needed a cow's eye?!

5. What psychophysical phenomenon does the sound of a Volvo horn blowing at 30 miles per hour demonstrate?

Progress Test 1

Multiple-Choice Questions

Circle your answers to the following questions and check them with the answers on page 158. If your answer is incorrect, read the explanation for why it is correct and then consult the appropriate pages of the text (in parentheses following the correct answer).

1. Which of the following is true?
   a. The absolute threshold for any stimulus is a constant.
   b. The absolute threshold for any stimulus varies somewhat.
   c. The absolute threshold is defined as the minimum amount of stimulation necessary for a stimulus to be detected 75 percent of the time.
   d. The absolute threshold is defined as the minimum amount of stimulation necessary for a stimulus to be detected 60 percent of the time.

2. Nearsightedness is a condition in which the:
   a. lens has become inflexible.
   b. lens is too thin.
   c. eyeball is longer than normal.
   d. eyeball is shorter than normal.

3. If you can just notice the difference between 10- and 11-pound weights, which of the following weights could you differentiate from a 100-pound weight?
   a. 101-pound weight
   b. 105-pound weight
   c. 110-pound weight
   d. There is no basis for prediction.

4. A decrease in sensory responsiveness accompanying an unchanging stimulus is called:
   a. sensory fatigue.
   b. accommodation.
   c. sensory restriction.
   d. sensory adaptation.
   e. sensory interaction.

5. The size of the pupil is controlled by the:
   a. lens.   c. cornea.
   b. retina.   d. iris.

6. The process by which the lens changes its curvature is:
   a. accommodation.   c. focusing.
   b. sensory adaptation. d. transduction.

7. The receptor of the eye that functions best in dim light is the:
   a. fovea.   d. bipolar cell.
   b. ganglion cell. e. rod.
   c. cone.

8. The Young-Helmholtz theory proposes that:
   a. there are three different types of color-sensitive cones.
   b. retinal cells are excited by one color and inhibited by its complementary color.
   c. there are four different types of cones.
   d. rod, not cone, vision accounts for our ability to detect fine visual detail.

9. Frequency is to pitch as _____ is to
   _____ .
   a. wavelength; loudness
   b. amplitude; loudness
   c. wavelength; intensity
   d. amplitude; intensity

10. The receptors for hearing are located in:
    a. the outer ear. c. the inner ear.
    b. the middle ear. d. all parts of the ear.

11. The place theory of pitch perception cannot account for how we hear:
    a. low-pitched sounds.
    b. middle-pitched sounds.
    c. high-pitched sounds.
    d. chords (three or more pitches simultaneously).

12. The hearing losses that occur with age are especially pronounced for:
    a. low-pitched sounds.
    b. middle-pitched sounds.
    c. high-pitched sounds.
    d. chords.

13. According to the gate-control theory, a way to alleviate chronic pain would be to stimulate the _____ nerve fibers that _____ the spinal gate.
    a. small; open   c. large; open
    b. small; close   d. large; close

14. The transduction of light energy into nerve impulses takes place in the:
    a. iris.   d. optic nerve.
    b. retina.   e. rods.
    c. lens.

15. The brain breaks vision into separate dimensions such as color, depth, movement, and form, and works on each aspect simultaneously. This is called:
    a. feature detection.
    b. parallel processing.
    c. accommodation.
    d. opponent processing.

16. Kinesthesis involves:
    a. the bones of the middle ear.
    b. information from the muscles, tendons, and joints.
    c. membranes within the cochlea.
    d. the body's sense of balance.

17. One light may appear reddish and another greenish if they differ in:
    a. wavelength.   c. opponent processes.
    b. amplitude.   d. brightness.

18. Which of the following explains why a rose appears equally red in bright and dim light?
    a. the Young-Helmholtz theory
    b. the opponent-process theory
    c. feature detection
    d. color constancy

19. Which of the following is an example of sensory adaptation?
    a. finding the cold water of a swimming pool warmer after you have been in it for a while
    b. developing an increased sensitivity to salt the more you use it in foods
    c. becoming very irritated at the continuing sound of a dripping faucet
    d. All of the above are examples.

20. Most color-deficient people will probably:
    a. lack functioning red- or green-sensitive cones.
    b. see the world in only black and white.
    c. also suffer from poor vision.
    d. have above-average vision to compensate for the deficit.

Matching Items

Match each of the structures with its function or description.

Structures or Conditions

_____ 1. lens
_____ 2. iris
_____ 3. pupil
_____ 4. rods
_____ 5. cones
_____ 6. middle ear
_____ 7. inner ear
_____ 8. large nerve fiber
_____ 9. small nerve fiber
_____ 10. semicircular canals
_____ 11. sensors in joints
_____ 12. acuity
_____ 13. farsightedness
_____ 14. nearsightedness

Functions or Descriptions

a. amplifies sounds
b. closes pain gate
c. vestibular sense
d. controls pupil
e. accommodation
f. eyeball is too short
g. opens pain gate
h. admits light
i. eyeball is too long
j. vision in dim light
k. transduction of sound
l. sharpness of vision
m. kinesthesis
n. color vision

Progress Test 2

Progress Test 2 should be completed during a final chapter review. Answer the following questions after you thoroughly understand the correct answers for the section reviews and Progress Test 1.

Multiple-Choice Questions

1. In his studies of the effects of sensory restriction, Peter Suedfeld found that:
   a. most people react negatively to reduced sensory stimulation.
   b. sensory restriction was experienced most negatively by people who were prone to addiction.
   c. sensory restriction helped smokers and overweight people modify their behavior.
   d. for most people, sensory restriction resulted in elevated absolute thresholds for vision and hearing.

2. Of the four distinct skin senses, the only one that has definable receptors is:
   a. warmth.   c. pressure.
   b. cold.   d. pain.

3. The process by which sensory information is converted into neural energy is:
   a. sensory adaptation.   d. transduction.
   b. feature detection.   e. parallel processing.
   c. signal detection.

4. The receptors for taste are located in the:
   a. taste buds.   c. fovea.
   b. cochlea.   d. cortex.

5. The inner ear contains receptors for:
   a. audition and kinesthesis.
   b. kinesthesis and the vestibular sense.
   c. audition and the vestibular sense.
   d. audition, kinesthesis, and the vestibular sense.

6. According to the opponent-process theory:
   a. there are three types of color-sensitive cones.
   b. the process of color vision begins in the cortex.
   c. neurons involved in color vision are stimulated by one color's wavelength and inhibited by another's.
   d. all of the above are true.

7. Nerve deafness is caused by:
   a. wax buildup in the outer ear.
   b. damage to the eardrum.
   c. blockage in the middle ear because of infection.
   d. damage to the cochlea.
   e. a puncture to the eardrum.

8. What enables you to feel yourself wiggling your toes even with your eyes closed?
   a. vestibular sense
   b. sense of kinesthesis
   c. the skin senses
   d. sensory interaction

9. The frequency theory of hearing is better than place theory at explaining our sensation of:
   a. the lowest pitches.
   b. pitches of intermediate range.
   c. the highest pitches.
   d. all of the above.

10. Hubel and Wiesel discovered feature detectors in the _____ of a monkey's visual system.
    a. fovea
    b. optic nerve
    c. iris
    d. cortex
    e. retina

11. Weber's law states that:
    a. the absolute threshold for any stimulus is a constant.
    b. the jnd for any stimulus is a constant.
    c. the absolute threshold for any stimulus is a constant proportion.
    d. the jnd for any stimulus is a constant proportion.

12. The principle that one sense may influence another is:
    a. transduction.
    b. sensory adaptation.
    c. Weber's law.
    d. sensory interaction.

13. Which of the following is the correct order of the structures through which light passes after entering the eye?
    a. lens, pupil, cornea, retina
    b. pupil, cornea, lens, retina
    c. pupil, lens, cornea, retina
    d. cornea, retina, pupil, lens
    e. cornea, pupil, lens, retina

14. In the opponent-process theory, the three pairs of processes are:
    a. red-green, blue-yellow, black-white.
    b. red-blue, green-yellow, black-white.
    c. red-yellow, blue-green, black-white.
    d. dependent upon the individual's past experience.

15. Wavelength is to _____ as _____ is to brightness.
    a. hue; intensity
    b. intensity; hue
    c. frequency; amplitude
    d. brightness; hue

16. Concerning the evidence for subliminal stimulation, which of the following is the best answer?
    a. The brain processes some information without our awareness.
    b. Stimuli too weak to cross our thresholds for awareness may trigger a response in our sense receptors.
    c. Because the "absolute" threshold is a statistical average, we are able to detect weaker stimuli some of the time.
    d. All of the above are true.

17. Which of the following is the most accurate description of how we process color?
    a. Throughout the visual system, color processing is divided into separate red, green, and blue systems.
    b. Red-green, blue-yellow, and black-white opponent processes operate throughout the visual system.
    c. Color processing occurs in two stages: (1) a three-color system in the retina and (2) opponent-process cells en route to the visual cortex.
    d. Color processing occurs in two stages: (1) an opponent-process system in the retina and (2) a three-color system en route to the visual cortex.

18. Which of the following is the most accurate explanation of how we discriminate pitch?
    a. For all audible frequencies, pitch is coded according to the place of maximum vibration on the cochlea's basilar membrane.
    b. For all audible frequencies, the rate of neural activity in the auditory nerve matches the frequency of the sound wave.
    c. For very high frequencies, pitch is coded according to place of vibration on the basilar membrane; for lower pitches, the rate of neural activity in the auditory nerve matches the sound's frequency.
    d. For very high frequencies, the rate of neural activity in the auditory nerve matches the frequency of the sound wave; for lower frequencies, pitch is coded according to the place of vibration on the basilar membrane.

19. One reason that your ability to detect fine visual details is greatest when scenes are focused on the fovea of your retina is that:
    a. there are more feature detectors in the fovea than in the peripheral regions of the retina.
    b. cones in the fovea are nearer to the optic nerve than those in peripheral regions of the retina.
    c. many rods, which are clustered in the fovea, have individual bipolar cells to relay their information to the cortex.
    d. many cones, which are clustered in the fovea, have individual bipolar cells to relay their information to the cortex.

20. Given normal sensory ability, a person can hear a watch ticking in a silent room from 20 feet away. This is a description of hearing's:
    a. difference threshold.
    c. absolute threshold.
    b. jnd.
    d. signal detection.

Thinking Critically About Chapter 5

Answer these questions the day before an exam as a final check on your understanding of the chapter's terms and concepts.

Multiple-Choice Questions

1. In shopping for a new stereo, you discover that you cannot differentiate between the sounds of models X and Y. The difference between X and Y is below your:
    a. absolute threshold.
    c. receptor threshold.
    b. signal detection.
    d. difference threshold.

2. In order to maximize your sensitivity to fine visual detail you should:
    a. stare off to one side of the object you are attempting to see.
    b. close one eye.
    c. decrease the intensity of the light falling upon the object.
    d. stare directly at the object.

3. The phantom limb sensation indicates that:
    a. pain is a purely sensory phenomenon.
    b. the central nervous system plays only a minor role in the experience of pain.
    c. pain involves the brain's interpretation of neural activity.
    d. all of the above are true.

4. While competing in the Olympic trials, marathoner Kirsten O'Brien suffered a stress fracture in her left leg. That she did not experience significant pain until the race was over is probably attributable to the fact that during the race:
    a. the pain gate in her spinal cord was closed by information coming from her brain.
    b. her body's production of endorphins decreased.
    c. an increase in the activity of small pain fibers closed the pain gate.
    d. a decrease in the activity of large pain fibers closed the pain gate.
    e. a decrease in the activity of large pain fibers opened the pain gate.

5. Which of the following is an example of sensory interaction?
    a. finding that despite its delicious aroma, a weird-looking meal tastes awful
    b. finding that food tastes bland when you have a bad cold
    c. finding it difficult to maintain your balance when you have an ear infection
    d. All of the above are examples.

6. In comparing the human eye to a camera, the film would be analogous to the eye's:
    a. pupil.
    c. cornea.
    b. lens.
    d. retina.

7. Sensation is to _____ as perception is to _____ .
    a. recognizing a stimulus; interpreting a stimulus
    b. detecting a stimulus; recognizing a stimulus
    c. interpreting a stimulus; detecting a stimulus
    d. seeing; hearing

8. I am a cell in the thalamus that is excited by red and inhibited by green. I am a(n):
    a. feature detector.
    d. opponent-process cell.
    b. cone.
    e. rod.
    c. bipolar cell.

9. Which of the following correctly lists the order of structures through which sound travels after entering the ear?
    a. auditory canal, eardrum, middle ear, cochlea
    b. eardrum, auditory canal, middle ear, cochlea
    c. eardrum, middle ear, cochlea, auditory canal
    d. cochlea, eardrum, middle ear, auditory canal
    e. auditory canal, middle ear, eardrum, cochlea

10. Dr. Frankenstein has forgotten to give his monster an important part; as a result, the monster cannot transduce sound. Dr. Frankenstein omitted the:
    a. eardrum.
    c. semicircular canals.
    b. middle ear.
    d. basilar membrane.

11. Seventy-five-year-old Claude has difficulty hearing high-pitched sounds. Most likely his hearing problem involves:
    a. his eardrum.
    b. his auditory canal.
    c. the bones of his middle ear.
    d. the hair cells of his inner ear.

12. Which of the following is *not* true of cones?
    a. Cones enable color vision.
    b. Cones are highly concentrated in the foveal region of the retina.
    c. Cones have a higher absolute threshold for brightness than rods.
    d. Each cone has its own bipolar cell.

13. Assuming that the visual systems of humans and other mammals function similarly, you would expect that the retina of a nocturnal mammal (one active only at night) would contain:
    a. mostly cones.
    b. mostly rods.
    c. an equal number of rods and cones.
    d. more bipolar cells than an animal active only during the day.

14. As the football game continued into the night, LeVar noticed that he was having difficulty distinguishing the colors of the players' uniforms. This is because the _____ , which enable color vision, have a _____ absolute threshold for brightness than the available light intensity.
    a. rods; higher   c. rods; lower
    b. cones; higher   d. cones; lower

15. After staring at a very intense red stimulus for a few minutes, Carrie shifted her gaze to a beige wall and "saw" the color _____ . Carrie's experience provides support for the _____ theory.
    a. green; trichromatic
    b. blue; opponent-process
    c. green; opponent-process
    d. blue; trichromatic

16. Elderly Mrs. Martinez finds that she must spice her food heavily or she cannot taste it. Unfortunately, her son often finds her cooking inedible because it is so spicy. What is the likely explanation for their taste differences?
    a. Women have higher taste thresholds than men.
    b. Men have higher taste thresholds than women.
    c. Being elderly, Mrs. Martinez probably has fewer taste buds than her son.
    d. All of the above are likely explanations.

17. When admiring the texture of a piece of fabric, Calvin usually runs his fingertips over the cloth's surface. He does this because:
    a. if the cloth were held motionless, sensory adaptation to its feel would quickly occur.
    b. the sense of touch does not adapt.

    c. a relatively small amount of brain tissue is devoted to processing touch from the fingertips.
    d. of all the above reasons.

18. Superman's eyes used _____ , while his brain used _____ .
    a. perception; sensation
    b. top-down processing; bottom-up processing
    c. bottom-up processing; top-down processing
    d. sensory adaptation; subliminal perception

19. How does pain differ from other senses?
    a. It has no identifiable receptors.
    b. It has no single stimulus.
    c. It is influenced by both physical and psychological phenomena.
    d. All the above are true.

20. Tamiko hates the bitter taste of her cough syrup. Which of the following would she find most helpful in minimizing the syrup's bad taste?
    a. tasting something very sweet before taking the cough syrup
    b. keeping the syrup in her mouth for several seconds before swallowing it
    c. holding her nose while taking the cough syrup
    d. gulping the cough syrup so that it misses her tongue

Essay Question

A dancer in a chorus line uses many sensory cues when performing. Discuss three senses that dancers rely on and explain why each is important. (Use the space below to list the points you want to make and organize them. Then write the essay on a separate sheet of paper.)

Summing Up

Use the diagrams to identify the parts of the eye and ear, then list them in the order in which they contribute to vision and hearing. Also, briefly explain the role of each structure.

The Eye

1. _____

2. _____

3. _____

4. _____

5. _____

6. _____

7. _____

The Ear

1. _____

2. _____

3. _____

4. _____

5. _____

6. _____

7. _____

8. _____

Key Terms

Writing Definitions

Using your own words, on a piece of paper write a brief definition or explanation of each of the following terms.

1. sensation

2. perception

3. bottom-up processing

4. top-down processing

5. psychophysics

6. absolute threshold

7. signal detection theory

8. subliminal stimulation

9. difference threshold (jnd)

10. Weber's law

11. sensory adaptation

12. transduction

13. wavelength and hue

14. intensity

15. pupil

16. iris

17. lens

18. accommodation

19. retina

20. acuity

21. nearsightedness

22. farsightedness

23. rods and cones

24. optic nerve

25. blind spot

26. fovea

27. feature detectors

28. parallel processing

29. Young-Helmholtz trichromatic (three-color) theory

30. opponent-process theory

31. color constancy

32. audition

33. pitch and frequency

34. middle ear

35. inner ear

36. cochlea

37. place theory

38. frequency theory

39. conduction hearing loss

40. sensorineural hearing loss

41. gate-control theory

42. sensory interaction

43. kinesthesis

44. vestibular sense

Cross-Check

As you learned in the Introduction, reviewing and overlearning of material are important to the learning process. After you have written the definitions of the key terms in this chapter, you should complete the crossword puzzle to ensure that you can reverse the process—recognize the term, given the definition.

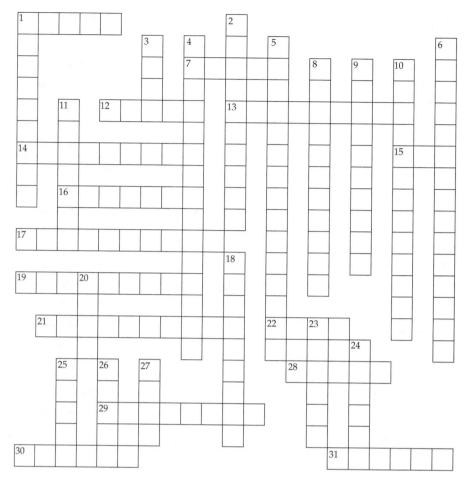

ACROSS

1. The retina's point of central focus.
7. Types of fibers that close the "pain gate."
12. Nerve that carries visual information to the brain.
13. Aspect of light and sound determined by the amplitude of energy waves.
14. Unit of measurement for electromagnetic energy.
15. The perceptual experience of color.
16. Membrane that lies at the end of the auditory canal.
17. Term for the color seen after staring at its opponent for a while.
19. Physical dimension of light and sound that determines brightness and loudness, respectively.
21. Type of deafness that results from damage in the mechanics of the outer or middle ear.
22. Membrane "window" at the entrance to the ear's cochlea.
28. Adjustable opening in the eye through which light enters.
29. Sense of hearing.
30. Transparent protective membrane through which light enters the eye.
31. Inner surface of the eye that contains the rods and cones.

DOWN

1. Theory of hearing that the rate of auditory nerve impulses matches the frequency of tones, enabling us to sense pitch.
2. Type of vision caused by a shorter-than-normal eyeball.
3. Acronym for type of sensory restriction designed to reduce stress and help people become more open to positive influence.
4. Energy spectrum that contains visible light.
5. Type of brain cell discovered by Hubel and Wiesel.
6. The basis of a "bionic ear."
8. Sense of the position and movement of body parts.
9. Ability of some brain-damaged patients to respond to something that is not consciously perceived.
10. Study of the relationship between the physical characteristics of stimuli and our psychological experience of them.
11. Perception of color is strongly influenced by the object's _____ .
18. Region of the retina where the optic nerve leaves the eye.
20. Part of the eye that changes shape to focus images on the retina.
23. Sharpness of vision.
24. Region of the ear that contains the hammer, anvil, and stirrup.
25. Region of the ear that contains the cochlea.
26. Theory that the region of maximum vibration along the basilar membrane is the basis of pitch discrimination.
27. Visual receptors that are concentrated in the periphery of the retina.

Answers

Introduction

Introduction Preview

1. Sensation refers to how we detect physical energy from the environment and encode it as neural signals. Perception refers to how we select, organize, and interpret sensory information. Sensory analysis, which works at the entry level, is called "bottom-up" processing. Perception, which draws on our experience and expectations, is called "top-down" processing.

Stepping Through the Introduction

1. sensation; perception
2. bottom-up processing; top-down processing
3. prosopagnosia

Sensing the World: Some Basic Principles

Section Preview

1. An absolute threshold is the minimum stimulation necessary to detect a particular environmental stimulus 50 percent of the time. A difference threshold, or just noticeable difference (jnd), is the minimum difference a person can detect between any two stimuli 50 percent of the time. Weber's law states that the difference threshold is a constant proportion of the stimulus.

   Signal detection studies indicate that thresholds depend not only on the strength of stimuli, but also on experience, expectations, motivation, and alertness. Thus, thresholds are not constant.

2. Stimuli at or above the "absolute" threshold are detected half the time; subliminal stimuli, which are below the absolute threshold, are therefore detected less than half the time. Experiments show that under certain conditions, a weak stimulus may reach a part of the brain where it evokes a feeling but not conscious awareness. Claims that subliminal stimulation may lead to thought persuasion have not been supported, however. While subliminal messages may have a fleeting effect on thinking, they do not have an enduring effect on behavior.

3. Sensory adaptation refers to our diminishing sensitivity to an unchanging stimulus. By allowing us to focus our attention on informative changes in the environment, it keeps us from being distracted by the uninformative, constant stimulation of unchanging stimuli.

Stepping Through the Section

1. psychophysics
2. absolute threshold; 50
3. signal detection; psychological
4. subliminal
5. conscious
6. difference threshold; just noticeable difference
7. Weber's law; stimulus
8. sensory adaptation

Although sensory adaptation reduces our sensitivity, it enables us to focus our attention on informative changes in the environment without being distracted by the uninformative, constant stimulation that bombards our senses.

Vision

Section Preview

1. Visible light is a small portion of the larger spectrum of electromagnetic radiation. Light can be described by two physical characteristics, wavelength, which determines hue, and intensity, which influences brightness.

   Vision begins when light enters the eye through the opening in the iris called the pupil. Light passes through the lens, which changes its curvature (accommodation) in order to focus light on the retina. Within the retina are the rods and cones, which are responsible for the transduction of light energy into neural impulses. The optic nerve carries neural impulses from the retina to visual processing centers in the brain.

2. Acuity, or sharpness of vision, is affected by distortions in the shape of the eye. In nearsightedness, the eyeball is longer than normal, causing light rays to converge in front of the retina. In farsightedness the eyeball is shorter than normal, causing light rays to reach the retina *before* they have converged to produce a sharp image.

3. The lowest level of visual information processing—the encoding and analyzing of sensory information—is at the retina. As we view a scene, the rods and cones of the retina transduce the reflected light into neural impulses that are relayed to bipolar and ganglion cells and then sent to the brain via the optic nerve. The brain—the source of most information processing—processes these visual stimuli relatively quickly by breaking them down into various subdimensions and working on each simultaneously (parallel processing). Thus, feature detectors break the

image into bars, edges, gradients of light, and other elementary features. Higher-level brain cells in the parietal and temporal lobes respond to specific visual scenes and then compare the resulting image with previously stored images until a match, and therefore recognition, occurs.

4. The Young-Helmholtz trichromatic (three-color) theory states that the retina has three types of color receptors, each sensitive to one of three colors: red, green, or blue. To "see" other hues, such as yellow, there must be a unique combination of activity in two or three of these color receptors (red and green, in this case). This theory explains color processing at the level of the retina.

   According to the opponent-process theory, some cells in the retina and in the thalamus of the brain analyze visual information in terms of the opponent colors red and green, blue and yellow, and black and white. This theory explains why we see afterimages following intense stimulation with a particular color.

5. Color constancy refers to the fact that, in an unvarying context, the color of an object remains roughly constant despite changes in lighting. If the context in which an object is viewed changes, the perceived color of the object changes. This demonstrates that the experience of color results not only from the light waves reflected from an object, but also from the light waves reflected by an object relative to surrounding objects.

Stepping Through the Section

1. neural; transduction
2. electromagnetic
3. wavelength; hue
4. intensity; amplitude; brightness
5. cornea; pupil; iris
6. lens; retina
7. accommodation; acuity
8. distant; in front of; nearby; distant; nearby; in back of; distant; nearby
9. rods; cones
10. bipolar; ganglion; optic nerve; brain
11. blind spot
12. fovea; peripheral; bipolar
13. cones
14. sensitive; 20
15. visual cortex; feature detectors
16. parietal; temporal; gaze; head angle; posture; body movement; perceives

17. simultaneously; parallel processing; blindsight; integration; gamma
18. reflects; construction
19. sex-linked
20. red; green; blue
21. opponent; afterimage
22. opponent-process; red; green; yellow; blue; black; white

In the first stage of color processing, the retina's red, green, and blue cones respond in varying degrees to different color stimuli, as suggested by the three-color theory. The resulting signals are then processed by red-green, blue-yellow, and black-white opponent-process cells, which are stimulated by one wavelength and inhibited by its opponent.

23. context
24. color constancy

Hearing

Section Preview

1. The stimulus energy for hearing is the sound waves of compressed and expanded air that are created by vibrating objects. The strength, or amplitude, of sound waves determines loudness; their length, or frequency, determines their pitch. Decibels are the measuring unit for sound energy. The absolute threshold for hearing is arbitrarily defined as 0 decibels.

   Hearing begins when the outer ear channels sound waves through the auditory canal to the eardrum. The middle ear transmits the eardrum's vibrations over three tiny bones (hammer, anvil, and stirrup) to the membrane entrance (oval window) of the fluid-filled cochlea of the inner ear. These vibrations cause ripples in the basilar membrane, which is lined with the hair cell receptors for audition. Movements of the basilar membrane cause the hair cells to bend, triggering impulses in the adjacent nerve fibers, which converge to form the auditory nerve.

2. According to the place theory, different sound wave frequencies trigger activity at different places along the cochlea's basilar membrane. The brain recognizes a sound's pitch by the place on the membrane from which it receives signals.

   Frequency theory suggests that the auditory nerve generates neural impulses at the same rate as a sound's frequency. The brain recognizes pitch from the frequency of these impulses. According to the volley principle, cells alternate their firing to match the frequencies of higher pitched sounds.

Place theory best explains how we sense high pitches and frequency theory explains low pitches. A combination of the two processes accounts for the sensing of intermediate pitches.

3. Because of the distance between the two ears, a sound coming from one side of the body will arrive sooner at one ear and be slightly louder. That differences in loudness and arrival time are used in locating sounds is demonstrated by the difficulty we have in locating a sound that comes from directly ahead, behind, overhead, or beneath us. Such sounds strike the two ears simultaneously and with equal intensity.

Damage to the eardrum or the bones of the middle ear cause conduction hearing loss, a problem in the mechanical system that conducts sound waves to the inner ear. A hearing aid that amplifies sound may restore hearing. Damage to the cochlea's hair cell receptors or their associated nerves due to disease, aging, or prolonged exposure to loud sounds can cause sensorineural hearing loss.

Stepping Through the Section

1. audition; air molecules
2. loudness
3. frequency
4. decibels; 0
5. outer; middle; inner
6. eardrum
7. hammer; anvil; stirrup
8. cochlea; oval window; basilar membrane; hair cells; number
9. less; stress; high blood pressure; anxiety; feelings of helplessness; unanticipated; uncontrollable
10. place; low
11. frequency; high; 1000
12. volley
13. speed (timing); loudness
14. harder
15. conduction hearing loss
16. sensorineural; aging
17. cochlear implant; chemically
18. is; with; seem to
19. higher
20. self-esteem; accepted

The Other Senses

Section Preview

1. The sense of touch is a mixture of at least four skin senses—pressure, warmth, cold, and pain. Of these, only pressure has identifiable neural receptors. Other skin sensations, such as tickle, itch, wetness, and hot, are variations of the four basic ones.

Pain is a property of the senses and the brain. Unlike other senses, pain has neither a single stimulus nor specialized receptors. According to the gate-control theory, the spinal cord contains a neural "gate" that either opens to permit pain signals to reach the brain or closes to prevent them from reaching the brain. This may explain why electrical stimulation, massage, and acupuncture relieve chronic pain—by triggering "gate-closing" activity in the spinal cord.

The gate-control theory also suggests that the pain gate can be closed by information from the brain. This may explain why thought distraction, hypnosis, and other psychological influences on pain are powerful.

2. Taste is a chemical sense comprised of four basic sensations—sweet, sour, salty, and bitter. Mixtures of these basic sensations give rise to other tastes. The receptors for taste (taste buds) are unevenly distributed so that different regions of the tongue are especially sensitive to one or more of the four basic tastes. Although the taste buds reproduce themselves every week or two, their number decreases with aging, smoking, and the use of alcohol.

Smell (olfaction) occurs when air-carried molecules of a substance reach receptor cells in the nasal cavity. Unlike other senses, olfaction is not based on a small set of basic odors from which all other odors derive. Exactly how the olfactory receptors work remains a mystery.

Sensors in the muscles, tendons, and joints of the body provide the brain with information about the position and movement of body parts (kinesthesis).

Receptors in the semicircular canals and the vestibular sacs of the inner ear monitor the position and movement of the whole body and enable us to maintain balance (the vestibular sense).

Sensory interaction is the principle that one sense may influence another. An example of sensory interaction is the enhancement of a food's taste that occurs when it smells delicious, or conversely the loss of taste when one has a cold.

3. Surprisingly, researchers have found that sensory restriction—controlled exposure to monotonous sensory environments—does not disturb most people. More often, it reduces stress and helps people become more open to positive influences that promote behavior modification. Sensory restriction has helped people increase their self-control, quit smoking, and reduce alcohol consumption.

Stepping Through the Section

1. pressure; warmth; cold; pain; variations
2. senses; brain
3. phantom limb
4. is not; does not
5. gate-control; gate; spinal cord; small; large; brain
6. social; physical; René Descartes; brain

The Lamaze method of prepared childbirth combines several pain control techniques, including distraction, deep breathing and muscle relaxation, and counterstimulation through gentle massage.

7. sweet; sour; salty; bitter
8. chemical; taste buds; pore
9. week or two
10. sensory interaction
11. olfaction; chemical; cannot
12. early adulthood
13. kinesthesis; muscles; tendons; joints
14. vestibular sense; semicircular canals; vestibular sacs
15. loss; monotony

Although early experiments reported disorientation and hallucinations, subsequent research has found that most people are not negatively affected by sensory restriction. In many instances, sensory restriction even seems to reduce stress and help people become more open to positive influence. For these reasons, sensory restriction may prove useful to people who want to modify their behavior, as indicated by experiments with smokers and overweight people.

Progress Test 1

Multiple-Choice Questions

1. **b.** is the answer. Psychological factors can affect the absolute threshold for a stimulus. (p. 173)

a. The absolute threshold for detecting a stimulus depends not only on the strength of the stimulus, but also on psychological factors such as experience, expectations, motivation, and fatigue. Thus, the threshold cannot be a constant.
c. & d. The absolute threshold is defined as the minimum stimulus that is detected 50 percent of the time.

2. **c.** is the answer. In nearsightedness, objects converge in front of the retina; one cause of this is an eyeball longer than normal in relation to the lens. (p. 179)

a. Inflexibility of the lens may cause the emergence of farsightedness as we get older.
b. Thinness of the lens is unrelated to near- or farsightedness.
d. A shorter-than-normal eyeball is related to farsightedness.

3. **c.** is the answer. According to Weber's law, the difference threshold is a constant proportion of the stimulus. There is a 10 percent difference between 10 and 11 pounds; since the difference threshold is a constant proportion, the weight closest to 100 pounds that can nonetheless be differentiated from it is 110 pounds (or 100 pounds plus 10 percent). (p. 175)

4. **d.** is the answer. (p. 176)
a. "Sensory fatigue" is not a term in psychology.
b. Accommodation refers to an adaptive change in shape by the lens of the eye.
c. Sensory restriction refers to restricted sensory input because of sensory monotony or loss of a sense.
e. Sensory interaction is the principle that one sense may influence another.

5. **d.** is the answer. (p. 179)
a. The lens lies behind the pupil and focuses light on the retina.
b. The retina is the inner surface of the eyeball and contains the rods and cones.
c. The cornea lies in front of the pupil and is the first structure that light passes through as it enters the eye.

6. **a.** is the answer. (p. 179)
b. Sensory adaptation is our diminishing sensitivity to an unchanging stimulus.
c. Focusing is the process through which light converges onto the retina as a sharp image. The image is focused because the lens accommodates its shape.
d. Transduction refers to the conversion of an environmental stimulus, such as light, into a neural impulse by a receptor—a rod or a cone.

7. **e.** is the answer. (p. 181)
    a. The fovea is not a receptor; it is a region of the retina that contains only cones.
    b. The ganglion cells' axons form the optic nerve.
    c. Cones have a higher threshold for brightness than rods and therefore do not function as well in dim light.
    d. Bipolar cells are not receptors; they are neurons in the retina that link rods and cones with ganglion cells, which make up the optic nerve.

8. **a.** is the answer. The Young-Helmholtz theory proposes that there are red-, green-, and blue-sensitive cones. (p. 186)
    b. This answer describes Hering's opponent-process theory.
    c. The Young-Helmholtz theory proposes that there are three types of cones, not four.
    d. The Young-Helmholtz theory concerns only color vision, not the detection of visual detail.

9. **b.** is the answer. Just as wave frequency determines pitch, so wave amplitude determines loudness. (p. 189)
    a. Amplitude is the physical basis of loudness; wavelength determines frequency and thereby pitch.
    c. & d. Wavelength, amplitude, and intensity are physical aspects of light and sound. Because the question is based on a relationship between a physical property (frequency) of a stimulus and its psychological attribute (pitch), these answers are incorrect.

10. **c.** is the answer. The receptors for hearing—those cells that transduce sound energy into neural impulses—are the hair cells lining the basilar membrane of the cochlea. (p. 190)

11. **a.** is the answer. (p. 192)
    b. & c. Although the localization of low-pitched sounds along the basilar membrane is poor, that for sounds of middle and, especially, high pitch is good. Therefore, place theory accounts well for high-pitched sounds and, together with frequency theory, can account for middle-pitched sounds.
    d. As long as the notes of a chord are within the range of responsiveness of the basilar membrane, chord perception can be accounted for by place theory.

12. **c.** is the answer. (p. 193)
    d. Chord perception, except for chords comprised exclusively of high-frequency notes, shows no age-dependent decline.

13. **d.** is the answer. The small fibers conduct most pain signals; the large fibers conduct most other sensory signals from the skin. The gate either allows pain signals to pass on to the brain or blocks them from passing. When the large fibers are stimulated, the pain gate is closed and other sensations are felt in place of pain. (p. 198)

14. **b.** is the answer. (p. 179)
    a. The iris controls the diameter of the pupil.
    c. The lens accommodates its shape to focus images on the retina.
    d. The optic nerve carries nerve impulses from the retina to the visual cortex.
    e. Rods are only one type of receptor cell in the retina.

15. **b.** is the answer. (p. 184)
    a. Feature detection is the process by which nerve cells in the brain respond to specific visual features of a stimulus, such as movement, angle, or shape.
    c. Accommodation is the process by which the lens changes its curvature to focus images on the retina.
    d. The opponent-process theory suggests that color vision depends on the response of brain cells to red-green, yellow-blue, and black-white opposing colors.

16. **b.** is the answer. Kinesthesis, or the sense of the position and movement of body parts, is based on information from the muscles, tendons, and joints. (p. 203)
    a. & c. The ear plays no role in kinesthesis.
    d. Equilibrium, or the sense of balance, is not involved in kinesthesis but is, rather, a companion sense.

17. **a.** is the answer. Wavelength determines hue, or color. (p. 178)
    b. & d. The amplitude of light determines its brightness.
    c. Opponent processes are neural systems involved in color vision, not properties of light.

18. **d.** is the answer. Color constancy is the perception that a familiar object has consistent color, even if changing illumination alters the wavelengths reflected by that object. (pp. 187–188)
    a. & b. These theories explain how the visual system detects color; they do not explain why colors do not seem to change when lighting does.
    c. Feature detection explains how the brain recognizes visual images by analyzing their distinctive features of shape, movement, and angle.

19. **a.** is the answer. Sensory adaptation means a diminishing sensitivity to an unchanging stimulus. Only the adjustment to cold water involves a decrease in sensitivity; the other examples involve an increase. (p. 176)

20. a. is the answer. Thus, they have difficulty discriminating these two colors. (p. 186)

b. Those who are color deficient are usually not "color blind" in a literal sense. Instead,

c. Failure to distinguish red and green is separate from, and does not usually affect, general visual ability.

d. Color deficiency does not enhance vision. A deficit in one sense often is compensated for by overdevelopment of another sense—for example, hearing in blind people.

Matching Items

1. e (p. 179)   **6.** a (p. 180)   **11.** m (p. 204)
2. d (p. 179)   **7.** k (p. 190)   **12.** l (p. 203)
3. h (p. 179)   **8.** b (p. 190)   **13.** f (p. 179)
4. j (p. 180)   **9.** g (p. 198)   **14.** i (p. 179)
5. n (p. 180)   **10.** c (p. 198)

Progress Test 2

Multiple-Choice Questions

1. c. is the answer. (p. 205)

a. In fact, researchers have found that most people are not affected negatively by sensory restriction.

b. & d. There is no evidence that sensory restriction has a more negative impact on people prone to addiction or that it elevates absolute thresholds.

2. c. is the answer. Researchers have identified receptors for pressure but have been unable to do so for the other skin senses. (p. 197)

3. d. is the answer. (p. 177)

a. Sensory adaptation refers to the diminished sensitivity that occurs with unchanging stimulation.

b. Feature detection refers to the process by which nerve cells in the brain respond to specific aspects of visual stimuli, such as movement or shape.

c. Signal detection is a task in which the observer must judge whether a faint signal is present.

e. Parallel processing refers to the simultaneous processing of several aspects of a problem.

4. a. is the answer. (p. 200)

b. The cochlea contains receptors for hearing.

c. The fovea contains receptors for vision (the cones).

d. The cortex is the outer layer of the brain, where information detected by the receptors is processed.

5. c. is the answer. The inner ear contains the receptors for audition (hearing) and the vestibular sense; those for kinesthesis are located in the muscles, tendons, and joints. (pp. 190, 204)

6. c. is the answer. After leaving the receptor cells, visual information is analyzed in terms of pairs of opponent colors; neurons stimulated by one member of a pair are inhibited by the other. (p. 187)

a. The idea that there are three types of color-sensitive cones is the basis of the Young-Helmholtz three-color theory.

b. According to the opponent-process theory, and all other theories of color vision, the process of color vision begins in the retina.

7. d. is the answer. Sensorineural hearing loss is caused by destruction of neural tissue as a result of problems with the cochlea's receptors or the auditory nerve. (p. 193)

a. & c. Wax buildup and blockage because of infection are temporary states; sensorineural hearing loss is permanent. Moreover, sensorineural hearing loss involves the inner ear, rather than the outer or middle ear.

b. Damage to the eardrum impairs the mechanical system that conducts sound waves; it could therefore cause conduction deafness, not sensorineural hearing loss.

8. b. is the answer. Kinesthesis, the sense of movement of body parts, would enable you to feel your toes wiggling. (p. 203)

a. The vestibular sense is concerned with movement and position, or balance, of the whole body, not of its parts.

c. The skin, or tactile, senses are pressure, pain, warmth, and cold; they have nothing to do with movement of body parts.

d. Sensory interaction, the principle that the senses influence each other, does not play a role in this example, which involves only the sense of kinesthesis.

9. a. is the answer. Frequency theory best explains the lowest pitches. Place theory best explains the highest pitches, and some combination of the two theories probably accounts for our sensation of intermediate-range pitches. (p. 192)

10. d. is the answer. Feature detectors are cortical neurons and hence are located in the visual cortex. (p. 182)

a. The fovea contains cones.

b. The optic nerve contains neurons that relay nerve impulses from the retina to higher centers in the visual system.

c. The iris is simply a ring of muscle tissue, which controls the diameter of the pupil.

e. The retina contains receptors that send information to the brain.

11. **d.** is the answer. Weber's law concerns difference thresholds (jnd's), not absolute thresholds, and states that these are constant proportions of the stimuli, not that they remain constant. (p. 175)

12. **d.** is the answer. (p. 201)

a. Transduction is the process by which stimulus energy is converted into nerve impulses.

b. Sensory adaptation is diminished sensitivity to unchanging stimulation.

c. Weber's law states that the jnd is a constant proportion of a stimulus.

13. **e.** is the answer. (p. 179)

14. **a.** is the answer. (p. 187)

15. **a.** is the answer. Wavelength determines hue, and intensity determines brightness. (p. 178)

16. **d.** is the answer. (pp. 173–175)

17. **c.** is the answer. (p. 187)

a. This answer is incorrect because separate red, green, and blue systems operate only in the retina.

b. This answer is incorrect because opponent-process systems operate en route to the brain, after visual processing in the receptors is completed.

d. This answer is incorrect because it reverses the correct order of the two stages of processing.

18. **c.** is the answer. (p. 192)

a. This answer describes how pitch is sensed in the case of high-pitched, but not low-pitched, sounds.

b. This answer describes how pitch is sensed in the case of low-pitched, but not high-pitched, sounds.

d. This answer is incorrect because it reverses the range of frequencies.

19. **d.** is the answer. (p. 181)

a. Feature detectors are nerve cells located in the visual cortex, not in the fovea of the retina.

b. The proximity of rods and cones to the optic nerve does not influence their ability to resolve fine details.

c. Rods are concentrated in the peripheral regions of the retina, not in the fovea; moreover, several rods share a single bipolar cell.

20. **c.** is the answer. The absolute threshold is the minimum stimulation needed to detect a stimulus. (pp. 172–173)

a. & b. The difference threshold, which is also known as the jnd, is the minimum difference between two stimuli that a person can detect. In this example, there is only one stimulus—the sound of the watch.

d. Signal detection is a research task, not a sensory phenomenon.

Thinking Critically About Chapter 5

Multiple-Choice Questions

1. **d.** is the answer. (p. 175)

a. The absolute threshold refers to whether a single stimulus can be detected, not to whether two stimuli can be differentiated.

b. Signal detection is a task in which one must determine whether or not a faint stimulus is present.

c. A receptor threshold is a minimum amount of energy that will elicit a neural impulse in a receptor cell.

2. **d.** is the answer. Greater sensitivity to fine visual detail is associated with the cones, which have their own bipolar cells to relay information to the cortex. The cones are concentrated in the fovea, the retina's point of central focus. For this reason, staring directly at an object maximizes sensitivity to fine detail. (p. 181)

a. If you stare off to one side, the image falls onto peripheral regions of the retina, where rods are concentrated and sensitivity to fine visual detail is poor.

b. Sensitivity to detail is not directly influenced by whether one or both eyes are stimulated.

c. Decreasing the intensity of light would only impair the functioning of the cones, which are sensitive to visual detail but have a high threshold for light intensity.

3. **c.** is the answer. Since pain is felt in the limb that does not exist, the pain is simply the brain's (mis)interpretation of neural activity. (p. 198)

a. If pain were a purely sensory phenomenon, phantom limb pain would not occur, since the receptors are no longer present.

b. That pain is experienced when a limb is missing indicates that the central nervous system, especially the brain, is where pain is sensed.

4. **a.** is the answer. (p. 198)

b. Since endorphins relieve pain, a decrease in their production would have made Kirsten more likely to experience pain. Moreover, because endorphins are released in response to pain, their production probably would have increased.

c. Neural activity in small fibers tends to open the pain gate.

d. & e. An *increase* in large-fiber activity would tend to *close* the pain gate.

5. **d.** is the answer. Each of these is an example of the interaction of two senses—vision and taste in the case of a., taste and smell in the case of b., and hearing and the vestibular sense in the case of c. (p. 201)

6. **d.** is the answer. Just as light strikes the film of a camera, visual images entering the eye are projected onto the retina. (p. 179)
   a. The pupil would be analogous to the aperture of a camera, since both control the amount of light permitted to enter.
   b. The lens of the eye performs a focusing function similar to the lens of the camera.
   c. The cornea would be analogous to a camera's lens cap in that both protect delicate inner structures.

7. **b.** is the answer. (p. 171)
   a. Both recognition and interpretation are examples of perception.
   c. This answer would have been correct if the question had read, "Perception is to sensation as _____ is to _____ ."
   d. Sensation and perception are important processes in both hearing and seeing.

8. **d.** is the answer. (p. 187)
   a. Feature detectors are located in the visual cortex and respond to features such as movement, shape, and angle.
   b. & c. Cones and bipolar cells are located in the retina. Moreover, neither are excited by some colors and inhibited by others.

9. **a.** is the answer. (p. 190)

10. **d.** is the answer. The hair cells, which transduce sound energy, are located on the basilar membrane. (p. 190)
    a. & b. The eardrum and bones of the middle ear merely conduct sound waves to the inner ear, where they are transduced.
    c. The semicircular canals are involved in the vestibular sense, not hearing.

11. **d.** is the answer. Hearing losses that result from aging are greatest in the higher frequencies and involve damage to the hair cells on the basilar membrane of the cochlea. (p. 193)
    a., b., & c. Damage to the eardrum, auditory canal, or bones of the middle ear would probably cause conduction deafness and reduced sensitivity to sounds of all frequencies.

12. **d.** is the answer. Many, but not all, cones are linked to their own bipolar cell. (p. 181)

13. **b.** is the answer. Rods and cones enable vision in dim and bright light, respectively. If an animal is active only at night, it is likely to have more rods than cones in its retinas. (p. 181)
    d. Bipolar cells link both cones and rods to ganglion cells. There is no reason to expect that a nocturnal mammal would have more bipolar cells than a mammal active both during the day and at night. If anything, because several rods share a single bipolar cell, whereas many cones have their own, a nocturnal animal (with a visual system consisting mostly of rods) might be expected to have fewer bipolar cells than an animal active during the day (with a visual system consisting mostly of cones).

14. **b.** is the answer. (p. 181)
    a. & c. It is the cones, rather than the rods, that enable color vision.
    d. If the cones' threshold were lower than the available light intensity, they would be able to function and therefore detect the colors of the players' uniforms.

15. **c.** is the answer. (p. 187)
    a. The trichromatic theory cannot account for the experience of afterimages.
    b. & d. Afterimages are experienced as the complementary color of a stimulus. Green, not blue, is red's complement.

16. **c.** is the answer. As people age they lose taste buds and their taste thresholds increase. For this reason, Mrs. Martinez needs more concentrated tastes than her son to find food palatable. (p. 201)
    a. & b. There is no evidence that women and men differ in their absolute thresholds for taste.

17. **a.** is the answer. (p. 176)
    b. The sense of touch (pressure) adapts very quickly.
    c. On the contrary, the extreme sensitivity of the fingertips is due to the relatively large amount of cortical tissue that processes neural impulses from the fingertips.

18. **c.** is the answer. (p. 171)

19. **d.** is the answer. (p. 198)

20. **c.** is the answer. Because of the powerful sensory interaction between taste and smell, eliminating the odor of the cough syrup should make its taste more pleasant. (p. 201)
    a. If anything, the contrasting tastes might make the bitter syrup even less palatable.

b. If Tamiko keeps the syrup in her mouth for several seconds, it will ensure that her taste pores fully "catch" the stimulus, thus intensifying the bitter taste.

d. It's probably impossible to miss the tongue completely.

Essay Question

The senses that are most important to dancers are vision, hearing, kinesthesis, and the vestibular sense. Your answer should refer to any three of these senses and include, at minimum, the following information.

Dancers rely on vision to gauge their body position relative to other dancers as they perform specific choreographed movements. Vision also helps dancers assess the audience's reaction to their performance. Whenever dance is set to music, hearing is necessary so that the dancers can detect musical cues for certain parts of their routines. Hearing also helps the dancers keep their movements in time with the music. Kinesthetic receptors in dancers' muscles, tendons, and joints provide their brains with information about the position and movement of body parts to determine if their hands, arms, legs, and heads are in the proper positions. Receptors for the vestibular sense located in the dancers' inner ears send messages to their brains that help them maintain their balance and determine the correctness of the position and movement of their bodies.

Summing Up

The Eye

1. Cornea. Light enters the eye through this transparent membrane, which protects the inner structures from the environment.
2. Iris. The colored part of the eye, the iris functions like the aperture of a camera, controlling the size of the pupil to optimize the amount of light that enters the eye.
3. Pupil. The adjustable opening in the iris, the pupil allows light to enter.
4. Lens. This transparent structure behind the pupil changes shape to focus images on the retina.
5. Retina. The light-sensitive inner surface of the eye, the retina contains the rods and cones, which transduce light energy into neural impulses.
6. Blind spot. The region of the retina where the optic nerve leaves the eye, the blind spot contains no rods or cones and so there is no vision here.
7. Optic nerve. This bundle of nerve fibers carries neural impulses from the retina to the brain.

The Ear

1. Outer ear. Hearing begins as sound waves enter the auditory canal of the outer ear.
2. Auditory canal. Sound waves passing through the auditory canal are brought to a point of focus at the eardrum.
3. Eardrum. Lying between the outer and middle ear, this membrane vibrates in response to sound waves.
4. Middle ear. Lying between the outer and inner ear, this air-filled chamber contains the hammer, anvil, and stirrup.
5. Hammer, anvil, and stirrup. These tiny bones of the middle ear concentrate the eardrum's vibrations on the cochlea's oval window.
6. Inner ear. This region of the ear contains the cochlea and the semicircular canals, which play an important role in balance.
7. Cochlea. This fluid-filled multichambered structure contains the hair cell receptors that transduce sound waves into neural impulses.
8. Auditory nerve. This bundle of fibers carries nerve impulses from the inner ear to the brain.

Key Terms

Writing Definitions

1. **Sensation** is the process by which we detect physical energy from the environment and encode it as neural signals. (p. 171)
2. **Perception** is the process by which the brain organizes and interprets sensory information. (p. 171)
3. **Bottom-up processing** is analysis that begins with the sense receptors and works up to the brain's integration of sensory information. (p. 171)
4. **Top-down processing** is information processing guided by higher-level mental processes. (p. 171)
5. **Psychophysics** is the study of relationships between the physical characteristics of stimuli and our psychological experience of them. (p. 172)
6. The **absolute threshold** is the minimum stimulation needed to detect a stimulus 50 percent of the time. (p. 173)
7. **Signal detection theory** explains precisely how and when we detect the presence of a faint stimulus ("signal"). Detection depends partly on experience, expectation, motivation, and alertness. (p. 173)
8. A stimulus that is **subliminal** is one that is below the absolute threshold for awareness. (p. 173)

Memory aid: Limen is the Latin word for "threshold." A stimulus that is **subliminal** is one that is *sub-* ("below") the *limen*, or threshold.

9. The **difference threshold**, or **just noticeable difference (jnd)**, is the minimum difference in two stimuli that a subject can detect 50 percent of the time. (p. 175)

10. **Weber's law** states that the just noticeable difference between two stimuli is a constant minimum proportion of the stimulus. (p. 175)

Example: If a difference of 10 percent in weight is noticeable, **Weber's law** predicts that a person could discriminate 10- and 11-pound weights or 50- and 55-pound weights.

11. **Sensory adaptation** refers to the decreased sensitivity that occurs with continued exposure to an unchanging stimulus. (p. 176)

12. In the study of sensation, **transduction** refers to the process by which receptor cells in the eye, ear, skin, and nose convert environmental stimuli into neural impulses. (p. 177)

13. **Wavelength**, which refers to the distance from the peak of one light (or sound) wave to the next, gives rise to the perceptual experiences of **hue**, or color, in vision (and **pitch** in sound). (p. 178)

14. The **intensity** of light and sound is determined by the amplitude of the waves and is experienced as brightness and loudness, respectively. (p. 178)

Example: Sounds that exceed 85 decibels in amplitude, or **intensity**, will damage the auditory system.

15. The **pupil** is the adjustable opening in the eye through which light enters. (p. 179)

16. The **iris** is a ring of muscle tissue that forms the colored part of the eye that controls the diameter of the pupil. (p. 179)

17. The **lens** is the transparent structure of the eye behind the pupil that changes shape to focus images on the retina. (p. 179)

18. **Accommodation** is the process by which the lens of the eye changes shape to focus near objects on the retina. (p. 179)

19. The **retina** is the light-sensitive, multilayered inner surface of the eye that contains the rods and cones, as well as neurons that form the beginning of the optic nerve. (p. 179)

20. Visual **acuity** refers to the sharpness of vision. (p. 179)

Example: If your **acuity** is 20/10, you are able to see clearly at a distance of 20 feet a visual detail that most people cannot see beyond a distance of 10 feet.

21. **Nearsightedness** is a condition in which nearby objects are seen clearly but distant objects are blurred because light rays reflecting from them converge in front of the retina. (p. 179)

22. **Farsightedness** is a condition in which distant objects are seen clearly but nearby objects are blurred because light rays reflecting from them strike the retina **before** converging. (p. 179)

Memory aid: To help you remember that farsightedness is caused by a shorter-than-normal eyeball, think of something falling "far short of the mark."

23. The **rods** and **cones** are visual receptors that transduce light into neural impulses. The rods are concentrated in the periphery of the retina, the cones in the fovea. The rods have poor sensitivity, detect black and white, and function well in dim light. The cones have excellent sensitivity, enable color vision, and function best in daylight or bright light. (p. 180)

24. Comprised of the axons of retinal ganglion cells, the **optic nerve** carries neural impulses from the eye to the brain. (p. 180)

25. The **blind spot** is the region of the retina where the optic nerve leaves the eye. Because there are no rods or cones in this area, there is no vision here. (p. 181)

24. The **fovea** is the retina's point of central focus. It contains only cones; therefore, images focused on the fovea are the clearest. (p. 181)

25. **Feature detectors**, located in the visual cortex of the brain, are nerve cells that selectively respond to specific visual features, such as movement, shape, or angle. Feature detectors are evidently the basis of visual information processing. (p. 182)

26. **Parallel processing** is information processing in which several aspects of a stimulus, such as light or sound, are processed simultaneously. (p. 184)

27. The **Young-Helmholtz trichromatic (three-color) theory** maintains that the retina contains red-, green-, and blue-sensitive color receptors that in combination can produce the perception of any color. This theory explains the first stage of color processing. (p. 186)

30. The **opponent-process theory** maintains that color vision depends on pairs of opposing retinal processes (red-green, yellow-blue, and white-black). This theory explains the second stage of color processing. (p. 187)

31. **Color constancy** is the perception that familiar objects have consistent color despite changes in illumination that shift the wavelengths they reflect. (p. 187)

32. **Audition** refers to the sense of hearing. (p. 189)

33. The **pitch** of a sound is determined by its **frequency**, that is, the number of complete wavelengths that can pass a point in a given time. Frequency, in turn, is directly related to wavelength: Longer waves produce lower pitch; shorter waves produce higher pitch. (p. 189)

34. The **middle ear** is the chamber between the eardrum and cochlea containing the three bones (hammer, anvil, and stirrup) that concentrate the eardrum's vibrations on the cochlea's oval window. (p. 190)

35. The **inner ear** contains the semicircular canals and the cochlea, which includes the receptors that transduce sound energy into neural impulses. Because it also contains the vestibular sac, the inner ear plays an important role in balance, as well as in audition. (p. 190)

36. The **cochlea** is the coiled, bony, fluid-filled tube of the inner ear where the transduction of sound waves into neural impulses occurs. (p. 190)

37. The **place theory** of hearing states that we hear different pitches because sound waves of various frequencies trigger activity at different places on the cochlea's basilar membrane. (p. 192)

    Memory aid: **Place theory** maintains that the *place* of maximum vibration along the cochlea's membrane is the basis of pitch discrimination.

38. The **frequency theory** of hearing presumes that the rate, or frequency, of nerve impulses in the auditory nerve matches the frequency of a tone, thus enabling us to sense its pitch. (p. 192)

39. **Conduction hearing loss** refers to the hearing loss that results from damage in the mechanics of the outer or middle ear, which impairs the conduction of sound waves to the cochlea. (p. 193)

40. **Sensorineural hearing loss** (*nerve deafness*) is hearing loss caused by damage to the auditory receptors of the cochlea or to the auditory nerve due to disease, aging, or prolonged exposure to ear-splitting noise. (p. 193)

41. Melzack and Wall's **gate-control theory** maintains that a "gate" in the spinal cord determines whether pain signals are permitted to reach the brain. Neural activity in small nerve fibers opens the gates; activity in large fibers or information from the brain closes the gate. (p. 198)

    Example: The **gate-control theory** gained support with the discovery of endorphins. Production of these opiatelike chemicals may be the brain's mechanism for closing the spinal gate.

42. **Sensory interaction** is the principle that one sense may influence another. (p. 201)

43. **Kinesthesis** is the sense of the position and movement of the parts of the body. (p. 203)

44. The sense of body movement, position, and balance is called the **vestibular sense**. (p. 204)

Cross-Check

ACROSS	DOWN
1. fovea	1. frequency
7. large	2. farsighted
12. optic	3. rest
13. intensity	4. electromagnetic
14. nanometer	5. feature detector
15. hue	6. cochlear implant
16. eardrum	8. kinesthesis
17. afterimage	9. blindsight
19. amplitude	10. psychophysics
21. conduction	11. context
22. oval	18. blindspot
28. pupil	20. lens
29. audition	23. acuity
30. cornea	24. middle
31. retina	25. inner
	26. place
	27. rods

FOCUS ON VOCABULARY AND LANGUAGE

Page 171: Shown her own face in the mirror she is again *stumped*. This person (E. H.) is suffering from *prosopagnosia* and cannot recognize faces and even fails (*she is stumped*) to recognize her own face in the mirror. What is interesting in this case is that she can process incoming sensory information (*bottom up*) but is unable to make any sense of it (*top down*). As Myers notes earlier, she has sensation (*bottom-up processing*), but her perception (*top-down processing*) is not working properly.

Sensing the World: Some Basic Principles

Page 172: A frog could starve to death *knee-deep* in motionless flies. But let one *zoom by* and the frog's *"bug detector"* cells *snap awake*. The frog's eyes and brain are organized in such a way that only fast moving (*zooming*), small, dark objects will cause these specialized feature detector nerve cells ("*bug detector*") to become active (*snap awake*). If the frog is surrounded by flies that don't move (*knee-deep in motionless flies*), it will die of hunger, completely unaware of the food at its feet.

Page 172: The *shades* on our senses are open just a *crack*, allowing us only a restricted awareness of this *vast sea* [of energy]. Just as sunblinds or curtains (*shades*) let only a little light in through any small opening (*a crack*), our sensory system is only able to detect a very small part of the large amount (*vast sea*) of the physical energy that exists in the world.

Page 173: Exhausted parents of a newborn will notice *the faintest whimper* from the *cradle*. . . . In **signal detection theory** there is no single absolute threshold for detecting stimuli; it all depends on the situation. Thus, parents who are sleeping soundly are more likely to become aware of the quietest cry of distress (*the faintest whimper*) from the infant in its small bed (*cradle*) than much louder but irrelevant noise.

Page 173: . . . "satanic messages" . . . It has been suggested that some rock music recordings have hidden or subliminal messages, and that behavior can be influenced or manipulated by them (i.e., *hidden persuasion*). Claims have been made that some of these messages are antireligious and promote devil worship (*diabolical* or *satanic*). As Myers makes clear, there is not a shred of evidence to support these ideas.

Page 175: . . . *hucksters* . . . A *huckster* is someone who sells merchandise that may be of dubious value. Those who promote and sell subliminal tapes (*hucksters*) make claims that are not supported by scientif-

ic research. In fact, the available evidence suggests that subliminal tapes do not have the profound, enduring effects on behavior claimed by their marketers; rather, the effect is zero (*zilch*).

Page 175: . . . it might take a £4000 *price hike* in a £40,000 Mercedes to *raise the eyebrows* of its potential buyers. *Raised eyebrows* express surprise. So a £4000 increase in the cost (*price hike*) of a luxury car (Mercedes-Benz), which normally costs £40,000, would be noticed by interested buyers (*would raise their eyebrows*). **Weber's law** states that a constant proportion of the original stimulus is needed in order for the difference to be detected, and the precise proportion will change depending on the stimulus. Thus, a $5 increase in the price of the car would not be a **just noticeable difference**, or **jnd**, but a $5 dollar increase (*price hike*) in the cost of a hamburger and fries would exceed a **jnd**.

Page 176: Thus, everywhere that Mary looks the scene is sure to go. In order to understand this sentence you need to be familiar with the old nursery rhyme: Mary had a little lamb, its fleece was white as snow, and *everywhere that Mary went the lamb was sure to go*. Myers is saying that if we were to project an unmoving image on our retinas by attaching contact lenses with a very small projector mounted on them, then whatever we look at (*the scene*) would disappear bit by bit and then reappear and disappear again.

Vision

Page 179: This fact was *baffling*. Scientists were puzzled (*baffled*) by the fact that although the retina receives an upside-down image, we experience the world right side up. We now know that the retina doesn't analyze the image as a total unit; rather, it transforms (*transduces*) the light energy into neural impulses which are transmitted to the brain via the optic nerve, and there it is put together to form the impression of a right-side-up world.

Page 181: . . . **blind spot** . . . You can use the suggestion in Figure 5.8 of your text to demonstrate that there are two small parts of your visual field (one in the left and one in the right) where you have no sight. These tiny areas (*blind spots*) are where the optic nerve exits the eye.

Page 181: Rods have no such *hotline* to the brain. . . . Cones, which are mostly clustered in the **fovea** and detect color and fine detail, have many more individual connections to the brain than the rods. Rods, which give us our black-and-white vision, have to share bipolar cells and so do not have as many individual connections (*hotlines*) to the brain.

Page 185: . . . blindsight . . . Blindsight refers to the fact that some people with neurological damage have the ability to see, to some degree, without any conscious awareness of the visual experience. They are blind, yet they can see (*blindsight*).

Page 186: Color, like all aspects of vision, resides not in the object but in the *theater of our brains.* Myers notes that when we view a colored object (for example, a blue balloon), it absorbs all the wavelengths except its own (blue) and reflects the wavelengths of blue back to us. The color we perceive is a product of our brain and exists only in the perceiver's mind (*theater of the brain*).

Hearing

Page 189: We also are remarkably sensitive to *faint sounds,* an obvious *boon* to our ancestors' survival when *hunting* or being *hunted* or detecting a *child's whimper.* Humans are very good at detecting very quiet noises (*faint sounds*), which was clearly beneficial (*a boon*) to our predecessors' ability to survive when they were both predator (*hunter*) and prey (*being hunted*). We are also very sensitive to changes in sounds and we have the ability to differentiate among thousands of human voices.

Page 189: A *piccolo* produces much shorter sound waves than does a *tuba.* Musical instruments produce stimulus energy called sound waves—molecules of air that bump and push each other along—and these may be long (low frequency) or short (high frequency). A *tuba* (a large, deep-toned, brass-wind instrument) produces low-frequency sound waves and thus has a lower pitch than a *piccolo* (a small flute), which produces high-frequency waves and has a higher pitch.

Page 191: At such times we may wish our ears had *earlids.* Myers makes it clear that prolonged exposure to loud and unpredictable noise can affect our well-being and seriously damage our hearing. So, in a noisy urban environment it would be nice if we could close our ears (*with earlids*) as we can our eyes (*with eyelids*).

Page 192: If a car to the right *honks,* your right ear receives a more *intense* sound slightly *sooner* than your left ear. We locate sounds because our ears are about 6 inches apart and there is a time, as well as a loudness difference, between auditory reception in each ear. If we hear the sound of a car horn (*it honks*) to our right, the left ear receives a less intense sound somewhat later than the right ear, and thus we locate the direction of the sound to the right.

Page 193: Occasionally, disease causes sensorineural hearing loss, but more often biological changes linked with aging (Figure 5.22, in your text) and prolonged exposure to *ear-splitting* noise or music are the *culprits.* Sensorineural hearing loss, or nerve deafness (cochlear damage), can sometimes be caused by illness, but the agents responsible (*the culprits*) are more likely to be age-related biological factors and extended encounters with extremely loud (*ear-splitting*) music or noise. There is only one-less-than-perfect partial remedy and that involves a cochlear implant.

The Other Senses

Page 197: As lovers, we *yearn* to touch—to kiss, to stroke, *to snuggle.* Our sense of touch involves a mixture of at least four distinct senses, pressure, warmth, cold, and pain. Intimate relations often involve a desire or longing (*we yearn*) to caress, kiss, and closely embrace each other (*snuggle*).

Page 198: Rubbing the area around your *stubbed toe* creates competing stimulation that will *block* some of the pain messages. If you hit your toe against a solid object (*stub your toe*), it really hurts. If, however, you massage (*rub*) the part around the sore spot, it makes you feel better because stimulation interferes with (*blocks*) some of the pain messages. This supports the **gate-control** model, which suggests that this stimulation (*rubbing*) will activate "gate-closing" in large neural fibers and, thus, will reduce pain.

Page 199: A well-trained nurse may distract *needle-shy* patients by chatting with them and asking them to look away when inserting the needle. One method of pain control is through distraction. If you are nervous or anxious about being injected with a hypodermic needle (*a needle-shy patient*), the nurse may talk to you about unimportant matters (*she chatters to you*) and request that you do not watch the procedure. This type of distraction can reduce the intensity of the pain.

Page 200 (caption): That evening he explained heat-diffusion principles that permit *firewalking,* then joined several others in *putting his feet where his mouth was* by leading 80 people across 12 feet of hot coals. The expression *"put your money where your mouth is"* means that you should be willing to back or support your words or claims with appropriate behavior. So Dr. Campbell was willing to support his explanation of firewalking, which was based on scientific facts, by taking the necessary action. By actually walking or stepping across the hot coals without burning his bare feet, he put his feet (*firewalking*) where his mouth was (his scientific explanation) and showed that the claims of the "mind over matter" promoters were wrong in this case.

Page 201: Taste buds are essential for taste, *but there is more to taste than meets the tongue.* The common expression *"there is more to this than meets the eye"* suggests that there is something extra going on over and above the obvious or apparent. Myers creates a variation of this expression using a different sense (taste). The flavors we experience are a function of more than just the taste buds in the tongue; they involve **sensory interaction** with the sense of smell (**olfaction**). Consequently, *there is more to taste than meets the tongue.*

Page 201: Each day, you inhale and exhale nearly 20,000 breaths of life-sustaining air, *bathing* your nostrils in a *stream of scent-laden molecules.* Smell (**olfaction**) is a chemical sense and as substances (flowers, feet, fish, fertilizer, etc.) release molecules, they are carried by the air we breathe (*a stream of scent-laden molecules*) and wash over (*bathe*) receptors in our nasal cavities (nostrils).

Page 203: Words more readily *portray* the sound of coffee brewing than its *aroma.* It is easier to talk about and describe (*portray*) the subtle aspects of the sound of a small flute (*piccolo*) than to put into words the sensory qualities involved in the smell (*aroma*) of coffee. Olfaction seems to be a more primitive sense than vision or audition.

Page 204: The biological *gyroscopes* for this sense of *equilibrium* are in the inner ear. A *gyroscope* is a mechanical device used as a stabilizer in navigation and scientific instruments. Likewise, we have biological stabilizers that monitor the movement and position of our bodies and provide us with a sense of balance (*equilibrium*). They are called the *semicircular canals* and the *vestibular sacs* and are located in the inner ear.

Page 204: Imagine that one of your *sensory windows* on the world *snapped shut.* Myers is asking you to think about what would happen to you if you lost one of your senses—say, if your vision or hearing (*sensory windows*) stopped working (*snapped shut*). To some extent loss of one sense can result in an increased sensitivity in other senses.

CHAPTER 6:

Perception

Chapter Overview

Chapter 6 explores how we select, organize, and interpret our sensations into meaningful perceptions. The chapter introduces a wide range of terminology, especially in the Perceptual Organization section. Each of the two sections that follow deals with an important issue. The first issue is the role of experience, as opposed to heredity, in perception. Make sure you understand the results of studies of recovery from blindness, early sensory restriction, adaptation to distorted environments, and perceptual set. The second is the possible existence of ESP, or perception without sensation. You should be able to discuss both the claims made for ESP and the criticisms of these claims.

NOTE: Answer guidelines for all Chapter 6 questions begin on page 180.

Selective Attention and Perceptual Illusions (pp. 209–213)

> David Myers at times uses idioms that are unfamiliar to some readers. If you do not know the meaning of any of the following words, phrases, or expressions in the context in which they appear in the text, refer to page 189 for an explanation: *your attentional spotlight shifts; you may draw a blank; sauntered; ventriloquist's dummy..*

Section Previews

First, skim the sections, noting headings and boldface items. Then read the following objectives and, as you read the text, search for the information that will enable you to meet each objective. Answer guidelines are provided on page 180.

1. Explain the concept of selective attention; give an example.

2. Explain how illusions help us to understand perception.

Stepping Through the Sections

After you have read the sections, complete the sentences and answer the questions. As you proceed, evaluate your performance by consulting the answers on page 181. Do not continue with the next section until you understand each answer. If you need to, review or reread the section in the textbook before continuing.

1. The philosopher _____ first proposed that we perceive objects through the senses, with the mind.

2. Our tendency to focus at any moment on only a limited aspect of all that we are capable of experiencing is called _____ _____ . One example of this is the _____ _____ _____ —the ability to attend selectively to only one voice among many.

3. The tendency of vision to dominate the other senses is referred to as _____ _____ .

Perceptual Organization (pp. 213–225)

> If you do not know the meaning of any of the following words, phrases, or expressions in the context in which they appear in the text, refer to pages 189–190 for an explanation: *There is far more to perception than meets the senses; yen; Sometimes, however, they can lead us astray; mothers then coaxed them to crawl out on the glass; The floating finger sausage; As we move, objects that are actually stable may appear to move; By flashing 24 still pictures; through a paper tube; carpentered; buffalo loomed.*

Section Preview

Answer guidelines are provided on page 181.

1. Discuss Gestalt psychology's contribution to our understanding of perception, including the figure-ground relationship and principles of perceptual grouping in form perception.

2. Discuss research on depth perception involving the use of the visual cliff.

3. Explain how 3-D movies are made, and describe the binocular and monocular cues in depth perception.

4. Describe the perceptual constancies, and show how they operate in visual illusions.

Stepping Through the Section

Answers are provided on page 181.

1. According to the _____ school of psychology, we tend to organize a cluster of sensations into a _____ , or form. This tendency can be illustrated using a figure called a _____ cube.

2. Our tendency to perceive complete forms involves sensory analysis, or _____-_____ processing of stimuli, as well as _____-_____ processing that uses our _____ and _____ to interpret our sensations. The distinction between sensation and perception in terms of these two types of information processing is _____ (clear cut/fuzzy).

3. When we view a scene, we see the central object, or _____ , as distinct from surrounding stimuli, or the _____ .

Identify the major contributions of Gestalt psychology to our understanding of perception.

4. Proximity, similarity, closure, continuity, and connectedness are examples of Gestalt rules of _____ .

5. The principle that we organize stimuli into smooth, continuous patterns is called _____ . The principle that we fill in gaps to create a complete, whole object is _____ . The grouping of items that are close to each other is the principle of _____ ; the grouping of items that look alike is the principle of _____ . The tendency to perceive uniform or attached items as a single unit is the principle of _____ .

6. The ability to see objects in three dimensions despite their two-dimensional representations on our retinas is called _____ _____ .

7. Gibson and Walk developed the _____ _____ to test depth perception in infants.

Summarize the results of Gibson and Walk's studies of depth perception.

For questions 8–19, identify the depth perception cue that is defined.

8. Any cue that requires both eyes:

   _____ .

9. Any cue that requires either eye alone:

   _____ .

10. The greater the difference between the images received by the two eyes, the nearer the object:

    _____ _____

    3-D movies simulate this cue by photographing each scene with _____ (how many?) cameras. This chapter's fundamental lesson is that our _____ are the constructions of our _____ .

11. The more our eyes focus inward when we view an object, the nearer the object:_____ .

12. An object partially covered by another is seen as farther away: _____ .

13. If two objects are presumed to be the same size, the one that casts a smaller retinal image is perceived as farther away:

    _____ _____ .

14. Objects that appear hazy are seen as farther away: _____ _____ .

15. As an object becomes increasingly distant, it appears progressively less distinct:

    _____ _____ .

16. Objects lower in the visual field are seen as nearer: _____ _____ .

17. As we move, objects at different distances appear to move at different rates:

    _____ _____ .

18. Parallel lines appear to converge in the distance:

    _____ _____ .

19. Dimmer, or shaded, objects seem farther away:

    _____ _____

    _____ .

20. The brain interprets a rapid series of slightly varying images as _____ . This phenomenon is called _____

    _____ .

21. The illusion of movement that results when two adjacent stationary spots of light blink on and off in quick succession is called the

_____ _____ .

22. Our tendency to see objects as unchanging while the stimuli from them change in size, shape, and lightness is called _____

_____ .

23. Several illusions, including the

_____ , _____ , and

_____-_____ illu-

sions, are explained by the interplay between per-

ceived _____ and perceived

_____ . When distance cues are

removed, these illusions are

_____ (diminished/strengthened).

Explain how the size-distance relationship accounts for the moon illusion.

24. People who have lived their lives in uncarpentered rural environments are _____ (more/less) susceptible to the Müller-Lyer illusion.

25. The brain computes an object's brightness _____ (relative to/independent of) surrounding objects. The amount of light an object reflects relative to its surroundings is called

_____ _____ .

Perceptual Interpretation (pp. 226–234)

> If you do not know the meaning of any of the following words, phrases, or expressions in the context in which they appear in the text, refer to page 190 for an explanation: *Ping-Pong ball; we may feel slightly disoriented and dizzy; to see is to believe . . . to believe is to see; a "monster" in Scotland's Loch Ness; from what's behind our eyes and between our ears; in the eyes of their beholders.*

Section Preview

Answer guidelines are provided on page 182.

1. Briefly describe the nature-nurture debate on the origins of perception.

2. Discuss research findings on sensory deprivation and restored vision.

3. Explain what the use of distorting goggles indicates regarding the adaptability of perception.

4. Discuss the effects of experiences, assumptions, expectations, schemas, and contexts on our perceptions.

Stepping Through the Section

Answers are provided on page 182.

1. The idea that knowledge comes from inborn ways of organizing sensory experiences was proposed by the philosopher _____ .

2. On the other side were philosophers who maintained that we learn to perceive the world by experiencing it. One philosopher of this school was _____ .

3. Studies of cases in which vision has been restored to a person who was blind from birth show that, upon *seeing* tactilely familiar objects for the first time, the person _____ (can/ cannot) recognize them.

4. Studies of sensory restriction demonstrate that visual experiences during _____ are crucial for perceptual development. Such experiences suggest that there is a _____ _____ for normal sensory and perceptual development. For this reason, human infants born with an opaque lens, called a _____ , typically have corrective surgery right away.

Summarize the results of Blakemore and Cooper's studies of visual deprivation in kittens.

5. Humans given glasses that shift or invert the visual field _____ (will/will not) adapt to the distorted perception. This is called _____ _____ .

6. A mental predisposition that influences perception is called a _____ _____ .

7. Through experience, people acquire perceptual _____ , as reflected in children's drawings at different ages.

8. How a stimulus is perceived depends on our perceptual schemas and the _____ in which it is experienced, which may be colored by _____ about gender or culture.

9. (Close-Up) Psychologists who study the importance of considering perceptual principles in the design of machines, appliances, and work settings are called _____ _____ .

Is There Extrasensory Perception? (pp. 201–205)

> If you do not know the meaning of any of the following words, phrases, or expressions in the context in which they appear in the text, refer to pages 190–191 for an explanation: *The media overflow with reports of psychic wonders; uncanny; one more dashed hope; clearing the decks; unsatisfied hunger . . . an itch.*

Section Preview

Answer guidelines are provided on page 182.

1. State the claims of ESP, and explain why most research psychologists remain skeptical.

Stepping Through the Section

Answers are provided on page 183.

1. Perception outside the range of normal sensation is called _____ _____ .

2. Psychologists who study ESP are called _____ .

3. The form of ESP in which people claim to be capable of reading others' minds is called _____ . A person who "senses" that a friend is in danger might claim to have the ESP ability of _____ . An ability to "see" into the future is called _____ . A person who claims to be able to levitate and move objects is claiming the power of _____ .

4. Analyses of psychic visions and premonitions reveal _____ (high/chance-level) accuracy. Nevertheless, some people continue to believe in their accuracy, because vague predictions often are later _____ to match events that have already occurred. In addition, people are more likely to recall or

_____ dreams that seem to have come true.

5. Critics point out that a major difficulty for parapsychology is that ESP phenomena are not consistently _____ .

6. Researchers Bem and Honorton used the _____ procedure to reduce external distractions between a "sender" and a "receiver" in an ESP experiment. Although these researchers reported performance levels that _____ (beat/did not beat) chance levels, a more recent analysis of 30 follow-up studies found _____ (no effect/a reliable effect). .

Progress Test 1

Multiple-Choice Questions

Circle your answers to the following questions and check them with the answers on page 183. If your answer is incorrect, read the explanation for why it is incorrect and then consult the appropriate pages of the text (in parentheses following the correct answer).

1. The historical movement associated with the statement "The whole may exceed the sum of its parts" is:
   a. parapsychology.
   b. behavioral psychology.
   c. functional psychology.
   d. Gestalt psychology.

2. Figures tend to be perceived as whole, complete objects, even if spaces or gaps exist in the representation, thus demonstrating the principle of:
   a. connectedness.
   b. similarity.
   c. continuity.
   d. proximity.
   e. closure.

3. The figure-ground relationship has demonstrated that:
   a. perception is largely innate.
   b. perception is simply a point-for-point representation of sensation.
   c. the same stimulus can trigger more than one perception.
   d. different people see different things when viewing a scene.

4. When we stare at an object, each eye receives a slightly different image, providing a depth cue known as:
   a. convergence.
   b. linear perspective.
   c. relative motion.
   d. retinal disparity.

5. As we move, viewed objects cast changing shapes on our retinas, although we do not perceive the objects as changing. This is part of the phenomenon of:
   a. perceptual constancy.
   b. relative motion.
   c. linear perspective.
   d. continuity.

6. Which of the following illustrates the principle of visual capture?
   a. We tend to form first impressions of other people on the basis of appearance.
   b. Because visual processing is automatic, we can pay attention to a visual image and any other sensation at the same time.
   c. We cannot simultaneously attend to a visual image and another sensation.
   d. When there is a conflict between visual information and that from another sense, vision tends to dominate.

7. A person claiming to be able to read another's mind is claiming to have the ESP ability of:
   a. psychokinesis.
   b. precognition.
   c. clairvoyance.
   d. telepathy.

8. Which philosopher maintained that knowledge comes from inborn ways of organizing our sensory experiences?
   a. Locke
   b. Kant
   c. Gibson
   d. Walk
   e. Neisser

9. Which of the following was *not* mentioned in the text as a criticism of parapsychology?
   a. ESP effects have not been consistently reproducible.
   b. Parapsychology has suffered from a number of frauds and hoaxes.
   c. The tendency of people to recall only events that confirm their expectations accounts for much of the belief in ESP.
   d. There have been no laboratory-controlled studies of ESP.

10. Which of the following depth cues creates the impression of a visual cliff?
    a. interposition
    b. relative height
    c. linear perspective
    d. texture gradient
    e. relative clarity

11. Kittens reared seeing only horizontal lines:
   a. later had difficulty perceiving both horizontal and vertical lines.
   b. later had difficulty perceiving vertical lines, but eventually regained normal sensitivity.
   c. later had difficulty perceiving vertical lines, and never regained normal sensitivity.
   d. showed no impairment in perception, indicating that neural feature detectors develop even in the absence of normal sensory experiences.

12. Adults who are born blind but later have their vision restored:
   a. are almost immediately able to recognize familiar objects.
   b. typically fail to recognize familiar objects.
   c. are unable to follow moving objects with their eyes.
   d. have excellent eye-hand coordination.

13. _____ processing refers to how the physical characteristics of stimuli influence their interpretation.
   a. Top-down
   b. Bottom-up
   c. Parapsychological
   d. Human factors

14. Which of the following is *not* a monocular depth cue?
   a. texture gradient
   b. relative height
   c. retinal disparity
   d. interposition
   e. light and shadow

15. The moon illusion occurs in part because distance cues at the horizon make the moon seem:
   a. farther away and therefore larger.
   b. closer and therefore larger.
   c. farther away and therefore smaller.
   d. closer and therefore smaller.

16. Figure is to ground as _____ is to _____ .
   a. night; day
   b. top; bottom
   c. cloud; sky
   d. sensation; perception

17. The study of perception is primarily concerned with how we:
   a. detect sights, sounds, and other stimuli.
   b. sense environmental stimuli.
   c. develop sensitivity to illusions.
   d. interpret sensory stimuli.

18. Which of the following influences perception?
   a. biological maturation
   b. the context in which stimuli are perceived
   c. expectations
   d. all of the above

19. Jack claims that he often has dreams that predict future events. He claims to have the power of:
   a. telepathy.
   b. clairvoyance.
   c. precognition.
   d. psychokinesis.

20. Using the ganzfeld procedure to investigate telepathy, researchers have found that:
   a. when external distractions are reduced, both the "sender" and the "receiver" become much more accurate in demonstrating ESP.
   b. Only "senders" become much more accurate.
   c. Only "receivers" become much more accurate.
   d. Over many studies, none of the above occur.

True-False Items

Indicate whether each statement is true or false by placing *T* or *F* in the blank next to the item.

_____ 1. Once we perceive an item as a figure, it is impossible to see it as ground.

_____ 2. Laboratory experiments have laid to rest all criticisms of ESP.

_____ 3. Six-month-old infants will cross a visual cliff if their mother calls.

_____ 4. Unlike other animals, humans have no critical period for visual stimulation.

_____ 5. Immanuel Kant argued that experience determined how we perceive the world.

_____ 6. People who live in a carpentered world are more likely than others to experience the Müller-Lyer illusion.

_____ 7. After a period of time, humans are able to adjust to living in a world made upside down by distorting goggles.

_____ 8. As different lights reflect off an object, the hue of the object seems to change.

_____ 9. Perception is influenced by psychological factors such as set and expectation as well as by physiological events.

_____ 10. John Locke argued that perception is inborn.

Progress Test 2

Progress Test 2 should be completed during a final chapter review. Answer the following questions after you thoroughly understand the correct answers for the section reviews and Progress Test 1.

1. The tendency to organize stimuli into smooth, uninterrupted patterns is called:
   a. closure.
   b. continuity.
   c. similarity.
   d. proximity.
   e. connectedness.

2. Which of the following is a monocular depth cue?
   a. light and shadow
   b. convergence
   c. retinal disparity
   d. All of the above are monocular depth cues.

3. Which of the following statements is consistent with the Gestalt theory of perception?
   a. Perception develops largely through learning.
   b. Perception is the product of heredity.
   c. The mind organizes sensations into meaningful perceptions.
   d. Perception results directly from sensation.

4. Experiments with distorted visual environments demonstrate that:
   a. adaptation rarely takes place.
   b. animals adapt readily, but humans do not.
   c. humans adapt readily, while lower animals typically do not.
   d. adaptation is possible during a critical period in infancy but not thereafter.

5. The phenomenon that refers to the ways in which an individual's expectations influence perception is called:
   a. perceptual set.
   b. retinal disparity.
   c. convergence.
   d. visual capture.

6. (Close-Up) Psychologists who study the importance of considering perceptual phenomena in the design of machines and work settings are called:
   a. parapsychologists.
   b. human factors psychologists.
   c. psychokineticists.
   d. Gestalt psychologists.

7. According to the philosopher _____ , we learn to perceive the world.
   a. Locke
   b. Kant
   c. Gibson
   d. Walk
   e. Neisser

8. The tendency to perceive hazy objects as being at a distance is known as _____ . This is a _____ depth cue.
   a. linear perspective; binocular
   b. linear perspective; monocular
   c. relative clarity; binocular
   d. relative clarity; monocular

9. The phenomenon of size constancy is based upon the close connection between an object's perceived _____ and its perceived _____ .
   a. size; shape
   b. size; distance
   c. size; brightness
   d. shape; distance
   e. shape; brightness

10. Which of the following statements best describes the effects of sensory restriction?
    a. It produces functional blindness when experienced for any length of time at any age.
    b. It has greater effects on humans than on animals.
    c. It has more damaging effects when experienced during infancy.
    d. It has greater effects on adults than on children.

11. Psychologists who study ESP are called:
    a. clairvoyants.
    b. telepaths.
    c. parapsychologists.
    d. levitators.

12. The depth cue that occurs when we watch stable objects at different distances as we are moving is:
    a. convergence.
    b. interposition.
    c. relative clarity.
    d. relative motion.

13. Which of the following statements concerning ESP is true?
    a. Most ESP researchers are quacks.
    b. There have been a large number of reliable demonstrations of ESP.
    c. Most research psychologists are skeptical of the claims of defenders of ESP.
    d. There have been reliable laboratory demonstrations of ESP, but the results are no different from those that would occur by chance.

14. Each time you see your car, it projects a different image on the retinas of your eyes, yet you do not perceive it as changing. This is because of:
    a. perceptual set.
    b. retinal disparity.
    c. perceptual constancy.
    d. convergence.

15. The term *gestalt* means:
    a. grouping.   d. whole.
    b. sensation.   e. visual capture.
    c. perception.

16. People asked to judge the distances of white disks under either clear or foggy conditions:
    a. estimated the disks to be more distant when viewed under clear conditions.
    b. estimated the disks to be nearer when viewed under clear conditions.
    c. took atmospheric conditions into consideration and judged the disks to be equally distant under the two viewing conditions.
    d. were much less accurate under foggy conditions.

17. Studies of the visual cliff have provided evidence that much of depth perception is:
    a. innate.
    b. learned.
    c. innate in lower animals, learned in humans.
    d. innate in humans, learned in lower animals.

18. All of the following are laws of perceptual organization *except*:
    a. proximity.   d. connectedness.
    b. closure.   e. simplicity.
    c. continuity.

    ●-● ● ● ●-●

19. You probably perceive the diagram above as three separate objects due to the principle of:
    a. proximity.   c. closure.
    b. continuity.   d. connectedness.

20. _____ processing refers to how our knowledge and expectations influence perception.
    a. Top-down   c. Parapsychological
    b. Bottom-up   d. Human factors

Thinking Critically About Chapter 6

Answer these questions the day before an exam as a final check on your understanding of the chapter's terms and concepts.

Multiple-Choice Questions

1. Although carpenter Smith perceived a briefly viewed object as a screwdriver, police officer Wesson perceived the same object as a knife. This illustrates that perception is guided by:
   a. linear perspective.   d. perceptual set.
   b. shape constancy.   e. convergence.
   c. retinal disparity.

2. Because the flowers in the foreground appeared coarse and grainy, the photographer decided that the picture was taken too near the subject. This conclusion was based on which depth cue?
   a. relative size   c. retinal disparity
   b. interposition   d. texture gradient

3. The fact that a white object under dim illumination appears lighter than a gray object under bright illumination is called:
   a. relative luminance.
   b. perceptual adaptation.
   c. color contrast.
   d. lightness constancy.

4. When two familiar objects of equal size cast unequal retinal images, the object that casts the smaller retinal image will be perceived as being:
   a. closer than the other object.
   b. more distant than the other object.
   c. larger than the other object.
   d. smaller than the other object.

5. If you slowly bring your finger toward your face until it eventually touches your nose, eye-muscle cues called _____ convey depth information to your brain.
   a. retinal disparity   d. proximity
   b. interposition   e. convergence
   c. continuity

6. Concluding her presentation on sensation and perception, Kelly notes that:
   a. sensation is bottom-up processing.
   b. perception is top-down processing.
   c. a. and b. are both true.
   d. sensation and perception blend into one continuous process.

7. As her friend Milo walks toward her, Noriko perceives his size as remaining constant because his perceived distance _____ at the same time that her retinal image of him _____ .
   a. increases; decreases
   b. increases; increases
   c. decreases; decreases
   d. decreases; increases

8. In the *absence* of perceptual constancy:
   a. objects would appear to change size as their distance from us changed.
   b. depth perception would be based exclusively on monocular cues.
   c. depth perception would be based exclusively on binocular cues.
   d. depth perception would be impossible.

9. The illusion that the St. Louis Gateway arch appears taller than it is wide (even though its height and width are equal) is based on our sensitivity to which monocular depth cue?
   a. relative size
   b. interposition
   c. relative height
   d. retinal disparity

10. How do we perceive a pole that partially covers a bush?
    a. as farther away
    b. as nearer
    c. as larger
    d. There is not enough information to determine the object's size or distance.

11. An artist paints a tree orchard so that the parallel rows of trees converge at the top of the canvas. Which cue has the artist used to convey distance?
    a. interposition
    b. relative clarity
    c. linear perspective
    d. texture gradient

12. Objects higher in our field of vision are perceived as _____ due to the principle of _____ .
    a. nearer; relative height
    b. nearer; linear perspective
    c. farther away; relative height
    d. farther away; linear perspective

13. According to the principle of light and shadow, if one of two identical objects reflects more light to your eyes it will be perceived as:
    a. larger.
    b. smaller.
    c. farther away.
    d. nearer.

14. Your friend tosses you a frisbee. You know that it is getting closer instead of larger because of:
    a. shape constancy.
    b. relative motion.
    c. size constancy.
    d. all of the above.

15. Which explanation of the Müller-Lyer illusion is offered by the text?
    a. The corners in our carpentered world teach us to interpret outward- or inward-pointing arrowheads at the end of a line as a cue to the line's distance from us and so to its length.
    b. The drawing's violation of linear perspective makes one line seem longer.
    c. Top-down processing of the illusion is prevented because of the stimuli's ambiguity.
    d. All of the above were offered as explanations.

16. When the traffic light changed from red to green, the drivers on both sides of Leon's vehicle pulled quickly forward, giving Leon the disorienting feeling that his car was rolling backward. Which principle explains Leon's misperception?

    a. relative motion
    b. continuity
    c. visual capture
    d. proximity

17. Regina claims that she can bend spoons, levitate furniture, and perform many other "mind over matter" feats. Regina apparently believes she has the power of:
    a. telepathy.
    b. clairvoyance.
    c. precognition.
    d. psychokinesis.

18. The predictions of leading psychics are:
    a. often ambiguous prophecies later interpreted to match actual events.
    b. no more accurate than guesses made by others.
    c. nearly always inaccurate.
    d. all of the above.

19. Studying the road map before her trip, Colleen had no trouble following the route of the highway she planned to travel. Colleen's ability illustrates the principle of:
    a. closure.
    b. similarity.
    c. continuity.
    d. proximity.
    e. connectedness.

20. The insensitivity of many rural Africans to the Müller-Lyer illusion proves that perception:
    a. is largely a "bottom-up" phenomenon.
    b. is unpredictable.
    c. is influenced by cultural experience.
    d. is characterized by all of the above.

Essay Question

In many movies from the 1930s, dancers performed seemingly meaningless movements which, when viewed from above, were transformed into intricate patterns and designs. Similarly, the formations of marching bands often create pictures and spell words. Identify and describe at least four Gestalt principles of grouping that explain the audience's perception of the images created by these types of formations. (Use the space below to list the points you want to make, and organize them. Then write the essay on a separate piece of paper.)

Key Terms

Writing Definitions

Using your own words, on a separate piece of paper write a brief definition or explanation of each of the following terms.

1. selective attention

2. visual capture

3. gestalt

4. figure-ground relationship

5. grouping

6. depth perception

7. visual cliff

8. binocular cue

9. monocular cue

10. retinal disparity

11. convergence

12. phi phenomenon

13. perceptual constancy

14. perceptual adaptation

15. perceptual set

16. extrasensory perception (ESP)

17. parapsychology

Cross-Check

As you learned in the Introduction, reviewing and overlearning of material are important to the learning process. After you have written the definitions of the key terms in this chapter, you should complete the crossword puzzle to ensure that you can reverse the process—recognize the term, given the definition.

ACROSS

1. Part of the visual field that surrounds the figure.
8. The tendency to perceive the convergence of parallel lines as indicating decreasing distance is the _____ perspective.
13. Depth cues that depend on information from both eyes.
15. Principle that we tend to group stimuli that are near one another.
16. Part of the visual field that stands out from its surroundings.
17. Philosopher who believed that all knowledge arises from experience.
18. Perceptual tendency to fill in incomplete figures to create the perception of a whole object.
19. Process by which we tend to organize stimuli in order to arrive at meaningful forms.
20. Means "organized whole."

DOWN

2. Figure-ground relationships are often _____ .
3. Creating three-dimensional perceptions from the two-dimensional images that strike the retina requires _____ perception.
4. The ability to attend to only one voice among many is the _____ effect.
5. Because of _____ attention, we focus our awareness on only a limited aspect of all that we are capable of experiencing.
6. Illusion of movement created by adjacent lights that blink off and on in succession.
7. Classic visual illusion involving the perception of line length.
9. Depth cue in which nearby objects partially obscure more distant objects.
10. The amount of light an object reflects relative to its surroundings.
11. Tendency of distant objects to appear hazier than nearer objects.
12. Gestalt principle that we perceive uniform and linked spots, lines, or areas as a single unit.
14. The irreversible effects of sensory restriction during infancy suggest the existence of a _____ for normal sensory and perceptual development.

Answers

Selective Attention and Perceptual Illusions

Section Previews

1. Although we are constantly being bombarded by various stimuli, we attend to only some of them at any one time. Thus, we have *selective attention*, which determines the stimuli we perceive. An example is the cocktail party effect, whereby we attend to only one voice among many. This ability, which we demonstrate in each of our senses, prevents us from becoming overwhelmed by the immense array of stimuli that bombard our senses at any moment.

2. Understanding illusions requires an understanding of how we transform sensations into mean-

ingful perceptions. Thus, for example, psychologists have learned a great deal about the interplay of size and distance from the Müller-Lyer illusion, about the principle of relative height from the horizontal-vertical illusion, and about principles of grouping and depth perception from the study of other illusions.

Stepping Through the Sections

1. Plato
2. selective attention; cocktail party effect
3. visual capture

Perceptual Organization

Section Preview

1. The Gestalt psychologists demonstrated that perception involves the organization of sensations into meaningful wholes, or gestalts, that may exceed the sum of their individual parts and be regrouped into more than one perception. They also showed that to recognize an object, we must first perceive it as a figure distinct from its surrounding stimuli, or ground. The Gestalt psychologists identified several principles by which sensations are organized into meaningful perceptions; these include proximity, similarity, continuity, closure, and connectedness.

2. The visual cliff is a miniature cliff with an apparent drop-off on one side of a table. Gibson and Walk found that infants as young as 6 months of age refused to crawl out on the glass, despite their mother's coaxing. Newborn animals with virtually no visual experience respond similarly, thus indicating that the ability to perceive depth is at least partly innate.

3. Three-dimensional movies create the impression of depth by simulating retinal disparity. Each scene is photographed with two cameras placed a few inches apart. Viewers wear spectacles that allow each eye to see only the image from one camera. The perceived depth occurs as each eye focuses on one of the two-dimensional images and the brain integrates them in a single 3-D image.

    The binocular (two-eye) cues to depth include retinal disparity and convergence, and the monocular (one-eye) cues to depth include relative size, interposition, relative clarity, texture gradient, relative height, relative motion, linear perspective, and light and shadow.

4. Thanks to perceptual constancy we perceive familiar objects as having a constant form (shape constancy), size (size constancy), and brightness (lightness or brightness constancy), even when our retinal images of them change.

    There is a close interplay between an object's perceived size and its distance. As the retinal image of a familiar object decreases, we perceive its distance as increasing rather than that its size has changed. This size-distance relationship partially explains the "moon illusion": Cues to objects' distances at the horizon make the moon behind them seem farther away, and seemingly larger, than when high in the sky. Similarly, one explanation of the Müller-Lyer illusion is that our experience with corners in our rectangularly carpentered world leads us to interpret a line segment ending in outward-pointing arrowheads as closer to us and therefore shorter than a line segment that ends in inward-pointing arrowheads.

Stepping Through the Section

1. Gestalt; whole; Necker
2. bottom-up; top-down; experiences; expectations; fuzzy
3. figure; ground

The Gestalt psychologists described some key principles of perceptual organization and, in so doing, demonstrated that perception is far more than a simple sensory process. The reversible figure-ground relationship, for example, demonstrates that a single stimulus can trigger more than one perception. As Gestalt psychologists showed, we continually filter sensory information and construct our perceptions in ways that make sense to us.

4. grouping
5. continuity; closure; proximity; similarity; connectedness
6. depth perception
7. visual cliff

Research on the visual cliff suggests that in many species the ability to perceive depth is present at, or very shortly after, birth.

8. binocular
9. monocular
10. retinal disparity; two; perceptions; brains
11. convergence
12. interposition
13. relative size
14. relative clarity
15. texture gradient

16. relative height

17. relative motion (motion parallax)

18. linear perspective

19. light and shadow

20. movement; stroboscopic movement

21. phi phenomenon

22. perceptual constancy

23. moon; Ponzo; Müller-Lyer; size; distance; diminished

A partial reason for the illusion that the moon at the horizon appears up to 50 percent larger than the moon directly overhead is that cues to the distance of objects at the horizon make the moon, behind them, seem farther away and therefore larger. When we see the moon overhead in the sky, these misleading cues are lacking.

24. less

25. relative to; relative luminance

Perceptual Interpretation

Section Preview

1. On one side of the nature-nurture debate, the German philosopher Immanuel Kant maintained that knowledge comes from our inborn ways of organizing sensory experiences. On the other side, the British philosopher John Locke argued that we learn how to perceive the world through our experiences of it.

2. In both humans and animals, infancy is a critical period during which normal visual stimulation must be experienced. Adults blinded with cataracts from birth, who later have their vision restored, are able to perceive figure, ground, and colors but are severely limited in their ability to recognize objects that were familiar by touch. Kittens and monkeys who were outfitted with goggles since infancy had similar visual impairments when the goggles were removed. Kittens raised in a restricted visual environment that allowed them to see only horizontal lines later had difficulty perceiving vertical lines. Research also shows that early visual experience is critical to the normal development of the feature detector cells of the brain.

3. Studies in which people and animals are given goggles that shift the world to the left, right, or even upside down demonstrate that vision is remarkably adaptable. After a relatively brief period of adjustment, most subjects are able to function normally in the distorted visual environment (chicks, fish, frogs, and salamanders, however, cannot adapt). When the goggles are first removed, subjects experience a brief perceptual aftereffect, as their perceptual systems continue to compensate for the shifted visual input.

4. Experiences, assumptions, expectations, schemas, and contexts may give us a perceptual set, or mental predisposition, that influences what we perceive. Perceptual sets, which are based on the concepts, or schemas, that we form through our experiences, help us organize and interpret unfamiliar or ambiguous information.

   The immediate context of a stimulus also influences how it is perceived. For example, a person or object is more quickly recognized in an expected context than in a novel one. The effects of context and perceptual sets show how our experiences help us to construct meaningful perceptions from our sensory experiences.

Stepping Through the Section

1. Kant

2. Locke

3. cannot

4. infancy; critical period; cataract

After raising kittens in darkness, except 5 hours each day during which the kittens were placed in a horizontally or vertically striped environment, Blakemore and Cooper found that perceptual impairment resulted. In particular, the kittens had difficulty perceiving the kind of line—horizontal or vertical—to which they had not been exposed. Moreover, in these kittens, feature-detecting cells were found to respond mostly to one or the other kind of line.

5. will; perceptual adaptation

6. perceptual set

7. schemas

8. context; stereotypes

9. human factors psychologists

Is There Extrasensory Perception?

Section Preview

1. Extrasensory perception refers to the controversial claim that perception can occur outside sensory input. Telepathy is the claimed ability of mind-to-mind communication between two people. Precognition refers to the claimed ability to perceive future events. Clairvoyance refers to the claimed ability to perceive remote events. Psychokinesis refers to the claimed ability to perform acts of "mind over matter."

   Despite the efforts of parapsychologists to

document ESP, most research psychologists argue that many so-called psychic demonstrations are nothing more than deceptive illusions that any magician could perform and that no one has ever discovered a reproducible ESP phenomenon.

Stepping Through the Section

1. extrasensory perception
2. parapsychologists
3. telepathy; clairvoyance; precognition; psychokinesis
4. chance-level; interpreted (retrofitted); reconstruct
5. reproducible
6. ganzfeld; beat; no effect

Progress Test 1

Multiple-Choice Questions

1. **d.** is the answer. Gestalt psychology, which developed in Germany at the turn of the twentieth century, was interested in how clusters of sensations are organized into "whole" perceptions. (p. 213)
   a. Parapsychology is the study of ESP and other paranormal phenomena.
   b. & c. Behavioral and functional psychology developed later in the United States.

2. **e.** is the answer. (p. 215)
   a. Connectedness refers to the tendency to see uniform and linked items as a unit.
   b. Similarity refers to the tendency to group similar items.
   c. Continuity refers to the tendency to group stimuli into smooth, continuous patterns.
   d. Proximity refers to the tendency to group items that are close to each other.

3. **c.** is the answer. Although we always differentiate a stimulus into figure and ground, those elements of the stimulus we perceive as figure and those as ground may change. In this way, the same stimulus can trigger more than one perception. (p. 214)
   a. The idea of a figure-ground relationship has no bearing on the issue of whether perception is innate.
   b. Perception cannot be simply a point-for-point representation of sensation, since in figure-ground relationships a single stimulus can trigger more than one perception.
   d. Figure-ground relationships demonstrate the existence of general, rather than individual, prin-

ciples of perceptual organization. Significantly, even the same person can see different figure-ground relationships when viewing a scene.

4. **d.** is the answer. The greater the retinal disparity, or difference between the images, the less the distance. (p. 216)
   a. Convergence is the extent to which the eyes move inward when looking at an object.
   b. Linear perspective is the monocular distance cue in which parallel lines appear to converge in the distance.
   c. Relative motion is the monocular distance cue in which objects at different distances change their relative positions in our visual image, with those closest moving most.

5. **a.** is the answer. Perception of constant shape, like perception of constant size, is part of the phenomenon of perceptual constancy. (p. 221)
   b. Relative motion is a monocular distance cue in which objects at different distances appear to move at different rates.
   c. Linear perspective is a monocular distance cue in which lines we know to be parallel converge in the distance, thus indicating depth.
   d. Continuity is the perceptual tendency to group items into continuous patterns.

6. **d.** is the answer. (p. 213)
   a., b., & c. Visual capture has nothing to do with forming impressions of people or whether we can attend to more than one stimulus at a time.

7. **d.** is the answer. (p. 234)
   a. Psychokinesis refers to the claimed ability to perform acts of "mind over matter."
   b. Precognition refers to the claimed ability to perceive future events.
   c. Clairvoyance refers to the claimed ability to perceive remote events.

8. **b.** is the answer. (p. 226)
   a. Locke argued that knowledge is not inborn but comes through learning.
   c. & d. Gibson and Walk studied depth perception using the visual cliff; they made no claims about the source of knowledge.
   e. Neisser studied selective attention.

9. **d.** is the answer. As discussed in the text, parapsychologists have conducted numerous experiments with both "psychic" and "normal" subjects. (pp. 236–238)
   a., b., & c. These are all valid criticisms of parapsychology mentioned in the text.

10. **d.** is the answer. There is, of course, no actual drop-off. The texture gradient of the checkerboard pattern beneath the glass table imparts the

impression of depth. The other cues mentioned would not be relevant to the situation in this experiment. (pp. 215, 218)

11. **c.** is the answer. (p. 227)
   a. & b. The kittens had difficulty only with lines they had never experienced, and never regained normal sensitivity.
   d. Both perceptual and feature-detector impairment resulted from visual deprivation.

12. **b.** is the answer. Because they have not had early visual experiences, these adults typically have difficulty learning to perceive objects. (p. 226)
   a. Such patients typically could not visually recognize objects with which they were familiar by touch, and in some cases this inability persisted.
   c. Being able to perceive figure-ground relationships, patients *are* able to follow moving objects with their eyes.
   d. This answer is incorrect because eye-hand coordination is an acquired skill and requires much practice.

13. **b.** is the answer. (p. 214)
   a. Top-down processing refers to how our knowledge and expectations influence perception.
   c. Parapsychology is the study of perception outside normal sensory input.
   d. Human factors psychology is concerned with how best to design machines and work settings to take into account human perception.

14. **c.** is the answer. Retinal disparity is a *binocular* cue; all the other cues mentioned are monocular. (pp. 216–218)

15. **a.** is the answer. The moon appears larger at the horizon than overhead in the sky because objects at the horizon provide distance cues that make the moon seem farther away and therefore larger. In the open sky, of course, there are no such cues. (p. 222)

16. **c.** is the answer. We see a cloud as a figure against the background of sky. (p. 214)
   a., b., & d. The figure-ground relationship refers to the organization of the visual field into objects (figures) that stand out from their surroundings (ground).

17. **d.** is the answer. (p. 209)
   a. & b. The study of sensation is concerned with these processes.
   c. Although studying illusions has helped psychologists understand ordinary perceptual mechanisms, it is not the primary focus of the field of perception.

18. **d.** is the answer. (pp. 228–230)

19. **c.** is the answer. (p. 234)
   a. This answer would be correct had Jack claimed to be able to read someone else's mind.
   b. This answer would be correct had Jack claimed to be able to sense remote events, such as a friend in distress.
   d. This answer would be correct had Jack claimed to be able to levitate objects or bend spoons without applying any physical force.

20. **d.** is the answer. (p. 237)
   a. The experiment involved written numerals, not thoughts.
   c. The experiment did not require students to "see the future."
   d. The experiment had nothing to do with the mental manipulation of matter.

True-False Items

1. F (p. 214)   5. F (p. 226)   8. F (p. 224)
2. F (p. 237)   6. T (p. 222)   9. T (pp. 228–230)
3. F (p. 215)   7. T (p. 228)   10. F (p. 226)
4. F (p. 227)

Progress Test 2

1. **b.** is the answer. (p. 215)
   a. Closure refers to the tendency to perceptually fill in gaps in recognizable objects in the visual field.
   c. Similarity refers to the tendency to group items that are similar.
   d. Proximity refers to the tendency to group items that are near one another.
   e. Connectedness refers to the tendency to group uniform and linked items.

2. **a.** is the answer. (p. 217)
   b. & c. Convergence and retinal disparity are both binocular cues that depend on information from both eyes.

3. **c.** is the answer. (p. 213)
   a. & b. The Gestalt psychologists did not deal with the origins of perception; they were more concerned with its form.
   d. In fact, they argued just the opposite: Perception is more than mere sensory experience.

4. **c.** is the answer. Humans and certain animals, such as monkeys, are able to adjust to upside-down worlds and other visual distortions, figuring out the relationship between the perceived and the actual reality; lower animals, such as chickens and fish, are typically unable to adapt. (pp. 227–228)

a. Humans and certain animals are able to adapt quite well to distorted visual environments (and then to readapt).

b. This answer is incorrect because humans are the most adaptable of creatures.

d. Humans are able to adapt at any age to distorted visual environments.

5. **a.** is the answer. (p. 228)

b. Retinal disparity is a binocular depth cue based on the fact that each eye receives a slightly different view of the world.

c. Convergence is a binocular depth cue based on the fact that the eyes swing inward to focus on near objects.

d. Visual capture refers to the tendency of vision to dominate the other senses.

6. **b.** is the answer. (p. 233)

a. Parapsychologists study claims of ESP.

c. Psychokineticists are people who claim ESP has the power of "mind over matter."

d. Gestalt psychologists emphasize the organization of sensations into meaningful perceptions.

7. **a.** is the answer. (p. 226)

b. Kant claimed that knowledge is inborn.

c. & d. Gibson and Walk make no claims about the origins of perception.

e. Neisser studied selective attention.

8. **d.** is the answer. (p. 217)

a. & b. Linear perspective, which is a monocular cue, refers to the tendency of parallel lines to converge in the distance.

c. Relative clarity requires only one eye and is therefore a monocular cue.

9. **b.** is the answer. (p. 221)

10. **c.** is the answer. There appears to be a critical period for perceptual development, in that sensory restriction has severe, even permanently, disruptive effects when it occurs in infancy but not when it occurs later in life. (p. 226)

a. & d. Sensory restriction does not have the same effects at all ages, and it is more damaging to children than to adults. This is because there is a critical period for perceptual development; whether functional blindness will result depends in part on the nature of the sensory restriction.

b. Research studies have not indicated that sensory restriction is more damaging to humans than to animals.

11. **c.** is the answer. (p. 234)

a., b., & d. These psychics claim to exhibit the phenomena studied by parapsychologists.

12. **d.** is the answer. When we move, stable objects we see also appear to move, and the distance and speed of the apparent motion cue us to the objects' relative distances. (p. 218)

a., b., & c. These depth cues are unrelated to movement and thus work even when we are stationary.

13. **c.** is the answer. (p. 234)

a. Many ESP researchers are sincere, reputable researchers.

b. & d. There have been no reliable demonstrations of ESP.

14. **c.** is the answer. Because of perceptual constancy, we see the car's shape and size as always the same. (p. 221)

a. Perceptual set is a mental predisposition to perceive one thing and not another.

b. Retinal disparity means that our right and left eyes each receive slightly different images.

d. Convergence is a form of neuromuscular feedback in which the eyes swing in, or out, as we view objects at different distances.

15. **d.** is the answer. Gestalt means a "form" or "organized whole." (p. 213)

16. **b.** is the answer. We perceive hazy objects as farther away than sharp, clear objects: This cue to depth is relative clarity. (pp. 212, 217)

a. & c. The disks were estimated to be *nearer* when viewed under clear conditions.

d. As shown by the chart on p. 212, foggy conditions increase the perceived distance but by no means necessarily reduce accuracy.

17. **a.** is the answer. Most infants refused to crawl out over the "cliff" even when coaxed, suggesting that much of depth perception is innate. Studies with the young of "lower" animals show the same thing. (p. 215)

18. **e.** is the answer. (pp. 214–215)

19. **d.** is the answer. (p. 215)

a. Proximity is the tendency to group objects near to one another. The diagram is perceived as three distinct units, even though the points are evenly spaced.

b. Continuity is the tendency to group stimuli into smooth, uninterrupted patterns. There is no such continuity in the diagram.

c. Closure is the perceptual tendency to fill in gaps in a form. In the diagram, three disconnected units are perceived rather than a single whole.

20. **a.** is the answer. (p. 214)

b. Bottom-up processing refers to the physical characteristics of stimuli rather than their perceptual interpretation.

b. Had the artist painted the trees so that the images of some were sharp and others hazy, the artist would have been using relative clarity.

d. Had the artist painted the trees so that there was a gradual change from a coarse, distinct to a fine, indistinct texture, texture gradient would have been used to convey depth.

12. **c.** is the answer. (p. 218)

   b. & d. Linear perspective is the apparent convergence of parallel lines as a cue to distance.

13. **d.** is the answer. Nearby objects reflect more light to the eyes. Thus, given two identical objects, the brighter one seems nearer. (p. 218)

   a. & b. Because of the principle of size constancy, an object's perceived size is unaffected by its distance, angle of viewing, or illumination.

14. **c.** is the answer. This is an illustration of the size-distance relationship in depth perception. (p. 221)

   a. Although the frisbee's shape is perceived as constant (even as the shape of its retinal image changes), this is not a cue to its distance.

   b. Relative motion is the perception that when we move, stationary objects at different distances change their relative positions in our visual image, with those closest moving most. In this example, only the frisbee is moving.

15. **a.** is the answer. (pp. 222–223)

16. **c.** is the answer. Although Leon's other senses would have told him his car was not moving, the visual images of the other cars moving forward "captured" his awareness and created the perception that he was rolling backward. (p. 213)

   a. Relative motion is a distance cue that occurs when stationary objects appear to move as we move. Just the opposite is happening to Leon.

   b. & d. Continuity and proximity are Gestalt principles of grouping, rather than cues to distance.

17. **d.** is the answer. (p. 234)

   a. Telepathy is the claimed ability to "read" minds.

   b. Clairvoyance refers to the claimed ability to perceive remote events.

   c. Precognition refers to the claimed ability to perceive future events.

18. **d.** is the answer. (p. 235)

19. **c.** is the answer. She perceives the line for the road as continuous, even though it is interrupted by lines indicating other roads. (p. 215)

   a. Closure refers to the perceptual filling in of gaps in a stimulus to create a complete, whole object.

   b. Similarity is the tendency to perceive similar objects as belonging together. On a road map, all the lines representing roads appear similar. Thus, this cue could not be the basis for Colleen's ability to trace the route of a particular road.

   d. Proximity is the tendency to group objects near to one another as a single unit.

   e. Connectedness is the tendency to group linked items. In this case, the roads often are not clearly linked.

20. **c.** is the answer. (pp. 222–223)

   a. If perception were entirely based on the physical characteristics of a stimulus ("bottom-up"), lack of experience with a carpentered environment would not reduce sensitivity to the illusion.

   b. Principles of grouping, depth perception, and sensitivity to illusions all demonstrate that perception often *is* predictable.

Essay Question

1. *Proximity.* We tend to perceive items that are near each other as belonging together. Thus, a small section of dancers or members of a marching band may separate themselves from the larger group in order to form part of a particular image.

2. *Similarity.* Because we perceive similar figures as belonging together, choreographers and band directors often create distinct visual groupings within the larger band or dance troupe by having the members of each group wear a distinctive costume or uniform.

3. *Continuity.* Because we perceive smooth, continuous patterns rather than discontinuous ones, dancers or marching musicians moving together (as in a column, for example) are perceived as a separate unit.

4. *Closure.* If a figure has gaps, we complete it, filling in the gaps to create a whole image. Thus, we perceptually fill in the relatively wide spacing between dancers or marching musicians in order to perceive the complete words or forms they are creating.

Key Terms

Writing Definitions

1. **Selective attention** is the focusing of conscious awareness on a particular stimulus out of all of those that we are capable of experiencing. (p. 209)

2. **Visual capture** is the tendency for vision to dominate the other senses. (p. 213)

3. **Gestalt** means "organized whole." The Gestalt psychologists emphasized our tendency to integrate pieces of information into meaningful wholes. (p. 213)

4. The **figure-ground relationship** refers to the organization of the visual field into two parts: the figure, which stands out from its surroundings, and the surroundings, or background. (p. 214)

5. **Grouping** is the perceptual tendency to organize stimuli in order to arrive at meaningful forms. Gestalt psychologists identified various principles of grouping. (p. 214)

6. **Depth perception** is the ability to see objects in three dimensions although the images that strike the retina are two-dimensional; it allows us to judge distance. (p. 215)

7. The **visual cliff** is a laboratory device for testing depth perception, especially in infants and young animals. In their experiments with the visual cliff, Gibson and Walk found strong evidence that depth perception is at least in part innate. (p. 215)

8. **Binocular cues** are depth cues that depend on information from both eyes. (p. 216)

   Memory aid: *Bi-* indicates "two"; *ocular* means something pertaining to the eye. **Binocular cues** are cues for the "two eyes."

9. **Monocular cues** are depth cues that depend on information from either eye alone. (p. 216)

   Memory aid: *Mono-* means one; a monocle is an eyeglass for one eye. A **monocular cue** is one that is available to either the left or the right eye.

10. **Retinal disparity** refers to the differences between the images received by the left eye and the right eye as a result of viewing the world from slightly different angles. It is a binocular depth cue, since the greater the difference between the two images, the nearer the object. (p. 216)

11. **Convergence** is a neuromuscular binocular depth cue based on the extent to which the eyes converge, or turn inward, when looking at near or distant objects. The more the eyes converge, the nearer the objects. (p. 217)

12. The **phi phenomenon** is an illusion of movement created when two or more adjacent lights blink on and off in succession. (p. 220)

13. **Perceptual constancy** is the perception that objects have consistent lightness, color, shape, and size, even as illumination and retinal images change. (p. 220)

14. **Perceptual adaptation** refers to our ability to adjust to an artificially displaced or even inverted visual field. Given distorting lenses, we perceive things accordingly but soon adjust by learning the relationship between our distorted perceptions and the reality. (p. 227)

15. **Perceptual set** is a mental predisposition to perceive one thing and not another. (p. 228)

16. **Extrasensory perception (ESP)** refers to the controversial claim that perception can occur without sensory input. Supposed ESP powers include telepathy, clairvoyance, and precognition. (p. 234)

    Memory aid: *Extra-* means "beyond" or "in addition to"; **extrasensory perception** is perception outside or beyond the normal senses.

17. **Parapsychology** is the study of ESP, psychokinesis, and other paranormal forms of interaction between the individual and the environment. (p. 234)

    Memory aid: *Para-*, like *extra-*, indicates "beyond"; thus, paranormal is beyond the normal and **parapsychology** is the study of phenomena beyond the realm of psychology and known natural laws.

Cross-Check

ACROSS	DOWN
1. ground	**2.** reversible
8. linear	**3.** depth
13. binocular	**4.** cocktail party
15. proximity	**5.** selective
16. figure	**6.** phi phenomenon
17. Locke	**7.** Müller-Lyer
18. closure	**9.** interposition
19. grouping	**10.** relative luminance
20. gestalt	**11.** relative clarity
	12. connectedness
	14. critical period

FOCUS ON VOCABULARY AND LANGUAGE

Selective Attention and Perceptual Illusions

Page 209: Now, suddenly, *your attentional spotlight shifts.* Your *feet feel encased, your nose stubbornly intrudes on the page* before you. **Selective attention** refers to our tendency to focus on only a small part of what is possible for us to experience. If you do attend to more aspects of your experience (*your attentional spotlight shifts*), you will be surprised at the amount of stimulation you process without awareness, such as the feel of the shoes on your feet (*your feet feel encased*) and the fact that your nose actually blocks your line of vision (*your nose stubbornly intrudes on the page*).

Page 209: . . . *you may draw a blank* . . . This means that you achieve no result, you don't succeed. When you attend to only one voice among many (*the cocktail party effect*), you may be *unable to say* (*you may draw a blank*) what someone else was saying within hearing range of you.

Page 210: . . . a young woman carrying an umbrella *sauntered* across the screen (Figure 6.2). In this experiment, subjects had to watch a video of basketball players and signal when the ball was passed. Because of their intense selective attention, they generally failed to notice a female walking slowly (*sauntering*) through the players.

Page 213: . . . (much as we perceive a voice from *the ventriloquist's dummy*). A ventriloquist is an entertainer who makes the audience believe his voice is coming from a silent doll (*dummy*). Due to the phenomenon of **visual capture** we assume that because the doll's mouth is moving and the ventriloquist's is not, the voice is coming from the dummy.

Perceptual Organization

Page 213: There is far more to perception than meets the senses. As noted earlier, *"there is more to this than meets the eye"* is a common expression meaning something is going on beyond the obvious or the apparent. In this variation of the expression, Myers is noting that we create our own reality, not only from the incoming stimulation (sensations), but also by imposing organization and structure (perceptual processes) to create a greater reality (*there is far more to perception than meets the senses*).

Page 214: . . . *yen* . . . This means to have a desire or deep need (*yen*) to do something. Myers notes that our brain's desire (*yen*) to put together bits and pieces of sensory input into coherent units involves both "bottom-up" and "top-down" processing. We actively impose structure and infer meaning (top-

down) and are not simply registering sensory stimulation (bottom-up) in a passive manner. Thus, there is no sharply defined line (the boundary is *fuzzy*) between sensory and perceptual processes.

Page 215: Usually, these grouping principles help us construct reality. Sometimes, however, they can *lead us astray.* . . . Although we put together elements of sensation through active organization (the Gestalt grouping principles) and end up with a unitary experience, we sometimes make mistakes in the process (*we are led astray*).

Pages 215–216: Their mothers then *coaxed* them to *crawl* out on the glass. In the experiment with the **visual cliff**, 6- to 14-month-old children were gently encouraged (*coaxed*) by their mothers to move, on their hands and knees (*crawl*), onto the invisible glass top on the "deep" side of the apparatus. Most could not be persuaded to do so, leading to the conclusion that depth perception may be innate (inborn).

Page 216: The floating *finger sausage* (Figure 6.8). Try the demonstration (page 216) and you will experience the effect of **retinal disparity** and see a tubular shape (*finger sausage*) made by your brain from the two different images of your fingers.

Page 218: As we move, objects that are actually *stable* may appear to move. Things that are stationary and do not move (*stable objects*) seem to move relative to us when we move.

Page 220: By flashing 24 *still pictures* each second, a motion picture creates perceived movement. When we view a film, we do not experience a rapid series of nonmoving images (*still pictures*); rather, our brain constructs the perceived motion. This is called stroboscopic movement.

Page 222: Take away these distance cues—by looking at the horizon moon (or each monster or each bar) through a *paper tube*—and it immediately shrinks. Observers have argued for centuries about why the moon near the horizon seems so much larger than the moon overhead in the sky. One explanation involves the interaction of perceived size and perceived distance. Distance cues at the horizon make the moon appear farther away than when it is overhead (where there are no distance cues). The moon casts the *same retinal image* in both situations, so the image that appears to be more distant (i.e., near the horizon) will therefore seem larger. We can eliminate the distance cues by looking at the moon through a rolled-up piece of paper (*paper tube*); the moon will appear much smaller (*it shrinks*).

Page 222: . . . carpentered . . . A carpenter is someone who constructs objects, houses, furniture, boats, etc., out of wood. In Western cultures many of these objects are angular, with 90° angles and corners, rather than circular or round. Our experiences with rectangular shapes (*carpentered context*) contributes to the Müller-Lyer illusion.

Page 223: As they were crossing a wide plain, buffalo *loomed* several miles away. As the wild oxen or bison (*buffalo*) came into sight (*loomed*) some distance away, Kenge, an African Pygmy, who had never been out of the dense forest before and was not used to judging size over large, flat, open expanses of land, thought they were insects. They cast small retinal images (the size of insects) at a distance of several miles; when they were much closer, the retinal images increased dramatically and Kenge became frightened and puzzled as the "insects" now seemed as big as oxen.

Perceptual Interpretation

Page 226: Most had been born with cataracts—clouded lenses that enabled them to see only diffused light, rather as you or I might see a diffuse fog through a *Ping-Pong* ball sliced in half. People born with cataracts cannot see clearly because the normally transparent lenses in their eyes are opaque. To understand what their vision is like, imagine what you would see if you had your eyes covered with half of a small, white, plastic ball that is used in table tennis (*Ping-Pong*). When cataract patients have their vision restored, after being blind since birth, they can distinguish colors and figures from ground (innate capacities), but they cannot visually recognize things that were familiar by touch.

Page 227: Given a new pair of glasses, we may feel slightly disoriented, even dizzy. When we start wearing ordinary eyeglasses or when we are fitted with a new pair, our initial reaction is a little confusion and vertigo (*dizziness*). However, we quickly adapt within a few days. We can also adapt to lenses that distort what we are looking at by 40° to one side, and even to distortion lenses that invert reality (turn the visual image upside down). Fish, frogs, salamanders, and young chickens cannot adapt in this way.

Page 228: As everyone knows, *to see is to believe.* As many people also know, but do not fully appreciate, *to believe is to see.* The expression *"seeing is believing"* means that we put much reliance on visual information when deciding (believing) what is true. Myers shows us that, on the contrary, what we believe may actually affect what we see. Our assumptions, expectations, and mental predispositions (**perceptual set**) determine, to a large extent, our perceptions.

Page 229: In 1972, a British newspaper published genuine, unretouched photographs of *a "monster"* in Scotland's Loch Ness. . . . People who had heard about, or believed in, the Loch Ness Monster before seeing a very ambiguous picture of a log were more inclined to see what they expected to see (i.e., a monster) because of their **perceptual set**.

Page 229: Clearly, much of what we perceive comes not just from the world "out there" but also *from what's behind our eyes and between our ears.* Myers is reiterating the point that our mental predispositions, expectations, beliefs, etc. (*what's behind our eyes and between our ears*) influence much more of what we perceive than the sensory stimulation received from the outside world.

Page 232: Some gender differences, it seems, exist merely in the eyes of their beholders. The familiar saying *"beauty is in the eye of the beholder"* means that what is perceived as beautiful has more to do with what the perceiver subjectively believes than with the absolute qualities of the person or object being judged. Likewise, our stereotypes (rigid, conventional ideas or beliefs) about gender or culture can greatly influence (*color*) what is perceived.

Is There Extrasensory Perception?

Page 234: The media overflow with reports of psychic wonders: crimes solved, dreams come true, futures foretold. About 50 percent of Americans believe in the ability to have perception in the absence of any sensory input (**extrasensory perception, or ESP**). Our media are filled (*overflow*) with stories about unexplained events, UFOs, alien abductions, and psychics (people who claim to have ESP) who allegedly solve crimes, predict the future, spy on military installations halfway around the world, etc., etc. There are TV shows devoted to the paranormal, and even a psychic telephone service (Dial-a-psychic). Most research psychologists are skeptical about the existence of ESP and point to the lack of evidence and especially to the inability of anyone to demonstrate a reproducible ESP effect.

Page 235: . . . uncanny . . . People who have dreams that coincide, by pure chance, with later events often have an eerie or strange (*uncanny*) feeling about the accuracy of their *apparent* precognitions.

Page 237: . . . one more dashed hope . . . This means that an optimistic expectation (*hope*) does not materialize or prove to be real (*it gets dashed*). Other researchers in other labs attempted to replicate the ganzfeld tests of ESP that had initially shown positive results. Milton and Wiseman's (1999) statistical analysis of 30 follow-up ganzfeld experiments found no effect (*one more dashed hope*).

Page 237: . . . clearing the decks . . . This means to put everything in readiness for a major activity and get rid of the unessentials. After examining the evidence and rejecting pseudoscientific accounts (*clearing the decks*), we can pursue the truth in a scientific manner and still keep a humble sense of wonder with respect to life's untestable mysteries.

Page 237: But some people also have an *unsatisfied hunger* for wonderment, *an itch* to experience the magical. Some people are predisposed to believe in ESP because they have a deeply felt need (*unsatisfied hunger*) for surprise and amazement, and a strong ambition or desire (*an itch*) to explore the mysterious and unknown.

CHAPTER 7:

States of Consciousness

Chapter Overview

Consciousness—our awareness of ourselves and our environment—can be experienced in various states. Chapter 7 examines not only waking consciousness, but also covers sleep and dreaming, daydreaming, fantasies, hypnotic states, drug-altered states, and near-death experiences.

Most of the terminology in this chapter is introduced in the sections on Sleep and Dreams and on Drugs and Consciousness. Among the issues discussed in the chapter are why we sleep and dream, whether hypnosis is a unique state of consciousness, and possible psychological and social roots of drug use.

NOTE: Answer guidelines for all Chapter 7 questions begin on page 208.

Waking Consciousness (pp. 241–244)

> David Myers at times uses idioms that are unfamiliar to some readers. If you do not know the meaning of any of the following words, phrases, or expressions in the context in which they appear in the text, refer to page 218 for an explanation (note that one item appears in the chapter introduction): *a fundamental yet slippery concept; Psychology had nearly lost consciousness; consciousness is but the tip of the information processing iceberg; to lag the brain events that evoke it.*

Section Preview

First, skim the section, noting headings and boldface items. Then read the following objectives and, as you read the text, search for the information that will enable you to meet each objective. Answer guidelines are provided on page 208.

1. Discuss the nature of consciousness and its significance in the history of psychology.

2. Discuss the different levels of information processing.

3. Discuss the nature and potential functions of daydreams and fantasies.

Stepping Through the Section

After you have read the sections, complete the sentences and answer the questions. As you proceed, evaluate your performance by consulting the answers on page 209. Do not continue with the next section until you understand each answer. If you need to, review or reread the section in the textbook before continuing.

1. The study of _____ was central in the early years of psychology and in recent decades, but for quite some time it was displaced by the study of observable

_____ .

Define consciousness in a sentence.

2. In comparison with unconscious processing, conscious processing has a(n) _____ (limited/unlimited) capacity, is relatively _____ (fast/slow), and processes pieces of information _____ (simultaneously/successively).

3. Tasks that are less habitual _____ (require/do not require) conscious attention.

4. Most people _____ (do/do not) daydream every day. Compared to older adults, young adults spend _____ (more/less) time daydreaming. About 4 percent of the population has such vivid fantasies and daydreams that they are referred to as

_____-_____

personalities.

Explain why some psychologists consider daydreaming to be adaptive.

Sleep and Dreams (pp. 245–260)

If you do not know the meaning of any of the following words, phrases, or expressions in the context in which they appear in the text, refer to pages 218–219 for an explanation: *move in concert; with a depressed body; we may fret over concerns: Does a lovers' spat signal a split?; Pulling an all-nighter; jet lag; the machine went wild . . . deep zigzags; in deep slumber; you ascend from your initial sleep dive; As the night wears on; drowsy; sleep patterns that thwart . . .; Teenagers . . . may fill this need by using home room for their first siesta and after-lunch study hall for a slumber party; riddle of sleep; the next-day blahs; snoozing is second only to boozing; a dream provides a psychic safety valve; it is time to wake up; brain weaves a story line.*

Section Preview

Answer guidelines are provided on page 209.

1. Differentiate the various biological rhythms of the human body.

2. Describe the cyclical nature of sleep.

3. Discuss possible functions of sleep and the effects of sleep deprivation.

4. Identify and describe the major sleep disorders.

5. Describe the normal content of dreams.

6. Discuss the possible functions of dreams as revealed in various theories.

Stepping Through the Section

Answers are provided on page 210.

1. Our bodies' internal "clocks" control several
_____ _____ .
Among these are _____
_____ , which may give rise to seasonal variations in _____
_____ . Some
people, especially those in far northern regions,
may experience a depressed winter mood called a
_____ _____
_____ . We may also experience
cycles lasting _____ days, such as
the female _____ _____ ;
_____-hour cycles of varying
_____ ;
and _____ -minute cycles such as
the various stages of sleep.

2. (Thinking Critically About PMS) Some
researchers believe that women who are more
depressed, tense, and irritable just before men-

struation begins are suffering from the so-called
_____ _____ . The
existence of this syndrome is _____
(questioned/endorsed) by the American
Psychological Association and by researchers
who report that women's physical and emotional
skills _____ (fluctuate/do not
fluctuate noticeably) with their menstrual cycles.
Moreover, PMS complaints _____
(vary/do not vary) from culture to culture.

3. The sleep-waking cycle follows a 24-hour clock
called the _____
_____ .

4. When people are at their daily peak in circadian
arousal, _____ is sharpest and
_____ is most accurate. In contrast
to university students, who often are at their peak
in the _____ (morning/evening),
older adults tend to peak in the
_____ .

5. We may experience _____
_____ if our circadian rhythm is
interrupted by travel across time zones. Resetting
of a disrupted biological clock is facilitated by
exposure to _____
_____ , which triggers proteins in
the _____ of the eyes to signal a
region of the brain that controls the circadian
clock. We can also reset our biological clocks by
adjusting our _____
_____ .

6. When clocks and daylight cues are absent, the
sleep-waking cycle shifts to a
_____ -hour day.

7. The sleep cycle consists of _____
distinct stages.

8. The rhythm of sleep cycles was discovered when
Aserinsky noticed that, at periodic intervals during the night, the _____ of a sleep-
ing child moved rapidly. This stage of sleep, during which _____ occur, is called
_____ _____ .

9. The relatively slow brain waves of the awake but relaxed state are known as _____ waves.

10. During Stage 1 sleep, which lasts about _____ , people often experience _____ sensations similar to _____ . These sensations may later be incorporated into _____ .

11. The bursts of brain-wave activity that occur during Stage 2 sleep are called _____ _____ .

12. Large, slow brain waves are called _____ waves. These predominate during Stage _____ sleep, which is therefore called _____-_____ sleep. A person in this stage of sleep generally will be _____ (easy/difficult) to awaken. It is during this stage that people may engage in sleep _____ .

Describe the bodily changes that accompany REM sleep.

13. During REM sleep, the motor cortex is _____ (active/relaxed), while the muscles are _____ (active/relaxed). For this reason, REM is often referred to as _____ sleep.

14. The rapid eye movements generally signal the beginning of a _____ .

15. The sleep cycle repeats itself about every _____ minutes. As the night progresses, Stage 4 sleep becomes _____ (longer/briefer) and REM periods become _____ (longer/briefer). Approximately _____ percent of a night's sleep is spent in REM sleep.

16. Newborns spend nearly _____ (how much?) of their day asleep, while adults spend no more than _____ .

17. Allowed to sleep unhindered, most people will sleep 9 or 10 hours a night. People who sleep less than that for several nights in a row often show signs of _____ _____ .

18. Teenagers typically need _____ hours of sleep but now average nearly _____ hours less sleep than teenagers at the turn of the century. To psychologist William _____ , this indicates that the vast majority of students are dangerously sleep-deprived. One indication of the hazards of this state is that the rate of _____ tends to increase immediately after the springtime change in Canada and the United States. Another is that sleep deprivation may suppress the functioning of the body's _____ system and alter metabolic functioning in ways that mimic _____ and promote _____ and _____ .

Describe the effects of sleep deprivation.

19. Two possible reasons for sleep are to keep us out of harm's way and to help restore body tissues, especially those of the _____ .

20. During sleep a growth hormone is released by the _____ gland. Adults spend _____ (more/less) time in deep sleep than children and so release _____ (more/less) growth hormone.

21. A persistent difficulty in falling or staying asleep is characteristic of _____ . Sleeping pills and alcohol may make the problem worse since they tend to _____ (increase/reduce) REM sleep.

22. The sleep disorder in which a person experiences uncontrollable sleep attacks is _____ . People with this disorder may collapse directly into _____ sleep and experience a loss of _____ _____ .

23. Individuals suffering from _____ _____ stop breathing while sleeping.

24. The sleep disorder characterized by extreme fright and rapid heartbeat and breathing is called _____ _____ . Unlike nightmares, these episodes usually happen early in the night, during Stage _____ sleep. The same is true of episodes of _____ and _____ , problems that _____ (run/do not run) in families. These sleep episodes are most likely to be experienced by _____ (young children/adolescents/older adults), in whom this stage tends to be the _____ and _____ .

25. During _____ dreams, the dreamer may be sufficiently aware to wonder whether he or she is, in fact, dreaming.

26. For both men and women, 8 in 10 dreams are marked by _____ (positive/negative) emotions, such as fears of being _____ .

27. Although females tend to dream equally often about males and females, males tend to dream more about _____ . This gender difference _____ (is/is not) found in cultures worldwide.

28. Freud referred to the actual content of a dream as its _____ content. Freud believed that this is a censored, symbolic version of the true meaning, or _____ _____ , of the dream.

29. According to Freud, most of the dreams of adults reflect _____ wishes and are the key to understanding inner _____ .

30. Freud's theory has given way to the theory that dreams serve an _____-processing function. Support for this theory is provided by the fact that after stressful or intense learning experiences, _____ (REM/Stage 4) sleep tends to increase.

31. Other theories propose that dreaming serves some _____ function, for example, that REM sleep provides the brain with needed _____ . Such an explanation is supported by the fact that _____ (infants/adults) spend the most time in REM sleep.

32. According to the _____-_____ theory, dreams are elicited by random bursts of _____ activity originating in lower regions of the brain, such as the _____ . These bursts are believed to be given their emotional tone by the brain's _____ system.

33. After being deprived of REM sleep, a person spends more time in REM sleep; this is the _____ _____ effect.

34. REM sleep _____ (does/does not) occur in other mammals. Animals such as fish, whose behavior is less influenced by learning, _____ (do/do not) dream. This finding supports the _____-_____ theory of dreaming.

Hypnosis (pp. 261–270)

> If you do not know the meaning of any of the following words, phrases, or expressions in the context in which they appear in the text, refer to page 220 for an explanation: —*or mesmerism, as it was then called; played a clever stunt; might the two views . . . be bridged?*

Section Preview

Answer guidelines are provided on page 210.

1. Define hypnosis, and discuss several popular misconceptions about hypnosis.

2. Discuss the controversy over whether hypnosis is an altered state of consciousness.

Stepping Through the Section

Answers are provided on page 211.

1. The suggestion that a person forget things that occurred while he or she was under hypnosis may produce _____

_____ .

2. The discovery of hypnosis is attributed to _____ , who claimed to have discovered an "_____ _____ ."

3. Most people are _____ (somewhat/not at all) hypnotically suggestible.

Describe people who are the most susceptible to hypnosis.

4. If people are led to expect that they are hypnotizable, their responsiveness under hypnosis _____ (will/will not) increase.

5. The hypnotic demonstration in which a subject supposedly relives earlier experiences is referred to as _____ _____ . Research studies show that the subjects in such demonstrations have memories that are _____ (more/no more) accurate than the memories of fully conscious persons.

6. The weight of research evidence suggests that hypnosis _____ (does/does not) allow a person to perform dangerous feats that are impossible in the normal waking state.

7. An _____ person in a legitimate _____ can induce people—hypnotized or not—to perform some unlikely acts.

8. Hypnotherapists have helped some people alleviate headaches through the use of _____ suggestions.

9. For _____ problems such as smoking, a subject's hypnotic responsiveness _____ (does/does not) make a difference in the effectiveness of hypnosis. As therapy for problems that are not related to will power, hypnosis _____ (is/is not) more effective in speeding recovery than techniques promoting relaxation and positive images.

10. Hypnosis _____ (can/cannot) relieve pain. One theory of hypnotic pain relief is that hypnosis separates, or _____ , the sensory and emotional aspects of pain. Another is that hypnotic pain relief is due to selective _____ , that is, to the person's focusing on stimuli other than pain.

Summarize the argument that hypnosis is not an altered state of consciousness.

11. Hilgard has advanced the idea that during hypnosis there is a _____ , or split, between different levels of consciousness. The existence of a separate consciousness, which is aware of what takes place during hypnosis, is expressed in the concept of the

_____ _____ .

Although this theory has provoked controversy, there is little doubt that _____ influences do play an important role in hypnosis.

Drugs and Consciousness (pp. 270–282)

If you do not know the meaning of any of the following words, phrases, or expressions in the context in which they appear in the text, refer to pages 220–221 for an explanation: *tipsy on one can of beer; tip more when tipsy; quicker pick-her-upper; one pays a price . . . gnawing craving for another fix; crack; "acid trip"; marijuana may spell relief; being stoned.*

Section Preview

Answer guidelines are provided on page 211.

1. Discuss the physical and psychological effects common to all psychoactive drugs and state three common misconceptions about addiction.

2. Describe the physiological and psychological effects of depressants, stimulants, and hallucinogens.

3. Discuss the biological, psychological, and social roots of drug use.

Stepping Through the Section

Answers are provided on page 212.

1. Drugs that alter moods and perceptions are called _____ drugs.

2. Drug users who require increasing doses to experience a drug's effects have developed _____ for the drug.

3. If a person begins experiencing withdrawal symptoms after ceasing to use a drug, the person has developed a physical _____ . Regular use of a drug to relieve stress is an example of a _____ dependence.

Briefly state three common misconceptions about addiction.

4. A person who is addicted to a dysfunctional partner has been said to be _____ . This idea, however, remains controversial.

5. The three broad categories of drugs discussed in the text include _____ , which tend to slow body functions; _____ , which speed body functions; and _____ , which alter perception. These drugs all work by mimicking or affecting the activity of the brain's _____ .

6. Low doses of alcohol, which is classified as a _____ , slow the activity of the _____ nervous system.

7. Alcohol may make a person more _____ , more _____ , more _____ , or more _____ daring; on the other hand, it reduces _____ . Alcohol affects memory by interfering with the process of transferring experiences into _____-_____ memory. Also, blackouts after drinking result from alcohol's suppression of _____ _____ .

Describe how a person's expectations can influence the behavioral effects of alcohol.

8. Tranquilizers, which are also known as
   _____ , have effects similar to those
   of alcohol.

9. Opium, morphine, and heroin all
   _____ (excite/depress) neural functioning. Together, these drugs are called the
   _____ . When they are present, the
   brain eventually stops producing
   _____ .

10. The most widely used stimulants are
    _____ , _____ ,
    _____ , and _____ .
    Stimulants _____ (are/are not)
    addictive.

11. Cocaine and crack deplete the brain's supply of
    the neurotransmitters _____ ,
    _____ , and _____ ,
    and result in depression as the drugs' effects
    wear off. Recent animal studies demonstrate that
    cocaine works by blocking the _____
    of _____ in nerve cells, which locks
    the brain's _____ switches into the
    "on" position.

12. Cocaine's psychological effects depend not only
    on dosage and form but also on
    _____ , _____ , and the
    _____ .

13. Hallucinogens are also referred to as
    _____ . Two common synthetic hal-
    lucinogens are _____ and
    LSD, which is chemically similar to the neuro-
    transmitter _____ .

14. The active ingredient in marijuana is abbreviated
    _____ . Marijuana has been used
    therapeutically with those who suffer from
    _____ and cancer. However, these
    medical uses are complicated by marijuana's toxi-
    city, which can cause _____
    _____ .

Describe some of the physical and psychological
effects of marijuana.

15. The negative aftereffects of drug use may be
    explained in part by the principle that emotions
    trigger _____ _____ .

16. Drug use by North American youth
    _____ (increased/declined) during
    the 1970s, then declined until the early 1990s due
    to increased _____
    _____ and efforts by the media to
    deglamorize drug use.

17. In the 1990s, drug use by North American teens
    _____ (continues to decline/has
    rebounded). At the same time, alcohol and tobac-
    co use is _____ (declining/on the
    rise).

18. Adopted individuals are more susceptible to alco-
    holism if they had an alcoholic
    _____ (adoptive/biological) parent.
    Boys who at age 6 are _____ (more/
    less) excitable are more likely as teens to smoke,
    drink, and use other drugs. Children whose par-
    ents abuse alcohol have a _____
    (higher/lower) tolerance for multiple drinks
    taken over an hour or two. They also show small-
    er evoked _____ response to certain
    types of _____ stimulation.

Identify some of the psychological and social roots of
drug use.

19. Among teenagers, drug use _____
    (varies/is about the same) across cultural groups.

20. African-American high school seniors report the
    _____ (highest/lowest) rates of
    drug use.

21. State three possible channels of influence for drug
    prevention and treatment programs.

    a. _____

    b. _____

    c. _____

Near-Death Experiences (pp. 283–284)

> If you do not know the meaning of any of the
> following words in the context in which they
> appear in the text, refer to page 221 for an
> explanation: *monists generally believe that death
> is real and that without bodies we truly are no-
> bodies.*

Section Preview

Answer guidelines are provided on page 212.

1. Describe the near-death experience and the controversy over the separability of mind and body.

Stepping Through the Section

Answers are provided on page 212.

1. The reports of people who have had near-death
   experiences are very similar to the
   _____ reported by drug users. These
   experiences may be the result of a deficient supply of _____ or other insults to the
   brain.

2. That the mind and body are distinct entities is the
   position of the theorists known as
   _____ . In contrast, the
   _____ believe that the mind and
   body are one.

Progress Test 1

Multiple-Choice Questions

Circle your answers to the following questions and
check them with the answers on page 213. If your
answer is incorrect, read the explanation for why it is
incorrect and then consult the appropriate pages of
the text (in parentheses following the correct answer).

1. As defined by the text, consciousness includes
   which of the following?
   a. daydreaming   c. hypnosis
   b. sleeping   d. all of the above

2. Which of the following groups tends to daydream the most?
   a. elderly men   d. middle-aged men
   b. elderly women   e. young adults
   c. middle-aged women

3. When our _____ is disrupted, we experience jet
   lag.
   a. daydreaming   d. Stage 4 sleep
   b. REM sleep   e. Stage 1 sleep
   c. circadian rhythm

4. Sleep spindles predominate during which stage
   of sleep?
   a. Stage 2   c. Stage 4
   b. Stage 3   d. REM sleep

5. During which stage of sleep does the body experience increased heart rate, rapid breathing, and
   genital arousal?
   a. Stage 2   c. Stage 4
   b. Stage 3   d. REM sleep

6. The sleep cycle is approximately _____ minutes.
   a. 30   c. 75
   b. 50   d. 90

7. The effects of chronic sleep deprivation include:
   a. suppression of the immune system.
   b. altered metabolic and hormonal functioning.
   c. misperceptions on monotonous tasks.
   d. increased accident proneness.
   e. all of the above.

8. One effect of sleeping pills is to:
   a. depress REM sleep.
   b. increase REM sleep.
   c. depress Stage 2 sleep.
   d. increase Stage 2 sleep.

9. Cocaine and crack produce a euphoric rush by:
   a. blocking the actions of serotonin.
   b. depressing neural activity in the brain.
   c. blocking the reuptake of dopamine in brain cells.
   d. stimulating the brain's production of endorphins.
   e. preventing the body from producing endorphins.

10. Which of the following is classified as a depressant?
    a. amphetamines   d. alcohol
    b. LSD   e. PCP
    c. marijuana

11. The modern discovery of hypnosis is generally attributed to:
    a. Freud.   c. Spanos.
    b. Mesmer.   d. Hilgard.

12. Which of the following statements concerning hypnosis is true?
    a. People will do anything under hypnosis.
    b. Hypnosis is the same as sleeping.
    c. Hypnosis is not associated with a distinct physiological state.
    d. Hypnosis improves memory recall.

13. The fact that animals such as fish, whose behavior is less influenced by learning, do not dream provides support for the _____ theory of dreaming.
    a. manifest content
    b. physiological
    c. information-processing
    d. activation-synthesis
    e. latent content

14. According to Freud, dreams are:
    a. a symbolic fulfillment of erotic wishes.
    b. the result of random neural activity in the brainstem.
    c. the brain's mechanism for self-stimulation.
    d. transparent representations of the individual's conflicts.

15. Psychoactive drugs affect behavior and perception through:
    a. the power of suggestion.
    b. the placebo effect.
    c. alteration of neural activity in the brain.
    d. psychological, not physiological, influences.

16. Which of the following is *not* a common *misconception* about addiction?
    a. To overcome an addiction a person almost always needs professional therapy.
    b. Psychoactive and medicinal drugs very quickly lead to addiction.
    c. Biological factors place some individuals at increased risk for addiction.
    d. Many other repetitive, pleasure-seeking behaviors fit the drug-addiction-as-disease-needing-treatment model.

17. At its beginning, psychology focused on the study of:
    a. observable behavior.
    b. consciousness.
    c. abnormal behavior.
    d. all of the above.

18. Which of the following is *not* a theory of dreaming mentioned in the text?
    a. Dreams facilitate information processing.
    b. Dreaming stimulates the developing brain.
    c. Dreams result from random neural activity originating in the brainstem.
    d. Dreaming is an attempt to escape from social stimulation.

19. The sleep-waking cycles of people isolated without clocks or daylight typically are _____ hours in duration.
    a. 23   c. 25
    b. 24   d. 26

20. The lowest rates of drug use among high school seniors is reported by:
    a. white males.
    b. white females.
    c. black males.
    d. Latinos.

Matching Items

Match each term with its appropriate definition or description.

Definitions or Descriptions

_____ 1. surface meaning of dreams
_____ 2. deeper meaning of dreams
_____ 3. stage of sleep associated with delta waves
_____ 4. stage of sleep associated with muscular relaxation
_____ 5. sleep disorder in which breathing stops
_____ 6. sleep disorder occurring in Stage 4 sleep
_____ 7. depressant
_____ 8. hallucinogen
_____ 9. stimulant
_____ 10. twilight stage of sleep associated with imagery resembling hallucinations
_____ 11. disorder in which sleep attacks occur

Terms

a. marijuana
b. alcohol
c. Stage 1 sleep
d. night terrors
e. manifest content
f. cocaine
g. narcolepsy
h. sleep apnea
i. Stages 3 and 4 sleep
j. REM sleep
k. latent content

Progress Test 2

Progress Test 2 should be completed during a final chapter review. Answer the following questions after you thoroughly understand the correct answers for the section reviews and Progress Test 1.

Multiple-Choice Questions

1. Which of the following statements regarding REM sleep is true?
   a. Adults spend more time than infants in REM sleep.
   b. REM sleep deprivation results in a REM rebound.
   c. People deprived of REM sleep adapt easily.
   d. After a stressful experience, a person's REM sleep decreases.
   e. REM sleep periods become shorter as the night progresses.

2. Which theorists believe that the mind and the body are separate entities?
   a. the behaviorists   c. the dualists
   b. the monists   d. the Freudians

3. Alcohol has the most profound effect on:
   a. the transfer of experiences to long-term memory.
   b. immediate memory.
   c. previously established long-term memories.
   d. all of the above.

4. A person whose EEG shows a high proportion of alpha waves is most likely:
   a. dreaming.   d. in Stage 4 sleep.
   b. in Stage 2 sleep.   e. awake and relaxed.
   c. in Stage 3 sleep.

5. Circadian rhythms are the:
   a. brain waves that occur during Stage 4 sleep.
   b. muscular tremors that occur during opiate withdrawal.
   c. regular body cycles that occur on a 24-hour schedule.
   d. brain waves that are indicative of Stage 2 sleep.

6. A person who requires increasing amounts of a drug in order to feel its effect is said to have developed:
   a. tolerance.
   b. physical dependency.
   c. psychological dependency.
   d. resistance.
   e. withdrawal symptoms.

7. Which of the following is *not* an example of a biological rhythm?
   a. feeling depressed during the winter months
   b. the female menstrual cycle
   c. the five sleep stages
   d. the peaking of body temperature during the day
   e. sudden sleep attacks during the day

8. Which of the following is characteristic of REM sleep?

   a. genital arousal

   b. increased muscular tension

   c. night terrors

   d. slow, regular breathing

   e. alpha waves

9. Which of the following is *not* a stimulant?

   a. amphetamines   **c.** nicotine

   b. caffeine   **d.** alcohol

10. Hypnotic responsiveness is:

   a. the same in all people.

   b. generally greater in women than men.

   c. generally greater in men than women.

   d. greater when people are led to *expect* it.

11. According to Hilgard, hypnosis is:

   a. no different from a state of heightened motivation.

   b. a hoax perpetrated by frauds.

   c. the same as dreaming.

   d. a dissociation between different levels of consciousness.

   e. a type of "animal magnetism."

12. Which of the following was *not* cited in the text as evidence that heredity influences alcohol use?

   a. Children whose parents abuse alcohol have a lower tolerance for multiple alcoholic drinks taken over a short period of time.

   b. Boys who are impulsive and fearless at age 6 are more likely to drink as teenagers.

   c. Laboratory mice have been selectively bred to prefer alcohol to water.

   d. Adopted children are more susceptible if one or both of their biological parents has a history of alcoholism.

13. As a form of therapy for relieving problems such as headaches, hypnosis is:

   a. ineffective.

   b. no more effective than positive suggestions given without hypnosis.

   c. highly effective.

   d. more effective with adults than children.

14. Which of the following is usually the most powerful determinant of whether teenagers begin using drugs?

   a. family strength   **c.** school adjustment

   b. religiosity   **d.** peer influence

15. THC is the major active ingredient in:

   a. nicotine.   **d.** cocaine.

   b. LSD.   **e.** amphetamine.

   c. marijuana.

16. Those who believe that hypnosis is a social phenomenon argue that "hypnotized" individuals are:

   a. consciously faking their behavior.

   b. merely acting out a role.

   c. underachievers striving to please the hypnotist.

   d. all of the above.

17. "Consciousness" is defined in the text as:

   a. mental life.

   b. selective attention to ongoing perceptions, thoughts, and feelings.

   c. information processing.

   d. a vague concept no longer useful to contemporary psychologists.

   e. our awareness of ourselves and our environment.

18. Which of the following is true?

   a. REM sleep tends to increase following intense learning periods.

   b. Non-REM sleep tends to increase following intense learning periods.

   c. REM-deprived people remember less presleep material than people deprived of Stages 1–4 sleep.

   d. Sleep control centers are located in the higher, association areas of the cortex, where memories are stored.

19. According to Seligman and Yellen, dreaming represents:

   a. the brain's efforts to integrate unrelated bursts of activity in the visual cortex with emotional tone provided by activity in the limbic system.

   b. a mechanism for coping with the stresses of daily life.

   c. a symbolic depiction of a person's unfulfilled wishes.

   d. an information-processing mechanism for converting the day's experiences into long-term memory.

20. How a particular psychoactive drug affects a person depends on:

   a. the dosage and form in which the drug is taken.

   b. the user's expectations and personality.

   c. the situation in which the drug is taken.

   d. all of the above.

Matching Items

Match each term with its appropriate definition or description.

Definitions or Descriptions

_____ 1. early name for hypnosis
_____ 2. drugs that increase energy and stimulate neural activity
_____ 3. brain wave of awake, relaxed person
_____ 4. brain-wave activity during Stage 2 sleep
_____ 5. sleep stage associated with dreaming
_____ 6. drugs that reduce anxiety and depress central nervous system activity
_____ 7. natural painkiller produced by the brain
_____ 8. neurotransmitter that LSD resembles
_____ 9. our awareness of ourselves and our environment
_____ 10. theory that dreaming reflects our erotic drives
_____ 11. a split between different levels of consciousness

Terms

a. Freud's theory
b. serotonin
c. mesmerism
d. alpha
e. dissociation
f. amphetamines
g. consciousness
h. sleep spindle
i. endorphin
j. REM
k. barbiturates

Thinking Critically About Chapter 7

Answer these questions the day before an exam as a final check on your understanding of the chapter's terms and concepts.

Multiple-Choice Questions

1. A person who falls asleep in the midst of a heated argument probably suffers from:
   a. sleep apnea.
   b. narcolepsy.
   c. night terrors.
   d. insomnia.

2. Which of the following was *not* suggested by the text as an important aspect of drug prevention and treatment programs?
   a. education about the long-term costs of a drug's temporary pleasures
   b. efforts to boost people's self-esteem and purpose in life
   c. attempts to modify peer associations
   d. "scare tactics" that frighten prepubescent children into avoiding drug experimentation

3. REM sleep is referred to as "paradoxical sleep" because:
   a. studies of people deprived of REM sleep indicate that REM sleep is unnecessary.
   b. the body's muscles remain relaxed while the brain and eyes are active.
   c. it is very easy to awaken a person from REM sleep.
   d. the body's muscles are very tense while the brain is in a nearly meditative state.
   e. erection during REM sleep indicates sexual arousal.

4. An attorney wants to know if the details and accuracy of an eyewitness's memory for a crime would be improved under hypnosis. Given the results of relevant research, what should you tell the attorney?
   a. Most hypnotically retrieved memories are either false or contaminated.
   b. Hypnotically retrieved memories are usually more accurate than conscious memories.
   c. Hypnotically retrieved memories are purely the product of the subject's imagination.
   d. Hypnosis only improves memory of anxiety-provoking childhood events.

5. Dan has recently begun using an addictive, euphoria-producing drug. Which of the following will probably occur if he repeatedly uses this drug?
   a. As tolerance to the drug develops, Dan will experience increasingly pleasurable "highs."
   b. The dosage needed to produce the desired effect will decrease.
   c. After each use, he will become more and more depressed.
   d. Dependence will become less of a problem.
   e. Both b. and c. will occur.

6. Although her eyes are closed, Adele's brain is generating bursts of electrical activity in the visual cortex. It is likely that Adele is:
   a. under the influence of a depressant.
   b. under the influence of an opiate.
   c. in NREM sleep.
   d. in REM sleep.
   e. having a near-death experience.

7. Concluding his presentation on levels of information processing, Miguel states that:
   a. humans process both conscious and subconscious information in parallel.
   b. conscious processing occurs in parallel, while subconscious processing is serial.
   c. conscious processing is serial, while subconscious processing is parallel.
   d. all information processing is serial in nature.

8. Roberto is moderately intoxicated by alcohol. Which of the following changes in his behavior is likely to occur?
   a. If angered, he is more likely to become aggressive than when he is sober.
   b. He will be less self-conscious about his behavior.
   c. If sexually aroused, he will be less inhibited about engaging in sexual activity.
   d. The next day he may be unable to remember what happened while he was drinking.
   e. All of the above are likely.

9. Jill dreams that her boyfriend pushes her in front of an oncoming car. Her psychoanalyst suggests that the dream might symbolize her fear that her boyfriend is rushing her into sexual activity prematurely. The analyst is evidently attempting to interpret the _____ content of Jill's dream.
   a. manifest   c. dissociated
   b. latent   d. overt

10. Barry has just spent four nights as a subject in a sleep study in which he was awakened each time he entered REM sleep. Now that the experiment is over, which of the following can be expected to occur?
    a. Barry will be extremely irritable until his body has made up the lost REM sleep.
    b. Barry will sleep so deeply for several nights that dreaming will be minimal.
    c. There will be an increase in sleep Stages 1–4.
    d. There will be an increase in Barry's REM sleep.

11. Of the following individuals, who is likely to be the most hypnotically suggestible?
    a. Bill, a reality-oriented stockbroker
    b. Janice, a fantasy-prone actress
    c. Megan, a sixth-grader who has trouble focusing her attention on a task
    d. Darren, who has never been able to really "get involved" in movies or novels

12. Which of the following statements concerning alcoholism is *not* true?
    a. Adopted individuals are more susceptible to alcoholism if they had an alcoholic adoptive parent.
    b. Having an alcoholic identical twin puts a male at increased risk of becoming alcoholic.
    c. Compared to children of nonalcoholics, children of alcoholics have a higher tolerance for multiple alcoholic drinks.
    d. Researchers have bred rats that prefer alcohol to water.

13. Research studies of the effectiveness of hypnosis as a form of therapy have demonstrated that:
    a. for problems of self-control, such as smoking, hypnosis is equally effective with subjects who can be deeply hypnotized and those who cannot.
    b. posthypnotic suggestions have helped alleviate headaches, asthma, warts, and certain skin disorders.
    c. positive suggestions given without hypnosis are often as effective as hypnosis as a form of therapy.
    d. all of the above are true.

14. As a child, Jane enjoyed intense make-believe play with dolls, stuffed animals, and imaginary companions. As an adult, she spends an unusually large amount of time fantasizing. She is sometimes uncertain whether an event was real or imagined. A psychologist would most likely describe Jane as:
    a. highly suggestible.
    b. a fantasy-prone personality.
    c. a daydreamer.
    d. a dissociator.

15. Levar believes that once the body has died, the mind also ceases to exist. Evidently, Levar is a(n):
    a. behaviorist.   d. atheist.
    b. monist.   e. mesmerist.
    c. dualist.

16. Which of the following statements concerning marijuana is *not* true?
    a. The by-products of marijuana are cleared from the body more quickly than the by-products of alcohol.
    b. Long-term marijuana use may depress male sex hormone and sperm levels.
    c. Marijuana is not as addictive as nicotine or cocaine.
    d. Large doses of marijuana hasten the loss of brain cells.

17. Which of the following statements concerning near-death experiences is true?
    a. Fewer than 1 percent of patients who come close to dying report having them.
    b. They typically consist of fantastic, mystical imagery.
    c. They are more commonly experienced by females than by males.
    d. They are more commonly experienced by males than by females.

18. Those who consider hypnosis a social phenomenon contend that:
    a. hypnosis is an altered state of consciousness.
    b. hypnotic phenomena are unique to hypnosis.
    c. if a hypnotist eliminates the motivation for acting, hypnotized subjects become unresponsive.
    d. all of the above are true.

19. Which of the following statements concerning the roots of drug use is *not* true?
    a. Heavy users of alcohol, marijuana, and cocaine often are depressed.
    b. If an adolescent's friends use drugs, odds are that he or she will, too.
    c. Teenagers who come from happy families and do well in school seldom use drugs.
    d. It is nearly impossible to predict whether or not a particular adolescent will experiment with drugs.

20. Which of the following statements concerning daydreaming is true?
    a. People prone to violence or drug use tend to have more frequent vivid daydreams.
    b. Most daydreaming involves the familiar details of our everyday lives.
    c. Psychologists consider children's daydreams to be unhealthy.
    d. All of the above are true.

Essay Question

You have just been assigned the task of writing an article tentatively titled "Alcohol and Alcoholism: Roots, Effects, and Prevention." What information should you include in your article? (Use the space below to list the points you want to make, and organize them. Then write the essay on a separate piece of paper.)

Key Terms

Writing Definitions

Using your own words, on a separate piece of paper write a brief definition or explanation of each of the following terms.

1. consciousness
2. fantasy-prone personality
3. biological rhythm
4. circadian rhythm
5. REM sleep
6. alpha waves
7. sleep
8. hallucinations
9. delta waves
10. insomnia
11. narcolepsy
12. sleep apnea
13. night terrors
14. dream

15. manifest content

16. latent content

17. REM rebound

18. hypnosis

19. posthypnotic amnesia

20. posthypnotic suggestion

21. dissociation

22. hidden observer

23. psychoactive drugs

24. tolerance

25. withdrawal

26. physical dependence

27. psychological dependence

28. depressants

29. stimulants

30. hallucinogens

31. barbiturates

32. opiates

33. amphetamines

34. LSD (lysergic acid diethylamide)

35. THC

36. near-death experience

37. dualism

38. monism

Cross-Check

As you learned in the Introduction, reviewing and overlearning of material are important to the learning process. After you have written the definitions of the key terms in this chapter, you should complete the crossword puzzle to ensure that you can reverse the process—recognize the term, given the definition.

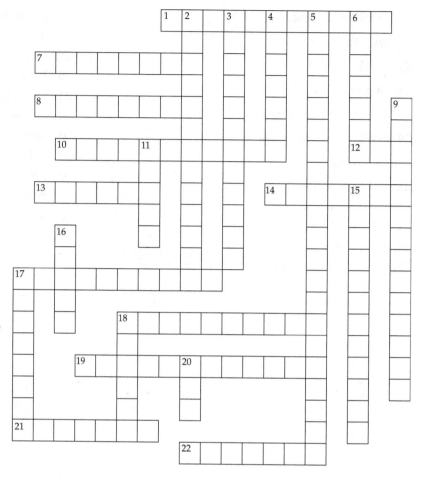

ACROSS

1. Term for REM sleep reflecting that the body is aroused but the muscles are relaxed.
7. Neurotransmitter whose reuptake is blocked by cocaine.
8. Widely used stimulant that is inhaled.
10. Dreams in which the dreamer is sufficiently aware to wonder if he or she is dreaming.
12. Powerful hallucinogen first used by Albert Hofmann.
13. Type of processing that describes how we deal with conscious information.
14. Type of brain wave that occurs during Stage 2 sleep.
17. Drug category that includes alcohol.
18. Stage 1 dream sensation similar to a hallucination.
19. Also known as tranquilizers.
21. Time of day at which the thinking and memory of older adults tends to be best.
22. Time of day at which the thinking and memory of college students tends to be best.

DOWN

2. In hypnosis, the supposed reliving of earlier experiences.
3. Drugs that "speed up" neural activity.
4. Drugs that depress neural activity, temporarily lessening pain.
5. Theory suggesting that dreams help fix daily experiences in our memories.
6. Drug that disrupts the processing of recent experiences into long-term memories.
9. Ernest Hilgard's term describing a hypnotized subject's awareness of unreported experiences.
11. Brain wave that predominates in Stage 4 sleep.
15. Divided consciousness (as during hypnosis).
16. Relatively slow brain waves of a relaxed, awake state.
17. Adaptive state of consciousness that may help us prepare for future events.

18. Depressant that causes a rush of euphoria.
20. Active ingredient in marijuana.

Answers

Waking Consciousness

Section Preview

1. At its beginning, psychology focused on the description and explanation of states of consciousness. The difficulty of scientifically studying consciousness and the emergence of the school of behaviorism, however, caused psychology to shift to the study of overt behavior. By 1960, advances in neuroscience made it possible to relate brain activity to various mental states; as a result, mental concepts began to reenter psychology.

   Contemporary psychologists define consciousness as "our awareness of ourselves and our environment" and conduct research on attention, sleeping, dreaming, and altered states of consciousness induced by hypnosis and drugs.

2. Research reveals that information processing occurs at many levels, depending on the difficul-

ty and familiarity of a task. Much information is processed without awareness. Less habitual tasks require conscious attention. Unlike the relatively slow, limited-capacity, serial processing of conscious information, subconscious information can be processed in parallel.

3. Daydreams help people prepare for future events by serving as mental rehearsals. For children, daydreaming is a form of imaginative play that fosters social and cognitive development. Daydreams may also substitute for impulsive behavior.

   Approximately 4 percent of people can be characterized as fantasy-prone. These individuals spend more than half their time fantasizing and may have trouble separating fantasy from reality.

Stepping Through the Section

1. consciousness; behavior

Consciousness can be defined as our awareness of ourselves and our environment.

2. limited; slow; successively

3. require

4. do; more; fantasy-prone

Daydreams help us prepare for future events by serving as mental rehearsals. For children, daydreaming in the form of imaginative play is important to social and cognitive development. Daydreams may also substitute for impulsive behavior (delinquents and drug users tend to have fewer vivid fantasies than most people).

Sleep and Dreams

Section Preview

1. Controlled by internal "biological clocks," our bodies' biological rhythms include annual cycles of appetite, sleep length, and mood; twenty-eight-day cycles such as the female menstrual cycle; twenty-four-hour cycles of varying alertness, body temperature, and growth hormone secretion; and ninety-minute cycles of the various stages of sleep.

2. The sleep-waking cycle is a circadian (24-hour) rhythm. The cycle of sleep is a 90- or 100-minute rhythm that consists of five distinct stages. During Stage 1 sleep, which lasts about 2 minutes, breathing rate slows, brain waves become slow and irregular, and people often experience hallucination-like and hypnogogic sensations. The approximately 20 minutes of Stage 2 sleep are characterized by bursts of brain-wave activity (sleep spindles). Starting in Stage 3 and increas-

ingly in Stage 4, the sleeper's brain emits large, slow delta waves, which last about 30 minutes. During Stage 4 sleep, it is difficult to awaken a sleeper. During REM sleep, brain waves, heart rate, and breathing become more rapid; genital arousal and rapid eye movements occur; and dreaming is common. Over the course of a night's sleep, REM sleep increases in duration, while Stages 3 and 4 become shorter.

3. Why people need sleep is not fully understood. Sleep may have evolved for two reasons. First, sleep kept our ancestors out of harm's way during the dangerous hours of darkness. Second, sleep helps restore body tissues, especially those of the brain. That sleep plays a role in the growth process is indicated by evidence that during deep sleep, the pituitary gland releases a growth hormone.

   The major effects of sleep deprivation are sleepiness and a general malaise. Other effects include impaired creativity and concentration, diminished immunity to disease, irritability, slight hand tremors, slowed performance, and occasional misperceptions on monotonous tasks. Some researchers believe that sleep deprivation is widespread and contributes to traffic deaths and other accidents. Sleep deprivation may also suppress the functioning of the immune system, making people more susceptible to infections, and alter metabolic and hormonal functioning in ways that mimic aging and promote obesity and hypertension.

4. Approximately 10 to 15 percent of adults suffer recurring problems in falling or staying asleep (insomnia). People with narcolepsy suffer overwhelming bouts of sleepiness and, in severe cases, collapse directly into a brief period of REM sleep. Those who suffer from sleep apnea intermittently stop breathing for a minute or so when they sleep. Unlike nightmares, which typically occur during early morning REM sleep, night terrors usually occur early in the night and during Stage 4 sleep; they are characterized by high arousal and an appearance of being terrified. Sleepwalking and sleeptalking are also Stage 4 phenomena, most often experienced by young children (who experience the lengthiest and deepest Stage 4 sleep).

5. REM dreams are vivid, emotional, and bizarre. Many dreams, however, are rather ordinary and deal with daily life events. People commonly dream of failure; of being attacked, pursued, or rejected; or of experiencing misfortune. Sexual imagery in dreams is less common than is popularly believed. Women dream of males and

females equally often, but 65 percent of men's dream characters are males. Occasionally, people experience "lucid dreams," in which they are sufficiently aware during a dream to wonder whether they are, in fact, dreaming and are able to test their state of consciousness.

6. Freud argued that dreams are a psychic safety valve that discharges threatening feelings. According to this view, a dream's manifest content is a symbolic version of its true underlying meaning (latent content), which consists of unacceptable drives and erotic wishes.

   According to the information-processing theory, dreams help with the processing and storage of daily experiences. In support of this theory is evidence that following stressful or intense learning periods, REM sleep increases.

   Another theory holds that dreams provide the brain with needed stimulation that promotes development of neural pathways. In support of this theory is evidence that infants spend more time in REM sleep than adults.

   According to Seligman and Yellen's activation-synthesis theory, dreams are the brain's attempt to integrate unrelated bursts of activity in the visual cortex, imposing meaning on meaningless stimuli. The emotional "tone" of dreams is provided by activity in the limbic system.

Stepping Through the Section

1. biological rhythms; annual cycles; appetite, sleep length, and moods; seasonal affective disorder; twenty-eight; menstrual cycle; twenty-four; alertness, body temperature, and growth hormone secretion; ninety

2. premenstrual syndrome (PMS); questioned; do not fluctuate noticeably; vary

3. circadian rhythm

4. thinking; memory; evening; morning

5. jet lag; bright light; retinas; sleep schedules

6. 25

7. 5

8. eyes; dreams; REM sleep

9. alpha

10. 2 minutes; hypnogogic; hallucinations; memories

11. sleep spindles

12. delta; 4; slow-wave; difficult; walking

During REM sleep, brain waves become as rapid as those of Stage 1 sleep, heart rate and breathing become more rapid and irregular, and genital arousal and rapid eye movements occur.

13. active; relaxed; paradoxical

14. dream

15. 90; briefer; longer; 20 to 25

16. two-thirds; one-third

17. sleep deprivation

18. 8 or 9; 2; Dement; accidents; immune; aging; obesity; hypertension

The major effect of sleep deprivation is sleepiness. Other effects include impaired creativity and concentration, diminished immunity to disease, slowed performance, irritability, and occasional misperceptions on monotonous tasks.

19. brain

20. pituitary; less; less

21. insomnia; reduce

22. narcolepsy; REM; muscular tension

23. sleep apnea

24. night terrors; 4; sleepwalking; sleeptalking; run; young children; lengthiest; deepest

25. lucid

26. negative; attacked, pursued, or rejected

27. males; is

28. manifest; latent content

29. erotic; conflicts

30. information; REM

31. physiological; stimulation; infants

32. activation-synthesis; neural; brainstem; limbic

33. REM rebound

34. does; do not; information-processing

Hypnosis

Section Preview

1. Hypnosis is a social interaction in which a hypnotist suggests to a subject that certain perceptions, feelings, thoughts, or behaviors will spontaneously occur. Approximately 20 percent of people are highly susceptible to hypnosis, although studies show that anyone can experience hypnotic responsiveness if led to expect it.

   Studies of hypnotic memory refreshment and age regression demonstrate that hypnosis does not boost memory. Age-regressed people merely act as they believe appropriate for a certain age.

   The belief that hypnosis can force people to act against their will, or perform acts that fully conscious people cannot, is also unsubstantiated.

   Posthypnotic suggestions have been used to help people alleviate headaches, asthma, warts, and stress-related skin disorders. But controlled studies demonstrate that giving patients positive suggestions without hypnosis is equally effective.

Hypnosis can relieve pain, perhaps by allowing a person to dissociate the pain from conscious awareness or by focusing attention elsewhere. Several studies have shown that hypnosis relieves pain no better than relaxing and distracting people without hypnosis.

2. Most studies have found that hypnosis does not produce any unique physiological changes that would indicate it is an altered state of consciousness. Nor is the behavior of hypnotized people fundamentally different from that of fully conscious people. Therefore, hypnosis may be mainly a social phenomenon, with hypnotized subjects acting out the role of a "good hypnotic subject."

The controversial divided-consciousness theory is based on Hilgard's idea that during hypnosis consciousness splits into a cooperating, suggestible component and a hidden observer that is passively aware of what is happening.

Stepping Through the Section

1. posthypnotic amnesia

2. Mesmer; animal magnetism

3. somewhat

Those who are most susceptible share with the fantasy-prone personality the capability of becoming deeply absorbed in the imaginary. They also tend to have rich fantasy lives.

4. will

5. age regression; no more

6. does not

7. authoritative; context

8. posthypnotic

9. self-control; does not; is not

10. can; dissociates; attention

Although the issue is still unsettled, most studies have found that hypnosis does not produce any unique changes in physiological processes—and we would expect such changes if hypnosis is an altered state of consciousness. Nor is the behavior of hypnotized subjects fundamentally different from that of other people. Therefore, hypnosis may be mainly a social phenomenon, with hypnotized subjects acting out the role of a "good hypnotic subject."

11. dissociation; hidden observer; social

Drugs and Consciousness

Section Preview

1. All psychoactive drugs can produce tolerance and both physical and psychological dependence. This dependence is made clear by the fact that when a user stops taking a psychoactive drug, he or she experiences the undesirable side effects of withdrawal.

There are several misconceptions about addiction, including the myth that psychoactive drugs automatically cause addiction, that addictions cannot be overcome without therapy, and that the addiction-as-disease-needing-treatment model can profitably be extended to many other pleasure-seeking behaviors.

2. Depressants such as alcohol, barbiturates, and opiates calm activity in the sympathetic nervous system and slow down body functions. Behaviorally, alcohol intake promotes aggressive, sexual, or helpful urges that the user's normal restraints might otherwise inhibit. Alcohol also disrupts the processing of recent experiences into long-term memories, reduces self-awareness, and suppresses REM sleep. The barbiturate drugs have effects similar to those of alcohol. With repeated use of artificial opiates, the brain stops producing endorphins, which leads to the agony of withdrawal when the drug is withdrawn.

The stimulants, which include caffeine, nicotine, amphetamines, and cocaine, speed up body functions. When stimulants wear off, there is a compensatory slowdown of behavior that includes symptoms of tiredness, headaches, irritability, and depression. Cocaine produces its effects by blocking the reabsorption of excess dopamine, norepinephrine, and serotonin.

Hallucinogens such as marijuana, PCP, and LSD distort perceptions and evoke unpredictable psychological effects. Many hallucinogens produce their effects by blocking the actions of the neurotransmitter serotonin. Like alcohol, marijuana relaxes, disinhibits, and impairs memory and perceptual and motor skills. Marijuana may also depress male sex hormones and hasten the loss of brain cells.

3. Drug use among teenagers and adults increased during the 1970s, then declined, indicating a changing national attitude toward drugs. Beginning in the early 1990s, however, drug use has rebounded.

That some people may be biologically vulnerable to drug use is indicated by evidence that heredity influences alcoholic tendencies. Males having an alcoholic identical twin, for example, or adopted individuals who have an alcoholic biological parent are at increased risk for problems.

Several psychological factors may promote addiction, including feeling that one's life is meaningless, experiencing significant stress or failure, and depression.

Especially for teenagers, social influences on drug use are strong. This is evident from differing rates of drug use across cultural groups. Peers influence attitudes about drugs, provide drugs, and establish the social context for their use. If an adolescent's friends use drugs, the odds are that he or she will, too.

Stepping Through the Section

1. psychoactive

2. tolerance

3. dependence; psychological

The following myths about addiction are false:
   a. Taking a psychoactive drug automatically leads to addiction.
   b. One cannot overcome an addiction without professional help.
   c. The addiction-as-disease-needing-treatment model is applicable to a broad spectrum of pleasure-seeking behaviors.

4. co-dependent

5. depressants; stimulants; hallucinogens; neurotransmitters

6. depressant; sympathetic

7. aggressive; helpful; self-disclosing; sexually; self-awareness; long-term; REM sleep

Studies have found that if people believe that alcohol affects social behavior in certain ways, then, when they drink alcohol (or even mistakenly think that they have been drinking alcohol), they will behave according to their expectations. For example, if people believe alcohol promotes sexual feeling, on drinking they are likely to behave in a sexually aroused way.

8. barbiturates

9. depress; opiates; endorphins

10. caffeine; nicotine; amphetamines; cocaine; are

11. dopamine; norepinephrine; serotonin; reuptake; dopamine; reward

12. expectations; personality; situation

13. psychedelics; PCP; serotonin

14. THC; AIDS; cancer, lung damage, and pregnancy complications

Like alcohol, marijuana relaxes, disinhibits, and may produce a euphoric feeling. Also like alcohol, marijuana impairs perceptual and motor skills. Marijuana is a mild hallucinogen; it can slow the perceived passage of time and amplify sensitivity to colors, sounds, tastes, and smells. Marijuana also interrupts memory formation.

15. opposing emotions

16. increased; drug education

17. has rebounded; declining

18. biological; more; higher; brain; sensory

A psychological factor in drug use is the feeling that one's life is meaningless and lacks direction. Regular users of psychoactive drugs often have experienced stress or failure and are somewhat depressed. Drug use often begins as a temporary way to relieve depression, anger, anxiety, or insomnia. A powerful social factor in drug use, especially among adolescents, is peer influence. Peers shape attitudes about drugs, provide drugs, and establish the social context for their use.

19. varies

20. lowest

21. **a.** education about the long-term costs of a drug's temporary pleasures
    b. efforts to boost people's self-esteem and purpose in life
    c. attempts to "inoculate" youth against peer pressures

Near-Death Experiences

Section Preview

1. Approximately 30 to 40 percent of people who have come close to death report some sort of near-death experience involving visions of tunnels, bright lights, out-of-body sensations, or replays of old memories. Dualists, who believe the mind can exist separate from the body, have glorified such experiences as evidence of life after death. Monists, who contend that the mind and body are inseparable, argue that near-death experiences are similar to the hallucinations people experience while using drugs, or when their brains are deprived of oxygen. Monists believe that near-death experiences mean nothing more than that the brain has been traumatized.

Stepping Through the Section

1. hallucinations; oxygen

2. dualists; monists

Progress Test 1

Multiple-Choice Questions

1. **d.** is the answer. (p. 242)

2. **e.** is the answer. (p. 243)

3. **c.** is the answer. Jet lag is experienced because, having traveled across time zones, we are awake at a time when our biological clock says, "Sleep!" This biological clock is the circadian rhythm. (p. 247)

4. **a.** is the answer. (p. 249)
   b. & c. Delta waves predominate during Stages 3 and 4. Stage 3 is the transition between Stages 2 and 4 and is associated with a pattern that has elements of both stages.
   d. Faster, nearly waking brain waves occur during REM sleep.

5. **d.** is the answer. (p. 251)
   a., b., & c. During non-REM Stages 1–4 heart rate and breathing are slow and regular and the genitals are not aroused.

6. **d.** is the answer. (p. 251)

7. **e.** is the answer. (p. 245)

8. **a.** is the answer. Like alcohol, sleeping pills carry the undesirable consequence of reducing REM sleep and may make insomnia worse in the long run. (p. 255)
   b., c., & d. Sleeping pills do not produce these effects.

9. **c.** is the answer. (p. 276)
   a. This answer describes the effect of LSD.
   b. Depressants such as alcohol have this effect. Cocaine and crack are classified as stimulants.
   d. None of the psychoactive drugs has this effect. Opiates, however, *suppress* the brain's production of endorphins.
   e. Use of opiates eventually does this.

10. **d.** is the answer. Alcohol, which slows body functions and neural activity, is a depressant. (p. 273)
    a. Amphetamines are stimulants.
    b., c., & e. LSD, PCP, and marijuana are hallucinogens.

11. **b.** is the answer. Hypnosis was originally referred to as "mesmerism." (p. 261)
    a. In the area of consciousness, Freud is best known for his theory of dreaming.
    c. Spanos is best known for his contention that hypnosis is an extension of everyday social behavior.
    d. Hilgard is known for his theory of dissociation and the hidden observer in hypnosis.

12. **c.** is the answer. (p. 267)
    a. Hypnotized subjects usually perform only acts they might perform normally.
    b. The brain waves of hypnotized subjects are like those seen in relaxed, awake states, not like those associated with sleeping.
    d. Hypnosis typically *disrupts*, or contaminates, memory.

13. **c.** is the answer. The very nature of learning is the processing of information. Since dreaming increases following intense learning periods, animals whose behavior is less influenced by learning have less need to dream. (p. 259)

14. **a.** is the answer. Freud saw dreams as psychic escape valves that discharge unacceptable feelings that are often related to erotic wishes. (p. 258)
    b. & c. These physiological theories of dreaming are not associated with Freud.
    d. According to Freud, dreams represent the individual's conflicts and wishes but in disguised, rather than transparent, form.

15. **c.** is the answer. Such drugs work primarily at synapses, altering neural transmission. (p. 272)
    a. What people believe will happen after taking a drug will likely have some effect on their individual reactions, but psychoactive drugs actually work by altering neural transmission.
    b. Since a placebo is a substance without active properties, this answer is incorrect.
    d. This answer is incorrect because the effects of psychoactive drugs on behavior, perception, and so forth have a physiological basis.

16. **c.** is the answer. This is true. Heredity, for example, influences tendencies toward alcoholism. (pp. 271–272)

17. **b.** is the answer. (p. 281)
    a. The behaviorists' emphasis on observable behavior occurred much later in the history of psychology.
    c. Psychology has never been primarily concerned with abnormal behavior.

18. **d.** is the answer. (pp. 257–259)
    a., b., & c. Each of these describes a valid theory of dreaming that was mentioned in the text.

19. **c.** is the answer. In the absence of these cues, the normal circadian (24-hour) rhythm shifts to a 25-hour cycle. (p. 247)

20. **c.** is the answer. (p. 280)

Matching Items

1. e (p. 257)   5. h (p. 256)   9. f (p. 275)
2. k (p. 258)   6. d (p. 256)   10. c (p. 248)
3. i (p. 249)   7. b (p. 273)   11. g (p. 255)
4. j (p. 248)   8. a (p. 277)

Progress Test 2

Multiple-Choice Questions

1. **b.** is the answer. Following REM deprivation, people temporarily increase their amount of REM sleep, in a phenomenon known as REM rebound. (p. 259)

   a. & e. Just the opposite is true: The amount of REM sleep is greatest in infancy, and the amount increases during the night.

   c. Deprived of REM sleep by repeated awakenings, people return more and more quickly to the REM stages after falling back to sleep. They by no means adapt easily to the deprivations.

   d. Just the opposite occurs: Following stressful experiences, REM sleep tends to increase.

2. **c.** is the answer. (p. 284)

   a. Behaviorists focus on observable behaviors and avoid concepts such as the mind.

   b. The monists believe that the mind and body are one.

   d. Freudians focus on unconscious and conscious aspects of the mind and have little to say regarding the mind-body relationship.

3. **a.** is the answer. Alcohol disrupts the processing of experiences into long-term memory but has little effect on either immediate or previously established memories. (p. 273)

4. **e.** is the answer. (p. 248)

   a. The brain waves of REM sleep (dream sleep) are more like those of Stage 1 sleepers.

   b. Stage 2 is characterized by sleep spindles.

   c. Stages 3 and 4 are characterized by slow, rolling delta waves.

5. **c.** is the answer. (p. 245)

6. **a.** is the answer. (p. 271)

   b. Physical dependence may occur in the absence of tolerance. The hallmark of physical dependence is the presence of withdrawal symptoms when the person is off the drug.

   c. Psychological dependence refers to a felt, or psychological, need to use a drug, for example, a drug that relieves stress.

   d. There is no such thing as drug "resistance."

   e. Withdrawal symptoms occur when the drug is no longer being taken.

7. **e.** is the answer. (p. 245)

8. **a.** is the answer. (p. 251)

   b. During REM sleep, muscular tension is low.

   c. Night terrors are associated with Stage 4 sleep.

   d. During REM sleep, respiration is rapid and irregular.

   e. Alpha waves are characteristic of Stage 1 sleep.

9. **d.** is the answer. Alcohol is a depressant. (p. 273)

10. **d.** is the answer. (pp. 262–263)

    a. Hypnotic responsiveness varies greatly from person to person.

    b. & c. There is no evidence of a gender difference in hypnotic responsiveness.

11. **d.** is the answer. Hilgard believes that hypnosis reflects a dissociation, or split, in consciousness, as occurs normally, only to a much greater extent. (p. 268)

12. **a.** is the answer. Compared with other children, children whose parents abuse alcohol have a *higher* tolerance for multiple drinks, making it more likely that they will, in fact, consume more alcohol. (p. 280)

13. **b.** is the answer. (p. 266)

    a. & c. Hypnosis *can* be helpful in treating these problems, but it is no more effective than other forms of therapy.

    d. Adults are not more responsive than children to hypnosis.

14. **d.** is the answer. If adolescents' friends use drugs, the odds are that they will, too. (p. 281)

    a., b., & c. These are also predictors of drug use but seem to operate mainly through their effects on peer association.

15. **c.** is the answer. (p. 277)

16. **b.** is the answer. (pp. 267–268)

    a. & c. There is no evidence that hypnotically responsive individuals fake their behaviors, or that they are underachievers.

17. **e.** is the answer. (p. 242)

18. **a.** is true. The fact that REM sleep tends to increase following intense learning periods has led to the theory that dreams may help sift, sort, and fix in memory the day's experiences. (p. 258)

    b. Non-REM sleep usually does *not* increase following intense learning periods.

    c. There is no evidence that REM-deprived people have poorer recall of presleep experiences than non-REM-deprived people.

    d. Sleep control centers are actually located in the lower centers of the brainstem, not in the association areas of the cortex.

19. **a.** is the answer. Seligman and Yellen believe that the brain's attempt to make sense of random neural activity is consistent with people's well-established tendencies to impose meaning on even meaningless stimuli. (pp. 258–259)

b. & c. These essentially Freudian explanations of the purpose of dreaming are based on the idea that a dream is a psychic safety valve that harmlessly discharges otherwise inexpressible feelings.

d. This explanation of the function of dreaming is associated with the information-processing viewpoint, but not with Seligman and Yellen.

20. **d.** is the answer. (pp. 280–281)

Matching Items

1. c (p. 261)	**5.** j (p. 248)	**9.** g (p. 242)
2. f (p. 275)	**6.** k (p. 275)	**10.** a (p. 258)
3. d (p. 248)	**7.** i (p. 275)	**11.** e (p. 266)
4. h (p. 249)	**8.** b (p. 277)	

Thinking Critically About Chapter 7

Multiple-Choice Questions

1. **b.** is the answer. Narcolepsy is characterized by uncontrollable sleep attacks. (p. 255)

    a. Sleep apnea is characterized by the temporary cessation of breathing while asleep.

    c. Night terrors are characterized by high arousal and terrified behavior, occurring during Stage 4 sleep.

    d. Insomnia refers to chronic difficulty in falling or staying asleep.

2. **d.** is the answer. (p. 282)

3. **b.** is the answer. Although the body is aroused internally, the messages of the activated motor cortex do not reach the muscles. (p. 251)

    a. Studies of REM-deprived subjects indicate just the opposite.

    c. It is difficult to awaken a person from REM sleep.

    d. Just the opposite occurs in REM sleep: The muscles are relaxed, yet the brain is aroused.

    e. Arousal is usually not caused by sexual dreams.

4. **a.** is the answer. Although people recall more under hypnosis, they "recall" a lot of fiction along with fact and appear unable to distinguish between the two. (p. 263)

    b. Hypnotically refreshed memories are usually no more accurate than conscious memories.

c. Although the hypnotized subject's imagination may influence the memories retrieved, some actual memory retrieval also occurs.

d. Hypnotically retrieved memories don't normally focus on anxiety-provoking events.

5. **e.** is the answer. Continued use of a drug produces a tolerance; to experience the same "high," Dan will have to use larger and larger doses. As the doses become larger, the negative aftereffects, or withdrawal symptoms, become worse. (p. 278)

6. **d.** is the answer. The rapid eye movements of REM sleep coincide with bursts of activity in the visual cortex. (p. 258)

7. **c.** is the answer. (p. 242)

8. **e.** is the answer. Alcohol reduces self-consciousness and it loosens inhibitions, making people more likely to act on their feelings of anger or sexual arousal. It also disrupts the processing of experience into long-term memory. (pp. 273–274)

9. **b.** is the answer. The analyst is evidently trying to go beyond the events in the dream and understand the dream's hidden meaning, or the dream's latent content. (p. 258)

    a. The manifest content of a dream is its actual story line.

    c. Dissociation refers to a split in levels of consciousness.

    d. There is no such term. In any case, "overt" would be the same as "manifest" content.

10. **d.** is the answer. Because of the phenomenon known as REM rebound, Barry, having been deprived of REM sleep, will now increase his REM sleep. (p. 259)

    a. Increased irritability is an effect of sleep deprivation in general, not of REM deprivation specifically.

    b. REM rebound will cause Barry to dream more than normal.

    c. The increase in REM sleep is necessarily accompanied by decreases in Stages 1–4 sleep.

11. **b.** is the answer. Fantasy-prone people have essentially the characteristics associated with hypnotic suggestibility: rich fantasy lives, the ability to become imaginatively absorbed, etc. The fact that Janice is an actress also suggests she possesses such traits. (p. 262)

    a. Bill's reality orientation makes him an unlikely candidate for hypnosis.

    c. The hypnotically suggestible are generally able to focus on tasks or on imaginative activities.

    d. People who are hypnotically suggestible tend to become deeply engrossed in novels and movies.

12. **a.** is the answer. Adopted individuals are more susceptible to alcoholism if they had an alcoholic *biological* parent. (p. 280)

b., c., & d. Each of these is true, which indicates that susceptibility to alcoholism is at least partially determined by heredity.

13. **d.** is the answer. (pp. 266–267)

14. **b.** is the answer. Although all people daydream, people with fantasy-prone personalities daydream far more and far more vividly. (p. 243)

a. Jane may very well also be suggestible to hypnosis; fantasy-prone personalities tend to be. The stated characteristics, however, do not necessarily indicate that she is.

c. The description indicates that Jane's behavior involves much more than simple daydreaming.

d. There is no such personality as a "dissociator." Dissociation refers to a split in consciousness that allows some thoughts and behaviors to occur simultaneously with others.

15. **b.** is the answer. Monists such as Levar believe that the mind and body are inseparable. Thus, when the body dies, the mind ceases to exist. (p. 284)

a. Behaviorists avoid references to the mind.

c. Dualists believe that the mind can exist apart from the body.

d. The text does not discuss the relationship between religious belief and near-death experiences.

e. This refers to followers of Mesmer, who was responsible for the early popularity of hypnosis.

16. **a.** is the answer. THC, the active ingredient in marijuana, and its by-products linger in the body for a month or more. (p. 278)

17. **b.** is the answer. (p. 283)

a. Approximately 30 to 40 percent of people who have come close to death report some sort of near-death experience.

c. & d. There is no gender difference in the prevalence of near-death experiences.

18. **c.** is the answer. (pp. 267–268)

19. **d.** is the answer. As answers a., b., & c. (which are true) indicate, it *is* possible to predict whether or not an adolescent will experiment with drugs. (pp. 280–281)

20. **b.** is the answer. (p. 243)

Essay Question

As a depressant, alcohol slows neural activity and body functions. Although low doses of alcohol may produce relaxation, with larger doses reactions slow, speech slurs, skilled performance deteriorates, and the processing of recent experiences into long-term memories is disrupted. Alcohol also reduces self-awareness and may facilitate sexual and aggressive urges the individual might otherwise resist.

Some people may be biologically vulnerable to alcoholism. This is indicated by the fact that individuals who have an alcoholic biological parent, or males who have an alcoholic identical twin, are more susceptible to alcoholism.

Stress, depression, and the feeling that life is meaningless and without direction are common feelings among heavy users of alcohol and may create a psychological vulnerability to alcoholism.

Especially for teenagers, peer group influence is strong. If an adolescent's friends use alcohol, odds are that he or she will too.

Research suggests three important channels of influence for drug prevention and treatment programs: (1) education about the long-term consequences of alcohol use; (2) efforts to boost people's self-esteem and purpose in life; and (3) attempts to counteract peer pressure that leads to experimentation with drugs.

Key Terms

Writing Definitions

1. The text defines **consciousness** as our awareness of ourselves and our environment. (p. 242)

2. The **fantasy-prone personality** is one who has a vivid imagination and spends an unusual amount of time fantasizing. (p. 243)

3. **Biological rhythms** are periodic fluctuations in our bodies' physiological states, including annual variations in appetite, ninety-minute sleep cycles, the twenty-eight-day menstrual cycle, and circadian rhythms. (p. 245)

4. A **circadian rhythm** is any regular biological rhythm, such as body temperature and sleep-wakefulness, that follows a 24-hour cycle. (p. 245)

   Memory aid: In Latin, *circa* means "about" and *dies* means "day." A **circadian rhythm** is one that is about a day, or 24 hours, in duration.

5. **REM sleep** is the sleep stage in which the brain and eyes are active, the muscles are relaxed, and vivid dreaming occurs; also known as paradoxical sleep. (p. 248)

   Memory aid: **REM** is an acronym for rapid eye movement, the distinguishing feature of this sleep stage that led to its discovery.

6. **Alpha waves** are the relatively slow brain waves characteristic of an awake, relaxed state. (p. 248)

7. **Sleep** is the natural, periodic, reversible loss of consciousness, on which the body and mind depend for healthy functioning. (p. 248)

8. **Hallucinations** are false sensory experiences that occur without any sensory stimulus. (p. 249)

9. **Delta waves** are the larger, slow brain waves associated with deep sleep. (p. 249)

10. **Insomnia** is a sleep disorder in which the person regularly has difficulty in falling or staying asleep. (p. 255)

11. **Narcolepsy** is a sleep disorder in which the victim suffers sudden, uncontrollable sleep attacks, often characterized by entry directly into REM. (p. 255)

12. **Sleep apnea** is a sleep disorder in which the person ceases breathing while asleep, briefly arouses to gasp for air, falls back asleep, and repeats this cycle throughout the night. (p. 256)

    Example: One theory of the Sudden Infant Death Syndrome is that it is caused by **sleep apnea**.

13. A person suffering from **night terrors** experiences episodes of high arousal with apparent terror. Night terrors usually occur during Stage 4 sleep. (p. 256)

14. **Dreams** are vivid sequences of images, emotions, and thoughts, the most vivid of which occur during REM sleep. (p. 257)

15. In Freud's theory of dreaming, the **manifest content** is the remembered story line. (p. 257)

16. In Freud's theory of dreaming, the **latent content** is the underlying but censored meaning of a dream. (p. 258)

    Memory aids for 15 and 16: Manifest means "clearly apparent, obvious"; *latent* means "hidden, concealed." A dream's **manifest content** is that which is obvious; its **latent content** remains hidden until its symbolism is interpreted.

17. **REM rebound** is the tendency for REM sleep to increase following deprivation. (p. 259)

18. **Hypnosis** is a social interaction in which one person (the hypnotist) suggests to another (the subject) that certain perceptions, feelings, thoughts, or behaviors will spontaneously occur. (p. 261)

19. **Posthypnotic amnesia** is the condition in which, in response to the hypnotist's suggestion, subjects are unable to recall what happened while they were under hypnosis. (p. 261)

20. A **posthypnotic suggestion** is a suggestion made during a hypnosis session that is to be carried out when the subject is no longer hypnotized. (p. 266)

21. **Dissociation** is a split between different levels of consciousness, allowing a person to divide attention between two or more thoughts. (p. 266)

22. According to Hilgard, the **hidden observer** is a part of a hypnotized person's consciousness that remains aware of happenings even under hypnosis. Hilgard believes the hidden observer is an example of dissociation. (p. 269)

23. **Psychoactive drugs**—which include stimulants, depressants, hallucinogens—are chemical substances that alter mood and perception. They work by affecting or mimicking the activity of neurotransmitters. (p. 270)

24. **Tolerance** is the diminishing of a psychoactive drug's effect that occurs with repeated use and the need for progressively larger doses in order to produce the same effect. (p. 271)

25. **Withdrawal** refers to the discomfort and distress that follow the discontinued use of addictive drugs. (p. 271)

26. **Physical dependence** is a physiological need for a drug that is indicated by the presence of withdrawal symptoms when the drug is not taken. (p. 271)

27. The psychological need to use a drug is referred to as **psychological dependence**. (p. 271)

28. **Depressants** are psychoactive drugs, such as alcohol, opiates, and barbiturates, that reduce neural activity and slow body functions. (p. 272)

29. **Stimulants** are psychoactive drugs, such as caffeine, nicotine, amphetamines, and cocaine, that excite neural activity and speed up body functions. (p. 272)

30. **Hallucinogens** are psychoactive drugs, such as LSD and marijuana, that distort perception and evoke sensory imagery in the absence of sensory input. (p. 272)

31. **Barbiturates** are depressants, sometimes used to induce sleep or reduce anxiety. (p. 275)

32. **Opiates** are depressants derived from the opium poppy, such as opium, morphine, and heroin; they reduce neural activity and relieve pain. Opiates are among the most strongly addictive of all psychoactive drugs. (p. 275)

33. **Amphetamines** are a type of stimulant and, as such, speed up body functions and neural activity. (p. 275)

34. **LSD** (lysergic acid diethylamide) is a powerful hallucinogen capable of producing vivid false perceptions and disorganization of thought pro-

cesses. LSD produces its unpredictable effects partially because it blocks the action of the neurotransmitter serotonin. (p. 277)

35. The active ingredient in marijuana, **THC** is classified as a mild hallucinogen. (p. 277)

36. The **near-death experience** is an altered state of consciousness that has been reported by some people who have had a close brush with death. (p. 283)

37. **Dualism** is the philosophical belief that the mind and body are distinct entities—the mind nonphysical, the body physical. (p. 284)

    Example: Those who believe that **near-death experiences** are proof of immortality are expressing the **dualist** position that mind and body are separate entities.

38. **Monism** is the philosophical belief that the mind and body are different aspects of the same thing. (p. 284)

Example: The belief that death is final and that no afterlife exists is a reflection of the **monist** position that mind and body are one.

Cross-Check

ACROSS

1. paradoxical	2. age regression
7. dopamine	3. amphetamines
8. nicotine	4. opiates
10. lucid dreams	5. information processing
12. LSD	6. alcohol
13. serial	9. hidden observer
14. spindle	11. delta
17. depressant	15. dissociation
18. hypnogogic	16. alpha
19. barbiturates	17. daydream
21. morning	18. heroin
22. evening	20. THC

FOCUS ON VOCABULARY AND LANGUAGE

Page 241: To psychologists, consciousness is similarly a *fundamental* yet *slippery* concept. In science many fundamental concepts are difficult to define (e.g., life, matter, energy). Consciousness is one of the most basic (*fundamental*) ideas in psychology, yet it is an elusive and difficult concept to grasp (*a slippery concept*).

Waking Consciousness

Page 241: Psychology had nearly *lost consciousness*. Myers is using a little humor here in order to illustrate the fact that changes (*swings*) have taken place during psychology's history. To *"lose consciousness"* can have two meanings in the above sentence: (1) to fall unconscious or pass out and (2) to fail to keep (lose) "consciousness" as the subject matter of psychology. Psychology started out as the study of conscious experience; then, because of problems in scientifically investigating the mind, overt behavior replaced consciousness in the 1920s. Finally, in the 1960s, psychology regained consciousness as a legitimate subject for psychologists to study.

Page 242: . . . yet *consciousness is but the tip of the information-processing iceberg*. Just as most of the mass or volume of an iceberg is below the surface of the ocean and out of sight, most mental functioning goes on without conscious awareness. Consciousness is a small part (*the tip of the iceberg*) of total information processing.

Page 242: . . . so, consciousness is known to *lag* the brain events that *evoke* it. *To lag* means to be late, to be behind, or to follow. So our conscious awareness always follows after (*lags*) the neural activities in the brain that give rise to, or create (*evoke*), it.

Sleep and Dreams

Page 245: . . . limbs often *move in concert*. . . . To *"move in concert"* is to move simultaneously or in synchrony. When we dream of doing something, our arms and legs do *not* move in synchrony (*do not move in concert*) with the activity in the dream.

Page 245: Awake at 4:00 A.M., with a *depressed body*, we may *fret* over concerns: Does a *lovers' spat signal a split*? Our body temperature drops after we go to sleep and begins to rise again toward morning. So if we wake up in the middle of the night our temperature may be low (*depressed body*). We may start to worry (*fret*) over problems. For example, if we've had a minor disagreement or argument with a loved one (*lovers' spat*), we may think this means the relationship is going to end (*signals a split*).

Page 247: *Pulling an all-nighter*, we feel *groggiest* about 4:00 A.M., but we feel a *second wind* as our normal wake-up time arrives. If we decide to stay up all night (*pull an all-nighter*), say, to finish a term paper by the deadline, we feel most mentally confused and uncoordinated (*groggiest*) around the middle of the night, but as our usual time for getting up approaches, we begin to feel renewed energy (*a second wind*).

Page 247: . . . *jet lag* . . . When we travel by plane across several time zones we may experience mental and physical fatigue (*jet lag*). Because our biological clocks naturally tend toward a 25-hour day, we may find it easier to jet west, which gives us a longer day, than to travel east.

Page 248: Before long, the machine *went wild*, tracing *deep zigzags* on the graph paper. The discovery of REM (Rapid Eye Movement) occurred accidentally. To see if an EEG (electroencephalograph) was working properly Aserinsky placed the electrodes near his 8-year-old son's eyes. Periodically during the night the machine responded vigorously (*went wild*), producing a pattern of high-frequency waves (*deep zigzags*) on the printout. These patterns were produced by rapid, jerky eye movements and accompanied by very frantic brain activity, and when awakened during one of these periods the boy said he was dreaming.

Page 248: Rather than continuing in deep *slumber*, you *ascend* from your initial *sleep dive*. During a typical night's sleep (*slumber*) you go through a number of distinct stages. If you are awake and relaxed, perhaps with your eyes closed, an EEG would show alpha waves. As you fall deeper and deeper into sleep (*sleep dive*), your brain waves continue to slow down. By Stage 4 your brain waves are long and slow (*delta waves*), but you don't stay here all night; instead, you go back up (*ascend*) through the stages into the most unique and interesting stage of all, REM (Rapid Eye Movement) sleep, where most dreams occur. Here, the brain waves resemble Stage 1 waves, but there is much more internal physiological arousal now, and, paradoxically, your muscles are almost paralyzed.

Page 251: As the night *wears on*, deep Stage 4 sleep gets progressively briefer and then disappears. As the night progresses (*wears on*), the time spent in Stage 4 deep sleep gets shorter (and eventually ceases altogether) and time spent in REM sleep gets longer.

Page 252: . . . *drowsy* . . . If you were deprived of sleep for a few nights, you would feel very tired and sleepy (*drowsy*).

Page 252: People today more than ever suffer from sleep patterns that *thwart* their having an energized feeling of well-being. Because of the pressures of work, school, social obligations, and so on, we often have sleep schedules that prevent (*thwart*) us from getting the amount of sleep we need. The consequence of this "sleep debt" (*accumulated insufficient sleep*) is a general lack of energy and discomfort (*malaise*), and a frequent feeling of sleepiness.

Page 252: Teenagers typically need 8 or 9 hours sleep, but they now average nearly 2 hours less sleep a night than their counterparts of 80 years ago (Holden, 1993; Maas, 1999). Many fill this need by using *home room* for their first *siesta* and after-lunch *study hall* for a *slumber party*. Today's young students often get much less sleep than they need and so, many end up using the classroom set aside for informal activities (*home room*) for a short sleep (*siesta*) and the quiet school area meant for study (*study hall*) may be occupied by whole groups of sleeping students (*slumber party*).

Page 255: These physiological discoveries are only beginning to solve the ongoing *riddle* of sleep. Recent research has shown that sleep helps us repair and restore body tissue (*recuperate*) and plays a part in physical growth. These findings are just starting to clear up the continuing puzzle (*riddle*) of sleep.

Page 255: Both [alcohol and sleeping pills] reduce REM sleep and can leave a person with the *next-day blahs*. The most popular fast remedies (*quick fixes*) for insomnia are sleeping pills and alcohol. Unfortunately, they can make the problem worse (*aggravate it*) by suppressing REM sleep; the next day the person may have less energy and feel very tired (*next-day blahs*). When these "remedies" are discontinued, the insomnia may get worse.

Page 256: As a traffic menace, *"snoozing is second only to boozing,"* says the American Sleep Disorders Association, and those with narcolepsy are especially at risk (Aldrich, 1989). Falling asleep (*snoozing*) while driving is almost as serious a problem as drinking (*boozing*) and driving. People with **narcolepsy** suffer from occasional periods of uncontrollable sleepiness often associated with emotional arousal, and are thus in danger, and dangerous, while driving.

Page 258: . . . He [Freud] argued that by fulfilling wishes, a dream provides a *psychic safety valve* that discharges otherwise unacceptable feelings. The story line of the dream (**manifest content**) is a disguised version of the real, but hidden, meaning of the dream (**latent content**). According to Freud, by symbolically expressing our hidden desires and exotic wishes, dreams allow us to ventilate unconscious drives that might otherwise be harmful (*acts as a psychic safety valve*). (A *safety valve* allows a system to dissipate built-up pressure and thus may prevent an explosion.)

Page 258: However, his critics say *it is time to wake up* from Freud's dream theory, which actually is one of his greatest failures. Dream interpretation, they say, is a *nightmare.* Myers is having some fun with a play on words here. The expression "it is time to wake up from something" means one should start paying attention to reality and facts, rather than fantasy, and to say something is "a nightmare" means that it is unruly, difficult, or even frightening. Most contemporary psychologists believe that REM sleep and dreams are important aspects of our life but that Freud's theory of dream interpretation is erroneous, unscientific, and misguided (*a nightmare*); thus, we should not place much reliance on its explanations (*it is time to wake up from it*).

Pages 258–259: . . . our ever-active brain *weaves a story line* from whatever is available. . . . The mind (*cognitive machinery*) reacts to meaningless stimuli by imposing meaning (*it weaves a story line*). Bursts of neural activity in the visual cortex, along with activity in the emotional limbic system, occur at the same time as rapid eye movements, and so it may be that dreams arise from the mind's ceaseless attempts to make sense of these unrelated events (*it weaves a story line*).

Hypnosis

Page 261: Thus, *hypnosis—or mesmerism,* as it was then called—became linked with *quackery.* Hypnosis—a social interaction in which a hypnotist suggests to a subject that certain perceptions, behaviors, and so on will spontaneously occur—was first referred to as *mesmerism* after the eighteenth-century physician Mesmer, who promoted its use. Because the Franklin commission found no scientific evidence for Mesmer's "cures," they concluded that hypnosis was fraudulent or bogus (*quackery*).

Page 263: . . . played a *clever stunt* on them. Researchers used a standard hypnotic induction with students, and then, in an attempt to make them believe they were hypnotizable, played an ingenious trick (*clever stunt*) on them. The happy trickster (*merry prankster*) experimenters secretly projected the stimuli (red light, green light, strange music, etc.) that the students had been led to believe they would see under hypnosis. Most were fooled by this strange (*weird*) experience and actually believed they were hypnotizable.

Page 266 (margin): "Hypnosis is not a psychological *truth serum,*" concludes researcher Kenneth Bowers (1987), "and to regard it as such has been a source of considerable *mischief.*" Research shows that hypnotists can subtly influence what people recall and they may inadvertently create false memories by making suggestions and asking leading questions. Thus, hypnosis is not like a so-called *truth serum* (a drug alleged to make people tell the truth) but rather has caused a great deal of annoying—and possibly harmful—effects (*considerable mischief*).

Page 270: So, might the two views—social influence and divided consciousness—*be bridged?* Although there are a number of different explanations about what hypnosis really is, Myers suggests that it may be possible to bring together some of these theories (*bridge the differences*). Thus, hypnosis may be both a part of normal aspects of social influence and our ability to have a divided (*or split*) consciousness.

Drugs and Consciousness

Page 271: A person who rarely drinks alcohol might get *tipsy* on one can of beer, but an experienced drinker may not get *tipsy* until the *second six-pack.* Prolonged use of a psychoactive drug produces an ability to take more and more of the substance (*tolerance*). Thus, an infrequent user of alcohol may get somewhat intoxicated (*tipsy*) from one beer, but for a regular drinker there might be little effect until 6 or more beers have been consumed (*until the second six-pack [of beer]*).

Page 273: . . . as when *tipsy* restaurant patrons leave extravagant tips. Alcohol can increase both harmful and helpful inclinations. Thus, it often happens that restaurant clientele give a larger gratuity (*extravagant tips*) when they are more intoxicated (*tipsy*). Whatever tendencies you have when sober will be more obvious when you are drunk.

Page 274: If, as commonly believed, liquor is the *quicker pick-her-upper,* the effect lies in that powerful sex organ, the mind. Alcohol (liquor) is thought by many to speed up the process of meeting members of the opposite sex and to lower sexual inhibitions. Thus, a male may believe that use of alcohol will facilitate his ability to initiate contact and get to know a female (a *quicker pick-her-upper*). Myers points out that not only alcohol is involved, but also our beliefs about its effects on sexual behavior (the effect lies partly in that *powerful sex organ, the mind*).

Page 275: But for short-term pleasure *one pays a long-term price,* which for the heroin users is the *gnawing craving* for another *fix* . . . . There is a cost (*one pays a long-term price*) for enjoying drug-induced pleasures, and for an addict this may be a persistent inner torment (*gnawing*) and an urgent, persistent desire (*craving*) for another dose of the drug (a *fix*).

Page 276: . . . *crack* . . . *Crack* is a very potent, synthetic form of cocaine which produces a feeling of euphoria (*a rush*) followed by deep depression, tiredness, and irritability (*a "crash"*).

Page 277: . . . *"acid trip"* . . . Taking any psychoactive drug is called a *trip* or *tripping out*. When LSD (acid) is used, it is called an *acid trip*; regular users are sometimes called *acid-heads*.

Page 277: . . . marijuana may *spell* relief. Although there are many reasons for not taking marijuana, it does have some therapeutic applications, such as alleviating the sick feelings that result from taking the drugs used to treat cancer (chemotherapy). Thus, it may provide (*spell*) relief for some patients.

Page 278: Clearly, being *stoned* is not conducive to learning. Marijuana use disrupts motor skills, perceptual abilities, memory formation, and short-term retention. Obviously, being under the influence of marijuana (*being stoned*) does not help memory and learning.

Near-Death Experiences

Page 284: Such monists generally believe that death is real and that without bodies we truly are *nobodies*. A *nobody* is someone of no importance. Myers is making a joke here: If mind and body are one (the monist position), then when we are dead and gone, there is nothing left, and we are *nobodies* (i.e., we have no bodies) and so have no afterlife existence.

Learning

Chapter Overview

"No topic is closer to the heart of psychology than learning, a relatively permanent change in an organism's behavior due to experience." Chapter 8 covers the basic principles of three forms of learning: classical, or respondent, conditioning, in which we learn associations between events; operant conditioning, in which we learn to engage in behaviors that are rewarded and to avoid behaviors that are punished; and observational learning, in which we learn by observing and imitating others.

The chapter also covers several important issues, including the generality of principles of learning, the role of cognitive processes in learning, and the ways in which learning is constrained by the biological predispositions of different species.

NOTE: Answer guidelines for all Chapter 8 questions begin on page 236.

Introducing Learning (pp. 287–290)

> David Myers at times uses idioms that are unfamiliar to some readers. If you do not know the meaning of any of the following words, phrases, or expressions in the context in which they appear in the text, refer to page 246 for an explanation: . . . *breeds hope; mugged; Japanese rancher reportedly herds cattle.*

Introduction Preview

First, skim the introduction. Then read the following objective and, as you read the text, search for the information that will enable you to meet that objective. Answer guidelines are provided on page 236.

1. Discuss the importance of experience in learning, and describe the role of association in learning.

Stepping Through the Introduction

After you have read the introduction, complete the sentences and answer the questions. As you proceed, evaluate your performance by consulting the answers on page 237. Do not continue with the next section until you understand each answer. If you need to, review or reread the section in the textbook before continuing.

1. A relatively permanent change in an organism's behavior due to experience is called

   _____ .

2. More than 200 years ago, philosophers such as John Locke and David Hume argued that an important factor in learning is our tendency to

   _____ events that occur in a sequence. Even simple animals, such as the sea snail *Aplysia*, can learn simple _

   _____ between stimuli. This type of learning is called _____

   _____ .

3. The type of learning in which the organism learns to associate two stimuli is _____ conditioning.

4. The tendency of organisms to associate a response and its consequence forms the basis of _____ conditioning.

5. Complex animals often learn behaviors merely by _____ others perform them.

6. Early in the twentieth century, psychologist _____ urged psychologists to discard references to mental concepts in favor of studying observable behavior. This view, called _____ , influenced American psychology during the first half of that century.

Classical Conditioning (pp. 290–300)

> If you do not know the meaning of any of the following words, phrases, or expressions in the context in which they appear in the text, refer to pages 246–247 for an explanation (note that some items appear in the chapter introduction): . . . *For many people, the name Ivan Pavlov rings a bell; drooled; sets your mouth to watering; red-light district; breaking up . . . fire-breathing heartthrob; willy-nilly; we stand on his shoulders; crack cocaine users; legendary significance.*

Section Preview

Answer guidelines are provided on page 237.

1. Describe the nature of classical conditioning, and show how it demonstrates associative learning.

2. Explain the processes of acquisition, extinction, spontaneous recovery, generalization, and discrimination.

3. Discuss the importance of cognitive processes and biological constraints in classical conditioning.

4. Discuss the importance of Pavlov's work in classical conditioning and explain how Pavlov paved the way for the behaviorist position.

Stepping Through the Section

Answers are provided on page 237.

1. Classical conditioning was first explored by the Russian physiologist _____ .

2. In Pavlov's classic experiment, a tone, or

_____ _____ ,

is sounded just before food, the

_____ _____ ,

is placed in the animal's mouth.

3. An animal will salivate when food is placed in its mouth. This salivation is called the

_____ _____ .

4. Eventually, the dogs in Pavlov's experiment would salivate on hearing the tone. This salivation is called the _____

_____ .

5. The initial learning of a conditioned response is called _____ . For many conditioning situations, the optimal interval between a neutral stimulus and the UCS is

_____ _____ .

6. When the UCS is presented prior to a neutral stimulus, conditioning _____ (does/does not) occur.

Explain why learning theorists consider classically conditioned behaviors to be biologically adaptive.

7. Michael Domjan's sexual conditioning studies with quail demonstrate that classical conditioning is highly adaptive because it helps animals _____ and _____ .

8. If a CS is repeatedly presented without the UCS, _____ soon occurs; that is, the CR diminishes.

9. Following a rest, however, the CR reappears in response to the CS; this phenomenon is called

_____ _____ .

10. Subjects often respond to a similar stimulus as they would to the original CS. This phenomenon is called _____ . Subjects can, however, also be trained not to respond to these similar stimuli. This learned ability is called

_____ .

11. Experiments by Rescorla and Wagner demonstrate that a CS must reliably _____ the UCS for an association to develop and, more generally, that _____ processes play a role in conditioning. It is as if the animal learns to _____ that the UCS will occur.

Describe two issues that have led to the recent reconsideration of behaviorism.

12. The importance of cognitive processes in human conditioning is demonstrated by the failure of classical conditioning as a treatment for

_____ .

13. Garcia discovered that rats would associate _____ with taste but not with other stimuli. Garcia found that taste-aversion conditioning _____ (would/would not) occur when the delay between the CS and the UCS was more than an hour.

14. Results such as these demonstrate that the principles of learning are constrained by the _____ predispositions of each animal species and that they help each species _____ to its environment.

Explain why the study of classical conditioning is important.

15. Research studies demonstrate that the body's immune system _____ (can/cannot) be classically conditioned. Other investigations of how classical conditioning can be applied reveal that older adults who condition easily, and whose brains do not have a shortage of the neurotransmitter _____ , rarely develop _____ disease.

Describe the Watson and Rayner experiment .

Operant Conditioning (pp. 300–313)

> If you do not know the meaning of any of the following words, phrases, or expressions in the context in which they appear in the text, refer to pages 247–248 for an explanation: *to pull habits out of a rat; . . . between Bach's music and Stravinsky's; pastes gold stars; snooze button; Billy throws a tantrum; goofing off; the kick that often comes within seconds; a sale with every pitch; paid on a piecework basis; pop quiz; loses a treat; drawbacks; hit with a couple of speeding tickets; backfire; piggy bank; stirred a hornet's nest; rule of thumb.*

Section Preview

Answer guidelines are provided on page 238.

1. Describe the process of operant conditioning, including the procedure of shaping.

2. Identify the different types of reinforcers, and describe the four major schedules of partial reinforcement.

3. Discuss the effects of punishment on behavior.

4. Discuss evidence of the importance of cognitive and biological processes in operant conditioning.

5. Describe some major applications of operant conditioning.

Stepping Through the Section

Answers are provided on page 238.

1. Classical conditioning associates _____ stimuli with stimuli that elicit responses that are _____ .

2. The reflexive responses of classical conditioning involve _____ behavior. In contrast, behavior that is more spontaneous and that is influenced by its consequences is called _____ behavior.

3. Using Thorndike's _____

_____ _____

as a starting point, Skinner developed a behavioral technology. He designed an apparatus, called the _____

_____ , to investigate learning in animals.

4. The procedure in which a person teaches an animal to perform an intricate behavior by building up to it in small steps is called _____ . This method involves reinforcing successive _____ of the desired behavior.

5. An event that increases the frequency of a preceding response is a _____ .

6. A stimulus that strengthens a response by presenting a stimulus after a response is a

_____ _____ .

7. A stimulus that strengthens a response by reducing or removing an aversive (unpleasant) stimulus is a _____

_____ .

8. Reinforcers, such as food and shock, that are related to basic needs and therefore do not rely on learning are called _____

_____ . Reinforcers that must be

conditioned and therefore derive their power through association are called

_____ _____ .

9. Children who are able to delay gratification tend to become _____ (more/less) socially competent and high achieving as adolescents.

10. Immediate reinforcement _____ (is/is not) more effective than its alternative, _____ reinforcement. This explains in part the difficulty that _____ users have in quitting their habits, as well as the tendency of some teens to engage in risky,

_____ _____ .

11. The procedure involving reinforcement of each and every response is called

_____ _____ .

Under these conditions, learning is _____ (rapid/slow). When this type of reinforcement is discontinued, extinction is _____ (rapid/slow).

12. The procedure in which responses are reinforced only part of the time is called _____ reinforcement. Under these conditions, learning is generally _____ (faster/slower) than it is with continuous reinforcement. Behavior reinforced in this manner is _____ (very/not very) resistant to extinction.

13. When behavior is reinforced after a set number of responses, a _____- _____ schedule is in effect.

14. Three-year-old Yusef knows that if he cries when he wants a treat, his mother will sometimes give in. When, as in this case, reinforcement occurs after an unpredictable number of responses, a

_____-_____

schedule is being used.

15. Reinforcement of the first response after a set interval of time defines the

_____-_____ schedule. An example of this schedule is

_____ .

16. When the first response after varying amounts of time is reinforced, a _____- _____ schedule is in effect.

Describe the typical patterns of response under fixed-interval, fixed-ratio, variable-interval, and variable-ratio schedules of reinforcement.

17. An aversive consequence that decreases the likelihood of the behavior that preceded it is called

_____ .

Describe some drawbacks to the use of physical punishment.

18. Skinner and other behaviorists resisted the growing belief that expectations, perceptions, and other _____ processes have a valid place in the science of psychology.

19. When a well-learned route in a maze is blocked, rats sometimes choose an alternative route, acting as if they were consulting a

_____ _____ .

20. Animals may learn from experience even when reinforcement is not available. When learning is not apparent until reinforcement has been provided, _____

_____ is said to have occurred.

21. When people are rewarded for doing what they already enjoy, their intrinsic motivation may be undermined; this is the _____ _____ .

22. Operant conditioning _____ (is/is not) constrained by an animal's biological predispositions.

23. The use of teaching machines and programmed textbooks was an early application of the operant conditioning procedure of _____ to education. Online _____ systems and software that is _____ are newer examples of this application of operant principles. Reinforcement principles can also be used to enhance _____ abilities by shaping successive approximations of new skills.

24. In boosting productivity in the workplace, positive reinforcement is _____ (more/less) effective when applied to specific behaviors than when given to reward general merit and when the desired performance is _____ . For such behaviors, immediate reinforcement is _____ (more/no more) effective than delayed reinforcement.

Learning by Observation (pp. 313–315)

> If you do not know the meaning of the following phrases in the context in which they appear in the text, refer to page 248 for an explanation: *children who observed the aggressive outburst were much more likely to lash out at the doll.*

Section Preview

Answer guidelines are provided on page 239.

1. Describe the process of observational learning.

Stepping Through the Section

Answers are provided on page 239.

1. Learning by observing and imitating others is called _____ , or _____ _____ . This form of learning _____ (occurs/does not occur) in species other than our own.

2. By age _____ , infants will imitate acts modeled on television.

3. The psychologist best known for research on observational learning is _____ . In one experiment, the child who viewed an adult punch an inflatable doll played _____ (more/less) aggressively than the child who had not observed the adult.

4. Children will also model positive, or _____ , behaviors.

5. Models are most effective when their words and actions are _____ and when they are perceived as _____ , _____ , or _____ .

Progress Test 1

Multiple-Choice Questions

Circle your answers to the following questions and check them with the answers on page 239. If your answer is incorrect, read the explanation for why it is incorrect and then consult the appropriate pages of the text (in parentheses following the correct answer).

1. Learning is best defined as:
   a. any behavior emitted by an organism without being elicited.
   b. a change in the behavior of an organism.
   c. a relatively permanent change in the behavior of an organism due to experience.
   d. behavior based on operant rather than respondent conditioning.

2. The type of learning associated with Skinner is:
   a. classical conditioning.
   b. operant conditioning.
   c. respondent conditioning.
   d. observational learning.

3. In Pavlov's original experiment with dogs, the meat served as a(n):
   a. CS.
   b. CR.
   c. UCS.
   d. UCR.

4. In Pavlov's original experiment with dogs, the tone was initially a(n) _____ stimulus; after it was paired with meat, it became a(n) _____ stimulus.
   a. conditioned; neutral
   b. neutral; conditioned
   c. conditioned; unconditioned
   d. unconditioned; conditioned

5. In order to obtain a reward a monkey learns to press a lever when a 1000-Hz tone is on but not when a 1200-Hz tone is on. What kind of training is this?
   a. extinction
   b. generalization
   c. classical conditioning
   d. spontaneous recovery
   e. discrimination

6. Which of the following statements concerning reinforcement is correct?
   a. Learning is most rapid with intermittent reinforcement, but continuous reinforcement produces the greatest resistance to extinction.
   b. Learning is most rapid with continuous reinforcement, but intermittent reinforcement produces the greatest resistance to extinction.
   c. Learning is fastest and resistance to extinction is greatest after continuous reinforcement.
   d. Learning is fastest and resistance to extinction is greatest following intermittent reinforcement.

7. Cognitive processes are:
   a. unimportant in classical and operant conditioning.
   b. important in both classical and operant conditioning.
   c. more important in classical than in operant conditioning.
   d. more important in operant than in classical conditioning.

8. The highest and most consistent rate of response is produced by a _____ schedule.
   a. fixed-ratio
   b. variable-ratio
   c. fixed-interval
   d. variable-interval

9. A response that leads to the removal of an unpleasant stimulus is one being:
   a. positively reinforced.
   b. negatively reinforced.
   c. punished.
   d. extinguished.

10. When a conditioned stimulus is presented without an accompanying unconditioned stimulus, _____ will soon take place.
    a. generalization
    b. discrimination
    c. extinction
    d. aversion
    e. spontaneous recovery

11. One difference between classical and operant conditioning is that:
    a. in classical conditioning the responses operate on the environment to produce rewarding or punishing stimuli.
    b. in operant conditioning the responses are triggered by preceding stimuli.
    c. in classical conditioning the responses are automatically elicited by stimuli.
    d. in operant conditioning the responses are reflexive.

12. In Garcia and Koelling's studies of taste-aversion learning, rats learned to associate:
    a. taste with electric shock.
    b. sights and sounds with sickness.
    c. taste with sickness.
    d. taste and sounds with electric shock.
    e. taste and sounds with electric shock, then sickness.

13. In Pavlov's original experiment with dogs, salivation to meat was the:
    a. CS.
    b. CR.
    c. UCS.
    d. UCR.

14. Learning by imitating others' behaviors is called _____ learning. The researcher best known for studying this type of learning is _____ .
    a. secondary; Skinner
    b. observational; Bandura
    c. secondary; Pavlov
    d. observational; Watson

15. When people are paid for performing tasks they enjoy, their self-motivation may decrease. This is called:
    a. latent learning.
    b. the overjustification effect.
    c. primary reinforcement.
    d. modeling.
    e. negative reinforcement.

16. Punishment is a controversial way of controlling behavior because:

   a. behavior is not forgotten and may return.
   b. punishing stimuli often create fear.
   c. punishment often increases aggressiveness.
   d. of all of the above reasons.

17. Classical conditioning experiments by Rescorla and Wagner demonstrate that an important factor in conditioning is:

   a. the subject's age.
   b. the strength of the stimuli.
   c. the predictability of an association.
   d. the similarity of stimuli.
   e. all of the above.

18. Which of the following is an example of reinforcement?

   a. presenting a positive stimulus after a response
   b. removing an unpleasant stimulus after a response

c. being told that you have done a good job
d. All of the above are examples.

19. Which of the following is a form of associative learning?

   a. classical conditioning
   b. operant conditioning
   c. observational learning
   d. all of the above

20. For the most rapid conditioning, a CS should be presented:

   a. about 1 second after the UCS.
   b. about one-half second before the UCS.
   c. about 15 seconds before the UCS.
   d. at the same time as the UCS.

Matching Items

Match each definition or description with the appropriate term.

Definitions or Descriptions

   _____ **1.** presentation of a desired stimulus
   _____ **2.** tendency for similar stimuli to evoke a CR
   _____ **3.** removal of an aversive stimulus
   _____ **4.** an innately reinforcing stimulus
   _____ **5.** an acquired reinforcer
   _____ **6.** responses are reinforced after an unpredictable amount of time
   _____ **7.** each and every response is reinforced
   _____ **8.** reinforcing closer and closer approximations of a behavior
   _____ **9.** the reappearance of a weakened CR
   _____ **10.** presentation of an aversive stimulus
   _____ **11.** learning that becomes apparent only after reinforcement is provided

Terms

   a. shaping
   b. punishment
   c. spontaneous recovery
   d. latent learning
   e. positive reinforcement
   f. negative reinforcement
   g. primary reinforcer
   h. generalization
   i. conditioned reinforcer
   j. continuous reinforcement
   k. variable-interval schedule

Progress Test 2

Progress Test 2 should be completed during a final chapter review. Answer the following questions after you thoroughly understand the correct answers for the section reviews and Progress Test 1.

Multiple-Choice Questions

1. During extinction, the _____ is omitted; as a result, the _____ seems to disappear.
   - **a.** UCS; UCR
   - **b.** CS; CR
   - **c.** UCS; CR
   - **d.** CS; UCR

2. In Watson and Rayner's experiment, the loud noise was the _____ and the white rat was the _____.
   - **a.** CS; CR
   - **b.** UCS; CS
   - **c.** CS; UCS
   - **d.** UCS; CR
   - **e.** UCR; CR

3. In which of the following may classical conditioning play a role?
   - **a.** emotional problems
   - **b.** the body's immune response
   - **c.** how animals adapt to the environment
   - **d.** helping drug addicts
   - **e.** all of the above

4. Shaping is a(n) _____ technique for _____ a behavior.
   - **a.** operant; establishing
   - **b.** operant; suppressing
   - **c.** respondent; establishing
   - **d.** respondent; suppressing

5. In Pavlov's studies of classical conditioning of a dog's salivary responses, spontaneous recovery occurred:
   - **a.** during acquisition, when the CS was first paired with the UCS.
   - **b.** during extinction, when the CS was first presented by itself.
   - **c.** when the CS was reintroduced following extinction of the CR and a rest period.
   - **d.** during discrimination training, when several conditioned stimuli were introduced.

6. For operant conditioning to be most effective, when should the reinforcers be presented in relation to the desired response?
   - **a.** immediately before
   - **b.** immediately after
   - **c.** at the same time as
   - **d.** at least a half hour before
   - **e.** in any of the above sequences

7. In distinguishing between negative reinforcers and punishment, we note that:
   - **a.** punishment, but not negative reinforcement, involves use of an aversive stimulus.
   - **b.** in contrast to punishment, negative reinforcement decreases the likelihood of a response by the presentation of an aversive stimulus.
   - **c.** in contrast to punishment, negative reinforcement increases the likelihood of a response by the presentation of an aversive stimulus.
   - **d.** in contrast to punishment, negative reinforcement increases the likelihood of a response by the termination of an aversive stimulus.

8. The "piecework," or commission, method of payment is an example of which reinforcement schedule?
   - **a.** fixed-interval
   - **b.** variable-interval
   - **c.** fixed-ratio
   - **d.** variable-ratio

9. Putting on your coat when it is cold outside is a behavior that is maintained by:
   - **a.** discrimination learning.
   - **b.** punishment.
   - **c.** negative reinforcement.
   - **d.** classical conditioning.
   - **e.** positive reinforcement.

10. On an intermittent reinforcement schedule, reinforcement is given:
   - **a.** in very small amounts.
   - **b.** randomly.
   - **c.** for successive approximations of a desired behavior.
   - **d.** only some of the time.

11. You teach your dog to fetch the paper by giving him a cookie each time he does so. This is an example of:
   - **a.** operant conditioning.
   - **b.** classical conditioning.
   - **c.** conditioned reinforcement.
   - **d.** partial reinforcement.

12. To be effective in promoting observational learning, models should be:
   - **a.** perceived as similar to the observers.
   - **b.** respected and admired.
   - **c.** consistent in their actions and words.
   - **d.** successful.
   - **e.** any of the above.

13. A cognitive map is a(n):
  a. mental representation of one's environment.
  b. sequence of thought processes leading from one idea to another.
  c. set of instructions detailing the most effective means of teaching a particular concept.
  d. biological predisposition to learn a particular skill.
  e. educational tool based on operant conditioning techniques.

14. After exploring a complicated maze for several days, a rat subsequently ran the maze with very few errors when food was placed in the goal box for the first time. This performance illustrates:
  a. classical conditioning.
  b. discrimination learning.
  c. observational learning.
  d. latent learning.

15. Leon's psychology instructor has scheduled an exam every third week of the term. Leon will probably study the most just before an exam and the least just after an exam. This is because the schedule of exams is reinforcing studying according to which schedule?
  a. fixed-ratio   **c.** fixed-interval
  b. variable-ratio **d.** variable-interval

16. Operant conditioning is to _____ as classical conditioning is to _____ .
  a. Pavlov; Watson   **c.** Pavlov; Skinner
  b. Skinner; Bandura **d.** Skinner; Pavlov

17. Online testing systems and interactive software are applications of the operant conditioning principles of:
  a. shaping and immediate reinforcement.
  b. immediate reinforcement and punishment.
  c. shaping and primary reinforcement.
  d. continuous reinforcement and punishment.

18. Fishing is reinforced according to which schedule?
  a. fixed-interval   **c.** variable-interval
  b. fixed-ratio   **d.** variable-ratio

19. Which of the following is the best example of a conditioned reinforcer?
  a. putting on a coat on a cold day
  b. relief from pain after the dentist stops drilling your teeth

  c. receiving a cool drink after washing your mother's car on a hot day
  d. receiving an approving nod from the boss for a job well done
  e. having a big meal after going without food all day

20. Experiments on taste-aversion learning demonstrate that:
  a. for the conditioning of certain stimuli, the UCS need not immediately follow the CS.
  b. any perceivable stimulus can become a CS.
  c. all animals are biologically primed to associate illness with the taste of a tainted food.
  d. all of the above are true.

True-False Items

Indicate whether each statement is true or false by placing *T* or *F* in the blank next to the item.

_____ **1.** Operant conditioning involves behavior that is primarily reflexive.

_____ **2.** The optimal interval between CS and UCS is about 15 seconds.

_____ **3.** Negative reinforcement decreases the likelihood that a response will recur.

_____ **4.** The learning of a new behavior proceeds most rapidly with continuous reinforcement.

_____ **5.** As a rule, variable schedules of reinforcement produce more consistent rates of responding than fixed schedules.

_____ **6.** Cognitive processes are of relatively little importance in learning.

_____ **7.** Although punishment may be effective in suppressing behavior, it can have several undesirable side effects.

_____ **8.** All animals, including rats and birds, are biologically predisposed to associate taste cues with sickness.

_____ **9.** Whether the CS or UCS is presented first seems not to matter in terms of the ease of classical conditioning.

_____ **10.** Spontaneous recovery refers to the tendency of extinguished behaviors to reappear suddenly.

Thinking Critically About Chapter 8

Answer these questions the day before an exam as a final check on your understanding of the chapter's terms and concepts.

Multiple-Choice Questions

1. You always rattle the box of dog biscuits before giving your dog a treat. As you do so, your dog salivates. Rattling the box is a(n) _____ ; your dog's salivation is a(n) _____ .
   a. CS; CR
   b. CS; UCR
   c. UCS; CR
   d. UCS; UCR

2. You are expecting an important letter in the mail. As the regular delivery time approaches you glance more and more frequently out the window, searching for the letter carrier. Your behavior in this situation typifies that associated with which schedule of reinforcement?
   a. fixed-ratio
   b. variable-ratio
   c. fixed-interval
   d. variable-interval

3. Jack finally takes out the garbage in order to get his father to stop pestering him. Jack's behavior is being influenced by:
   a. positive reinforcement.
   b. negative reinforcement.
   c. a primary reinforcer.
   d. punishment.

4. Mrs. Ramirez often tells her children that it is important to buckle their seat belts while riding in the car, but she rarely does so herself. Her children will probably learn to:
   a. use their seat belts and tell others it is important to do so.
   b. use their seat belts but not tell others it is important to do so.
   c. tell others it is important to use seat belts but rarely use them themselves.
   d. neither tell others that seat belts are important nor use them.

5. A pigeon can easily be taught to flap its wings in order to avoid shock but not for food reinforcement. According to the text, this is most likely so because:
   a. pigeons are biologically predisposed to flap their wings in order to escape aversive events and to use their beaks to obtain food.
   b. shock is a more motivating stimulus for birds than food is.

   c. hungry animals have difficulty delaying their eating long enough to learn *any* new skill.
   d. of all of the above reasons.

6. From a casino owner's viewpoint, which of the following jackpot-payout schedules would be the most desirable for reinforcing customer use of a slot machine?
   a. variable-ratio
   b. fixed-ratio
   c. variable-interval
   d. fixed-interval

7. After discovering that her usual route home was closed due to road repairs, Sharetta used her knowledge of the city and sense of direction to find an alternate route. This is an example of:
   a. latent learning.
   b. observational learning.
   c. shaping.
   d. using a cognitive map.
   e. discrimination.

For questions 8 to 11, use the following information. As a child, you were playing in the yard one day when a neighbor's cat wandered over. Your mother (who has a terrible fear of animals) screamed and snatched you into her arms. Her behavior caused you to cry. You now have a fear of cats.

8. Identify the CS.
   a. your mother's behavior
   b. your crying
   c. the cat
   d. your fear today

9. Identify the UCS.
   a. your mother's behavior
   b. your crying
   c. the cat
   d. your fear today

10. Identify the CR.
   a. your mother's behavior
   b. your crying
   c. the cat
   d. your fear today

11. Identify the UCR.
   a. your mother's behavior
   b. your crying
   c. the cat
   d. your fear today

12. The manager of a manufacturing plant wishes to use positive reinforcement to increase the productivity of workers. Which of the following procedures would probably be the most effective?
   a. Deserving employees are given a general merit bonus at the end of each fiscal year.
   b. A productivity goal that seems attainable, yet is unrealistic, is set for each employee.
   c. Employees are given immediate bonuses for specific behaviors related to productivity.
   d. Employees who fail to meet standards of productivity receive pay cuts.

13. Which of the following would be most likely to result in the overjustification effect?
    a. Each day that her son fails to clean his room, Mrs. Shih adds an additional chore he must complete.
    b. Kim's mother decides to reward her daughter's enjoyment of karate by paying her 75 cents for each hour that she practices.
    c. The manager of a shoe store decides to give a bonus to the employee who sells the most shoes each week.
    d. After her soccer team's poor performance, the coach scolds the players.
    e. Greg's father "pays" himself 2 dollars a day for not smoking.

14. Bill once had a blue car that was in the shop more than it was out. Since then he will not even consider owning blue- or green-colored cars. Bill's aversion to green cars is an example of:
    a. discrimination.
    b. generalization.
    c. latent learning.
    d. the overjustification effect.

15. After watching coverage of the Olympics on television recently, Lynn and Susan have been staging their own "summer games." Which of the following best accounts for their behavior?
    a. classical conditioning   d. shaping
    b. observational learning   e. discrimination
    c. latent learning

16. Two groups of rats receive classical conditioning trials in which a tone and electric shock are presented. For Group 1 the electric shock always follows the tone. For Group 2 the tone and shock occur randomly. Which of the following is likely to result?
    a. The tone will become a CS for Group 1 but not for Group 2.
    b. The tone will become a CS for Group 2 but not for Group 1.
    c. The tone will become a CS for both groups.
    d. The tone will not become a CS for either group.

17. Last evening May-ling ate her first cheeseburger and french fries at an American fast-food restaurant. A few hours later she became ill. It can be expected that:
    a. May-ling will develop an aversion to the sight of a cheeseburger and french fries.
    b. May-ling will develop an aversion to the taste of a cheeseburger and french fries.

    c. May-ling will not associate her illness with the food she ate.
    d. May-ling will associate her sickness with something she experienced immediately before she became ill.

18. Reggie's mother tells him that he can watch TV after he cleans his room. Evidently, Reggie's mother is attempting to use _____ to increase room cleaning.
    a. operant conditioning
    b. secondary reinforcement
    c. positive reinforcement
    d. all of the above

19. Which of the following is an example of shaping?
    a. A dog learns to salivate at the sight of a box of dog biscuits.
    b. A new driver learns to stop at an intersection when the light changes to red.
    c. A parrot is rewarded first for making any sound, then for making a sound similar to "Laura," and then for "speaking" its owner's name.
    d. A psychology student reinforces a laboratory rat only occasionally, to make its behavior more resistant to extinction.

20. Lars, a shoe salesman, is paid every two weeks, whereas Tom receives a commission for each pair of shoes he sells. Evidently, Lars is paid on a _____ schedule of reinforcement, and Tom on a _____ schedule of reinforcement.
    a. fixed-ratio; fixed-interval
    b. continuous; intermittent
    c. fixed-interval; fixed-ratio
    d. variable-interval; variable-ratio
    e. variable-ratio; variable-interval

Essay Question

Describe the best way for a pet owner to condition her dog to roll over. (Use the space below to list the points you want to make, and organize them. Then write the essay on a separate piece of paper.)

Key Terms

Writing Definitions

Using your own words, on a piece of paper write a brief definition or explanation of each of the following terms.

1. learning
2. associative learning
3. behaviorism
4. classical conditioning
5. unconditioned response (UCR)
6. unconditioned stimulus (UCS)
7. conditioned response (CR)
8. conditioned stimulus (CS)
9. acquisition
10. extinction
11. spontaneous recovery
12. generalization
13. discrimination
14. operant conditioning
15. respondent behavior
16. operant behavior
17. law of effect
18. operant chamber (Skinner box)
19. shaping
20. reinforcer
21. primary reinforcers
22. conditioned reinforcers
23. continuous reinforcement
24. partial (intermittent) reinforcement
25. fixed-ratio schedule
26. variable-ratio schedule
27. fixed-interval schedule
28. variable-interval schedule
29. punishment
30. cognitive map
31. latent learning
32. overjustification effect
33. observational learning
34. modeling
35. prosocial behavior

Summing Up

Complete the following flow charts.

CLASSICAL CONDITIONING

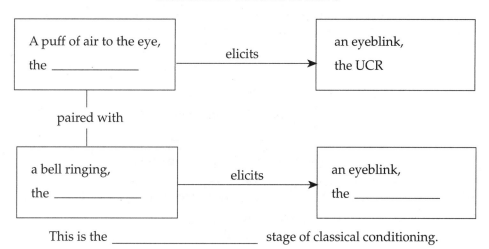

A puff of air to the eye,
the _____   elicits →   an eyeblink,
the UCR

paired with

a bell ringing,
the _____   elicits →   an eyeblink,
the _____

This is the _____ stage of classical conditioning.

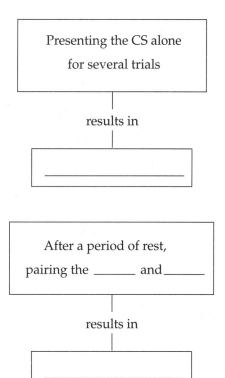

Presenting the CS alone
for several trials

results in

_____

After a period of rest,
pairing the _____ and _____

results in

_____

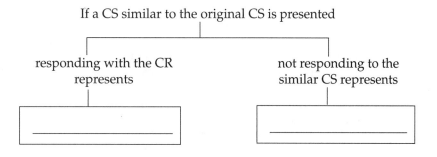

If a CS similar to the original CS is presented

responding with the CR
represents

not responding to the
similar CS represents

_____   _____

OPERANT CONDITIONING

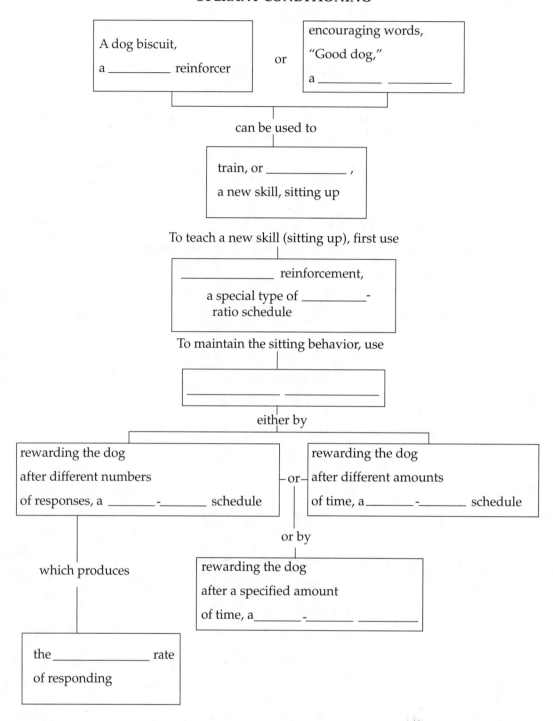

Answers

Introduction

Introduction Preview

1. Experience is the key to learning, which is defined as a relatively permanent change in an organism's behavior due to experience. This ability to learn from experience is the foundation for adaptability—the capacity to learn new behaviors that enable humans and animals to cope with ever-changing circumstances.

   As such philosophers as Aristotle, Locke, and Hume noted, our minds naturally link events that we have experienced together. This is the basis for associative learning, in which two stimuli (as in classical conditioning) or a response and a rewarding or punishing stimulus (as in operant conditioning) become linked because of their co-occurrence.

Stepping Through the Introduction

1. learning
2. associate; associations; associative learning
3. classical
4. operant
5. observing
6. John Watson; behaviorism

Classical Conditioning

Section Preview

1. In associative learning, organisms learn that certain events occur together. Through classical conditioning, organisms learn to anticipate and prepare for significant events, such as the delivery of food or a painful stimulus. In other words, they learn to associate two events. Classical conditioning occurs when a neutral stimulus becomes associated with an unconditioned stimulus (UCS). By itself, the UCS will automatically trigger a reflexive, unconditioned response (UCR). If the association between the CS and UCS is predictable, conditioning will occur and the CS alone will eventually elicit a conditioned response (CR) similar to the UCR.

2. Acquisition refers to the initial stage of learning, during which the CR is established and gradually strengthened. Extinction refers to the diminishing of a CR when the CS is repeatedly presented without a UCS. Spontaneous recovery refers to the reappearance, after a period of rest, of a weakened CR. Generalization is the tendency for stimuli similar to the CS to evoke a CR. Discrimination is the ability to distinguish between an actual CS and similar stimuli that have not been associated with the UCS.

3 Pavlov, Watson, and the early behaviorists underestimated the importance of cognitive processes and biological constraints on learning.

Research by Rescorla and Wagner demonstrated that classical conditioning occurs best when the association between a CS and UCS is predictable. This indicates that subjects develop a cognitive expectancy, or an awareness of how likely it is that the UCS will follow the CS.

Garcia and Koelling's studies of conditioned taste aversion demonstrated that animals are biologically primed to learn to associate certain CSs with certain UCSs. Rats, for example, develop aversions to the taste, but not the appearance, of tainted foods. In contrast, birds are biologically primed to develop aversions to the sight of tainted food. This violates the behaviorist tenet that any perceivable stimulus can become a CS.

4. Pavlov's work showed that virtually all organisms can learn to adapt to their environment. It also showed how a significant internal process, such as learning, could be studied objectively. Finally, Pavlov's findings also provided a basis for the behaviorist idea that human behavior consists, in part, of stimulus-response connections.

The original behaviorist philosophy, as stated by John Watson, was that psychology should be an objective science that studied only observable behaviors and avoided references to all mental processes. Watson argued that by studying how organisms respond to stimuli in their environments, psychologists would eventually become able to understand, predict, and control behavior.

Stepping Through the Section

1. Ivan Pavlov
2. conditioned stimulus; unconditioned stimulus
3. unconditioned response
4. conditioned response
5. acquisition; one-half second
6. does not

Learning theorists consider classical conditioning to be adaptive because conditioned responses help organisms to prepare for good or bad events (unconditioned stimuli) that are about to occur.

7. survive; reproduce
8. extinction
9. spontaneous recovery
10. generalization; discrimination
11. predict; cognitive; expect

The early behaviorists believed that all learned behavior could be reduced to stimulus-response mechanisms. This discounting of mental (cognitive) processes has been strongly challenged by experiments suggesting that even in animals cognition is important for learning. Second, the behaviorists' belief that learning principles would generalize from one response to another and from one species to another has been questioned by research indicating that conditioning principles are constrained by each organism's biological predispositions.

12. alcoholism
13. sickness; would
14. biological; adapt

Classical conditioning led to the discovery of general principles of learning that are the same for all species tested, including humans. Classical conditioning also provided an example to the young field of psychology of how complex, internal processes could be studied objectively. In addition, classical conditioning has proven to have many helpful applications to human health and well-being.

15. can; acetylcholine; Alzheimer's

In Watson and Rayner's experiment, classical conditioning was used to condition fear of a rat in Albert, an 11-month-old infant. When Albert touched the white rat (neutral stimulus), a loud noise (unconditioned stimulus) was sounded. After several pairings of the rat with the noise, Albert began crying at the mere sight of the rat. The rat had become a conditioned stimulus, eliciting a conditioned response of fear.

Operant Conditioning

Section Preview

1. In contrast to classical conditioning, which works on automatic responses to stimuli, *operant* conditioning works on behaviors that *operate* on the environment to produce consequences that influence the future occurrence of those behaviors. Behaviors followed by favorable events (reinforcers) tend to be repeated. Behaviors followed by unpleasant stimuli (punishers) tend not to be repeated.

   Shaping is a systematic technique for establishing a new response in which successive approximations of a desired behavior are reinforced.

2. A positive reinforcer is a stimulus that strengthens a response that leads to its presentation. A negative reinforcer is an aversive stimulus that strengthens a response that leads to its removal. Primary reinforcers are innately reinforcing stimuli that satisfy biological needs. Conditioned reinforcers acquire their effectiveness by being associated with primary reinforcers.

   Fixed-ratio schedules deliver reinforcement after a set number of responses. Variable-ratio schedules deliver reinforcement after an unpredictable number of responses. Fixed-interval schedules deliver reinforcement for the first response that follows a specified amount of time. Variable-interval schedules deliver reinforcement for a response that follows an unpredictable time interval.

3. A punisher is any consequence that decreases the frequency of a behavior that it follows. Although punishment may be effective in the short run, it has its drawbacks. Because punished behavior is merely suppressed rather than forgotten, it may reappear in safe settings. Punishment may also promote aggressiveness as a way of coping with problems; fear of the person who administers it; fear of the situation in which it occurs; or, when it is unpredictable, a sense that events are beyond the person's control. Because punishment does not teach positive behaviors, it is usually more effective when used in combination with positive reinforcement.

4. Latent learning is learning that occurs without reinforcement. Rats allowed to explore a maze without reinforcement nevertheless learn a cognitive map of its layout. When they later are rewarded, they immediately perform as well as rats that have been reinforced with food all along.

   Overjustification occurs when people, who are offered a reward for a task they already enjoy, lose their intrinsic motivation for the task.

   Latent learning and overjustification demonstrate that there is more to learning than the association of a response with a reinforcer. Cognitive processes must be taken into consideration.

   Evidence for biological processes in operant conditioning comes from studies demonstrating that animals have biologically predisposed response patterns that influence the effectiveness of operant procedures with certain behaviors.

5. Operant principles of shaping and immediate reinforcement have been applied in school settings through the use of online testing systems, interactive software, and Internet resources. Reinforcement principles have been used to enhance sports abilities, especially in golf and baseball. Operant principles have also helped business managers increase productivity among their employees. Operant principles also have helped people take charge of their own behavior by creating self-management programs to stop smoking, lose weight, study, or exercise.

Stepping Through the Section

1. neutral; automatic
2. respondent; operant
3. law of effect; Skinner box
4. shaping; approximations
5. reinforcer
6. positive reinforcer
7. negative reinforcer
8. primary reinforcers; conditioned reinforcers
9. more

10. is; delayed; drug; unprotected sex

11. continuous reinforcement; rapid; rapid

12. partial (intermittent); slower; very

13. fixed-ratio

14. variable-ratio

15. fixed-interval; checking the mail as delivery time approaches

16. variable-interval

Following reinforcement on a fixed-interval schedule, there is a pause in responding and then an increasing rate of response as time for the next reinforcement draws near. On a fixed-ratio schedule there also is a post-reinforcement pause, followed, however, by a return to a consistent, high rate of response. Both kinds of variable schedules produce steadier rates of response, without the pauses associated with fixed schedules. In general, schedules linked to responses produce *higher* response rates and fixed schedules produce *higher* response rates than the related variable schedules.

17. punishment

Because punished behavior is merely suppressed, it may reappear. Punishment can lead to fear and a sense of helplessness, as well as to the association of the aversive event with the person who administers it. Punishment also often increases aggressiveness. Finally, punishment alone does not guide the organism toward more desirable behavior.

18. cognitive

19. cognitive map

20. latent learning

21. overjustification effect

22. is

23. shaping; testing; interactive; athletic

24. more; achievable; more

Observational Learning

Section Preview

1. Observational learning, in which people observe and imitate, or model, others' behaviors, explains how many social behaviors are acquired. Research studies have shown that children will imitate both antisocial and prosocial models. Models are most effective when their actions and words are consistent. We are most likely to imitate people we respect, those we perceive as similar to ourselves, and those we perceive as successful.

Stepping Through the Section

1. modeling; observational learning; occurs

2. 14 months

3. Bandura; more

4. prosocial

5. consistent; similar; successful; admirable

Progress Test 1

Multiple-Choice Questions

1. **c.** is the answer. (p. 287)
   a. This answer is incorrect because it simply describes any behavior that is automatic rather than being triggered, or elicited, by a specific stimulus.
   b. This answer is too general, since behaviors can change for reasons other than learning.
   d. Respondently conditioned behavior also satisfies the criteria of our definition of learning.

2. **b.** is the answer. (p. 301)
   a. & c. Classical conditioning is associated with Pavlov; respondent conditioning is another name for classical conditioning.
   d. Observational learning is most closely associated with Bandura.

3. **c.** is the answer. Meat automatically triggers the response of salivation and is therefore an unconditioned stimulus. (p. 291)
   a. A conditioned stimulus acquires its response-eliciting powers through learning. A dog does not learn to salivate to meat.
   b. & d. Responses are behaviors elicited in the organism, in this case the dog's salivation. The meat is a stimulus.

4. **b.** is the answer. Prior to its pairing with meat (the UCS), the tone did not elicit salivation and was therefore a neutral stimulus. Afterward, the tone elicited salivation (the CR) and was therefore a conditioned stimulus (CS). (pp. 291–292)
   c. & d. Unconditioned stimuli, such as meat, innately elicit responding. Pavlov's dogs had to learn to associate the tone with the food.

5. **e.** is the answer. In learning to distinguish between the conditioned stimulus and another, similar stimulus, the monkey has received training in discrimination. (p. 294)
   a. In extinction training, a stimulus and/or response is allowed to go unreinforced.
   b. Generalization training involves responding to stimuli similar to the conditioned stimulus; here the monkey is being trained not to respond to a similar stimulus.

c. This cannot be classical conditioning since the monkey is acting in order to obtain a reward. Thus, this is an example of operant conditioning.
d. Spontaneous recovery refers to the reappearance, after a period of rest, of a weakened CR.

6. **b.** is the answer. A continuous association will naturally be easier to learn than one that occurs on only some occasions, so learning is most rapid with continuous reinforcement. Yet, once the continuous association is no longer there, as in extinction training, extinction will occur more rapidly than it would have had the organism not always experienced reinforcement. (p. 304)

7. **b.** is the answer. (pp. 295, 307)
c. & d. The text does not present evidence regarding the relative importance of cognitive processes in classical and operant conditioning.

8. **b.** is the answer. (p. 305)
a. Response rate is high with fixed-ratio schedules, but there is a pause following each reinforcement.
c. & d. Because reinforcement is not contingent on the rate of response, interval schedules, especially fixed-interval schedules, produce lower response rates than ratio schedules.

9. **b.** is the answer. (p. 303)
a. Positive reinforcement involves presenting a favorable stimulus following a response.
c. Punishment involves presenting an unpleasant stimulus following a response.
d. In extinction, a previously reinforced response is no longer followed by reinforcement. In this situation, a response causes a stimulus to be terminated or removed.

10. **c.** is the answer. In this situation, the CR will decline, a phenomenon known as extinction. (p. 293)
a. Generalization occurs when the subject makes a CR to stimuli similar to the original CS.
b. Discrimination is when the subject does not make a CR to stimuli other than the original CS.
d. An aversion is a CR to a CS that has been associated with an unpleasant UCS, such as shock or a nausea-producing drug.
e. Spontaneous recovery is the reappearance, after a rest period, of a CR.

11. **c.** is the answer. (p. 301)
a. In *operant* conditioning the responses operate on the environment.
b. In *classical* conditioning responses are triggered, or elicited, by preceding stimuli.
d. In *classical* conditioning responses are reflexive.

12. **c.** is the answer. (pp. 295–296)

a., d., & e. These studies also indicated that rats are biologically predisposed to associate visual and auditory stimuli, but not taste, with shock.
b. Rats are biologically predisposed to associate taste with sickness.

13. **d.** is the answer. A dog does not have to learn to salivate to food; therefore, this response is unconditioned. (p. 291)
a. & c. Salivation is a response, not a stimulus.

14. **b.** is the answer. (p. 313)
a. Skinner is best known for studies of *operant* learning. Moreover, there is no such thing as secondary learning.
c. Pavlov is best known for classical conditioning.
d. Watson is best known as an early proponent of behaviorism.

15. **b.** is the answer. (p. 308)
a. Latent learning is learning that occurs but is not apparent until there is an incentive to demonstrate it.
c. Primary reinforcement involves the presentation of a stimulus that satisfies some biological need. Money is an acquired, or conditioned, reinforcer.
d. Modeling is the process of learning by watching and imitating the behavior of others.
e. Negative reinforcement is the removal of an aversive stimulus following a response.

16. **d.** is the answer. (pp. 306–307)

17. **c.** is the answer. (p. 295)
a., b., & d. Rescorla and Wagner's research did not address the importance of these factors in classical conditioning.

18. **d.** is the answer. a. is an example of positive reinforcement, b. is an example of negative reinforcement, and c. is an example of conditioned reinforcement. (p. 303)

19. **d.** is the answer. (pp. 288–289)

20. **b.** is the answer. (p. 292)
a. Backward conditioning, in which the UCS precedes the CS, is ineffective.
c. This interval is longer than is optimum for the most rapid acquisition of a CS-UCS association.
d. Simultaneous presentation of CS and UCS is ineffective because it does not permit the subject to anticipate the UCS.

Matching Items

1. e (p. 303)   5. i (p. 303)   9. c (p. 293)
2. h (p. 294)   6. k (p. 305)   10. b (p. 306)
3. f (p. 303)   7. j (p. 304)   11. d (p. 308)
4. g (p. 303)   8. a (p. 302)

Progress Test 2

Multiple-Choice Questions

1. **c.** is the answer. (p. 293)

2. **b.** is the answer. The loud noise automatically elicited Albert's fear and therefore functioned as a UCS. After being associated with the UCS, the white rat acquired the power to elicit fear and thus became a CS. (p. 298)

3. **e.** is the answer. (pp. 297–298)

4. **a.** is the answer. Shaping works on operant behaviors by reinforcing successive approximations to a desired goal. (p. 302)

5. **c.** is the answer. (p. 293)
   a., b., & d. Spontaneous recovery occurs after a CR has been extinguished, and in the absence of the UCS. The situations described here all involve the continued presentation of the UCS and, therefore, the further strengthening of the CR.

6. **b.** is the answer. (pp. 303–304)
   a., c., & d. Reinforcement that is delayed, presented before a response, or at the same time as a response, does not increase the response's frequency of occurrence.

7. **d.** is the answer. (pp. 303, 306)
   a. Both involve an aversive stimulus.
   b. All reinforcers, including negative reinforcers, increase the likelihood of a response.
   c. In negative reinforcement, an aversive stimulus is withdrawn following a desirable response.

8. **c.** is the answer. Payment is given after a fixed number of pieces have been completed. (p. 305)
   a. & b. Interval schedules reinforce according to the passage of time, not the amount of work accomplished.
   d. Fortunately for those working on commission, the work ratio is fixed and therefore predictable.

9. **c.** is the answer. By learning to put on your coat before going outside, you have learned to reduce the aversive stimulus of the cold. (p. 303)
   a. Discrimination learning involves learning to make a response in the presence of the appropriate stimulus and not other stimuli.
   b. Punishment is the suppression of an undesirable response by the presentation of an aversive stimulus.
   d. Putting on a coat is a response that is willfully emitted by the person. Therefore, this is an example of operant, not classical, conditioning.
   e. Positive reinforcement involves the *presentation* of a stimulus.

10. **d.** is the answer. (p. 304)
    a. Intermittent reinforcement refers to the ratio of responses to reinforcers, not the overall quantity of reinforcement delivered.
    b. Unlike intermittent reinforcement, in which the delivery of reinforcement is contingent on responding, random reinforcement is delivered independently of the subject's behavior.
    c. This defines the technique of shaping, not intermittent reinforcement.

11. **a.** is the answer. You are teaching your dog by rewarding him when he produces the desired behavior. (p. 301)
    b. This is not classical conditioning because the cookie is a primary reinforcer presented after the operant behavior of the dog fetching the paper.
    c. Food is a primary reinforcer; it satisfies an innate need.
    d. Rewarding your dog each time he fetches the paper is continuous reinforcement.

12. **e.** is the answer. (p. 314)

13. **a.** is the answer. (p. 307)

14. **d.** is the answer. The rat had learned the maze but did not display this learning until reinforcement became available. (p. 308)
    a. Negotiating a maze is clearly operant behavior.
    b. This example does not involve learning to distinguish between stimuli.
    c. This is not observational learning because the rat has no one to observe!

15. **c.** is the answer. Because reinforcement (earning a good grade on the exam) is available according to the passage of time, studying is reinforced on an interval schedule. Because the interval between exams is constant, this is an example of a fixed-interval schedule. (p. 305)

16. **d.** is the answer. (pp. 290, 301)
    a. Pavlov and Watson are both associated with classical conditioning.
    b. Skinner is associated with operant conditioning, and Bandura is associated with observational learning.

17. **a.** is the answer. Online testing systems apply operant principles such as reinforcement, immediate feedback, and shaping to the teaching of new skills. (p. 310)
    b. & d. Online testing systems provide immediate, and continuous, reinforcement for correct responses, but does not use aversive control procedures such as punishment.
    c. Online testing systems are based on feedback for correct responses; this feedback constitutes conditioned, rather than primary, reinforcement.

18. **c.** is the answer. In fishing, an unpredictable amount of time passes between catches. (p. 305)

19. **d.** is the answer. An approving nod from the boss is a conditioned reinforcer in that it doesn't satisfy an innate need but has become linked with desirable consequences. Cessation of cold, cessation of pain, and a drink are all primary reinforcers, which meet innate needs. (p. 303)

20. **a.** is the answer. Taste-aversion experiments demonstrate conditioning even with CS-UCS intervals as long as several hours. (p. 296)
    b. Despite being perceivable, a visual or auditory stimulus cannot become a CS for illness in some animals, such as rats.
    c. Some animals, such as birds, are biologically primed to associate the *appearance* of food with illness.

True-False Items

1. F (p. 301)   5. T (p. 304)   9. F (p. 292)
2. F (p. 292)   6. F (pp. 295, 307)   10. T (p. 293)
3. F (p. 303)   7. T (pp. 306–307)
4. T (p. 304)   8. F (p. 296

Thinking Critically About Chapter 8

Multiple-Choice Questions

1. **a.** is the answer. Your dog had to learn to associate the rattling sound with the food. Rattling is therefore a conditioned, or learned, stimulus, and salivation in response to this rattling is a learned, or conditioned, response. (pp. 291–292)

2. **c.** is the answer. Reinforcement (the letter) comes after a fixed interval, and as the likely end of the interval approaches, your behavior (glancing out the window) becomes more frequent. (p. 305)
   a. & b. These answers are incorrect because with ratio schedules, reinforcement is contingent upon the number of responses rather than on the passage of time.
   d. Assuming that the mail is delivered at about the same time each day, the interval is fixed rather than variable. Your behavior reflects this, since you glance out the window more often as the delivery time approaches.

3. **b.** is the answer. By taking out the garbage, Jack terminates an aversive stimulus—his father's nagging. (p. 303)
   a. Positive reinforcement would involve a desirable stimulus that increases the likelihood of the response that preceded it.
   c. This answer would have been correct if Jack's

father had rewarded Jack for taking out the garbage by providing his favorite food.
   d. Punishment suppresses behavior; Jack is emitting a behavior in order to obtain reinforcement.

4. **c.** is the answer. Studies indicate that when a model says one thing but does another, subjects do the same and learn not to practice what they preach. (p. 314)

5. **a.** is the answer. As in this example, conditioning must be consistent with the particular organism's biological predispositions. (p. 309)
   b. Some behaviors, but certainly not all, are acquired more rapidly than others when shock is used as negative reinforcement.
   c. Pigeons are able to acquire many new behaviors when food is used as reinforcement.

6. **a.** is the answer. Ratio schedules maintain higher rates of responding—gambling in this example—than do interval schedules. Furthermore, variable schedules are not associated with the pause in responding following reinforcement that is typical of fixed schedules. The slot machine would therefore be used more often, and more consistently, if jackpots were scheduled according to a variable-ratio schedule. (p. 305)

7. **d.** is the answer. Sharetta is guided by her mental representation of the city, or cognitive map. (p. 307)
   a. & e. Latent learning, or learning in the absence of reinforcement that is demonstrated when reinforcement becomes available, has no direct relevance to the example. The same is true of discrimination.
   b. Observational learning refers to learning from watching others.
   c. Shaping is the technique of reinforcing successive approximations of a desired behavior.

8. **c.** is the answer. Because the cat was associated with your mother's scream, it elicited a fear response, and is thus the CS. (p. 292)

9. **a.** is the answer. Your mother's scream and evident fear, which naturally caused you to cry, was the UCS. (p. 291)

10. **d.** is the answer. Your fear of cats is the CR. An acquired fear is always a conditioned response. (p. 292)

11. **b.** is the answer. Your crying, automatically elicited by your mother's scream and fear, was the UCR. (p. 291)

12. **c.** is the answer. (p. 310)
    a. Positive reinforcement is most effective in boosting productivity in the workplace when specific behavior, rather than vaguely defined gener-

al merit, is rewarded. Also, immediate reinforcement is much more effective than the delayed reinforcement described in a.

b. Positive reinforcement is most effective in boosting productivity when performance goals are achievable, rather than unrealistic.

d. The text does not specifically discuss the use of punishment in the workplace. However, it makes the general point that although punishment may temporarily suppress unwanted behavior, it does not guide one toward more desirable behavior. Therefore, workers who receive pay cuts for poor performance may learn nothing about how to improve their productivity.

13. **b.** is the answer. Paying a person for doing what he or she already enjoys may undermine the person's intrinsic motivation for the task and lead to the overjustification effect. (p. 308)

a. This negative reinforcement of room cleaning may motivate the son to get the job done, but since the job apparently is not intrinsically rewarding, it is doubtful that Mrs. Shih's additional incentives will lead to an overjustification effect.

c. Presumably the salespeople work to make money; a bonus should therefore serve as additional positive reinforcement for selling shoes.

d. The coach's scolding may make soccer less enjoyable for the players, but not as a result of overjustification provided by additional reinforcement.

e. This answer is incorrect because it is unclear whether Greg's father enjoys not smoking.

14. **b.** is the answer. Not only is Bill extending a learned aversion to a specific blue car to all blue cars but also to cars that are green. (p. 294)

a. Whereas discrimination involves responding only to a particular stimulus, Bill is extending his aversive response to other stimuli (green cars) as well.

c. Latent learning is learning that becomes apparent only after reinforcement becomes available.

d. The overjustification effect refers to the counterproductive effects of reinforcement on behavior that is self-reinforcing.

15. **b.** is the answer. The girls are imitating behavior they have observed and admired. (p. 313)

a. Because these behaviors are clearly willful rather than elicited, classical conditioning plays no role.

c. Latent learning plays no role in this example.

d. Shaping is a procedure for teaching the acquisition of a new response by reinforcing successive approximations of the behavior.

e. Discrimination involves responding to certain stimuli but not to others. In this example, only

one stimulus (the televised Olympic games) is described.

16. **a.** is the answer. Classical conditioning proceeds most effectively when the CS and UCS are reliably paired and therefore appear predictably associated. Only for Group 1 is this likely to be true. (p. 292)

17. **b.** is the answer. (p. 296)

a., c., & d. Taste-aversion research demonstrates that humans and some other animals, such as rats, are biologically primed to associate illness with the taste of tainted food, rather than with other cues, such as the food's appearance. Moreover, taste aversions can be acquired even when the interval between the CS and the illness is several hours.

18. **d.** is the answer. By making a more preferred activity (watching TV) contingent on a less preferred activity (room cleaning), Reggie's mother is employing the operant conditioning technique of positive reinforcement. (pp. 300–301, 303)

19. **c.** is the answer. The parrot is reinforced for making successive approximations of a goal behavior. This defines shaping. (p. 302)

a. Shaping is an operant conditioning procedure; salivation at the sight of dog biscuits is a classically conditioned response.

b. Shaping involves the systematic reinforcement of successive approximations of a more complex behavior. In this example there is no indication that the response of stopping at the intersection involved the gradual acquisition of simpler behaviors.

d. This is an example of the partial reinforcement of an established response, rather than the shaping of a new response.

20. **c.** is the answer. Whereas Lars is paid (reinforced) after a fixed period of time (fixed-interval), Tom is reinforced for each sale (fixed-ratio) he makes. (p. 305)

Essay Question

The first step in shaping an operant response, such as rolling over, is to find an effective reinforcer. Some sort of biscuit or dog treat is favored by animal trainers. This primary reinforcement should be accompanied by effusive praise (secondary reinforcement) whenever the dog makes a successful response.

Rolling over (the goal response) should be divided into a series of simple approximations, the first of which is a response, such as lying down on command, that is already in the dog's repertoire. This response should be reinforced several times. The next step is to issue a command, such as "Roll over," and withhold reinforcement until the dog (usually out of frustration) makes a closer approximation (such as rotating slightly in one direction). Following this example, the trainer should gradually require closer and closer approximations until the goal response is attained. When the new response has been established, the trainer should switch from continuous to partial reinforcement, in order to strengthen the skill.

Key Terms

Writing Definitions

1. **Learning** is any relatively permanent change in an organism's behavior due to experience. (p. 287)

2. In **associative learning**, organisms learn that certain events occur together. Two variations of associative learning are classical conditioning and operant conditioning. (p. 288)

3. **Behaviorism** is the school of thought maintaining that psychology should be an objective science, study only observable behaviors, and avoid references to mental processes. (p. 290)

   Example: Because he was an early advocate of the study of observable behavior, John Watson is often called the father of **behaviorism**.

4. Also known as Pavlovian conditioning, **classical conditioning** is a type of learning in which a neutral stimulus becomes capable of eliciting a conditioned response after having become associated with an unconditioned stimulus. (p. 290)

5. In classical conditioning, the **unconditioned response (UCR)** is the unlearned, involuntary response to the unconditioned stimulus. (p. 291)

6. In classical conditioning, the **unconditioned stimulus (UCS)** is the stimulus that naturally and automatically elicits the reflexive unconditioned response. (p. 291)

7. In classical conditioning, the **conditioned response (CR)** is the learned response to a previously neutral conditioned stimulus, which results from the acquired association between the CS and UCS. (p. 292)

8. In classical conditioning, the **conditioned stimulus (CS)** is an originally neutral stimulus that comes to elicit a CR after association with an unconditioned stimulus. (p. 292)

9. In a learning experiment, **acquisition** refers to the initial stage of conditioning in which the new response is established and gradually strengthened. In operant conditioning, it is the strengthening of a reinforced response. (p. 292)

10. **Extinction** refers to the weakening of a CR when the CS is no longer followed by the UCS; in operant conditioning extinction occurs when a response is no longer reinforced. (p. 293)

11. **Spontaneous recovery** is the reappearance of an extinguished CR after a rest period. (p. 293)

12. **Generalization** refers to the tendency, once a response has been conditioned, for stimuli similar to the original CS to evoke a CR. (p. 294)

13. **Discrimination** in classical conditioning refers to the ability to distinguish the CS from similar stimuli that do not signal a UCS. In operant conditioning, responding differently to stimuli that signal a behavior will be reinforced or will not be reinforced. (p. 294)

14. **Operant conditioning** is a type of learning in which behavior is strengthened if followed by reinforcement or diminished if followed by punishment. (pp. 300–301)

    Example: Unlike classical conditioning, which works on automatic behaviors, **operant conditioning** works on behaviors that are willfully emitted by an organism.

15. **Respondent behavior** is that which occurs as an automatic response to some stimulus. (p. 301)

    Example: In classical conditioning, conditioned and unconditioned responses are examples of **respondent behavior** in that they are automatic responses elicited by specific stimuli.

16. **Operant behavior** is behavior the organism emits that operates on the environment to produce reinforcing or punishing stimuli. (p. 301)

17. E. L. Thorndike proposed the **law of effect**, which states that rewarded behavior is likely to recur. (p. 301)

18. An **operant chamber (Skinner box)** is an experimental chamber for the operant conditioning of an animal such as a pigeon or rat. The controlled environment enables the investigator to present visual or auditory stimuli, deliver reinforcement or punishment, and precisely measure simple responses such as bar presses or key pecking. (p. 301)

19. **Shaping** is the operant conditioning procedure for establishing a new response by reinforcing successive approximations of the desired behavior. (p. 302)

20. In operant conditioning, a **reinforcer** is any event that strengthens the behavior it follows. (p. 303)

21. The powers of **primary reinforcers** are inborn and do not depend on learning. (p. 303)

22. **Conditioned reinforcers** are stimuli that acquire their reinforcing power through their association with a primary reinforcer. (p. 303)

23. **Continuous reinforcement** is the operant procedure of reinforcing the desired response every time it occurs. In promoting the acquisition of a new response it is best to use continuous reinforcement. (p. 304)

24. **Partial (intermittent) reinforcement** is the operant procedure of reinforcing a response intermittently. A response that has been partially reinforced is much more resistant to extinction than one that has been continuously reinforced. (p. 304)

25. In operant conditioning, a **fixed-ratio schedule** is one in which reinforcement is presented after a set number of responses. (p. 305)

    Example: Continuous reinforcement is a special kind of **fixed-ratio schedule**: Reinforcement is presented after *each* response, so the ratio of reinforcements to responses is one to one.

26. In operant conditioning, a **variable-ratio schedule** is one in which reinforcement is presented after a varying number of responses. (p. 305)

27. In operant conditioning, a **fixed-interval schedule** is one in which a response is reinforced after a specified time has elapsed. (p. 305)

28. In operant conditioning, a **variable-interval schedule** is one in which responses are reinforced after varying intervals of time. (p. 305)

29. In operant conditioning, **punishment** is the presentation of an aversive stimulus, such as shock, which decreases the behavior it follows. (p. 306)

    Memory aid: People often confuse negative reinforcement and **punishment**. The former strengthens behavior, while the latter weakens it.

30. A **cognitive map** is a mental picture of one's environment. (p. 307)

31. **Latent learning** is learning that occurs in the absence of reinforcement but only becomes apparent when there is an incentive to demonstrate it. (p. 308)

32. The undermining effect of being rewarded for something enjoyable is called the **overjustification effect**. (p. 308)

33. **Observational learning** is learning by watching and imitating the behavior of others. (p. 313)

34. **Modeling** is the process of watching and then imitating a specific behavior and is thus an important means through which observational learning occurs. (p. 313)

35. The opposite of antisocial behavior, **prosocial behavior** is positive, helpful, and constructive, and is subject to the same principles of observational learning as is undesirable behavior, such as aggression. (p. 314)

Summing Up

Classical Conditioning

The flow chart reads as follows: A puff of air to the eye, the *UCS*, elicits an eye blink, the UCR. When the puff of air is paired with a bell ringing, a *CS*, the CS comes to elicit an eyeblink, a *CR*. This is the *acquisition* stage of classical conditioning. Presenting the CS alone for several trials results in *extinction*. After a period of rest, pairing the *CS* and *UCS* results in *spontaneous recovery*. If a CS similar to the original CS is presented, responding with the CR represents *generalization*, not responding to the similar CS represents *discrimination*.

Operant Conditioning

A dog biscuit, the *primary* reinforcer, or conditioned encouraging words such as "Good dog," the *conditioned reinforcer*, can be used to train, or *shape*, a new skill such as sitting up. To teach a new skill (sitting), first use *continuous* reinforcement, a special kind of *fixed-ratio* schedule. To maintain the skill, use *partial reinforcement* either by rewarding the dog after different numbers of responses, a *variable-ratio* schedule (which produces the *steadiest* rate of responding) or rewarding the dog after different amounts of time, a *variable-interval* schedule, or by rewarding the dog after a specified amount of time, a *fixed-interval* schedule.

FOCUS ON VOCABULARY AND LANGUAGE

Page 287: Learning in all such realms *breeds hope.* The fact that we can change and adapt as a result of experience (*learn*) in so many different areas (*realms*) gives rise to optimism (*breeds hope*) about our future prospects.

Page 287: . . . watching a TV character get *mugged* . . . This means to be attacked, (sometimes) beaten, and robbed. The term is used here to describe how associations are formed between events, such as between the sounds that precede an attack and the *mugging* itself. In movies and on TV, a certain type of music is often played before a frightening event or scene. After a few such associations, the music itself can elicit fear before you actually see the frightening or scary event. This is an example of classical conditioning.

Page 289: A clever Japanese *rancher* reportedly *herds* cattle by outfitting them with electronic *pagers*, which he calls from his portable phone. In this example of conditioning, the cattle farmer (*rancher*) has trained his animals to gather together and move (*he herds them*) to the feeding station (*food trough*). They have learned to associate the sound of the tone (*the beep*) made by the signaling device (*electronic pager*) with the delivery of food (classical conditioning), and they have also learned that moving fast (*hustling*) to the trough is followed by the good feeling of satiating their hunger (operant conditioning).

Classical Conditioning

Page 290: For many people, the name Ivan Pavlov rings a bell. Myers is making a little joke here. A common expression when hearing something familiar but vague is to say, *"That rings a bell."* Pavlov's name is familiar to many people, who may also be vaguely aware that his research involved dogs and ringing bells (classical conditioning).

Page 291: . . . what the dog was thinking . . . as it *drooled.* . . . To drool means to salivate or produce spit. When food (UCS) is placed in a dog's mouth, the dog will automatically salivate or *drool* (UCR). If a tone (CS) is sounded before (or precedes) the UCS over a number of trials, then the CS alone (the tone) will be able to elicit salivation (CR).

Page 292: (margin note): If the *aroma* of cake baking *sets your mouth to watering,* what is the UCS? The CS? The CR? When you bake a cake in the oven, there is a lovely smell (*aroma*) which makes you salivate or drool (*sets your mouth to watering*). This is an example of classical conditioning: The taste of the cake in your mouth is the UCS (this automatically produces saliva, the UCR), the aroma is the CS, and, because of its past associations with the UCS, it can now, by itself, elicit saliva (the CR).

Page 292: Moreover, the male quail developed a general liking for their cage's *red-light district.* Traditionally, a red lamp hung in the window identified the house as a brothel, and the area of town populated by many brothels became known as the *red-light district.* In Domjan's experiments with male quail a red light (CS) was used to signal the arrival of a receptive female quail (UCS), which elicited sexual arousal (CR). Eventually, the red light (CS) alone elicited sexual arousal (CR), and the male quail appeared to develop a general liking for the cage with the red light (*the red-light district*).

Page 294: After *breaking up* with his *fire-breathing heartthrob,* Tirrell also experienced extinction and spontaneous recovery. He recalls that "the smell of onion breath (CS), no longer paired with the kissing (UCS), lost its ability to *shiver my timbers."* This paragraph describes the end of the relationship (*breaking up*) with his girlfriend (*heartthrob*) who loved to eat onions and thus had hot, smelly breath (*fire-breathing*). The repeated smell of onions or onion breath (CS) without the UCS (kissing) resulted in extinction of his conditioned aroused state (CR), and, consequently, the CS lost its ability to get him excited (*shiver his timbers*). He later experienced spontaneous recovery (the extinguished CR returned briefly) when he smelled onion breath once more. (The idiom *"shiver my timbers"* has no simple explanation; it is probably an old expression dating back to the days of wooden [timbered] sailing ships that would tremble or shiver in a storm.)

Page 295: . . . the organism *willy-nilly* . . . This means without any forethought, intention, or purpose—at random. An organism does not randomly (*willy-nilly*) form associations. The associations have to be meaningful; the CS needs to have informational value and be able to reliably predict the occurrence of the UCS.

Page 297: But if we *see further* than Pavlov did, it is because we *stand on his shoulders.* This phrase is not to be taken literally; it simply means that we now know more than Pavlov did (*see further*) because we can build and expand on his great work (*stand on his shoulders*).

Page 297: . . . *crack cocaine users* . . . This term refers to drug addicts who use a drug that is a synthetic, but very potent, form of cocaine.

Page 299: . . . *legendary significance* . . . Watson and Rayner's work with Little Albert was the first investigation of how phobias or irrational fears might develop through the process of classical conditioning. Thus, the story was passed on to future generations of psychologists (it became a *legend*) and influenced their research.

Operant Conditioning

Page 301: . . . to pull habits out of a rat. David Myers is having fun playing with the English language here. The expression "to pull rabbits out of a hat" refers to stage magicians who are able to extract rabbits from a seemingly empty hat. Can you see the way Myers has twisted this expression? Both classical and operant conditioning involve teaching new habits to various organisms, including rats. Following classical conditioning the CS elicits a new response from the animal (i.e., the CS *"pulls a habit out of the rat"*), or the sight of the lever may elicit the habit of lever pressing (operant conditioning).

Page 302: With training, pigeons have even been taught to discriminate between *Bach's music and Stravinsky's.* Bach and Stravinsky were composers whose styles of musical composition were quite different. Through shaping (rewarding behaviors that are closer and closer to the target or desired response), psychologists have been able to train pigeons to discriminate (or choose) between the two musical sounds. For example, pigeons may be rewarded for pecking a disk when Bach is playing and for refraining from pecking when Stravinsky is playing. They can be trained to discriminate, or tell the difference, between the two.

Page 303: On a wall chart, the teacher pastes *gold stars* after the names of children scoring 100 percent on spelling tests. Teachers often use extrinsic rewards such as small, bright stickers (*gold stars*) for, say, the very best spellers in the class. Unfortunately, if only the top few students (*academic all-stars*) are recognized in this way, the rest of the students may lose motivation because, even if they improve their spelling and work very hard (but still don't get 100%), they don't get any reinforcers. Myers recommends a shaping procedure that rewards even small improvements and recognizes the child for making the effort to do better and better.

Page 256: Pushing the *snooze button,* silences the annoying alarm. When your radio alarm goes off in the morning, you may press the switch (*snooze button*) which turns off the irritating tone for a brief period of time. The ensuing quiet period, which may allow you to go back to sleep for a while (*snooze*),

and the absence of the buzzer are negative reinforcers for pushing the snooze button. (Your button-pushing behavior has been strengthened because it removed an aversive event, the alarm.)

Page 303: . . . Billy throws a tantrum . . . A child screams and shouts in an uncontrollable manner when his or her desires are blocked or thwarted. For example, a parent goes shopping and takes a child along. Once in the store the child sees some candy and asks for it. The parent says "no!" Immediately, the child starts screaming and crying (*throws a tantrum*), so the parent gives the child the candy. The child's behavior has been positively reinforced and the parent's behavior (giving in) has been strengthened by negative reinforcement.

Page 303: . . . goofing off and getting a bad exam grade . . . Students may score poorly on an exam because they were doing something unproductive, such as watching TV, instead of studying (they were *goofing off*). As a consequence, they may decide to change their behavior and work hard to avoid further exam anxiety and the unpleasant possibility of getting a low grade. The new behavior may be strengthened if it avoids the aversive consequences of anxiety (negative reinforcement); in addition, getting a good score on the exam can positively reinforce good study habits. Remember, reinforcers of either kind (positive or negative) always strengthen behavior.

Page 304: . . . the kick that often comes within seconds [after taking drugs] . . . The term *kick* as used here refers to a jolt of pleasure (not as in "to kick the ball"). Myers is making the point that behaviors such as smoking, drinking, and drug taking, in general, are followed by some immediate pleasurable consequence, which controls the behavior more than does the delayed consequence (e.g., lung cancer, memory loss, cognitive impairment, etc.).

Page 304: A salesperson does not make a sale with every *pitch,* nor does an *angler* get a bite with every *cast.* The *pitch* referred to here is the sales talk (*pitch*) that the salesperson uses to promote the product or service. The bite the angler (fisherman) does not get refers to the fact that throwing out the line (*casting*) does not always result in fish biting the bait. The idea is that much of our behavior is not continuously reinforced but persists, nevertheless, by being partially reinforced (you make a sale or catch a fish only once in a while despite many responses).

Page 305: . . . paid on a piecework basis . . . This refers to situations in which someone is paid for the number of items produced (and not by the hour or the week). A worker gets paid only if he or she produces, so the number of responses (i.e., the number of items produced) is reinforced on a **fixed-ratio schedule**. An example would be factory worker sewing shirts who would be paid 5 dollars for each finished shirt (*piecework*). The more shirts she makes, the more money she earns, and thus the rate of responding is usually high.

Page 305: . . . pop quiz . . . If your professor gives brief tests at unpredictable intervals (*pop quizzes*), you never know when the next exam is going to be. Thus, your best strategy would be to study on a regular basis and prepare for a test before *every* class. If you do this, your study habits will be reinforced on a **variable-interval schedule.**

Page 306: . . . the child who *loses a treat* after running into the street . . . Here the phrase *"loses a treat"* refers to the withholding of some pleasant consequence such as a candy bar or piece of cake (appetitive stimulus) following some unwanted behavior. This is one type of punishment; it decreases the probability of the behavior being repeated. Another example is *time out*, in which the child is put in a situation (such as in the corner) in which no reinforcement is available.

Page 306: . . . drawbacks . . . This means problems or bad consequences. One problem (*drawback*) with using punishment is that the behavior may be temporarily suppressed in the presence of the punisher but may reappear in other, safer settings. In addition, punishment may elicit aggression, create fear and apprehension, and generate avoidance behavior in those being punished. As Myers notes, punishment teaches what not to do, whereas positive reinforcement teaches what to do.

Page 306: The driver who is *hit with* a couple of speeding tickets. . . . The phrase *"hit with"* means issued or given, but "hit" is associated with punitive, aversive, or bad consequences. A driver who is issued (*hit with*) a speeding ticket may feel punished and, instead of changing the speeding behavior, may find ways to avoid getting tickets by using a radar detector. The point Myers is making is that punishment may not be the best way to change behavior.

Page 308: Actually, promising children a reward for a task they already enjoy can *backfire*. If children enjoy doing something because it is fun (intrinsic motivation), they may lose interest in the task if they are promised a reward for it (extrinsic motivation). Thus, in some circumstances offering material gains (a *payoff*) may have an effect opposite to the one expected (it can *backfire*). This phenomenon is called the **overjustification effect**.

Page 309: . . . piggy bank . . . This is a small container for saving money (usually coins) that is often in the shape of a pig. Children can learn to save their money by putting it in their *piggy bank*. However, as Myers points out, pigs who were trained to put big wooden coins in a large *piggy bank* soon reverted to their natural behavior of pushing the coins with their snouts (noses) despite the fact that they received no reward for doing this. This is an example of the biological constraints on learning.

Page 309: . . . stirred a hornet's nest. . . . A hornet is a large yellow and black stinging insect belonging to the wasp family. Up to 200 hornets live together in a sheltered home (*nest*); if disturbed or agitated (*stirred*), they will attack in an angry and aggressive manner. B. F. Skinner aroused a great deal of anger and hostility and was vehemently attacked by many people (*he stirred a hornet's nest*) for insisting that mental events and free will (internal events) were of little relevance as determinants of behavior compared to environmental factors such as rewards and punishments (external influences).

Page 311: . . . rule of thumb . . . This is a simple guide or principle that is true in general. Applying the principles of operant conditioning to economics, Al Gore noted that, as a general principle (*rule of thumb*), whatever is taxed tends to decrease and whatever is subsidized tends to increase.

Learning by Observation

Page 314: Compared with children not exposed to the adult model, children who observed the *aggressive outburst* were much more likely to *lash out* at the doll. Bandura's experiments on observational learning demonstrated that children who saw an adult engage in (*model*) violent behavior (an *aggressive outburst*) were more inclined to attack and beat up (*lash out at*) a Bobo doll and copy (*imitate*) the words and gestures used by the role model.

CHAPTER 9:

Memory

Chapter Overview

Chapter 9 explores human memory as a system that processes information in three steps. Encoding refers to the process of putting information into the memory system. Storage is the purely passive mechanism by which information is maintained in memory. Retrieval is the process by which information is accessed from memory through recall or recognition.

Chapter 9 also discusses the important role of meaning, imagery, and organization in encoding new memories, how memory is represented physically in the brain, and how forgetting may result from failure to encode or store information or to find appropriate retrieval cues. The final section of the chapter discusses the issue of memory construction. How "true" are our memories of events? A particularly controversial issue in this area involves suspicious claims of long-repressed memories of sexual abuse and other traumas that are "recovered" with the aid of hypnosis and other techniques. As you study this chapter, try applying some of the memory and studying tips discussed in the text.

NOTE: Answer guidelines for all Chapter 9 questions begin on page 266.

The Phenomenon of Memory
(pp. 318–320)

> David Myers at times uses idioms that are unfamiliar to some readers. If you do not know the meaning of any of the following words, phrases, or expressions in the context in which they appear in the text, refer to pages 275–276 for an explanation: . . . *mind's storehouse, the reservoir; medal winners in a memory Olympics; memory feats; shine the flashlight beam of attention on.*

Section Preview

First, skim the section, noting headings and boldface items. Then read the following objectives and, as you read the text, search for the information that will enable you to meet each objective. Answer guidelines are provided on page 266.

1. Explain memory in terms of information processing.

Stepping Through the Section

After you have read the section, complete the sentences and answer the questions. As you proceed, evaluate your performance by consulting the answers on page 266. Do not continue with the next section until you understand each answer. If you need to, review or reread the section in the textbook before continuing.

1. Learning that persists over time indicates the existence of _____ for that learning.
2. Memories for surprising, significant moments that are especially clear are called _____ memories.
3. Both human memory and computer memory can be viewed as _____-_____ systems that perform three tasks: _____ , _____ , and _____ .

4. The most influential model of memory in recent years has been Atkinson and Shiffrin's _____-_____ _____ model. According to this model, we first record information as a fleeting _____ _____ , from which it is processed into a _____-_____ memory, where the information is _____ into a _____-_____ memory for later retrieval.

5. The phenomenon of short-term memory has been expanded into the concept of _____ memory, which is similar to a computer's _____ memory, which integrates incoming information with material retrieved from long-term storage. This form of memory is _____ (unlimited/limited) and has both _____ and _____ subsystems.

Encoding: Getting Information In
(pp. 321–327)

> If you do not know the meaning of any of the following words, phrases, or expressions in the context in which they appear in the text, refer to page 276 for an explanation: _boost; nonsense syllables; a raw script . . . finished stage production; mental snapshots; peg-word; motionless while learning the numbers._

Section Preview

Answer guidelines are provided on page 266.

1. Explain the process of encoding, and distinguish between automatic and effortful processing.

2. Discuss the importance of rehearsal, spacing, and serial position in encoding.

3. Explain the importance of meaning, imagery, and organization in the encoding process.

Stepping Through the Section

Answers are provided on page 266.

1. A distinction is made between encoding that does not require conscious attention and is therefore _____ and that which is _____ .

Give examples of material encoded by automatic processing and by effortful processing.

2. With novel information, conscious repetition, or _____ , boosts memory.

3. A pioneering researcher in verbal memory was _____ . In one experiment, he found that the longer he studied a list of nonsense syllables, the _____ (fewer/greater) the number of repetitions he required to relearn it later.

4. After material has been learned, additional repetition, or _____ , usually will increase retention.

5. When people go around a circle reading words, their poorest memories are for the _____ (least/most) recent information heard. This phenomenon is called the _____-_____ _____ effect.

6. Memory studies also reveal that distributed rehearsal is more effective for retention; this is called the _____ _____ .

7. The tendency to remember the first and last items in a list best is called the _____ _____ _____ .

Following a delay, first items are remembered ____ (better/less well) than last items.

8. Encoding the meaning of words is referred to as _____ encoding; encoding by sound is called _____ encoding; encoding the image of words is _____ encoding.

9. Craik and Tulving's study comparing visual, acoustic, and semantic encoding showed that memory was best with _____ encoding.

10. Our excellent recall of information that relates to ourselves is called the _____ _____ effect.

11. Memory that consists of mental pictures is based on the use of _____ .

12. Your earliest memories are most likely of events that occurred when you were about _____ years old.

13. Concrete, high-imagery words tend to be remembered _____ (better/less well) than abstract, low-imagery words.

14. Memory aids are known as _____ devices. One such device involves forming associations between a familiar series of locations and to-be-remembered words; this technique is called the "_____ _____ _____ ."

15. Using a jingle, such as the one that begins "one is a bun," is an example of the "_____-_____" system.

16. Memory may be aided by grouping information into meaningful units called _____ . An example of this technique involves forming words from the first letters of to-be-remembered words; the resulting word is called an _____ .

17. In addition, material may be processed into _____ , which are composed of a few broad concepts divided into lesser concepts, categories, and facts.

Storage: Retaining Information
(pp. 328–334)

> If you do not know the meaning of any of the following words, phrases, or expressions in the context in which they appear in the text, refer to pages 276–277 for an explanation: *flashes of lightning; Sherlock Holmes; champion memorist; memory "software"; with tongue only partially in cheek; arousal sears the events onto the brain; mirror-image writing . . . jigsaw puzzle.*

Section Preview

Answer guidelines are provided on page 266.

1. Distinguish between iconic and echoic memory.

2. Describe memory capacity and duration.

3. Discuss research findings on the physical basis of memory.

4. Discuss what research with amnesics and animal conditioning studies reveals about the brain mechanisms involved in the dual explicit-implicit memory system.

Stepping Through the Section

Answers are provided on page 267.

1. If you are able to retrieve something from memory, you must have engaged in the passive process of _____ .

2. Stimuli from the environment are first recorded in _____ memory.

3. George Sperling found that when people were briefly shown three rows of letters, they could recall _____ (virtually all/about half) of them. When Sperling sounded a tone immediately after a row of letters was flashed to indicate which letters were to be recalled, the subjects were much _____ (more/less) accurate. This suggests that people have a brief photographic, or _____ , memory lasting about a few tenths of a second.

4. Sensory memory for sounds is called _____ memory. This memory fades _____ (more/less) rapidly than photographic memory, lasting for as long as _____ .

5. Peterson and Peterson found that when _____ was prevented by asking subjects to count backward, memory for letters was gone after 12 seconds. Without _____ processing, short-term memories have a limited life.

6. Our short-term memory capacity is about _____ chunks of information.

7. Short-term memory for random _____ (digits/letters) is slightly better than for random _____ (digits/letters) and memory for information we hear is somewhat _____ (better/worse) than that for information we see.

8. Both children and adults have short-term recall for roughly as many words as they can speak in _____ (how many?) seconds.

9. In contrast to short-term memory—and contrary to popular belief—the capacity of permanent memory is essentially _____ .

10. Penfield's electrically stimulated patients _____ (do/do not) provide reliable evidence that our stored memories are precise and durable.

11. It is likely that forgetting occurs because new experiences _____ with our retrieval of old information and that the physical memory trace _____ with the passage of time.

12. Lashley attempted to locate memory by cutting out pieces of rats' _____ after they had learned a maze. He found that no matter where he cut, the rats _____ (remembered/forgot) the maze.

13. Gerard found that a hamster's memory remained even after its body temperature was lowered to a point where the brain's _____ activity stopped.

14. Researchers believe that memory involves a strengthening of certain neural connections, which occurs at the _____ between neurons.

15. Kandel and Schwartz have found that when learning occurs in the sea snail *Aplysia*, the neurotransmitter _____ is released in greater amounts, making synapses more efficient.

16. After learning has occurred, a sending neuron needs _____ (more/less) prompting to fire, and the number of _____ _____ it stimulates may increase. This phenomenon, called _____-_____ _____ , may be the neural basis for learning and memory. Blocking this process with a specific _____ , or by genetic engineering that causes the absence of an _____ , interferes with learning. Rats given a drug that enhances _____ will learn a maze _____ (faster/more slowly).

17. A blow or an electric shock to the brain _____ (will/will not) disrupt old memories and _____ (will/will not) wipe out recent experiences.

18. Alcohol impairs memory _____ (formation/retrieval) by disrupting the neurotransmitter _____ .

19. Hormones released when we are excited or under stress often _____ (facilitate/impair) learning and memory. Drugs that block the effects of stress hormones _____ (facilitate/disrupt) memories of emotional events. Stress that is prolonged, however, may cause an area of the brain that is vital for laying down memories to _____ .

20. The loss of memory is called _____ . Studies of people who have lost their memory suggest that there _____ (is/is not) a single unified system of memory.

21. Although amnesics typically _____ (have/have not) lost their capacity for learning, which is called _____ memory, they _____ (are/are not) able to declare their memory, suggesting a deficit in their _____ memory systems.

22. Amnesic patients typically have suffered damage to the _____ of their limbic system. This brain structure is important in the processing and storage of _____ memories. Damage on the left side of this structure impairs _____ memory; damage on the right side impairs memory for _____ designs and locations.

23. The hippocampus seems to function as a zone where the brain _____ (temporarily/permanently) stores the elements of a memory. It also serves as a _____-_____ system that reactivates the _____ that fired when an event was first experienced.

24. The cerebellum is important in the processing of _____ memories.

25. The dual explicit-implicit memory system helps explain _____ amnesia. We do not have explicit memories of our first three years because the _____ is one of the last brain structures to mature.

Retrieval: Getting Information Out
(pp. 335–338)

> If you do not know the meaning of any of the following words, phrases, or expressions in the context in which they appear in the text, refer to page 277 for an explanation: *buoyant mood . . . rose-colored glasses; morph from devils into angels.*

Section Preview

Answer guidelines are provided on page 267.

1. Contrast recall, recognition, and relearning measures of memory.

2. Describe the importance of retrieval cues, noting the effects of priming, contexts, and moods on retrieval.

Stepping Through the Section

Answer guidelines are provided on page 268.

1. The ability to retrieve information not in conscious awareness is called _____ .

2. Bahrick found that 25 years after graduation, people were not able to _____ (recall/recognize) the names of their classmates but were able to _____ (recall/recognize) 90 percent of their names and their yearbook picture.

3. If you have learned something and then forgotten it, you will probably be able to

_____ it _____ (more/less) quickly than you did originally.

4. The process by which associations can lead to retrieval is called _____ .The best retrieval cues come from the associations formed at the time we _____ a memory.

5. Studies have shown that retention is best when learning and testing are done in _____ (the same/different) contexts.

Summarize the text's explanation of the déjà vu experience.

6. The type of memory in which emotions serve as retrieval cues is referred to as

_____-_____

memory.

Describe the effects of mood on memory.

7. People who are currently depressed may recall their parents as _____ . People who have recovered from depression typically recall their parents about the same as do people who

_____ .

Forgetting (pp. 338–344)

If you do not know the meaning of any of the following words, phrases, or expressions in the context in which they appear in the text, refer to page 277 for an explanation: *applause for memory; may lie poised on the tip of the tongue; mental attic; sheepishly.*

Section Preview

Answer guidelines are provided on page 268.

1. Broadly describe Schacter's seven sins of memory as a categorization of the ways in which we forget.

2. Discuss forgetting as either a form of encoding failure or storage decay.

3. Discuss the roles of interference and motivated forgetting in the process of retrieval failure.

Stepping Through the Section

Answers are provided on page 268.

1. Memory researcher Daniel Schacter has identified the seven sins of memory, divided into three categories that identify the ways in which our memory can fail: the three sins of _____ , the three sins of _____ , and the one sin of _____ .

2. The first category of sins refers to forgetting caused by _____ failure,

_____ _____ , and
_____ _____ . The
second category has to do with memory
_____ , and the third category
deals with _____ memories.

3. Encoding failure occurs because some of the
information that we sense _____
_____ . One reason for age-
related memory decline is that the brain areas
responsible for _____ new information are _____ (more/less) responsive in older adults.

4. Studies by Ebbinghaus and by Bahrick indicate
that most forgetting occurs _____
(soon/a long time) after the material is learned.
This type of forgetting is known as

_____ _____ .

5. When information that is stored in memory temporarily cannot be found, _____
failure has occurred.

6. Research suggests that memories are also lost as a
result of _____ , which is especially
possible if we simultaneously learn similar, new
material.

7. The disruptive effect of previous learning on current learning is called _____
_____ . The disruptive effect of
learning new material on efforts to recall material
previously learned is called _____

_____ .

8. Jenkins and Dallenbach found that if subjects
went to sleep after learning, their memory for a
list of nonsense syllables was _____
(better/worse) than it was if they stayed awake.

9. In some cases, old information facilitates our
learning of new information. This is called

_____ _____ .

10. Freud proposed that motivated forgetting, or
_____ , may protect a person from
painful memories. Increasing numbers of memory researchers think that motivated forgetting is
_____ (less/more) common than
Freud believed.

Memory Construction (pp. 345–353)

> If you do not know the meaning of any of the
> following words, phrases, or expressions in the
> context in which they appear in the text, refer
> to page 278 for an explanation: _reconstruction as
> well as reproduction; hypnotically refreshed; sin-
> cerely wrong._

Section Preview

Answer guidelines are provided on page 268.

1. Discuss the evidence for memory's being constructive.

2. Identify several ways in which real memories differ from false memories, and discuss whether
children are credible eyewitnesses.

3. Explain why memory researchers are suspicious
of claims of long-repressed memories "recovered" with the aid of a therapist.

Stepping Through the Section

Answers are provided on page 269.

1. Research has shown that recall of an event is
often influenced by past experiences and present
assumptions. The workings of these influences
illustrate the process of memory

_____ .

2. When witnesses to an event receive misleading
information about it, they may experience a
_____ _____ and
misremember the event. A number of experi-

ments have demonstrated that false memories _____ (can/cannot) be created when people are induced to imagine nonexistent events.

Describe what Loftus's studies have shown about the effects of misleading postevent information on eyewitness reports.

3. At the heart of many false memories is _____ _____ , which occurs when we _____ an event to the wrong source.

4. The persistence of a memory _____ (does/does not) reveal whether or not it derives from an actual experience. Whereas real memories have more _____ , gist memories are more _____ .

5. PET scans comparing brain activity when a subject is truly or falsely recalling a word reveal different activity patterns in an area of the _____ _____ _____ , but not in the _____ .

6. Eyewitnesses' confidence in their memories _____ (is/is not) related to the accuracy of those memories.

7. Memory construction explains why memories "refreshed" under _____ are often inaccurate.

8. Research studies of children's eyewitness recall reveals that preschoolers _____ (are/are not) more suggestible than older children or adults. For this reason, whether a child produces an accurate eyewitness memory depends heavily on how he or she is _____ .

9. A person whose identity centers around a false but strongly believed traumatic memory is said to

be suffering from the _____ _____ _____ .

10. Memories of events that happened before age _____ are unreliable. This phenomenon is called _____ _____ .

Improving Memory (pp. 354–355)

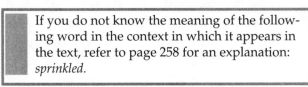

If you do not know the meaning of the following word in the context in which it appears in the text, refer to page 258 for an explanation: *sprinkled*.

Section Preview

Answer guidelines are provided on page 269.

1. Discuss strategies for improving memory.

Web Sighting

As noted in the text, memory researchers have become increasingly skeptical about Freud's concept of memory repression and are challenging its validity. At the same time, a rash of new court cases have involved therapeutically "recovered" memories of traumatic childhood events. After reading the chapter, you can understand how memory construction, source amnesia, and the misinformation effect contribute to this social problem.

To further your studies of these phenomena, use internet resources to see what you can learn about *recovered memory therapy (RMT)* and the *False Memory Syndrome (FMS)*. (Hint: Use your favorite search engine to locate web sites that pertain to RMT and FMS. One that will help you get started is the web site of the FMS Foundation, a nonprofit organization founded in 1992 to find out why FMS is spreading, try to prevent new cases of FMS, and provide assistance to all victims of FMS.)

Try to find answers to the following questions:

1. How did the False Memory Syndrome Foundation start?

2. What are "body memories"?

3. Are traumatic memories more accurate than non-traumatic memories?

4. What are the symptoms of FMS?

5. How does recovered memory therapy allegedly work?

6. What are the American Medical Association and American Psychological Association's positions regarding FMS?

Progress Test 1

Multiple-Choice Questions

Circle your answers to the following questions and check them with the answers on page 269. If your answer is incorrect, read the explanation for why it is incorrect and then consult the appropriate pages of the text (in parentheses following the correct answer).

1. The three steps in memory information processing are:
   a. input, processing, output.
   b. input, storage, output.
   c. input, storage, retrieval.
   d. encoding, storage, retrieval.
   e. encoding, retrieval, storage.

2. Visual sensory memory is referred to as:
   a. iconic memory.   c. photomemory.
   b. echoic memory.   d. semantic memory.

3. Echoic memories fade after approximately:
   a. 1 hour.   d. 1 second.
   b. 1 minute.   e. 3 to 4 seconds.
   c. 30 seconds.

4. Which of the following is *not* a measure of retention?
   a. recall   c. relearning
   b. recognition   d. retrieval

5. Our short-term memory span is approximately _____ items.
   a. 2   c. 7
   b. 5   d. 10

6. Memory techniques such as the method of loci, acronyms, and the peg-word system are called:
   a. consolidation devices.
   b. imagery techniques.
   c. encoding strategies.
   d. mnemonic devices.

7. One way to increase the amount of information in memory is to group it into larger, familiar units. This process is referred to as:
   a. consolidating.   d. encoding.
   b. organization.   e. chunking.
   c. memory construction.

8. Kandel and Schwartz have found that when learning occurs, more of the neurotransmitter _____ is released into synapses.
   a. ACh   c. serotonin
   b. dopamine   d. noradrenaline

9. Research on memory construction reveals that memories:
   a. are stored as exact copies of experience.
   b. reflect a person's biases and assumptions.
   c. may be chemically transferred from one organism to another.
   d. even if long term, usually decay within about five years.

10. In a study on context cues, people learned words while on land or when they were underwater. In a later test of recall, those with the best retention had:
    a. learned the words on land, that is, in the more familiar context.
    b. learned the words underwater, that is, in the more exotic context.
    c. learned the words and been tested on them in different contexts.
    d. learned the words and been tested on them in the same context.

11. PET scans taken when a person is truly or falsely recalling a word reveal different patterns of activity in an area of the:
    a. hippocampus.   c. cerebellum.
    b. left temporal lobe. d. thalamus.

12. The spacing effect means that:
    a. distributed study yields better retention than cramming.
    b. retention is improved when encoding and retrieval are separated by no more than 1 hour.
    c. learning causes a reduction in the size of the synaptic gap between certain neurons.
    d. delaying retrieval until memory has consolidated improves recall.

13. Studies demonstrate that learning causes permanent neural changes in the _____ of animals' neurons.
    a. myelin   c. synapses
    b. cell bodies d. all the above

14. In Sperling's memory experiment, subjects were shown three rows of three letters, followed immediately by a low-, medium-, or high-pitched tone. The subjects were able to report:
    a. all three rows with perfect accuracy.
    b. only the top row of letters.
    c. only the middle row of letters.
    d. any one of the three rows of letters.

15. Studies of amnesics suggest that:
    a. memory is a single, unified system.
    b. there are two distinct types of memory.
    c. there are three distinct types of memory.
    d. memory losses following brain trauma are unpredictable.
    e. brain trauma eliminates the ability to learn.

16. Memory for skills is called:
    a. explicit memory.   c. episodic memory.
    b. declarative memory. d. implicit memory.

17. The eerie feeling of having been somewhere before is an example of:
    a. state dependency.   c. priming.
    b. encoding failure.   d. déjà vu.

18. When Gordon Bower presented subjects with words grouped by category or in random order, recall was:
    a. the same for all words.
    b. better for the categorized words.
    c. better for the random words.
    d. improved when subjects developed their own mnemonic devices.

19. Which of the following has been proposed as a neurophysiological explanation of infantile amnesia?
    a. The slow maturation of the hippocampus leaves the infant's brain unable to store images and events.
    b. The deficient supply of serotonin until about age 3 makes encoding very limited.
    c. The limited availability of association areas of the cortex until about age 3 impairs encoding and storage.
    d. All of the above explanations have been proposed.

20. Hypnotically "refreshed" memories may prove inaccurate—especially if the hypnotist asks leading questions—because of:
    a. encoding failure.
    b. state-dependent memory.
    c. proactive interference.
    d. memory construction.

21. Which area of the brain is most important in the processing of implicit memories?
    a. hippocampus
    b. cerebellum
    c. hypothalamus
    d. amygdala

22. Which of the following terms does *not* belong with the others?
    a. misattribution
    b. blocking
    c. suggestibility
    d. bias

Matching Items

Match each definition or description with the appropriate term.

Definitions or Descriptions

_____ 1. sensory memory that decays more slowly than visual sensory memory
_____ 2. the process by which information gets into the memory system
_____ 3. mental pictures that aid memory
_____ 4. the blocking of painful memories
_____ 5. the phenomenon in which one's mood can influence retrieval
_____ 6. memory for a list of words is affected by word order
_____ 7. "one is a bun, two is a shoe" mnemonic device
_____ 8. matching each of a series of locations with a visual representation of to-be-remembered items
_____ 9. new learning interferes with previous knowledge
_____ 10. a measure of memory
_____ 11. old knowledge interferes with new learning
_____ 12. misattributing the origin of an event
_____ 13. the fading of unused information over time
_____ 14. the lingering effects of misinformation
_____ 15. a memory sin of intrusion

Terms

a. repression
b. relearning
c. serial position effect
d. persistence
e. peg-word system
f. method of loci
g. proactive interference
h. transience
i. retroactive interference
j. source amnesia
k. suggestibility
l. imagery
m. mood-congruent memory
n. echoic memory
o. encoding

Progress Test 2

Progress Test 2 should be completed during a final chapter review. Answer the following questions after you thoroughly understand the correct answers for the section reviews and Progress Test 1.

Multiple-Choice Questions

1. Which of the following best describes the typical forgetting curve?
   a. a steady, slow decline in retention over time
   b. a steady, rapid decline in retention over time
   c. a rapid initial decline in retention becoming stable thereafter
   d. a slow initial decline in retention becoming rapid thereafter

2. Jenkins and Dallenbach found that memory was better in subjects who were _____during the retention interval, presumably because _____ was reduced.
   a. awake; decay
   b. asleep; decay
   c. awake; interference
   d. asleep; interference

3. Which of the following measures of retention is the least sensitive in triggering retrieval?
   a. recall   c. relearning
   b. recognition   d. déjà vu

4. Amnesics typically have experienced damage to the _____ of the brain.
   a. frontal lobes   d. hippocampus
   b. cerebellum   e. cortex
   c. thalamus

5. According to the serial position effect, when recalling a list of words you should have the greatest difficulty with those:
   a. at the beginning of the list.
   b. at the end of the list.
   c. at the end and in the middle of the list.
   d. at the beginning and end of the list.
   e. in the middle of the list.

6. Craik and Watkins gave subjects a list of words to be recalled. When subjects were tested after a delay, the items that were best recalled were those:
   a. at the beginning of the list.
   b. in the middle of the list.
   c. at the end of the list.
   d. at the beginning and the end of the list.

7. Craik and Tulving had subjects process words visually, acoustically, or semantically. In a subsequent recall test, which type of processing resulted in the greatest retention?
   a. visual
   b. acoustic
   c. semantic
   d. Acoustic and semantic processing were equally beneficial.

8. Lashley's studies, in which rats learned a maze and then had various parts of their brains surgically removed, showed that the memory:
   a. was lost when surgery took place within 1 hour of learning.
   b. was lost when surgery took place within 24 hours of learning.
   c. was lost when any region of the brain was removed.
   d. remained no matter which area of the brain was tampered with.

9. The disruption of memory caused by excessive consumption of alcohol provides evidence for the importance of:
   a. neurotransmitters in the formation of new memories.
   b. neurotransmitters in the retrieval of long-term memories.
   c. nutrition in normal neural functioning.
   d. all of the above.

10. *Long-term potentiation* refers to:
    a. the disruptive influence of old memories on the formation of new memories.
    b. the disruptive influence of recent memories on the retrieval of old memories.
    c. our tendency to recall experiences that are consistent with our current mood.
    d. the increased efficiency of synaptic transmission between certain neurons following learning.
    e. our increased ability to recall long-ago events as we grow older.

11. Repression is an example of:
    a. encoding failure.   c. motivated forgetting.
    b. memory decay.   d. all of the above.

12. Studies by Loftus and Palmer, in which subjects were quizzed about a film of an accident, indicate that:
    a. when quizzed immediately, subjects can recall very little, due to the stress of witnessing an accident.
    b. when questioned as little as one day later, their memory was very inaccurate.
    c. most subjects had very accurate memories as much as 6 months later.
    d. subjects' recall may easily be affected by misleading information.

13. Which of the following was *not* recommended as a strategy for improving memory?
    a. active rehearsal
    b. distributed study
    c. speed reading
    d. encoding meaningful associations
    e. use of mnemonic devices

14. The process of getting information out of memory storage is called:
    a. encoding.   c. rehearsal.
    b. retrieval.   d. storage.

15. Amnesic patients typically experience disruption of:
    a. implicit memories.   c. iconic memories.
    b. explicit memories.   d. echoic memories.

16. Information is maintained in short-term memory only briefly unless it is:
    a. encoded.   c. iconic or echoic.
    b. rehearsed.   d. retrieved.

17. Textbook chapters are often organized into _____ in order to facilitate information processing.
    a. mnemonic devices
    c. hierarchies
    b. chunks
    d. recognizable units

18. Memory researchers are suspicious of long-repressed memories of traumatic events that are "recovered" with the aid of drugs or hypnosis because:
    a. such experiences usually are vividly remembered.
    b. such memories are unreliable, and easily influenced by misinformation.
    c. memories of events happening before about age 3 are especially unreliable.
    d. of all of the above reasons.

19. It is easier to recall information that has just been presented when the information:
    a. consists of random letters rather than words.
    b. is seen rather than heard.
    c. is heard rather than seen.
    d. is experienced in an unusual context.

20. The misinformation effect provides evidence that memory:
    a. is constructed during encoding.
    b. is unchanging once established.
    c. may be reconstructed during recall according to how questions are framed.
    d. is highly resistant to misleading information.

21. According to memory researcher Daniel Schacter, blocking occurs when:
    a. our inattention to details produces encoding failure.
    b. we confuse the source of information.
    c. our beliefs influence our recollections.
    d. information is on the tip of our tongue, but we can't get it out.

22. The three-stage processing model of memory was proposed by:
    a. Atkinson and Shifrin.
    b. Herman Ebbinghaus.
    c. Loftus and Palmer.
    d. George Sperling.

True-False Items

Indicate whether each statement is true or false by placing *T* or *F* in the blank next to the item.

_____ 1. Studying that is distributed over time produces better retention than cramming.

_____ 2. Generally speaking, memory for pictures is better than memory for words.

_____ 3. Recall of childhood abuse through hypnosis indicates that memory is permanent, due to the reliability of such reports.

_____ 4. Most people do not have memories of events that occurred before the age of 3.

_____ 5. Studies by Ebbinghaus show that most forgetting takes place soon after learning.

_____ 6. The persistence of a memory is a good clue as to whether or not it derives from an actual experience.

_____ 7. Recall of newly acquired knowledge is no better after sleeping than after being awake for the same period of time.

_____ 8. Time spent in developing imagery, chunking, and associating material with what you already know is more effective than time spent repeating information again and again.

_____ 9. Although repression has not been confirmed experimentally, most clinical psychologists believe that it happens.

_____ 10. Overlearning material by continuing to restudy it beyond mastery often disrupts recall.

Thinking Critically About Chapter 9

Answer these questions the day before an exam as a final check on your understanding of the chapter's terms and concepts.

Multiple-Choice Questions

1. Complete this analogy: Fill-in-the-blank test questions are to multiple-choice questions as:
    a. encoding is to storage.
    b. storage is to encoding.
    c. recognition is to recall.
    d. recall is to recognition.
    e. encoding is to recall.

2. The above figure depicts the recall of a list of words under two conditions. Which of the following best describes the difference between the conditions?
   a. In *A*, the words were studied and retrieved in the same context; in *B*, the contexts were different.
   b. In *B*, the words were studied and retrieved in the same context; in *A*, the contexts were different.
   c. The delay between presentation of the last word and the test of recall was longer for *A* than for *B*.
   d. The delay between presentation of the last word and the test of recall was longer for *B* than for *A*.

3. Darren was asked to memorize a list of letters that included *v*, *q*, *y*, and *j*. He later recalled these letters as *e*, *u*, *i*, and *k*, suggesting that the original letters had been encoded:
   a. automatically.   c. semantically.
   b. visually.   d. acoustically.

4. After finding her old combination lock, Janice can't remember its combination because she keeps confusing it with the combination of her new lock. She is experiencing:
   a. proactive interference.
   b. retroactive interference.
   c. encoding failure.
   d. storage failure.
   e. repression.

5. Which of the following sequences would be best to follow if you wanted to minimize interference-induced forgetting in order to improve your recall on the psychology midterm?
   a. study, eat, test
   b. study, sleep, test
   c. study, listen to music, test
   d. study, exercise, test

6. Being in a bad mood after a hard day of work, Susan could think of nothing positive in her life. This is best explained as an example of:
   a. priming.
   b. memory construction.
   c. mood-congruent memory.
   d. retrieval failure.
   e. repression.

7. In an effort to remember the name of the classmate who sat behind her in fifth grade, Martina mentally recited the names of other classmates who sat near her. Martina's effort to refresh her memory by activating related associations is an example of:
   a. priming.   c. encoding.
   b. déjà vu.   d. relearning.

8. Walking through the halls of his high school 10 years after graduation, Tom experienced a flood of old memories. Tom's experience showed the role of:
   a. state-dependent memory.
   b. context effects.
   c. retroactive interference.
   d. echoic memory.
   e. iconic memory.

9. The first thing Karen did when she discovered that she had misplaced her keys was to re-create in her mind the day's events. That she had little difficulty in doing so illustrates:
   a. automatic processing.
   b. effortful processing.
   c. state-dependent memory.
   d. priming.

10. Which of the following is the best example of a flashbulb memory?
    a. suddenly remembering to buy bread while standing in the checkout line at the grocery store
    b. recalling the name of someone from high school while looking at his or her yearbook snapshot
    c. remembering to make an important phone call
    d. remembering what you were doing the day high school students were killed in Littleton, Colorado

11. When Carlos was promoted, he moved into a new office with a new phone extension. Every time he is asked for his phone number, Carlos first thinks of his old extension, illustrating the effects of:
    a. proactive interference.
    b. retroactive interference.
    c. encoding failure.
    d. storage failure.

12. Elderly Mr. Flanagan can easily recall his high school graduation, but he cannot remember the name of the president of the United States. Evidently, Mr. Flanagan's _____ memory is better than his _____ memory.
    a. implicit; explicit
    b. explicit; implicit
    c. episodic; semantic
    d. semantic; episodic

13. Although you can't recall the answer to a question on your psychology midterm, you have a clear mental image of the textbook page on which it appears. Evidently, your _____ encoding of the answer was _____ .
    a. semantic; automatic
    b. visual; automatic
    c. semantic; effortful
    d. visual; effortful

14. At your high school reunion you cannot remember the last name of your homeroom teacher. Your failure to remember is most likely the result of:
    a. encoding failure.
    b. storage failure.
    c. retrieval failure.
    d. state-dependent memory.

15. Brenda has trouble remembering her new five-digit ZIP plus four-digit address code. What is the most likely explanation for the difficulty Brenda is having?
    a. Nine digits are at or above the upper limit of most people's short-term memory capacity.
    b. Nine digits are at or above the upper limit of most people's iconic memory capacity.
    c. The extra four digits cannot be organized into easily remembered chunks.
    d. Brenda evidently has an impaired implicit memory.

16. Lewis cannot remember the details of the torture he experienced as a prisoner of war. According to Freud, Lewis's failure to remember these painful memories is an example of:
    a. repression.
    b. retrieval failure.
    c. state-dependent memory.
    d. flashbulb memory.
    e. implicit memory.

17. Which of the following illustrates the constructive nature of memory?
    a. Janice keeps calling her new boyfriend by her old boyfriend's name.
    b. After studying all afternoon and then getting drunk in the evening, Don can't remember the material he studied.
    c. After getting some good news, elated Kareem has a flood of good memories from his younger years.
    d. Although elderly Mrs. Harvey, who has Alzheimer's disease, has many gaps in her memory, she invents sensible accounts of her activities so that her family will not worry.

18. To help him remember the order of ingredients in difficult recipes, master chef Giulio often associates them with the route he walks to work each day. Giulio is using which mnemonic technique?
    a. peg-word system   c. the method of loci
    b. acronyms   d. chunking

19. During basketball practice Jan's head was painfully elbowed. If the trauma to her brain disrupts her memory, we would expect that Jan would be most likely to forget:
    a. the name of her teammates.
    b. her telephone number.
    c. the name of the play during which she was elbowed.
    d. the details of events that happened shortly after the incident.

20. After suffering damage to the hippocampus, a person would probably:
    a. lose memory for skills such as bicycle riding.
    b. be incapable of being classically conditioned.
    c. lose the ability to store new facts.
    d. experience all of the above changes.

21. When he was 8 years old, Frank was questioned by the police about a summer camp counselor suspected of molesting children. Even though he was not, in fact, molested by the counselor, today 19-year-old Frank "remembers" the counselor touching him inappropriately. Frank's false memory is an example of which "sin" of memory?
    a. blocking
    b. transience
    c. misattribution
    d. suggestibility

22. The concept of working memory is analogous to a computer's:
    a. read-only (ROM) memory.
    b. random-access (RAM) memory.
    c. mouse.
    d. keyboard.

Essay Question

Discuss the points of agreement among experts regarding the validity of recovered memories of child abuse. (Use the space below to jot down notes for your essay; then write the essay on a separate piece of paper.)

Key Terms

Writing Definitions

Using your own words, on a separate piece of paper write a brief definition or explanation of each of the following terms.

1. memory
2. flashbulb memory
3. encoding
4. storage
5. retrieval
6. sensory memory
7. short-term memory
8. long-term memory
9. automatic processing
10. effortful processing
11. rehearsal
12. spacing effect
13. serial position effect
14. semantic encoding
15. acoustic encoding
16. visual encoding
17. imagery
18. mnemonics
19. chunking
20. iconic memory
21. echoic memory
22. long-term potentiation (LTP)
23. amnesia
24. implicit memory
25. explicit memory
26. hippocampus
27. recall
28. recognition
29. relearning
30. priming
31. déjà vu
32. mood-congruent memory
33. proactive interference
34. retroactive interference
35. repression
36. misinformation effect
37. source amnesia

Summing Up

Complete the following flow chart.

INFORMATION PROCESSING

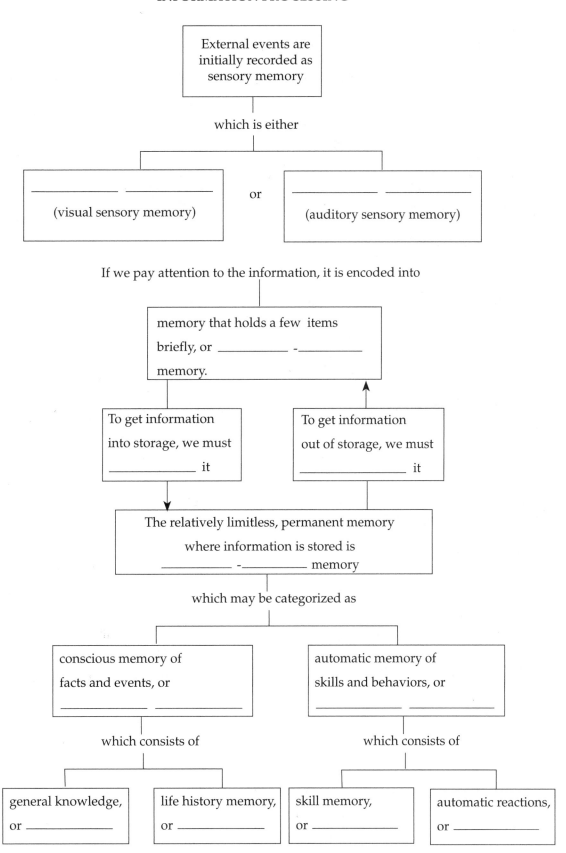

External events are initially recorded as sensory memory

which is either

_____ _____

(visual sensory memory)

or

_____ _____

(auditory sensory memory)

If we pay attention to the information, it is encoded into

memory that holds a few items briefly, or _____ -_____ memory.

To get information into storage, we must _____ it

To get information out of storage, we must _____ it

The relatively limitless, permanent memory where information is stored is _____ -_____ memory

which may be categorized as

conscious memory of facts and events, or _____ _____

automatic memory of skills and behaviors, or _____ _____

which consists of

which consists of

general knowledge, or _____

life history memory, or _____

skill memory, or _____

automatic reactions, or _____

Answers

The Phenomenon of Memory

Section Preview

1. To remember any event requires that we somehow get information into our brain (encoding), retain it (storage) as short- or long-term memory, and get it back out (retrieval). These three steps apply not only to human memory but also to other information-processing systems, such as computers. According to Atkinson and Shiffrin's three-stage processing model, we first record to-be-remembered information as a brief sensory memory, from which it is processed into a short-term, or working, memory and then encoded into a durable long-term memory.

Stepping Through the Section

1. memory
2. flashbulb
3. information-processing; encoding; storage; retrieval
4. three-stage processing; sensory memory; short-term; encoded; long-term
5. working; RAM; limited; visual; verbal

Encoding: Getting Information In

Section Preview

1. Encoding is the process by which sensory information is transferred into the memory system. Information about space, time, and frequency, as well as well-learned information, is encoded with little or no effort (automatic processing). Encoding of most other types of information requires attention and conscious rehearsal (effortful processing).

2. Ebbinghaus demonstrated that the amount of material remembered depends on the time spent rehearsing it. Even after material is learned, additional rehearsal (overlearning) increases retention.

   Experiments show that distributed study yields better long-term retention than cramming (spacing effect).

   The serial position effect refers to the finding that people often remember the first and last items in a list better than they do middle items.

3. Studies by Craik and Tulving demonstrate that the processing of meaning (semantic encoding) yields better memory of verbal information than does the processing of images (visual encoding) or sounds (acoustic encoding). Recall of informa-

tion we relate to ourselves is particularly good.

The imagery principle—that people have excellent memory for pictures and picture-evoking words—is at the heart of memory-enhancing mnemonic devices. In the method of loci and the "peg-word" system, we associate to-be-remembered items with visual codes.

Organizing information into meaningful units, or chunks, also improves memory. The use of acronyms and hierarchies, for example, can facilitate both retention and retrieval.

Stepping Through the Section

1. automatic; effortful

Automatic processing includes the encoding of information about space, time, and frequency. It also includes the encoding of word meaning, a type of encoding that appears to be learned. Effortful processing, or encoding that requires attention and effort, is used to encode material like telephone numbers, word lists, textbook chapters, and so on.

2. rehearsal
3. Ebbinghaus; fewer
4. overlearning
5. most; next-in-line
6. spacing effect
7. serial position effect; better
8. semantic; acoustic; visual
9. semantic
10. self-reference
11. imagery
12. 3 or 4
13. better
14. mnemonic; method of loci
15. peg-word
16. chunks; acronym
17. hierarchies

Storage: Retaining Information

Section Preview

1. Iconic memory is momentary photographic memory in which the eyes register an exact representation of a scene. George Sperling first demonstrated the existence of this type of sensory memory, which lasts for only about a few tenths of a second. Sensory memory for sound, called echoic memory, disappears after 3 or 4 seconds.

2. Studies by Peterson and Peterson demonstrate that short-term memory stores approximately seven chunks of information. This type of memo-

ry is slightly better for random digits than for random letters and is slightly better for information we hear rather than see. Without some form of active processing, the duration of short-term memory is limited. In contrast, our capacity for storing long-term memories is essentially limitless. However, we do not store long-term memories with the exactness of a tape recorder. Rather, forgetting occurs as new experiences interfere with retrieval and as the physical memory trace gradually decays.

3. Lashley's studies demonstrated that memories do not reside in single, specific parts of the cortex. Gerard demonstrated that lowering animals' body temperatures until their brains' electrical activity ceased did not disrupt long-term memories. Kandel and Schwartz found that when learning occurs in sea snails, more of the neurotransmitter serotonin is released at certain synapses, and neural transmission is more efficient. This increased efficiency, called long-term potentiation, may be the neural basis for learning and memory. Other studies have shown that when neurotransmitters are blocked by alcohol and other drugs, memory formation is disrupted. Conversely, learning and retention are boosted by emotion-triggered hormonal changes.

4. Although amnesics often can't recall new facts or recent experiences, most are capable of learning new skills. This suggests that there are two distinct types of memory: implicit (or nondeclarative) memory of skills, preferences, and dispositions; and explicit (declarative) memory of facts and experiences that are consciously known.

   The fact that most amnesics have suffered damage to the hippocampus suggests that this limbic structure plays a crucial role in the processing of explicit memories. Because older memories remain intact in amnesics, the hippocampus cannot be the permanent storehouse for such memories. It is likely that the hippocampus functions as a relay station that feeds new information to other brain circuits for permanent storage. In contrast, the cerebellum seems to be the site of implicit memories. Animal conditioning studies and studies of human patients with a damaged cerebellum demonstrate that when this area of the brain is not functioning, learning is disrupted.

Stepping Through the Section

1. storage
2. sensory
3. about half; more; iconic
4. echoic; less; 3 or 4 seconds
5. rehearsal; active
6. 7
7. digits; letters; better
8. 2
9. unlimited (limitless)
10. do not
11. interfere; decays
12. cortexes; remembered
13. electrical
14. synapses
15. serotonin
16. less; receptor sites; long-term potentiation; drug; enzyme; LTP; faster
17. will not; will
18. formation; serotonin
19. facilitate; disrupt; shrink
20. amnesia; is not
21. have not; implicit; are not; explicit
22. hippocampus; explicit; verbal; visual
23. temporarily; play-back; neurons
24. implicit
25. infantile; hippocampus

Retrieval: Getting Information Out

Section Preview

1. Recall is the ability to retrieve information not in conscious awareness. Recognition is a measure of memory in which one need only identify previously learned information. Relearning measures the amount of time saved when previously learned information is learned for a second time. Tests of recognition and relearning typically reveal that people remember more than they can recall. Recognition tests of memory are "easier" because they provide retrieval cues that serve as reminders of information that could not otherwise be recalled.

2. Priming and context effects indicate the importance of retrieval cues in memory. Emotions also trigger memories. State-dependent memory is the phenomenon that things learned in one emotional state are more easily recalled when we are again in the same state. Another aspect of this phenomenon is that our current mood influences our retrieval of past experiences. Mood also influences how we interpret other people's behavior and how attentive we are to new information.

Stepping Through the Section

1. recall
2. recall; recognize
3. relearn; more
4. priming; encode
5. the same

The déjà vu experience is most likely the result of being in a context similar to one that we *have* actually been in before. If we have previously been in a similar situation, though we cannot recall what it was, the current situation may present cues that unconsciously help us to retrieve the earlier experience.

6. state-dependent

When happy, for example, we perceive things in a positive light and recall happy events; these perceptions and memories, in turn, prolong our good mood. Moods also influence how we interpret other people's behavior.

7. rejecting or punitive; have never suffered depression

Forgetting

Section Preview

1. Daniel Schacter's seven sins of memory are grouped into three categories: sins of forgetting, sins of distortion, and a sin of intrusion. Broadly, these identify the different ways people forget. The first category can be applied to encoding failure, storage decay, and retrieval failure. The second refers to the ways in which our memory reconstructs reality. The final category deals with motivated forgetting of unwanted memories, for example.

2. Much of the material we think of as having been forgotten was never "remembered." Although it was sensed, it never entered the memory system because it was not encoded; therefore, its "loss" can be attributed to encoding failure. The areas of the brain responsible for encoding become less responsive as we age, which is one reason that older people tend to recall less than younger adults do.

    Even when information has been encoded well, it may gradually fade with time. Ebbinghaus' famous "forgetting curve" and Bahrick's study of long-term retention of Spanish vocabulary showed that most forgetting occurs relatively soon after learning.

3. Another explanation for the forgetting curve is that experiences interfere with retrieval. Proactive interference refers to the disruptive effect of previous learning on the recall of new information. Retroactive interference refers to the disruptive effect of new information on the recall of previous information. Jenkins and Dallenbach's classic study demonstrated that retroactive interference was reduced when subjects slept following a learning episode, presumably because the number of potentially interfering events was minimized.

    Motivated forgetting refers to the irretrievability of memories that are embarrassing to remember. Similarly, with his concept of repression Freud proposed that memory is self-censoring. According to this viewpoint, repressed memories remain intact and may be retrieved at some later time.

Stepping Through the Section

1. forgetting; distortion; intrusion
2. encoding; storage decay; retrieval failure; construction; unwanted
3. never actually enters the memory system; encoding; less
4. soon; storage decay
5. retrieval
6. interference
7. proactive interference; retroactive interference
8. better
9. positive transfer
10. repression; less

Memory Construction

Section Preview

1. Memory retrieval does not consist merely of a literal reporting of stored information. Instead, memories are constructed as we encode them, then alter them in the face of new experiences. Loftus and Palmer have shown that after exposure to subtle misinformation, eyewitnesses to an incident incorrectly recalled the actual incident (the misinformation effect). Another phenomenon, *source amnesia*, is at the heart of many false memories. This occurs whenever we misattribute an event that we experienced, read about, or imagined to the wrong source. Memory construction also explains why "hypnotically refreshed" memories often incorporate false information.

2. Although false memories created by misinformation and misattribution feel as though they are real, confidence does not equate with accuracy in memory. Furthermore, PET scans reveal that the

brain responds differently to true and false memories. Finally, real memories that derive from experience have more detail than memories derived from imagination.

Recent studies of eyewitness memory demonstrate that young children are more suggestible to memory plants than older children or adults. However, children are especially credible when questioned by a neutral person who asks nonleading questions.

3. Researchers are skeptical of such claims because, although recovered memories are commonplace, memories of things happening before age 3, as well as those "recovered" under hypnosis or the influence of drugs are unreliable. In addition, the "recovery" of painful memory rests on the assumption that the human mind commonly represses traumatic experiences—an assumption that increasingly is being challenged by contemporary researchers.

Stepping Through the Section

1. construction

2. misinformation effect; can

When subjects viewed a film of a traffic accident and were quizzed a week later, misleading postevent information was found to influence recall of the event (although it did not affect people's ability to recognize what they had witnessed). Phrasing of questions affected answers; the word "smashed," for instance, made subjects mistakenly think they had seen broken glass.

3. source amnesia; misattribute

4. does not; details; durable

5. left temporal lobe; hippocampus

6. is not

7. hypnosis

8. are; questioned

9. false memory syndrome

10. 3; infantile amnesia

Improving Memory

Section Preview

1. Suggestions for improving memory include rehearsing material over many separate and distributed study sessions with the objective of overlearning material. Studying should also involve active rehearsal, rather than mindless repetition of information. Organizing information, relating material to what is already known, developing numerous retrieval cues, and using mnemonic devices that incorporate vivid imagery are helpful too. Frequent activation of retrieval cues, such as the context and mood in which the original learning occurred, can also help strengthen memory, as can recalling events while they are fresh, before possible misinformation is encountered. Studying should also be arranged to minimize potential sources of interference. Finally, self-tests in the same format (recall or recognition) that will later be used on the actual test are useful. (The PRTR technique described in the Introduction of the text incorporates several of these strategies.)

Progress Test 1

Multiple-Choice Questions

1. **d.** is the answer. Information must be encoded, or put into appropriate form; stored, or retained over time; and retrieved, or located and gotten out when needed. (p. 319)

2. **a.** is the answer. Iconic memory is our fleeting memory of visual stimuli. (p. 328)
   b. Echoic memory is auditory sensory memory.
   c. There is no such thing as photomemory.
   d. Semantic memory is memory for meaning, not a form of sensory memory.

3. **e.** is the answer. Echoic memories last 3 to 4 seconds. (p. 328)

4. **d.** is the answer. Retrieval refers to the *process* of remembering. (p. 335)

5. **c.** is the answer. (p. 329)

6. **d.** is the answer. (p. 325)
   a. There is no such term as "consolidation techniques."
   b. & c. Imagery and encoding strategies are important in storing new memories, but mnemonic device is the general designation of techniques that facilitate memory, such as acronyms and the peg-word system.

7. **e.** is the answer. (p. 326)
   a. There is no such process of "consolidating."
   b. Organization *does* enhance memory but it does so through hierarchies, not grouping.
   c. Memory construction refers to the ways in which memories are altered by the individual's basic assumptions and experiences.
   d. Encoding refers to the processing of information into the memory system.

8. **c.** is the answer. Kandel and Schwartz found that when learning occurred in the sea snail *Aplysia*, serotonin was released at certain synapses, which

then became more efficient at signal transmission. (p. 331)

9. **b.** is the answer. In essence, we construct our memories, bringing them into line with our biases and assumptions, as well as with our subsequent experiences. (pp. 345–346)

a. If this were true, it would mean that memory construction does not occur. Through memory construction, memories may deviate significantly from the original experiences.

c. There is no evidence that such chemical transfers occur.

d. Many long-term memories are apparently unlimited in duration.

10. **d.** is the answer. In general, being in a context similar to that in which you experienced something will tend to help you recall the experience. (p. 336)

a. & b. The learning environment per se—and its familiarity or exoticness—did not affect retention.

11. **b.** is the answer. (348)

a. In fact, brain activity in the hippocampus does *not* differentiate true and false word recognition memories.

c. & d. These brain areas are not implicated in this type of memory.

12. **a.** is the answer. (p. 322)

b. & d. The text does not suggest that there is an optimal interval between encoding and retrieval.

c. Learning increases the efficiency of synaptic transmission in certain neurons, but not by altering the size of the synapse.

13. **c.** is the answer. (pp. 330–331)

14. **d.** is the answer. When asked to recall all the letters, subjects could recall only about half; however, if immediately after the presentation they were signaled to recall a particular row, their recall was near perfect. This showed that they had a brief photographic memory—so brief that it faded in less time than it would have taken to say all nine letters. (p. 328)

15. **b.** is the answer. Because amnesics lose their fact (explicit) memories but not their skill (implicit) memories or their capacity to learn, it appears that human memory can be divided into two distinct types. (p. 332)

d. As studies of victims of amnesia show, memory losses following damage to the hippocampus are quite predictable.

16. **d.** is the answer. (p. 332)

a. & b. Explicit memory (also called declarative memory) is memory of facts and experiences that one can consciously know and declare.

c. Episodic memory is explicit memory for personally experienced events.

17. **d.** is the answer. (p. 337)

a. State-dependent memory is the phenomenon in which information is best retrieved when the person is in the same emotional or physiological state he or she was in when the material was learned.

b. Encoding failure occurs when a person has not processed information sufficiently for it to enter the memory system.

c. Priming is the process by which a memory is activated through retrieval of an associated memory.

18. **b.** is the answer. When the words were organized into categories, recall was two to three times better, indicating the benefits of hierarchical organization in memory. (p. 327)

d. This study did not examine the use of mnemonic devices by subjects.

19. **a.** is the answer. We remember skills acquired in infancy, as such memories are recorded in earlier developing brain regions, but declarative memories involve the hippocampus. (p. 334)

b., c., & d. There is no evidence that serotonin levels or association areas are deficient until age 3. Moreover, such proposals are unlikely, as they wouldn't explain why we remember skills learned in infancy while forgetting events experienced.

20. **d.** is the answer. It is in both encoding and retrieval that we construct our memories, and as Loftus's studies showed, leading questions affect people's memory construction. (p. 348)

a. The memory encoding occurred at the time of the event in question, not during questioning by the hypnotist.

b. State-dependent memory refers to the influence of one's own emotional or physiological state on encoding and retrieval, and would not apply here.

c. Proactive interference is the interfering effect of prior learning on the recall of new information.

21. **b.** is the answer. (p. 334)

a. The hippocampus is a temporary processing site for *explicit memories*.

c. & d. These areas of the brain are not directly involved in the memory system.

22. **b.** is the answer. Blocking is an example of retrieval failure. Each of the others is an example of a "sin of distortion," in which memories, although inaccurate, are retrieved (p. 339)

Matching Items

1. n (p. 328)	**6.** c (p. 322)	**11.** g (p. 342)
2. o (p. 319)	**7.** e (p. 325)	**12.** j (p. 347)
3. l (p. 325)	**8.** f (p. 325)	**13.** h (p. 339)
4. a (p. 344)	**9.** i (p. 342)	**14.** k (p. 339)
5. m (p. 337)	**10.** b (p. 335)	**15.** d (p. 339)

Progress Test 2

Multiple-Choice Questions

1. **c.** is the answer. As Ebbinghaus and Bahrick both showed, most of the forgetting that is going to occur happens soon after learning. (p. 340)

2. **d.** is the answer. (p. 343)
   a. & b. This study did not find evidence that memories fade (decay) with time.
   c. When one is awake, there are many *more* potential sources of memory interference than when one is asleep.

3. **a.** is the answer. A test of recall presents the fewest retrieval cues and usually produces the most limited retrieval. (p. 335)

4. **d.** is the answer. (p. 337)

5. **e.** is the answer. According to the serial position effect, items at the beginning and end of a list tend to be remembered best. (p. 322)

6. **a.** is the answer. (pp. 322–323)
   b. In the serial position effect, the items in the middle of the list always show the *poorest* retention.
   c. & d. Delayed recall erases the memory facilitation for items at the end of the list.

7. **c.** is the answer. Processing a word in terms of its meaning (semantic encoding) produces much better retention than does visual or acoustic encoding. (pp. 323–324)

8. **d.** is the answer. Surprisingly, Lashley found that no matter where he cut, the rats had at least a partial memory of how to solve the maze. (p. 330)
   a. & b. Lashley's studies did not investigate the significance of the interval between learning and cortical lesioning.

9. **a.** is the answer. Alcohol disrupts memory by interfering with the neurotransmitter serotonin. (p. 331)
   b. The disruptive effects of alcohol are on the formation, rather than the retrieval, of memories.
   c. Although nutrition plays an important role in brain chemistry, the effects of alcohol are independent of nutrition.

10. **d.** is the answer. (p. 331)

11. **c.** is the answer. According to Freud, we repress painful memories to preserve our self-concepts. (p. 344)
    a. & b. The fact that repressed memories can sometimes be retrieved suggests that they were encoded and have not decayed with time.

12. **d.** is the answer. When misled by the phrasings of questions, subjects incorrectly recalled details of the film and even "remembered" objects that weren't there. (p. 345)

13. **c.** is the answer. Speed reading, which entails little active rehearsal, yields poor retention. (p. 354)

14. **b.** is the answer. (p. 319)
    a. Encoding is the process of getting information *into* memory.
    c. Rehearsal is the conscious repetition of information in order to maintain it in memory.
    d. Storage is the maintenance of encoded material over time.

15. **b.** is the answer. Amnesics typically have suffered damage to the hippocampus, a brain structure involved in processing explicit memories for facts. (p. 333)
    a. Amnesics do retain implicit memories for how to do things; these are processed in the more ancient parts of the brain.
    c. & d. Amnesics generally do not experience impairment in their iconic and echoic sensory memories.

16. **b.** is the answer. (p. 321)
    a. Information in short-term memory has *already* been encoded.
    c. Iconic and echoic are types of *sensory* memory.
    d. Retrieval is the process of getting material out of storage and into conscious, short-term memory. Thus, all material in short-term memory has either already been retrieved or is about to be placed in storage.

17. **c.** is the answer. By breaking concepts down into subconcepts and yet smaller divisions and showing the relationships among these, hierarchies facilitate information processing. Use of main heads and subheads is an example of the organization of textbook chapters into hierarchies. (p. 327)
    a. Mnemonic devices are the method of loci, acronyms, and other memory *techniques* that facilitate retention.
    b. Chunks are organizations of knowledge into familiar, manageable units.
    d. Recognition is a measure of retention.

18. **d.** is the answer. (pp. 351–352)

19. **c.** is the answer. Short-term recall is slightly better for information we hear rather than see, because echoic memory momentarily outlasts iconic memory. (p. 328)

a. Meaningful stimuli, such as words, are usually remembered more easily than meaningless stimuli, such as random letters.

b. Iconic memory does not last as long as echoic memory in short-term recall.

d. Although context is a powerful retrieval cue, there is no general facilitation of memory in an unusual context.

20. **c.** is the answer. Loftus and Palmer found that eyewitness testimony could easily be altered when questions were phrased to imply misleading information. (p. 345)

a. Although memories *are* constructed during encoding, the misinformation effect is a retrieval, rather than an encoding, phenomenon.

b. & d. In fact, just the opposite is true.

21. **d.** is the answer. (p. 339)

a. This defines absent-mindedness.

b. This is misattribution.

c. This is bias.

22. **a.** is the answer. (p. 319)

b. Herman Ebbinghaus conducted pioneering studies of verbal learning and memory.

c. Loftus and Palmer conducted influential research studies of eyewitness memory.

d. George Sperling is known for his research studies of iconic memory.

True-False Items

1. T (p. 354)	**6.** F (p. 348)
2. T (p. 325)	**7.** F (p. 343)
3. F (p. 348)	**8.** T (p. 354)
4. T (p. 352)	**9.** F (p. 344)
5. T (p. 340)	**10.** F (p. 354)

Thinking Critically About Chapter 9

Multiple-Choice Questions

1. **d.** is the answer. (p. 335)

a., b., & e. In order to correctly answer either type of question, the knowledge must have been encoded and stored.

c. With fill-in-the-blank questions, the answer must be recalled with no retrieval cues other than the question. With multiple-choice questions, the correct answer merely has to be recognized from among several alternatives.

2. **d.** is the answer. (pp. 322–323)

a. & b. A serial position effect would presumably occur whether the study and retrieval contexts were the same or different.

c. As Craik and Watkins found, when recall is delayed, only the first items in a list are recalled more accurately than the others. With immediate recall, both the first and last items are recalled more accurately.

3. **d.** is the answer. That all four mistakes are based on a sound confusion suggests that the letters were encoded acoustically. (p. 323)

a. Memorizing a list of letters would involve effortful, rather than automatic, processing.

b. The mistakes do not involve letters that are similar in appearance.

c. Semantic encoding would have been suggested by errors based on similarities in meaning.

4. **b.** is the answer. Retroactive interference is the disruption of something you once learned by new information. (p. 342)

a. Proactive interference occurs when old information makes it difficult to correctly remember new information.

c. & d. Interference produces forgetting even when the forgotten material was effectively encoded and stored. Janice's problem is at the level of retrieval.

e. There is no reason to believe that Janice's old locker combination is a painful memory.

5. **b.** is the answer. (p. 343)

a., c., & d. Involvement in other activities, even just eating or listening to music, is more disruptive than sleeping.

6. **c.** is the answer. Susan's memories are affected by her bad mood. (p. 337)

a. Priming refers to the conscious or unconscious activation of particular associations in memory.

b. Memory construction refers to changes in memory as new experiences occur.

d. Although Susan's difficulty in recalling the good could be considered retrieval failure, it is caused by the mood-congruent effect, which is therefore the best explanation.

e. Repression involves the suppression of *painful* memories.

7. **a.** is the answer. Priming is the conscious or unconscious activation of particular associations in memory. (p. 336)

b. Déjà vu is the false impression of having previously experienced a current situation.

c. That Martina is able to retrieve her former classmates' names implies that they already have been encoded.

d. Relearning is a measure of retention based on how long it takes to relearn something already mastered. Martina is recalling her former class-mates' names, not relearning them.

8. **b.** is the answer. Being back in the context in which the original experiences occurred triggered memories of these experiences. (p. 337)
a. The memories were triggered by similarity of place, not mood.
c. Retroactive interference would involve difficulties in retrieving old memories.
d. Echoic memory refers to momentary memory of auditory stimuli.
e. Iconic memory refers to momentary memory of visual stimuli.

9. **a.** is the answer. Time and space—and therefore sequences of events—are often automatically processed. (p. 321)
b. That she had *little difficulty* indicates that the processing was automatic, rather than effortful.
c. & d. State-dependent memory and priming have nothing to do with the automatic processing of space and time.

10. **d.** is the answer. Flashbulb memories are unusually clear memories of emotionally significant moments in life. (p. 319)

11. **a.** is the answer. Proactive interference occurs when old information makes it difficult to recall new information. (p. 342)
b. If Carlos were having trouble remembering the old extension, this answer would be correct.
c. & d. Carlos has successfully encoded and stored the extension; he's just having problems retrieving it.

12. **c.** is the answer. Episodic memory is memory for personal life experiences, such as a high school graduation; semantic memory is memory for facts, such as the name of the president. (p. 333)
a. & b. Implicit memories are memories for skills. Both of these examples involve explicit memory, which is memory for facts and experiences.

13. **b.** is the answer. (pp. 321, 323)
a. & c. Your failure to recall the answer indicates that it was never encoded semantically.
d. Spatial information, such as the location of an answer (but not the actual answer) on a textbook page, is often encoded automatically.

14. **c.** is the answer. (p. 341)
a. & b. The name of your homeroom teacher, which you probably heard at least once each day of school, was surely processed into memory (encoded) and maintained there for some time (stored).
d. State-dependent memory is the tendency to recall information best in the same emotional or

physiological state as when it was learned. It is unlikely that a single state was associated with learning your homeroom teacher's name.

15. **a.** is the answer. Short-term memory capacity is approximately seven digits. (p. 329)
b. Because iconic memory lasts no more than a second or so, regardless of how much material is experienced, this cannot be the explanation for Brenda's difficulty.
c. The final four digits should be no more difficult to organize into chunks than the first five digits of the address code.
d. Memory for digits is an example of explicit, rather than implicit, memory.

16. **a.** is the answer. (p. 344)
b. Although Lewis's difficulty in recalling these memories could be considered retrieval failure, it is caused by repression, which is therefore the *best* explanation.
c. This answer is incorrect because it is clear that Lewis fails to remember these experiences because they are painful memories and not because he is in a different emotional or physiological state.
d. Flashbulb memories are especially *vivid* memories for emotionally significant events. Lewis has no memory at all.
e. Implicit memories are memories of skills.

17. **d.** is the answer. (p. 346)
a. This is an example of proactive interference.
b. This is an example of the disruptive effects of depressant drugs, such as alcohol, on the formation of new memories.
c. This is mood-congruent memory.

18. **c.** is the answer. (p. 325)
a. The peg-word system involves developing associations between rhyming words in a jingle and to-be-remembered items.
b. Acronyms are words created from the first letters of to-be-remembered words.
d. Chunking is the organization of information into meaningful units, such as acronyms.

19. **c.** is the answer. Blows to the head usually disrupt the most recent experiences, such as this one, rather than long-term memories like those in choices a. and b., or new learning such as that in choice d. (p. 331)

20. **c.** is the answer. The hippocampus is involved in processing new facts for storage. (p. 333)
a., b., & d. Studies of amnesics with hippocampal damage show that neither classical conditioning nor skill memory are impaired, indicating that these aspects of memory are controlled by more primitive regions of the brain.

21. **d.** is the answer. In this example, the questions Frank was asked to answer created misinformation that later became part of his memory.

   a. This answer would have been correct if Frank had been molested by the counselor but had failed to encode it in his memory.

   b. This answer would have been correct if Frank had been molested, but the memory trace had faded with time.

   c. Misattribution might have occurred if Frank had witnessed another camper being molested and later recalled himself as the actual victim.

22. **b.** is the answer. Like a computer's RAM, working memory integrates information coming in from a mouse (c.) or keyboard (d) with that retrieved from long-term storage. (p. 320)

Essay Question

Experts agree that child abuse is a real problem that can have long-term adverse effects on individuals. They also acknowledge that forgetting of isolated events, both good and bad, is an ordinary part of life. Although experts all accept the fact that recovered memories are commonplace, they warn that memories "recovered" under hypnosis or with the use of drugs are unreliable, as are memories of events before age 3. Finally, they agree that memories can be traumatic, whether real or false.

Key Terms

1. **Memory** is the persistence of learning over time via the storage and retrieval of information. (p. 318)

2. A **flashbulb memory** is an unusually vivid memory of an emotionally important moment in one's life. (p. 319)

3. **Encoding** is the first step in memory; information is translated into some form that enables it to enter our memory system. (p. 319)

4. **Storage** is the passive process by which encoded information is maintained over time. (p. 319)

5. **Retrieval** is the process of bringing to consciousness information from memory storage. (p. 319)

6. **Sensory memory** is the immediate, initial recording of sensory information in the memory system. (p. 320)

7. **Short-term memory** is conscious memory, which can hold about seven items for a short time; also called working memory. (p. 320)

8. **Long-term memory** is the relatively permanent and unlimited capacity memory system into which information from short-term memory may pass. (p. 320)

9. **Automatic processing** refers to our unconscious encoding of incidental information such as space, time, and frequency, and of well-learned information. (p. 321)

10. **Effortful processing** is encoding that requires attention and some degree of conscious effort. (p. 321)

11. **Rehearsal** is the conscious, effortful repetition of information that you are trying either to maintain in consciousness or to encode for storage. (p. 321)

12. The **spacing effect** is the tendency for distributed practice to yield better long-term retention than massed practice, or cramming. (p. 322)

13. The **serial position effect** is the tendency for items at the beginning and end of a list to be more easily retained than those in the middle. (p. 322)

14. **Semantic encoding** is the processing of information into memory according to its meaning. (p. 323)

15. **Acoustic encoding** is the processing of information into memory according to its sound. (p. 323)

16. **Visual encoding** is the use of imagery to process information into memory. (p. 323)

17. **Imagery** refers to mental pictures and can be an important aid to effortful processing. (p. 325)

18. **Mnemonics** are memory aids (the method of loci, acronyms, peg-words, etc.), which often use visual imagery. (p. 325)

19. **Chunking** is the memory technique of organizing material into familiar, meaningful units. (p. 326)

20. **Iconic memory** is the visual sensory memory consisting of a perfect photographic memory, which lasts no more than a few tenths of a second. (p. 328)

   Memory aid: Icon means "image" or "representation." **Iconic memory** consists of brief visual images.

21. **Echoic memory** is the momentary sensory memory of auditory stimuli, lasting about 3 or 4 seconds. (p. 328)

22. **Long-term potentiation (LTP)** is an increase in a synapse's firing potential following brief, rapid stimulation. LTP is believed to be the neural basis for learning and memory. (p. 331)

23. **Amnesia** is the loss of memory. (p. 332)

24. **Implicit memories** are memories of skills, preferences, and dispositions. These memories are evidently processed, not by the hippocampus, but by a more primitive part of the brain, the cerebellum. They are also called procedural or nondeclarative memories. (p. 332)

25. **Explicit memories** are memories of facts, including names, images, and events. They are also called declarative memories. (p. 332)

26. The **hippocampus** is a neural region within the limbic system that is important in the processing of explicit memories for storage. (p. 333)

27. **Recall** is a measure of retention in which the person must remember, with few retrieval cues, information learned earlier. (p. 335)

28. **Recognition** is a measure of retention in which one need only identify, rather than recall, previously learned information. (p. 335)

29. **Relearning** is also a measure of retention in that the less time it takes to relearn information, the more that information has been retained. (p. 335)

30. **Priming** is the activation, often unconscious, of a web of associations in memory in order to retrieve a specific memory. (p. 336)

31. **Déjà vu** is the false sense that you have already experienced a current situation. (p. 337)

32. **Mood-congruent memory** is the tendency to recall experiences that are consistent with our current mood. (p. 337)

33. **Proactive interference** is the disruptive effect of something you already have learned on your efforts to learn or recall new information. (p. 342)

34. **Retroactive interference** is the disruptive effect of something recently learned on old knowledge. (p. 342)

Memory aid: *Retro* means "backward." **Retroactive interference** is "backward-acting" interference.

35. **Repression** is an example of motivated forgetting in that painful and unacceptable memories are prevented from entering consciousness. (p. 344)

36. The **misinformation effect** is the tendency of eyewitnesses to an event to incorporate misleading information about the event into their memories. (p. 345)

37. At the heart of many false memories, **source amnesia** refers to misattributing an event to the wrong source. (p. 347)

Summing Up

Information Processing

External events are initially recorded as sensory memory, which is either *iconic memory* (visual sensory memory) or *echoic memory* (auditory sensory memory). If we pay attention to the information, it is encoded into memory that holds a few items briefly, or *short-term* memory. To get information into storage, we must *encode* it. To get information out of storage, we must *retrieve* it. The relatively limitless, permanent memory where information is stored is *long-term* memory, which is categorized as *explicit memory* (conscious memory of facts and events) or *implicit memory* (automatic memory of skills and behaviors). Explicit memory consists of *semantic memory* (general knowledge) and *episodic memory* (life history memory). Implicit memory includes *skills* and *dispositions* (or automatic reactions).

FOCUS ON VOCABULARY AND LANGUAGE

The Phenomenon of Memory

Page 318: Your memory is your mind's *storehouse*, the *reservoir* of your accumulated learning. Myers is using an analogy to help you understand the general concept of memory. Both *storehouses* and *reservoirs* are used to keep materials (water, food, etc.) until we need them. Likewise, your memory system retains most of the things you experienced (*accumulated learning*), and items can be recalled or retrieved as required.

Page 318: . . . medal winners in a memory Olympics. . . . People with exceptional memories are being likened

or compared to the top athletes in the Olympic Games. S, for example, would clearly receive the top prize (*medal winner*) in any competition in which remembering vast amounts of information was being tested (*memory Olympics*).

Page 318: Do these memory *feats* make your own memory seem *feeble*? Myers is pointing out that although S may have demonstrated spectacular abilities in remembering all sorts of things (*memory feats*), normal memory in the average person is no less astounding in many ways. Despite our occasional failures, our ordinary memory accomplishments, which we tend to take for granted, are quite remarkable (*they are far from being feeble*).

Page 320: Instead we *shine the flashlight beam of attention on* certain incoming stimuli—often novel or important stimuli. One model of memory suggests that we only focus on (*shine the flashlight beam of attention on*) and process one part or aspect of the total sensory input, particularly new (*novel*) or important stimuli. We can also locate and bring back stored information from long-term memory (**LTM**) into short-term memory (**STM**).

Encoding: Getting Information In

Page 321: . . . *boost* . . . One way to improve and increase the power of our memory is to use **rehearsal**. Thus, actively repeating some new information (such as a stranger's name or new terminology) will help strengthen (*boost*) our ability to remember this material. As Myers notes it is important for effective retention to space out or distribute practice (rehearsal) over time rather than doing the repetitions all at once (massed practice or cramming).

Page 321: His [Ebbinghaus's] solution was to form a list of all possible *nonsense syllables* created by *sandwiching* a vowel between two consonants. In order to avoid using meaningful words with prior associations, Hermann Ebbinghaus invented three letter words that made no sense and had no meaning (*nonsense syllables*). He did this by putting a vowel (*sandwiching it*) between two consonants. His nonsense (*meaningless*) syllables were consonant (C), vowel (V), Consonant (C), or CVCs.

Page 323: Gordon Bower and Daniel Morrow (1990) liken our minds to theater directors who, *given a raw script*, imagine a *finished stage production*. This suggests that what we remember is not an exact replica of reality. We construct some mental representation or model (*finished stage production*) from the basic sensory information (*raw script*) available to us, and so, when we recall something, it is our own version (*mental model*) that comes to mind and not the real thing.

Page 325: Thanks to the durability of our most vivid images, we recall our experiences with *mental snapshots* of their best or worst moments. The use of imagery or mental pictures (*snapshots*) is one way to enhance recall. We have exceptionally good memory for pictures and ideas that are encoded using visual imagery. As Myers notes, "imagery is at the heart of many memory aids" (e.g., method of loci, peg-word, etc.).

Page 325: For example, the *"peg-word"* system requires that you first memorize a *jingle*. A *jingle* is an easily remembered succession of words that ring or resound against each other due to alliteration or rhyme and are often used in radio or TV commercials. The mnemonic (memory aid) called the *"peg-word"* method is based on memorizing a short 10-item poem (*jingle*) that can be associated with a new list of 10 items through visual imagery. The new items are hung on, or pegged to, the familiar items.

Page 326: *Motionless while learning the numbers,* Donatelli then *sprang alive. He whispered numbers, rubbed his chin, tapped his feet, counted on his fingers, and ran his hands through his hair.* By **chunking** (organizing material into meaningful units) we can increase the amount of information we can remember. Donatelli was able to recall up to 106 numbers read to him only once, one digit per second, by using chunking and hierarchies (clusters of chunks, organized from small to big). He was quiet while listening to the list but became very active and agitated as he used his mnemonic technique.

Storage: Retaining Information

Page 328: It was harder than reading by *flashes of lightning.* In his investigation of sensory storage, George Sperling showed his subjects an array of 9 letters for a very brief period (for about the length of a *flash of lightning*). He demonstrated that this was sufficient time for them to briefly view (*glimpse*) all 9 letters and that an image remained for less than half a second before fading away; he called this sensory image **iconic memory.**

Page 329: . . . *Sherlock Holmes* . . . Mystery writer Sir Arthur Conan Doyle's most popular character was a very intelligent and logical private detective named Sherlock Holmes. Holmes believed, as did many others, that our memory capacity was limited, much like an empty room can only hold so much furniture before it overflows. Contemporary psychologists now believe that our ability to store long-term memories is basically without any limit.

Page 329 (caption): Among animals, one contender for *champion memorist* would be a mere *birdbrain*—the Clark's nutcracker. . . . Clark's nutcracker is a small bird with a small brain (*birdbrain*) but a phenomenal memory (*champion memorist*) of where it buries its food. It can recall, after a period of more than 6 months, 6000 different locations of hidden food.

Page 330: While cognitive psychologists study our memory *"software,"* neuroscientists are gaining new insights into our memory *"hardware."* . . . Throughout this chapter Myers uses the analogy of the computer as a model for how memory works. In attempting to understand memory, cognitive psychologists study the mind and how it works (*the computer "software"*) and neuroscientists study the physical aspect of the brain and the functioning of its neurons (*the computer "hardware"*).

Page 330: . . . with tongue only partially in cheek. When someone makes a statement that is not meant to be taken seriously, we note that it was said *with tongue in cheek*. When researchers stated that "memories are more of a spiritual than a physical reality," they were somewhat serious (*tongue only partially in cheek*).

Page 331: The arousal *sears* the events onto the brain. When arousal level rises because of stress so too do the levels of certain hormones. These in turn signal the brain that something important has happened and the events that triggered the arousal make an indelible impression on the brain much as a hot grill burns (*sears*) its shape on the surface of the meat placed on it.

Page 332: They [amnesic people] can be classically conditioned. . . . They can learn to read *mirror-image writing* or do a *jigsaw puzzle*. . . . People who have lost the ability to remember new information (*amnesics*) may nevertheless be capable of learning through association (classical conditioning) and of learning to solve problems (e.g., *jigsaw puzzles*) even if they are not aware of having done so. Myers notes that these findings suggest that memory is not a single, unified system. Amnesics can learn how to *do* something (**implicit memory**) without any knowledge of this learning (**explicit**, or **declarative**, **memory**).

Retrieval: Getting Information Out

Page 337: Conversely, if people are put in a *buoyant mood . . .* they recall the world through *rose-colored glasses*. . . . Our memories are affected by our emotional states (*moods*). Thus, if we are in a good or happy (*buoyant*) mood, we are more likely to view the total situation in a more optimistic and hopeful way (through *rose-colored glasses*). Memory of events and people is influenced by the particular mood we are in, whether it is good or bad, and we tend to remember the events accordingly.

Page 338: When teenagers are *down*, their world, including their parents, seems inhuman; as their mood *brightens*, their parents *morph from devils into angels*. Because our memories tend to be **mood-congruent**, we are likely to explain our present emotion-

al state by remembering events and people as being consistent (*congruent*) with how we now feel. In one study when young adolescents were in a bad mood (*down*), they viewed their parents as cruel and uncaring (inhuman), but later when they were in a much better (*brighter*) mood their parents were described in much nicer terms. It seemed as though their parents had undergone an amazing change in character (*morphing from devils to angels*), but the change was simply in the teenagers' mood. As Myers notes, *"passions [or emotions] exaggerate."*

Forgetting

Page 338: Amidst all the *applause for memory . . .* have any voices been heard in praise of forgetting? If we could not forget, we would be like the Russian memory expert (*memory whiz*) S who was overwhelmed by the amount of useless information he had stored (*haunted by his junk heap of memories*). Thus, many people, from William James to contemporary cognitive psychologists, acknowledge the importance of forgetting.

Page 341: A name *may lie poised on the tip of the tongue*, waiting to be retrieved. The expression *"it's on the tip of my tongue"* refers to the feeling you get when you are trying to remember something (a name, place, etc.) but can't, even though you feel you know it and can *almost* say it (*it's on the tip of your tongue*). Given an appropriate retrieval cue (such as the first letter of the name, or something it rhymes with, etc.) we can often remember the item.

Page 342: As you collect more and more information, your *mental attic* never fills, but it certainly gets *cluttered*. We may have an unlimited amount of space in our memory system or *mental attic* (a room at the top of a house), but with a constant flow of new information coming in, the storage can become disorganized (*cluttered*). The new information may get in the way of recalling old material (**retroactive interference**), or old material may block or disrupt recall of new information (**proactive interference**).

Page 343: We *sheepishly* accepted responsibility for 89 cookies. Still, we had not come close; there had been 160. The Myers family obviously loves chocolate chip cookies, and the story of how all 160 were devoured within 24 hours (*not a crumb was left*) is quite funny but makes an important point. Embarrassed, guilty, and feeling a little foolish (*sheepish*), they could only account for and remember eating 89. This illustrates the self-serving nature of memory and how, unknowingly, we change and revise our own histories.

Memory Construction

Page 347: Because memory is *reconstruction* as well as *reproduction*, we can't be sure whether a memory is real by how real it feels. It is difficult to determine if a memory is real simply by noting how real it feels or how confident we are about its accuracy. We not only recall and retrieve real memories (*reproduction*) but we also manufacture false memories (*reconstruction*).

Page 348: Memory construction helps explain why *"hypnotically refreshed"* memories of crimes so easily incorporate errors, some of which originate with the hypnotist's leading questions. Because of the tendency to manufacture events without being consciously aware of doing so (*memory construction*), people are likely to be influenced by suggestions and biased questions while under hypnosis. Their subsequent recollections (*"hypnotically refreshed"*) may therefore be a mixture of fact and fiction.

Page 349: If memories can be *sincere*, yet so *sincerely wrong*, might children's recollections of sexual abuse err? The evidence suggests that under appropriate conditions children's memories can be reliable and accurate (*sincere*), but that they are also prone to the misinformation effect and can be misled by biased questions and suggestions; later, the children are not able to reliably separate real from false memories (*sincerely wrong*).

Improving Memory

Page 354: Sprinkled throughout this chapter and summarized here for easy reference are *concrete* suggestions for improving memory. This chapter on memory has many good ideas for memory improvement scattered or interspersed (*sprinkled*) throughout it, and Myers has pulled them altogether in an easy to understand format—the **PRTR** (**P**review, **R**ead, **T**hink critically, **R**eview) method. These are real and tangible (*concrete*) ways that will help you improve your memory. Use them!!!

CHAPTER 10:

Thinking and Language

Chapter Overview

Most of Chapter 10 deals with thinking, with emphasis on how people logically—or at times illogically—use tools such as algorithms and heuristics when making decisions and solving problems. Also discussed are several common obstacles to problem solving, including fixations that prevent us from taking a fresh perspective on a problem and our bias to search for information that confirms rather than challenges existing hypotheses.

The chapter also explores how computer systems have been constructed to simulate the neural networks of the human brain. By mimicking the ways in which human neural networks interconnect, computers enable scientists to study how human systems process sensations and memories and how the thought process works.

The rest of the chapter is concerned with language, including its structure, development in children, relationship to thinking, and use by animals. Two theories of language acquisition are evaluated: Skinner's theory that language acquisition is based entirely on learning and Chomsky's theory that humans have a biological predisposition to acquire language.

NOTE: Answer guidelines for all Chapter 10 questions begin on page 293.

Thinking (pp. 358–372)

> David Myers at times uses idioms that are unfamiliar to some readers. If you do not know the meaning of any of the following words, phrases, or expressions in the context in which they appear in the text, refer to pages 301–302 for an explanation: *kin to; birdier bird; stumbling upon one that worked; rule-of-thumb; Try your hand . . . brainteasers; shoot the basketball; seat-of-the-pants; snap judgment; a broken promise; mere statistics on some world health ledger; plagues; flip-flop; hunches; fuels social conflict; filled with straw; hybrid; computers shine; mind-boggling.*

Section Preview

First, skim the section, noting headings and boldface items. Then read the following objectives and, as you read the text, search for the information that will enable you to meet each objective. Answer guidelines are provided on page 293.

1. Describe the nature, function, and formation of concepts.

2. Discuss the major problem-solving strategies, and describe the nature of insight.

3. Identify obstacles to problem solving.

4. Describe the heuristics that guide decision making, and explain how overconfidence and framing can affect judgment.

5. Describe how our beliefs influence our logical reasoning.

6. Contrast the human mind and the computer as information processors, and describe recent advances in artificial intelligence.

Stepping Through the Section

After you have read the section, complete the sentences and answer the questions. As you proceed, evaluate your performance by consulting the answers on page 293. Do not continue with the next section until you understand each answer. If you need to, review or reread the section in the textbook before continuing.

1. Thinking, or _____ , can be defined as _____
_____ .
Scientists who study these mental activities are called _____ _____ .

2. People tend to organize specific items into mental groupings called_____ , and many such groupings often are further organized into _____ . Animals such as pigeons _____ (are/are not) capable of forming such mental groupings.

3. Concepts are typically formed through the development of a best example, or _____ , of a category. For example, people more easily detect _____ (male/female) prejudice against _____ (male/female) than vice versa.

4. Humans are especially capable of using their reasoning powers for coping with new situations, and thus for _____
_____ .

5. Finding a problem's solution by trying each possibility is called _____
_____ _____ .

6. Logical, methodical, step-by-step procedures for solving problems are called
_____ .

7. Rule-of-thumb strategies that provide us with problem-solving shortcuts are referred to as
_____ .

8. When you suddenly realize a problem's solution, _____ has occurred.

9. The tendency of people to look for information that verifies their preconceptions is called the
_____ _____ .

10. Not being able to take a new perspective when attempting to solve a problem is referred to as _____ . One example of this obstacle to problem solving is the tendency to repeat solutions that have worked previously; this phenomenon is known as the development of a
_____ _____ .

11. When a person is unable to envision using an object in an atypical way, _____
_____ is operating.

12. People judge how well something matches a particular prototype; this is the _____
_____ .

13. When we judge the likelihood of something occurring in terms of how readily it comes to mind, we are using the _____
_____ .

Explain how these two heuristics may lead us to make judgmental errors.

14. The tendency of people to overestimate the accuracy of their knowledge results in _____ . Warning people against this tendency _____ (does/does not) reduce it. Exposing people to other's differing judgments about events _____ (does/does not) reduce this tendency.

15. Overconfidence has _____ value because self-confident people tend to live _____ (more/less) happily and find it _____ (easier/harder) to make tough decisions. Furthermore, research has shown that when subjects are given feedback on the accuracy of their judgments, such feedback generally _____ (does/does not) help them become more realistic about how much they know.

16. Decision making can be significantly affected by the phrasing, or _____ , of an issue.

17. The tendency for our beliefs to distort logical reasoning is called _____
_____ . This phenomenon makes it _____ (easier/more difficult) for us to see the illogic of conclusions that run counter to our beliefs.

18. Research has shown that once we form a belief or a concept, it may take more convincing evidence for us to change the concept than it did to create it; this is because of _____
_____ .

19. The science involving the development of computers and programs that mimic human thinking is called _____
_____ .

20. Unlike the computer, which processes information _____ (serially/simultaneously), humans can process many bits of information _____ (serially/simultaneously).

21. Computer systems that imitate the brain's neural organization are called _____
_____ _____ . Such systems increase the computer's capacity for _____ processing _____ (and so/but do not) enable the computer to "learn" simple concepts.

Language (pp. 373–380)

> If you do not know the meaning of any of the following words, phrases, or expressions in the context in which they appear in the text, refer to pages 302–303 for an explanation: *catapulting our species forward; They are hunting dogs; read lips; a Martian scientist; grammar switches are thrown.*

Section Preview
Answer guidelines are provided on page 294.

1. Describe the structure of language.

2. Trace the course of language acquisition, and discuss alternative theories of language development.

3. Discuss the impact of early experience on language development as revealed by cognitive neuroscience.

Stepping Through the Section

Answers are provided on page 294.

1. The basic sound units of language are its _____ . English has approximately _____ of these units. The basic units of sign language are defined by _____ _____ and _____ .

2. Phonemes are grouped into units of meaning called _____ .

3. The system of rules that enables us to use our language to speak to and understand others is called _____ .

4. The system by which meaning is derived from morphemes, words, and sentences is the _____ of a language.

5. The system of rules we use to combine words into grammatically sensible sentences is called _____ .

6. The first stage of language development, in which children spontaneously utter different sounds, is the _____ stage. This stage typically begins at about _____ months of age. The sounds

children make during this stage _____ (do/do not) include only the phonemes of the language that they hear.

7. Deaf infants _____ (do/do not) babble.

8. At 6 months, infants _____ (can/cannot) perceive phoneme differences from other languages. By about _____ months of age, infant babbling begins to resemble the household language. By _____ months, the ability to perceive phoneme differences is _____ (lost/acquired).

9. During the second stage, called the _____-_____ stage, children convey complete thoughts using single words. This stage begins at about _____ year(s) of age.

10. During the _____-_____ stage children speak in sentences containing mostly nouns and verbs. This type of speech is called _____ speech.

11. After this stage, children quickly begin to utter longer phrases that _____ (do/ do not) follow the rules of syntax.

12. Skinner believed that language development follows the general principles of learning, including _____ , _____ , and _____ .

13. Other theorists believe that humans are biologically predisposed to learn language. One such theorist is _____ , who believes that we all are born with a _____ _____ in which _____ switches are thrown as children experience their language.

Give several examples of linguistic behavior in children that support the argument that humans are biologically predisposed to acquire language.

14. With no "inborn" linguistic rules, computer neural networks _____ (can/are unable to) learn a language's statistical structure.

15. Research by Jenny Saffran has demonstrated that even before _____ year(s) of age, infants are able to discern _____ _____ by analyzing which syllables most often go together.

16. Research studies of infants' knack for soaking up language _____ (challenges/supports) Chomsky's concept of an inborn _____ _____ . On the other hand, a recent study of twins indicates that genes _____ (do/do not) play a role in determining how quickly children learn language.

17. Those who learn a second language as adults usually speak it with the _____ of their first language. Moreover, they typically show _____ (poorer/better) mastery of the _____ of the second language.

18. Considering the two theories together, we can say that although we are born with a readiness to learn language, _____ is also important, as shown in linguistically stunted children who have been isolated from language during the _____ _____ for its acquisition.

Thinking and Language (pp. 380–384)

> If you do not know the meaning of the following phrase in the context in which it appears in the text, refer to page 303 for an explanation: *chicken-and-egg questions.*

Section Preview

Answer guidelines are provided on page 294.

1. Discuss the relationship between thought and language.

Stepping Through the Section

Answers are provided on page 295.

1. According to the _____ _____ hypothesis, language shapes our thinking. The linguist who proposed this hypothesis is _____ .

2. In several studies, researchers have found that using the pronoun "he" (instead of "he or she") _____ (does/does not) influence people's thoughts concerning gender.

3. Bilingual children outperform monolinguals on _____ tests. Bilingual education may also improve the _____- _____ of children who are in a linguistic minority.

4. It appears that thinking _____ (can/cannot) occur without the use of language. Athletes often supplement physical with _____ practice.

5. In one study of psychology students preparing for a midterm exam, the greatest benefits were achieved by those who visualized themselves _____ (receiving a high grade/studying effectively.).

Summarize the probable relationship between thinking and language.

Animal Thinking and Language (pp. 384–389)

> If you do not know the meaning of the following phrase in the context in which it appears in the text, refer to page 303 for an explanation: *rhapsodized; Spying the short stick; Were the chimps language champs or were the researchers chumps?*

Section Preview

Answer guidelines are provided on page 295.

1. Describe the research on animal communication, and discuss the controversy over whether animals have language.

Stepping Through the Section

Answers are provided on page 295.

1. Recent research has shown that monkeys can learn a simple form of _____ , in which they touch pictures of objects in ascending _____ order. Wolfgang Köhler demonstrated that chimpanzees also exhibit the "aha" reaction that characterizes reasoning by _____ .

2. Forest-dwelling chimpanzees learn to use branches, stones, and other objects as _____ . These behaviors, along with behaviors related to grooming and courtship, _____ (vary/do not vary) from one group to another, suggesting the transmission of _____ customs.

3. Deception and mirror usage by chimpanzees and other apes suggests to some researchers that these animals may possess a rudimentary understanding of mental states called a _____ _____ _____ .

4. Honeybees communicate by means of a _____ , which researchers _____ (do/do not) consider to have the complexity and flexibility of human language.

5. The Gardners attempted to communicate with the chimpanzee Washoe by teaching her _____ _____ .

6. Human language appears to have evolved from _____ communications.

Summarize some of the arguments of skeptics of the "talking apes" research.

Progress Test 1

Multiple-Choice Questions

Circle your answers to the following questions and check them with the answers on page 295. If your answer is incorrect, read the explanation for why it is incorrect and then consult the appropriate pages of the text (in parentheses following the correct answer).

1. The text defines cognition as:
    a. silent speech.
    b. all mental activity.
    c. mental activity associated with processing, understanding, and communicating information.
    d. logical reasoning.
    e. problem solving.

2. A mental grouping of similar things, events, or people is called a(n):
    a. prototype.   d. heuristic.
    b. concept.   e. mental set.
    c. algorithm.

3. When forming a concept, people often develop a best example, or _____ , of a category.
    a. denoter   c. prototype
    b. heuristic   d. algorithm

4. Confirmation bias refers to the tendency to:
    a. allow preexisting beliefs to distort logical reasoning.
    b. cling to one's initial conceptions after the basis on which they were formed has been discredited.
    c. search randomly through alternative solutions when problem solving.
    d. look for information that is consistent with one's beliefs.

5. The English language has approximately _____ phonemes.

   a. 25   d. 45
   b. 30   e. 50
   c. 40

6. Which of the following is *not* true of babbling?

   a. It is imitation of adult speech.
   b. It is the same in all cultures.
   c. It typically occurs from about age 4 months to 1 year.
   d. Babbling increasingly comes to resemble a particular language.
   e. Deaf babies babble with gestures.

7. Mental set and functional fixedness are two types of:

   a. algorithms.   c. fixation.
   b. heuristics.   d. insight.

8. Which of the following has been argued by critics of ape language research?

   a. Ape language is merely imitation of the trainer's behavior.
   b. There is little evidence that apes can equal even a 3-year-old's ability to order words with proper syntax.
   c. By seeing what they wish to see, trainers attribute greater linguistic ability to apes than actually exists.
   d. All of the above have been argued.

9. Whorf's linguistic relativity hypothesis states that:

   a. language is primarily a learned ability.
   b. language is partially an innate ability.
   c. the size of a person's vocabulary reflects his or her intelligence.
   d. our language shapes our thinking.

10. Which of the following *best* describes Chomsky's view of language development?

   a. Language is an entirely learned ability.
   b. Language is an innate ability.
   c. Humans have a biological predisposition to acquire language.
   d. There are no cultural influences on the development of language.

11. Failing to solve a problem that requires using an object in an unusual way illustrates the phenomenon of:

   a. mental set.   d. belief perseverance.
   b. functional fixedness. e. overconfidence.
   c. framing.

12. Which of the following is an example of the use of heuristics?

   a. trying every possible letter ordering when unscrambling a word
   b. considering each possible move when playing chess
   c. using the formula "area = length × width" to find the area of a rectangle
   d. playing chess using a defensive strategy that has often been successful for you

13. The chimpanzee Sultan used a short stick to pull a longer stick that was out of reach into his cage. He then used the longer stick to reach a piece of fruit. Researchers hypothesized that Sultan's discovery of the solution to his problem was the result of:

   a. trial and error.   d. mental set.
   b. heuristics.   e. insight.
   c. functional fixedness.

14. You hear that one of the Smith children is an outstanding Little League player and immediately conclude it's their one son rather than any of their four daughters. You reached your quite possibly erroneous conclusion as the result of:

   a. the confirmation bias.
   b. the availability heuristic.
   c. the representativeness heuristic.
   d. belief perseverance.

15. Because of their lightning speed, computers can retrieve and manipulate stored data faster than people can, but the human brain beats the computer hands down when it comes to:

   a. using heuristics.
   b. following algorithms.
   c. serial processing.
   d. simultaneous processing.

16. Deaf children who are not exposed to sign language until they are teenagers:

   a. are unable to master the basic words of sign language.
   b. learn the basic words but not how to order them.
   c. are unable to master either the basic words or syntax of sign language.
   d. never become as fluent as those who learned to sign at a younger age.

17. According to the text, language acquisition is best described as:
    a. the result of conditioning and reinforcement.
    b. a biological process of maturation.
    c. an interaction between biology and experience.
    d. a mystery of which researchers have no real understanding.

18. Biologist Karl von Frisch won the Nobel prize for his discovery that honeybees communicate with each other by:
    a. varying the acoustic pitch of their buzzing noises.
    b. secreting chemical odors called pheromones.
    c. performing an intricate dance.
    d. leading other worker bees on lengthy flights to find nectar.

19. The linguistic relativity hypothesis is challenged by the finding that:
    a. chimps can learn to communicate spontaneously by using sign language.
    b. people with no word for a certain color can still perceive that color accurately.
    c. the Eskimo language contains a number of words for snow, whereas English has only one.
    d. infants' babbling contains many phonemes that do not occur in their own language and that they therefore cannot have heard.

20. Several studies have indicated that the generic pronoun "he":
    a. tends for children and adults alike to trigger images of both males and females.
    b. tends for adults to trigger images of both males and females, but for children to trigger images of males.
    c. tends for both children and adults to trigger images of males but not females.
    d. for both children and adults triggers images of females about one-fourth of the time it is used

21. Researchers who are convinced that animals can think point to evidence that:
    a. monkeys demonstrate the ability to "count" by learning to touch pictures of objects in ascending numerical order.
    b. chimpanzees regularly use branches, stones, and other objects as tools in their natural habitats.
    c. chimps invent grooming and courtship customs and pass them on to their peers.
    d. all of the above occur.

Matching Items

Match each definition or description with the appropriate term.

Definitions or Descriptions

_____ 1. the basic units of sound in a language
_____ 2. the way an issue or question is posed
_____ 3. rules for combining words into sentences
_____ 4. the rules by which meaning is derived from sentences
_____ 5. presuming that something is likely if it comes readily to mind
_____ 6. the tendency to overestimate the accuracy of one's judgments
_____ 7. being unable to see a problem from a different angle
_____ 8. haphazard problem solving by trying one solution after another
_____ 9. the sudden realization of the solution to a problem
_____ 10. the tendency to repeat problem-solving techniques that worked in the past even though a fresh approach may be more appropriate.
_____ 11. the basic units of meaning in a language

Terms

a. syntax
b. morphemes
c. mental set
d. trial and error
e. availability heuristic
f. phonemes
g. semantics
h. insight
i. framing
j. overconfidence
k. fixation

Progress Test 2

Progress Test 2 should be completed during a final chapter review. Answer the following questions after you thoroughly understand the correct answers for the section reviews and Progress Test 1.

Multiple-Choice Questions

1. A common problem in everyday reasoning is our tendency to:
   a. accept as logical those conclusions that agree with our own opinions.
   b. accept as logical those conclusions that disagree with our own opinions.
   c. underestimate the accuracy of our knowledge.
   d. accept as logical conclusions that involve unfamiliar concepts.

2. Phonemes are the basic units of _____ in language.
   a. sound
   b. meaning
   c. grammar
   d. semantics
   e. syntax

3. Syntax refers to the:
   a. sounds in a word.
   b. rules for grouping words into sentences.
   c. rules by which meaning is derived from sentences.
   d. overall rules of a language.

4. Skinner and other behaviorists have argued that language development is the result of:
   a. imitation.
   b. reinforcement.
   c. association.
   d. all of the above.

5. Many psychologists are skeptical of claims that chimpanzees can acquire language because the chimps have not shown the ability to:
   a. use symbols meaningfully.
   b. acquire speech.
   c. acquire even a limited vocabulary.
   d. use syntax in communicating.

6. Representativeness and availability are examples of:
   a. mental sets.
   b. belief bias.
   c. algorithms.
   d. fixation.
   e. heuristics.

7. The basic units of cognition are:
   a. phonemes.
   b. concepts.
   c. prototypes.
   d. morphemes.

8. Which of the following describes artificial intelligence?
   a. the science of low-temperature phenomena
   b. the study of animal behavior in its natural habitat
   c. the study of control processes in electronic and biological systems
   d. the science that explores human thought by attempting to model it on the computer
   e. the best example of a category

9. Assume that Congress is considering revising its approach to welfare and to this end is hearing a range of testimony. A member of Congress who uses the availability heuristic would be most likely to:
   a. want to experiment with numerous possible approaches to see which of these seems to work best.
   b. want to cling to approaches to welfare that seem to have had some success in the past.
   c. refuse to be budged from his or her beliefs despite persuasive testimony to the contrary.
   d. base his or her ideas on the most vivid, memorable testimony given, even though many of the statistics presented run counter to this testimony.

10. If you want to be absolutely certain that you will find the solution to a problem you know *is* solvable, you should use:
    a. a heuristic.
    b. an algorithm.
    c. insight.
    d. trial and error.

11. Complete the following: *-ed* is to *sh* as _____ is to _____.
    a. phoneme; morpheme
    b. morpheme; phoneme
    c. grammar; syntax
    d. syntax; grammar

12. Which of the following is *not* cited by Chomsky as evidence that language acquisition cannot be explained by learning alone?
    a. Children master the complicated rules of grammar with ease.
    b. Children create sentences they have never heard.
    c. Children make the kinds of mistakes that suggest they are attempting to apply rules of grammar.
    d. Children raised in isolation from language spontaneously begin speaking words.

13. Telegraphic speech is typical of the _____ stage.
    a. babbling
    b. one-word
    c. two-word
    d. three-word

14. Children first demonstrate a rudimentary understanding of syntax during the _____ stage.
    a. babbling
    b. one-word
    c. two-word
    d. three-word

15. The study in which people who immigrated to the United States at various ages were compared in terms of their ability to understand English grammar found that:
    a. age of arrival had no effect on mastery of grammar.
    b. those who immigrated as children understood grammar as well as native speakers.
    c. those who immigrated as adults understood grammar as well as native speakers.
    d. whether or not English was spoken in the home was the most important factor in mastering the rules of grammar.

16. Researchers taught the chimpanzee Washoe and the gorilla Koko to communicate by using:
    a. various sounds.
    b. plastic symbols of various shapes and colors.
    c. sign language.
    d. all of the above.

17. Neural network computers:
    a. can be programmed to mimic excitatory and inhibitory neural messages.
    b. have a greater capacity than conventional computers to learn from experience.
    c. are not limited to serial processing.
    d. can do all of the above.
    e. can do none of the above.

18. The rules most directly involved in permitting a person to derive meaning from words and sentences are rules of:
    a. syntax.
    b. grammar.
    c. phonemic structure.
    d. semantics.

19. Which of the following is true regarding the relationship between thinking and language?
    a. "Real" thinking requires the use of language.
    b. People sometimes think in images rather than in words.
    c. A thought that cannot be expressed in a particular language cannot occur to speakers of that language.
    d. All of the above are true.

20. One reason an English-speaking adult may have difficulty pronouncing Russian words is that:

   a. the vocal tracts of English- and Russian-speaking people develop differently in response to the demands of the two languages.

   b. although English and Russian have very similar morphemes, their phonemic inventories are very different.

   c. although English and Russian have very similar phonemes, their morphemic inventories are very different.

   d. after the babbling stage, a child who hears only English stops uttering other phonemes.

21. Researchers who believe that some primates possess a rudimentary theory of mind point to evidence that:

   a. chimpanzees have been observed using mirrors to inspect themselves.

   b. vervet monkeys have different alarm calls for different predators.

   c. orangutans in the wild frequently use stones as tools.

   d. honeybees communicate the direction and distance of a food source by performing an intricate dance.

   e. all of the above occur.

True-False Items

Indicate whether each statement is true or false by placing *T* or *F* in the blank next to the item.

   1. The order in which children acquire an understanding of various morphemes is unpredictable.

   2. According to the confirmation bias, people often interpret ambiguous evidence as support for their beliefs.

   3. Most human problem solving involves the use of heuristics rather than reasoning that systematically considers every possible solution.

   4. When asked, most people underestimate the accuracy of their judgments.

   5. Studies have shown that even animals may sometimes have insight reactions.

   6. Mental set is the tendency to repeat problem-solving solutions that have worked in the past.

   7. Although the morphemes differ from language to language, the phonemes for all languages are the same.

   8. Children of all cultures babble using the same phonemes.

   9. Thinking without using language is not possible.

   10. Unlike computers, which are limited to processing information serially, humans can process many different bits of information simultaneously.

Thinking Critically About Chapter 10

Answer these questions the day before an exam as a final check on your understanding of the chapter's terms and concepts.

Multiple-Choice Questions

1. The word "predates" contains _____ phonemes and _____ morphemes.

   a. 7; 3   **c.** 7; 2

   b. 3; 7   **d.** 3; 2

2. Which of the following utterances is an example of overgeneralization of a grammatical rule?

   a. "We goed to the store."

   b. "Ball pretty."

   c. "The sky is crying."

   d. "We eat 'paghetti."

3. A listener hearing a recording of Japanese, Spanish, and North American children babbling would:

   a. not be able to tell them apart.

   b. be able to tell them apart if they were older than 6 months.

   c. be able to tell them apart if they were older than 8 to 10 months.

   d. be able to tell them apart at any age.

4. Which of the following illustrates belief perseverance?

   a. Your belief remains intact even in the face of evidence to the contrary.

   b. You refuse to listen to arguments counter to your beliefs.

   c. You tend to become flustered and angered when your beliefs are refuted.

   d. You tend to search for information that supports your beliefs.

   e. Your beliefs tend to distort logical reasoning.

5. Complete the following analogy: Rose is to flower as:

   a. concept is to prototype.

   b. prototype is to concept.

   c. concept is to hierarchy.

   d. hierarchy is to concept.

6. Your stand on an issue such as the use of nuclear power for electricity involves personal judgment. In such a case, one memorable occurrence can weigh more heavily than a bookful of data, thus illustrating:
   a. belief perseverance.
   b. confirmation bias.
   c. the representativeness heuristic.
   d. the availability heuristic.
   e. belief bias.

7. A dessert recipe that gives you the ingredients, their amounts, and the steps to follow is an example of a(n):
   a. prototype.   c. heuristic.
   b. algorithm.   d. mental set.

8. Marilyn was asked to solve a series of five math problems. The first four problems could only be solved by a particular sequence of operations. The fifth problem could also be solved following this sequence; however, a much simpler solution was possible. Marilyn did not realize this simpler solution and solved the problem in the way she had solved the first four. Her problem-solving strategy was hampered by:
   a. functional fixedness.
   b. the overconfidence phenomenon.
   c. mental set.
   d. her lack of a prototype for the solution.

9. Dr. Mendoza is studying the mental strategies people use when solving problems. Dr. Mendoza is clearly a(n):
   a. cognitive psychologist.
   b. experimental psychologist.
   c. organizational psychologist.
   d. developmental psychologist.

10. Boris the chess master selects his next move by considering moves that would threaten his opponent's queen. His opponent, a chess-playing computer, selects its next move by considering *all* possible moves. Boris is using a(n) _____ and the computer is using a(n) _____ .
    a. algorithm; heuristic
    b. prototype; mental set
    c. mental set; prototype
    d. heuristic; algorithm

11. During a televised political debate, the Republican and Democratic candidates each argued that the results of a recent public opinion poll supported their party's platform regarding sexual harassment. Because both candidates saw the information as supporting their belief, it is clear that both were victims of:
    a. functional fixedness.   c. belief bias.
    b. mental set.   d. confirmation bias.

12. The child who says "Milk gone" is engaging in _____ . This type of utterance demonstrates that children are actively experimenting with the rules of _____ .
    a. babbling; syntax
    b. telegraphic speech; syntax
    c. babbling; semantics
    d. telegraphic speech; semantics

13. Experts in a field prefer heuristics to algorithms because heuristics:
    a. guarantee solutions to problems.
    b. prevent mental sets.
    c. often save time.
    d. prevent fixation.
    e. do all of the above.

14. Rudy is 6 feet 6 inches tall, weighs 210 pounds, and is very muscular. If you think that Rudy is more likely to be a basketball player than a computer programmer, you are a victim of:
    a. belief bias.
    b. the availability heuristic.
    c. mental set.
    d. functional fixedness.
    e. the representativeness heuristic.

15. Failing to see that an article of clothing can be inflated as a life preserver is an example of:
    a. belief bias.
    b. the availability heuristic.
    c. the representativeness heuristic.
    d. functional fixedness.

16. Airline reservations typically decline after a highly publicized airplane crash because people overestimate the incidence of such disasters. In such instances, people's decisions are being influenced by:
    a. belief bias.
    b. the availability heuristic.
    c. the representativeness heuristic.
    d. functional fixedness.

17. Most people tend to:
    a. accurately estimate the accuracy of their knowledge and judgments.
    b. underestimate the accuracy of their knowledge and judgments.
    c. overestimate the accuracy of their knowledge and judgments.
    d. lack confidence in their decision-making strategies.

18. In relation to ground beef, consumers respond more positively to an ad describing it as "75 percent lean" than to one referring to its "25 percent fat" content. This is an example of:
    a. the framing effect.   c. mental set.
    b. confirmation bias.   d. overconfidence.

19. The sentence "Blue jeans wear false smiles" has correct _____ but incorrect _____ .
    a. morphemes; phonemes
    b. phonemes; morphemes
    c. semantics; syntax
    d. syntax; semantics

20. Regarding the relationship between thinking and language, which of the following most accurately reflects the position taken in the text?
    a. Language determines everything about our thinking.
    b. Language determines the way we think.
    c. Thinking without language is not possible.
    d. Thinking affects our language, which then affects our thought.

21. In preparing her class presentation, "Updating Chomsky's Understanding of Language Development," Britney's outline includes all of the following evidence *except* that:
    a. computer neural networks programmed to learn to form the past tense of irregular verbs can learn to do so, even without "inborn" linguistic rules.
    b. infants rapidly learn to detect subtle differences between simple sequences of syllables.
    c. infants can recognize color differences even before they can name different colors.
    d. children isolated from language during the first seven years of life never fully develop language.

Essay Question

The lectures of your linguistics professor, who happens to be a staunch behaviorist, clearly imply that she believes language development can be explained according to principles of conditioning. What evidence should you present to convince her that she is wrong? (Use the space below to list the points you want to make and organize them. Then write the essay on a separate piece of paper.)

Key Terms

Writing Definitions

Using your own words, on a piece of paper write a brief definition or explanation of each of the following terms.

1. cognition
2. concept
3. prototype
4. algorithm
5. heuristic
6. insight
7. confirmation bias
8. fixation
9. mental set
10. functional fixedness
11. representativeness heuristic
12. availability heuristic
13. overconfidence
14. framing
15. belief bias
16. belief perseverance
17. artificial intelligence (AI)

18. computer neural networks
19. language
20. phonemes
21. morphemes
22. grammar
23. semantics

24. syntax
25. babbling stage
26. one-word stage
27. two-word stage
28. telegraphic speech
29. linguistic relativity

Cross-Check

As you learned in the Introduction, reviewing and overlearning of material are important to the learning process. After you have written the definitions of the key terms in this chapter, you should complete the crossword puzzle to ensure that you can reverse the process—recognize the term, given the definition.

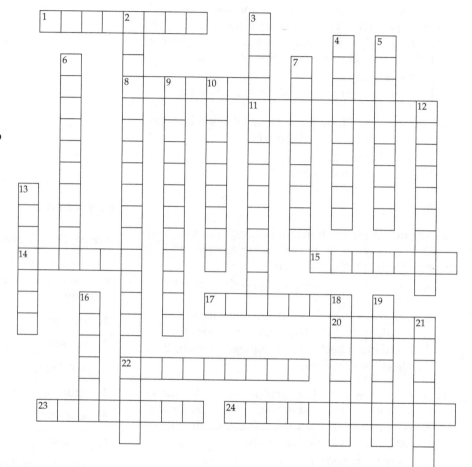

ACROSS

1. Stage of speech development characterized by the spontaneous utterance of speech sounds.
8. System of rules that enables us to communicate with and understand others.
11. Methodical problem-solving strategy that guarantees success.
14. Chimp that was taught sign language by the Gardners.
15. Theorist who believed that language development could be explained by principles of learning.
17. Sudden and often creative solution to a problem.
20. Theorist who formulated the linguistic relativity hypothesis.
22. Nobel prize-winning biologist who studied honeybee communication.
23. Inability to approach a problem in a new way.
24. The economical speech of children in the two-word stage.

DOWN

2. The idea that language determines the way we think.
3. Computer circuits that simulate the brain's interconnected nerve cells are called computer _____.
4. Problem-solving strategy based on rules of thumb.

5. The best example of a particular category.
6. Tendency for preexisting beliefs to distort reasoning.
7. Mental activity associated with processing, understanding, and communicating information.
9. Heuristic based on estimating the probability of events in terms of how readily they come to mind.
10. Tendency to continue applying a particular problem-solving strategy even when it is no longer helpful.
12. Smallest units of language that convey meaning.
13. Stage of language development that occurs between 1 and 2 years of age.
16. Aspect of grammar specifying the rules for combining words into grammatical sentences.

18. Stage of language development that begins about age 2.
19. Mental grouping of similar objects, events, or people.
21. How an issue or question is posed.

Answers

Thinking

Section Preview

1. Concepts are mental groupings of similar objects, events, and people. Because they provide a great deal of information with minimal cognitive effort, concepts are the basic units of thinking. Most concepts are formed around a best example, or prototype, of a particular category. Concepts are often organized into hierarchies that further increase cognitive efficiency.

2. Trial and error is a haphazard strategy for solving problems, in which one solution after another is tried until success is achieved. Algorithms are methodical and logical rules for solving problems; they often are laborious and inefficient. Heuristics are based on rules of thumb. Although formally not a problem-solving strategy, a sudden flash of inspiration (insight) often helps us to solve problems. Insight has been seen in chimpanzees given challenging problems to solve.

3. The confirmation bias is an obstacle to problem solving in which people search for information that confirms their preconceptions. Another common obstacle to problem solving is fixation, an inability to approach a familiar problem in a new way. One example of fixation is the tendency to continue applying a particular problem-solving strategy even when it is no longer useful (mental set). Another example is functional fixedness, whereby a person is unable to perceive unusual functions for familiar objects.

4. The representativeness heuristic is the tendency to judge the likelihood of things in terms of how well they represent particular prototypes. With the availability heuristic, we base our judgments on how readily information comes to mind.

   The overconfidence phenomenon is the tendency of people to overestimate the accuracy of their knowledge and judgments. Although overconfidence may blind us to our vulnerability to errors in reasoning, it has adaptive value in that it makes decision making somewhat easier.

   Framing refers to the way an issue or question is posed, which can greatly influence our perception of the issue or answer to the question.

5. Belief bias is the tendency for our beliefs to distort logical reasoning. An example of this common error is our tendency to accept as logical those conclusions that agree with our opinions. Belief perseverance is our tendency to cling to our beliefs even in the face of contrary evidence. Once beliefs are formed, it takes stronger evidence to change them than it did to create them.

6. Although both the mind and the computer process input from the environment, only humans truly think and feel. Computers excel at tasks that require the manipulation of large amounts of data. Unlike the human brain, which can process unrelated bits of information simultaneously, most computers process information serially (in sequence). A new generation of computer neural networks has been designed to more closely simulate the brain's interconnected neural units and their functions. Compared with conventional artificial intelligence systems, neural network computers show greater capacity for parallel processing and "learning" from experience.

Stepping Through the Section

1. cognition; the mental activity associated with processing, understanding, and communicating knowledge; cognitive psychologists
2. concepts; hierarchies; are
3. prototype; male; female
4. problem solving
5. trial and error
6. algorithms
7. heuristics
8. insight
9. confirmation bias
10. fixation; mental set
11. functional fixedness
12. representativeness heuristic
13. availability heuristic

Using these heuristics often prevents us from processing other relevant information; because we overlook this information, we make judgmental errors. Thus, in the text example, the representativeness heuristic leads people to overlook the fact that there are many more truck drivers than Ivy League classics professors and, as a result, to wrongly conclude that the poetry reader is more likely to be an Ivy League classics professor. Also as noted in the text, the availability heuristic leads us to incorrectly think that words beginning with *k* are more common than words having *k* as their third letter.

14. overconfidence; does not; does

15. adaptive; more; easier; does

16. framing

17. belief bias; easier

18. belief perseverance

19. artificial intelligence

20. serially; simultaneously

21. computer neural networks; parallel; and so

Language

Section Preview

1. Phonemes are the basic units of sound in a language. Morphemes are the smallest units of speech that convey meaning. Most morphemes are combinations of two or more phonemes. Each language has a system of rules, or grammar, that enables people to use and understand it. Semantics refers to the grammatical rules used to derive meaning from the elements of language. Syntax specifies the rules for combining words into sentences.

2. At about 4 months of age, babies enter a babbling stage in which they spontaneously utter phonemes of all languages. By 1 year, children enter the one-word stage. In this stage, single-syllable words are used to name things and may even be inflected to convey the meaning of an entire sentence. By age 2, most children enter the two-word stage. At this time. their speech consists of telegraphic utterances containing mostly nouns and verbs, yet placed in a sensible syntactic order. Children then quickly begin uttering longer and more complex phrases and sentences.

   According to B. F. Skinner, language development can be explained according to the learning principles of association, imitation, and reinforcement. In contrast, Noam Chomsky believes that children are biologically prepared to learn language as they interact with their caregivers. Most theorists today believe that language development is the product of both hereditary and environmental influences.

3. Cognitive neuroscientists emphasize the importance of grammatical learning that occurs during the first few years of life. Human infants display a remarkable knack for soaking up language and discerning statistical aspects of human speech. The impact of early experiences is also evident in comparisons of children and adults who attempt to master a second language, whether spoken or gestured. Those who learn as adults typically speak with the accent of their first language and do not as easily (or accurately) master the grammar of the second language. This evidence for the importance of early learning challenges Chomsky's concept of an innate universal grammar. However, research with twins indicates that genes may be involved.

Stepping Through the Section

1. phonemes; 40; hand shapes; movements

2. morphemes

3. grammar

4. semantics

5. syntax

6. babbling; 4; do not

7. do

8. can; 10; 12; lost

9. one-word; 1

10. two-word; telegraphic

11. do

12. association; imitation; reinforcement

13. Chomsky; language acquisition device; grammar

The rate at which children acquire vocabulary and grammar is too rapid to be explained solely by learning. Children create sentences that they have never heard and, therefore, could not be imitating. Children learn grammatical rules in a predictable order. Children's linguistic errors are often logical overextensions of grammatical rules.

14. can

15. 1; word breaks

16. challenges; universal grammar; do

17. accent; poorer; grammar

18. experience; critical period

Thinking and Language

Section Preview

1. According to Whorf's linguistic relativity hypothesis, language determines the way we think. Critics of this idea claim that our language *reflects* rather than creates the way we think. Studies of the ability of vocabulary enrichment to enhance thinking reveal that it is more accurate to say that language *influences*, rather than determines, thought. Some thoughts, such as the imagery involved in art, music, and athletics, do not depend on language.

Stepping Through the Section

1. linguistic relativity; Whorf
2. does
3. intelligence; self-esteem
4. can; mental
5. studying effectively

The relationship is probably a two-way one: The linguistic relativity hypothesis suggests that language helps shape thought; that words come into the language to express new ideas indicates that thought also shapes language.

Animal Thinking and Language

Section Preview

1. Numerous studies demonstrate that animals have remarkable capacities for thinking. Studies with chimpanzees and other primates reveal counting abilities, reasoning by insight, tool use, transmission of cultural traditions, and perhaps even a rudimentary theory of mind.

    Although animals communicate effectively among themselves, the question of whether these communications make up a language remains controversial. Karl von Frisch, for example, discovered that explorer bees convey to other bees the direction and distance of a food source by means of an intricate dance. But the inflexibility of this dance clearly limits its linguistic significance.

    Several attempts have been made to teach sign language and other symbolic languages to chimpanzees. Although apes have a capacity to learn a relatively large vocabulary of sign words, critics contend that much of their signing is nothing more than imitation of their trainer's signs and shows little evidence of syntax.

Stepping Through the Section

1. counting; numerical; insight
2. tools; vary; cultural
3. theory of mind
4. dance; do not
5. sign language
6. gestural

Chimps have acquired only limited vocabularies and—in contrast to children—have acquired these vocabularies only with great difficulty. Also in contrast to children, it's unclear that chimps can use syntax to express meaning. Even simpler animals, such as birds, are capable of learning behavioral sequences that some chimp researchers consider language. The signing of chimps is often nothing more than imitation of the trainer's actions. People tend to interpret such ambiguous behavior in terms of what they want to see.

Progress Test 1

Multiple-Choice Questions

1. **c.** is the answer. (p. 358)
2. **b.** is the answer. (p. 358)
    a. A prototype is the best example of a particular category, or concept.
    c. & d. Algorithms and heuristics are problem-solving strategies.
    e. Mental set is an obstacle to problem solving.
3. **c.** is the answer. (p. 358)
    a. There is no such thing as a "denoter."
    b. & d. Heuristics and algorithms are problem-solving strategies.
4. **d.** is the answer. It is a major obstacle to problem solving. (p. 360)
    a. & b. These refer to belief bias and belief perseverance, respectively.
    c. This is trial-and-error problem solving.
5. **c.** is the answer. (p. 373)
6. **a.** is the answer. Babbling is not the imitation of adult speech since babbling infants produce phonemes from languages they have not heard and could not be imitating. (pp. 374–375)
7. **c.** is the answer. Both involve failing to see a problem from a new perspective. (pp. 360–361)
    a. & b. Algorithms and heuristics are problem-solving strategies.
    d. Insight is the sudden realization of a problem's solution.
8. **d.** is the answer. (p. 387)
9. **d.** is the answer. (p. 381)
    a. This is Skinner's position regarding language development.
    b. This is Chomsky's position regarding language development.
    c. The linguistic relativity hypothesis is concerned with the content of thought, not intelligence.
10. **c.** is the answer. (p. 376)
    a. This is Skinner's position.
    b. According to Chomsky, although the *ability* to acquire language is innate, the child can only acquire language in association with others.
    d. Cultural influences are an important example of the influence of learning on language development, an influence Chomsky fully accepts.

11. **b.** is the answer. Functional fixedness is the tendency to think of things only in terms of their usual functions. (p. 361)

   a. Mental set is the tendency to approach a problem in a particular way that worked previously.

   c. Framing refers to the way an issue is posed; this often influences our judgment.

   d. Belief perseverance is the tendency to cling to one's beliefs even after they have been refuted.

   e. Overconfidence is the tendency to think we know more than we do.

12. **d.** is the answer. Heuristics are rule-of-thumb strategies—such as playing chess defensively—that are based on past successes in similar situations. (p. 359)

   a., b., & c. These are all algorithms.

13. **e.** is the answer. Sultan suddenly arrived at a novel solution to his problem, thus displaying apparent insight. (p. 385)

   a. Sultan did not randomly try various strategies of reaching the fruit; he demonstrated the "light bulb" reaction that is the hallmark of insight.

   b. Heuristics are rule-of-thumb strategies.

   c. & d. Functional fixedness and mental set are impediments to problem solving. Sultan obviously solved his problem.

14. **c.** is the answer. Your conclusion is based on sex stereotypes, that is, athletic ability and participation are for you more *representative* of boys. Your conclusion is by no means necessarily right, however, especially since the Smiths have four daughters and only one son. (p. 362)

   a. The confirmation bias is the tendency to look for information that confirms one's preconceptions.

   b. The availability heuristic involves judging the probability of an event in terms of how readily it comes to mind.

   d. Belief perseverance is the tendency to cling to beliefs, even when the evidence has shown that they are wrong.

15. **d.** is the answer. People can process millions of different bits of information at the same time; computers, except for the new neural networks, must generally process information one step at a time. (pp. 370–371)

   a., b., & c. Both computers and people are capable of these.

16. **d.** is the answer. Compared with deaf children exposed to sign language from birth, those who learn to sign as teens have the same grammatical difficulties as do hearing adults trying to learn a second spoken language. (p. 379)

17. **c.** is the answer. Children are biologically prepared to learn language as they and their caregivers interact. (p. 380)

   a. This is Skinner's position.

   b. No psychologist, including Chomsky, believes that language is entirely a product of biological maturation.

   d. Although language acquisition is not completely understood, research has shed sufficient light on it to render it less than a complete mystery.

18. **c.** is the answer. The dance's direction and duration inform worker bees of the direction and distance of a food source. (p. 386)

19. **b.** is the answer. The evidence that absence of a term for a color does not affect ability to perceive the color challenges the idea that language always shapes thought. (p. 381)

   a. & d. These findings are not relevant to the linguistic relativity hypothesis, which addresses the relationship between language and thought.

   c. This finding is in keeping with the linguistic relativity hypothesis.

20. **c.** is the answer. The generic pronoun *he* evidently tends, for both adults and children, to conjure up images of males. (p. 381)

21. **d.** is the answer. (pp. 384–385)

Matching Items

1. f (p. 373)	**5.** e (p. 363)	**9.** h (p. 359)
2. i (p. 366)	**6.** j (p. 365)	**10.** c (p. 361)
3. a (p. 374)	**7.** k (p. 361)	**11.** b (p. 373)
4. g (p. 374)	**8.** d (p. 359)	

Progress Test 2

Multiple-Choice Questions

1. **a.** is the answer. Reasoning in daily life is often distorted by our beliefs, which may lead us, for example, to accept conclusions that haven't been arrived at logically. (pp. 367–368)

   b., c., & d. These are just the opposite of what we tend to do.

2. **a.** is the answer. (p. 373)

   b. Morphemes are the basic units of meaning.

   c., d., & e. The text does not refer to basic units of grammar, semantics, or syntax.

3. **b.** is the answer. (p. 374)

   a. Phonemes are the sounds in a word.

   c. Such rules are known as semantics.

   d. Such rules are the language's grammar, which would include its syntax as well as its semantics.

4. **d.** is the answer. These are all basic principles of

learning and, according to Skinner, explain language development. (p. 376)

5. **d.** is the answer. Syntax is one of the fundamental aspects of language, and chimps seem unable, for example, to use word order to convey differences in meaning. (p. 387)

a. & c. Chimps' use of sign language demonstrates both the use of symbols and the acquisition of fairly sizable vocabularies.

b. No psychologist would require the use of speech as evidence of language; significantly, all the research and arguments focus on what chimps are and are not able to do in acquiring other facets of language.

6. **e.** is the answer. Both are rule-of-thumb strategies that allow us to make quick judgments. (pp. 362–363)

a. & d. Mental sets and fixation are obstacles to problem solving, in which the person tends to repeat solutions that have worked in the past and is unable to conceive of other possible solutions.

b. Belief bias is the tendency for preexisting beliefs to distort logical reasoning.

c. Algorithms are methodical strategies that guarantee a solution to a particular problem.

7. **b.** is the answer. (p. 358)

a. & d. Phonemes and morphemes are units of sound and meaning in language, respectively.

c. Prototypes are the best examples of specific categories.

8. **d.** is the answer. Artificial intelligence researchers attempt to design and program computers to do things that appear "intelligent." (p. 370)

9. **d.** is the answer. If we use the availability heuristic, we base judgments on the availability of information in our memories, and more vivid information is often the most readily available. (p. 363)

a. This would exemplify use of the trial-and-error approach to problem solving.

b. This would exemplify a mental set.

c. This would exemplify belief perseverance.

10. **b.** is the answer. Because they involve the systematic examination of all possible solutions to a problem, algorithms guarantee that a solution will be found. (p. 359)

a., c., & d. None of these methods guarantees that a problem's solution will be found.

11. **b.** is the answer. The morpheme *-ed* changes the *meaning* of a regular verb to form its past tense; the phoneme *sh* is a unique *sound* in the English language. (p. 373)

c. & d. Syntax, which specifies rules for combining words into grammatical sentences, is one aspect of the grammar of a language.

12. **d.** is the answer. Chomsky believes that the inborn capacity for language acquisition must be activated by exposure to language. And, in fact, children raised in isolation will *not* begin to speak spontaneously. (pp. 376–377)

13. **c.** is the answer. (p. 376)

14. **c.** is the answer. Although the child's utterances are only two words long, the words are placed in a sensible order. In English, for example, adjectives are placed before nouns. (p. 376)

a. & b. Syntax specifies rules for *combining* two or more units in speech.

d. There is no three-word stage.

15. **b.** is the answer. (pp. 378–379)

16. **c.** is the answer. (pp. 386–387)

17. **d.** is the answer. (p. 371)

18. **d.** is the answer. Semantic rules are directly concerned with the derivation of meaning from morphemes, words, and sentences. (p. 374)

a. Syntax is the set of rules for a language that permits the combination of words into sentences.

b. Grammar is the overall system of rules for using a language and, as such, includes syntax as well as semantics.

c. Phonemic structure concerns the basic sounds, or phonemes, of a language.383

19. **b.** is the answer. (p. 330)

a. Researchers do not make a distinction between "real" and other thinking, nor do they consider nonlinguistic thinking less valid than linguistic thinking.

c. As indicated by several studies cited in the text, this is not true.

20. **d.** is the answer. Following the babbling stage, the child's ability to produce all phonemes becomes in a sense shaped and limited to the ability to produce those phonemes he or she hears. (p. 375)

a. The vocal tract of *Homo sapiens* does not develop in specialized ways for different languages.

b. & c. English and Russian differ significantly in both their phonemes and their morphemes. Nor is there any reason why differences in morphemes would in and of themselves cause pronunciation difficulties.

21. **a.** is the answer. (p. 385)

b. & c. Alarm-calling and tool use are clear indicators of animal communication and thinking, respectively. However, they reveal nothing about the ability to infer mental states in oneself or another.

d. Honeybees are insects, not primates!

True-False Items

1. F (p. 375)	**6.** T (p. 361)
2. T (p. 360)	**7.** F (p. 373)
3. T (p. 359)	**8.** T (p. 374)
4. F (p. 365)	**9.** F (p. 383)
5. T (p. 385)	**10.** T (p. 371)

Thinking Critically About Chapter 10

Multiple-Choice Questions

1. **a.** is the answer. Each sound of the word is a phoneme (note that the second letter "e" does not itself represent a sound); the morphemes are "pre," which means before, "date," and "s," which indicates the plural. (p. 373)

2. **a.** is the answer. Adding *-ed* to the irregular verb *go* results in the ungrammatical *goed*—an overgeneralization of the rule by which the past tense of regular verbs is formed. (p. 377)
   b. This is an example of telegraphic speech.
   c. This is a grammatical statement.
   d. "'paghetti" is simply an immature pronunciation of "spaghetti"; young children often have difficulty with consonant clusters like "sp."

3. **a.** is the answer. (p. 374)

4. **a.** is the answer. (p. 368)
   b. & c. These may very well occur, but they do not define belief perseverance.
   d. This is the confirmation bias.
   e. This is belief bias.

5. **b.** is the answer. A rose is a prototypical example of the concept *flower.* (p. 358)
   c. & d. Hierarchies are organized clusters of concepts. In this example, there is only the single concept *flower.*

6. **d.** is the answer. The availability heuristic is the judgmental strategy that estimates the likelihood of events in terms of how readily they come to mind, and the most vivid information is often the most readily available. (p. 363)

7. **b.** is the answer. Follow the directions precisely and you can't miss! (p. 359)
   a. A prototype is the best example of a concept.
   c. Heuristics are rules of thumb that help solve problems but, in contrast to a recipe that is followed precisely, do not guarantee success.
   d. A mental set is a tendency to approach a problem in a way that has been successful in the past.

8. **c.** is the answer. By simply following a strategy that has worked well in the past, Marilyn is hampered by the type of fixation called mental set. (p. 361)
   a. Functional fixedness is being unable to conceive of an unusual function for an object.
   b. Overconfidence is exhibited by the person who overestimates the accuracy of his or her judgments.
   d. Prototypes are best examples of categories, not strategies for solving problems.

9. **a.** is the answer. Cognitive psychologists study how we process, understand, and communicate knowledge. Problem solving involves processing information and is therefore a topic explored by cognitive psychologists. (p. 358)
   b. Cognitive psychologists often use experimentation to study phenomena but, because not all experimental psychologists study cognition, a. is the best answer.
   c. Organizational psychologists study behavior in the workplace.
   d. Developmental psychologists study the ways in which behavior changes over the life span.

10. **d.** is the answer. (p. 359)
    b. & c. If Boris always attacks his opponent's queen when playing chess, he is a victim of mental set; prototypes, however, have nothing to do with chess playing.

11. **d.** is the answer. The confirmation bias is the tendency to search for information that confirms one's preconceptions. In this example, the politicians' preconceptions are biasing their interpretation of the survey results. (p. 360)
    a. Functional fixedness is the inability to perceive an unusual use for a familiar object.
    b. Mental set is the tendency to approach a problem in a particular way. There is no problem per se in this example.
    c. Belief bias is the tendency for one's preexisting beliefs to distort logical reasoning. This answer is incorrect because it is not clear, in this example, whether either politician is reasoning illogically.

12. **b.** is the answer. Such utterances, characteristic of a child of about 2 years, are like telegrams, in that they consist mainly of nouns and verbs and show use of syntax. (pp. 375–376)
    a. & c. Babbling consists of phonemes, not words.
    d. Semantics refers to the rules by which meaning is derived from sentences; this speech example indicates nothing in particular about the child's understanding of semantics.

13. **c.** is the answer. (p. 359)

a., b., & d. Heuristics do not guarantee solutions or prevent mental sets.

14. **e.** is the answer. Your conclusion is based on the stereotype that muscular build is more *representative* of athletes than computer programmers. (p. 362)

a. Belief bias is the tendency for one's preexisting beliefs to distort logical reasoning.

b. The availability heuristic involves judging the probability of an event in terms of how readily it comes to mind.

c. Mental set is the tendency to repeat solutions that have worked in the past.

d. Functional fixedness is the tendency to think of things only in terms of their usual functions.

15. **d.** is the answer. (p. 361)

16. **b.** is the answer. The publicity surrounding disasters makes such events vivid and seemingly more probable than they actually are. (p. 363)

a. The belief bias is the tendency for preexisting beliefs to distort logical thinking.

c. The representativeness heuristic operates when we judge the likelihood of things in terms of how well they represent particular prototypes. This example does not involve such a situation.

d. Functional fixedness operates in situations in which effective problem solving requires using an object in an unfamiliar manner.

17. **c.** is the answer. This is referred to as overconfidence. (p. 365)

18. **a.** is the answer. In this example, the way the issue is posed, or framed, has evidently influenced consumers' judgments. (p. 366)

b. Confirmation bias is the tendency to search for information that confirms one's preconceptions.

c. Mental set is the tendency to approach a problem in a particular way.

d. Overconfidence is the tendency to be more confident than correct.

19. **d.** is the answer. This sentence, although semantically meaningless, nevertheless follows the grammatical rules of English syntax for combining words into sentences. (p. 374)

a. & b. The phonemes (smallest units of sound) and morphemes (smallest units of meaning) of this sentence are equally correct.

20. **d.** is the answer. (p. 384)

21. **c.** is the answer. This fact challenges the linguistic relativity hypothesis; it neither supports nor refutes Chomsky's concept of an inborn universal grammar. (pp. 376–377, 381)

Essay Question

You should point out that the rate at which children acquire words and grammar is too extraordinary to be explained solely according to principles of learning. Children also utter all sorts of word forms they have never heard and could not, therefore, be imitating. Furthermore, children begin using morphemes in a predictable order, which learning theorists would not expect since each child experiences a unique linguistic environment. Children also make predictable errors that result from overuse of grammatical rules, rather than from imitation. It therefore seems clear that children are biologically prepared to acquire language and that the behaviorist position is incorrect.

Key Terms

1. Thinking, or **cognition**, refers to the mental activity associated with processing, understanding, and communicating information. (p. 358)

2. A **concept** is a mental grouping of similar objects, events, or people. (p. 358)

3. A **prototype** is the best example of a particular category. (p. 358)

4. An **algorithm** is a methodical, logical procedure that, while sometimes slow, guarantees success. (p. 359)

5. A **heuristic** is any problem-solving strategy based on rules of thumb. Although heuristics are more efficient than algorithms, they do not guarantee success and sometimes even impede problem solving. (p. 359)

6. **Insight** is a sudden and often novel realization of the solution to a problem. Insight contrasts with trial and error and, indeed, may often follow an unsuccessful episode of trial and error. (p. 359)

7. The **confirmation bias** is an obstacle to problem solving in which people tend to search for information that validates their preconceptions. (p. 360)

8. **Fixation** is an inability to approach a problem in a new way. (p. 361)

9. **Mental set** refers to the tendency to continue applying a particular problem-solving strategy even when it is no longer helpful. (p. 361)

10. **Functional fixedness** is a type of fixation in which a person can think of things only in terms of their usual functions. (p. 361)

11. The **representativeness heuristic** is the tendency to judge the likelihood of things in terms of how well they conform to one's prototypes. (p. 362)

12. The **availability heuristic** is based on estimating the probability of certain events in terms of how readily they come to mind. (p. 363)

13. Another obstacle to problem solving, **overconfidence** refers to the tendency to overestimate the accuracy of one's beliefs and judgments. (p. 365)

14. **Framing** refers to the way an issue or question is posed. It can affect people's perception of the issue or answer to the question. (p. 366)

15. **Belief bias** is the tendency for a person's preexisting beliefs to distort his or her logical reasoning. (p. 367)

16. **Belief perseverance** is the tendency for people to cling to a particular belief even after the information that led to the formation of the belief is discredited. (p. 368)

17. **Artificial intelligence (AI)** is the science of designing and programming computers to do "intelligent" things and to simulate human thought processes. (p. 370)

18. **Computer neural networks** are computer circuits that simulate the brain's interconnected nerve cells and perform tasks such as learning to recognize visual patterns. (p. 371)

19. **Language** refers to spoken, written, or gestured words and how we combine them to communicate meaning. (p. 373)

20. **Phonemes** are the smallest units of sound in a language that are distinctive for speakers of the language. (p. 373)

21. **Morphemes** are the smallest units of language that convey meaning. (p. 373)

    Example: The word "dogs," which contains four phonemes, contains only two **morphemes**—"dog" and "-s." Although most morphemes are combinations of two or more phonemes, the plural "-s" conveys a distinctive meaning of "more than one."

22. **Grammar** is a system of rules that enables us to communicate with and understand others. (p. 374)

23. **Semantics** is the aspect of grammar that specifies the rules used to derive meaning from morphemes, words, and sentences. (p. 374)

    Example: One **semantic** rule of English is that adding *-ed* to a verb gives the verb a past-tense meaning.

24. **Syntax** is the aspect of grammar specifying the rules for combining words into grammatical sentences. (p. 374)

    Example: One **syntactic** rule of English is that adjectives are positioned before nouns.

25. The **babbling stage** of speech development, which begins at 3 to 4 months, is characterized by the spontaneous utterance of speech sounds. During the babbling stage, children the world over sound alike. (p. 374)

26. Between 1 and 2 years of age children speak mostly in single words; they are therefore in the **one-word stage** of linguistic development. (p. 375)

27. Beginning about age 2, children are in the **two-word stage** and speak mostly in two-word sentences. (p. 376)

28. **Telegraphic speech** is the economical, telegram-like speech of children in the two-word stage. Utterances consist mostly of nouns and verbs; however, words occur in the correct order, showing that the child has learned some of the language's syntactic rules. (p. 376)

29. **Linguistic relativity** is Benjamin Whorf's hypothesis that language determines the way we think. (p. 381)

Cross-Check

ACROSS

1. babbling
8. grammar
11. algorithm
14. Washoe
15. Skinner
17. insight
20. Whorf
22. von Frisch
23. fixation
24. telegraphic

DOWN

2. linguistic relativity
3. neural networks
4. heuristic
5. prototype
6. belief bias
7. cognition
9. availability
10. mental set
12. morphemes
13. one-word
16. syntax
18. two-word
19. concept
21. framing

FOCUS ON VOCABULARY AND LANGUAGE

Page 357: . . . our species is *kin to* . . . Myers notes that we are biological creatures related to (*kin to*) other species of animals. We have exceptional abilities for innovation, learning, memory, and rational thinking; yet, at the same time we are prone to making mistakes and thinking and acting irrationally.

Thinking

Page 358: For most of us, the robin is the *birdier bird* . . . We develop our ideas of how things go together (*concepts*) from definitions or by using **prototypes**. The best example (*prototype*) of a bird is a robin (*the birdier bird*) rather than a penguin or an ostrich.

Page 359: Thomas Edison tried thousands of light-bulb filaments before *stumbling upon one that worked*. Edison was a famous inventor and he used a trial-and-error method in developing the metal filament that makes the light bulb glow brightly. Using trial and error, he came upon the solution by chance (*stumbled upon one that worked*). Myers contrasts this method with following an **algorithm** (a step-by-step method that always ends with the answer and is typical of computer programs).

Page 359: . . . *rule-of-thumb* strategies . . . A rule of thumb is a simple guide or principle that is true in general. Rather than using the longer step-by-step procedure (an **algorithm**), we frequently use **heuristics** (*rule-of-thumb* strategies) to help us find the solution more quickly.

Page 360: Try your hand at these *brainteasers* drawn from classic experiments. Myers offers you a chance to attempt (*try your hand at*) some intriguing mental puzzles (*brainteasers*) taken from (*drawn from*) well-known experiments. If you encounter problems in solving these puzzles, it may be due to **fixation** (our inability to see things from a new or different perspective), **mental set** (repeating old solutions that worked before), or **functional fixedness** (our tendency to see things as having only one function or use).

Page 362: Should I *shoot* the basketball or pass to the player who's *hot*?—we seldom take the time and effort to reason systematically. (Don't take this sentence literally.) For example, in a game of basketball, the player holding the ball has to decide to throw it through the hoop (*shoot the basketball*) or pass it to a player who has scored frequently (*who's hot*). We usually follow our subjective feelings (*intuitions*) rather than taking the time to use logic and reason.

Page 362: . . . *seat-of-the-pants* decisions. When we make decisions based on subjective or intuitive reasons, rather than using logical, reflective problem-solving strategies, we are using *seat-of-the-pants* judgments. Thus, when we employ **heuristics** (quick rule-of-thumb strategies), we may make wrong (*dumb*) decisions.

Page 362: The **representativeness heuristic** enabled you to make a *snap* judgment. We can make quick (*snap*) judgments using a strategy that allows us to determine the probability of things by how well they appear to be typical of some prototype (*representativeness heuristic*). For example, is person A, who is intelligent, unimaginative, compulsive, and generally lifeless, more likely to (a) play jazz for a hobby or (b) play jazz for a hobby and work as an accountant? The representativeness heuristic leads most people to incorrectly pick (b) as the answer.

Page 363: The faster people can remember an instance of some event (*"a broken promise"*), the more they expect it to recur. We tend to use whatever information is accessible in our memories when making decisions and judgments; similarly, events or mistakes that are easiest to access (i.e., those that most readily come to mind) will most likely be used. This is called the **availability heuristic.** So, if on one occasion, someone did not keep his or her word (*broke a promise*) about doing something, we tend to remember that event and use it in predicting future behavior. Sometimes the availability heuristic can cause errors in judgment.

Page 365: During those three days, more than 100,000 invisible children—*mere statistics on some world health ledger*—died of preventable starvation, diarrhea, and disease (Gore, 1992). There was worldwide media attention to the 3-day rescue of a small child trapped in a deep hole (a well) in Texas. Due to the availability heuristic we tend to remember the vivid pictures associated with the danger to one child and ignore the statistics which showed that more than 100,000 children we did not observe (*invisible*) died during the same period. They were mere numbers (*statistics*) on some world health accounting book (*ledger*).

Page 365: Overconfidence *plagues* decisions outside the laboratory, too. Many factors combine to produce the tendency to overestimate the accuracy of our decisions, judgments, and knowledge (**overconfidence**). In everyday life, as well as in lab experiments, our judgments are greatly afflicted (*plagued*) by overconfidence.

Page 367: That our judgments *flip-flop* so dramatically is startling. Presenting the same information in two different ways can cause people to react more negatively or positively depending on how the (logically equivalent) information was **framed**. The framing effect can cause alarming and dramatic reversals (*flip-flops*) in people's decisions and judgments. For example, a very fatty food product made by grinding meat (*ground beef*) will be seen more positively if described as "75% lean" as opposed to "25% fat," despite the fact that exactly the same information is conveyed in each case.

Page 367: . . . hunches . . . We have a propensity to make mistakes because we seek information that will confirm our intuitive feelings (*hunches*) about situations, people, or future events. We rely on heuristics, we are overconfident in our estimates, and we are easily influenced by the framing effect. Myers notes that it is difficult to escape bias even by use of forceful logic.

Page 368: Belief perseverance often *fuels social conflict*. Our irrationality also shows when we persist (*persevere*) in our views despite evidence to the contrary (**belief perseverance**). This can lead to an increase in strong feelings or passions over controversial issues (*fuels social conflict*). Myers suggests one solution for those who wish to restrain (*rein in*) the effect of belief perseverance, and that is to give serious consideration to beliefs *opposite* to your own.

Page 369: From this we might conclude that our heads are indeed *filled with straw*. The discussion about human irrationality might lead to the conclusion that we have ineffective and inefficient cognitions (*heads filled with straw*). Myers, however, is optimistic and suggests that we can learn about our irrational propensities (tendencies) and be alert to the dangers that can result in poor or foolish (*dumb*) decisions.

Page 370: A *hybrid* of cognitive psychology and computer science, **AI** has two facets, one practical, the other theoretical. Artificial intelligence (**AI**) is an integrated science (a *hybrid*), combining elements of cognitive psychology with aspects of computer technology, whose goal is to create systems and programs that imitate (*mimic*) human mental operations and intelligent behaviors. The result is twofold, applied or practical products on one hand, and theoretical or basic science on the other.

Page 370: . . . computers shine. Computers can easily do many things we find difficult, such as processing large volumes of numerical data, making quick decisions using algorithms, rapidly retrieving information from storage, etc.; compared to our dull or slow performance, the computer is exceptional (*it shines*).

Page 371: The computer system's complex interaction is *mind-boggling*, but the basic idea is simple. Neural networks (systems designed to imitate the brain's interconnected neural circuitry) are extremely intricate and complicated. Although it is difficult for us to comprehend fully (*it is mind-boggling*), the underlying principle is simple.

Language

Page 373: When the human vocal tract evolved the capacity to utter vowels, *our capacity for language exploded, catapulting our species forward.* When the physiological ability for complex vocalization evolved, the ability to communicate orally expanded exponentially (*exploded*). This new linguistic capacity propelled (*catapulted*) our species to new levels of accomplishments, enabling us to communicate from person to person and to transmit civilization's accumulated knowledge from generation to generation.

Page 374: They are hunting dogs. The sentence "*They are hunting dogs*" is syntactically correct, but its meaning (semantics) is derived from the context. In one context it could mean that people (*they*) are out looking (*hunting*) for dogs, and in another it could refer to dogs that are used to track or seek (*hunt*) animals.

Page 374: Yet by 4 months of age, babies can *read lips* and *discriminate* speech sounds. When people speak, their lips move in ways that correspond to the sounds they utter. Many deaf people can understand what is being said by watching how the lips move (*lip reading*). Very young children can not only tell the difference (*discriminate*) between sounds, but can also recognize lip movements that correspond with certain sounds (*read lips*).

Page 376: Surely, says Chomsky, *a Martian scientist* observing children in a single-language community would conclude that language is almost entirely inborn. The famous linguist Chomsky believes that the behaviorist's views (as exemplified by Skinner) are simplistic (*naive*). He argues that language acquisition could not be simply a function of experience or learning. Instead, he contends that any unbiased observer (e.g., *an imaginary scientist from the planet Mars*) would have to arrive at the inescapable fact that our capacity for language is almost totally biologically inherited (*inborn*). The specific language you speak is a product of your environment which builds on your innate capacity for language. As Myers puts it, "*we are born with the hardware and an operating system; experience writes the software.*"

Page 379: Chomsky would say that once the *grammar*

switches are thrown during a child's developing years, mastering another grammar becomes more difficult. Chomsky likens learning a particular grammar during early childhood to turning on (*throwing*) switches that influence language acquisition. When they have been turned on for one grammar, it becomes much harder to master a second grammar.

Thinking and Language

Page 380: Thinking and language intricately intertwine. Asking which comes first is one of psychology's *chicken-and-egg* questions. "Which came first: the chicken or the egg?" Clearly, you need an egg to produce a chicken, but you also need a chicken to lay the egg. So, like this age-old conundrum (riddle), psychologists have argued over which comes first, our ideas and thoughts, or the words we use to name and verbalize them. Myers concludes that language influences (but does not determine) thought, and our thinking affects our language, which in turn affects thought.

Animal Thinking and Language

Page 384: If in our use of language we humans are, as the psalmist *rhapsodized*, "little lower than God," where do other animals fit in the scheme of things? The psalmist (an author of religious or sacred songs)

spoke in an extravagantly enthusiastic manner (*rhapsodized*) about human nature, and Myers notes that it is our use of human language that elevates us above nonhumans. Nevertheless, we do share a capacity for language with other animals.

Page 385: Spying the short stick, Sultan grabbed it and tried to reach the fruit with it. Kohler's experiment with the chimpanzee Sultan showed that our closest relatives are capable of cognition. When the fruit was out of reach, Sultan noticed (*spied*) the short stick and used it to pull a longer stick into the cage, which he then used to get the fruit.

Page 387: Were the chimps *language champs* or were the researchers *chumps*? Critics of "ape language" argue that for animals, language acquisition is painfully slow, resembles conditioned responses, does not follow syntax, and is little more than imitation. In addition, demonstrations of animal language are always subjectively interpreted by their trainers. Myers asks: Were the chimps exceptionally talented (*language champs*) or were the researchers being biased and foolish (*chumps*)? The answer is that the controversy has led to further research and progress, and a renewed appreciation of our own, as well as our closest relatives', capacity for communication and language.

Intelligence

Chapter Overview

An enduring controversy in psychology involves attempts to define and measure intelligence. Chapter 11 describes the historical origins of intelligence tests and discusses several important issues concerning their use. These include the methods by which intelligence tests are constructed and whether such tests are valid, reliable, and free of bias. The chapter also discusses whether intelligence is a single general ability or several specific ones, the stability of intelligence, research that attempts to assess the neurological basis of intelligence, and the extent of genetic and environmental influences on intelligence.

NOTE: Answer guidelines for all Chapter 11 questions begin on page 319.

The Origins of Intelligence Testing
(pp. 391–394)

> David Myers at times uses idioms that are unfamiliar to some readers. If you do not know the meaning of any of the following words, phrases, or expressions, in the context in which they appear in the text, refer to pages 327–328 for an explanation: *sparked debate; heirs . . . ponder; "dull" child; "mental orthopedics"; out of whack; lamented.*

Section Preview

First, skim the section, noting headings and boldface items. Then read the following objectives and, as you read the text, search for the information that will enable you to meet each objective. Answer guidelines are provided on page 319.

1. Trace the origins of intelligence tests.

Stepping Through the Section

After you have read the section, complete the sentences and answer the questions. As you proceed, evaluate your performance by consulting the answers on page 319. Do not continue with the next section until you understand each answer. If you need to, review or reread the section in the textbook before continuing.

1. Tests that assess a person's mental capacities and compare them to others', using numerical scores, are called _____ tests.

2. The early Greek philosopher_____ concluded that individuals differed in their natural endowments.

3. The French psychologist who devised a test to predict the success of children in school was _____ . Predictions were made by comparing children's chronological ages with their _____ ages, which were determined by the test. This test _____ (was/was not) designed to measure inborn intelligence.

4. Lewis Terman's revision of Binet's test is referred to as the _____-_____ .

This test enables one to derive a(n)
_____ _____ for an
individual.

Give the original formula for computing IQ and
explain any items used in the formula.

5. Today's tests compute _____ (IQ/
   a mental ability score) by comparing the individual's performance to the average performance of
   people of _____ (the same/differ-
   ent) age(s). These tests are designed so that a
   score of _____ is considered
   average.

6. When given intelligence tests in the early 1900s,
   immigrants arriving in the United States often
   scored _____ (above/below) aver-
   age. This is because the tests were based on a particular _____ background.

What Is Intelligence? (pp. 394–400)

> If you do not know the meaning of any of the
> following words, phrases, or expressions in the
> context in which they appear in the text, refer
> to pages 328–329 for an explanation: *slippery
> concept; dumbfounded; island of brilliance; street-
> smart adolescent; how to read people; quick-witted;
> in its heyday.*

Section Preview

Answer guidelines are provided on page 320.

1. Describe intelligence, and discuss two controversies regarding its nature.

2. Describe the factor-analysis approach to understanding intelligence, and discuss evidence
   regarding intelligence as a general mental ability
   and/or as many specific abilities.

3. Discuss neurological approaches to the measurement of intelligence.

Stepping Through the Section

Answers are provided on page 320.

1. Psychologists _____ (do/do not)
   agree on a definition of intelligence.

2. To regard an abstract concept as a concrete entity
   is to commit the error known as

   _____ .

3. Intelligence is a _____ constructed
   concept.

4. In any context, intelligence can be defined as ____
   _____ .

5. One controversy regarding the nature of intelligence centers on whether intelligence is one
   _____ ability or several
   _____ abilities.

6. The statistical procedure used to identify groups
   of items that appear to measure a common ability
   is called _____
   _____ . Charles Spearman, one of
   the developers of this technique, believed that a
   factor called g, or _____
   _____ , runs through the more
   specific aspects of intelligence.

7. Opposing Spearman, _____
   identified eight clusters of _____
   _____ _____ .

8. People with _____
   _____ score at the low end of

intelligence tests but possess extraordinary specific skills.

9. Howard Gardner proposes that there are _____ _____ , each independent of the others. However, critics point out that the world is not so just: People with mental disadvantages often have lesser _____ abilities as well, and that some abilities, such as _____ and _____ skills, are more crucial than others.

10. Sternberg and Wagner distinguish three types of intelligence: _____ intelligence, _____ intelligence, and _____ intelligence. Similarly, Cantor and Kihlstrom distinguish between _____ intelligence and _____ intelligence. Support for this distinction comes from evidence that college grades _____ (accurately/only modestly/do not) predict later achievement in careers.

11. A critical part of social intelligence is _____ _____ —the ability to _____ , _____ , _____ , and _____ emotions.
Briefly describe emotionally intelligent people.

12. Some scholars believe that the recent concepts of _____ intelligence and _____ intelligence are stretching the idea of multiple intelligences too far.

13. Although general intelligence is most important in occupations that are mentally demanding, successful people usually have other traits as well, such as _____ and being well connected and extremely energetic.

14. Some experts predict that ultimately there will be _____ tests of intelligence.

15. The phrenologist _____ attempted to link intelligence to _____ _____ .

16. Modern studies reveal a _____ (small/large) _____ (positive/negative) correlation between head size (relative to body size) and intelligence score. Newer studies that measure brain _____ using _____ scans reveal a _____ (more/less) significant correlation between brain size (adjusted for body size) and intelligence score.

17. As adults age, brain size and _____ intelligence test scores decrease together. A recent study of Einstein's brain revealed that it was 15 percent larger in the the lower _____ lobe—known to be an important neural center for processing _____ and _____ information.

18. Using _____ scans, researchers have found that the brains of people with high ability on a cognitive task are _____ (more/less) active—use _____ (more/less) glucose—than those of people with low ability.

19. Studies looking at a range of tasks have found that people with high intelligence scores tend to process and retrieve information _____ (faster/more slowly) than people with low intelligence scores.

20. Other studies have found that the brain waves of highly intelligent people register stimuli more _____ and with greater _____ .

Assessing Intelligence (pp. 401–405)

If you do not know the meaning of any of the following words, phrases, or expressions in the context in which they appear in the text, refer to page 329 for an explanation: *clear-cut; clustered; baffled.*

Section Preview

Answer guidelines are provided on page 320.

1. Distinguish between aptitude and achievement tests, and describe modern tests of mental abilities.

2. Identify the major principles of good test construction and illustrate their application to intelligence tests.

Stepping Through the Section

Answers are provided on page 321.

1. Tests designed to predict your ability to learn something new are called _____ tests. Tests designed to measure what you already have learned are called _____ tests.

2. The most widely used intelligence test is the

_____ _____

_____ _____ .

Consisting of 11 subtests, it provides not only a general intelligence score but also _____ and _____ intelligence scores.

3. Three requirements of a good test are

_____ , _____ ,

and _____ .

4. The process of defining meaningful scores relative to a pretested comparison group is called

_____ .

5. When scores on a test are compiled, they generally result in a bell-shaped pattern, or _____ distribution.

Describe the normal curve and explain its significance in the standardization process.

6. The Stanford-Binet and the Wechsler Scales _____ (are/are not) periodically restandardized, thereby keeping the average score near _____ .

7. During the 1960s and 1970s, college entrance aptitude scores showed a steady _____ (increase/decline). At the same time, intelligence test performance _____ (improved/decreased). This phenomenon is called the

_____ _____ .

8. The recent performance gains on the WAIS are greatest on _____ (verbal/nonverbal) tests, which schooling should _____ (most/least) affect.

Cite several proposed reasons for these trends.

9. If a test yields consistent results, it is said to be

_____ .

10. When a test is administered more than once to the same people, the psychologist is determining its _____-_____ reliability.

11. For example, when a person's scores for the odd- and even-numbered questions on a test are compared, _____ -_____ reliability is being assessed.

12. The Stanford-Binet, WAIS, and WISC have reliabilities of about _____ .

13. The degree to which a test measures or predicts what it is supposed to is referred to as the test's _____ .

14. The degree to which a test measures the behavior it was designed to measure is referred to as the test's _____ _____ .

15. The degree to which a test predicts future performance of a particular behavior, called the test's _____ , is referred to as the test's _____ _____ .

Choose a specific example and use it to illustrate and explain the concept of criterion and its relationship to predictive validity.

16. Generally speaking, the predictive validity of general aptitude tests _____ (is/is not) as high as their reliability. The predictive validity of these tests _____ (increases/diminishes) as individuals move up the educational ladder.

The Dynamics of Intelligence
(pp. 405–410)

> If you do not know the meaning of any of the following words, phrases, or expressions in the context in which they appear in the text, refer to page 329 for an explanation: *has left few stones unturned; the pendulum of opinion . . . complete swing.*

Section Preview

Answer guidelines are provided on page 321.

1. Discuss the stability of intelligence test scores and the two extremes of intelligence.

2. Identify the factors associated with creativity.

Stepping Through the Section

Answers are provided on page 321.

1. Two- to 7-month-old infants who quickly become bored when looking at a picture score _____ (higher/lower) on tests of brain speed and intelligence up to 11 years later.

2. Traditional intelligence tests before age _____ generally do not predict future scores.

3. During childhood, the stability of intelligence scores _____ (increases/ decreases) with age. By late adolescence, intelligence scores are _____ (extremely/not very) stable.

4. Individuals whose intelligence scores fall below 70 and who have difficulty adapting to life may be labeled _____ _____ . This label applies to approximately _____ percent of the population.

5. Severe retardation sometimes has a physical basis, such as _____ _____ , a genetic disorder caused by an extra chromosome.

Discuss criticisms of programs that sort children into gifted and nongifted tracks.

6. The ability to produce ideas that are both novel and valuable is called _____ . The relationship between intelligence and creativity holds only up to a certain point—an intelligence score of about _____ .

Describe five components of creativity other than intelligence.

Section Preview

Answer guidelines are provided on page 322.

1. Discuss evidence for genetic influences on intelligence.

2. Discuss evidence for environmental influences on intelligence.

3. Describe group differences in intelligence test scores, and show how they can be explained in terms of environmental factors.

4. Discuss whether intelligence tests are biased and/or discriminatory.

Genetic and Environmental Influences on Intelligence (pp. 410–421)

If you do not know the meaning of any of the following words, phrases, or expressions in the context in which they appear in the text, refer to pages 329–330 for an explanation: *virtual carbon copies of each other; bludgeoning native intelligence; capture our attention; sharpest at the extremes; computer camps; Differences are not deficits.*

Stepping Through the Section

Answers are provided on page 322.

1. The position that both heredity and environment exert some influence on intelligence is _____ (controversial/generally accepted) among psychologists.

2. The intelligence scores of identical twins reared together are _____ (more/no more) similar than those of fraternal twins.

3. A gene located on chromosome _____ (what number?) may occur more often in children with very high intelligence scores than those with average scores.

4. By inserting an extra gene that engineers a neural receptor involved in _____ into fertilized mouse eggs, researchers have created smarter mice.

5. The intelligence test scores of fraternal twins are _____ (more alike/no more alike) than the intelligence test scores of other siblings. This provides evidence of a(n) _____ (genetic/environmental) effect because fraternal twins, being the same _____ , are treated more alike.

6. Studies of adopted children and their adoptive and biological families demonstrate that with age, genetic influences on intelligence become _____ (more/less) apparent. Thus, children's intelligence scores are more like those of their _____ (biological/adoptive) parents than their _____ (biological/adoptive) parents.

7. The amount of variation in a trait within a group that is attributed to genetic factors is called its _____ . For intelligence, this has been estimated at _____ percent.

8. If we know a trait has perfect heritability, this knowledge _____ (does/does not) enable us to rule out environmental factors in explaining differences between groups.

9. Studies indicate that neglected children _____ (do/do not) show signs of recovery in intelligence and behavior when placed in more nurturing environments.

10. High-quality programs for disadvantaged children, such as the government-funded _____ _____ program, produce at least short-term cognitive gains, even on intelligence tests.

Identify several qualities shared by the most effective day-care programs, according to research studies of poor and uneducated families.

11. Intelligence scores _____ (rise/fall/remain stable) during the school year and _____ (rise/fall/remain stable) over the summer. The Flynn effect of rising IQ scores is partly due to the increasing years of _____ over the last fifty years.

12. Research evidence suggests that group differences in intelligence may be entirely _____ (genetic/environmental).

Explain why heredity may contribute to individual differences in intelligence but not necessarily contribute to group differences.

13. Group differences in intelligence scores _____ (do/do not) provide an accurate basis for judging individuals. Individual differences within a race are _____ (greater than/less than) between-race differences.

14. Although Asian students on the average score _____ (higher/lower) than North American students on math tests, this difference may be due to the fact that _____ _____ _____ .

15. On an infant intelligence measure (preference for looking at novel stimuli), black infants score _____ (lower than/higher than/about the same as) white infants.

16. Gender similarities in math and verbal ability are _____ (smaller/greater) than gender differences. Girls tend to outscore boys on _____ tests and are more _____ fluent. Although girls have an edge in math _____ , boys score higher in math _____ _____ . Boys tend to outscore girls on tests of _____ _____ .

17. Working from an _____ perspective, some theorists speculate that these gender differences helped our ancestors survive.

18. There is evidence that spatial abilities are enhanced by high levels of _____ _____ _____ during prenatal development.

19. The gender gap in math is _____ (increasing/decreasing/remaining steady), perhaps because _____ expectations for boys and girls are changing.

20. In the sense that they detect differences caused by cultural experiences, intelligence tests probably _____ (are/are not) biased.

21. Most psychologists agree that, in terms of predictive validity, the major aptitude tests _____ (are/are not) racially biased.

Web Sighting

The World Wide Web is chock full of resources related to various aspects of intelligence, including intelligence testing, theories of intelligence, animal intelligence, and artificial intelligence. For example, use *Yahoo*, *WebCrawler*, or your favorite search engine to find the 30-minute Mensa intelligence-test workout. Consult an "on-line oracle" to hone your intuition. Play an interactive web game with a cybertherapist. To get started, try to find the answers to the following questions.

1. Who is Dr. Werner Wilhelm Webowitz? How can he help you? Is he related to ELIZA?

2. Do you have a pet dog? Where is your dog's breed in the ranking of dogs for working intelligence? If you don't own a dog, can you find which breed ranks highest in working intelligence?

3. Can you find Daniel Goleman's sample emotional intelligence test? What is your EQ?

4. What is Mensa? Can you pass their test of wisdom?

Progress Test 1

Multiple-Choice Questions

Circle your answers to the following questions and check them with the answers on page 323. If your answer is incorrect, read the explanation for why it is incorrect and then consult the appropriate pages of the text (in parentheses following the correct answer).

1. Studies of adopted children and their biological and adoptive families demonstrate that with age, genetic influences on intelligence:
   a. become more apparent.
   b. become less apparent.
   c. become more difficult to disentangle from environmental influences.
   d. become easier to disentangle from environmental influences.

2. A 6-year-old child has a mental age of 9. The child's IQ is:
   a. 96.   d. 150.
   b. 100.   e. 166.
   c. 125.

3. Which of the following is *not* true?
   a. In math grades, the average girl typically equals or surpasses the average boy.
   b. The gender gap in math and science scores is increasing.
   c. Women are better than men at detecting emotions.
   d. Males score higher than females on tests of spatial abilities.

4. Most psychologists believe that racial gaps in test scores:
   a. have been exaggerated when they are, in fact, insignificant.
   b. indicate that intelligence is in large measure inherited.
   c. are in large measure caused by environmental factors.
   d. are increasing.

5. Standardization refers to the process of:
   a. determining the accuracy with which a test measures what it is supposed to.
   b. defining meaningful scores relative to a representative pretested group.
   c. determining the consistency of test scores obtained by retesting people.
   d. measuring the success with which a test predicts the behavior it is designed to predict.

6. Down syndrome is normally caused by:
   a. an extra chromosome in the person's genetic makeup.
   b. a missing chromosome in the person's genetic makeup.
   c. malnutrition during the first few months of life.
   d. prenatal exposure to an addictive drug.

7. Which of the following is *not* a requirement of a good test?
   a. reliability
   b. standardization
   c. reification
   d. validity
   e. criterion

8. First-time parents Geena and Brad want to give their baby's intelligence a jump-start by providing a super enriched learning environment. Experts would suggest that the new parents should:
   a. pipe stimulating classical music into the baby's room.
   b. hang colorful mobiles and artwork over the baby's crib.
   c. take the child to one of the new "superbaby" preschools that specialize in infant enrichment.
   d. relax, since there is no surefire environmental recipe for giving a child a superior intellect.

9. Which of the following statements is true?
   a. The predictive validity of intelligence tests is not as high as their reliability.
   b. The reliability of intelligence tests is not as high as their predictive validity.
   c. Modern intelligence tests have extremely high predictive validity and reliability.
   d. The predictive validity and reliability of most intelligence tests is very low.

10. Before about age _____ , intelligence tests generally do not predict future scores.
    a. 1
    b. 3
    c. 5
    d. 10
    e. 15

11. Sorting children into gifted and nongifted educational groups:
    a. presumes that giftedness is a single trait.
    b. does not result in higher academic achievement scores.
    c. promotes racial segregation and prejudice.
    d. sometimes creates self-fulfilling prophecies.
    e. has all of the above effects.

12. Which of the following best describes the relationship between creativity and intelligence?
    a. Creativity appears to depend on the ability to think imaginatively and has little if any relationship to intelligence.
    b. Creativity is best understood as a certain kind of intelligence.
    c. The more intelligent a person is, the greater his or her creativity.
    d. A certain level of intelligence is necessary but not sufficient for creativity.

13. Studies of 2- to 7-month-old babies show that babies who quickly become bored with a picture:
    a. often develop learning disabilities later on.
    b. score lower on infant intelligence tests.
    c. score higher on intelligence tests several years later.
    d. score very low on intelligence tests several years later.

14. The existence of _____ reinforces the generally accepted notion that intelligence is a multidimensional quality.
    a. adaptive skills
    b. mental retardation
    c. general intelligence
    d. savant syndrome

15. Which of the following provides the strongest evidence of the role of heredity in determining intelligence?
    a. The IQ scores of identical twins raised separately are very similar.
    b. The intelligence scores of fraternal twins are more similar than those of ordinary siblings.
    c. The intelligence scores of identical twins raised together are more similar than those of identical twins raised apart.
    d. The intelligence scores of adopted children show relatively weak correlations with scores of adoptive as well as biological parents.

16. Current estimates are that _____ percent of the total variation among intelligence scores can be attributed to genetic factors.
    a. less than 10
    b. approximately 25
    c. between 50 and 70
    d. over 75

17. Over the past 50 years, college aptitude test scores have _____ and WAIS scores have _____ .
    a. declined; remained stable
    b. remained stable; declined
    c. risen; declined
    d. declined; risen

18. Reported racial gaps in average intelligence scores are most likely attributable to:
    a. the use of biased tests of intelligence.
    b. the use of unreliable tests of intelligence.
    c. genetic factors.
    d. environmental factors.

19. The bell-shaped distribution of intelligence scores in the general population is called a:
    a. g distribution.
    b. standardization curve.
    c. bimodal distribution.
    d. normal distribution.

20. Research on the effectiveness of Head Start suggests that enrichment programs:
    a. produce permanent gains in intelligence scores.
    b. improve school readiness, but have no measurable impact on intelligence scores.
    c. improve intelligence scores but not school readiness.
    d. produce temporary gains in intelligence scores.

Matching Items

Match each term with its definition or description.

Terms

_____ 1. mental ability score
_____ 2. g
_____ 3. eugenics
_____ 4. savant syndrome
_____ 5. factor analysis
_____ 6. aptitude test
_____ 7. achievement test
_____ 8. Stanford-Binet
_____ 9. criterion
_____ 10. content validity
_____ 11. reliability

Definitions or Descriptions

a. a test designed to predict a person's ability to learn something new
b. a test designed to measure current knowledge
c. the consistency with which a test measures performance
d. the degree to which a test measures what it is designed to measure
e. Terman's revision of Binet's original intelligence test
f. the behavior that a test is designed to predict
g. an underlying, general intelligence factor
h. a person's score on an intelligence test based on performance relative to the average performance of people the same age
i. a very low intelligence score accompanied by one extraordinary skill
j. a program for the selective breeding of the most intelligent individuals
k. a statistical technique that identifies related items on a test

Progress Test 2

Progress Test 2 should be completed during a final chapter review. Answer the following questions after you thoroughly understand the correct answers for the section reviews and Progress Test 1.

Multiple-Choice Questions

1. The test created by Alfred Binet was designed specifically to:
   a. measure inborn intelligence in adults.
   b. measure inborn intelligence in children.
   c. predict school performance in children.
   d. identify mentally retarded children so that they could be institutionalized.
   e. do all of the above.

2. Which of the following provides the strongest evidence of environment's role in intelligence?
   a. Adopted children's intelligence scores are more like their adoptive parents' scores than their biological parents'.
   b. Children's intelligence scores are more strongly related to their mothers' scores than to their fathers'.
   c. Children moved from a deprived environment into an intellectually enriched one show gains in intellectual development.
   d. The intelligence scores of identical twins raised separately are no more alike than those of siblings.

3. If a test designed to indicate which applicants are likely to perform the best on the job fails to do so, the test has:
   a. low reliability.
   b. low content validity.
   c. low predictive validity.
   d. not been standardized.

4. By creating a label such as "gifted," we begin to act as if all children are naturally divided into two categories, gifted and nongifted. This logical error is referred to as:
   a. rationalization.
   b. nominalizing.
   c. factor analysis.
   d. reification.
   e. heritability.

5. The formula for the intelligence quotient was devised by:
   a. Sternberg.   d. Terman.
   b. Gall.   e. Stern.
   c. Binet.

6. Current intelligence tests compute an individual's intelligence score as:
   a. the ratio of mental age to chronological age multiplied by 100.
   b. the ratio of chronological age to mental age multiplied by 100.
   c. the amount by which the test-taker's performance deviates from the average performance of others the same age.
   d. the ratio of the test-taker's verbal intelligence score to his or her nonverbal intelligence score.

7. J. McVicker Hunt found that institutionalized children given "tutored human enrichment":
   a. showed no change in intelligence test performance compared with institutionalized children who did not receive such enrichment.
   b. responded so negatively as a result of their impoverished early experiences that he felt it necessary to disband the program.
   c. thrived intellectually and socially on the benefits of positive caregiving.
   d. actually developed greater intelligence than control subjects who had lived in foster homes since birth.

8. The concept of a *g* factor implies that intelligence:
   a. is a single overall ability.
   b. is several specific abilities.
   c. cannot be defined or measured.
   d. is both a. and c.
   e. is a dynamic rather than stable phenomenon.

9. Gerardeen has superb social skills, manages conflicts well, and has great empathy for her friends and co-workers. Peter Salovey and John Mayer would probably say that Gerardeen possesses a high degree of:
   a. *g*.
   b. social intelligence.
   c. practical intelligence.
   d. emotional intelligence.

10. By what age does a child's performance on an intelligence test become stable?
    a. 2   d. 7
    b. 4   e. 12
    c. 6

11. The Flynn effect refers to the fact that:
    a. White and black infants score equally well on measures of infant intelligence.
    b. Asian students outperform North American students on math achievement tests.

c. The IQ scores of today's better fed and educated population exceed that of the 1930s population.

d. Individual differences within a race are much greater than between-race differences.

12. In his study of children with high intelligence scores, Terman found that:

a. the children were more emotional and less healthy than a control group.

b. the children were ostracized by classmates.

c. the children were healthy and well-adjusted, and did well academically.

d. later, as adults, they nearly all achieved great vocational success.

13. When performing a task, the brains of highly skilled people:

a. require less glucose energy.

b. register simple stimuli more quickly.

c. demonstrate a more complex brain-wave response to stimuli.

d. do all of the above.

14. Most experts view intelligence as a person's:

a. ability to perform well on intelligence tests.

b. innate mental capacity.

c. ability to learn from experience, solve problems, and adapt to new situations.

d. diverse skills acquired throughout life.

15. Which of the following statements is true?

a. About 1 percent of the population is mentally retarded.

b. More males than females are mentally retarded.

c. A majority of the mentally retarded can learn basic reading skills.

d. Many of the mentally retarded are mainstreamed into regular classrooms.

e. All of the above are true.

16. High levels of male hormones during prenatal development may enhance:

a. verbal reasoning.

b. spatial abilities.

c. overall intelligence.

d. all of the above.

17. Which of the following is *not* cited as evidence of the reciprocal relationship between schooling and intelligence?

a. Neither education level nor intelligence scores accurately predict income.

b. Intelligence scores tend to rise during the school year.

c. High school graduates have higher intelligence scores than do those who drop out early.

d. High intelligence is conducive to prolonged schooling.

18. Originally, IQ was defined as:

a. mental age divided by chronological age and multiplied by 100.

b. chronological age divided by mental age and multiplied by 100.

c. mental age subtracted from chronological age and multiplied by 100.

d. chronological age subtracted from mental age and multiplied by 100.

19. Tests of _____ measure what an individual can do now, whereas tests of _____ predict what an individual will be able to do later.

a. aptitude; achievement

b. achievement; aptitude

c. reliability; validity

d. validity; reliability

20. Which of the following statements most accurately reflects the text's position regarding the relative contribution of genes and environment in determining intelligence?

a. Except in cases of a neglectful early environment, each individual's basic intelligence is largely the product of heredity.

b. With the exception of those with genetic disorders such as Down syndrome, intelligence is primarily the product of environmental experiences.

c. Both genes and life experiences significantly influence performance on intelligence tests.

d. Because intelligence tests have such low predictive validity, the question cannot be addressed until psychologists agree on a more valid test of intelligence.

True–False Items

Indicate whether each statement is true or false by placing *T* or *F* in the blank next to the item.

_____ 1. In the current version of the Stanford-Binet intelligence test, one's performance is compared only with the performance of others the same age.

_____ 2. Intelligence scores in the United States have been dropping over the past 50 years.

_____ 3. Most of the major aptitude tests have higher validity than reliability.

_____ 4. People with high intelligence scores tend to process sensory information more quickly.

_____ 5. The gap in intelligence scores between black and white children is increasing.

_____ 6. The intelligence scores of adopted children are more similar to those of their adoptive parents than their biological parents.

_____ 7. The consensus among psychologists is that most intelligence tests are extremely biased.

_____ 8. Most psychologists agree that intelligence is mainly determined by heredity.

_____ 9. The Stanford-Binet test and the Wechsler scales are periodically restandardized.

_____ 10. The variation in intelligence scores within a racial group is much larger than that between racial groups.

Thinking Critically About Chapter 11

Answer these questions the day before an exam as a final check on your understanding of the chapter's terms and concepts.

Multiple-Choice Questions

1. Vanessa is a very creative sculptress. We would expect that Vanessa also:
   a. has an exceptionally high intelligence score.
   b. is quite introverted.
   c. has a venturesome personality and is intrinsically motivated.
   d. lacks expertise in most other skills.
   e. is more successful than other sculptors.

2. To say that the heritability of a trait is approximately 50 percent means:
   a. that genes are responsible for 50 percent of the trait in an individual, and the environment is responsible for the rest.
   b. that the trait's appearance in a person will reflect approximately equal genetic contributions from both parents.
   c. that of the variation in the trait within a group of people, 50 percent can be attributed to heredity.
   d. all of the above.

3. Twenty-two-year-old Dan has an intelligence score of 63 and the academic skills of a fourth-grader, and is unable to live independently. Dan *probably*:

   a. has Down syndrome.
   b. has savant syndrome.
   c. is mentally retarded.
   d. will eventually achieve self-supporting social and vocational skills.

4. At age 16, Angel's intelligence score was 110. What will her score probably be at age 32?
   a. 105
   b. 110
   c. 115
   d. There is no basis for predicting an individual's future IQ.

5. A school psychologist found that 85 percent of those who scored above 115 on an aptitude test were "A" students and 75 percent of those who scored below 85 on the test were "D" students. The psychologist concluded that the test had high _____ validity because scores on it correlated highly with the _____ behavior.
   a. content; criterion
   b. predictive; criterion
   c. content; target
   d. predictive; target

6. When Amelia performed a complex perceptual task, a PET scan showed that she used less glucose than Herman did while performing the same task. Which of the following is most likely true of Amelia, as compared to Herman?
   a. As a female, she has better perceptual abilities.
   b. She scores higher on verbal intelligence tests.
   c. Based on her upbringing, she was better trained to perform such tasks.
   d. She is older and better educated.

7. Benito was born in 1937. In 1947, he scored 130 on an intelligence test. What was Benito's mental age when he took the test?
   a. 9   c. 11
   b. 10   d. 13
   e. It cannot be determined from the information provided.

8. Melvin has been diagnosed as having savant syndrome, which means that he:
   a. has an IQ of 120 or higher.
   b. would score high on a test of analytical intelligence.
   c. is mentally retarded but has one exceptional ability.
   d. was exposed to high levels of testosterone during prenatal development.

9. The contribution of environmental factors to racial gaps in intelligence scores is indicated by:
   a. evidence that individual differences within a race are much greater than differences between races.
   b. evidence that white and black infants score equally well on certain measures of infant intelligence.
   c. the fact that Asian students outperform North American students on math achievement and aptitude tests.
   d. all of the above.

10. Hiroko's math achievement score is considerably higher than that of most American students her age. Which of the following is true regarding this difference between Asian and North American students:
    a. It is a recent phenomenon.
    b. It may be due to the fact that Asian students have a longer school year.
    c. It holds only for girls.
    d. Both a. and b. are true.
    e. a., b., and c. are true.

11. Jack takes the same test of mechanical reasoning on several different days and gets virtually identical scores. This suggests that the test has:
    a. high content validity.
    b. high reliability.
    c. high predictive validity.
    d. been standardized.
    e. all of the above qualities.

12. You would not use a test of hearing acuity as an intelligence test because it would lack:
    a. content reliability.
    b. predictive reliability.
    c. predictive validity.
    d. content validity.

13. Before becoming attorneys, law students must pass a special licensing exam, which is an _____ test. Before entering college, high school students must take the SAT, which is an _____ test.
    a. achievement; aptitude
    b. aptitude; achievement
    c. achievement; achievement
    d. aptitude; aptitude

14. If you compare the same trait in people of similar heredity who live in very different environments, heritability for that trait will be _____ ; heritability for the trait is most likely to be _____ among people of very different heredities who live in similar environments.
    a. low; high
    b. high; low
    c. environmental; genetic
    d. genetic; environmental

15. A high-school psychologist who is looking at a student's intelligence score finds a jump of 30 points between the earliest score at age 2 and the most recent at age 17. The psychologist's knowledge of testing would probably lead her to conclude that such a jump:
    a. indicates that different tests were used, creating an apparent change in intelligence level, although it actually remained stable.
    b. signals a significant improvement in the child's environment over this period.
    c. is unsurprising, since intelligence scores do not become stable until late adolescence.
    d. is mainly the result of the age at which the first test was taken.

16. If you wanted to develop a test of musical aptitude in North American children, which would be the appropriate standardization group?
    a. children all over the world
    b. North American children
    c. children of musical parents
    d. children with known musical ability

17. Don's intelligence scores were only average, but he has been enormously successful as a corporate manager. Psychologists Sternberg and Wagner would probably suggest that Don's _____ intelligence exceeds his _____ intelligence.
    a. verbal; performance
    b. performance; verbal
    c. academic; practical
    d. practical; academic

18. According to the text, what can be concluded from early intelligence testing in the United States?
    a. Most European immigrants were "feeble-minded."
    b. Army recruits of other than West European heritage were intellectually deficient.
    c. The tests were biased against people who did not share the culture assumed by the test.
    d. Both a. and b. could be concluded.

19. If asked to guess the intelligence score of a stranger, your best guess would be:
    a. 75.
    b. 100.
    c. 125.
    d. "I don't know, intelligence scores vary too widely."

20. Which of the following is true of people who score high on aptitude tests?
    a. They achieve greater career success.
    b. They are likely to be happier.
    c. They always do well in college.
    d. None of the above is true.
    e. All of the above are true.

Essay Question

You have been asked to devise a Psychology Achievement Test (PAT) that will be administered to freshmen who declare psychology as their major. What steps will you take to ensure that the PAT is a good intelligence test? (Use the space below to list the points you want to make and organize them. Then write the essay on a separate sheet of paper.)

Key Terms

Writing Definitions

Using your own words, write on a separate piece of paper a brief definition or explanation of each of the following terms.

1. intelligence test
2. mental age
3. Stanford-Binet
4. intelligence quotient (IQ)
5. intelligence
6. factor analysis
7. general intelligence (*g*)
8. savant syndrome
9. emotional intelligence
10. aptitude tests
11. achievement tests
12. Wechsler Adult Intelligence Scale—(WAIS)
13. standardization
14. normal curve (normal distribution)
15. reliability
16. validity
17. content validity
18. criterion
19. predictive validity
20. mental retardation
21. Down syndrome
22. creativity

Cross-Check

As you learned in the Introduction, reviewing and overlearning of material are important to the learning process. After you have written the definitions of the key terms in this chapter, you should complete the crossword puzzle to ensure that you can reverse the process—recognize the term, given the definition.

ACROSS

5. Type of intelligence assessed by standard intelligence tests.
7. Theorist who distinguished among three intelligences.
9. Type of intelligence often required for everyday tasks.
10. Theorist who proposed a large number of distinct types of intelligence.
11. Psychologist who revised Binet's original intelligence test.
17. The most widely used adult intelligence test.
18. Term that refers to viewing an abstract concept as if it were a real, concrete thing.
19. Most widely used intelligence test for children.
21. French psychologist who initiated the modern intelligence-testing movement.

DOWN

1. The age that typically corresponds to a given level of performance.
2. Statistical procedure that identifies clusters of related items on a test.
3. A condition of limited mental ability, as indicated by an IQ score below 70.
4. A condition of limited mental ability caused by an extra chromosome.
6. The behavior that a test is designed to predict.
8. The proportion of variation among individuals that is attributed to genes.
12. Type of test that is designed to measure what a person has already learned.
13. The success with which a test predicts the behavior it is designed to predict is its _____ validity.
14. Bell-shaped distribution that describes many physical and psychological traits.
15. The extent to which a test yields consistent results.
16. The phenomenon of rising intelligence-test performance.

20. The extent to which a test samples the behavior that is of interest is its _____ validity.

Answers

The Origins of Intelligence Testing

Section Preview

1. Modern intelligence testing began when Alfred Binet developed a test to predict children's future school performance. Binet's test was designed to compute a mental age for each child. Lewis Terman's revision of Binet's test, known as the Stanford-Binet, computed an IQ score as the ratio of mental age to chronological age. Modern intelligence tests no longer compute an intelligence quotient; instead, they produce a mental ability score based on the test-taker's performance relative to the average of others the same age.

Stepping Through the Section

1. intelligence
2. Plato
3. Binet; mental; was not

4. Stanford-Binet; intelligence quotient

In the original formula for IQ, measured mental age is divided by chronological age and multiplied by 100. "Mental age" refers to the chronological age that most typically corresponds to a given level of performance.

5. a mental ability score; the same; 100

6. below; cultural

What Is Intelligence?

Section Preview

1. Intelligence is a socially constructed concept defined as the ability to learn from experience, solve problems, and use knowledge to adapt to new situations. The two controversies regarding intelligence are (a) whether intelligence is a single overall ability or several specific abilities and (b) whether intelligence can neurologically be measured as the brain's information-processing speed.

2. Factor analysis is a statistical technique used to identify clusters of test items that measure a common ability, such as spatial or reasoning ability.

   Although psychologists agree that people have specific abilities, such as verbal or mathematical intelligence, they do not agree about the existence of an underlying general intelligence factor. People with savant syndrome, who score very low on intelligence tests but possess extraordinary specific abilities, provide support for the viewpoint that there are multiple intelligences, each independent of the others. Sternberg and Wagner, for example, distinguish among three intelligences—academic, practical, and creative— while Cantor and Kihlstrom distinguish between academic and social intelligence (including emotional intelligence) and Gardner among seven different intelligences.

3. Efforts to link brain structure and cognition continue. Recent studies using MRI and PET scans reveal modest correlations between brain size (adjusted for body size) and intelligence, and between ability on a specific cognitive task and neurological efficiency. Other researchers have found that people with high intelligence scores have faster perceptual and neurological reactions on tests that measure speed of processing simple information.

Stepping Through the Section

1. do not

2. reification

3. socially

4. the ability to learn from experience, solve problems, and use knowledge to adapt to new situations

5. overall (general); specific

6. factor analysis; general intelligence

7. Thurstone; primary mental abilities

8. savant syndrome

9. multiple intelligences; physical; verbal; reasoning

10. academic; practical; creative; academic; social; only modestly

11. emotional intelligence; perceive; express; understand; regulate

Emotionally intelligent people are self-aware. They can manage their emotions and they can delay gratification. They handle others' emotions skillfully.

12. emotional; moral

13. conscientiousness

14. neurological

15. Gall; brain structure

16. small; positive; volume; MRI; more

17. nonverbal; temporal; mathematical; spatial

18. PET; less; less

19. faster

20. quickly; complexity

Assessing Intelligence

Section Preview

1. Aptitude tests, such as a college entrance exam, are intended to predict a person's ability to learn new skills. Achievement tests, such as a final exam in a college course, are intended to measure what already has been learned.

   The most widely used intelligence tests, the WAIS and the WISC, consist of 11 subtests and yield an overall intelligence score, as well as separate verbal and performance scores.

2. Good intelligence tests have been standardized and are reliable and valid. Standardization is the process of defining meaningful scores on the test relative to a pretested group. A random group of test results should form a normal distribution depicted on a normal curve.

   Reliability is the extent to which a test yields consistent results. To check a test's reliability, people are tested twice using the same or a different form of the test. If the scores correlate, the test is reliable. The Stanford-Binet, WAIS, WISC, and American college aptitude tests all have high reliabilities of about +.9.

Validity is the extent to which a test actually measures the behavior (content validity) it claims to, or predicts some criterion, such as future performance (predictive validity). The predictive validity of general aptitude tests is not as high as their reliability.

Stepping Through the Section

1. aptitude; achievement
2. Wechsler Adult Intelligence Scale; verbal; performance
3. standardization; reliability; validity
4. standardization
5. normal

The normal curve describes the distribution of many physical phenomena and psychological attributes (including IQ scores), with most scores falling near the average and fewer and fewer near the extremes. When a test is standardized on a normal curve, individual scores are assigned according to how much they deviate above or below the distribution's average.

6. are; 100
7. decline; improved; Flynn effect
8. nonverbal; least

Part of the decline in college aptitude test scores has been attributed to the greater academic diversity of students who began taking the test during the 1960s. In contrast, the WAIS has always been taken by a diverse group of people. Americans as a whole have become more literate and better educated since the 1930s. Thus, while performance on the more complex college aptitude tests has declined, performance on the basic skills tested by the WAIS has improved.

9. reliable
10. test-retest
11. split-half
12. +.9
13. validity
14. content validity
15. criterion; predictive validity

The criterion is the particular behavior that a predictive test, such as an aptitude test, is intended to predict. For example, performance in a relevant job situation would be the criterion for a test measuring managerial aptitude. The criterion determines whether a test has predictive validity. For example, the on-the-job success of those who do well on a job aptitude test would indicate the test has predictive validity.

16. is not; diminishes

The Dynamics of Intelligence

Section Preview

1. The stability of intelligence test scores increases with age. Infants who become quickly bored with a picture score higher on intelligence tests several years later. By age 3, children's performances on intelligence tests begin to predict their adolescent and adult scores. After age 7, intelligence test scores, though not fixed, stabilize. By late adolescence, aptitude scores are quite stable.

    Approximately 1 percent of the population have very low intelligence scores, experience difficulty adapting to the normal demands of living independently, and are labeled as mentally retarded. Severe mental retardation sometimes results from physical causes, such as Down syndrome.

    Approximately 3 to 5 percent of children are labeled "gifted." Contrary to popular myth, gifted children are not frequently maladjusted. The segregation of children into gifted and nongifted educational tracks remains controversial. Critics of ability tracking contend that it does not result in higher achievement scores, that it lowers all students' self-concepts and sometimes creates a self-fulfilling prophecy, and that it promotes segregation and prejudice. Ability tracking also is based on the possibly erroneous notion that giftedness is a single trait rather than any one of many specific abilities.

2. Creativity is the ability to produce novel and valuable ideas. Although people with high intelligence scores do well on tests of creativity, beyond an intelligence score of about 120, the correlation between intelligence scores and creativity disappears.

    Studies suggest five components to creativity other than intelligence: expertise, imaginative thinking skills, a venturesome personality, intrinsic motivation, and a creative environment.

Stepping Through the Section

1. higher
2. 3
3. increases; extremely
4. mentally retarded; 1
5. Down syndrome

By labeling and segregating "gifted" and "nongifted" groups we presume that giftedness is a single objective trait rather than one of many potentials. Critics of ability tracking contend that it does not result in higher intelligence scores, that it lowers students' self-esteem and sometimes creates self-fulfilling prophecies, and that it promotes racial segregation and prejudice.

6. creativity; 120

Creative people tend to have *expertise*, or a solid base of knowledge; *imaginative thinking skills*, which allow them to see things in new ways, to recognize patterns, and to make connections; *intrinsic motivation*, or the tendency to focus on the pleasure and challenge of their work; and a *venturesome personality* that tolerates ambiguity and risk and seeks new experiences. Creative people also have generally benefited from living in *creative environments*.

Genetic and Environmental Influences on Intelligence

Section Preview

1. Studies of twins and adopted children point to the influence of heredity. For example, the most genetically similar people have the most similar intelligence scores, and adopted children's intelligence scores are more like their biological parents' scores than their adoptive parents' scores. Moreover, with age, genetic influences become even more apparent. Researchers have identified a gene located on chromosome 6 that is found more often in children with very high intelligence scores; they have also produced smarter mice by inserting an extra gene into fertilized mouse eggs. It is estimated that the *heritability* of intelligence is about 50 to 70 percent; that is, 50 to 70 percent of the variation in intelligence within a *group* of people can be attributed to heredity.

2. Research studies that compare children reared in neglectful environments—including those associated with poverty and malnutrition—with those who have been reared in normal environments point to the impact of environmental experiences on intelligence scores. However, there is no sure-fire environmental recipe for producing a child with superior intellect, beyond normal exposure to sights, sounds, and speech. Findings regarding Head Start and other preschool programs indicate that high-quality programs can generate short-term cognitive gains and long-term positive effects. Recent studies also provide evidence that schooling and intelligence have a positive, reciprocal effect on each other.

3. Individual differences within a race are much greater than differences between races. However, on average, there *are* group differences in intelligence scores. For example, Asian students outperform North American students on math

achievement and aptitude tests, females score higher than males in math computation, and white Americans tend to score higher than black Americans on IQ tests.

Although heredity contributes to individual differences in intelligence, it does not necessarily contribute to group differences. Most experts believe that the intelligence score gaps between groups are the result of differences between privileged and disadvantaged groups around the world, as well as differences in educational enrichment.

4. In the sense that intelligence scores are sensitive to differences caused by cultural experience, aptitude tests are certainly biased. In terms of predictive validity, however, most experts agree that the major intelligence tests are not racially biased.

Because intelligence tests are designed to distinguish different levels of aptitude, their purpose in this sense *is* to discriminate among individuals. In another sense, however, intelligence tests reduce discrimination by reducing the use of subjective criteria in school and job placement.

Stepping Through the Section

1. generally accepted
2. more
3. 6
4. memory
5. more alike; environmental; age
6. more; biological; adoptive
7. heritability; 50 to 70
8. does not
9. do
10. Head Start

The most effective programs begin earlier and continue longer, are more intensive, provide direct educational experiences, and offer support programs for maintaining positive attitudes and behaviors.

11. rise; fall; schooling
12. environmental

Because of the impact of environmental factors such as education and nutrition on intelligence test performance, even if the heritability of intelligence is high within a particular group, differences in intelligence *among* groups may be environmentally caused. One group may, for example, thrive in an enriched environment while another of the same genetic predisposition may falter in an impoverished one.

13. do not; greater than

14. higher; Asian students have a longer school year and spend more time studying math.

15. about the same as

16. greater; spelling; verbally; computation; problem solving; mental rotation

17. evolutionary

18. male sex hormones

19. decreasing; social

20. are

21. are not

Progress Test 1

Multiple-Choice Questions

1. **a.** is the answer. (p. 412)

    c. & d. Separating genetic from environmental influences is difficult *at any age.*

2. **d.** is the answer. If we divide 9, the measured mental age, by 6, the chronological age, and multiply the result by 100, we obtain 150. (p. 393)

3. **b.** is the answer. As social expectations have changed, the gender gap in math and science scores is narrowing. (pp. 417–418)

4. **c.** is the answer. (pp. 415–416)

    a. On the contrary, many *group* differences are highly significant, even though they tell us nothing about specific *individuals.*

    b. Although heredity contributes to individual differences in intelligence, it does not necessarily contribute to group differences.

    d. In fact, the difference has diminished somewhat in recent years.

5. **b.** is the answer. (p. 402)

    a. This answer refers to a test's content validity.

    c. This answer refers to test-retest reliability.

    d. This answer refers to predictive validity.

6. **a.** is the answer. (p. 407)

    b. Down syndrome is normally caused by an extra, rather than a missing, chromosome.

    c. & d. Down syndrome is a genetic disorder that is manifest during the earliest stages of prenatal development, well before malnutrition and exposure to drugs would produce their harmful effects on the developing fetus.

7. **c.** is the answer. Reification is a reasoning error, in which an abstract concept such as IQ is regarded as though it were real. (pp. 402–405)

8. **d.** is the answer. (p. 413)

9. **a.** is the answer. (p. 404)

    c. & d. Most modern tests have high reliabilities of about +.9; their validity scores are much lower.

10. **b.** is the answer. (p. 406)

11. **e.** is the answer. (p. 408)

12. **d.** is the answer. Up to an intelligence score of about 120, there is a positive correlation between intelligence and creativity. But beyond this point the correlation disappears, indicating that factors other than intelligence are also involved. (p. 409)

    a. The ability to think imaginatively and intelligence are *both* components of creativity.

    b. Creativity, the capacity to produce ideas that are novel and valuable, is related to and depends in part on intelligence but cannot be considered simply a kind of intelligence.

    c. Beyond an intelligence score of about 120 there is no correlation between intelligence scores and creativity.

13. **c.** is the answer. (p. 406)

14. **d.** is the answer. That people with savant syndrome excel in one area but are intellectually retarded in others suggests that there are multiple intelligences. (pp. 395–396)

    a. The ability to adapt defines the capacity we call intelligence.

    b. Mental retardation is an indicator of the range of human intelligence.

    c. A general intelligence factor was hypothesized by Spearman to underlie each specific factor of intelligent behavior, but its existence is controversial and remains to be proved.

15. **a.** is the answer. Identical twins who live apart have the same genetic makeup but different environments; if their scores are similar, this is evidence for the role of heredity. (p. 411)

    b. Since fraternal twins are no more genetically alike than ordinary siblings, this could not provide evidence for the role of heredity.

    c. That twins raised together have more similar scores than twins raised apart provides evidence for the role of the environment.

    d. As both sets of correlations are weak, little evidence is provided either for or against the role of heredity.

16. **c.** is the answer. Recent estimates are generally in the range of 50 to 70 percent. (p. 411)

17. **d.** is the answer. College aptitude tests are complex tests that are not periodically restandardized. The WAIS, a more basic test that is periodically restandardized so that the average is always 100, also reflects the performance of a more diverse group. (p. 403)

18. **d.** is the answer. Findings from a range of studies—including studies related to the Flynn effect and adoption studies—have led experts to focus on the influence of environmental factors. (p. 416)

a. Most experts believe that in terms of predictive validity, the major tests are not racially biased.

b. The reliability of the major tests is actually very high.

c. The bulk of the evidence on which experts base their findings points to the influence of environmental factors.

19. **d.** is the answer. (p. 402)

a. *g* is Spearman's term for "general intelligence"; there is no such thing as a "*g* distribution."

b. There is no such thing.

c. A bimodal distribution is one having two (bi-) modes, or averages. The normal distribution has only one mode.

20. **d.** is the answer. The benefits for intelligence scores of enrichment programs such as Head Start dissipate over time. (p. 414)

b. & c. Enrichment programs do improve school readiness and result in measurable, but temporary, gains in intelligence scores.

Matching Items

1. h (p. 393)   5. k (p. 395)   9. f (p. 404)
2. g (p. 395)   6. a (p. 401)   10. d (p. 404)
3. j (p. 393)   7. b (p. 401)   11. c (p. 404)
4. i (pp. 395–396) 8. e (p. 393)

Progress Test 2

Multiple-Choice Questions

1. **c.** is the answer. French compulsory education laws brought more children into the school system, and the government didn't want to rely on teachers' subjective judgments to determine which children would require special help. (p. 392)

a. & b. Binet's test was intended for children, and Binet specifically rejected the idea that his test measured inborn intelligence, which is an abstract capacity that cannot be quantified.

d. This was not a purpose of the test, which dealt with children in the school system.

2. **c.** is the answer. (p. 413)

a., b., & d. None of these is true.

3. **c.** is the answer. Predictive validity is the extent to which tests predict what they are intended to predict. (p. 404)

a. Reliability is the consistency with which a test samples the particular behavior of interest.

b. Content validity is the degree to which a test measures what it is designed to measure.

d. Standardization is the process of defining meaningful test scores based on the performance of a representative group.

4. **d.** is the answer. Reification is the error of creating a concept and then assuming the created concept has a concrete reality. (pp. 394, 408)

a. To rationalize is to develop self-satisfying explanations of one's behavior.

b. The term "nominalizing" has no relevance to psychology.

c. Factor analysis is a statistical procedure that identifies clusters of related items, or factors, on a test.

e. Heritability is the proportion of variation among individuals in a trait that is attributable to genes.

5. **e.** is the answer. (p. 393)

6. **c.** is the answer. (p. 393)

a. This is William Stern's original formula for the intelligence quotient.

b. & d. Neither of these formulas is used to compute the score on current intelligence tests.

7. **c.** is the answer. Enrichment led to dramatic results and thereby testified to the importance of environmental factors. (p. 413)

a. & d. The study involved neither intelligence tests nor comparisons with control groups.

b. The children showed a dramatic positive response.

8. **a.** is the answer. (p. 395)

9. **d.** is the answer. (p. 398)

a. The concept of general intelligence pertains more to academic skills.

b. Although emotional intelligence *is* a key component of social intelligence, Salovey and Mayer coined the newer term "emotional intelligence" to refer to skills such as Gerardeen's.

c. Practical intelligence is that which is required for everyday tasks, not all of which involve emotions.

10. **d.** is the answer. Intelligence test performances begin to become predictive at about age 3 and become stable by about age 7. (p. 406)

11. **c.** is the answer. (p. 403)

12. **c.** is the answer. (p. 407)

a. & b. There was no evidence of either of these in Terman's subjects.

d. Vocational success in adulthood varied.

13. **d.** is the answer. (p. 399)

14. **c.** is the answer. (p. 394)

a. Performance ability and intellectual ability are separate traits.

b. This has been argued by some, but certainly not most, experts.

d. Although many experts believe that there are multiple intelligences, this would not be the same thing as diverse acquired skills.

15. e. is the answer. (p. 407)

16. b. is the answer. (p. 418)

17. a. is the answer. Both schooling and intelligence enhance later income. (p. 414)

b., c., & d. The issues of whether intelligence is innate and whether it is a single entity or multi-faceted have relatively little bearing on the question of the potential for culture-free tests.

18. a. is the answer. (p. 393)

19. b. is the answer. (p. 401)

c. & d. Reliability and validity are characteristics of good tests.

20. c. is the answer. (p. 413)

a. & b. Studies of twins, family members, and adopted children point to a significant hereditary contribution to intelligence scores. These same studies, plus others comparing children reared in neglectful or enriched environments, indicate that life experiences also significantly influence test performance.

d. Although the issue of how intelligence should be defined is controversial, intelligence tests generally have predictive validity, especially in the early years.

True–False Items

1. T (p. 393)	**6.** F (p. 412)
2. F (p. 403)	**7.** F (pp. 419–420)
3. F (p. 404)	**8.** F (pp. 411–413)
4. T (p. 399)	**9.** T (p. 403)
5. F (p. 415)	**10.** T (p. 416)

Thinking Critically About Chapter 11

Multiple-Choice Questions

1. c. is the answer. (p. 409)

a. Beyond an intelligence score of about 120, creativity and intelligence scores are not correlated.

b. & d. There is no evidence that creative people are more likely to be introverted.

e. This may be true, but it cannot be assumed to be a result of creativity.

2. c. is the answer. Heritability is a measure of the extent to which a trait's variation within a group of people can be attributed to heredity. (p. 412)

a. & b. Heritability is *not* a measure of how much of an *individual's* behavior is inherited, nor of the relative contribution of genes from that person's mother and father. Further, the heritability of any trait depends on the context, or environment, in which that trait is being studied.

3. c. is the answer. To be labeled mentally retarded a person must have a test score below 70 and experience difficulty adapting to the normal demands of living independently. (p. 407)

a. Down syndrome is a common cause of *severe* mental retardation; Dan's test score places him in the range of mild retardation.

b. There is no indication that Dan possesses one extraordinary skill, as do people with savant syndrome.

d. The text does not suggest that mentally retarded people eventually become self-supporting.

4. b. is the answer. Intelligence scores become quite stable during adolescence. (p. 406)

5. b. is the answer. (p. 404)

a., c., & d. Content validity is the degree to which a test measures what it claims to measure. Furthermore, "target behavior" is not a term used by intelligence researchers.

6. b. is the answer. PET scans have shown that quick-witted people, who tend to score higher on verbal intelligence tests, use less glucose in solving problems. (p. 399)

a. In fact, the opposite tends to be true.

c. & d. Gender, age, and education have not been shown to be related to glucose use and speed of performance.

7. d. is the answer. At the time he took the test, Benito's chronological age (CA) was 10. Knowing that IQ = 130 and CA = 10, solving the equation for mental age yields a value of 13. (p. 393)

8. c. is the answer. People with savant syndrome tend to score low on intelligence tests but have one exceptional ability. (pp. 395–396)

9. d. is the answer. These reasons, along with other historical and cross-cultural reasons, all argue for the role of environment in creating and perpetuating the gap. (p. 416)

10. d. is the answer. (p. 416)

c. The racial gap is found in both girls and boys.

11. b. is the answer. (p. 404)

12. d. is the answer. Because the hearing acuity test would in no way sample behaviors relevant to intelligence, it would not have content validity as a test of intelligence. (p. 404)

a. & b. There is no such thing as content reliability or predictive reliability.

c. There is nothing to indicate that, used to test hearing, this test would lack predictive validity.

13. **a.** is the answer. An exam for a professional license is intended to measure whether you have gained the overall knowledge and skill to practice the profession. The SAT is designed to predict ability, or aptitude, for learning a new skill. (p. 401)

14. **a.** is the answer. If everyone has nearly the same heredity, then heritability—the variation in a trait attributed to heredity—must be low. If individuals within a group come from very similar environments, environmental differences cannot account for variation in a trait; heritability, therefore, must be high. (p. 412)

15. **d.** is the answer. It is not until after age 3 that intelligence-test performance begins to predict adult scores. (p. 406)
a. Such a conclusion is unlikely, given the high validity of the commonly used intelligence tests.
b. No such conclusion is possible, because intelligence-test performance before age 3 does not predict later aptitude.
c. Stability in intelligence scores is generally established by age 7—long before adulthood.

16. **b.** is the answer. A standardization group provides a representative comparison for the trait being measured by a test. Since this test will measure musical aptitude in North American children, the standardization group should be limited to North American children but should include children of all degrees of musical aptitude. (p. 402)

17. **d.** is the answer. Sternberg and Wagner distinguish among *academic* intelligence, as measured by intelligence tests; *practical* intelligence, which is involved in everyday life and tasks, such as managerial work; and *creative* intelligence. (p. 397)
a. & b. Verbal and performance intelligence are both measured by standard intelligence tests such as the WAIS and would be included in Sternberg and Wagner's academic intelligence.
c. Academic intelligence refers to skills assessed by intelligence tests; practical intelligence applies to skills required for everyday tasks and, often, for occupational success.

18. **c.** is the answer. (p. 393)
a. & b. Although at the time the tests were administered some individuals reached these conclusions, they were of course misled.

19. **b.** is the answer. Modern intelligence tests are periodically restandardized so that the average remains near 100. (p. 403)

20. **d.** is the answer. (p. 401)

Essay Question

The first step in constructing the test is to create a valid set of questions that measure psychological knowledge and therefore give the test content validity. If your objective is to predict students' future achievement in psychology courses, the test questions should be selected to measure a criterion, such as information faculty members expect all psychology majors to master before they graduate.

To enable meaningful comparisons, the test must be standardized. That is, the test should be administered to a representative sample of incoming freshmen at the time they declare psychology to be their major. From the scores of your pretested sample you will then be able to assign an average score and evaluate any individual score according to how much it deviates above or below the average.

To check your test's reliability you might retest a sample of people using the same test or another version of it. If the two scores are correlated, your test is reliable. Alternatively, you might split the test in half and determine whether scores on the two halves are correlated.

Key Terms

Writing Definitions

1. **Intelligence tests** measure people's mental aptitudes and compare them to others' through numerical scores. (p. 391)

2. A concept introduced by Binet, **mental age** is the chronological age that most typically corresponds to a given level of performance. (p. 392)

3. The **Stanford-Binet** is Lewis Terman's widely used revision of Binet's original intelligence test. (p. 393)

4. The **intelligence quotient**, or **IQ**, was defined originally as the ratio of mental age to chronological age multiplied by 100. Contemporary tests of intelligence assign a score of 100 to the average performance for a given age and define other scores as deviations from this average. (p. 393)

5. Most experts define **intelligence** as the ability to learn from experience, solve problems, and use knowledge to adapt to new situations. (p. 394)

6. **Factor analysis** is a statistical procedure that identifies factors, or clusters of items, that seem to define a common ability. Using this procedure, psychologists have identified several clusters, including verbal intelligence, spatial ability, and reasoning ability factors. (p. 395)

7. **General intelligence**, or *g*, factor underlies each of the more specific intelligence clusters identified through factor analysis. (p. 395)

8. A person with **savant syndrome** has a very low intelligence score, yet possesses one exceptional ability, for example, in music or drawing. (pp. 395–396)

9. **Emotional intelligence** is the ability to perceive, express, understand, and regulate emotions. (p. 398)

10. **Aptitude tests** are designed to predict future performance. They measure your capacity to learn new information, rather than measuring what you already know. (p. 401)

11. **Achievement tests** measure a person's current knowledge. (p. 401)

12. The **Wechsler Adult Intelligence Scale (WAIS)** is the most widely used intelligence test. It is individually administered, contains 11 subtests, and yields separate verbal and performance intelligence scores, as well as an overall intelligence score. (p. 401)

13. **Standardization** is the process of defining meaningful scores on a test by pretesting a large, representative sample of people. (p. 402)

14. The **normal curve** is a bell-shaped curve that represents the distribution (frequency of occurrence) of many physical and psychological attributes. The curve is symmetrical, with most scores near the average and fewer near the extremes. (p. 402)

15. **Reliability** is the extent to which a test produces consistent results. (p. 404)

16. **Validity** is the degree to which a test measures or predicts what it is supposed to. (p. 404)

17. The **content validity** of a test is the extent to which it samples the behavior that is of interest. (p. 404)

18. A test's **criterion** is the behavior the test is designed to predict. (p. 404)

19. **Predictive validity** is the extent to which a test predicts the behavior it is designed to predict. (p. 404)

20. The two criteria that designate **mental retardation** are an IQ below 70 and difficulty adapting to the normal demands of independent living. (p. 407)

21. A common cause of severe retardation and associated physical disorders, **Down syndrome** is usually the result of an extra chromosome in the person's genetic makeup. (p. 407)

22. Most experts agree that **creativity** refers to an ability to generate novel and valuable ideas. People with high IQs may or may not be creative, which indicates that intelligence is only one component of creativity. (p. 408)

Cross-Check

ACROSS	DOWN
5. academic	1. mental age
7. Sternberg	2. factor analysis
9. practical	3. mental retardation
10. Gardner	4. Down syndrome
11. Terman	6. criterion
17. WAIS	8. heritability
18. reification	12. achievement
19. WISC	13. predictive
21. Binet	14. normal curve
	15. reliability
	16. Flynn effect
	20. content

FOCUS ON VOCABULARY AND LANGUAGE

Page 391: In the last decade, three huge controversies have *sparked debate* in and beyond psychology. The topic of intelligence (along with gender differences and the nature of repressed, recovered, and false memories) has provoked emotionally charged discussions (*sparked debate*) not only within psychology but in the larger community as well.

The Origins of Intelligence Testing

Page 391: As *heirs* to Plato's individualism, people in Western societies *ponder* how and why individuals differ. Western culture has inherited Plato's individualism. Thus, we are the recipients (*heirs*) of his ideas regarding the origins of individual differences and we think carefully and deeply (*ponder*) about how and why these differences occur. The scientific attempt to investigate this phenomenon began seriously (*in earnest*) about a century ago.

Page 392: On tests, therefore, a *"dull"* child should perform as does a typical younger child, and a *"bright"* child as does a typical older child. Children develop intellectually at different rates and so Binet and Simon developed the concept of **mental age**. Children who performed below the average level of other children the same age (e.g., a 10-year-old who performed as the average 8-year-old did) would be considered retarded or slow in development ("*dull*"). Those who performed above the average (e.g., a 10-year-old who scored as the average 12-year-old did) would be considered developmentally advanced or precocious ("*bright*").

Page 392: To raise the capacities of low-scoring children, he recommended "*mental orthopedics*" that would train them to develop their attention span and self-discipline. Binet did not believe that intellectual capacity was wholly genetic. Rather, he believed that intellectual capacity could be improved with remedial work. Once children who were likely to have problems in school were identified, he suggested the use of "*mental orthopedics.*" (*Orthopedics* is concerned with the prevention and cure of physical deformities of bones, joints, and muscles, especially in children; "*mental orthopedics*" would apply the same principles to the mind.)

Page 393: Obviously, something is *out of whack*. This means that something is not right or correct. The formula for calculating IQ scores (mental age divided by chronological age and multiplied by 100) works for children but produces scores that are clearly absurd (*out of whack*) for adults.

Page 393: In sympathy with the eugenics movement, . . . Terman (1916, pp. 91–92) *lamented* what he believed was the "*dullness*" and "*unusually prolific breeding*" of certain ethnic groups. His belief that mental capacity was inherited and that only the smartest should be allowed to procreate (*eugenics*) prompted Terman to complain (*lament*) about the lack of intelligence of ("*feeble mindedness*" or "*dullness*") and the many children produced ("*unusually prolific breeding*") by certain ethnic groups. He believed that the widespread use of intelligence tests would reduce crime, poverty (*pauperism*), and low productivity.

What Is Intelligence?

Page 394: Intelligence is a *slippery* concept. There is much controversy around the issue of intelligence. It is a concept and not a tangible (concrete) variable such as height or eye color; but is it tied to specific cultures? Is it a single attribute or many? Is it related to quick thinking and can it be observed at the biological level? Agreement about this construct is difficult to come by (it is a *slippery concept*).

Page 395: Perhaps you have known a talented artist who is *dumbfounded by* the simplest mathematical problems . . . . Researchers have used a statistical approach (factor analysis) to identify groups of test items that measure a common ability. So, someone who has a group, or cluster, of abilities in one area

may be very puzzled by and completely unable to solve (*dumbfounded by*) a relatively simple problem in a different area. Spearman argued that there was a common factor (*general intelligence,* or *g*) underlying particular abilities.

Pages 395–396: People with **savant syndrome**, for example, often score low on intelligence tests but have an *island of brilliance*—some incredible ability, as in computation, drawing, or musical memory. Some people are functionally retarded in almost every aspect except for one very specific ability (*island of brilliance*) in which they are exceptionally gifted (**savant syndrome**). Despite having very poor language skills and other cognitive dysfunctions, they may be capable of outstanding performance in computation, memory for music heard only once, drawing, etc. Some psychologists argue that this is evidence for the notion of multiple intelligences.

Page 396: . . . the *street-smart* adolescent who becomes a *crafty* executive. Myers is attempting to simplify Howard Gardner's eight intelligences, referring to *word smarts, number smarts,* and so on. As an example of one of these intelligences, he uses the adolescent who has the ability to survive in urban environments (*street smart*) becoming a clever (*crafty*) executive.

Page 397: . . . how to read people . . . People who have good practical managerial intelligence may not score high on academic ability but will be good at motivating people; assigning work to others appropriately; and knowing and understanding peoples' needs, desires, and ambitions (*knowing how to read people*). They will also be alert, astute, and wise (*shrewd*) in their approach to life in general. Other people may demonstrate different types of intelligences (for example, academic, creative, or emotional intelligence).

Page 399: . . . quick-witted? This means being able to rapidly assess a situation or problem and respond appropriately without delay. Research shows that there is a positive correlation between intelligence-test scores and the speed demonstrated on a number of perceptual and neurological tests.

Page 400: The neurological approach to understanding intelligence (and so many other things in psychology) is currently *in its heyday*. Today, neurological psychology is enjoying unprecedented prosperity and growth (is *in its heyday*) and is vigorously researching many areas in psychology, including intelligence. Myers wonders if we will ultimately be able to describe and explain general intelligence (*g* factor) in pure biological terms, or if we are simply clinging obstinately to mistaken or inaccurate notions (are we *wrongheaded*). Perhaps intelligence is not a single trait but a combination of multiple abilities. The intense debate about what intelligence really is still continues.

Assessing Intelligence

Page 401: Actually, the differences between *aptitude* tests and *achievement* tests are not so *clear-cut.* Some tests measure your present ability and knowledge (*achievement*), as well as predict your future capacity to learn and develop (*aptitude*). Because what you know influences what you can learn in the future and what you are capable of learning is related to what you already know, there is no definite (*clear-cut*) distinction between aptitude and achievement tests. It is a practical matter; a test can be used either to predict future progress or to measure your present ability and skill.

Page 402: . . . scores often form a roughly symmetrical, bell-shaped distribution *clustered* around the average. Many variables that we measure (weight, height, intelligence, etc.) follow a bell-shaped curve when plotted on a frequency distribution. On intelligence tests, the average is 100; most scores (68%) are between 85 and 115, so they are gathered close together (*clustered*) near the mean (*average*).

Page 404: . . . *baffled* . . . This means to be confused, perplexed, or bewildered. James Flynn, who first calculated the size (*magnitude*) of the worldwide phenomenon of rising intelligence test scores (the *Flynn effect*), is uncertain as to how to account for the data (he is *baffled*).

The Dynamics of Intelligence

Page 405: The search for indicators of infants' later intelligence *has left few stones unturned.* Can we predict later level of intelligence from observing the behavior of infants and very young children? Researchers have examined every possible variable (*they have left no stone unturned*) for accurate predictors. One test, which provides a rough (*crude*) indicator of later intelligence, involves observing how quickly children habituate to (*get bored* with) looking at a previously seen picture compared to a new one.

Page 407: During the last two centuries, *the pendulum of opinion* about how best to care for the mentally challenged has made a *complete swing.* Over time and in different ways we have taken care of the mentally retarded—first at home, then in small residential schools, then in massive institutions (*warehouses* for keeping people), and now back to a more normal situation in which they are integrated (mainstreamed) into regular classrooms. The way we have cared has moved from one extreme to the other (*the pendulum of opinion . . . has made a complete swing*).

Genetic and Environmental Influences on Intelligence

Page 411: Even identical twins whose parents do not dress or treat them identically are *virtual carbon copies of each other* in intelligence test scores. Those who believe that heredity powerfully influences intelligence-test performance argue that even when parents treat their identical twins very differently, the twins are still, in essence, identical (*virtual carbon copies of each other*). Genes are more important than environment. Those who believe that the environment is more influential point out the flaws or bias in many of these studies and report evidence that supports the view that genes are less important than life experiences.

Page 413: Extreme deprivation was *bludgeoning native intelligence.* In this investigation of a destitute orphanage, Hunt (1982) found that the effect of extreme neglect was severe depression and a general mental and physical passivity (the children became *"glum lumps"*). Their inborn (*native*) intellectual capacity was taking a severe beating (*bludgeoning*) due to the physical and emotional neglect. Hunt's intervention program had dramatic results. This points to the strong influence of environment.

Page 417: Similarly, in the psychological domain, gender similarities vastly outnumber gender differences, but the differences often *capture our attention.* Males and females are alike in many more ways than they are different. Although the similarities overwhelm (*vastly outnumber*) the dissimilarities, we are more intrigued by the dissimilarities (*they capture our attention*).

Page 417: The score differences are *sharpest* at the *extremes.* Although the variability in ability is greater within the two groups, people tend to focus on the between-group male-female differences. The differences in scores between males and females on the SAT test are more noticeable (*sharpest*) at the high and low ends of the distribution (*extremes*) than in the middle. Thus, among the very highest scorers in math, the majority are likely to be male.

Page 418: . . . *computer camps* . . . Because math and science have historically been viewed as male subjects, boys have been encouraged to become involved in special science activities and computer workshops (*computer camps*), whereas girls have been urged to take an interest in English. Today, a greater and greater number of females are involved in math and science, and the male-female difference in scores in these subjects is becoming smaller and smaller (*the gender gap is narrowing*).

Page 420: Differences are not deficits. Individual differences in abilities exist, but need not be seen as deficiencies. Scores on an intelligence test (important but not everything) reflect only one aspect of our total array of capabilities and we should capitalize on the variety of differences whatever their origins. We should view the differences as beneficial and valuable aspects of human adaptability (*differences are not deficits*).

12 :

Motivation

Chapter Overview

Perhaps no topic is more fundamental to psychology than motivation—the study of forces that energize and direct our behavior. Chapter 12 discusses various motivational concepts and looks closely at three motives: hunger, sex, and achievement. Research on hunger points to the interplay between physiological and psychological (internal and external) factors in motivation. Sexual motivation in men and women is triggered less by physiological factors and more by external incentives. Achievement motivation, in particular, demonstrates that a drive-reduction theory is of limited usefulness in explaining human behavior: Although this motivation serves no apparent physiological need, it may be extremely forceful nonetheless.

NOTE: Answer guidelines for all Chapter 12 questions begin on page 347.

Introducing Motivation (p. 423)

> David Myers at times uses idioms that are unfamiliar to some readers. If you do not know the meaning of the following words in the context in which it appears in the text, refer to page 356 for an explanation: *truant officer.*

Introduction Preview

First, skim the introduction. Then read the following objective and, as you read the text, search for the information that will enable you to meet that objective. Answer guidelines are provided on page 347.

1. Define motivation.

Motivational Concepts (pp. 424–427)

> If you do not know the meaning of any of the following words, phrases, or expressions, in the context in which they appear in the text, refer to pages 356–357 for an explanation: *this fad for naming instincts collapsed under its own weight; feedback loops; monkey around.*

Section Preview

First, skim the section, noting headings and boldface items. Then read the following objectives and, as you read the text, search for the information that will enable you to meet each objective. Answer guidelines are provided on page 347.

1. Discuss the three perspectives that have influenced our understanding of motivation.

2. Discuss Maslow's hierarchy of needs.

Stepping Through the Section

After you have read the section, complete the sentences and answer the questions. As you proceed, evaluate your performance by consulting the answers on page 348. Do not continue with the next section until you understand each answer. If you need to, review or reread the section in the textbook before continuing.

1. As a result of Darwin's influence, many behaviors were classified as rigid, unlearned behavior patterns that are characteristic of a species, called _____ .

Discuss why early instinct theory failed as an explanation of human behavior.

2. The idea underlying the theory that _____ predispose species-typical behavior remains popular.

3. According to another view of motivation, organisms may experience a physiological _____ , which creates a state of arousal, or _____ .

4. The aim of drive reduction is to maintain a constant internal state, called _____ . Behavior is often not so much pushed by our drives as it is pulled by _____ in the environment.

5 Rather than reduce a physiological need, some motivated behaviors actually _____ arousal. This demonstrates that human motives _____

(do/do not) always satisfy some biological need.

6. Starting from the idea that some needs take precedence over others, Maslow constructed a _____ of needs.

7. According to Maslow, the _____ needs are the most pressing, whereas the highest-order needs relate to _____ . A criticism of Maslow's theory is that the sequence is _____ and not _____ experienced.

8. Surveys of life satisfaction reveal that _____ satisfaction is strongly predictive of subjective well-being in poorer nations, whereas _____-_____ satisfaction matters more in wealthy nations and _____ in individualist nations.

Hunger (pp. 427–434)

> If you do not know the meaning of any of the following words, phrases, or expressions in the context in which they appear in the text, refer to page 357 for an explanation: *feasted their eyes on delectable forbidden foods; keeping tabs; miser; munching . . . M&Ms; steak . . . crackling; binge-purge.*

Section Preview

Answer guidelines are provided on page 348.

1. Discuss the basis of hunger in terms of physiology and external incentives and explain how taste preferences are determined.

2. Describe the symptoms and possible causes of anorexia nervosa and bulimia nervosa.

Stepping Through the Section

Answers are provided on page 348.

1. Ancel Keys observed that men became preoccupied with thoughts of food when they underwent _____ .

2. Cannon and Washburn's experiment using a balloon indicated that there is an association between hunger and _____ _____ .

3. When an animal has had its stomach removed, hunger _____ (does/does not) continue.

4. Increases in the hormone _____ diminish blood _____ , partly by converting it to stored fat, which causes hunger to _____ .

5. The brain area that plays a role in hunger and other bodily maintenance functions is the _____ . Animals will begin eating when the _____ _____ is electrically stimulated. When this region is destroyed, hunger _____ (increases/decreases). Animals will stop eating when the _____ _____ is stimulated. When this area is destroyed, animals _____ (overeat/undereat). Human patients with tumors in the _____ will eat excessively and become fat. Feedback from this area of the brain is sent to the _____ _____ , which decide behavior.

6. To estimate body fat, the hypothalamus monitors levels of the protein _____ . When levels of this protein rise in mice, eating _____ (increases/decreases) and activity _____ (increases/decreases).

7. The weight level at which an individual's body is programmed to stay is referred to as the body's _____ _____ . A person whose weight goes beyond this level will tend to feel _____ (more/less) hungry than usual and expend _____ (more/less) energy.

8. The rate of energy expenditure in maintaining basic functions when the body is at rest is the _____ _____ rate. When food intake is reduced, the body compensates by _____ (raising/lowering) this rate.

9. The concept of a precise body set point that drives hunger _____ (is accepted/is not accepted) by all researchers.

10. Some researchers believe that set point can be altered by _____ _____ . In support of this idea is evidence that when people and other animals are given unlimited access to tasty foods, they tend to _____ and _____ _____ .

11. Research with amnesia patients indicates that part of knowing when to eat is our _____ of our last meal.

12. Rodin refers to people whose eating is more affected by food stimuli than by internal cues as _____ . Rodin found that such individuals showed a particularly marked increase in blood _____ level when confronted with the sight, smell, and sound of a steak being grilled.

13. Carbohydrates boost levels of the neurotransmitter _____ , which _____ (calms/arouses) the body.

14. Taste preferences for sweet and salty are _____ (genetic/learned). Other influences on taste include _____ and _____ .

15. Eating disorders are perhaps the best example of the influence of _____ factors on eating behavior.

16. The disorder in which a person becomes significantly underweight and yet feels fat is known as _____ _____ . In terms of sex and age, this disorder tends to develop in _____ who are in their _____ .

17. A more common disorder is

    _____ _____ ,

    which is characterized by repeated

    _____-_____

    episodes and by feelings of depression or anxiety.

18. The families of bulimia patients have a high inci-

    dence of _____ ,

    _____ , and _____ .

    The families of anorexia patients tend to be

    _____ , _____-

    _____ , and _____ .

    Eating disorders _____ (pro-

    vide/do not provide) a telltale sign of childhood

    sexual abuse.

19. Genetic factors _____ (may/do

    not) influence susceptibility to eating disorders.

    People with eating disorders may also have

    abnormal supplies of certain

    _____ that put them at risk for

    _____ or _____ .

20. A female whose _____ body

    weight is well above her _____

    weight is especially vulnerable to eating

    disorders.

21. Vulnerability to eating disorders

    _____ (increases/does not

    increase) with greater body dissatisfaction.

22. Fallon and Rozin found a discrepancy between

    _____ (men's/women's) ideal

    body weight and the weight actually preferred by

    members of the opposite sex.

23. Stice and Shaw found that when young women

    were shown pictures of unnaturally thin models,

    they felt more and _____ ,

    _____ , and

    _____ with their own bodies.

24. Women with low _____ are

    especially vulnerable to eating disorders.

25. Women students in _____ rate

    their actual shape as closer to the cultural ideal.

    In _____ cultures, however, the

    rise in eating disorders has coincided with an

increasing number of women having a poor

_____ _____ .

Sexual Motivation (pp. 435–447)

> If you do not know the meaning of any of the following words, phrases, or expressions in the context in which they appear in the text, refer to pages 357–358 for an explanation: *rapid-fire questions; faithful attractions . . . fatal attractions; shift it into high gear; the pendulum of sexual values has swung; fired; neither willfully chosen nor willfully changed; swung the pendulum toward; double-edged sword.*

Section Preview

Answer guidelines are provided on page 349.

1. Discuss whether survey research has contributed to our understanding of sexual behavior, and describe the human sexual response cycle.

2. Discuss the basis of sexual motivation in terms of both internal physiology and external incentives.

3. (Close-Up) Identify some common sexual disorders and their possible treatment.

4. Discuss cultural and historical variations in adolescent sexuality, and identify several factors that contribute to the high rate of unprotected sex.

5. Describe research findings on the nature of sexual orientation.

6. Discuss the origins of homosexuality, including both myths and recent research findings.

7. Discuss the place of values in research and education about sexual behavior.

Stepping Through the Section

Answers are provided on page 350.

1. In the 1940s and 1950s, a biologist named _____ surveyed the sexual practices of thousands of men and women. One of his major findings was that there _____ (was/was not) great diversity in "normal" sexual behavior.

2. Many popular sexual surveys cannot be taken seriously because they are based on _____ samples of respondents. Recent surveys indicate that marital infidelity is _____ (more/less) common than indicated by earlier surveys.

3. The two researchers who identified a four-stage sexual response cycle are _____ and _____ . In order, the stages of the cycle are the _____ phase, the _____ phase, _____ , and the _____ phase.

4. During resolution, males experience a _____ _____ , during which they are incapable of another orgasm.

5. In most mammals, females are sexually receptive only during ovulation, when the hormone _____ has peaked.

6. The importance of the hormone _____ to male sexual arousal is confirmed by the fact that sexual interest declines in animals if their _____ are removed. In women, low levels of the hormone _____ may cause a waning of sexual interest.

7. Normal hormonal fluctuations in humans have _____ (little/significant) effect on sexual motivation. In later life, frequency of intercourse _____ (increases/ decreases) as sex hormone levels _____ (increase/decline).

8. The region of the brain through which hormones help trigger sexual arousal is the _____ .

9. Studies by Heiman have shown that erotic stimuli _____ (are/are not) as arousing for women as for men.

Explain some of the possible harmful consequences of sexually explicit material.

_____ _____ .

State five factors that contribute to the high rate of unprotected sex among teenagers.

10. The importance of the brain in sexual motivation is indicated by the fact that people who, because of injury, have no genital sensation _____ (do/do not) feel sexual desire.

11. Most women and men _____ (have/ do not have) sexual fantasies. Compared to women's fantasies, men' sexual fantasies are more _____

_____ .

Sexual fantasies do not indicate sexual _____ or _____ .

12. (Close-Up) Problems that consistently impair sexual functioning are called _____

_____ . Examples of such problems include _____

_____ , _____ ,

and _____ _____ .

Personality disorders _____ (have/have not) been linked with most of the problems impairing sexual functioning, and so the usual psychotherapeutic methods _____ (are/are not) effective.

13. Attitudes toward premarital sex vary widely from one _____ to another and with the passage of _____ .

Rates of teen intercourse in the United States and _____ _____

are much higher than those in _____ and _____ countries.

14. Approximately one-third of sexually active male teens use condoms consistently. This has led to an increase in adolescent _____ and rates of _____

15. A person's sexual attraction toward members of a particular gender is referred to as

_____ _____ .

16. Historically, _____ (all/a slight majority) of the world's cultures have been predominantly heterosexual. Most homosexuals begin thinking of themselves as gay or lesbian around age _____ .

17. Studies in Europe and the United States indicate that approximately _____ percent of men and _____ percent of women are exclusively homosexual. This finding suggests that popular estimates of the rate of homosexuality are _____ (high/low/accurate).

18. A person's sexual orientation _____ (does/does not) appear to be voluntarily chosen.

19. Childhood events and family relationships _____ (are/are not) important factors in determining a person's sexual orientation.

20. Homosexuality _____ (does/does not) involve a fear of the other gender that leads people to direct their sexual desires toward members of their own gender.

21. Sex hormone levels _____ (do/do not) predict sexual orientation.

22. As children, most homosexuals _____ (were/were not) sexually victimized.

23. The sons of homosexual fathers _____ (are/are not) more likely to become gay if they live with their fathers.

24. Homosexual people appear more often in certain populations, including men who live in

_____ _____ ;

_____ , _____ ,

_____ , and _____ ;

and men who have older _____ .

25. One theory proposes that people develop a homosexual orientation if they are segregated with _____ (their own/the other) gender at the time their sex drive matures. The fact that early homosexual behavior _____ (does/does not) make people homosexual _____ (supports/conflicts with) this theory.

26. Researcher Simon LeVay discovered a cluster of cells in the _____ that is larger in _____ men than in all others. Other studies have found a section of fibers connecting the brain's _____ and

_____ _____ that is larger in homosexual men than in heterosexual men.

27. Studies of twins suggest that genes probably _____ (do/do not) play a role in homosexuality.

28. In animals and some rare human cases, sexual orientation has been altered by abnormal _____ conditions during prenatal development. In humans, prenatal exposure to hormone levels typical of _____ , particularly between _____ and _____ months after conception, may predispose an attraction to males.

29. Gay males and lesbians may have certain physical traits more typical of those of the other gender, including _____ patterns and anatomical traits of the _____ within the hearing system.

30. Most psychiatrists now believe that _____ (nature/nurture) plays the larger role in predisposing sexual orientation. Those who believe that sexual orientation is determined by _____ express more accepting attitudes toward homosexual persons.

The Need to Belong (pp. 448–449)

> If you do not know the meaning of any of the following words, phrases, or expressions in the context in which they appear in the text, refer to page 358 for an explanation: *colors our thoughts and emotions; to be shunned—given the cold shoulder . . . .*

Section Preview

Answer guidelines are provided on page 350.

1. Discuss the significance of the need to belong, including its origins and benefits.

Stepping Through the Section

Answers are provided on page 350.

1. From an evolutionary standpoint, social bonds in humans boosted our ancestors' _____ rates. If those who felt this need to _____ survived and reproduced more successfully, their _____ would in time predominate.

2. When asked what makes life meaningful, most people mention _____

_____ .

3. Feeling accepted and loved by others boosts our

_____ .

4. Much of our _____ behavior aims to increase our belonging. For most people, familiarity leads to _____ (liking/disliking).

5. People who perceive strong social support from others live with better _____ than those who lack social support. They also have a lower risk of _____ disorder and premature _____ .

Achievement Motivation (pp. 450–456)

> If you do not know the meaning of any of the following words, phrases, or expressions in the context in which they appear in the text, refer to page 359 for an explanation: *daredevils ... thrills; ring toss game; superstar achievers; teaspoon of inspiration with a gallon of perspiration; avoid snuffing out ... controlling extrinsic rewards; Different strokes for different folks; "great person" ... share certain traits; exude a self-confident "charisma."*

Section Preview

Answer guidelines are provided on page 351.

1. Describe the nature and origin of achievement motivation.

2. Distinguish between extrinsic and intrinsic motivation, focusing on their relative effectiveness in promoting achievement motivation.

3. Discuss how managers can create a motivated, productive, and satisfied work force.

Stepping Through the Section

Answers are provided on page 351.

1. The biological perspective on motivation is contradicted by the existence of many behaviors that appear to satisfy no apparent biological

_____ . An example is the desire for significant accomplishments, mastering skills, and attaining a high standard—which psychologists refer to as _____

_____ .

2. Psychologists Murray, McClelland, and Atkinson studied achievement motivation by having people create _____ about ambiguous pictures.

3. In experiments, individuals who chose extremely difficult tasks tended to have a _____ (low/high) need for achievement.

4. The parents of highly motivated children tend to encourage their _____ and _____ and _____ them for the successes.

5. Achievement motivation has both _____ roots and _____ roots.

6. Motivation to perform a behavior for its own sake is referred to as _____ _____ . Motivation based on external rewards and punishments is called _____ _____ . Of the two, _____ _____ appears to be more successful in fueling achievement.

7. Excessive external pressures and incentives can undermine _____ motivation.

8. People who are intrinsically religious tend to score lower on tests of _____ and _____ ; they also tend to live with a greater sense of _____ over their lives.

9. The field of _____ / _____ psychology studies how managers might best motivate employees.

10. Studies have shown that rewards lower intrinsic motivation when they are used to _____ but raise it when they are used to _____ . Studies of schoolchildren show that intrinsic motivation is enhanced when teachers praise _____ more than _____ .

11. Managers who are directive, set clear standards, organize work, and focus attention on specific goals are said to employ _____ . More democratic managers who aim to build teamwork and mediate conflicts in the work force employ

_____ _____ .

12. In experiments, women tended to excel at _____ leadership, whereas men tended to excel at _____ leadership.

Give several pieces of advice offered in the text to managers who wish to motivate employees.

13. The most effective style of leadership _____ (varies/does not vary) with the situation and/or the person.

14. Effective managers _____ (rarely/often) exhibit a high degree of both task and social leadership.

15. McGregor refers to managers who assume that workers are basically lazy and motivated only by money as _____ managers. Managers who assume that people are intrinsically motivated in their work are referred to as _____ managers.

Progress Test 1

Multiple-Choice Questions

Circle your answers to the following questions and check them with the answers on page 351. If your answer is incorrect, read the explanation for why it is incorrect and then consult the appropriate pages of the text (in parentheses following the correct answer).

1. Motivation is best understood as a state that:
   a. reduces a drive.
   b. aims at satisfying a biological need.
   c. energizes an organism to act.
   d. energizes and directs behavior.

2. Which of the following is a difference between a drive and a need?
   a. Needs are learned; drives are inherited.
   b. Needs are physiological states; drives are psychological states.
   c. Drives are generally stronger than needs.
   d. Needs are generally stronger than drives.

3. One problem with the idea of motivation as drive reduction is that:
   a. because some motivated behaviors do not seem to be based on physiological needs, they cannot be explained in terms of drive reduction.
   b. it fails to explain any human motivation.
   c. it cannot account for homeostasis.
   d. it does not explain the hunger drive.

4. Recent evidence makes a preliminary link between homosexuality and:
   a. late sexual maturation.
   b. the age of an individual's first erotic experience.
   c. atypical prenatal hormones.
   d. early problems in relationships with parents.
   e. all of the above.

5. Increases in insulin will:
   a. lower blood sugar and trigger hunger.
   b. raise blood sugar and trigger hunger.
   c. lower blood sugar and trigger satiety.
   d. raise blood sugar and trigger satiety.

6. Electrical stimulation of the lateral hypothalamus will cause an animal to:
   a. begin eating.
   b. stop eating.
   c. become obese.
   d. begin copulating.
   e. stop copulating.

7. The text suggests that a "neophobia" for unfamiliar tastes:
   a. is more common in children than in adults.
   b. protected our ancestors from potentially toxic substances.
   c. may be an early warning sign of an eating disorder.
   d. only grows stronger with repeated exposure to those tastes.
   e. does all of the above.

8. Rodin found that, in response to the sight and smell of a steak being grilled:
   a. overweight people had a greater insulin response than people of normal weight.
   b. people of normal weight had a greater insulin response than overweight people.
   c. externals had a greater insulin response than internals.
   d. internals had a greater insulin response than externals.

9. Instinct theory and drive-reduction theory both emphasize _____ factors in motivation.
   a. environmental   d. social
   b. cognitive   e. biological
   c. psychological

10. The correct order of the stages of Masters and Johnson's sexual response cycle is:
    a. plateau; excitement; orgasm; resolution.
    b. excitement; plateau; orgasm; resolution.
    c. excitement; orgasm; resolution; refractory.
    d. plateau; excitement; orgasm; refractory.
    e. excitement; orgasm; plateau; resolution.

11. Few human behaviors are sufficiently automatic to qualify as:
    a. needs.   c. instincts.
    b. drives.   d. incentives.

12. Theory _____ managers tend to adopt a style of _____ leadership.
    a. X; task   c. Y; autocratic
    b. X; social   d. Y; directive

13. In his study of men on a semistarvation diet, Keys found that:
    a. the metabolic rate of the subjects increased.
    b. the subjects eventually lost interest in food.
    c. the subjects became obsessed with food.
    d. the subjects' behavior directly contradicted predictions made by Maslow's hierarchy of needs.

14. When asked what makes life meaningful, most people first mention:
    a. good health.
    b. challenging work.
    c. satisfying relationships.
    d. serving others.

15. Bulimia nervosa involves:
    a. binging.   d. a. and b.
    b. purging.   e. a., b., and c.
    c. dramatic weight loss.

16. Castration of male rats results in:
    a. reduced testosterone and sexual interest.
    b. reduced testosterone, but no change in sexual interest.
    c. reduced estrogen and sexual interest.
    d. reduced estrogen, but no change in sexual interest.

17. (Close-Up) Which of the following has been found to be most effective in treating sexual disorders?
    a. psychoanalysis.
    b. cognitive therapy.
    c. drug therapy.
    d. behavior therapy.

18. It has been said that the body's major sex organ is the brain. With regard to sex education:
    a. transmission of value-free information about the wide range of sexual behaviors should be the primary focus of the educator.
    b. transmission of technical knowledge about the biological act should be the classroom focus, free from the personal values and attitudes of researchers, teachers, and students.
    c. the home, not the school, should be the focus of all instruction about reproductive behavior.
    d. people's attitudes, values, and morals cannot be separated from the biological aspects of sexuality.

19. Kinsey's studies of sexual behavior showed that:
    a. males enjoy sex more than females.
    b. females enjoy sex more than males.
    c. premarital sex is less common than is popularly believed.
    d. sexual behavior is enormously varied.

20. To increase employee productivity, industrial/organizational psychologists advise managers to:
    a. adopt a directive leadership style.
    b. adopt a democratic leadership style.
    c. instill competitiveness in each employee.
    d. deal with employees according to their individual motives.

Matching Items

Match each term with its definition or description.

Terms

_____ 1. intrinsic motivation
_____ 2. set point
_____ 3. drive
_____ 4. orgasmic disorder
_____ 5. extrinsic motivation
_____ 6. estrogen
_____ 7. homeostasis
_____ 8. sexual orientation
_____ 9. need
_____ 10. incentive
_____ 11. impotence

Definitions or Descriptions

a. a hormone secreted more by females than by males
b. the body's tendency to maintain a balanced internal state
c. an environmental stimulus that motivates behavior
d. a person's attraction to members of a particular sex
e. the motivation to perform a behavior for its own sake
f. a desire to perform a behavior due to promised rewards
g. an inability to have or maintain an erection
h. an inability to experience orgasm
i. an aroused state arising from some physiological need
j. a state of deprivation
k. the body's weight-maintenance setting

Progress Test 2

Progress Test 2 should be completed during a final chapter review. Answer the following questions after you thoroughly understand the correct answers for the section reviews and Progress Test 1.

Multiple-Choice Questions

1. Obese mice eat less, become more active, and lose weight after they have been injected with:
   a. insulin.
   b. glucose.
   c. leptin.
   d. estrogen
   e. testosterone.

2. Homeostasis refers to:
   a. the tendency to maintain a steady internal state.
   b. the tendency to seek external incentives for behavior.
   c. the setting of the body's "weight thermostat."
   d. a theory of the development of sexual orientation.

3. Which of the following tends to foster a high need for achievement?
   a. the frequent use of extrinsic controls on behavior
   b. encouraging young children to remain dependent
   c. the use of punishment for failures
   d. giving rewards that provide feedback

4. Of the following parts of the world, teen intercourse rates are highest in:
   a. Western Europe
   b. Canada.
   c. The United States.
   d. Asia.
   e. Arab countries.

5. Although the cause of eating disorders is still unknown, explanations that have been proposed focus on all of the following *except*:
   a. metabolic factors.
   b. genetic factors.
   c. family background factors.
   d. cultural factors.

6. The brain area that when stimulated suppresses eating is the:
   a. lateral hypothalamus.
   b. ventromedial hypothalamus.
   c. lateral thalamus.
   d. ventromedial thalamus.

7. Exposure of a fetus to the hormones typical of females between _____ and _____ months after conception may predispose the developing human to become attracted to males.

   a. 1; 3
   b. 2; 5
   c. 4; 7
   d. 6; 9
   e. 9; 11

8. Which of the following statements concerning homosexuality is true?

   a. Homosexuals have abnormal hormone levels.
   b. As children, most homosexuals were molested by an adult homosexual.
   c. Homosexuals had a domineering opposite-sex parent.
   d. New research indicates that sexual orientation may be at least partly physiological.

9. Investigations of how men and women view body image found that:

   a. men and women alike expressed significant self-dissatisfaction.
   b. men and women alike accurately assessed the body weight for their own sex that the other sex preferred.
   c. men tended to rate their current weight as corresponding both to their ideal weight and to women's ideal weight for men.
   d. women tended to be satisfied with their current body weight but to think that men preferred a thinner body shape for women.

10. According to Maslow's theory:

    a. the most basic motives are based on physiological needs.
    b. needs are satisfied in a specified order.
    c. the highest motives relate to self-actualization.
    d. all of the above are true.

11. Which of the following is *inconsistent* with the drive-reduction theory of motivation?

    a. When body temperature drops below 98.6° Fahrenheit, blood vessels constrict to conserve warmth.
    b. A person is driven to seek a drink when his or her cellular water level drops below its optimum point.
    c. Monkeys will work puzzles even if not given a food reward.
    d. A person becomes hungry when body weight falls below its biological set point.
    e. None of the above is inconsistent.

12. Which of the following is true concerning eating disorders?

    a. Genetic factors may influence susceptibility.
    b. Abnormal levels of certain neurotransmitters may play a role.
    c. People with eating disorders are at risk for anxiety or depression.
    d. Family background is a significant factor.
    e. All of the above are true.

13. Sexual orientation refers to:

    a. a person's tendency to display behaviors typical of males or females.
    b. a person's sense of identity as a male or female.
    c. a person's enduring sexual attraction toward members of a particular gender.
    d. all of the above.

14. Which of the following is *not* an aspect of Murray's definition of achievement motivation?

    a. the desire to master skills
    b. the desire for control
    c. the desire to gain approval
    d. the desire to attain a high standard

15. The power of external stimuli in sexual motivation is illustrated in Julia Heiman's experiment, in which subjects' responses to various romantic, erotic, or neutral audio tapes were recorded. Which of the following was among the findings of her research?

    a. The women were more aroused by the romantic tape; the men were more aroused by the sexually explicit tape.
    b. The sexually experienced subjects reported greater arousal when the tape depicted a sexual encounter in which a woman is overpowered by a man and enjoys being dominated.
    c. Whereas the men's physical arousal was both obvious and consistent with their verbal reports, the women's verbal reports did not correspond very directly with their measured physical arousal.
    d. Both men and women were aroused most by the sexually explicit tape.

16. According to Masters and Johnson, the sexual response of males is most likely to differ from that of females during:

    a. the excitement phase.
    b. the plateau phase.
    c. orgasm.
    d. the resolution phase.

17. In animals, destruction of the lateral hypothalamus results in _____ , whereas destruction of the ventromedial hypothalamus results in _____ .
    a. overeating; loss of hunger
    b. loss of hunger; overeating
    c. an elevated set point; a lowered set point
    d. increased thirst; loss of thirst
    e. increased metabolic rate; weight loss

18. Why do people with a high need for achievement prefer tasks of moderate difficulty?
    a. They are afraid of failing at more difficult tasks.
    b. They want to avoid the embarrassment of failing at easy tasks.
    c. Moderately difficult tasks present an attainable goal in which success is attributable to their own skill.
    d. They have high extrinsic motivation.

19. Beginning with the most basic needs, which of the following represents the correct sequence of needs in the hierarchy described by Maslow?
    a. safety; physiological; esteem; belongingness and love; self-fulfillment
    b. safety; physiological; belongingness and love; esteem; self-fulfillment
    c. physiological; safety; esteem; belongingness and love; self-fulfillment
    d. physiological; safety; belongingness and love; esteem; self-fulfillment
    e. physiological; safety; self-fulfillment; esteem; belongingness and love

20. Which of the following is currently true regarding first-year college students' opinions of casual sex?
    a. The majority feel that sex between persons who know each other for only a short time is acceptable.
    b. The majority feel that condom use is unnecessary, because they know when the safe times are.
    c. The majority feel that sex between persons who know each other for only a short time is unacceptable.
    d. The majority feel that they will be ostracized by their peers if they don't do "what everyone else is doing."

True-False Items

Indicate whether each statement is true or false by placing *T* or *F* in the blank next to the item.

_____ 1. When body weight rises above set point, hunger increases.

_____ 2. According to Masters and Johnson, only males experience a plateau period in the cycle of sexual arousal.

_____ 3. Testosterone affects the sexual arousal of the male only.

_____ 4. Unlike men, women tend not to be aroused by sexually explicit material.

_____ 5. All taste preferences are conditioned.

_____ 6. Married people are less at risk for depression than are unattached people.

_____ 7. An increase in insulin increases blood glucose levels and triggers hunger.

_____ 8. Most types of sexual disorder are associated with personality disorders.

_____ 9. Intrinsic motivation fuels achievement more than does extrinsic motivation.

_____ 10. One's sexual orientation is not voluntarily chosen.

Thinking Critically About Chapter 12

Answer these questions the day before an exam as a final check on your understanding of the chapter's terms and concepts.

Multiple-Choice Questions

1. Because Brent believes that his employees are intrinsically motivated to work for reasons beyond money, Brent would be described as a(n) _____ manager.
    a. directive
    b. autocratic
    c. theory X
    d. theory Y

2. Execuvac Company subscribes to _____ idea that employees are happier and more productive if they are _____ .
    a. McGregor's; given simple tasks and monitored closely
    b. Maslow's; paid enough to fulfill basic needs for food and shelter
    c. Lewin's; allowed to participate in managerial decision making
    d. Keys's; allowed to set their own work hours

3. Mary loves hang-gliding. It would be most difficult to explain Mary's behavior according to:
   a. incentives.
   b. achievement motivation.
   c. drive-reduction theory.
   d. Maslow's hierarchy of needs.

4. For two weeks, Orlando has been on a hunger strike in order to protest his country's involvement in what he perceives as an immoral war. Orlando's willingness to starve himself in order to make a political statement conflicts with the theory of motivation advanced by:
   a. Kinsey.   d. Masters and Johnson.
   b. Murray.   e. Maslow.
   c. Keys.

5. Kathy has been undergoing treatment for bulimia. There is an above-average probability that one or more members of Kathy's family are:
   a. high-achieving.   c. alcoholic.
   b. overprotective.   d. all of the above.

6. Which of the following was not identified as a contributing factor in the high rate of unprotected sex among adolescents?
   a. alcohol use
   b. mass media sexual norms
   c. guilt related to sexual activity
   d. ignorance
   e. thrill-seeking

7. One shortcoming of the instinct theory of motivation is that it:
   a. places too much emphasis on environmental factors.
   b. focuses only on cognitive aspects of motivation.
   c. applies only to animal behavior.
   d. does not explain human behaviors; it simply names them.

8. Which of the following is not typical of both anorexia and bulimia?
   a. far more frequent occurrence in women than in men
   b. preoccupation with food and fear of being overweight
   c. weight significantly and noticeably outside normal ranges
   d. low self-esteem and feelings of depression

9. Which of the following is not an example of homeostasis?
   a. perspiring in order to restore normal body temperature
   b. feeling hungry and eating to restore the level of blood glucose to normal
   c. feeling hungry at the sight of an appetizing food
   d. All of the above are examples of homeostasis.

10. Two rats have escaped from their cages in the neurophysiology lab. The technician needs your help in returning them to their proper cages. One rat is grossly overweight; the other is severely underweight. You confidently state that the overweight rat goes in the "_____-lesion" cage, while the underweight rat goes in the "_____-lesion" cage.
    a. hippocampus; amygdala
    b. amygdala; hippocampus
    c. lateral hypothalamus; ventromedial hypothalamus
    d. ventromedial hypothalamus; lateral hypothalamus

11. Two students are shown the same picture of a diver standing at the edge of a diving board. They each write a story describing what they see. One says the diver is concentrating on making a successful dive that will qualify her for her country's Olympic team. The other student sees the diver as balking from the intense pressure and training required to be a competitive diver. The two students probably differ in their:
    a. intrinsic motivation.
    b. extrinsic motivation.
    c. need for achievement.
    d. self-actualization.

12. Ali's parents have tried hard to minimize their son's exposure to sweet, fattening foods. If Ali has the occasion to taste sweet foods in the future, which of the following is likely?
    a. He will have a strong aversion to such foods.
    b. He will have a neutral reaction to sweet foods.
    c. He will display a preference for sweet tastes.
    d. It is impossible to predict Ali's reaction.

13. Darren, a sales clerk at a tire store, enjoys his job, not so much for the money as for its challenge and the opportunity to interact with a variety of people. The store manager asks you to recommend a strategy for increasing Darren's motivation. Which of the following is most likely to be effective?

 a. Create a competition among the salespeople so that whoever has the highest sales each week receives a bonus.

 b. Put Darren on a week-by-week employment contract, promising him continued employment only if his sales increase each week.

 c. Leave Darren alone unless his sales drop and then threaten to fire him if his performance doesn't improve.

 d. Involve Darren as much as possible in company decision making and use rewards to inform him of his successful performance.

14. Summarizing her report on the need to belong, Rolanda states that:

 a. "Cooperation amongst our ancestors was uncommon."

 b. "Social bonding is not in our nature; it is a learned human trait."

 c. "Because bonding with others increased our ancestors' success at reproduction and survival, it became part of our biological nature."

 d. both a. and b. are true.

15. Of the following individuals, who might be most prone to developing an eating disorder?

 a. Jason, an adolescent boy who is somewhat overweight and is unpopular with his peers

 b. Jennifer, a teenage girl who has a poor self-image and a fear of not being able to live up to her parents' high standards

 c. Susan, a 35-year-old woman who is a "workaholic" and devotes most of her energies to her high-pressured career

 d. Bill, a 40-year-old man who has had problems with alcoholism and is seriously depressed after losing his job of 20 years

16. Lucille has been sticking to a strict diet but can't seem to lose weight. What is the most likely explanation for her difficulty?

 a. Her body has a very low set point.

 b. Her prediet weight was near her body's set point.

 c. Her weight problem is actually caused by an underlying eating disorder.

 d. Lucille is an "external."

17. Randy, who has been under a lot of stress lately, has intense cravings for sugary junk foods, which tend to make him feel more relaxed. Which of the following is the most likely explanation for his craving?

 a. Randy feels that he deserves to pamper himself with sweets because of the stress he is under.

 b. The extra sugar gives Randy the energy he needs to cope with the demands of daily life.

 c. Carbohydrates boost levels of serotonin, which has a calming effect.

 d. The extra sugar tends to lower blood insulin level, which promotes relaxation.

18. A course that Janice wants very much to take is being offered by three instructors. Janice chooses the instructor with a reputation for being moderately difficult over one perceived as impossibly difficult and another viewed as very easy. It is most likely that Janice's choice reflects her having a(n):

 a. optimum level of arousal.

 b. low need for achievement.

 c. high need for achievement.

 d. high level of extrinsic motivation.

19. Nancy decided to take introductory psychology because she has always been interested in human behavior. Jack enrolled in the same course because he thought it would be easy. Nancy's behavior was motivated by _____ , Jack's by _____ .

 a. extrinsic motivation; intrinsic motivation

 b. intrinsic motivation; extrinsic motivation

 c. drives; incentives

 d. incentives; drives

20. For as long as she has been the plant manager, Juanita has welcomed input from employees and has delegated authority. Bill, in managing his department, takes a more authoritarian, iron-fisted approach. Juanita's style is one of _____ leadership, whereas Bill's is one of _____ leadership.

 a. task; social

 b. social; task

 c. directive; democratic

 d. democratic; participative

Essay Question

Differentiate the three major theories of motivation, discuss their origins, and explain why they cannot fully account for human behavior. (Use the space below to list the points you want to make and organize them. Then write the essay on a separate sheet of paper.)

Key Terms

Writing Definitions

Using your own words, write on a separate piece of paper a brief definition or explanation of each of the following terms.

1. motivation
2. instinct
3. drive-reduction theory
4. homeostasis
5. incentives
6. hierarchy of needs
7. glucose
8. set point
9. basal metabolic rate
10. anorexia nervosa
11. bulimia nervosa
12. sexual response cycle
13. refractory period
14. estrogen
15. sexual disorder
16. sexual orientation
17. achievement motivation
18. intrinsic motivation
19. extrinsic motivation
20. industrial/organizational psychology
21. task leadership
22. social leadership
23. theory X
24. theory Y

Cross-Check

As you learned in the Introduction, reviewing and overlearning of material are important to the learning process. After you have written the definitions of the key terms in this chapter, you should complete the crossword puzzle to ensure that you can reverse the process—recognize the term, given the definition.

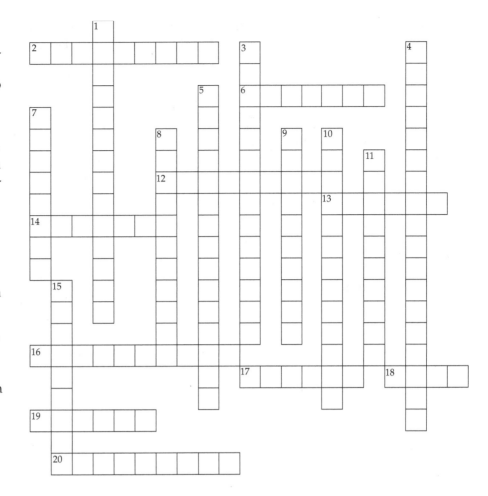

ACROSS

2. Type of motivation that reflects the desire to perform a behavior for its own sake.
6. Region of the hypothalamus that, when electrically stimulated, causes an animal to eat.
12. In Maslow's theory, human needs are organized into a
_____ .
13. In Maslow's theory, the needs that follow physiological needs in order of priority.
14. Major energy source for the body.
16. Final stage of the sexual response cycle.
17. Group-oriented leadership.
18. Goal-oriented leadership.
19. Early researcher on sexual behavior patterns.
20. Type of motivation that reflects the desire to perform a behavior in order to obtain a reward or avoid a punishment.

DOWN

1. Theory that explains behavior as arising from physiological needs and the states of tension they create.
3. Eating disorder characterized by repeated "binge-purge" episodes.
4. The body's rate of energy expenditure at rest.
5. Eating disorder in which a person restricts food intake to become significantly underweight and yet still feels fat.
7. Sex hormone secreted in greater amount by females than by males.
8. Type of motivation that reflects the degree to which a person is motivated by a desire for significant accomplishment.

9. Initial stage of the sexual response cycle.
10. In Maslow's theory, the most basic types of needs.
11. The resting period after orgasm, during which a male cannot be aroused to another orgasm.
15. A positive or negative stimulus that motivates behavior.

Answers

Introduction

Section Preview

1. Motivation is a need or desire that energizes behavior and directs it toward a goal.

Motivational Concepts

Section Preview

1. The earliest theory classified motivated behavior as instinctive and unlearned; more recently, the evolutionary perspective contends that genes predispose species-typical behavior. Drive-reduction theory argues that a physiological need—not nec-

essarily an instinct—creates a psychological state. People are not only pushed by the need to reduce drives but also pulled by incentives. Arousal theory emphasizes the urge for an optimum level of stimulation.

2. Maslow's hierarchy of needs expresses the idea that some needs are more fundamental than others. Maslow proposed that physiological needs, such as for food, water, and shelter, are the most basic and must be met before we are motivated to meet "higher" needs for safety, belongingness and love, self-esteem, and self-actualization. Critics of Maslow's theory contend that the proposed sequence of needs is arbitrary and not universally fixed.

Stepping Through the Section

1. instincts

According to instinct theory, any human behavior could be regarded as an instinct. The only evidence for each such "instinct" was the behavior used to identify it. Thus, instinct theory offered only circular explanations; it labeled behaviors but did not explain them.

2. genes

3. need; drive

4. homeostasis; incentives

5. increase; do not

6. hierarchy

7. physiological; self-actualization; arbitrary; universally

8. financial; home-life; self-esteem

Hunger

Section Preview

1. Although stomach pangs correlate with feelings of hunger, they are not the only source. Hunger also increases when increases in insulin diminish the secretion of glucose into the bloodstream. Blood chemistry is monitored by the lateral and ventromedial areas of the hypothalamus, which therefore control body weight. The hypothalamus also monitors levels of the hormone leptin to estimate body fat. Animal research shows that when the LH is electrically stimulated, hunger increases; when the LH is destroyed, hunger decreases. Stimulation of the VMH depresses hunger, while its destruction will increase hunger and trigger rapid weight gain. The body also adjusts its basal metabolic rate to maintain its weight set point.

Our preferences for sweet and salty tastes are

genetic and universal. Culture and learning also affect taste, as when people given highly salted foods or foods common only in certain societies develop preferences for these tastes. Studies by Judith Rodin indicate that, especially in "external" people, the sights and smells of food can increase hunger, in part because these stimuli trigger increases in blood levels of insulin.

2. Anorexia nervosa is a disorder in which a person becomes significantly underweight yet feels fat. The disorder usually develops in adolescent females. Anorexia patients tend to come from high-achieving and protective families.

   Bulimia nervosa is a more common disorder characterized by repeated episodes of overeating followed by vomiting or using a laxative ("binge-purge" episodes). The families of bulimia patients have a higher than usual incidence of alcoholism, obesity, and depression.

   Several factors may contribute to these eating disorders—for example, genetics or the presence of abnormal supplies of certain neurotransmitters may be implicated. Socially, a factor may be the increasingly stringent cultural standards of thinness for women. In addition, studies have demonstrated that, in Western societies such as the United States, women's self-reported ideal weights tend to be lighter than their current weights and that women tend to think that men prefer them to weigh less than the weight men actually prefer. Another indication of the impact of psychological factors is evidence that women with low self-esteem and those with greater body dissatisfaction are especially vulnerable to eating disorders.

Stepping Through the Section

1. semistarvation

2. stomach contractions

3. does

4. insulin; glucose; increase

5. hypothalamus; lateral hypothalamus; decreases; ventromedial hypothalamus; overeat; hypothalamus; frontal lobes

6. leptin; decreases; increases

7. set point; less; more

8. basal metabolic; lowering

9. is not accepted

10. slow, sustained changes in body weight; overeat; gain weight

11. memory

12. externals; insulin

13. serotonin; calms
14. genetic; conditioning; culture
15. psychological
16. anorexia nervosa; females; teens
17. bulimia nervosa; binge-purge
18. alcoholism; obesity; depression; competitive; high-achieving; protective; do not provide
19. may; neurotransmitters; anxiety; depression
20. current; ideal
21. increases
22. women's
23. ashamed; depressed; dissatisfied
24. self-esteem
30. India; Western; body image

Sexual Motivation

Section Preview

1. Biologist Alfred Kinsey interviewed 18,000 men and women in an effort to describe human sexual behavior. Although Kinsey's sample was not random, his statistics showed that sexual behavior is enormously varied. Other sex reports have been prepared, but because they were based on biased samples of people, they cannot be taken seriously. Better information is only now starting to become available.

   Masters and Johnson outlined four stages in the sexual response cycle. During the initial excitement phase, the genital areas become engorged with blood, causing the penis and clitoris to swell and the vagina to expand and secrete lubricant. In the plateau phase, breathing, pulse, and blood pressure rates increase along with sexual excitement. During orgasm, rhythmic genital contractions create a pleasurable feeling of sexual release. During the resolution phase, the body gradually returns to its unaroused state and males enter a refractory period during which they are incapable of another orgasm.

2. Sex hormones direct the development of male and female sex characteristics and (especially in nonhuman animals) they activate sexual behavior. In most mammals, sexual activity coincides with ovulation and peak level of estrogen in the female. Sexual behavior in male animals is directly related to the level of testosterone in their bodies.

   In humans, normal fluctuations in hormone levels have little effect on sex drive once the pubertal surge in sex hormones has occurred. A woman's sexual interest may wane if her testosterone level is low, but this can easily be restored by a replacement drug. In later life, however, for both women and men, the frequency of sexual fantasies and intercourse decreases as sex hormone levels decline.

   External stimuli, such as touch and erotic material, can trigger sexual arousal in both men and women, although sexually explicit materials may lead people to devalue their partners. Our imagination—in dreams and fantasies—can also lead to arousal.

3. (Close-Up) Sexual disorders are problems that consistently impair sexual arousal or functioning, such as premature ejaculation, the inability to have or maintain an erection (impotence), or infrequent orgasms (orgasmic disorder).

   Sexual disorders do not appear to be linked to personality disorders; it is therefore not surprising that traditional psychotherapy is ineffective in treating them. Sexual disorders are most effectively treated by methods that assume that people can learn and therefore modify their sexual responses.

4. Sexual attitudes vary widely from one culture to another, and across time within the same culture. For example, teen intercourse rates are higher in the United States and Western Europe than in Arab and Asian countries, and much higher among American teens today than in the past.

   Increased sexual activity has led to increases in teen pregnancies and sexually transmitted diseases (STDs). Several factors contribute to the alarmingly high rate of unprotected sex among teens, including ignorance about the menstrual cycle, guilt, lack of communication about birth control, alcohol use, and mass media norms of unprotected promiscuity.

5. Sexual orientation is an individual's enduring sexual attraction toward members of a particular sex. Although virtually all cultures in all times have been predominantly heterosexual, studies suggest that 3 or 4 percent of men and 1 or 2 percent of women are exclusively homosexual.

   Most homosexuals report first being aware of same-gender sexual feelings around puberty, but they typically do not think of themselves as gay or lesbian until around age 20. The ostracism homosexuals often face may cause them to struggle with their sexual motivation. Because sexual orientation is neither willfully chosen nor willfully changed, however, homosexual feelings generally persist.

6. There are many myths about the causes of homosexuality, including that it is linked with levels of sex hormones; as a child, being molested or seduced by an adult homosexual; having a domineering mother and an ineffectual father; or fearing or hating members of the opposite sex. Recent evidence suggests genetic influence plays a role, possibly through the inheritance of a particular gene. In animals and some exceptional human cases, sexual orientation has been altered by abnormal prenatal hormone conditions, leading some researchers to suggest that exposure to hormone levels typical of females during a critical period of brain development may predispose the male to become attracted to males.

   The consistency of genetic, prenatal, and brain research findings has caused most psychiatrists to now believe that nature more than nurture predisposes sexual orientation.

7. Most sex educators and researchers aim for objectivity and strive to keep their writings on sexuality value-free. Critics contend that the study of sex cannot, and should not, be free of values. For example, the words we use to describe sexual behavior often reflect our personal values. Second, when sexual information is separated from the context of human values, young people are sent a message that sexual behavior is merely recreational activity. Therefore, sex-related values should be discussed openly, rather than avoided.

Stepping Through the Section

1. Kinsey; was
2. biased; less
3. Masters; Johnson; excitement; plateau; orgasm; resolution
4. refractory period
5. estrogen
6. testosterone; testes; testosterone
7. little; decreases; decline
8. hypothalamus
9. are

Erotic material may increase the viewer's acceptance of the false idea that women enjoy rape, may increase men's willingness to hurt women, and may lead people to devalue their partners and relationships.

10. do
11. have; frequent, physical, and less romantic; problems; dissatisfaction
12. sexual disorders; premature ejaculation; impotence; orgasmic disorder; have not; are not

13. culture; time; Western Europe; Asian; Arab
14. pregnancies; sexually transmitted disease (STD)

Among the factors that contribute to unprotected sex among adolescence are (1) ignorance about the safe and risky times of the menstrual cycle, (2) guilt related to sexual activity, (3) minimal communication about birth control, (4) alcohol use that influences judgment, and (5) mass media norms of unprotected promiscuity.

15. sexual orientation
16. all; 20
17. 3 or 4; 1 or 2; high
18. does not
19. are not
20. does not
21. do not
22. were not
23. are not
24. large cities; poets; writers; musicians; brothers
25. their own; does not; conflicts with
26. hypothalamus; heterosexual; right; left hemispheres
27. do
28. hormone; females; 2; 5
29. fingerprint; cochlea
30. nature; nature

The Need to Belong

Section Preview

1. Humans have a need to feel connected to others in enduring, close relationships. This need boosted our ancestors' success at survival and reproduction. Today, it influences our thoughts, emotions, and much of our social nature. By conforming to group standards and striving to make favorable impressions, we shape our social behavior to increase our social acceptance and inclusion.

   Children and adults who are denied others' acceptance and inclusion become withdrawn and may feel more depression, anxiety, jealousy, and loneliness. Those who have close friends and perceive strong social support live with better health and lower risk of psychological disorder and premature death.

Stepping Through the Section

1. survival; belong; genes

2. close, satisfying relationships with family, friends, or romantic partners

3. self-esteem

4. social; liking

5. health; psychological; death

Achievement Motivation

Section Preview

1. As defined by Henry Murray, achievement motivation is the desire for significant accomplishment, for mastering skills or ideas, for control, and for rapidly attaining a high standard. People with a low need for achievement prefer very easy or very difficult tasks, where failure is either unlikely or unembarrassing. People with a high need for achievement prefer moderately difficult tasks, where success is attainable and attributable to their own effort.

   Children with a high need for achievement often have parents who encourage their independence from an early age and praise them for their successes. Achievement motivation has both emotional and cognitive roots, as children learn to associate achievement with positive emotions and to attribute their achievements to their own competence.

   Analyses of accomplished scientists, writers, musicians, and political leaders confirm that great achievement depends more on hard work and disciplined motivation than on inspiration alone.

2. Intrinsic motivation is the desire to perform a behavior for its own sake. Extrinsic motivation is seeking external rewards and avoiding punishments. Intrinsic motivation promotes high achievement, as does the use of extrinsic rewards that *inform* people of their successes. Extrinsic rewards that are delivered to *control* people's behaviors, however, undermine intrinsic motivation.

3. Effective managers assess workers' motives (accomplishment, recognition, affiliation, power, etc.) and adjust their managerial style accordingly. What workers value also varies from culture to culture. Regardless of the managerial style, setting clear objectives, establishing challenging goals, and providing feedback on progress motivate high productivity.

   The appropriate leadership style depends on the situation, the strengths of the manager, and his or her assumptions about employees' motives. Those who excel at task leadership are directive, goal-oriented managers who are good at keeping a group centered on its mission. Those who excel at social leadership take a more democratic approach as they promote teamwork, mediate conflicts, and support their work force. Theory X managers, who assume that workers are basically lazy and extrinsically motivated, monitor employees closely and provide incentives to work harder. Theory Y managers, who assume that workers are intrinsically motivated, encourage employee participation in decision making. Effective managers combine goal-oriented task leadership with group-oriented social leadership, adjusting their managerial style in response to workers' motives.

Stepping Through the Section

1. need; achievement motivation

2. stories

3. low

4. independence; praise; reward

5. emotional; cognitive

6. intrinsic motivation; extrinsic motivation; intrinsic motivation

7. intrinsic

8. prejudice; anxiety; control

9. industrial/organizational

10. control; inform; effort; ability

11. task leadership; social leadership

12. social; task

Effective managers use extrinsic rewards to *inform* employees of their successes and boost intrinsic motivation. They also adjust their managerial style to suit their employees, assessing workers' motives (accomplishment, recognition, affiliation, power), challenging them with clear objectives and specific goals, and rewarding them accordingly.

13. varies

14. often

15. theory X; theory Y

Progress Test 1

Multiple-Choice Questions

1. **d.** is the answer. (p. 423)

   a. & b. Although motivation is often aimed at reducing drives and satisfying biological needs, this is by no means always the case, as achievement motivation illustrates.

   c. Motivated behavior not only is energized but also is directed at a goal.

2. b. is the answer. A drive is the psychological consequence of a physiological need. (p. 425)
a. Needs are unlearned states of deprivation.
c. & d. Since needs are physical and drives psychological, their strengths cannot be compared directly.

3. a. is the answer. The curiosity of a child or a scientist is an example of behavior apparently motivated by something other than a physiological need. (p. 425)
b. & d. Some behaviors, such as thirst and hunger, are partially explained by drive reduction.
c. Drive reduction is directly based on the principle of homeostasis.

4. c. is the answer. (p. 445)
a., b., & d. None of these is linked to homosexuality.

5. a. is the answer. Increases in insulin increase hunger indirectly by lowering blood sugar, or glucose. (p. 429)

6. a. is the answer. This area of the hypothalamus seems to elevate hunger. (p. 429)
b. Stimulating the ventromedial hypothalamus has this effect.
c. Lesioning the ventromedial hypothalamus has this effect.
d. The hypothalamus is involved in sexual motivation, but not in this way.

7. b. is the answer. (p. 431)
a. Neophobia for taste is typical of all age groups.
c. Neophobia for taste is *not* an indicator of an eating disorder.
d. With repeated exposure, our appreciation for a new taste typically *increases*.

8. c. is the answer. Externals—those whose eating is especially triggered by food stimuli—showed a greater insulin response than did internals. (p. 431)
a. & b. The greater insulin response occurred in people who were especially sensitive to external cues, regardless of whether they were overweight.
d. Blood insulin levels rose less in internal subjects.

9. e. is the answer. (pp. 424–425)

10. b. is the answer. (pp. 436–437)

11. c. is the answer. (p. 424)
a. & b. Needs and drives are biologically based states that stimulate behaviors but are not themselves behaviors.

d. Incentives are the external stimuli that motivate behavior.

12. a. is the answer. Because they assume that workers are basically lazy and extrinsically motivated, theory X managers tend to be task-oriented. (p. 455)
c. & d. Theory Y managers tend to be democratic/participative leaders.

13. c. is the answer. The deprived subjects focused on food almost to the exclusion of anything else. (p. 428)
a. In order to conserve energy, the men's metabolic rate actually *decreased*.
b. & d. Far from losing interest in food, the subjects came to care only about food—a finding consistent with Maslow's hierarchy, in which physiological needs are at the base.

14. c. is the answer. (p. 448)

15. d. is the answer. (p. 432)

16. a. is the answer. (p. 437)
c. & d. Castration of the testes, which produce testosterone, does not alter estrogen levels.

17. d. is the answer. (p. 439)
a. Anderson was not successful in treating sexual disorder as though it were a personality disorder.
b. & c. Neither type of therapy is discussed in the text. However, it seems likely that they would be as unsuccessful as more traditional methods.

18. d. is the answer. Sex is much more than just a biological act, and its study therefore inherently involves values, attitudes, and morals, which should thus be discussed openly. (pp. 446–447)

19. d. is the answer. (p. 435)
a., b., & c. Kinsey's data do not support any of these statements.

20. d. is the answer. As different people are motivated by different things, in order to increase motivation and thus productivity, managers are advised to learn what motivates individual employees and to challenge and reward them accordingly. (p. 452)
a. & b. The most effective management style will depend on the situation.
c. This might be an effective strategy with some, but not all, employees.

Matching Items

1. e (p. 451)	**5.** f (p. 451)	**9.** j (p. 425)
2. k (p. 430)	**6.** a (p. 437)	**10.** c (p. 425)
3. i (p. 425)	**7.** b (p. 425)	**11.** g (p. 439)
4. h (p. 439)	**8.** d (p. 442)	

Progress Test 2

Multiple-Choice Questions

1. **c.** is the answer. (p. 430)
   a. Insulin increases hunger.
   b. Rising glucose levels cause insulin levels to increase.
   d. & e. These hormones affect sexual motivation; their effect on body weight was not discussed.

2. **a.** is the answer. (p. 425)
   b. This describes extrinsic motivation.
   c. This describes set point.
   d. Homeostasis has nothing to do with sexual orientation.

3. **d.** is the answer. If used to inform rather than to control, rewards can increase intrinsic motivation and the need for achievement. (p. 452)
   a., b., & c. Each of these has been shown to *discourage* the development of intrinsic motivation.

4. **a.** is the answer. (p. 440)

5. **a.** is the answer. The text does not indicate whether their metabolism is higher or lower than most. (pp. 432–433)
   b., c., & d. Genes, family background, and cultural influence have all been proposed as factors in eating disorders.

6. **b.** is the answer. (p. 429)
   a. Stimulation of the lateral hypothalamus triggers eating.
   c. & d. The thalamus is a sensory relay station; stimulation of it has no effect on eating.

7. **b.** is the answer. The time between 2 and 5 months after conception may be a critical period for the brain's neuro-hormonal control system. Exposure to abnormal hormonal conditions at other times has no effect on sexual orientation. (p. 445)

8. **d.** is the answer. Researchers have not been able to find any clear differences, psychological or otherwise, between homosexuals and heterosexuals. Thus, the basis for sexual orientation remains unknown, although recent evidence points more to a physiological basis. (pp. 443, 444)

9. **c.** is the answer. (p. 433)
   a. It has been found that women tend to express greater dissatisfaction with their body image than do men.
   b. Men tend to judge more accurately the body weight they think women prefer.
   d. Women tend to be dissatisfied with their body weight, and to think, erroneously, that men would prefer them thinner.

10. **d.** is the answer. (p. 426)

11. **c.** is the answer. Such behavior, presumably motivated by curiosity rather than any biological need, is inconsistent with a drive-reduction theory of motivation. (p. 425)
    a., b., & d. Each of these examples is consistent with a drive-reduction theory of motivation.

12. **e.** is the answer. (pp. 432–433)

13. **c.** is the answer. (p. 442)

14. **c.** is the answer. (p. 450)

15. **d.** is the answer. (p. 438)

16. **d.** is the answer. During the resolution phase males experience a refractory period. (p. 437)
    a., b., & c. The male and female responses are very similar in each of these phases.

17. **b.** is the answer. (p. 429)
    a. & e. These effects are the reverse of what takes place.
    c. If anything, set point is lowered by destruction of the lateral hypothalamus and elevated by destruction of the ventromedial hypothalamus.
    d. These effects do not occur.

18. **c.** is the answer. (p. 450)

19. **d.** is the answer. (p. 426)

20. **c.** is the answer. (p. 442)

True-False Items

1. F (p. 430)		**6.** T (p. 449)	
2. F (p. 436)		**7.** F (p. 429)	
3. F (p. 437)		**8.** F (p. 439)	
4. F (p. 438)		**9.** T (p. 452)	
5. F (p. 431)		**10.** T (p. 443)	

Thinking Critically About Chapter 12

Multiple-Choice Questions

1. **d.** is the answer. (p. 455)
   a. Directive managers are likely to favor theory X assumptions regarding worker motivation.
   b. Although this is not mentioned in the text, it is a characteristic of the task leadership style.
   c. Theory X managers assume that workers are basically lazy, error-prone, and extrinsically motivated by money.

2. **c.** is the answer. (pp. 455–456)
   a. McGregor identified the two leadership styles—theory X and theory Y—but did not specify which was most effective.
   b. Maslow's hierarchy of needs was not directed at a specific task.

d. Keys studied the role of physiological needs in hunger.

3. **c.** is the answer. Drive-reduction theory maintains that behavior is motivated when a biological need creates an aroused state, driving the individual to satisfy the need. It is difficult to believe that Mary's hang-gliding is satisfying a biological need. (p. 425)

a., b., & d. Mary may enjoy hang-gliding because it is a challenge that "is there" (incentive), because it satisfies a need to accomplish something challenging (achievement), or because it increases her self-esteem and sense of fulfillment in life (Maslow's hierarchy of needs).

4. **e.** is the answer. According to Maslow's theory, physiological needs, such as the need to satisfy hunger, must be satisfied before a person pursues loftier needs, such as making political statements. (p. 426)

a. Kinsey and Masters and Johnson were concerned with sexual behavior.

b. Murray was concerned with achievement motivation.

c. Keys was concerned with hunger.

5. **c.** is the answer. (p. 432)

a. & b. These are more typical of the families of anorexia patients.

6. **e.** is the answer. (p. 441)

7. **d.** is the answer. (p. 424)

a. & b. Instinct theory emphasizes biological factors, rather than environmental or cognitive factors.

c. Instinct theory applies to both humans and other animals.

8. **c.** is the answer. Although anorexics are significantly underweight, bulimics often are not unusually thin or overweight. (p. 432)

a., b., & d. Both anorexics and bulimics are more likely to be women than men, preoccupied with food, fearful of becoming overweight, and suffer from depression or low self-esteem.

9. **c.** is the answer. This is an example of salivating in response to an incentive rather than to maintain a balanced internal state. (p. 425)

a. & b. Both of these are examples of behavior that maintains a balanced internal state (homeostasis).

10. **d.** is the answer. Lesions of the ventromedial hypothalamus produce overeating and rapid weight gains. Lesions of the lateral hypothalamus suppress hunger and produce weight loss. (p. 429)

a. & b. The hippocampus and amygdala are not involved in regulating eating behavior.

11. **c.** is the answer. Achievement researchers regard people whose stories about ambiguous pictures express fantasies about the pursuit of goals, performing heroic acts, or feeling pride in success, as indicating achievement concerns. (p. 450)

a., b., & d. There is nothing in the stated information that would allow us to conclude that the students differ in their intrinsic or extrinsic orientation, or in their need to belong.

12. **c.** is the answer. Our preferences for sweet and salty tastes are genetic and universal. (p. 431)

13. **d.** is the answer. Because Darren evidently has high intrinsic motivation, giving him feedback about his work and involving him in participative management are probably all he needs to be very satisfied with his situation. (pp. 453, 456)

a., b., & c. Creating competitions and using controlling, rather than informing, rewards may have the opposite effect and actually undermine Darren's intrinsic motivation.

14. **c.** is the answer. (p. 448)

15. **b.** is the answer. Adolescent females with low self-esteem and high-achieving families seem especially prone to eating disorders such as anorexia nervosa. (pp. 432–433)

a. & d. Eating disorders occur much more frequently in women than in men.

c. Eating disorders usually develop during adolescence, rather than during adulthood.

16. **b.** is the answer. The body acts to defend its set point, or the weight to which it is predisposed. If Lucille was already near her set point, weight loss would prove difficult. (p. 430)

a. If the weight level to which her body is predisposed is low, weight loss upon dieting should not be difficult.

c. The eating disorders relate to eating behaviors and psychological factors and would not explain a difficulty with weight loss.

d. Externals might have greater problems losing weight, since they tend to respond to food stimuli, but this can't be the explanation in Lucille's case, since she has been sticking to her diet.

17. **c.** is the answer. Serotonin is a neurotransmitter that is elevated by the consumption of carbohydrates and has a calming effect. (p. 431)

a. & b. These answers do not explain the feelings of relaxation that Randy associates with eating junk food.

d. The consumption of sugar tends to elevate insulin level rather than lower it.

18. c. is the answer. Individuals with a high need for achievement tend to choose moderately difficult tasks at which they can succeed if they work at it. (p. 450)

a. Janice may be at her optimum level of arousal but that is not the reason for her choosing the course.

b. People with a low need for achievement might be more likely to prefer either the easy or the very difficult course.

d. That she chooses the course because it interests her implies that she is *intrinsically* motivated.

19. b. is the answer. Wanting to do something for its own sake is intrinsic motivation; wanting to do something for a reward (in this case, presumably, a high grade) is extrinsic motivation. (p. 451)

a. The opposite is true. Nancy was motivated to take the course for its own sake, whereas Jack was evidently motivated by the likelihood of a reward in the form of a good grade.

c. & d. A good grade, such as the one Jack is expecting, is an incentive. Drives, however, are aroused states that result from physical deprivation; they are not involved in this example.

20. b. is the answer. (p. 454)

a. Bill's style is one of task leadership, whereas Juanita's is one of social leadership.

c. Juanita's style is democratic/participative, whereas Bill's is directive.

d. The terms democratic and participative refer to the same style of leadership.

Essay Question

Under the influence of Darwin's evolutionary theory, it became fashionable to classify all sorts of behaviors as instincts. Instinct theory fell into disfavor for several reasons. First, instincts do not explain behaviors, they merely name them. Second, to qualify as an instinct, a behavior must have a fixed and automatic pattern and occur in all people, regardless of differing cultures and experiences. Apart from a few simple reflexes, however, human behavior is not sufficiently automatic and universal to meet these criteria. Although instinct theory failed to explain human motives, the underlying assumption that genes predispose many behaviors is as strongly believed as ever.

Instinct theory was replaced by drive-reduction theory and the idea that biological needs create aroused drive states that motivate the individual to satisfy these needs and preserve homeostasis. Drive-reduction theory failed as a complete account of human motivation because many human motives do not satisfy any obvious biological need. Instead, such behaviors are motivated by environmental incentives.

Arousal theory emerged in response to evidence that some motivated behaviors *increase*, rather than decrease, arousal.

Key Terms

Writing Definitions

1. **Motivation** is a need or desire that energizes and directs behavior. (p. 423)

2. An **instinct** is a complex behavior that is rigid, patterned throughout a species, and unlearned. (p. 424)

3. **Drive-reduction theory** attempts to explain behavior as arising from a physiological need that creates an aroused tension state (drive) that motivates an organism to satisfy the need. (p. 425)

4. **Homeostasis** refers to the body's tendency to maintain a balanced or constant internal state. (p. 425)

5. **Incentives** are positive or negative environmental stimuli that motivate behavior. (p. 425)

6. Maslow's **hierarchy of needs** proposes that human motives may be ranked from the basic, physiological level through higher-level needs for safety, love, esteem, and self-actualization, and that until they are satisfied, the more basic needs are more compelling than the higher-level ones. (p. 426)

7. **Glucose**, or blood sugar, is the major source of energy for the body's tissues. Elevating the level of glucose in the body will reduce hunger. (p. 429)

8. **Set point** is an individual's regulated weight level, which is maintained by adjusting food intake and energy output. (p. 430)

9. **Basal metabolic rate** is the body's base rate of energy expenditure when resting. (p. 430)

10. **Anorexia nervosa** is an eating disorder, most common in adolescent females, in which a person restricts food intake to become significantly underweight and yet still feels fat. (p. 432)

11. **Bulimia nervosa** is an eating disorder characterized by private "binge-purge" episodes of overeating followed by vomiting or laxative use. (p. 432)

12. The **sexual response cycle** described by Masters and Johnson consists of four stages of bodily reaction: excitement, plateau, orgasm, and resolution. (p. 436)

13. The **refractory period** is a resting period after orgasm, during which a male cannot be aroused to another orgasm. (p. 437)

14. **Estrogen** is a sex hormone secreted in greater amounts by females than by males. In mammals other than humans, estrogen levels peak during ovulation and trigger sexual receptivity. (p. 437)

15. A **sexual disorder** is a problem—such as impotence, premature ejaculation, and orgasmic disorder—that consistently impairs sexual arousal or functioning. (p. 439)

16. **Sexual orientation** refers to a person's enduring attraction to members of either the same or the opposite gender. (p. 442)

17. **Achievement motivation** is the degree to which a person is motivated internally by a desire for significant accomplishment; mastery of things, people, or ideas; and attaining a high standard. (p. 450)

18. **Intrinsic motivation** is the desire to perform a behavior for its own sake, rather than for some external reason, and to be effective. (p. 451)

    Memory aid: In*trinsic means "*in*ternal": A person who is **intrinsically** motivated is motivated from within.

19. **Extrinsic motivation** is the desire to perform a behavior in order to obtain a reward or avoid a punishment. (p. 451)

    Memory aid: Ex*trinsic means "*ex*ternal": A person who is **extrinsically** motivated is motivated by some outside factor.

20. **Industrial/organizational psychology** is a subfield of psychology that studies and advises on issues related to behavior in the workplace, including employee selection, training, productivity, and morale. (452 387)

21. **Task leadership** is goal-oriented leadership that sets standards, organizes work, and often is adopted by theory X managers. (p. 454)

22. **Social leadership** is group-oriented leadership that builds teamwork, mediates conflict, offers support, and often is adopted by theory Y managers. (p. 454)

23. **Theory X** managers assume that employees are basically lazy, error-prone, and extrinsically motivated by money. (p. 455)

24. **Theory Y** managers assume that, under the proper conditions, employees are intrinsically motivated to achieve self-esteem and to demonstrate their competence and creativity. (p. 455)

Cross-Check

ACROSS
2. intrinsic
6. lateral
12. hierarchy
13. safety
14. glucose
16. resolution
17. social
18. task
19. Kinsey
20. extrinsic

DOWN
1. drive-reduction
3. bulimia nervosa
4. basal metabolic rate
5. anorexia nervosa
7. estrogen
8. achievement
9. excitement
10. physiological
11. refractory
15. incentive

FOCUS ON VOCABULARY AND LANGUAGE

Page 423:. . . truant officer . . . A *truant* is a child who stays away from school without permission, and government officials who enforce compulsory education policy are called *truant officers*. Alfredo was forced to go to school and was spanked (*paddled*) for speaking Spanish. He decided to learn English and work hard to get good grades in school and college and he was successful. As a well-educated college administrator, Alfredo now tries to motivate others to become aware of (*wake up to*) their own potential and ability to do well.

Motivational Concepts

Page 424: Before long, *this fad for naming instincts collapsed under its own weight.* The fact that categorizing a very broad range of behaviors as instincts (*instinct-naming fad*) became very popular (*fashionable*) provides a good example of the misuse of a theory. In Darwinian theory, an **instinct** is an *unlearned* behavior that follows a fixed pattern in all members of the species. This fashion (*fad*) of naming thousands of behaviors as instincts grew so large and cumbersome that it was finally abandoned as a useful explanatory system (*collapsed under its own weight*).

Page 425: Both systems operate through *feedback loops. . . .* A thermostat in a house and the body's temperature-regulation system are both examples of **homeostasis**. If temperature drops, the change is detected and the information is directed (*fed*) to the system so that necessary steps are taken to bring the temperature back up to its original position. This information is then transmitted back to the system, so that there is a continuous cycle of cooling down and heating up (*feedback loop*) in an attempt to maintain a steady state. This is the basis of **drive-reduction theory**.

Page 425: Curiosity drives monkeys to *monkey around* trying to figure out how to unlock a latch that opens nothing, or how to open a window that allows them to see outside their room (Butler, 1954). The expression *"monkey around"* means to play or fool around (*meddle*) with something. Monkeys and young children have a very great need to explore and find out about their surroundings. Arousal theory suggests that we are driven to seek stimulation and increase our level of arousal to some comfortable state which is neither too high nor too low (*optimum level*).

Hunger

Page 428: They talked food. They daydreamed food. They collected recipes, read cookbooks, and *feasted their eyes on delectable forbidden foods.* In this experiment, subjects were given only half their normal intake of food, and the men became lethargic (*listless*), focused all their thoughts on the topic of food, and looked longingly at (*feasted their eyes on*) pictures of delicious, but unobtainable, foods (*delectable forbidden foods*). This behavior is consistent with Maslow's theory that there is a hierarchy of needs.

Page 429: This suggests that the body is somehow, somewhere, *keeping tabs on* its available resources. People and other animals naturally and automatically tend to control food intake in order to keep a relatively constant body weight. This indicates that there is a mechanism, or mechanisms, which monitor (*keep tabs on*) energy fluctuations. Levels of the blood sugar glucose and certain brain chemicals such as the neurotransmitter serotonin may play a role in this process.

Page 429: . . . rather like a *miser* who runs a bit of extra money to the bank and resists taking any out. The idea of a **set point** suggests that two parts of the hypothalamus, the lateral hypothalamus (LH) and ventromedial hypothalamus (VMH), regulate hunger. Stimulation of the LH increases hunger, while activity in the VMH depresses hunger. If the VMH is destroyed (*lesioned*), rats tend to create and store more fat, just as a person who loves money more than anything else (*a miser*) will keep banking money and use as little of it as possible.

Page 431: During the first week of [summer] camp, some could not resist *munching* readily visible *M&Ms*, even after a full meal. People who tend to eat because tasty food is available rather than because they are hungry are called *externals*. Those girls who continued to eat (*munch*) candies (*M&Ms*), which were made available after they had eaten a complete meal, were the ones who gained the most weight by the end of 8 weeks.

Page 431: While blood samples were being taken, a large, juicy steak was wheeled in, *crackling* as it finished grilling. When very hungry subjects were exposed to the smell (*aroma*) and sight of an appetizing food stimulus (a tender piece of beef barbecuing on the grill [*crackling steak*] was brought into the room), externals showed the largest increase in insulin levels and associated hunger response. This shows how external stimuli (the steaks) can create psychological incentives that interact with internal physiological processes.

Page 432: . . . binge-purge . . . People who have an eating disorder called **bulimia nervosa** may have episodes of overeating (*binging*) similar to those who engage in drinking bouts (*spurts of drinking*). The bulimic person (typically females in their teens or twenties) usually follows the overeating episode (*gorging*) with self-induced vomiting and excessive laxative use (*purging*).

Sexual Motivation

Page 435: . . . asked more than 350 *rapid-fire questions.* Kinsey and Pomeroy were the first sex researchers to systematically interview a large sample of the American population. Their technique (*tactic*) involved starting with easy-to-answer questions (e.g., age, education, health, gender, etc.) and then moving on to questions that required subjects to divulge personal sexual information. These questions were asked in an aggressive interrogative style (*rapid-fire questions*) and that fact, along with a nonrepresentative sample, may have biased their results.

Page 436: Faithful attractions overwhelmingly outnumber *fatal attractions.* Recent research (based on more random representative samples) has shown that couples are more monogamous and committed to their partners (*faithful attractions*) than previous, less valid or reliable surveys have suggested. (*Fatal*

Attraction is the title of a movie about a married man who has an affair with a woman who becomes obsessed with him, and this eventually leads to her death, thus the title *Fatal Attraction*.)

Page 438: The hormonal fuel is essential, but so are the psychological stimuli that *turn on the engine*, keep it running, and *shift it into high gear*. Myers makes an analogy between sex hormones and the fuel that propels a car. We need the hormones to be sexually motivated just as a car needs fuel to operate. In humans, however, there is a two-way interaction between the chemicals and sexuality. In addition to hormones, psychological factors are needed to initiate sexual desire (*turn on the engine*) and produce the associated behaviors (*shift it into high gear*).

Page 438: Viewing *X-rated sex films* similarly tends to diminish people's satisfaction with their own sexual partners (Zillmann, 1989). All films are rated by a censor, and those with an *X-rating* because of their sexually explicit content are restricted to adults only. There is much debate over the influence of such films on people, and some research suggests that there may be adverse effects. For example, they may create the false impression that females enjoy rape; they may increase men's willingness to hurt women; they tend to lead both males and females to devalue their partners and their relationships; and they may reduce people's feeling of fulfillment with their lovers.

Page 442: Throughout history, the *pendulum* of sexual values has swung—from the European eroticism of the early 1800s to the *conservative Victorian era* of the late 1800s, from the *libertine flapper era* of the 1920s to the family values period of the 1950s. The *pendulum* of a mechanical clock swings back and forth from one side, or extreme, to the other. Myers is pointing out that our views of sexuality tend to move from restrictive (*conservative Victorian*) at one extreme to those with fewer restraints (*libertine flapper*) at the other, during different periods of time (*eras*). Today's generation may be moving toward an era in which commitment and restraint are more important than sexual expression. (Note: A *flapper* was an emancipated young woman in the 1920s.)

Page 442: . . . *fired* . . . To be *fired* means to lose your job (*to be laid off, let go, or sacked*). Myers suggests that one way for heterosexual people to understand how a homosexual feels in a predominantly heterosexual society is to imagine what it would be like if the situation were reversed and homosexuality was the norm. How would it feel as a heterosexual to be ostracized (*ignored*), to lose one's job (*be fired*), to be

confronted by media that showed or indicated homosexuality as the societal norm.

Page 443: Most psychologists today view sexual orientation as neither *willfully chosen* nor *willfully changed*. Myers compares sexual orientation to handedness. You don't deliberately decide (*willfully choose*) to be right-handed or left-handed and you can't intentionally alter (*willfully change*) your inherent inclination to use one hand over the other. Like handedness, sexual orientation is not linked to criminality nor is it associated with personality or psychological disorder.

Page 446: Regardless of the process, the consistency of the genetic, prenatal, and brain findings has *swung the pendulum toward* a physiological explanation. The debate over what causes different sexual orientations has continued for many years. Recent evidence from the research seems to favor (*has swung the pendulum toward*) a biologically based account.

Page 446: To gay and lesbian activists, the new biological research is a *double-edged sword* (Diamond, 1993). The research supporting a physiological explanation of sexual orientation has both positive and negative aspects (*a double-edged sword*). On the one hand, if sexual orientation is genetically influenced, there is a basis for claiming equal civil rights and there is no need to attribute blame. On the other hand, these findings create a nagging anxiety (*haunting possibility*) that sexual orientation may be controlled through genetic engineering or fetal abortions.

The Need to Belong

Page 448: The need to belong *colors our thoughts and emotions*. As humans, we have a desire to be connected to others and to develop close, long-lasting relationships, and this need to belong affects the way we think and feel (*colors our thoughts and emotions*).

Page 449: To be *shunned—given the cold shoulder or the silent treatment*, with others' eyes avoiding yours—is to have one's *need to belong threatened*. . . . For both adults and children, to be ignored (*shunned*), treated with disdain (*given the cold shoulder*), or to be deprived of verbal interactions with others (*given the silent treatment*) is very distressing and hurtful; this type of social ostracism makes us feel isolated and abandoned (*threatens our need to belong*) and can lead to depression and withdrawal.

Achievement Motivation

Page 450: Billionaire entrepreneurs may be motivated to make ever more money . . . *daredevils* to seek *greater thrills.* A person who tries very hard to be successful, by being better than others at whatever task is undertaken, has a high need for achievement **(achievement motivation)**. For instance, some people are high risk-takers (*daredevils*) and they frequently look for activities that produce ever higher levels of stimulation or arousal (*greater thrills*).

Page 450: In a *ring toss game* they often stand at an *intermediate distance* from the *stake*; this enables some successes, yet provides a suitable challenge. When faced with the task of throwing a small rubber ring onto a vertical post (*stake*) some distance away (*ring toss game*), those with a high need for achievement tend to stand neither too near nor too far away (*intermediate distance*). This makes the game somewhat difficult (*challenging*), yet ensures some correct responses which can then be attributed to skill and concentration. Those with low achievement motivation pick either a very close or a very far position from the stake.

Page 451: These *superstar achievers* were distinguished not so much by their extraordinary *natural talent* as by their extraordinary daily discipline. Studies of people who were outstanding artists, scientists, athletes, etc. (*superstar achievers*) found that they were not different because of intelligence or innate skills (*natural talent*) but because of exceptional motivation and very high levels of self-discipline in relation to the daily pursuit of their goals.

Page 451: Great achievement, it seems, mixes *a teaspoon of inspiration* with *a gallon of perspiration.* The main point here is that success and achievement are the result of a lot of hard work and sweat (*a gallon of perspiration*) combined with a little genius, talent, creativity, or imagination (*a teaspoon of inspiration*).

Page 453: Second, *avoid snuffing out* people's sense of self-determination with an overuse of *controlling extrinsic rewards* (Deci & Ryan, 1987). **Industrial/ organizational psychologists** are interested in how best to motivate people to realize their potential, and to be productive and contented workers. One thing that leaders (managers, coaches, teachers, etc.) can do is to make sure that people are intellectually challenged and that their curiosity is aroused. In addition, it is important to encourage intrinsic motivation and preclude inhibiting (*avoid snuffing out*) people's feelings of control in their lives by imposing too many externally restraining incentives (*controlling extrinsic rewards*).

Page 453: Different *strokes* for different *folks*, but for each a way to motivate. Good leaders change their managerial style depending on the needs of the people they are working with. They tend to create challenges for people who need to feel they have accomplished something, they pay attention and give praise to those who need recognition, they create a feeling of teamwork for those who have a need to belong, and they provide some competitive challenges and opportunities for success for those who value power. There are different incentives (*strokes*) for different people (*folks*), but each has the ability to motivate.

Page 454: Because effective leadership styles vary with the situation and the person, the once-popular *"great person"* theory of leadership—that all great leaders *share certain traits—fell out of favor.* It was once believed that good management or leadership was a function of common characteristics (*shared traits*) possessed by some people (*"great persons"*). This notion is no longer popular (*it fell out of favor*), but recent research suggests that effective managers typically demonstrate high levels of *both* **task leadership** (organizing work, focusing on goals, and being directive) *and* **social leadership** (developing cooperation, settling conflicts, and being democratic).

Page 455: Effective leaders of laboratory groups, work teams, and large corporations also tend to *exude a self-confident "charisma."* . . . Competent managers who lead groups of people in an effective and productive manner typically exhibit an ability to rely on their own capacities (*exude self-confidence*), project their vision of what needs to be done, and inspire others to follow them (*"charisma"*).

Emotion

Chapter Overview

Emotions are responses of the whole individual, involving physiological arousal, expressive behaviors, and conscious experience. Chapter 13 examines these components in detail, particularly as they relate to the emotions of fear, anger, and happiness. In addition, the chapter discusses several theoretical controversies concerning the relationship and sequence of the components of emotion, primarily regarding whether the body's response to a stimulus causes the emotion that is felt and whether thinking is necessary to and must precede the experience of emotion.

NOTE: Answer guidelines for all Chapter 13 questions begin on page 375.

Introducing Emotion (p. 459)

> David Myers at times uses idioms that are unfamiliar to some readers. If you do not know the meaning of any of the following words, phrases, or expressions in the context in which they appear in the text, refer to page 383 for an explanation: *add color to your life.*

Introduction Preview

First, skim the introduction. Then read the following objective and, as you read the text, search for the information that will enable you to meet that objective. Answer guidelines are provided on page 375.

1. Identify the three components of emotion.

Theories of Emotion (pp. 459–465)

> David Myers at times uses idioms that are unfamiliar to some readers. If you do not know the meaning of any of the following words, phrases, or expressions in the context in which they appear in the text, refer to page 383 for an explanation:*rumble of an engine . . . stalking you; lash out; Which is the chicken and which the egg?; testy; The heart is not always subject to the mind.*

Section Preview

First, skim the section, noting headings and boldface items. Then read the following objectives and, as you read the text, search for the information that will enable you to meet each objective. Answer guidelines are provided on page 375.

1. Contrast and critique the James-Lange and Cannon-Bard theories of emotion, and describe Schachter's two-factor theory of emotion.

2. Discuss evidence suggesting that some emotional reactions involve no conscious thought, and describe the two dimensions of emotion.

Stepping Through the Section

After you have read the section, complete the sentences and answer the questions. As you proceed, evaluate your performance by consulting the answers on page 375. Do not continue with the next section until you understand each answer. If you need to, review or reread the section in the textbook before continuing.

1. According to the James-Lange theory, emotional states _____ (precede/follow) body arousal.

Describe two problems that Walter Cannon identified with the James-Lange theory.

2. Cannon proposed that emotional stimuli in the environment are routed simultaneously to the _____ , which results in awareness of the emotion, and to the _____ nervous system, which causes the body's reaction. Because another scientist concurrently proposed similar ideas, this theory has come to be known as the _____-_____ theory.

3. For victims of spinal cord injuries who have lost all feeling below the neck, the intensity of emotions tends to _____ . This result supports the _____-_____ theory of emotion.

4. Most researchers _____ (agree/disagree) with Cannon and Bard's position that emotions involve _____ as well as arousal.

5. The two-factor theory of emotion proposes that emotion has two components: _____ arousal and a _____ label. This theory was proposed by _____ .

6. Schachter and Singer found that physically aroused subjects told that an injection would cause arousal _____ (did/did not) become emotional in response to an accomplice's aroused behavior. Physically aroused subjects not expecting arousal _____ (did/did not) become emotional in response to an accomplice's behavior.

7. Robert Zajonc believes that the feeling of emotion _____ (can/cannot) precede our cognitive labeling of that emotion.

Cite two pieces of evidence that support Zajonc's position.

8. The researcher who disagrees with Zajonc and argues that most emotions require cognitive processing is _____ . According to this view, emotions arise when we _____ an event as beneficial or harmful to our well-being.

Express some general conclusions that can be drawn about cognition and emotion.

9. Throughout the world, people place emotions along two dimensions: _____ , which refers to whether a feeling is _____ or _____ , and high versus low _____ .

The Physiology of Emotion (pp. 465–470)

> If you do not know the meaning of any of the following words, phrases, or expressions in the context in which they appear in the text, refer to page 383 for an explanation: *your stomach develops butterflies; shooting free throws; clutching, sinking sensation; peppy left hemisphere . . . perky disposition; Pinocchio . . . telltale sign.*

Section Preview

Answer guidelines are provided on page 375.

1. Describe the physiological changes that occur during emotional arousal, noting the relationship between arousal and performance.

2. Discuss the research findings on the relationship between body states and specific emotions.

3. (Thinking Critically) Discuss the effectiveness of the polygraph in detecting lies.

Stepping Through the Section

Answers are provided on page 376.

1. Describe the major physiological changes that each of the following undergoes during emotional arousal:

    a. heart: _____

    b. muscles: _____

    c. liver: _____

    d. breathing: _____

    e. digestion: _____

    f. pupils: _____

    g. blood: _____

    h. skin: _____

2. The responses of arousal are activated by the _____ nervous system. In response to its signal, the _____ glands release the hormones _____ and _____ , which increase heart rate, blood pressure, and blood sugar.

3. When the need for arousal has passed, the body is calmed through activation of the _____ nervous system.

Explain the relationship between performance and arousal.

4.. The various emotions are associated with _____ (similar/different) forms of physiological arousal.

5. The emotions _____ and _____ are accompanied by differing _____ temperatures and _____ secretions.

6. The brain circuits underlying different emotions _____ (are/are not) different. For example, negative emotions are accompanied by increased activity in the _____ hemisphere, whereas positive emotions are accompanied by increased activity in the _____ hemisphere.

7. Individuals with more active _____ (right/left) _____ lobes tend to be more cheerful than those in whom this pattern of brain activity is reversed.

8. The physical accompaniments of emotion _____ (are/are not) innate and universal.

9. The technical name for the "lie detector" is the _____ .

Explain how lie detectors supposedly indicate whether a person is lying.

10. How well the lie detector works depends on whether a person exhibits _____ while lying.

11. Those who criticize lie detectors feel that the tests are particularly likely to err in the case of the _____ (innocent/guilty), because different _____ all register as _____ .

12. By and large, experts _____ (agree/do not agree) that lie detector tests are highly accurate.

13. A test that assesses a suspect's knowledge of details of a crime that only the guilty person should know is the _____ _____ .

Expressing Emotion (pp. 470–476)

> If you do not know the meaning of any of the following words, phrases, or expressions in the context in which they appear in the text, refer to pages 383–384 for an explanation: *good enough at reading; Fidgeting; Ditto; sneer; Fake a big grin.*

Section Preview

Answer guidelines are provided on page 376.

1. Discuss gender and personality differences in nonverbal communication, and describe people's varying abilities to detect deceit.

2. Discuss whether nonverbal expressions of emotion are universally understood, and describe the effects of facial expressions on emotion.

Stepping Through the Section

Answers are provided on page 376.

1. Emotions may be communicated in words and/or through body expressions, referred to as _____ communication.

2. Most people are especially good at interpreting nonverbal _____ . We read fear and _____ mostly from the _____ , and happiness from the _____ .

3. Introverts are _____ (better/worse) at reading others' emotions, whereas extraverts are themselves _____ (easier/harder) to read.

4. Women are generally _____ (better/worse) than men at detecting nonverbal signs of emotion. Although women are _____ (more/less) likely than men to describe themselves as empathic, physiological measures reveal a much _____ (smaller/larger) gender difference. Women are _____ (more/less) likely than men to express empathy.

5. Women are also better at conveying

_____ (which emotion?), whereas men surpass women in conveying their

_____ .

6. Various emotions may be linked with specific

_____ _____ .

Most people _____ (are/are not) very accurate at detecting lying. Accuracy varies, however, with a person's _____ and training. For example, _____ _____ (people in which professions?) seem to be especially good at detecting lying.

7. The absence of nonverbal cues to emotion is one reason that communications sent as

_____ are easy to misread.

8. Gestures have _____ (the same/different) meanings in different cultures.

9. Studies of adults indicate that in different cultures facial expressions have

_____ (the same/different) meanings. Studies of children indicate that the meaning of their facial expressions

_____ (varies/does not vary) across cultures.

10. According to _____ , human emotional expressions evolved because they helped our ancestors communicate before language developed. It has also been adaptive for us to _____ faces in particular

_____ .

11. In cultures that encourage

_____ , emotional expressions are often intense and prolonged. In cultures that emphasize _____ , emotions such as _____ , _____ , and _____ are more common than in the _____ (East/West).

12. Darwin believed that when an emotion is accompanied by an outward facial expression, the emotion is _____ (intensified/ diminished).

13. In one study, students who were induced to smile _____ (found/did not find) cartoons more humorous.

14. Studies have found that imitating another person's facial expressions

_____ (leads/does not lead) to greater empathy with that person's feelings.

Experiencing Emotion (pp. 477–487)

> If you do not know the meaning of any of the following words, phrases, or expressions in the context in which they appear in the text, refer to pages 384–385 for an explanation: *poisonous; Stone Age fears; hostile outbursts; "blowing off steam"; rush of euphoria; machines galore; lob a bombshell; run amuck; with every kick comes a kickback; passively vegetating.*

Section Preview

Answer guidelines are provided on page 377.

1. Discuss the significance of environmental and biological factors in the acquisition of fear.

2. Discuss the catharsis hypothesis and identify some of the advantages and disadvantages of openly expressing anger.

3. Identify some potential causes and consequences of happiness, and discuss reasons for the relativity of happiness.

4. (Close-Up) Explain the opponent-process theory of emotion.

Stepping Through the Section

Answers are provided on page 377.

1. Izard believes that there are _____ basic emotions, most of which _____ (are/are not) present in infancy.

2. Fear can by and large be seen as a(n) _____ (adaptive/maladaptive) response.

3. Most human fears are acquired through _____ . In addition, some fears are acquired by _____ parents and friends.

Explain why researchers think that some fears are biologically predisposed.

4. A key to fear learning lies in the _____ , a neural center in the _____ system. Following damage to this area, humans who have been conditioned to fear a loud noise will _____ the conditioning but show no _____ effect of it.

5. Conversely, people who have suffered damage to the _____ will show the _____ _____ but _____ (will/will not) be able to remember why.

6. Patients who have lost use of the _____ are unusually trusting of scary-looking people.

7. Fears that fall outside the average range are called _____ .

8. Averill has found that most people become angry several times per _____

9. The belief that expressing pent-up emotion is adaptive is most commonly found in cultures that emphasize _____ . This is the _____ hypothesis. In cultures that emphasize _____ , such as those of _____ or _____ , expressions of anger are less common.

10. Psychologists have found that when anger has been provoked, retaliation may have a calming effect under certain circumstances. List the circumstances.
   a. _____
   b. _____
   c. _____

Identify some potential problems with expressing anger.

11. List two suggestions offered by experts for handling anger.
   a. _____
   b. _____

12. Happy people tend to perceive the world as _____ . They are also _____ (more/less) willing to help others. This is called the _____-_____ , _____-_____ phenomenon. An individual's self-perceived happiness or satisfaction with life is called his or her _____ _____ .

13. Most people tend to _____ (underestimate/overestimate) the long-term emotional consequences of very bad news. After experiencing tragedy or dramatically positive events, people generally _____ (regain/do not regain) their previous degree of happiness.

14. Researchers have found that levels of happiness _____ (do/do not) mirror differences in standards of living. During the last four decades, spendable income in the United States has more than doubled; personal happiness has _____ (increased/decreased/remained unchanged).

15. Recent studies demonstrate that people generally experience a higher quality of life and greater well-being when they strive for _____ _____ than _____ when they strive for _____ .

16. The idea that happiness is relative to one's recent experience is stated by the _____-_____ phenomenon.

Explain how this principle accounts for the fact that, for some people, material desires can never be satisfied.

17. The principle that one feels worse off than others is known as _____ _____ .

18. (Close-Up) The idea that "every emotion triggers its opposite" is the basis of the _____-_____ theory of emotion. According to this theory, the opposing emotion is most intense immediately _____ (before/after) an emotion-arousing event. With repeated experience of the event, the primary emotion becomes _____ (weaker/stronger) and the opposing emotion becomes _____ (weaker/stronger).

19. List six factors that have been shown to be positively correlated with feelings of happiness.

   _____
   _____
   _____
   _____
   _____
   _____

20. List five factors that are evidently unrelated to happiness.

   _____
   _____
   _____
   _____
   _____

21. When people were interrupted during their daily activities and asked to report their feelings, they reported being happier when they were engaged in _____ _____ or _____ _____ .

22. Research studies of identical and fraternal twins have led to the estimate that _____ percent of the variation in people's happiness ratings is heritable.

Progress Test 1

Multiple-Choice Questions

Circle your answers to the following questions and check them with the answers on page 378. If your answer is incorrect, read the explanation for why it is incorrect and then consult the appropriate pages of the text (in parentheses following the correct answer).

1. Which of the following is correct regarding the relationship between arousal and performance?
   a. Generally, performance is optimal when arousal is low.
   b. Generally, performance is optimal when arousal is high.
   c. On easy tasks, performance is optimal when arousal is low.
   d. On easy tasks, performance is optimal when arousal is high.

2. Which division of the nervous system is especially involved in bringing about emotional arousal?

   a. skeletal nervous system
   b. peripheral nervous system
   c. sympathetic nervous system
   d. parasympathetic nervous system
   e. central nervous system

3. Concerning emotions and their accompanying body responses, which of the following appears to be true?

   a. Each emotion has its own body response and underlying brain circuit.
   b. All emotions involve the same body response as a result of the same underlying brain circuit.
   c. Many emotions involve similar body responses but have different underlying brain circuits.
   d. All emotions have the same underlying brain circuits but different body responses.

4. The Cannon-Bard theory of emotion states that:

   a. emotions have two ingredients: physical arousal and a cognitive label.
   b. the conscious experience of an emotion occurs at the same time as the body's physical reaction.
   c. emotional experiences are based on an awareness of the body's responses to an emotion-arousing stimulus.
   d. emotional ups and downs tend to balance in the long run.

5. Electrical stimulation of which brain region can produce terror or rage in cats?

   a. limbic system   c. cortex
   b. hypothalamus   d. cerebellum

6. The body's response to danger is triggered by the release of _____ by the _____ glands.

   a. acetylcholine; adrenal
   b. epinephrine and norepinephrine; adrenal
   c. acetylcholine; pituitary
   d. epinephrine and norepinephrine; pituitary

7. Which of the following was *not* raised as a criticism of the James-Lange theory of emotion?

   a. The body's responses are too similar to trigger the various emotions.
   b. Emotional reactions occur before the body's responses can take place.
   c. The cognitive activity of the cortex plays a role in the emotions we experience.
   d. People with spinal cord injuries at the neck typically experience less emotion.

8. (Thinking Critically) Current estimates are that the polygraph is inaccurate approximately _____ of the time.

   a. three-fourths   d. one-fourth
   b. one-half   e. one-tenth
   c. one-third

9. In the Schachter-Singer experiment, which subjects reported feeling an emotional change in the presence of the experimenter's highly emotional confederate?

   a. those receiving epinephrine and expecting to feel physical arousal
   b. those receiving a placebo and expecting to feel physical arousal
   c. those receiving epinephrine but not expecting to feel physical arousal
   d. those receiving a placebo and not expecting to feel physical arousal

10. Which of the following is true?

    a. People with more education tend to be happier.
    b. Whites tend to be happier than Latinos.
    c. Women tend to be happier than men.
    d. People with children tend to be happier.
    e. People who are socially outgoing or who exercise regularly tend to be happier.

11. Catharsis will be most effective in reducing anger toward another person if:

    a. you wait until you are no longer angry before confronting the person.
    b. the target of your anger is someone you feel has power over you.
    c. your anger is directed specifically toward the person who angered you.
    d. the other person is able to retaliate by also expressing anger.

12. Emotions are:

    a. physiological reactions.
    b. behavioral expressions.
    c. conscious feelings.
    d. all of the above.

13. Law enforcement officials sometimes use a lie detector to assess a suspect's responses to details of the crime believed to be known only to the perpetrator. This is known as the:

    a. inductive approach.
    b. deductive approach.
    c. guilty knowledge test.
    d. screening examination.
    e. prevarication probe.

14. Research on nonverbal communication has revealed that:
    a. it is easy to hide your emotions by controlling your facial expressions.
    b. facial expressions tend to be the same the world over, while gestures vary from culture to culture.
    c. most authentic expressions last between 7 and 10 seconds.
    d. most gestures have universal meanings; facial expressions vary from culture to culture.

15. In laboratory experiments, facial expressions of fear and anger have been found to result in:
    a. an increase in skin temperature.
    b. increases in skin temperature and heart rate.
    c. strong feelings of fear and anger.
    d. subtly different body reactions.
    e. all of the above.

16. Research suggests that people generally experience the greatest well-being when they strive for:
    a. wealth.
    b. modest income increases from year to year.
    c. slightly higher status than their friends, neighbors, and co-workers.
    d. intimacy and personal growth.

17. Research indicates that a person is most likely to be helpful to others if he or she:
    a. is feeling guilty about something.
    b. is happy.
    c. recently received help from another person.
    d. recently offered help to another person.

18. Darwin believed that:
    a. the expression of emotions helped our ancestors to survive.
    b. all humans express basic emotions using similar facial expressions.
    c. human facial expressions of emotion retain elements of animals' emotional displays.
    d. all of the above are true.

19. Research supporting the opponent-process theory of emotion suggests that:
    a. the price of pleasure is pain.
    b. with repetition a task that arouses fear will become more tolerable.
    c. suffering can pay emotional dividends.
    d. all of the above are true.

20. Evidence that changes in facial expression can directly affect people's feelings and body states has convinced Robert Zajonc that:
    a. the heart is always subject to the mind.
    b. emotional reactions involve deliberate rational thinking.
    c. cognition is not necessary for emotion.
    d. the interpretation of facial expressions is a learned skill.

Matching Items

Match each definition or description with the appropriate term.

Definitions or Descriptions

_____ 1. the tendency to react to changes on the basis of recent experience

_____ 2. an individual's self-perceived happiness

_____ 3. emotional release

_____ 4. the tendency to evaluate our situation negatively against that of other people

_____ 5. the reason emotions may balance in the short run

_____ 6. emotions consist of physical arousal *and* a cognitive label

_____ 7. an emotion-arousing stimulus triggers cognitive and body responses simultaneously

_____ 8. the division of the nervous system that calms the body following arousal

_____ 9. the division of the nervous system that activates arousal

_____ 10. a device that measures the physiological correlates of emotion

_____ 11. the tendency of people to be helpful when they are in a good mood

_____ 12. we are sad because we cry

Terms
   a. adaptation-level phenomenon
   b. opponent-process theory
   c. two-factor theory
   d. catharsis
   e. sympathetic nervous system
   f. James-Lange theory
   g. polygraph
   h. Cannon-Bard theory
   i. parasympathetic nervous system
   j. relative deprivation principle
   k. feel-good, do-good phenomenon
   l. subjective well-being

Progress Test 2

Progress Test 2 should be completed during a final chapter review. Answer the following questions after you thoroughly understand the correct answers for the section reviews and Progress Test 1.

Multiple-Choice Questions

1. Which of the following most accurately describes emotional arousal?
   a. Emotions prepare the body to fight or flee.
   b. Emotions are voluntary reactions to emotion-arousing stimuli.
   c. Because all emotions have the same physiological basis, emotions are primarily psychological events.
   d. Emotional arousal is always accompanied by cognition.
   e. All are accurate descriptions.

2. Schachter's two-factor theory emphasizes that emotion involves both:
   a. the sympathetic and parasympathetic divisions of the nervous system.
   b. verbal and nonverbal expression.
   c. physical arousal and a cognitive label.
   d. universal and culture-specific aspects.

3. Dermer found that students who had studied others who were worse off than themselves felt greater satisfaction with their own lives; this is the principle of:
   a. relative deprivation.
   b. adaptation level.
   c. behavioral contrast.
   d. opponent processes.

4. Which theory of emotion emphasizes the simultaneous experience of body response and emotional feeling?
   a. James-Lange theory
   b. Cannon-Bard theory
   c. two-factor theory
   d. opponent-process theory

5. Izard believes that there are _____ basic emotions.
   a. 3   d. 10
   b. 5   e. 12
   c. 7

6. (Thinking Critically) The polygraph measures:
   a. lying.
   b. brain rhythms.
   c. chemical changes in the body.
   d. physiological indexes of arousal.

7. (Close-Up) According to the opponent-process theory, as an emotion is repeatedly experienced:
   a. the primary emotional experience becomes stronger.
   b. the opposing emotional experience becomes weaker.
   c. both a. and b. occur.
   d. the primary emotional experience becomes weaker; the opposing emotional experience becomes stronger.

8. Which of the following is true?
   a. Gestures are universal; facial expressions, culture-specific.
   b. Facial expressions are universal; gestures, culture-specific.
   c. Both gestures and facial expressions are universal.
   d. Both gestures and facial expressions are culture-specific.

9. Which theory of emotion implies that every emotion is associated with a unique physiological reaction?
   a. James-Lange theory
   b. Cannon-Bard theory
   c. two-factor theory
   d. opponent-process theory

10. For which of the following fears do humans appear to be biologically prepared?
    a. fear of electricity   d. fear of flying
    b. fear of cliffs   e. fear of bombs
    c. fear of flowers

11. Which of the following was *not* presented in the text as evidence that some emotional reactions involve no deliberate, rational thinking?
    a. Some of the neural pathways involved in emotion are separate from those involved in thinking and memory.
    b. Emotional reactions are sometimes quicker than our interpretations of a situation.
    c. People can develop an emotional preference for visual stimuli to which they have been unknowingly exposed.
    d. Arousal of the sympathetic nervous system will trigger an emotional reaction even when artificially induced by an injection of epinephrine.

12. Concerning the catharsis hypothesis, which of the following is true?
    a. Expressing anger can be temporarily calming if it does not leave one feeling guilty or anxious.
    b. The arousal that accompanies unexpressed anger never dissipates.
    c. Expressing one's anger always calms one down.
    d. Psychologists agree that under no circumstances is catharsis beneficial.

13. In an emergency situation, emotional arousal will result in:
    a. increased rate of respiration.
    b. increased blood sugar.
    c. a slowing of digestion.
    d. pupil dilation.
    e. all of the above.

14. A relatively high level of arousal would be most likely to facilitate:
    a. remembering the lines of a play.
    b. shooting free throws in basketball.
    c. sprinting 100 meters.
    d. taking a final exam in introductory psychology.

15. Several studies have shown that physical arousal can intensify just about any emotion. For example, when people who have been physically aroused by exercise are insulted, they often misattribute their arousal to the insult. This finding illustrates the importance of:
    a. cognitive labels of arousal in the conscious experience of emotions.
    b. a minimum level of arousal in triggering emotional experiences.
    c. the simultaneous occurrence of physical arousal and cognitive labeling in emotional experience.
    d. all of the above.

16. (Thinking Critically) Psychologist David Lykken is opposed to the use of lie detectors because:
    a. they represent an invasion of a person's privacy and could easily be used for unethical purposes.
    b. there are often serious discrepancies among the various indicators such as perspiration and heart rate.
    c. polygraphs cannot distinguish the various possible causes of arousal.
    d. they are accurate only about 50 percent of the time.

17. Most human fears are:
- **a.** universal.
- **c.** present at birth.
- **b.** biologically determined.
- **d.** learned.

18. Averill found that most people become angry:
- **a.** once a day.
- **b.** once a week.
- **c.** several times a week.
- **d.** several times a month.
- **e.** There is no common pattern to anger.

19. Which of these factors have researchers *not* found to correlate with happiness?
- **a.** a satisfying marriage or close friendship
- **b.** high self-esteem
- **c.** religious faith
- **d.** intelligence

20. In cultures that emphasize social interdependence:
- **a.** emotional displays are typically intense.
- **b.** emotional displays are typically prolonged.
- **c.** negative emotions are rarely displayed.
- **d.** all of the above are true.

True-False Items

Indicate whether each statement is true or false by placing *T* or *F* in the blank next to the item.

_____ **1.** For easy tasks, the optimal level of arousal is higher than for difficult tasks.

_____ **2.** Men are generally better than women at detecting nonverbal emotional expression.

_____ **3.** The sympathetic nervous system triggers physiological arousal during an emotion.

_____ **4.** The adrenal glands produce the hormones epinephrine and norepinephrine.

_____ **5.** When one imitates an emotional facial expression, the body may experience physiological changes characteristic of that emotion.

_____ **6.** People who have lost sensation only in their lower bodies experience a considerable decrease in the intensity of their emotions.

_____ **7.** Wealthy people tend to be much happier than middle-income people.

_____ **8.** Physical arousal can intensify emotion.

_____ **9.** All emotions involve conscious thought.

_____ **10.** The two-factor theory states that emotions are given a cognitive label before physical arousal occurs.

Thinking Critically About Chapter 13

Answer these questions the day before an exam as a final check on your understanding of the chapter's terms and concepts.

Multiple-Choice Questions

1. You are on your way to school to take a big exam. Suddenly, on noticing that your pulse is racing and that you are sweating, you feel nervous. With which theory of emotion is this experience most consistent?
- **a.** Cannon-Bard theory
- **b.** James-Lange theory
- **c.** opponent-process theory
- **d.** adaptation-level theory

2. When Professor Simon acquired a spacious new office, he was overjoyed. Six months later, however, he was taking the office for granted. His behavior illustrates the:
- **a.** relative deprivation principle.
- **b.** adaptation-level phenomenon.
- **c.** opponent-process theory.
- **d.** optimum arousal principle.

3. After Brenda scolded her brother for forgetting to pick her up from school, the physical arousal that had accompanied her anger diminished. Which division of her nervous system mediated her physical *relaxation*?
- **a.** sympathetic division
- **b.** parasympathetic division
- **c.** skeletal division
- **d.** peripheral nervous system

4. Two years ago Maria was in an automobile accident in which her spinal cord was severed, leaving her paralyzed from her neck down. Today, Maria finds that she experiences emotions less intensely than she did before her accident. This tends to support which theory of emotion?
- **a.** James-Lange theory
- **b.** Cannon-Bard theory
- **c.** opponent-process theory
- **d.** adaptation-level theory
- **e.** relative deprivation theory

5. The candidate stepped before the hostile audience, panic written all over his face. It is likely that the candidate's facial expression caused him to experience:
- **a.** a lessening of his fear.
- **b.** an intensification of his fear.
- **c.** a surge of digestive enzymes in his body.
- **d.** increased body temperature.

6. Jane was so mad at her brother that she exploded at him when he entered her room. That she felt less angry afterward is best explained by the principle of:
   a. adaptation level.
   b. opponent processes.
   c. relative deprivation.
   d. catharsis.

7. After hitting a grand-slam home run, Mike noticed that his heart was pounding. Later that evening, after nearly having a collision while driving on the freeway, Mike again noticed that his heart was pounding. That he interpreted this reaction as fear, rather than as ecstasy, can best be explained by the:
   a. James-Lange theory.
   b. Cannon-Bard theory.
   c. opponent-process theory.
   d. two-factor theory.
   e. adaptation-level theory.

8. As part of her job interview, Jan is asked to take a lie-detector test. Jan politely refuses and points out that:
   a. a guilty person can be found innocent by the polygraph.
   b. an innocent person can be found guilty.
   c. a liar can learn to fool a lie-detector test.
   d. these tests err one-third of the time.
   e. all of the above are true.

9. A subject in an experiment concerned with physical responses that accompany emotions reports that her mouth is dry, her heart is racing, and she feels flushed. What emotion is the subject experiencing?
   a. anger
   b. fear
   c. ecstasy
   d. It cannot be determined from the information given.

10. Who will probably be angrier after learning that he or she has received a parking ticket?
    a. Bob, who has just awakened from a nap
    b. Veronica, who has just finished eating a big lunch
    c. Dan, who has just completed a tennis match
    d. Alicia, who has been reading a romantic novel
    e. It cannot be determined from the information given.

11. Children in New York, Nigeria, and New Zealand smile when they are happy and frown when they are sad. This suggests that:
    a. the Cannon-Bard theory is correct.
    b. some emotional expressions are learned at a very early age.
    c. the two-factor theory is correct.
    d. facial expressions of emotion are universal and biologically determined.

12. Who is the *least* likely to display negative emotions openly?
    a. Paul, a game warden in Australia
    b. Niles, a stockbroker in Belgium
    c. Deborah, a physicist in Toronto
    d. Yoko, a dentist in Japan

13. Nine-month-old Nicole's left frontal lobe is more active than her right frontal lobe. We can expect that, all other things being equal, Nicole:
    a. may suffer from mild depression for most of her life.
    b. may have trouble "turning off" upsetting feelings later in her life.
    c. may be more cheerful than those with more active right frontal lobes.
    d. may have trouble expressing feelings later in her life.

14. Julio was extremely angry when he came in for a routine EEG of his brain activity. When he later told this to the doctor, she was no longer concerned about the:
    a. increased electrical activity in Julio's right hemisphere.
    b. increased electrical activity in Julio's left hemisphere.
    c. decreased electrical activity in Julio's amygdala.
    d. increased electrical activity in Julio's amygdala.

15. When the scientist electrically stimulated one area of a monkey's brain, the monkey became enraged. When another electrode was activated, the monkey cowered in fear. The electrodes were most likely implanted in the:
    a. pituitary gland.
    b. adrenal glands.
    c. limbic system.
    d. right hemisphere.

16. As elderly Mr. Hooper crosses the busy intersection, he stumbles and drops the packages he is carrying. Which passerby is most likely to help Mr. Hooper?
    a. Drew, who has been laid off from work for three months
    b. Leon, who is on his way to work
    c. Bonnie, who graduated from college the day before
    d. Nancy, whose father recently passed away

17. Expressing anger can be adaptive when you:
    a. retaliate immediately.
    b. have mentally rehearsed all the reasons for your anger.
    c. count to ten, then blow off steam.
    d. first wait until the anger subsides, then deal with the situation in a civil manner.

18. Cindy was happy with her promotion until she found out that Janice, who has the same amount of experience, receives a higher salary. Cindy's feelings are *best* explained according to the:
    a. adaptation-level phenomenon.
    b. opponent-process theory.
    c. catharsis hypothesis.
    d. principle of relative deprivation.

19. (Close-Up) The first time Rosalina used cocaine she enjoyed it. After taking the drug several times a day for several months, she no longer enjoys its effects; she continues to take it, however, in order not to feel shaky and depressed. Which theory best accounts for her behavior?
    a. James-Lange theory
    b. Cannon-Bard theory
    c. opponent-process theory
    d. two-factor theory

20. Margaret is a finalist in the U.S. Ice Skating Championship. She is very excited about the competition and is feeling energized. More than likely, the two dimensions of her current emotion would be a _____ and _____ .
    a. positive valence; low arousal
    b. negative valence; low arousal
    c. positive valence; high arousal
    d. negative valence; high arousal

Essay Question

Discuss biological and cultural influences on emotions. (Use the space below to list the points you want to make and organize them. Then write the essay on a separate sheet of paper.)

Key Terms

Writing Definitions

Using your own words, on a separate piece of paper write a brief definition or explanation of each of the following terms.

1. emotion
2. James-Lange theory
3. Cannon-Bard theory
4. two-factor theory
5. polygraph
6. catharsis
7. feel-good, do-good phenomenon
8. subjective well-being
9. adaptation-level phenomenon
10. relative deprivation

Summing Up

Complete the flow chart on the following page.

THEORIES OF EMOTION

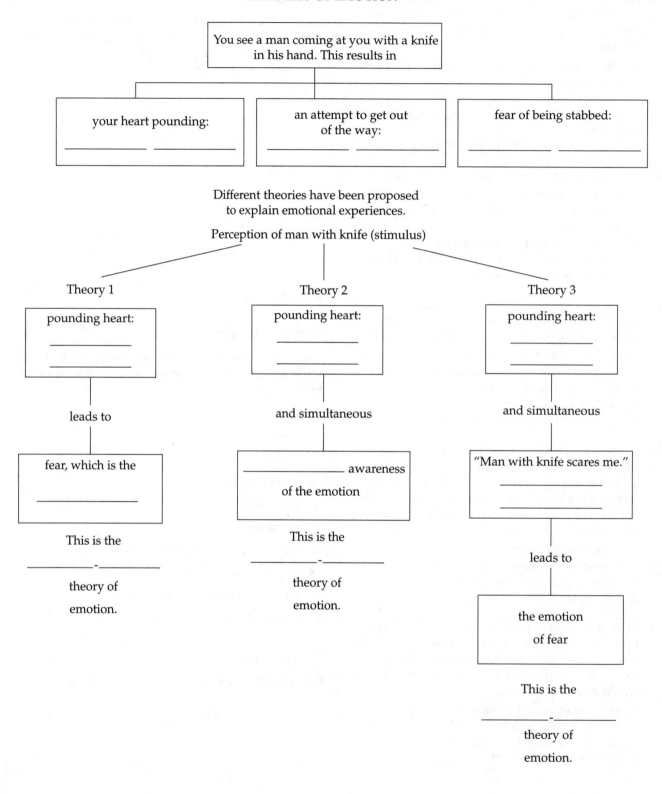

You see a man coming at you with a knife in his hand. This results in

your heart pounding:
_____ _____

an attempt to get out of the way:
_____ _____

fear of being stabbed:
_____ _____

Different theories have been proposed to explain emotional experiences.

Perception of man with knife (stimulus)

Theory 1

pounding heart:
_____
_____

leads to

fear, which is the
_____

This is the
_____-_____
theory of
emotion.

Theory 2

pounding heart:
_____
_____

and simultaneous

_____ awareness
of the emotion

This is the
_____-_____
theory of
emotion.

Theory 3

pounding heart:
_____
_____

and simultaneous

"Man with knife scares me."
_____
_____

leads to

the emotion
of fear

This is the
_____-_____
theory of
emotion.

Answers

Introducing Emotion

Introduction Preview

1. Emotions involve a mixture of physiological arousal, expressive behaviors, and conscious experience.

Theories of Emotion

Section Preview

1. According to the James-Lange theory, the experience of emotion results from awareness of the physiological responses to emotion-arousing stimuli. According to the Cannon-Bard theory, an emotion-arousing stimulus is simultaneously routed to the cortex, which causes the subjective experience of emotion, and to the sympathetic nervous system, which causes the body's physiological arousal.

   In criticizing the James-Lange theory, Walter Cannon argued that the body's responses were not sufficiently distinct to trigger the different emotions. The James-Lange theory has recently received support from evidence showing that there are physiological distinctions among the emotions and that emotions are diminished when the brain's awareness of the body's reactions is reduced. However, many researchers continue to agree with Cannon and Bard that the experience of emotion also involves cognitive activity.

   Schachter's two-factor theory of emotion proposes that emotions have two components: physical arousal and a cognitive label. Like the James-Lange theory, the two-factor theory presumes that our experience of emotion stems from our awareness of physical arousal. Like the Cannon-Bard theory, the two-factor theory presumes that emotions are physiologically similar and require a conscious interpretation of the arousal.

2. Although complex emotions, such as guilt, happiness, and love, clearly arise from conscious thought, there is evidence that some simple emotional responses may not involve conscious thinking. When people repeatedly view stimuli they are not consciously aware of (subliminal stimuli), for example, they come to prefer those stimuli. Furthermore, some neural pathways involved in emotion, such as the one that links the eye to the amygdala, bypass cortical areas involved in thinking and enable an automatic emotional response.

   Worldwide, people experience emotions along two dimensions: pleasant versus unpleasant (the emotion's valence) and high versus low arousal. For people who are energized by arousal, arousal has a positive valence; if arousal causes fear in the person, it has a negative valence.

Stepping Through the Section

1. follow

Cannon argued that the body's responses were not sufficiently distinct to trigger the different emotions and, furthermore, that physiological changes occur too slowly to trigger sudden emotion.

2. cortex; sympathetic; Cannon-Bard

3. diminish; James-Lange

4. agree; cognition

5. physiological; cognitive; Schachter

6. did not; did

7. can

First, experiments on subliminal perception indicate that although stimuli are not consciously perceived, subjects later prefer these stimuli to others they have never been exposed to. Second, there is some separation of the neural pathways involved in emotion and cognition.

8. Lazarus; appraise

It seems that some emotional responses—especially simple likes, dislikes, and fears—involve no conscious thinking. Other emotions are greatly affected by our interpretations and expectations.

9. valence; pleasant (positive valence); unpleasant (negative valence); arousal

The Physiology of Emotion

Section Preview

1. Physiological arousal occurs when the sympathetic nervous system directs the adrenal glands to release epinephrine and norepinephrine. These hormones trigger increased heart rate, blood pressure, and blood sugar levels.

   Our performance on a task is usually best when arousal is moderate. However, the difficulty of the task affects optimum arousal level. A relatively high level of arousal is best on easy or well-learned tasks; a relatively low level of arousal is best on difficult or unrehearsed tasks.

2. Although the autonomic arousal that accompanies the different emotions often is similar, there are real, if subtle, physiological differences. For example, different brain circuits underlie differ-

ent emotions. Limbic stimulation will trigger rage or terror in an animal. These emotions are also accompanied by different finger temperatures and hormone secretions. Negative emotions and positive emotions tend to be accompanied by greater activity in the right and left hemispheres, respectively. Infants and adults with greater activity in their left frontal lobes tend to be more cheerful than those with more active right frontal lobes.

3. (Thinking Critically) The polygraph, or lie detector, measures the physiological responses that accompany emotions. How well the polygraph works depends on whether liars become anxious and exhibit detectable physiological arousal. Critics of the use of lie detectors argue that the tests are inaccurate about one-third of the time because they can't distinguish among anxiety, irritation, and guilt. Thus, they may label the innocent guilty when a question is upsetting. The polygraph may be somewhat more effective in criminal investigations that use the guilty knowledge test, which assesses a subject's response to details of the crime known only to the police and the guilty person.

Stepping Through the Section

1. **a.** Heart rate increases.

   b. Muscles become tense.

   c. The liver pours extra sugar into the bloodstream.

   d. Breathing rate increases.

   e. Digestion slows.

   f. Pupils dilate.

   g. Blood tends to clot more rapidly.

   h. Your skin perspires.

2. sympathetic; adrenal; epinephrine (adrenaline); norepinephrine (noradrenaline)

3. parasympathetic

Performance on a task is usually best when arousal is moderate. However, the difficulty of the task affects optimum arousal level. A relatively high level of arousal is best on easy and well-learned tasks; a relatively low level of arousal is best on difficult tasks.

4. similar

5. fear; rage; finger; hormone

6. are; right; left

7. left; frontal

8. are

9. polygraph

The polygraph measures several of the physiological responses that accompany emotion, such as changes in breathing, pulse rate, blood pressure, and perspiration. The assumption is that lying is stressful, so a person who is lying will become physiologically aroused.

10. anxiety

11. innocent; emotions; arousal

12. do not agree

13. guilty knowledge test

Expressing Emotion

Section Preview

1. People differ in their abilities to detect nonverbal expressions of emotion; introverts and women are better at reading others' emotions, and extraverts are easier to read. Women express happiness best, but men are better at expressing anger. Women are also more likely to express empathy when observing someone in distress.

   Unless trained in detecting lying, most people are not very accurate in spotting subtle facial indicators of deception. U.S. Secret Service agents, federal law officers, and clinical psychologists interested in lying research are more skilled lie-catchers. However, we generally are much more accurate at detecting facial indicators of other emotions.

2. Although there are many cultural variations in the meaning of gestures, facial expressions have universal meaning. Cultures differ in how and how much they use nonverbal expressions, however. In cultures that encourage individuality, emotional displays often are more intense and prolonged than in communal cultures that value interdependence.

   Research demonstrates that facial expressions intensify emotions and also trigger physiological changes in the autonomic nervous system. Imitating others' expressions also promotes empathy with others' feelings.

Stepping Through the Section

1. nonverbal

2. threats; anger; eyes; mouth

3. better; easier

4. better; more; smaller; more

5. happiness; anger

6. facial muscles; are not; experience; law enforcement (U.S. Secret Service agents and federal law officers)

7. e-mail

8. different

9. the same; does not vary

10. Darwin; interpret; contexts

11. individuality; interdependence; sympathy; respect; shame; West

12. intensified

13. found

14. leads

Experiencing Emotion

Section Preview

1. Fear is an adaptive response that prepares the body to flee from danger, protects us from harm, and constrains us from harming other people. Although most fears are the product of learning, we are biologically prepared to acquire certain fears, such as those that probably helped our ancestors to survive. Biological factors also influence specific emotional tendencies, such as a person's level of fearfulness. The amygdala in the brain plays an important role in associating various emotions with certain situations. Following fear conditioning, subjects who have suffered amygdala damage will *remember* the conditioning but no longer show the emotional reaction. If the hippocampus is damaged, however, subjects will show the emotional reaction but won't remember the conditioning trials.

2. The catharsis hypothesis maintains that expressing emotion results in emotional release. Research shows that the cathartic expression of anger is most likely to reduce anger *temporarily* when it is specifically directed against the provoker, when it is justifiable, and when the provoker is not intimidating. Other studies show that openly expressing anger can have the opposite effect and amplify underlying hostility. Angry outbursts may also be habit-forming if they temporarily calm the individual.

   Anger experts recommend that the best way to handle anger is to first bring down the level of physiological arousal by waiting, then deal with the anger in a way that involves neither being chronically angry nor passively sulking.

3. People who are happy perceive the world as safer, make decisions more easily, rate job applicants more favorably, report greater satisfaction with their lives, and are more willing to help others. Factors that predict happiness include having high self-esteem, a close friendship or a satisfying marriage, a meaningful religious faith, being optimistic and outgoing, sleeping well, exercising,

and engaging in challenging work and leisure activities.

The effect of dramatically positive or negative events on happiness is typically temporary. Happiness is also relative to our recent experiences (adaptation-level phenomenon) and to how we compare ourselves with others (relative deprivation principle). These principles help explain why middle- and upper-income people in a given country tend to be slightly more satisfied with life than the relatively poor, even though happiness does not directly increase with affluence.

4. (Close-Up) According to the opponent-process theory, every emotion triggers an opposing emotion that causes our emotions to balance. Repetitions of the event that arouses the primary emotion strengthen the opposing emotion and weaken the experience of the primary emotion, explaining why with repetition the afterreaction, such as the pain of drug withdrawal, becomes stronger.

Stepping Through the Section

1. 10; are

2. adaptive

3. learning (conditioning); observing

The fact that humans quickly learn and slowly unlearn to fear snakes, spiders, and cliffs—fears that were presumably very useful to our ancestors—suggests that these are biologically predisposed fears that develop with little or no learning.

4. amygdala; limbic; remember; emotional

5. hippocampus; emotional reaction; will not

6. amygdala

7. phobias

8. week

9. individuality; catharsis; interdependence; Tahiti; Japan

10. a. Retaliation must be directed against the person who provoked the anger.
    b. Retaliation must be justifiable.
    c. The target of the retaliation must not be someone who is intimidating.

One problem with expressing anger is that it breeds more anger, in part because it may trigger retaliation. Expressing anger can also magnify anger and reinforce its occurrence.

11. a. Wait to calm down.
    b. Deal with anger in a civil way that promotes reconciliation rather than retaliation.

12. safer; more; feel-good, do-good; subjective well-being

13. overestimate; regain

14. do not; remained unchanged

15. intimacy, personal growth, and contribution to the community; wealth

16. adaptation-level

If we acquire new possessions, we feel an initial surge of pleasure. But we then adapt to having these new possessions, come to see them as normal, and require other things to give us another surge of happiness.

17. relative deprivation

18. opponent-process; after; weaker; stronger

19. high self-esteem; satisfying marriage or close friendships; meaningful religious faith; optimistic outgoing personality; good sleeping habits; regular exercise

20. age; race; gender; education; parenthood

21. challenging tasks; active leisure

22. 50

Progress Test 1

Multiple-Choice Questions

1. **d.** is the answer. Generally speaking, performance is optimal when arousal is moderate; for easy tasks, however, performance is optimal when arousal is high. For difficult tasks, performance is optimal when arousal is low. (p. 466)

2. **c.** is the answer. (p. 466)
   a. The skeletal division of the peripheral nervous system carries sensory and motor signals to and from the central nervous system.
   b. The peripheral nervous system is too general an answer, since it includes the sympathetic and parasympathetic divisions, as well as the skeletal division.
   d. The parasympathetic nervous system restores the body to its unaroused state.
   e. The central nervous system is involved in the labeling of emotional arousal.

3. **c.** is the answer. Although many emotions have the same general body arousal, resulting from activation of the sympathetic nervous system, they appear to be associated with different brain circuits. (p. 467)

4. **b.** is the answer. (p. 460)
   a. This expresses the two-factor theory.
   c. This expresses the James-Lange theory.
   d. This expresses the opponent-process theory.

5. **a.** is the answer. (p. 467)
   b. The hypothalamus is involved in eating, thirst, and sexual motivation.

c. The cortex is the center of higher cognitive functions, such as memory and thinking.
   d. The cerebellum is involved in motor coordination.

6. **b.** is the answer. (p. 466)
   a. & c. Acetylcholine, a neurotransmitter involved in motor responses, is not a hormone and therefore is not secreted by a gland.

7. **d.** is the answer. The finding that people whose brains can't sense the body's responses experience considerably less emotion in fact supports the James-Lange theory, which claims that experienced emotion follows from body responses. (pp. 460–461)
   a., b., & c. All these statements go counter to the theory's claim that experienced emotion is essentially just an awareness of the body's response.

8. **c.** is the answer. (p. 468)

9. **c.** is the answer. Subjects who received epinephrine without an explanation felt arousal and experienced this arousal as whatever emotion the experimental confederate in the room with them was displaying. (p. 462)
   a. Epinephrine recipients who expected arousal attributed their arousal to the drug and reported no emotional change in reaction to the confederate's behavior.
   b. & d. In addition to the two groups discussed in the text, the experiment involved placebo recipients; these subjects were not physically aroused and did not experience an emotional change.

10. **e.** is the answer. Education level, race, parenthood, and gender seem unrelated to happiness. (p. 487)

11. **c.** is the answer. (p. 480)
    a. This would not be an example of catharsis, since catharsis involves releasing, rather than suppressing, aggressive energy.
    b. Expressions of anger in such a situation tend to cause the person anxiety and thus tend not to be effective.
    d. One danger of expressing anger is that it will lead to retaliation and an escalation of anger.

12. **d.** is the answer. These are the three components of emotions identified in the textbook. (p. 460)

13. **c.** is the answer. If the suspect becomes physically aroused while answering questions about details only the perpetrator of the crime could know, it is presumed that he or she committed the crime. (p. 469)

14. **b.** is the answer. (pp. 473–474)
    a. The opposite is true; relevant facial muscles are hard to control voluntarily.

c. Authentic facial expressions tend to fade within 4 or 5 seconds.

d. Facial expressions are generally universal; many gestures vary from culture to culture.

15. **d.** is the answer. Facial expressions of fear were associated with increased heart rate only, facial expressions of anger with increases in both heart rate and finger temperature. (p. 467)

a. & b. Skin temperature increases were associated only with expressions of anger.

c. Such feelings did not occur.

16. **d.** is the answer. (p. 483)

17. **b.** is the answer. (p. 481)

a., c., & d. Research studies have not found these factors to be related to altruistic behavior.

18. **d.** is the answer. (p. 474)

19. **d.** is the answer. According to the opponent-process theory, with repeated stimulations the primary emotion becomes weaker and the opponent emotion becomes stronger. (p. 486)

20. **c.** is the answer. (pp. 463)

a. & b. These answers imply that cognition *always* precedes emotion.

d. That changes in facial expression can directly affect people's feelings and body states does not imply a learned ability to interpret facial expressions. In fact, facial expressions apparently speak a universal language, which implies that the ability to interpret them is inborn.

Matching Items

1. a (p. 484)
2. l (p. 481)
3. d (p. 480)
4. j (p. 485)
5. b (p. 486)
6. c (p. 462)
7. h (p. 460)
8. i (p. 466)
9. e (p. 466)
10. g (p. 468)
11. k (p. 481)
12. f (p. 460)

Progress Test 2

Multiple-Choice Questions

1. **a.** is the answer. Emotional arousal activates the sympathetic nervous system, causing the release of sugar into the blood for energy, pupil dilation, and the diverting of blood from the internal organs to the muscles, all of which help prepare the body to meet an emergency. (pp. 465–466)

b. Being autonomic responses, most emotions are *involuntary* reactions.

c. All emotions do *not* have the same physiological basis.

d. Some emotions occur without cognitive awareness.

2. **c.** is the answer. According to Schachter, the two factors in emotion are (1) body arousal and (2) conscious interpretation of the arousal. (p. 462)

3. **a.** is the answer. The principle of relative deprivation states that happiness is relative to others' attainments. This helps explain why those who are relatively well off tend to be slightly more satisfied than the relatively poor, with whom the better-off can compare themselves. (pp. 485–486)

b. Adaptation level is the tendency for our judgments to be relative to our prior experience.

c. This phenomenon has nothing to do with the interpretation of emotion.

d. Opponent processes are opposing emotional states that tend to balance each other.

4. **b.** is the answer. (p. 460)

a. The James-Lange theory states that the experience of an emotion is an awareness of one's physical response to an emotion-arousing stimulus.

c. The two-factor theory states that to experience emotion one must be physically aroused and attribute the arousal to an emotional cause.

d. The opponent-process theory states that every emotion tends to trigger an opposing emotion.

5. **d.** is the answer. (p. 477)

6. **d.** is the answer. No device can literally measure lying. The polygraph measures breathing, pulse rate, blood pressure, and perspiration for changes indicative of physiological arousal. (p. 468)

7. **d.** is the answer. (p. 486)

8. **b.** is the answer. Whereas the meanings of gestures vary from culture to culture, facial expressions seem to have the same meanings around the world. (pp. 473–474)

9. **a.** is the answer. If, as the theory claims, emotions are triggered by physiological reactions, then each emotion must be associated with a unique physiological reaction. (p. 460)

b. According to the Cannon-Bard theory, the same general body response accompanies many emotions.

c. The two-factor theory states that the cognitive interpretation of a general state of physical arousal determines different emotions.

d. The opponent-process theory states that every emotion triggers its opposite emotion.

10. **b.** is the answer. The fears for which humans seem biologically prepared are fears that probably were useful to our ancestors. (p. 478)

11. **d.** is the answer. As the Schachter-Singer study indicated, physical arousal is not always accompanied by an emotional reaction. Only when arousal was attributed to an emotion was it expe-

rienced as such. The results of this experiment, therefore, support the viewpoint that conscious interpretation of arousal must precede emotion. (pp. 462–463)

a., b., & c. Each of these was presented as a supporting argument in the text.

12. **a.** is the answer. (p. 480)

b. The opposite is true. Any emotional arousal will simmer down if you wait long enough.

c. Catharsis often magnifies anger, escalates arguments, and leads to retaliation.

d. When counterattack is justified and can be directed at the offender, catharsis may be helpful.

13. **e.** is the answer. (pp. 465–466)

14. **c.** is the answer. Easy or well-rehearsed tasks, such as sprinting, are best performed when arousal is high; more difficult tasks are best performed when arousal is lower. (p. 466)

15. **a.** is the answer. That physical arousal can be misattributed demonstrates that it is the cognitive interpretation of arousal, rather than the intensity or specific nature of the body's arousal, that determines the conscious experience of emotions. (pp. 462–463)

b. & c. The findings of these studies do not indicate that a minimum level of arousal is necessary for an emotional experience nor that applying a cognitive label must be simultaneous with the arousal.

16. **c.** is the answer. As heightened arousal may reflect feelings of anxiety or irritation rather than of guilt, the polygraph, which simply measures arousal, may easily err. (p. 469)

a. Misuse and invasion of privacy are valid issues, but Lykken primarily objects to the use of lie detectors because of their inaccuracy.

b. Although there are discrepancies among the various measures of arousal, this was not what Lykken objected to.

d. The lie detector errs about one-third of the time.

17. **d.** is the answer. (p. 478)

a. Because most fears are acquired through learning, people acquire highly individual fears.

b. & c. Only a few basic fears are biologically determined and present at birth.

18. **c.** is the answer. (p. 479)

19. **d.** is the answer. (p. 487)

20. **c.** is the answer. (p. 475)

a. & b. These are true of cultures that emphasize individuality rather than interdependence.

True-False Items

1. T (p. 466)
2. F (p. 471)
3. T (p. 466)
4. T (p. 466)
5. T (pp. 475–476)
6. F (pp. 460–461)
7. F (p. 483)
8. T (p. 462)
9. F (p. 463)
10. F (p. 462)

Thinking Critically About Chapter 13

Multiple-Choice Questions

1. **b.** is the answer. The James-Lange theory proposes that the experienced emotion is an awareness of a prior body response: Your pulse races, and so you feel nervous. (p. 460)

a. According to the Cannon-Bard theory, your body's reaction would occur simultaneously with, rather than before, your experience of the emotion.

c. The opponent-process theory states that each time an emotion occurs, an opposing emotion is triggered as well.

d. The adaptation-level phenomenon concerns our tendency to judge stimuli on the basis of recent experience.

2. **b.** is the answer. Professor Simon's judgment of his office is affected by his recent experience: When that experience was of a smaller office, his new office seemed terrific; now, however, it is commonplace. (p. 484)

a. Relative deprivation is the sense that one is worse off than those with whom one compares oneself.

c. This is the theory that every emotion triggers an opposing emotion.

d. This is the principle that there is an inverse relationship between the difficulty of a task and the optimum level of arousal.

3. **b.** is the answer. The parasympathetic division is involved in calming arousal. (p. 466)

a. The sympathetic division is active during states of arousal and hence would not be active in the situation described.

c. The skeletal division is involved in transmitting sensory information and controlling skeletal muscles; it is not involved in arousing and calming the body.

d. This answer is too general, since the peripheral nervous system includes not only the parasympathetic division but also the sympathetic division and the skeletal division.

4. **a.** is the answer. According to the James-Lange theory, Maria's emotions should be greatly diminished since her brain is unable to sense physical arousal. (p. 460)

b. Cannon and Bard would have expected Maria to experience emotions normally because they believed that the experiencing of emotions occurs separately from the body's responses.

c., d., & e. The opponent-process theory, the adaptation-level phenomenon, and the relative deprivation principle make no particular prediction regarding the importance of physical arousal in the conscious experience of emotion.

5. **b.** is the answer. Expressions may amplify the associated emotions. (pp. 475–476)

   a. Laboratory studies have shown that facial expressions *intensify* emotions.

   c. Arousal of the sympathetic nervous system, such as occurs when one is afraid, slows digestive function.

   d. Increased body temperature accompanies anger but not fear.

6. **d.** is the answer. In keeping with the catharsis hypothesis, Jane feels less angry after releasing her aggression. (p. 480)

   a. Adaptation level is our tendency to judge things relative to our experiences.

   b. The opponent-process theory states that every emotion triggers its opposing emotion and that, with repeated stimulation, the former becomes weaker and the latter stronger.

   c. Relative deprivation is the sense that one is worse off relative to those with whom one compares oneself.

7. **d.** is the answer. According to the two-factor theory, it is cognitive interpretation of the same general physiological arousal that distinguishes the two emotions. (p. 462)

   a. According to the James-Lange theory, if the same physical arousal occurred in the two instances, the same emotions should result.

   b. The Cannon-Bard theory argues that conscious awareness of an emotion and body reaction occur at the same time.

   c. The opponent-process theory, which states that every emotion triggers an opposing emotion, has no particular relevance to the example.

   e. Adaptation level concerns our tendency to judge things relative to our experiences.

8. **e.** is the answer. (pp. 468–469)

9. **d.** is the answer. (p. 467)

10. **c.** is the answer. Because physical arousal tends to intensify emotions, Dan (who is likely to be physically aroused after playing tennis) will probably be angrier than Bob or Veronica, who are in more relaxed states. (p. 462)

11. **d.** is the answer. (p. 474)

    a. & c. The Cannon-Bard and two-factor theories

of emotion do not address the universality of emotional expressions.

   b. Even if it is true that emotional expressions are acquired at an early age, this would not necessarily account for the common facial expressions of children from around the world. If anything, the different cultural experiences of the children might lead them to express their feelings in very *different* ways.

12. **d.** is the answer. In Asian and other cultures that emphasize human connections and interdependence, negative emotional displays are rare and typically brief. (p. 475)

    a., b., & c. In cultures that encourage individuality, as in Western Europe, Australia, and North America, emotional displays often are intense and prolonged.

13. **c.** is the answer. (p. 467)

    a. Individuals with more active right frontal lobes tend to be less cheerful and are more likely to be depressed.

    b. In fact, just the opposite is true: People with greater left frontal activity tend to be better able to turn off upsetting feelings.

    d. The text does not suggest that greater left or right frontal activity influences a person's ability to express his or her feelings.

14. **a.** is the answer. As people experience negative emotions, such as anger, the right hemisphere becomes more electrically active. (p. 467)

    c. & d. The EEG measures electrical activity on the surface of the cortex, not at the level of structures deep within the brain, such as the amygdala.

15. **c.** is the answer. (p. 467)

    a., b., & d. Direct stimulation of these brain areas will not trigger fear or rage.

16. **c.** is the answer. People who are in a good mood are more likely to help others. Bonnie, who is probably pleased with herself following her graduation from college, is likely to be in a better mood than Drew, Leon, or Nancy. (p. 481)

17. **d.** is the answer. (p. 480)

    a. Venting anger immediately may lead you to say things you later regret and/or may lead to retaliation by the other person.

    b. Going over the reasons for your anger merely prolongs the emotion.

    c. Counting to ten may give you a chance to calm down, but "blowing off steam" may rekindle your anger.

18. **d.** is the answer. Cindy is unhappy with her promotion because she feels deprived relative to Janice. (p. 485)

a. The adaptation-level phenomenon would predict that Cindy's raise would cause an increase in her happiness, since her most recent experience was to earn a lower salary.

b. The opponent-process theory states that every emotion triggers an opposing emotion that lingers after the first emotion is extinguished. Cindy's mood change, however, is the result of comparing herself to Janice, not the extinction of her pleasure at being promoted.

c. The catharsis hypothesis maintains that venting one's anger may relieve aggressive urges.

19. **c.** is the answer. (p. 486)

   a., b., & d. The James-Lange, Cannon-Bard, and two-factor theories of emotion do not address situations such as Rosalina's, in which conflicting emotions are experienced.

20. **c.** is the answer. (p. 464)

Essay Question

All emotions involve some degree of physiological arousal of the sympathetic nervous system. Although the arousal that occurs with different emotions is in most ways undifferentiated, there may be subtle differences in the brain pathways and hormones associated with different emotions.

Other examples of the influence of biological factors on emotion are the universality of facial expressions of emotion and the fact that humans seem biologically predisposed to learn some fears more quickly than others.

Unlike facial expressions of emotion, the meaning of many gestures is culturally determined. Culture also influences how people express their feelings. In cultures that encourage individuality, for example, emotional displays often are intense and prolonged. In cultures that emphasize human interdependence, negative emotions that might disrupt group harmony are rarely expressed, while displays of "other-sensitive" emotions such as sympathy, respect, and shame are more common than in the West.

Key Terms

1. **Emotion** is a response of the whole organism involving three components: (1) physical arousal, (2) expressive behaviors, and (3) conscious experience. (p. 460)

2. The **James-Lange theory** states that emotional experiences are based on an awareness of the body's responses to emotion-arousing stimuli: a stimulus triggers the body's responses that in turn trigger the experienced emotion. (p. 460)

3. The **Cannon-Bard theory** states that the conscious, subjective experience of an emotion occurs at the same time as the body's physical reaction. (p. 460)

4. The **two-factor theory** of emotion proposes that emotions have two ingredients: physical arousal and a cognitive label. Thus, physical arousal is a necessary, but not a sufficient, component of emotional change. For an emotion to be experienced, arousal must be attributed to an emotional cause. (p. 462)

5. The **polygraph**, or lie detector, is a device that measures several of the physiological responses accompanying emotion. (p. 468)

6. **Catharsis** is emotional release; according to the catharsis hypothesis, by expressing our anger, we can reduce it. (p. 480)

7. The **feel-good, do-good phenomenon** is the tendency of people to be helpful when they are in a good mood. (p. 481)

8. **Subjective well-being** refers to a person's sense of satisfaction with his or her life. (p. 481)

9. The **adaptation-level phenomenon** refers to our tendency to judge things relative to our prior experience. (p. 484)

10. The principle of **relative deprivation** is the sense that we are worse off relative to those with whom we compare ourselves. (p. 485)

Summing Up

You see a man coming at you with a knife in his hand. This results in your heart pounding (*physiological arousal*), an attempt to get out of the way (*expressive behaviors*), and fear of being stabbed (*conscious experience*).

Different theories have been proposed to explain emotional experiences.

Perception of man with knife (stimulus): Theory 1: pounding heart (*physiological arousal*) leads to fear: the *emotion*. This is the *James-Lange* theory of emotion. Theory 2: pounding heart (*physiological arousal*) and simultaneous *subjective* awareness of emotion. This is the *Cannon-Bard* theory of emotion. Theory 3: pounding heart (*physiological arousal*) and simultaneous thought that "Man with knife scares me" lead to the emotion of fear. This is the *two-factor* theory of emotion.

FOCUS ON VOCABULARY AND LANGUAGE

Page 459: No one needs to tell you that feelings add *color* to your life. . . . Without emotions we would experience a very dull and uninteresting existence; we would have no feelings of intense happiness or excitement nor would we experience depression and sadness. Thus, emotions add a variety of interesting qualities (*color*) to our lives.

Theories of Emotion

Page 459: . . . *rumble* of an engine and think someone in a car is *stalking* you. Motorcycles make a vibrating, roaring sound (*rumble*), and if you believed the cyclist was pursuing or hunting you in an ominous and stealthy manner (*stalking you*), you would feel frightened (*scared*); your heart rate would increase (*physiological arousal*), you would walk faster (*behavioral expression*), and you would wonder what was going on (*cognition*).

Page 460: Common sense tells most of us that we cry because we are sad, *lash out* because we are angry, *tremble* because we are afraid. The James-Lange theory states that physiological arousal precedes the experience of emotion. Thus, we cry first, then feel sad; we strike someone (*lash out*), then experience the anger; we shiver and shake (*tremble*), then feel fear. The Cannon-Bard theory proposes that physiological arousal and the experience of emotion occur at the same time but separately. One does not cause the other.

Page 462: Which is the chicken and which the egg? The old riddle asks, "Which came first, the chicken or the egg?" Myers asks which comes first, our cognitions or our emotions? The two-factor theory suggests that physiological arousal has to be cognitively interpreted in order for one to experience different emotions. Stanley Schachter's research showed that the same arousal (*stirred-up state*) can be experienced as two very different emotional states (e.g., euphoria or irritation) depending on how we interpret and label it. Thus, thinking comes before feeling.

Page 462: . . . *testy* . . . This means to be ill-tempered or irritable. Those subjects who were physiologically aroused but did not know why were affected by (*"caught"*) the apparent emotional state of the person they were with. They made different attributions about their aroused (*stirred-up*) state ("I'm happy" or "I'm feeling testy") on the basis of whether the accomplice acted in a euphoric or irritated way.

Page 463: The *heart* is not always subject to the *mind*. Robert Zajonc proposed that some emotional states are not preceded by cognitions. The emotions (*heart*) are not determined by our thoughts (*mind*). We can have *some* feelings, at least, without thinking first.

The Physiology of Emotion

Page 465: . . . *your stomach develops butterflies* . . . When you are apprehensive, fearful, and nervous, you have visceral (internal) sensations that may feel as though small flying insects (*butterflies*) are fluttering around in your stomach (*it develops butterflies*).

Page 466: Basketball players *shooting free throws*—a less automatic skill—may not perform quite as well if a *packed fieldhouse* makes them *hyperaroused* (Sokoll & Mynatt, 1984). When a basketball player is allowed (without interference) to throw the ball through the hoop (*shooting free throws*), it requires a lot of concentration because it is not a usual part of the game. If the player gets anxious and is overaroused (*hyperaroused*) because of the attention of a large crowd (*packed fieldhouse*), he is more likely to make a mistake. A high level of arousal is beneficial for the performance of easy, routine tasks.

Page 467: If you are terrified, you may feel a *clutching, sinking sensation* in your chest and a *knot in your stomach*. Different emotions (anger, fear, sadness) feel different. Someone who is extremely afraid may have certain visceral (internal) reactions such as tightness in the upper abdomen (*a clutching, sinking sensation*) and a feeling of a lump (*knot*) in the stomach.

Page 467: The frontal lobe's rich supply of dopamine receptors may help explain why a *peppy* left hemisphere correlates with a *perky* disposition. For some people, the left frontal lobe has more lively electrical activity (*it is peppy*), compared to the right, and these particular individuals tend to have more cheerful and happier personalities (*preppy dispositions*).

Page 468 (Box): Given the physical indicators of emotion, might we, like *Pinocchio*, give some *telltale sign* whenever we lie? Pinocchio is a fictional character in a children's story whose nose grows longer every time he tells a lie. The polygraph, or lie detector, does not detect lies; rather, it measures a number of physiological reactions (heart rate, blood pressure, and perspiration) (*telltale signs*) which indicate a change in emotional state. Unlike Pinocchio, people display no reliable or valid indicators of whether they are lying or telling the truth.

Expressing Emotion

Page 470: Most of us are good enough at *reading* nonverbal cues to decipher the emotions in an old *silent film.* We communicate our feelings with words (verbally) and through body language (nonverbally). Without hearing a single word, as in a movie with no soundtrack (*silent film*), we can discern much about someone's emotional state by observing (*reading*) his or her bodily actions and facial expressions. As Myers notes, when we look at a large group of faces, a single angry one will be extremely noticeable (*it will "pop out"*) and will be detected more quickly than a single happy one.

Page 473: Fidgeting, for example, may reveal *anxiety* or *boredom.* Many popular books and articles suggest what to look for in body language during interviews, business meetings, and so on. However, specific interpretations of gestures or posture cannot be made accurately or reliably. For example, restlessness, accompanied by frequent small movements (*fidgeting*), may be indicative of either disinterest (*boredom*) or extreme nervousness (*anxiety*).

Page 474: Ditto for anger, and to a lesser extent the other basic expressions. There is a great deal of consistency across cultures in the interpretation of different emotional expressions. In tests, people the world over could reliably tell which face expressed happiness; this result was found over and over again (*ditto*), and similar results were found for other fundamental expressions (e.g., anger and fear).

Page 474: A sneer, for example, retains elements of an animal's baring its teeth in *a snarl.* Darwin believed that all humans have inherited the ability to express emotions through very similar facial expressions. Thus, a person's scornful or contemptuous grimace (*sneer*) has many aspects of the fierce growl with teeth showing (*a snarl*) typical of dogs and other animals. Emotional expressions are one form of social communication.

Page 475: Fake a big grin. Now scowl. Can you feel the difference? Clearly, our moods affect how we look, but Myers is inviting you to test the idea that your facial expression can affect your mood. Make a large, false smile (*fake a grin*). Next, wrinkle or furrow your brow, frown and look sullen (*scowl*). Subjects in numerous experiments felt different emotions under these conditions. Smile and inside you feel happy, scowl and you may see the world as more miserable than it is.

Experiencing Emotion

Page 477: Fear can be *poisonous.* To be very afraid is an adaptive emotion (it prepares our bodies for fight or flight, it creates cohesion in groups, it can protect us from harm, and it can constrain us from behaving badly). On the other hand, fear can obsess us, keep us awake at night, and keep us constantly worried (*a poisonous emotion*).

Page 478: Stone Age fears leave us unprepared for high-tech dangers. Because of our evolutionary past we seem to be biologically inclined to learn some fears much more easily and quickly than others. Fear of heights, snakes, spiders, and so forth is easier to condition than fear of furniture, appliances, cars, electricity, and so on. Fears that were adaptive in the past (*Stone Age fears*) are not necessarily beneficial in today's technological era.

Page 479: Popular books and articles on aggression at times advise that even releasing angry feelings as *hostile outbursts* can be better than internalizing them. The idea is that expressing your anger openly (*hostile outbursts or "venting your anger"*) provides some form of emotional release (*catharsis*) and that this is better than not expressing your feelings and holding your anger inside (*internalizing it*). Under certain circumstances, this may provide temporary relief, but the evidence also suggests that expressing anger can increase or magnify (*breed more*) anger.

Page 480: . . . *"blowing off steam"* . . . This means to openly express your anger and rage. Myers notes that doing this can increase or amplify your hostile emotions, but it may also be reinforcing because it releases some of the frustration. Consequently, the next time these feelings arise, the more likely it is that the hostile behavior (*explosive outbursts*) will be repeated.

Page 481: We have inherited any number of *contradictory maxims* concerning happiness. . . . Over the centuries wise people have passed on to us a variety of principles (*maxims*) on the topic of happiness. Most of these are inconsistent and often in opposition to each other (*contradictory*). As Myers points out, to sort out (*sift*) the real predictors of happiness from the seemingly believable guesses (*plausible hunches*) requires research.

Page 482: Once their *rush of euphoria* wears off, state lottery winners typically find their overall happiness unchanged. . . . We probably all dream of winning large amounts of money through gambling (*state lottery winners*) and then living happily ever after. However, once the initial feelings of excitement (*rush of euphoria*) diminish, most winners discover that they are no happier. Myers puts it succinctly: "Wealth is like health. Its utter absence breeds misery, yet having it is no guarantee of happiness."

Page 483: . . . machines *galore* . . . To have high-tech gadgets, such as VCRs, TVs, CDs, and other material possessions in plentiful supply (*galore*) does not make people happier.

Page 483: The findings *lob a bombshell* at modern materialism. . . . The contemporary tendency to accumulate wealth and possessions (*modern materialism*) in industrialized and affluent countries has not resulted in greater happiness. This finding challenges and destroys (*lobs a bombshell at*) the myth that riches (*affluence*) bring happiness and social well-being.

Page 485: When the victor belongs to the spoils and the possessor is possessed by possessions, adaptation level has *run amuck.* An old adage states that "to the victor belongs the spoils of the enemy." Myers has humorously and alliteratively rephrased this piece of wisdom. He points out that when we no longer own our belongings (*possessions*) but are owned (*possessed*) by them, then adaptation level is totally out of control (*has run amuck*). The **adaptation-level principle** states that happiness is relative to our prior experience.

Page 486 (Close-Up): With every *kick* comes a *kickback.* . . . With most *pain* comes a *gain.* The *opponent-process theory* proposes that for every feeling we experience, an opposite emotion is elicited. If we feel pleasure (*get a kick*), it will also trigger the opposite effect (*a kickback*), and with repeated exposure to the stimulus, there will be diminished positive feelings. Likewise, if we experience suffering, there will also be an opposite emotion elicited (*a gain*) that will linger after the painful stimulus is gone. Thus, the unpleasant experience of fear before some dangerous activity (e.g., jumping out of a plane with a parachute on) will be replaced by elation once you land safely, and this feeling will last for some time.

Page 486: Usually, they felt happier if mentally engaged by work or active leisure than if *passively vegetating.* In a study in which subjects were asked at random intervals (by use of electronic pagers) to report their present emotional state and the activities they were engaged in, they reported being happiest when busy and involved in some activity (work or leisure) that was relatively inexpensive; they were most content when totally and actively absorbed compared to when they were indifferent and mindlessly preoccupied (*passively vegetating*), such as when watching TV.

CHAPTER 14: Personality

Chapter Overview

Personality refers to each individual's characteristic pattern of thinking, feeling, and acting. Chapter 14 examines four perspectives on personality. Psychoanalytic theory emphasizes the unconscious and irrational aspects of personality. Trait theory led to advances in techniques for evaluating and describing personality. Humanistic theory draws attention to the concept of self and to human potential for healthy growth. The social-cognitive perspective emphasizes the effects of our interactions with the environment. The text first describes and then evaluates the contributions and shortcomings of each perspective. In addition, within each section is a brief description of some of the techniques used by the perspective in analyzing personality.

NOTE: Answer guidelines for all Chapter 14 questions begin on page 405.

Introducing Personality (p. 489)

Introduction Preview

First, skim the introduction. Then read the following objective and, as you read the text, search for the information that will enable you to meet that objective. Answer guidelines are provided on page 405.

1. Define personality, and explain how its study differs from that of other psychological research interests.

The Psychoanalytic Perspective
(pp. 490–501)

> David Myers at times uses idioms that are unfamiliar to some readers. If you do not know the meaning of any of the following words, phrases, or expressions in the context in which they appear in the text, refer to pages 415–416 for an explanation: *ran up a bookstore debt; mind running; glimpse; virtuous . . . wantonly; twig of personality is bent; act out . . . willy-nilly; icebreaker; sparks flew; scientific shortcomings.*

Section Preview

First, skim the section, noting headings and boldface items. Then read the following objectives and, as you read the text, search for the information that will enable you to meet each objective. Answer guidelines are provided on page 405.

1. Describe how Freud's search for the psychological roots of nervous disorders led to his study of the unconscious, and explain psychoanalysis.

2. Describe Freud's views of personality structure.

3. Outline and describe Freud's psychosexual stages of personality development.

4. Explain Freud's view of maladaptive behavior and describe how defense mechanisms operate.

5. Explain how projective tests are used to assess personality, and describe research findings regarding their validity and reliability.

6. Discuss the major ideas of the neo-Freudians and today's psychodynamic theorists.

7. Evaluate the psychoanalytic perspective.

Stepping Through the Section

After you have read the section, complete the sentences and answer the questions. As you proceed, evaluate your performance by consulting the answers on page 406. Do not continue with the next section until you understand each answer. If you need to, review or reread the section in the textbook before continuing.

1. The psychoanalytic perspective on personality was proposed by _____ _____ .

2. The technique used by Freud, in which the patient relaxes and says whatever comes to mind, is called _____ _____ .

3. Freud called his theory and associated techniques, whereby painful unconscious memories are exposed, _____ .

4. According to this theory, the mind is like an iceberg in that many of a person's thoughts, wishes, and feelings are hidden in a large _____ region. Some of the thoughts in this region can be retrieved at will into consciousness; these thoughts are said to be _____ . Many of the memories of this region, however, are blocked, or _____ , from consciousness.

5. Freud believed that a person's _____ wishes are often reflected in his or her dreams and _____ of the tongue or pen. Freud called the remembered content of dreams the _____ _____ , which he believed to be a censored version of the dream's true _____ .

6. Freud believed that all facets of personality arise from conflict between our _____ impulses and the _____ restraints against them.

7. According to Freud, personality consists of three interacting structures: the _____ , the _____ , and the _____ .

8. The id is a reservoir of energy that is primarily _____ (conscious/unconscious) and operates according to the _____ principle.

9. The ego develops _____ (before/after) the id and consists of perceptions, thoughts, and memories that are mostly _____ (conscious/unconscious).

The ego operates according to the
_____ principle.

Explain why the ego is considered the "executive" of personality.

Explain how this complex of feelings is resolved through the process of identification.

10. The personality structure that reflects moral values is the _____ .

11. A person with a _____ (strong/weak) superego may be self-indulgent; one with an unusually _____ (strong/weak) superego may be continually guilt-ridden.

12. According to Freud, personality is formed as the child passes through a series of _____ stages.

13. The first stage is the _____ stage, which takes place during the first 18 months of life. During this stage, the id's energies are focused on behaviors such as _____ .

14. The second stage is the _____ stage, which lasts from about age _____ months to _____ years.

15. The third stage is the _____ stage, which lasts roughly from ages _____ to _____ . During this stage the id's energies are focused on the _____ . Freud also believed that during this stage children develop sexual desires for the _____ (same/opposite)-sex parent. Freud referred to these feelings as the _____ in boys. Some psychologists believe that girls experience a parallel _____ _____ .

16. Freud believed that _____ with the same-sex parent is the basis for _____ _____ .

17. During the next stage, sexual feelings are repressed: this phase is called the _____ stage and lasts until adolescence.

18. The final stage of development is called the _____ stage.

19. According to Freud, it is possible for a person's development to become blocked in any of the stages; in such an instance, the person is said to be _____ .

20. The ego attempts to protect itself against anxiety through the use of _____ _____ . The process underlying each of these mechanisms is _____ .

21. Dealing with anxiety by returning to an earlier stage of development is called _____ .

22. When a person reacts in a manner opposite that of his or her true feelings, _____ _____ is said to have occurred.

23. When a person attributes his or her own feelings to another person, _____ has occurred.

24. When a person offers a false, self-justifying explanation for his or her actions, _____ has occurred.

25. When impulses are directed toward an object other than the one that caused arousal, _____ has occurred.

26. When a person rechannels an unacceptable impulse into a socially approved activity, _____ has occurred.

Matching Items

Match each defense mechanism in the following list with the proper example of its manifestation.

Defense Mechanisms

_____ **1.** displacement
_____ **2.** projection
_____ **3.** reaction formation
_____ **4.** rationalization
_____ **5.** regression
_____ **6.** sublimation

Manifestations

a. nail biting or thumb sucking in an anxiety-producing situation

b. overzealous crusaders against "immoral behaviors," who don't want to acknowledge their own sexual desires

c. saying you drink "just to be sociable" when in reality you have a drinking problem

d. thinking someone hates you when in reality you hate that person

e. a child who is angry at his parents and vents this anger on the family pet, a less threatening target

f. a musician who channels her anger over social injustices into songwriting

27. Defense mechanisms are _____ (conscious/unconscious) processes.

28. Tests that provide subjects with ambiguous stimuli for interpretation are called _____ tests.

29. Henry Murray introduced the personality assessment technique called the _____ _____ Test.

30. The most widely used projective test is the _____ , in which subjects are shown a series of _____ . Generally, these tests appear to have _____ (little/significant) validity and reliability.

31. The theorists who established their own, modified versions of psychoanalytic theory are called _____-_____ . These theorists typically place _____ (more/less) emphasis on the conscious mind than Freud did and _____ (more/less) emphasis on sex and aggression.

Briefly summarize how each of the following theorists departed from Freud.

a. Adler _____

_____

b. Horney _____

_____

_____

c. Jung _____

_____

32. Today's psychologists _____ (accept/reject) the idea that people inherit a common reservoir of experiences, which _____ (which theorist?) called a _____ .

33. More recently, some of Freud's ideas have been incorporated into _____ theory. Unlike Freud, the theorists advocating this perspective do not believe that _____ is the basis of personality. They do agree, however, that much of mental life is _____ , that _____ shapes personality, and that we often struggle with _____ _____ .

34. Contrary to Freud's theory, research indicates that human development is _____ (fixed in childhood/life-long), children gain their gender-identity at a(n) _____ (earlier/later) age, and the presence of a same-sex parent _____ (is/is not) necessary for the child to become strongly masculine or feminine. Freud's ideas about the natural superiority of men _____ (have/have not) been thoroughly discounted. Another Freudian idea that is no longer widely accepted is that psychological disorders are caused by _____ _____ .

35. Psychoanalytic theory rests on the assumption that the human mind often _____ painful experiences. Many of today's researchers think that this process is much _____ (more common/rarer) than Freud believed. They also believe that when it does occur, it is a reaction to terrible _____ .

36. Recent researchers primarily perceive the unconscious not as the site of instinctual urges, but as where _____ is processed without awareness.

Explain the views held by contemporary researchers regarding the contents of the unconscious.

37. Recent research _____ (supports/does not support) Freud's idea that we defend ourselves against anxiety.

38. Recent research provides some support for two Freudian defense mechanisms: _____ and _____ . More supportive evidence exists for defenses that defend _____ than for defenses tied to _____ _____ such as _____ and _____ .

39. Criticism of psychoanalysis as a scientific theory centers on the fact that it provides after-the-fact explanations and does not offer _____ _____ .

The Trait Perspective (pp. 502–511)

> If you do not know the meaning of any of the following words, phrases, or expressions in the context in which they appear in the text, refer to pages 416–417 for an explanation: *Flabbergasted; dubbed the Big Five; blind date; spoofing; the acid test; scoff; suckering methods; "stock spiel"; labeling and pigeonholing.*

Section Preview

Answer guidelines are provided on page 407.

1. Discuss trait theories of personality and trace their history.

2. Identify the Big Five personality factors, and discuss recent research findings regarding them.

3. Describe the assessment techniques associated with the trait perspective.

4. Evaluate the trait perspective on personality, and describe research findings regarding the consistency of behavior over time and across situations.

Stepping Through the Section

Answers are provided on page 407.

1. Gordon Allport developed trait theory, which defines personality in terms of people's characteristic _____ and conscious _____ .

2. Trait theorists are generally less interested in _____ individual traits than they are in _____ them.

3. The ancient Greeks classified people according to four types: _____ , or depressed; _____ , or cheerful; _____ , or unemotional; and _____ , or irritable.

4. Sheldon identified three body types: the jolly _____ type, the bold _____ type, and the high-strung _____ type.

5. The _____-_____ _____ _____ classifies people according to Carl Jung's personality types. Although recently criticized for its lack of predictive value, this test has been widely used in _____ and _____ counseling.

6. To reduce the number of traits to a few basic ones, psychologists use the statistical procedure of _____ _____ . The Eysencks think that two or three genetically influenced personality dimensions are sufficient; these include _____-_____ and emotional _____-_____ .

7. More recently, researchers have arrived at a cluster of five factors that seem to describe the major features of personality. List and briefly describe the Big Five.
   a. _____
   b. _____
   c. _____
   d. _____
   e. _____

8. In adulthood, the Big Five traits are quite _____ (stable/variable), with heritability estimated at _____ percent or more for each dimension. Moreover, these traits _____ (describe/do not describe) personality in other cultures and _____ (predict/do not predict) other personal attributes.

9. Genetic predispositions _____ (do/do not) influence most personality traits.

10. Some researchers believe that extraverts seek stimulation because their level of _____ is relatively low. PET scans reveal an area of the brain's _____ lobe that is less active in _____ (extraverts/introverts) than in _____ (extraverts/introverts.

11. Emotionally _____ (stable/unstable) people react calmly because their _____ _____ _____ are not as reactive as those of _____ (stable/unstable) people.

12. Jerome Kagan attributes differences in children's _____ and _____ to autonomic nervous system reactivity. Research increasingly reveals that our _____ play an important role in defining our

_____ and _____
style.

(Thinking Critically) Explain several techniques used by astrologers to persuade people to accept their advice.

13. Questionnaires that categorize personality traits are called _____
_____ . The most widely used of all such personality tests is the

_____ _____

_____ _____ .

This test was developed by testing a large pool of items and selecting those that differentiated particular individuals; in other words, the test was _____ derived.

14. Although personality tests that are based on _____-reports are the most widely used, some psychologists believe that _____ reports are more trustworthy.

15. Human behavior is influenced both by our inner _____ and by the external _____ .

16. To be considered a personality trait a characteristic must persist over _____ and across _____ . Research on children's propensity to cheat, for example, indicates that people's behavior on different occasions is generally quite _____ (variable/consistent).

17. An individual's score on a personality test _____ (is/is not) very predictive of his or her behavior in any given situation.

Defend trait theory against the criticism that people seem not to have clear, consistent personalities.

The Humanistic Perspective (pp. 512–521)

> If you do not know the meaning of any of the following words, phrases, or expressions in the context in which they appear in the text, refer to pages 417–418 for an explanation: *crippled spirits; acorn, primed for growth; negative about themselves; prowess; Lake Wobegon; pride does often go before a fall; swelled head; put-downs; provides one's bearings; lose face; rugged individual; playing possum.*

Section Preview

Answer guidelines are provided on page 408.

1. Describe the humanistic perspective on personality, and discuss the basic ideas of Maslow and Rogers.

2. Describe recent research on the way people view themselves.

3. Discuss how culture affects one's sense of self, including research findings on stigmatized groups and differences between individualist and collectivist cultures.

4. Evaluate the humanistic perspective.

Stepping Through the Section

Answers are provided on page 408.

1. Two influential theories of humanistic psychology were proposed by _____ and _____ .

2. According to Maslow, humans are motivated by needs that are organized into a _____ . Maslow refers to the process of fulfilling one's potential as _____ .

List some of the characteristics Maslow associated with those who fulfilled their potential.

3. According to Rogers, a person nurtures growth in a relationship by being _____ , _____ , and _____ . People who are accepting of others offer them _____ _____ _____ .

4. For both Maslow and Rogers, an important feature of personality is how an individual perceives himself or herself; this is the person's _____ .

5. Hazel Markus and colleagues introduced the concept of an individual's _____ _____ to emphasize how our aspirations motivate us through specific goals.

6. According to the humanists, personality development hinges on our feelings of self-worth, or _____ . People who feel good about themselves are relatively

_____ (dependent on/independent of) outside pressures, while people who fall short of their ideals are more prone to _____ and _____ .

7. People who are vulnerable to depression often feel they are falling short of their _____ . Those vulnerable to anxiety often feel they are falling short of what they _____ .

8. In a series of experiments, researchers found that people who were made to feel insecure were _____ (more/less) critical of other persons or tended to express heightened _____ _____ .

9. Research studies demonstrate that ethnic minorities, people with disabilities, and women generally _____ (have/do not have) lower self-esteem.

10. Members of stigmatized groups maintain self-esteem in three ways:

    a. _____

    b. _____

    c. _____

11. Research has shown that most people tend to have _____ (low/high) self-esteem.

12. The tendency of people to judge themselves favorably is called the _____ bias.

13. Responsibility for success is generally accepted _____ (more/less) readily than responsibility for failure.

14. Most people perceive their own behavior and traits as being _____ (above/below) average.

15. Bushman and Baumeister found that students with unrealistically _____ (low/high) self-esteem were most likely to become exceptionally aggressive after criticism.

16. People who give priority to personal goals and define their identity in terms of personal attributes are members of _____ cultures. People who give priority to the goals of their groups belong to _____ cultures.

Contrast the influences of individualism and collectivism on personal identity.

17. Direct confrontation and blunt honesty are rare in _____ cultures. People in _____ cultures have more personal _____ , but they also experience more _____ , more _____ , more _____ , and more _____-_____ disease. Within individualist cultures, people with the strongest _____ _____ express the greatest satisfaction with their lives.

18. In recent decades, Western individualism has _____ (increased/decreased).

State three criticisms of humanistic psychology.

The Social-Cognitive Perspective
(pp. 522–528)

> If you do not know the meaning of any of the following words, phrases, or expressions in the context in which they appear in the text, refer to page 418 for an explanation: *cold shoulder; leaping a hurdle; put an optimistic spin on setbacks; bombing the upcoming exam; flunking out.*

Section Preview

Answer guidelines are provided on page 409.

1. Describe the social-cognitive perspective, and define reciprocal determinism, giving three examples.

2. Discuss research findings on personal control.

3. Describe how social-cognitive researchers study behavior, and evaluate this perspective on personality.

Stepping Through the Section

Answers are provided on page 409.

1. Social-cognitive theorists focus on how the individual and the _____ interact. One such theorist is _____ .

2. Social-cognitive theorists propose that personality is shaped by the mutual influence of our

_____ , _____
factors, and _____ factors. This is
the principle of _____

_____ .

Describe three different ways in which the environment and personality interact.

9. It follows from the social-cognitive perspective
that the best means of predicting people's future
behavior is their _____

_____ .

Describe a criticism of the social-cognitive perspective.

3. Individuals who believe that they control their
own destinies are said to perceive an

_____ _____

_____ _____ .

Individuals who believe that their fate is determined by outside forces are said to perceive an

_____ _____

_____ _____ .

4. Seligman found that exposure to inescapable
punishment produced a passive resignation in
behavior, which he called _____

_____ .

5. People become happier when they are given
_____ (more/less) control over
what happens to them.

6. One measure of a person's feelings of effectiveness is their degree of _____ .

7. (Close-Up) During its first century, psychology
focused primarily on understanding and alleviating _____ _____ . In
the future, however, thriving Western cultures
may create a more _____ psycholo-
gy, focused on three pillars:

   a. _____
   b. _____
   c. _____

8. Our natural positive thinking tends to vanish
when we are about to face _____ .

10. List the major contributions of each perspective to
our understanding of personality.

   a. Psychoanalytic _____

   _____

   b. Trait _____

   _____

   c. Humanistic _____

   _____

   d. Social-Cognitive _____

   _____

   _____

Web Sightings

Many excellent web sites are available for exploring
personality. For example, there are web pages for all
the major theorists that present overviews of their
understanding of personality, biographical sketches,
and critical evaluations of their contributions to psychology. Other sites allow you to view samples of the
major personality tests. Be careful, however. Remember to be skeptical in your inquiry and always consider the scientific credibility of the source of information you find on the Web. A good way to get started
is to pick several key words or phrases that are related to personality and, using _Yahoo_, _Webcrawler_,
PsychCrawler, or your favorite search engine, try to
find relevant pages. For example, try searching for
"personality theory," "projective test," or "Carl
Rogers." When you have exhausted this approach,

access the American Psychological Association's *Frequently Asked Questions (FAQ)* page (**http://www. apa.org/science/test.html**). Then, using this site, try to find the answers to the following questions.

1. What is graphoanalysis? Can it help illuminate the mysteries of human nature?

2. Identify three scientific journals that publish theory and research articles about personality. Pick one, then find the table of contents of its most recent issue.

3. Learn as much as you can about the life of a major personality theorist.

4. Where would you find a test to measure the self-concept? Who is qualified to administer such a test? What are some of the responsibilities of those who administer personality tests?

5. What is the difference between *phrenology* and *craniology*? When were these approaches to personality popular? Are they still around?

Progress Test 1

Multiple-Choice Questions

Circle your answers to the following questions and check them with the answers on page 409. If your answer is incorrect, read the explanation for why it is incorrect and then consult the appropriate pages of the text (in parentheses following the correct answer).

1. The text defines *personality* as:
   a. the set of personal attitudes that characterizes a person.
   b. an individual's characteristic pattern of thinking, feeling, and acting.
   c. a predictable set of responses to environmental stimuli.
   d. an unpredictable set of responses to environmental stimuli.

2. Which of the following places the greatest emphasis on the unconscious mind?
   a. the humanistic perspective
   b. the social-cognitive perspective
   c. the trait perspective
   d. the psychoanalytic perspective

3. Which of the following is the correct order of psychosexual stages proposed by Freud?
   a. oral; anal; phallic; latency; genital
   b. anal; oral; phallic; latency; genital
   c. oral; anal; genital; latency; phallic
   d. anal; oral; genital; latency; phallic
   e. oral; phallic; anal; genital; latency

4. According to Freud, defense mechanisms are methods of reducing:
   a. anger.   c. anxiety.
   b. fear.   d. lust.

5. Collectivist cultures:
   a. give priority to the goals of their groups.
   b. value the maintenance of social harmony.
   c. foster social interdependence.
   d. are characterized by none of the above.
   e. are characterized by a., b., and c.

6. Neo-Freudians such as Adler and Horney believed that:
   a. Freud placed too great an emphasis on the conscious mind.
   b. Freud placed too great an emphasis on sexual and aggressive instincts.
   c. the years of childhood were more important in the formation of personality than Freud had indicated.
   d. Freud's ideas about the id, ego, and superego as personality structures were incorrect.

7. Research on locus of control indicates that internals are _____ than externals.
   a. more dependent
   b. more intelligent
   c. better able to cope with stress
   d. more sociable
   e. more depressed

8. Which two dimensions of personality have the Eysencks emphasized?
   a. extraversion–introversion and emotional stability–instability
   b. internal–external locus of control and extraversion–introversion
   c. internal–external locus of control and emotional stability–instability
   d. melancholic–phlegmatic and choleric–sanguine

9. With regard to personality, it appears that:
   a. there is little consistency of behavior from one situation to the next and little consistency of traits over the life span.
   b. there is little consistency of behavior from one situation to the next but significant consistency of traits over the life span.
   c. there is significant consistency of behavior from one situation to the next but little consistency of traits over the life span.
   d. there is significant consistency of behavior from one situation to the next and significant consistency of traits over the life span.

10. The humanistic perspective on personality:
    a. emphasizes the driving force of unconscious motivations in personality.
    b. emphasizes the growth potential of "healthy" individuals.
    c. emphasizes the importance of interaction with the environment in shaping personality.
    d. describes personality in terms of scores on various personality scales.

11. According to Rogers, three conditions are necessary to promote growth in personality. These are:
    a. honesty, sincerity, and empathy.
    b. high self-esteem, honesty, and empathy.
    c. high self-esteem, genuineness, and acceptance.
    d. high self-esteem, acceptance, and honesty.
    e. genuineness, acceptance, and empathy.

12. Regarding the self-serving bias, humanistic psychologists have emphasized that self-affirming thinking:
    a. is generally maladaptive to the individual because it distorts reality by overinflating self-esteem.
    b. is generally adaptive to the individual because it maintains self-confidence and minimizes depression.
    c. tends to prevent the individual from viewing others with compassion and understanding.
    d. tends not to characterize people who have experienced unconditional positive regard.

13. Which of Freud's ideas would not be accepted by most contemporary psychologists?
    a. Development is essentially fixed in childhood.
    b. Sexuality is a potent drive in humans.
    c. The mind is an iceberg with consciousness being only the tip.
    d. Repression can be the cause of forgetting.

14. Individualist cultures:
    a. value communal solidarity.
    b. emphasize personal achievement and identity.
    c. are less competitive than collectivist cultures.
    d. are characterized by none of the above.
    e. are characterized by a., b., and c.

15. Projective tests such as the Rorschach inkblot test have been criticized because:
    a. their scoring system is too rigid and leads to unfair labeling.
    b. they were standardized with unrepresentative samples.
    c. they have low reliability and low validity.
    d. it is easy for people to fake answers in order to appear healthy.

16. A major criticism of trait theory is that it:
    a. places too great an emphasis on early childhood experiences.
    b. overestimates the consistency of behavior in different situations.
    c. underestimates the importance of heredity in personality development.
    d. places too great an emphasis on positive traits.

17. For humanistic psychologists, many of our attitudes and behaviors are ultimately shaped by whether our _____ is _____ or _____ .
    a. ego; strong; weak
    b. locus of control; internal; external
    c. personality structure; introverted; extraverted
    d. self-concept; positive; negative

18. In studying personality, a trait theorist would most likely:
    a. use a projective test.
    b. observe a person in a variety of situations.
    c. use a personality inventory.
    d. use the method of free association.

19. Id is to ego as _____ is to _____ .
    a. reality principle; pleasure principle
    b. pleasure principle; reality principle
    c. conscious forces; unconscious forces
    d. conscience; "personality executive"

20. Which of the following is a major criticism of the social-cognitive perspective?
   a. It focuses too much on early childhood experiences.
   b. It focuses too little on the inner traits of a person.
   c. It provides descriptions but not explanations.
   d. It lacks appropriate assessment techniques.

21. Recent research has provided more support for defense mechanisms such as _____ than for defense mechanisms such as _____ .
   a. displacement; reaction formation
   b. reaction formation; sublimation
   c. displacement; sublimation
   d. sublimation; displacement

Matching Items

Match each definition or description with the appropriate term.

Definitions or Descriptions

_____ **1.** redirecting impulses to a less threatening object
_____ **2.** test consisting of a series of inkblots
_____ **3.** the conscious executive of personality
_____ **4.** personality inventory
_____ **5.** disguising an impulse by imputing it to another person
_____ **6.** switching an unacceptable impulse into its opposite
_____ **7.** the unconscious repository of instinctual drives
_____ **8.** a statistical technique that identifies clusters of personality traits
_____ **9.** personality structure that corresponds to a person's conscience
_____ **10.** providing self-justifying explanations for an action
_____ **11.** a projective test consisting of a set of ambiguous pictures

Terms

a. id
b. ego
c. superego
d. reaction formation
e. rationalization
f. displacement
g. factor analysis
h. projection
i. TAT
j. Rorschach
k. MMPI

Progress Test 2

Progress Test 2 should be completed during a final chapter review. Answer the following questions after you thoroughly understand the correct answers for the section reviews and Progress Test 1.

Multiple-Choice Questions

1. Which perspective on personality emphasizes the interaction between the individual and the environment in shaping personality?
   a. psychoanalytic   **c.** humanistic
   b. trait   **d.** social-cognitive

2. According to Freud's theory, personality arises in response to conflicts between:
   a. our unacceptable urges and our tendency to become self-actualized.
   b. the process of identification and the ego's defense mechanisms.
   c. the collective unconscious and our individual desires.
   d. our biological impulses and the social restraints against them.

3. The _____ classifies people according to Carl Jung's personality types.
   a. Myers-Briggs Type Indicator
   b. MMPI
   c. Locus of Control Scale
   d. Kagan Temperament Scale
   e. TAT

4. Seligman has found that humans and animals who are exposed to aversive events they cannot escape may develop:
   a. an internal locus of control.
   b. a reaction formation.
   c. learned helplessness.
   d. neurotic anxiety.
   e. displacement.

5. Research has shown that individuals who are made to feel insecure are subsequently:
   a. more critical of others.
   b. less critical of others.
   c. more likely to display a self-serving bias.
   d. less likely to display a self-serving bias.

6. An example of the self-serving bias described in the text is the tendency of people to:
   a. see themselves as better than average on nearly any desirable dimension.
   b. accept more responsibility for successes than failures.
   c. be overly critical of other people.
   d. be overly sensitive to criticism.
   e. do both a. and b.

7. The Minnesota Multiphasic Personality Inventory (MMPI) is a(n):
   a. projective personality test.
   b. empirically derived and objective personality test.
   c. personality test developed mainly to assess job applicants.
   d. personality test used primarily to assess locus of control.

8. Trait theory attempts to:
   a. show how development of personality is a lifelong process.
   b. describe and classify people in terms of their predispositions to behave in certain ways.
   c. determine which traits are most conducive to individual self-actualization.
   d. explain how behavior is shaped by the interaction between traits, behavior, and the environment.

9. With which of the following statements would a social-cognitive psychologist agree?
   a. People with an internal locus of control achieve more in school.
   b. "Externals" are better able to cope with stress than "internals."
   c. "Internals" are less independent than "externals."
   d. All of the above are true.

10. Which of the following statements about self-esteem is *not* correct?
   a. People with low self-esteem tend to be negative about others.
   b. People with high self-esteem are less prone to drug addiction.
   c. People with low self-esteem tend to be non-conformists.
   d. People with high self-esteem suffer less from insomnia.
   e. People with high self-esteem are more persistent at difficult tasks.

11. The Oedipus and Electra complexes have their roots in the:
   a. anal stage.   d. phallic stage.
   b. oral stage.   e. genital stage.
   c. latency stage.

12. Which of the following is a common criticism of the humanistic perspective?
   a. Its concepts are vague and subjective.
   b. The emphasis on the self encourages selfishness in individuals.
   c. Humanism fails to appreciate the reality of evil in human behavior.
   d. All of the above are common criticisms.

13. In studying personality, a social-cognitive theorist would *most likely* make use of:
   a. personality inventories.
   b. projective tests.
   c. observing behavior in different situations.
   d. factor analyses.

14. A major difference between the psychoanalytic and trait perspectives is that:
   a. trait theory defines personality in terms of behavior; psychoanalytic theory, in terms of its underlying dynamics.
   b. trait theory describes behavior but does not attempt to explain it.
   c. psychoanalytic theory emphasizes the origins of personality in childhood sexuality.
   d. all of the above are differences.

15. Compared to those in collectivist cultures, people in individualist cultures:

a. are less geographically bound to elderly parents.

b. tend to be lonelier.

c. are more vulnerable to stress-related disease.

d. have all of the above characteristics.

16. The Big Five personality factors are:

a. emotional stability, openness, introversion, sociability, locus of control.

b. neuroticism, extraversion, openness, emotional stability, sensitivity.

c. neuroticism, gregariousness, extraversion, impulsiveness, conscientiousness.

d. emotional stability, extraversion, openness, agreeableness, conscientiousness.

e. emotional stability, extraversion, openness, locus of control, sensitivity.

17. Which of the following was *not* mentioned in the text as a criticism of Freud's theory?

a. The theory is sexist.

b. It offers few testable hypotheses.

c. There is no evidence of anything like an "unconscious."

d. The theory ignores the fact that human development is lifelong.

18. According to Freud, _____ is the process by which children incorporate their parents' values into their _____ .

a. reaction formation; superegos

b. reaction formation; egos

c. identification; superegos

d. identification; egos

19. Which of the following groups tend to suffer from relatively low self-esteem?

a. women

b. ethnic minorities

c. disabled persons

d. all of the above

e. none of the above

20. In promoting personality growth, the person-centered perspective emphasizes all but:

a. empathy.   **c.** genuineness.

b. acceptance.   **d.** altruism.

21. Recent research on the Big Five personality factors provides evidence that:

a. some tendencies decrease during adulthood, while others increase.

b. these traits only describe personality in Western, individualist cultures.

c. the heritability of individual differences in these traits generally runs about 25 percent or less.

d. all of the above are true.

Matching Items
Match each term with the appropriate definition or description.

Terms

_____ 1. projective test
_____ 2. identification
_____ 3. collective unconscious
_____ 4. reality principle
_____ 5. psychosexual stages
_____ 6. pleasure principle
_____ 7. empirically derived test
_____ 8. reciprocal determinism
_____ 9. personality inventory
_____ 10. Oedipus complex
_____ 11. preconscious

Definitions or Descriptions

a. the id's demand for immediate gratification
b. a boy's sexual desires toward the opposite-sex parent
c. information that is retrievable but currently not in conscious awareness
d. stages of development proposed by Freud
e. questionnaire used to assess personality traits
f. the two-way interactions of behavior with personal and environmental factors
g. personality test that provides ambiguous stimuli
h. the repository of universal memories proposed by Jung
i. the process by which children incorporate their parents' values into their developing superegos
j. the process by which the ego seeks to gratify impulses of the id in nondestructive ways
k. developed by testing a pool of items and then selecting those that discriminate the group of interest

Thinking Critically About Chapter 14

Answer these questions the day before an exam as a final check on your understanding of the chapter's terms and concepts.

Multiple-Choice Questions

1. Bill is muscular and physically strong. Sheldon would classify him as a(n):
   a. endomorphic type.
   b. mesomorphic type.
   c. ectomorphic type.
   d. dysmorphic type.

2. A psychoanalyst would characterize a person who is impulsive and self-indulgent as possessing a strong _____ and a weak _____ .
   a. id and ego; superego
   b. id; ego and superego
   c. ego; superego
   d. id; superego
   e. superego; ego

3. Because Ramona identifies with her politically conservative parents, she chose to enroll in a conservative college. After four years in this environment Ramona's politics have become even more conservative. Which perspective best accounts for the mutual influences of Ramona's upbringing, choice of school, and political viewpoint?
   a. psychoanalytic
   b. trait
   c. humanistic
   d. social-cognitive

4. Jill has a biting, sarcastic manner. According to Freud, she is:
   a. projecting her anxiety onto others.
   b. fixated in the oral stage of development.
   c. fixated in the anal stage of development.
   d. displacing her anxiety onto others.

5. James attributes his failing grade in chemistry to an unfair final exam. His attitude exemplifies:
   a. internal locus of control.
   b. unconditional positive regard.
   c. the self-serving bias.
   d. reciprocal determinism.

6. Being fed up with your cultural background, you decide to move to a culture that places greater value on maintaining social harmony and family identity. To which of the following countries should you move?
   a. the United States
   b. Canada
   c. Australia
   d. Japan
   e. Great Britain

7. Because you have a relatively low level of brain arousal, a trait theorist would suggest that you are a(n) _____ who would naturally seek _____ .
   a. introvert; stimulation
   b. introvert; isolation
   c. extravert; stimulation
   d. extravert; isolation

8. A psychologist at the campus mental health center administered an empirically derived personality test to diagnose an emotionally troubled student. Which test did the psychologist *most likely* administer?
   a. the MMPI
   b. the TAT
   c. the Rorschach
   d. the Locus of Control Scale

9. The personality test Teresa is taking involves her describing random patterns of dots. What type of test is she taking?
   a. an empirically derived test
   b. the MMPI
   c. a personality inventory
   d. the Myers-Briggs Type Indicator
   e. a projective test

10. Dr. Gonzalez believes that most students can be classified as "Type A" or "Type B" according to the intensities of their personalities and competitiveness. Evidently, Dr. Gonzalez is working within the _____ perspective.
    a. psychoanalytic   c. humanistic
    b. trait   d. social-cognitive

11. According to the psychoanalytic perspective, a child who frequently "slips" and calls her teacher "mom" *probably*:
    a. has some unresolved conflicts concerning her mother.
    b. is fixated in the oral stage of development.
    c. did not receive unconditional positive regard from her mother.
    d. can be classified as having a weak sense of personal control.

12. Isaiah is sober and reserved; Rashid is fun-loving and affectionate. The Eysencks would say that Isaiah _____ and Rashid _____ .
    a. has an internal locus of control; has an external locus of control
    b. has an external locus of control; has an internal locus of control

   c. is an extravert; is an introvert
   d. is an introvert; is an extravert

13. In high school, Britta and Debbie were best friends. They thought they were a lot alike, as did everyone else who knew them. After high school, they went on to very different colleges, careers, and life courses. Now, at their twenty-fifth reunion, they are shocked at how little they have in common. Bandura would suggest that their differences reflect the interactive effects of environment, personality, and behavior, which he refers to as:
    a. reciprocal determinism.
    b. personal control.
    c. identification.
    d. the self-serving bias.

14. For his class presentation, Bruce plans to discuss the Big Five personality factors used by people throughout the world to describe others or themselves. Which of the following is *not* a factor that Bruce will discuss?
    a. extraversion   d. conscientiousness
    b. openness   e. agreeableness
    c. independence

15. Dayna is not very consistent in showing up for class and turning in assignments when they are due. Research studies would suggest that Dayna's inconsistent behavior:
    a. indicates that she is emotionally troubled and may need professional counseling.
    b. is a sign of learned helplessness.
    c. is not necessarily unusual.
    d. probably reflects a temporary problem in another area of her life.

16. Andrew's grandfather, who has lived a rich and productive life, is a spontaneous, loving, and self-accepting person. Maslow might say that he:
    a. has an internal locus of control.
    b. is an extravert.
    c. has resolved all the conflicts of the psychosexual stages.
    d. is a self-actualizing person.

17. The school psychologist believes that having a positive self-concept is necessary before students can achieve their potential. Evidently, the school psychologist is working within the _____ perspective.
    a. psychoanalytic   c. humanistic
    b. trait   d. social-cognitive

18. Wanda wishes to instill in her children an accepting attitude toward other people. Maslow and Rogers would probably recommend that she:
    a. teach her children first to accept themselves.
    b. use discipline sparingly.
    c. be affectionate with her children only when they behave as she wishes.
    d. do all of the above.

19. Suzy bought a used, high-mileage automobile because it was all she could afford. Attempting to justify her purchase, she raves to her friends about the car's attractiveness, good acceleration, and stereo. According to Freud, Suzy is using the defense mechanism of:
    a. displacement.   c. rationalization.
    b. reaction formation. d. projection.

20. Nadine has a relatively low level of brain arousal. Trait theorists would probably predict that she is:
    a. an extravert.   c. an unstable person.
    b. an introvert.   d. both a. and c.

21. During a class discussion, Trevor argues that the recent "positive psychology" is sure to wane in popularity, since it suffers from the same criticisms as humanistic psychology. You counter his argument by pointing out that, unlike humanistic psychology, positive psychology:
    a. focuses on advancing human fulfillment.
    b. is rooted in science.
    c. is not based on the study of individual characteristics.
    d. has all of the above characteristics.

Essay Question

You are an honest, open, and responsible person. Discuss how these characteristics would be explained according to the four major perspectives on personality. (Use the space below to list points you want to make and organize them. Then write the essay on a separate piece of paper.)

Key Terms

Writing Definitions

Using your own words, on a separate piece of paper write a brief definition or explanation of each of the following terms.

1. personality
2. free association
3. psychoanalysis
4. unconscious
5. preconscious
6. id
7. ego
8. superego
9. psychosexual stages
10. Oedipus complex
11. identification
12. fixation
13. defense mechanisms
14. repression
15. regression
16. reaction formation
17. projection
18. rationalization
19. displacement
20. sublimation
21. projective test
22. Thematic Apperception Test (TAT)
23. Rorschach inkblot test
24. collective unconscious
25. traits
26. personality inventory
27. Minnesota Multiphasic Personality Inventory-2 (MMPI-2)
28. empirically derived test
29. self-actualization
30. unconditional positive regard
31. self-concept
32. self-esteem

33. self-serving bias
34. individualism
35. collectivism
36. reciprocal determinism
37. personal control

38. external locus of control
39. internal locus of control
40. learned helplessness
41. positive psychology

Cross-Check

As you learned in the Introduction, reviewing and overlearning of material are important to the learning process. After you have written the definitions of the key terms in this chapter, you should complete the crossword puzzle to ensure that you can reverse the process—recognize the term, given the definition.

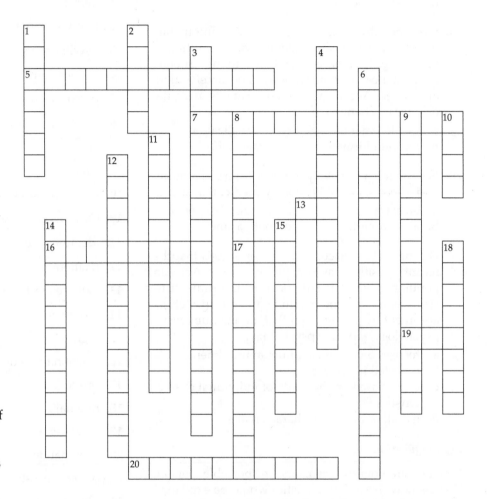

ACROSS

5. Defense mechanism in which an impulse is shifted to an object other than the one that originally aroused the impulse.
7. A cultural emphasis on personal goals over group goals.
13. In Freud's theory, the personality system consisting of basic sexual and aggressive drives.
16. Locus of control that reflects the belief that one's fate is determined by forces not under personal control.
17. In Freud's theory, the conscious division of personality.
19. Projective test consisting of ambiguous pictures about which people are asked to make up stories.
20. Defense mechanism in which a person reverts to a less mature pattern of behavior.

DOWN

1. In Freud's theory, the complex developed by boys in which they are sexually attracted to their mother and resent their father.
2. People's characteristic patterns of behavior and conscious motives.
3. Type of test developed by testing many items to see which best distinguish between groups of interest.
4. A person's sense of being male or female.
6. The passive resignation a person or animal develops from repeated exposure to inescapable aversive events.
8. The ego's methods of unconsciously protecting itself against anxiety.
9. In Freud's theory, the process by which the child's superego develops and incorporates the parents' values.
10. The most widely used personality inventory.
11. In Freud's theory, the area of the unconscious containing material that is retrievable into conscious awareness.
12. The TAT and Rorschach are examples of a _____.
14. An individual's characteristic pattern of thinking, feeling, and acting.

15. A widely used test in which people are asked to interpret ten inkblots.
18. According to Freud, _____ occurs when development becomes arrested in an immature psychosexual stage.

Answers

Introducing Personality

Section Preview

1. Personality is your characteristic pattern of thinking, feeling, and acting. Unlike other areas of study in psychology, which focus on similarities among people, personality emphasizes the uniqueness of the individual.

The Psychoanalytic Perspective

Section Preview

1. Freud discovered that, under hypnosis, his patients were sometimes able to talk freely about their neurological symptoms, which led to their improvement. He later began using free association instead of hypnosis, believing that this technique triggered a chain of thoughts leading into a patient's unconscious, thereby retrieving and releasing painful unconscious memories.

   Psychoanalysis is based on Freud's belief that below our surface consciousness is a much larger, unconscious region that contains thoughts, feelings, wishes, and memories of which we are unaware. Although some of these thoughts are held in a preconscious area and can be retrieved at will into consciousness, some unacceptable thoughts and wishes are forcibly blocked, or repressed, from consciousness. These unconscious thoughts and urges often are expressed in troubling symptoms.

2. To Freud, personality is composed of three interacting, and often conflicting, systems: the id, ego, and superego. Operating on the pleasure principle, the unconscious id strives to satisfy basic drives to survive, reproduce, and aggress. Operating on the reality principle, the ego seeks to gratify the id's impulses in realistic and nondestructive ways. The superego, which represents the individual's internalization of the morals and values of parents and culture, forces the ego to consider not only the real but also the ideal. Because the ego must intervene among the impulsive demands of the id, the restraining demands of the superego, and those of the external world, it is the personality "executive."

3. Freud believed that children pass through a series of psychosexual stages during which the id's pleasure-seeking energies focus on particular erogenous zones. Between birth and 18 months (oral stage), pleasure centers on the mouth. Between 18 and 36 months (anal stage), pleasure focuses on bowel and bladder retention and elimination. Between 3 and 6 years (phallic stage), the pleasure zone shifts to the genitals, and boys develop unconscious sexual desires for their mothers and the fear that their fathers will punish them (Oedipus complex). Children eventually cope with these threatening feelings by repressing them and identifying with their same-sex parent.

   Between 6 years of age and puberty (latency stage), sexual feelings are repressed and redirected. At puberty, sexual interests mature as youths begin to experience sexual feelings toward others (genital stage).

4. According to Freud, maladaptive adult behavior results from unresolved conflicts during earlier psychosexual stages. Such unresolved conflicts may cause the person's pleasure-seeking energies to become fixated in one psychosexual stage, leading to later problem behaviors or distinctive personality characteristics.

   Defense mechanisms are the ego's attempt to reduce or redirect anxiety by distorting reality. Examples of defense mechanisms include the banishing of thoughts from consciousness (repression), retreating to behavior characteristic of an earlier stage (regression), turning threatening impulses into their opposites (reaction formation) or attributing them to others (projection), self-justification of unacceptable actions (rationalization), diverting sexual or aggressive impulses to a more acceptable object (displacement), and transforming unacceptable impulses into socially valued activities (sublimation).

5. Projective tests, such as the Thematic Apperception Test and the Rorschach inkblot test, ask people to describe or tell a story about an ambiguous stimulus that has no inherent meaning. In doing so, people presumably project their own interests and conflicts and provide a sort of psychological "x-ray" of their personalities. Despite their widespread use, projective tests are considered by most researchers to be lacking in validity and reliability. For example, there is no single accepted scoring system for interpreting the Rorschach, so two raters may not interpret a subject's responses similarly (although a new computer-aided scoring and interpretation tool is improving agreement among raters and enhanc-

ing validity). Furthermore, the test is not very successful at predicting future behavior or discriminating between groups.

6. The neo-Freudians placed more emphasis than Freud on the role of the conscious mind in determining personality, and less emphasis on sex and aggression as all-consuming motivations. Alfred Adler and Karen Horney emphasized the importance of social rather than sexual tensions in the formation of the child's personality. Horney also countered the male bias inherent in Freud's theory. Carl Jung expanded Freud's view of the unconscious into the idea of a collective unconscious, a common reservoir of thoughts derived from the experiences of our ancestors.

   Psychodynamic theorists downplay the importance of sex in personality formation. They do agree with Freud, however, that much of mental life is unconscious, that childhood shapes personality and attachment, and that we often struggle with inner conflicts.

7. Freud's idea that development is fixed in childhood has been contradicted by research showing that development is lifelong. It is also clear that children gain their gender identity earlier than Freud believed and become strongly feminine or masculine even without a same-sex parent present. Freud's theory of dreams, memory losses, and defense mechanisms as disguising unfulfilled or repressed urges also has been disputed, as has his idea about the natural superiority of men. Today's researchers contend that repression is actually quite rare and, contrary to Freud's views, occurs as a mental response to terrible trauma. In addition, Freud's theory has been criticized for offering after-the-fact explanations of behavior, yet failing to generate testable predictions of those behaviors. Freud's ideas concerning our limited access to all that goes on in the mind, the importance of sexuality, our attempts to defend ourselves against anxiety, and the tension between our biological impulses and our social well-being have endured, however. Recent evidence has provided some support for defense mechanisms that defend self-esteem such as reaction formation.

Stepping Through the Section

1. Sigmund Freud
2. free association
3. psychoanalysis
4. unconscious; preconscious; repressed
5. unconscious; slips; manifest content; latent

content
6. biological; social
7. id; ego; superego
8. unconscious; pleasure
9. after; conscious; reality

The ego is considered the executive of personality because it directs our actions as it intervenes among the impulsive demands of the id, the reality of the external world, and the ideals of the superego.

10. superego
11. weak; strong
12. psychosexual
13. oral; sucking (also biting, chewing)
14. anal; 18; 3
15. phallic; 3; 6; genitals; opposite; Oedipus complex; Electra complex
16. identification; gender identity

Children eventually cope with their feelings for the opposite-sex parent by repressing them and by identifying with the rival (same-sex) parent. Through this process children incorporate many of their parents' values, thereby strengthening the superego.

17. latency
18. genital
19. fixated
20. defense mechanisms; repression
21. regression
22. reaction formation
23. projection
24. rationalization
25. displacement
26. sublimation

Matching Items

1. e
2. d
3. b
4. c
5. a
6. f
27. unconscious
28. projective
29. Thematic Apperception
30. Rorschach; inkblots; little
31. neo-Freudians; more; less
   a. Adler emphasized the social, rather than the sexual, tensions of childhood.

b. Horney questioned the male bias in Freud's theory, such as the assumptions that women have weak egos and suffer "penis envy." Like Adler, she emphasized social tensions.

c. Jung emphasized an inherited collective unconscious.

32. reject; Jung; collective unconscious

33. psychodynamic; sex; unconscious; childhood; inner conflicts

34. lifelong; earlier; is not; have; sexual repression

35. represses; rarer; trauma

36. information

Contemporary researchers contend that the unconscious involves schemas that control our perceptions, implicit memories, the priming effect of stimuli, emotions that are activated before conscious analysis, our self-concept, and stereotypes that automatically influence how we process information about ourselves and others.

37. supports

38. reaction formation; projection; self-esteem; instinctual energy; displacement; sublimation

39. testable predictions

The Trait Perspective

Section Preview

1. Trait theories define personality in terms of identifiable behavior patterns and conscious motives. As compared with psychoanalytic theories, they are less concerned with explaining personality and more concerned with its description.

The ancient Greeks classified people according to four bodily "humors": melancholic (depressed), sanguine (cheerful), phlegmatic (unemotional), and choleric (irritable). William Sheldon classified people according to their body types, as endomorphs (relaxed and jolly), mesomorphs (bold and physically active), or ectomorphs (high strung and solitary).

A popular procedure today, especially in business and career counseling, is to classify people according to Carl Jung's personality types using the Myers-Briggs Type Indicator.

The statistical technique called factor analysis is used to identify clusters of personality test items that make up basic traits. Hans and Sybil Eysenck believe that many of the personality traits researchers have identified using factor analysis can be reduced to two genetically influenced dimensions: extraversion-introversion and emotional stability-instability.

2. Across the world, people describe others in terms roughly consistent with these five trait dimensions: emotional stability, extraversion, openness, agreeableness, and conscientiousness. Recent research provides evidence that these traits are quite stable in adulthood, apply to various cultures, predict other personal attributes, and have heritability values of approximately 50 percent. Most personality traits are subject to genetic influences. Extraverts, for example, seek stimulation because their level of arousal in an area of the frontal lobe is lower than in introverts, while emotionally stable people have less active autonomic nervous systems than do unstable people.

3. To assess traits, psychologists use trait scales that measure single traits or personality inventories that assess several traits at once. In contrast to the subjectivity of projective tests, personality inventories are scored objectively. The most widely used personality inventory is the Minnesota Multiphasic Personality Inventory-2 (MMPI-2) for assessing psychological disorders. The MMPI-2 is an empirically derived test that contains 10 clinical scales, several validity scales, and 15 content scales.

4. To be a genuine personality trait, a characteristic must persist over time and across situations. Critics of this perspective question the consistency of traits. Although people's traits do seem to persist over time, research has revealed much less consistency of specific behaviors from one situation to another. However, although people do not act with perfect consistency, their *average* behavior over *many* situations is predictable.

Stepping Through the Section

1. behaviors; motives

2. explaining; describing

3. melancholic; sanguine; phlegmatic; choleric

4. endomorph; mesomorph; ectomorph

5. Myers-Briggs Type Indicator; business; career

6. factor analysis; extraversion–introversion; stability–instability

7. a. Emotional stability: calm vs. anxious; secure vs. insecure
   b. Extraversion: sociable vs. retiring
   c. Openness: preference for variety vs. routine
   d. Agreeableness: soft-hearted vs. ruthless
   e. Conscientiousness: disciplined vs. impulsive

8. stable; 50; describe; predict

9. do

10. brain arousal; frontal; extraverts; introverts

11. stable; autonomic nervous systems; unstable

12. shyness; inhibition; genes; temperament; behavioral

Astrologers use a "stock spiel" that includes information that is generally true of almost everyone. The willingness of people to accept this type of phony information is called the "Barnum effect." A second technique used by astrologers is to "read" a person's clothing, features, reactions, etc. and build their advice from these observations.

13. personality inventories; Minnesota Multiphasic Personality Inventory; empirically

14. self; peer

15. traits (or dispositions); situation (or environment)

16. time; situations; variable

17. is not

At any given moment a person's behavior is powerfully influenced by the immediate situation, so that it may appear that the person does not have a consistent personality. But averaged over many situations a person's outgoingness, happiness, and carelessness, for instance, are more predictable.

The Humanistic Perspective

Section Preview

1. The humanistic perspective emerged as a reaction against several other perspectives on personality. In contrast to Freud's study of the negative motives of "sick" people, the humanistic psychologists have focused on the strivings of "healthy" people. Unlike the trait theorists, they view people as whole persons, rather than as collections of individual traits.

   Maslow proposed that people are motivated by a hierarchy of needs and that if basic needs are fulfilled, people will strive to reach their highest potential (self-actualization). Carl Rogers agreed with much of Maslow's thinking, adding that people nurture others' actualizing tendencies by being genuine, accepting, and empathic. For both theorists a central feature of personality is a person's self-concept.

2. Research on the self documents the concept of possible selves, including people's visions of the self or selves they would like to become in motivating their behavior. Another finding is that people with high self-esteem have fewer physical problems, strive more at difficult tasks, and are happier than people with low self-esteem. One of the most firmly established findings is people's readiness to perceive themselves favorably through the self-serving bias. This bias is revealed in the willingness of people to accept responsibility for good deeds and successes more readily

than for bad deeds and failures, and in the tendency of people to see themselves as better than average on nearly any desirable dimension.

3. Contrary to popular belief, and despite discrimination and lower social status, ethnic minorities, people with disabilities, and women do not suffer lower self-esteem.

   Individualist cultures nurture the development of personal goals and define identity in terms of individual attributes. Collectivist cultures give priority to the goals of their groups—often the family, clan, or work group. While individualists easily move in and out of social groups, collectivists have fewer but deeper, more stable attachments to their groups and friends. Collectivist cultures also place a premium on maintaining harmony and allowing others to save face. People in individualist cultures have greater personal freedom and more privacy. But compared to collectivists, individualists also tend to be lonelier, more likely to divorce, more homicidal, and more vulnerable to stress-related diseases.

4. The ideas of humanistic psychologists have influenced counseling, education, child-rearing, and management. Critics contend, however, that the concepts of humanistic psychology are vague, subjective, and so focused on the individual that they promote self-indulgence, selfishness, and an erosion of moral restraints. Furthermore, the humanistic psychologists have been accused of being naively optimistic and unrealistic, and failing to appreciate the human capacity for evil.

Stepping Through the Section

1. Maslow; Rogers

2. hierarchy; self-actualization

For Maslow, such people were self-aware, self-accepting, open, spontaneous, loving, caring, secure, and problem-centered rather than self-centered.

3. genuine; accepting; empathic; unconditional positive regard

4. self-concept

5. possible selves

6. self-esteem; independent of; anxiety; depression

7. hopes; think they ought to be

8. more; racial prejudice

9. do not have

10. **a.** They value the things at which they excel.
    b. They attribute problems to prejudice.
    c. They compare themselves to those in their own group.

11. high

12. self-serving

13. more

14. above

15. high

16. individualist; collectivist

Individualists identify themselves in terms of their personal convictions and values. They strive for personal control and individual achievement. Collectivists give priority to their groups and define their identity accordingly. They place a premium on maintaining harmony and allowing others to save face.

17. collectivist; individualist; freedom; loneliness; divorce; homicide; stress-related; social ties

18. increased

Humanistic psychology is criticized for being vague and subjective, for encouraging self-indulgence and selfishness, and for failing to appreciate the capacity of humans for evil.

The Social-Cognitive Perspective

Section Preview

1. The social-cognitive perspective applies principles of learning, cognition, and social behavior to personality and emphasizes the ways in which our personalities shape and are shaped by external events. Reciprocal determinism refers to the ways in which our personalities are influenced by the interaction of our situations, our thoughts and feelings, and our behaviors. There are many examples of reciprocal determinism. For one, different people choose different environments. For another, our personalities shape how we interpret and react to events. Finally, our personalities help create situations to which we react.

2. Whether people see themselves as controlling, or being controlled by, their environments is an important aspect of their personalities. Research reveals that people who perceive an internal locus of control achieve more in school and are more independent, less depressed, better able to delay gratification, and better able to cope with various life stresses than people who perceive an external locus of control. Seligman found that animals and people who experience uncontrollable negative events may perceive a lack of control in their lives and develop the passive resignation of learned helplessness. One measure of how helpless or effective people feel is whether they generally are optimistic or pessimistic.

3. Social-cognitive researchers study personality by exploring the effect of differing situations on people's behavior patterns and attitudes. This perspective has increased our awareness of how social situations influence, and are influenced by, individuals. Critics contend, however, that the theory explains behavior after the fact and that it focuses so much on the situation that it ignores the importance of people's inner traits, unconscious motives, and emotions in the formation of personality.

Stepping Through the Section

1. environment; Bandura

2. behaviors; personal/cognitive; environmental; reciprocal determinism

Different people choose different environments partly on the basis of their dispositions. Our personality shapes how we interpret and react to events. It also helps create the situations to which we react.

3. internal locus of control; external locus of control

4. learned helplessness

5. more

6. optimism

7. negative states; positive
   a. positive subjective well-being
   b. positive character
   c. positive groups, communities, and cultures

8. feedback

9. past behavior in similar situations

One criticism is that the theory has overemphasized situational influences to the neglect of inner traits.

10. a. The psychoanalytic perspective has drawn attention to the unconscious and irrational aspects of personality.
    b. The trait perspective has systematically described and measured important components of personality.
    c. The humanistic perspective emphasizes the healthy potential of personality and the importance of our sense of self.
    d. The social-cognitive perspective emphasizes that we always act in the context of situations that we help to create.

Progress Test 1

Multiple-Choice Questions

1. **b.** is the answer. Personality is defined as patterns of response—of thinking, feeling, and acting—that are relatively consistent across a variety of situations. (p. 489)

2. **d.** is the answer. (p. 491)

a. & b. Conscious processes are the focus of these perspectives.

c. The trait perspective focuses on the description of behaviors.

3. **a.** is the answer. (pp. 492–493)

4. **c.** is the answer. According to Freud, defense mechanisms reduce anxiety unconsciously, by disguising one's threatening impulses. (p. 494)

a., b., & d. Unlike these specific emotions, anxiety need not be focused. Defense mechanisms help us cope when we are unsettled but are not sure why.

5. **e.** is the answer. (pp. 517–519)

6. **b.** is the answer. (p. 496)

a. According to most neo-Freudians, Freud placed too great an emphasis on the *unconscious* mind.

c. Freud placed great emphasis on early childhood, and the neo-Freudians basically agreed with him.

d. The neo-Freudians accepted Freud's ideas about the basic personality structures.

7. **c.** is the answer. (p. 523)

a., d., & e. In fact, just the opposite is true.

b. Locus of control is not related to intelligence.

8. **a.** is the answer. (p. 504)

b. & c. Locus of control is emphasized by the social-cognitive perspective.

d. This is how the ancient Greeks described personality.

9. **b.** is the answer. Studies have shown that people do not act with predictable consistency from one situation to the next. But, over a number of situations, consistent patterns emerge, and this basic consistency of traits persists over the life span. (pp. 509–510)

10. **b.** is the answer. (p. 512)

a. This is true of the psychoanalytic perspective.

c. This is true of the social-cognitive perspective.

d. This is true of the trait perspective.

11. **e.** is the answer. (p. 512)

12. **b.** is the answer. Humanistic psychologists emphasize that for the individual, self-affirming thinking is generally adaptive (therefore, not a.); such thinking maintains self-confidence, minimizes depression, and enables us to view others with compassion and understanding (therefore, not c.); unconditional positive regard tends to promote self-esteem and thus self-affirming thinking (therefore, not d.). (p. 517)

13. **a.** is the answer. Developmental research indicates that development is lifelong. (p. 497)

b., c., & d. To varying degrees, research has par-

tially supported these Freudian ideas.

14. **b.** is the answer. (pp. 517–518)

a. & c. These are characteristics of collectivist cultures.

15. **c.** is the answer. As scoring is largely subjective and the tests have not been very successful in predicting behavior, their reliability and validity have been called into question. (p. 495)

a. This is untrue.

b. Unlike empirically derived personality tests, projective tests are not standardized.

d. Although this may be true, it was not mentioned as a criticism of projective tests.

16. **b.** is the answer. In doing so it underestimates the influence of the environment. (pp. 509–511)

a. The trait perspective does not emphasize early childhood experiences.

c. This criticism is unlikely since trait theory does not seek to explain personality development.

d. Trait theory does not look on traits as being "positive" or "negative."

17. **d.** is the answer. (p. 513)

a. & c. Personality structure is a concern of the psychoanalytic perspective.

b. Locus of control is a major focus of the social-cognitive perspective.

18. **c.** is the answer. (p. 505)

a. & d. A psychoanalytic theorist would be most likely to use a projective test or free association.

b. This would most likely be the approach taken by a social-cognitive theorist.

19. **b.** is the answer. In Freud's theory, the id operates according to the pleasure principle; the ego operates according to the reality principle. (p. 492)

c. The id is presumed to be unconscious.

d. The superego is, according to Freud, the equivalent of a conscience; the ego is the "personality executive."

20. **b.** is the answer. The social-cognitive theory has been accused of putting so much emphasis on the situation that inner traits are neglected. (p. 528)

a. Such a criticism has been made of the psychoanalytic perspective but is not relevant to the social-cognitive perspective.

c. Such a criticism might be more relevant to the trait perspective; the social-cognitive perspective offers an explanation in the form of reciprocal determinism.

d. There are assessment techniques appropriate to the theory, namely, questionnaires and observations of behavior in situations.

21. **b.** is the answer. (pp. 499–500)

a. The evidence supports defenses that defend self-esteem, rather than those that are tied to instinctual energy.

c. & d. Neither of these defense mechanisms has received much supportive evidence.

Matching Items

1. f (p. 494)
2. j (p. 495)
3. b (p. 492)
4. k (p. 508)
5. h (p. 494)
6. d (p. 494)
7. a (p. 492)
8. g (p. 503)
9. c (p. 492)
10. e (p. 494)
11. i (p. 495)

Progress Test 2

Multiple-Choice Questions

1. **d.** is the answer. (p. 522)

   a. This perspective emphasizes unconscious dynamics in personality.

   b. This perspective is more concerned with *describing* than *explaining* personality.

   c. This perspective emphasizes the healthy, self-actualizing tendencies of personality.

2. **d.** is the answer. (p. 491)

   a. Self-actualization is a concept of the humanistic perspective.

   b. Through identification, children *reduce* conflicting feelings as they incorporate their parents' values.

   c. Jung, rather than Freud, proposed the concept of the collective unconscious.

3. **a.** is the answer. (p. 503)

4. **c.** is the answer. In such situations, passive resignation, called learned helplessness, develops. (p. 524)

   a. This refers to the belief that one controls one's fate; the circumstances described lead to precisely the opposite belief.

   b. Reaction formation is a defense mechanism in which unacceptable impulses are channeled into their opposites.

   d. Seligman did not specify that neurotic anxiety occurs.

5. **a.** is the answer. Feelings of insecurity reduce self-esteem, and those who feel negative about themselves tend to feel negative about others as well. (p. 515)

6. **e.** is the answer. (p. 516)

7. **b.** is the answer. The MMPI was developed by selecting from many items those that differentiated between the groups of interest; hence, it was empirically derived. That it is an objective test is shown by the fact that it can be scored by computer. (p. 508)

   a. Projective tests present ambiguous stimuli for people to interpret; the MMPI is a questionnaire.

   c. Although sometimes used to assess job applicants, the MMPI was developed to assess emotionally troubled people.

   d. The MMPI does not focus on control but, rather, measures various aspects of personality.

8. **b.** is the answer. Trait theory attempts to describe behavior and not to develop explanations or applications. The emphasis is more on consistency than on change. (p. 502)

9. **a.** is the answer. "Internals," or those who have a sense of personal control, have been shown to achieve more in school. Relative to externals, they also cope better with stress and are more independent. (p. 523)

10. **c.** is the answer. In actuality, people with *high* self-esteem are generally more independent of pressures to conform. (p. 514)

11. **d.** is the answer. (p. 493)

12. **d.** is the answer. (pp. 520–521)

13. **c.** is the answer. In keeping with their emphasis on interactions between people and situations, social-cognitive theorists would most likely make use of observations of behavior in relevant situations. (p. 527)

    a. & d. Personality inventories and factor analyses would more likely be used by a trait theorist.

    b. Projective tests would more likely be used by a psychologist working within the psychoanalytic perspective.

14. **d.** is the answer. Trait theory defines personality in terms of behavior and is therefore interested in describing behavior; psychoanalytic theory defines personality as dynamics underlying behavior and therefore is interested in explaining behavior in terms of these dynamics. (pp. 491, 493, 502)

15. **d.** is the answer. (p. 519)

16. **d.** is the answer. (p. 504)

17. **c.** is the answer. Although many researchers think of the unconscious as information processing without awareness rather than as a reservoir of repressed information, they agree with Freud that we do indeed have limited access to all that goes on in our minds. (pp. 497–498, 500–501)

18. **c.** is the answer. (p. 493)

    a. & b. Reaction formation is the defense mechanism by which people transform unacceptable impulses into their opposites.

    d. It is the superego, rather than the ego, that represents parental values.

19. e. is the answer. (p. 515)

20. d. is the answer. (p. 512)

21. a. is the answer. Neuroticism, extraversion, and openness tend to decrease, while agreeableness and conscientiousness tend to increase. (p. 505)

b. The Big Five dimensions describe personality in various cultures reasonably well.

c. Heritability generally runs 50 percent or more for each dimension.

Matching Items

1. g (p. 495)	**5.** d (p. 492)	**9.** e (p. 505)
2. i (p. 493)	**6.** a (p. 492)	**10.** b (p. 493)
3. h (p. 497)	**7.** k (p. 508)	**11.** c (p. 491)
4. j (p. 492)	**8.** f (p. 522)	

Thinking Critically About Chapter 14

Multiple-Choice Questions

1. b. is the answer. (p. 503)
a. Endomorphs are overweight.
c. Ectomorphs are thin.
d. This is not one of Sheldon's types.

2. d. is the answer. Impulsiveness is the mark of a strong id; self-indulgence is the mark of a weak superego. Because the ego serves to mediate the demands of the id, the superego, and the outside world, its strength or weakness is judged by its decision-making ability, not by the character of the decision—so the ego is not relevant to the question asked. (p. 492)

3. d. is the answer. The social-cognitive perspective emphasizes the reciprocal influences between people and their situations. In this example, Ramona's parents (situational factor) helped shape her political beliefs (internal factor), which influenced her choice of colleges (situational factor), and created an environment that fostered her predisposed political attitudes. (p. 522)

4. b. is the answer. Sarcasm is said to be an attempt to deny the passive dependence characteristic of the oral stage. (p. 493)
a. A person who is projecting attributes his or her own feelings to others.
c. Such a person might be either messy and disorganized or highly controlled and compulsively neat.
d. Displacement involves diverting aggressive or sexual impulses onto a more acceptable object than that which aroused them.

5. c. is the answer. (p. 516)
a. A person with an internal locus of control

would be likely to *accept* responsibility for a failing grade.
b. Unconditional positive regard is an attitude of total acceptance directed toward others.
d. Reciprocal determinism refers to the mutual influences among personality, environment, and behavior.

6. d. is the answer. Of the countries listed, only Japan has a collectivist culture that emphasizes family identity and social harmony. (pp. 517–518)

7. c. is the answer. (p. 505)
a. & b. According to this theory, introverts have relatively *high* levels of arousal, causing them to crave solitude.
d. Isolation might lower arousal level even further.

8. a. is the answer. (p. 508)
b. & c. The TAT and Rorschach are projective tests that were not empirically derived.
d. A personality test that measures locus of control would not be helpful in identifying troubled behaviors.

9. e. is the answer. Projective tests provide ambiguous stimuli, such as random dot patterns, in an attempt to trigger in the test-taker projection of his or her personality. (p. 495)

10. b. is the answer. (p. 502)
a. The psychoanalytic perspective emphasizes unconscious processes in personality dynamics.
c. The humanistic perspective emphasizes each person's potential for healthy growth and self-actualization.
d. The social-cognitive perspective emphasizes the reciprocal influences of personality and environment.

11. a. is the answer. Freud believed that dreams and such slips of the tongue reveal unconscious conflicts. (p. 491)
b. A person fixated in the oral stage might have a sarcastic personality; this child's slip of the tongue reveals nothing about her psychosexual development.
c. & d. Unconditional positive regard and personal control are not psychoanalytic concepts.

12. d. is the answer. (p. 504)
a. & b. The traits of Isaiah and Rashid reveal nothing about their sense of personal control.

13. a. is the answer. Reciprocal determinism refers to the mutual influences among personal factors, environmental factors, and behavior. (p. 522)
b. Personal control is one's sense of controlling, or being controlled by, the environment.
c. In Freud's theory, identification is the process

by which children incorporate parental values into their developing superegos.

d. The self-serving bias describes our readiness to perceive ourselves favorably.

14. **c.** is the answer. (p. 504)

15. **c.** is the answer. (pp. 509–510)

16. **d.** is the answer. (p. 512)

a. & b. These are concepts used by trait theorists rather than humanistic theorists such as Maslow.

c. This reflects Freud's viewpoint.

17. **c.** is the answer. (p. 513)

a., b., & d. The self-concept is not relevant to the psychoanalytic, trait, or social-cognitive perspectives.

18. **a.** is the answer. (p. 513)

b. The text does not discuss the impact of discipline on personality.

c. This would constitute *conditional*, rather than unconditional, positive regard and would likely cause the children to be *less* accepting of themselves and others.

19. **c.** is the answer. Suzy is trying to justify her purchase by generating (inaccurate) explanations for her behavior. (p. 494)

a. Displacement is the redirecting of impulses toward an object other than the one responsible for them.

b. Reaction formation is the transformation of unacceptable impulses into their opposites.

d. Projection is the attribution of one's own unacceptable thoughts and feelings to others.

20. **a.** is the answer. The Eysencks believe that extraverts are predisposed to seek stimulation because their normal level of brain arousal is relatively low. (p. 505)

c. Nadine's low level of brain arousal would, if anything, be related to a *stable* personality, according to the Eysencks.

21. **b.** is the answer. (p. 525)

a. Both positive psychology and humanistic psychology focus on advancing human fulfillment.

c. Both perspectives focus, at least partly, on individual characteristics.

Essay Question

Since you are apparently in good psychological health, according to the psychoanalytic perspective you must have experienced a healthy childhood and successfully passed Freud's stages of psychosexual development. Freud would also say that your ego is functioning well in balancing the demands of your id with the restraining demands of your superego and reality. Freud might also say that your honest nature reflects a well-developed superego, while Jung might say it derives from a universal value found in our collective unconscious.

Trait theorists would be less concerned with explaining these specific characteristics than with describing them, determining their consistency, and classifying your personality type. Some trait theorists, such as Allport, Eysenck, and Kagan, attribute certain trait differences to biological factors such as autonomic reactivity and heredity.

According to the humanistic perspective, your open and honest nature indicates that your basic needs have been met and you are in the process of self-actualization (Maslow). Furthermore, your openness indicates that you have a healthy self-concept and were likely nurtured by genuine, accepting, and empathic caregivers (Rogers).

According to the social-cognitive perspective, your personal/cognitive factors, behavior, and environmental influences interacted in shaping your personality and behaviors. The fact that you are a responsible person indicates that you perceive yourself as controlling, rather than being controlled by, your environment.

Key Terms

Writing Definitions

1. **Personality** is an individual's characteristic pattern of thinking, feeling, and acting. (p. 489)

2. **Free association** is the Freudian technique in which the person is encouraged to say whatever comes to mind as a means of exploring the unconscious. (p. 490)

3. In Freud's theory, **psychoanalysis** refers to the treatment of psychological disorders by seeking to expose and interpret the tensions within a patient's unconscious, using methods such as free association. (p. 490)

4. In Freud's theory, the **unconscious** is the repository of mostly unacceptable thoughts, wishes, feelings, and memories. According to contemporary psychologists, it is a level of information processing of which we are unaware. (p. 491)

5. In Freud's theory, the **preconscious** area is a region of the unconscious that contains material that is retrievable at will into conscious awareness. (p. 491)

Example: The Freudian notion of a **preconscious** is similar to the concept of long-term memory: Material is accessible but not currently in our awareness.

6. In Freud's theory, the **id** is the unconscious system of personality, consisting of basic sexual and aggressive drives, that supplies psychic energy to personality. (p. 492)

7. In psychoanalytic theory, the **ego** is the conscious division of personality that attempts to mediate between the demands of the id, the superego, and reality. (p. 492)

8. In Freud's theory, the **superego** is the division of personality that contains the conscience and develops by incorporating the perceived moral standards of society. (p. 492)

9. Freud's **psychosexual stages** are developmental periods children pass through during which the id's pleasure-seeking energies are focused on different erogenous zones. (p. 492)

10. According to Freud, boys in the phallic stage develop a collection of feelings, known as the **Oedipus complex**, that center on sexual attraction to the mother and resentment of the father. Some psychologists believe girls have a parallel Electra complex. (p. 493)

11. In Freud's theory, **identification** is the process by which the child's superego develops and incorporates the parents' values. Freud saw identification as crucial, not only to resolution of the Oedipus complex, but also to the development of gender identity. (p. 493)

12. In Freud's theory, **fixation** occurs when development becomes arrested, due to unresolved conflicts, in an immature psychosexual stage. (p. 493)

13. In Freud's theory, **defense mechanisms** are the ego's methods of unconsciously protecting itself against anxiety by distorting reality. (p. 494)

14. The basis of all defense mechanisms, **repression** is the unconscious exclusion of anxiety-arousing thoughts, feelings, and memories from the conscious mind. Repression is an example of motivated forgetting: One "forgets" what one really does not wish to remember. (p. 494)

15. **Regression** is the defense mechanism in which a person faced with anxiety reverts to a less mature pattern of behavior. (p. 494)

16. **Reaction formation** is the defense mechanism in which the ego converts unacceptable impulses into their opposites. (p. 494)

17. In psychoanalytic theory, **projection** is the unconscious attribution of one's own unacceptable feelings, attitudes, or desires to others. (p. 494)

    Memory aid: To project is to thrust outward. **Projection** is an example of thrusting one's own feelings outward to another person.

18. **Rationalization** is the defense mechanism in which one devises self-justifying but incorrect reasons for one's behavior. (p. 494)

19. **Displacement** is the defense mechanism in which a sexual or aggressive impulse is shifted to a more acceptable object other than the one that originally aroused the impulse. (p. 494)

20. **Sublimation** is the defense mechanism in which one rechannels unacceptable impulses into socially approved activities. (p. 494)

21. **Projective tests**, such as the TAT and Rorschach, present ambiguous stimuli onto which people supposedly *project* their own inner feelings. (p. 495)

22. The **Thematic Apperception Test (TAT)** is a projective test that consists of ambiguous pictures about which people are asked to make up stories. (p. 495)

23. The **Rorschach inkblot test**, the most widely used projective test, consists of ten inkblots that people are asked to interpret. (p. 495)

24. The **collective unconscious** is Jung's concept of an inherited unconscious shared by all people and deriving from our early ancestors' universal experiences. (p. 497)

25. **Traits** are people's characteristic patterns of behavior. (p. 502)

26. **Personality inventories**, associated with the trait perspective, are questionnaires used to assess personality traits. (p. 505)

27. Consisting of ten clinical scales, the **Minnesota Multiphasic Personality Inventory (MMPI)** is the most widely used personality inventory. (p. 508)

28. An **empirically derived test** is one developed by testing many items to see which best distinguish between groups of interest. (p. 508)

29. In Maslow's theory, **self-actualization** describes the process of fulfilling one's potential and becoming spontaneous, loving, creative, and self-accepting. Self-actualization is at the very top of Maslow's need hierarchy and therefore becomes active only after the more basic physical and psychological needs have been met. (p. 512)

30. **Unconditional positive regard** is, according to Rogers, an attitude of total acceptance and one of the three conditions essential to a "growth-promoting" climate. (p. 513)

31. **Self-concept** refers to one's personal awareness of "who I am." In the humanistic perspective, the self-concept is a central feature of personality; life

happiness is significantly affected by whether the self-concept is positive or negative. (p. 513)

32. In humanistic psychology, **self-esteem** refers to an individual's sense of self-worth. (p. 514)

33. The **self-serving bias** is the tendency to perceive oneself favorably. (p. 516)

34. **Individualism** is a cultural emphasis on personal goals over group goals, and defining one's identity in terms of personal attributes rather than group identifications. (p. 517)

35. **Collectivism** is a cultural emphasis on the goals of one's group, and defining one's identity accordingly. (p. 517)

36. According to the social-cognitive perspective, personality is shaped through **reciprocal determinism**, or the interaction between personality and environmental factors. (p. 522)

37. **Personal control** refers to a person's sense of controlling the environment. (p. 523)

38. **External locus of control** is the perception that one's fate is determined by forces not under personal control. (p. 523)

39. **Internal locus of control** is the perception that to a great extent one controls one's own destiny. (p. 523)

40. **Learned helplessness** is the passive resignation and perceived lack of control that a person or animal develops from repeated exposure to inescapable aversive events. (p. 524)

41. Focusing on subjective well-being, character virtues such as creativity and compassion, and healthy families and neighborhoods, **positive psychology** is the scientific study of optimal human functioning. (p. 525)

Cross-Check

ACROSS

5. displacement	1. Oedipus
7. individualism	2. trait
13. id	3. empirically derived
16. external	4. gender identity
17. ego	6. learned helplessness
19. TAT	8. defense mechanisms
20. regression	9. identification
	10. MMPI
	11. preconscious
	12. projective test
	14. personality
	15. Rorschach
	18. fixation

FOCUS ON VOCABULARY AND LANGUAGE

The Psychoanalytic Perspective

Page 490: He [Freud] had a prodigious memory and so loved serious reading plays, poetry, and philosophy that he once *ran up a bookstore debt* beyond his means. When he was young, Freud was a very serious student with an exceptionally good (*prodigious*) memory and an intense interest in a variety of topics. He obtained many books which he could not afford to pay for (*ran up a bookstore debt*) in order to satisfy his curiosity about literature and the natural sciences.

Page 490: Freud's search for a cause for such disorders set his *mind running* in a direction that was destined to change human self-understanding. Patients came to Freud with strange neurological (*nervous*) disorders which had no obvious physiological explanation. Freud suspected that the problems were psychological in nature, and the questions raised by this theorizing caused him to think (*set his mind running*) in a way that changed the way we view human nature.

Page 491: He [Freud] believed he could *glimpse* the

seepage of the unconscious not only in people's free associations, beliefs, habits, and symptoms but also in their dreams and *slips of the tongue and pen* while reading, writing, and speaking. Freud used the technique of free association to gain access to the unconscious. He also thought he got a fleeting look at (*glimpse of*) the unconscious in the content of people's dreams and in the inadvertent verbal mistakes we make in speech and writing (*slips of the tongue and pen*).

Page 492: Someone with an exceptionally strong superego may be *virtuous* yet, ironically, guilt-ridden; another with a weak superego may be *wantonly* self-indulgent and remorseless. In Freud's theory, the superego (our conscience) develops when the 4-to-5-year-old child incorporates society's values through identification with the parent of the opposite sex. A person with a well-developed superego may behave in an appropriately moral way (*virtuous*) yet still feel ashamed and anxious (*guilt-ridden*); someone with a poorly developed superego may be excessively and willfully (*wantonly*) selfish and aggressive.

Page 493: In such ways, believed Freud, the *twig of*

personality is *bent* at an early age. Freud believed that adult personality was formed during the first 4 or 5 years of life and was a function of the way the conflicts of the first three psychosexual stages (oral, anal, and phallic) were handled. Just as the shape of the grown tree is the result of how the young tree (*twig*) was twisted (*bent*), adult personality is a function of early childhood experiences.

Page 494: To live in social groups, we cannot spontaneously *act out* our sexual and aggressive impulses *willy-nilly.* Anxiety results when the ego senses that it may lose control of the battle between the insatiable demands of the id and the morality of the superego. We cannot do whatever we want, whenever we want (*act out our impulses willy-nilly*); in order to deal with this unsettled feeling, the ego controls the anxiety with **defense mechanisms.**

Page 496: Other clinicians use the test [Rorschach inkblot test] as an *icebreaker* and a revealing interview technique. Because of problems in scoring and interpreting the Rorschach inkblot test, most researchers question its validity and reliability. Some clinicians use the test to help generate hypotheses about the client's problems, and others use it as a point of departure to help get the interview under way (*as an icebreaker*).

Page 496: From time to time *sparks flew,* and one member or another would leave or be *cast out.* Freud was not very tolerant of dissent or criticism and he and some of his early followers had very intense arguments (*the sparks flew*); as a result, the follower left the group or was told to depart (*cast out*). Although those who left were influenced by Freud, they did not adhere directly to his teaching (*they veered away*).

Page 500: Psychologists also criticize Freud's theory for its *scientific shortcomings.* In order for a theory to be considered scientifically acceptable, it must be able to explain observations and provide testable hypotheses. Freud's theory fails on this account. In addition, his theory offers explanations only after the events or behaviors have occurred (*after-the-fact explanations*). Freud's theory does not meet acceptable or desired scientific standards (*it has scientific shortcomings*).

The Trait Perspective

Page 502: Flabbergasted . . . This means to be shocked with overwhelming surprise. When Allport interviewed Freud in Vienna, he was astounded and confused (*flabbergasted*) by Freud's mistaken suggestion about the trivial story he told him. In fact, he was

simply telling Freud about the events on the bus in order to start the conversation (*conversational gambit*). Nevertheless, it aroused Allport's interest in personality (*started a deep train of thought*), which finally led to his development of a trait theory.

Page 504: A slightly expanded set of factors—*dubbed* the Big Five—does a better job. . . . The Eysencks use two prime personality dimensions, or factors—extraversion–introversion and emotional stability–instability. Other researchers offer another three dimensions (openness, agreeableness, and conscientiousness), bringing the total to five factors, which they named (*dubbed*) the Big Five.

Page 505: . . . *blind date* . . . If a social outing (*a date*) is arranged with a person you have never seen before, this is called a *blind date.* Having the person ranked on the Big Five dimensions would tell you a lot about the person's character and personality.

Page 506 (Thinking Critically): . . . *scoff* . . . This means to have a contemptuously mocking attitude toward something. Astronomers who study the universe scientifically *scoff* at astrologers who believe that the planets and stars determine human affairs.

Page 506 (Thinking Critically): . . . *suckering methods* . . . To get suckered means to be easily fooled and exploited. Psychologists, such as Ray Hyman, show us how astrologers, palm (hand) readers, graphologists (who allegedly analyze handwriting to reveal personality), and others fool and exploit people by use of a few simple techniques (*suckering methods*).

Page 506 (Thinking Critically): . . . "*stock spiel*" . . . A "stock spiel" is a well-rehearsed and glib story. Astrologers, horoscope writers, and such often use statements that are generally true of almost everybody (*their "stock spiel"*), and most people find it hard to resist believing the flattering descriptions of themselves; consequently, many view astrology as an authentic art.

Page 508: . . . people have had fun *spoofing* the MMPI with their own *mock* items . . . Some items on the MMPI may appear nonsensical (*sound silly*), but they differentiated, say, depressed from nondepressed people, and so were retained in the form. Some authorities have created some humorous but false (*mock*) items for a personality test that is a parody (*spoof*) of the MMPI.

Page 509: . . . *the acid test* . . . Self-report personality tests are the most commonly used form of trait assessment, but some psychologists (e.g., David Funder) believe that peer reports are more accurate and that they provide the ultimate description (*acid test*) of personality. Although self-reports and peer assessments usually agree, David Funder would support, or bet, on the latter (*he'd put his money on peer reports*).

Page 510: If we remember such results, says Mischel, we will be more cautious about *labeling* and *pigeonholing* individuals. Research has shown that some behavior can be context specific (i.e., determined by the situation and not by the personality) and that personality test scores are poorly correlated with people's actual behavior on any particular occasion. Mischel warns that we should be careful about classifying individuals (*labeling*) and concluding that they belong in one particular slot (*pigeonholing*).

The Humanistic Perspective

(*Page 512, caption*): . . . *crippled spirits*. Abraham Maslow, a humanistic psychologist, studied healthy, motivated, creative people and came to the conclusion that once our basic needs are met, we all seek **self-actualization.** He believed that any theory of personality and motivation must be based on more than the study of psychologically impaired individuals (*crippled spirits*); rather, it should also include those who have achieved or fulfilled their innate potential (*self-actualized people*).

Page 512: Unless *thwarted* by an environment that inhibits growth, each of us is like an *acorn, primed* for growth and fulfillment. Carl Rogers was another pioneer in humanistic psychology. We are born with an innate striving (*we are primed*) for achieving our potential and like the seed (*acorn*) of the oak tree we will grow and develop unless we are blocked (*thwarted*) by an uncaring and unaccepting environment. As Rogers puts it, genuineness, acceptance, and empathy are the water, sun, and nutrients that enable people to grow like vigorous oak trees.

Page 515: Those who are *negative about themselves* also tend to be *thin-skinned* and *judgmental*. . . . People who have low self-esteem (*are negative about themselves*) are more likely to be anxious, depressed, insecure, and very sensitive to criticism (*thin-skinned*). In addition, they are also more likely to disparage and be critical (*judgmental*) of others.

Page 516: Athletes often privately credit their victories to their own *prowess* and their losses to *bad breaks, lousy officiating,* or the other team's exceptional performance. Athletes, like the rest of us, want to feel that desirable outcomes are due to their own abilities (*prowess*) and that failures are due to factors beyond their control such as poor luck (*bad breaks*), unfair refereeing (*lousy officiating*), or their opponents' unexpectedly outstanding efforts. This is called the **self-serving bias.**

Page 516: The world, it seems, is Garrison Keillor's *Lake Wobegon* writ large—a place where "all the women are strong, all the men are good-looking, and all the children are above average." Lake Wobegon is a fictional but ideal community satirized by comedian Garrison Keillor. Most abilities follow a bell-shaped distribution (the normal curve), so approximately half the population will be below average and half above on any given trait, such as strength, looks, or intelligence. The **self-serving bias**, which prompts most of us to rate ourselves as above average, appears to be almost universal, and the world is a magnified reflection of the Lake Wobegon community.

Page 516: Moreover, *pride does often go before a fall.* Our conceit and self-important attitudes (*pride*) often precede a harsh lesson from reality (*a fall*). As Myers notes, it was nationalistic pride (the conceited belief that the Aryan race was superior) that facilitated and fostered (*fueled*) the growth of the Nazi movement and legitimized their inhumane and cruel deeds (*atrocities*).

Page 517: Someone with a *swelled head* that gets deflated by insult or rejection is potentially dangerous. Overly self-confident people with high self-esteem (*swelled heads or large egos*) do more than retaliate in kind (*put down others*) when criticized, insulted, or rejected. Instead, they are more likely to react violently and aggressively (they are potentially dangerous). Researchers suggest that this negative aspect (*dark side*) of self-esteem is the result of threatened egotism and not low self-esteem.

Page 517: Sometimes self-directed *put-downs* are subtly strategic: They *elicit* reassuring *strokes*. When people disparage themselves with criticisms aimed at themselves (*self-directed put-downs*), they sometimes have an insidious or hidden purpose (*are subtly strategic*). They may want to have people reassure them that the opposite is true (*they want strokes*), or they may want to prepare for the worst possible outcome and have a rationalization for failure ready, just in case.

Page 518: . . . *a social network provides one's bearings.* Collectivist cultures emphasize the family, the group, and the community, rather than individual needs. Thus, the interconnectedness of people (*social network*) gives the collectivist a sense of belonging and place (*provides one's bearings*).

Page 518: . . . *lose face.* This means public disgrace or injury to one's pride or self-esteem. In collectivist cultures, people observe the rules (*norms*) that emphasize pleasant and nonconfrontational relationships. In order to maintain group cohesion, they avoid publicly embarrassing others (they make sure others never *lose face*), do not bring up sensitive issues, give way to others' opinions, and show proper respect to those who are older and those who are in charge. Happiness is being concerned with and sensitive (*attuned*) to others.

Page 520 . . . the popular media have celebrated the *rugged* individual. Humanistic psychology has been popular because it is consistent with Western cultural values, which emphasize strong, capable (*rugged*) individuals who follow their own beliefs and ambitions and oppose (*they buck*) social norms and restrictions. This popular reception of the humanistic movement has elicited a strongly adverse and disapproving reaction (*set off a backlash of criticism*).

Page 521: May agreed with critics who see people joining the humanistic movement seeking "a community of like-minded persons who also are *playing possum* to the evils about us." Rollo May, a humanistic psychologist, disagreed with Carl Rogers's hopeful or optimistic viewpoint and pointed out that adopting the humanistic perspective was like joining a group of people who reinforced each other's beliefs and seemed to be oblivious to, and pretended not to notice (*played possum to*), the problems in the world.

The Social-Cognitive Perspective

Page 523: If we expect someone to be angry with us, we may give the person a *cold shoulder, touching off* the very behavior we expect. The way we are (our personalities) may influence how we are treated by others. If we believe that someone has hostile intentions toward us, we may ignore and treat the person with indifference (*give the person a cold shoulder*), and this in turn may cause (*touch off*) the angry behavior we predicted or expected from that person. As Myers notes, we are both the results (*products*) and the creators (*architects*) of our environments.

Page 523: Later placed in another situation where they *could* escape the punishment by merely *leaping*

a hurdle, they cowered without hope. In Seligman's experiments, dogs learned that nothing they did had any effect on what happened to them (**learned helplessness**), so they would not make even a minimal effort, such as jumping over a small barrier (*leaping a hurdle*), to escape being shocked. People, too, who feel they have no control over what happens to them may become depressed and feel hopeless and helpless.

Page 525: Those who *put an optimistic spin on setbacks* —by seeing them as *flukes* or as suggesting a new approach, rather than viewing them as signs of incompetence—. . . . People who view unwelcome reversals of fortune (*setbacks*) as just pure chance (*flukes*) or see them as challenges and as an opportunity to try something different (*put an optimistic spin on them*) are more likely to be successful and content. As Myers points out, positive thinking when confronted by problems (*in the face of adversity*) has many benefits (*pays dividends*).

Page 526: . . . *bombing* the upcoming exam . . . Students who are excessively optimistic and overconfident may not do as well as those who are concerned about failing (*bombing*) the exam and consequently study extremely hard. Extreme optimism may prevent us from becoming aware of potential hazards (*blind us to real risks*).

Page 527: . . . so many low-scoring students are *dumbfounded* after doing badly on an exam. People often are most overconfident when most incompetent, mainly because it is difficult for them to recognize incompetence without having competence in the first place. Consequently, many students who do not recognize that they are having problems are often astounded (*dumbfounded*) when they find they are not in the top half of the class. (As Myers notes, like pride, illusory or blind optimism may precede a negative outcome or fall.)

CHAPTER **15:**

Psychological Disorders

Chapter Overview

Although there is no clear-cut line between normal and abnormal behavior, we can characterize as abnormal those behaviors that are atypical, disturbing, maladaptive, and unjustifiable. Chapter 15 discusses types of anxiety, dissociative, mood, schizophrenia, and personality disorders, as classified by the *Diagnostic and Statistical Manual of Mental Disorders* (DSM-IV). Although this classification system follows a medical model, in which disorders are viewed as illnesses, the chapter discusses psychological as well as physiological factors, as advocated by the current biopsycho-social perspective. Thus, psychoanalytic theory, learning theory, social-cognitive theory, and other psychological perspectives are drawn on when relevant. The chapter concludes with a discussion of the incidence of serious psychological disorders in society today.

Your major task in this chapter is to learn about psychological disorders, their various subtypes and characteristics, and their possible causes. Since the material to be learned is extensive, it may be helpful to rehearse it by mentally completing the Chapter Review several times.

NOTE: Answer guidelines for all Chapter 15 questions begin on page 435.

Perspectives on Psychological Disorders (pp. 532–538)

> David Myers at times uses idioms that are unfamiliar to some readers. If you do not know the meaning of any of the following words, phrases, or expressions in the context in which they appear in the text, refer to pages 443–444 for an explanation: *eerie sense of self-recognition; draw the line; The devil made him do it; handy shorthand; faulted the manual; self-fulfilling prophecies; Hinckley Insane, Public Mad.*

Section Preview

First, skim the section, noting headings and boldface items. Then read the following objectives and, as you read the text, search for the information that will enable you to meet each objective. Answer guidelines are provided on page 435.

1. List the criteria for judging whether behavior is disordered.

2. Explain and contrast two perspectives on psychological disorders.

3. Describe the system used to classify psychological disorders, and explain the reasons for its development.

4. Discuss the controversy surrounding the use of diagnostic labels.

Stepping Through the Section

After you have read the section, complete the sentences and answer the questions. As you proceed, evaluate your performance by consulting the answers on page 435. Do not continue with the next section until you understand each answer. If you need to, review or reread the section in the textbook before continuing.

1. Psychologically disorders are

   _____ _____

   that must be judged to be _____ ,

   _____ , _____ ,

   and _____ . This definition emphasizes that standards of acceptability for behavior are _____ (constant/variable).

2. The view that psychological disorders are sicknesses is the basis of the _____ model. According to this view, psychological disorders are viewed as mental _____ , or _____ .

3. One of the first reformers to advocate this position and call for providing more humane living conditions for the mentally ill was

   _____ .

4. Today's psychologists recognize that all behavior arises from the interaction of _____ and _____ . To presume that a person is "mentally ill" attributes the condition solely to an _____ problem.

5. Major psychological disorders such as

   _____ and

   _____ are universal; others, such

   as _____ _____

   and _____ , are culture-bound. These culture-bound disorders may share an underlying _____ , such as

   _____ , yet differ in their

   _____ .

6. Most mental health workers today work from the

   _____-_____-

   _____ perspective, which assumes that disorders are influenced by

   _____ _____ ,

   inner _____

   _____ , and

   _____ and _____

   circumstances.

7. The most widely used system for classifying psychological disorders is the American Psychiatric Association manual, commonly known by its abbreviation, _____ . This manual defines 400 categories of "mental disorder," divided into _____ (how many?) major categories.

8. Psychological illnesses that are severely impairing, called _____

   _____ , are contrasted with

   _____ _____ , or psychological illnesses that allow the person to function socially. In general, DSM-IV now seeks to list and _____ the disorders, rather than attempting to _____ their causes.

9. Independent diagnoses made with the current manual generally _____ (show/do not show) agreement.

10. One criticism of DSM-IV is that as the number of disorder categories has _____ (increased/decreased), the number of adults who meet the criteria for at least one psychiatric ailment has _____ (increased/ decreased).

11. Studies have shown that labeling has _____ (little/a significant) effect on our interpretation of individuals and their behavior.

Outline the pros and cons of labeling psychological disorders.

Anxiety Disorders (pp. 539–544)

> If you do not know the meaning of any of the following words, phrases, or expressions in the context in which they appear in the text, refer to page 444 for an explanation: *ringing in the ears . . . fidgeting; road tested in the Stone Age; flashbacks and nightmares; Grooming gone wild.*

Section Preview

Answer guidelines are provided on page 435.

1. Describe the various anxiety disorders.

2. Discuss anxiety disorders from the psychoanalytic, learning, and biological perspectives.

Stepping Through the Section

Answers are provided on page 436.

1. When a person tends to feel anxious for no apparent reason, he or she is diagnosed as suffering from a _____ _____ disorder.

2. In generalized anxiety disorder, the body reacts physiologically with the arousal of the _____ nervous system. In some instances, anxiety may intensify dramatically and be accompanied by trembling or dizziness; people with these symptoms are said to have _____ _____ .

3. People who fear situations in which escape or help might not be possible when panic strikes suffer from _____ .

4. When a person has an irrational fear of a specific object, activity, or situation, the diagnosis is a _____ . Although in many situations, the person can live with the problem, some _____ _____ , such as a fear of thunderstorms, are incapacitating.

5. When a person has an intense fear of being scrutinized by others, the diagnosis is a _____ _____ .

6. When a person cannot control repetitive thoughts and actions, an _____ _____ disorder is diagnosed. Older people are _____ (more/less) likely than teens and young adults to suffer from this disorder.

7. Freud assumed that anxiety disorders are symptoms of submerged mental energy that derives from intolerable impulses that were _____ during childhood.

8. Learning theorists, drawing on research in which rats are given unpredictable shocks, link general anxiety with _____ conditioning of _____ .

9. Some fears arise from _____ _____ , such as when a person who fears heights after a fall also comes to fear airplanes.

10. Phobias and compulsive behaviors reduce anxiety and thereby are _____ . Through _____ learning, some-

one might also learn fear by seeing others display their own fears.

11. Humans probably _____ (are/are not) biologically prepared to develop certain fears. Compulsive acts typically are exaggerations of behaviors that contributed to our species' _____ .

12. The anxiety response probably _____ (is/is not) genetically influenced.

13. PET scans of persons with obsessive-compulsive disorder reveal excessive activity in a region of the _____ lobes. Antidepressant drugs may reduce this activity by influencing the neurotransmitter _____ .

14. (Close-Up)) Traumatic stress, such as that associated with witnessing atrocities or combat, can produce _____-_____ _____ disorder, symptoms of which include _____ _____.

Despite such symptoms, some psychologists believe this disorder is a _____ diagnosis.

Mood Disorders (pp. 545–553)

If you do not know the meaning of any of the following words, phrases, or expressions in the context in which they appear in the text, refer to pages 444–445 for an explanation: *To grind temporarily to a halt; blue mood; slow motion . . . fast forward; view life through dark glasses; sour our thinking; two-way traffic; company does not love another's misery.*

Section Preview

Answer guidelines are provided on page 436.

1. Describe two principal mood disorders.

2. Discuss the alternative explanations of mood disorders.

Stepping Through the Section

Answers are provided on page 436.

1. The experience of prolonged depression with no discernible cause is called _____ _____ disorder.

2. When a person's mood alternates between depression and the hyperactive state of _____ , a _____ disorder is diagnosed.

3. Although _____ are more common, _____ is the number one reason that people seek mental health services.

4. In between the temporary blue moods everyone experiences and major depression is a condition called _____ _____ , in which a person feels down-in-the-dumps nearly every day for two years or more.

5. The possible signs of depression include _____ _____ .

6. Major depression occurs when its signs last _____ _____ or more with no apparent cause.

7. Depressed persons usually _____ (can/cannot) recover without therapy.

8. Symptoms of mania include _____ _____ .

The bipolar disorder occurs in approximately _____ percent of men and women.

9. Compared with men, women are _____ (more/less) vulnerable to major depression. In general, women are most vulnerable to

_____ (active/passive) disorders, such as _____
_____ .

Men's disorders tend to be _____ (active/passive) and include _____
_____ .

Among college students, the gender difference in depression is _____ (quite small/much larger).

10. It usually _____ (is/is not) the case that a depressive episode has been triggered by a stressful event.

11. With each new generation, the rate of depression is _____ (increasing/decreasing) and the disorder is striking _____ (earlier/later).

State the psychoanalytic explanation of depression.

12. Mood disorders _____ (tend/do not tend) to run in families. Studies of _____ also reveal that genetic influences on mood disorders are _____ (weak/strong).

13. To determine which genes are involved in depression, researchers use
_____ _____ , in which they examine the _____ of both affected and unaffected family members.

14. Depression may also be caused by _____ (high/low) levels of two neurotransmitters, _____ or
_____ .

15. Drugs that alleviate mania reduce _____ ; drugs that relieve depression increase _____ or _____ by blocking their _____ or their chemical _____ .

16. The brains of depressed people tend to be _____ (more/less) active, especially in an area of the _____ _____ lobe of the brain. In severely depressed patients, this brain area may also be _____ (smaller/larger) in size.

17. According to the social-cognitive perspective, depression may be linked with beliefs that are _____ . Such beliefs may arise from _____
_____ , the feeling that can arise when the individual repeatedly experiences uncontrollable, painful events.

18. Gender differences in _____
_____ help explain why women have been twice as vulnerable to depression.

Describe how depressed people differ from others in their explanations of failure and how such explanations tend to feed depression.

19. Research studies suggest that depressing thoughts usually _____ (precede/follow/coincide with) a depressed mood.

20. Depression-prone people respond to bad events in an especially _____ , _____ way.

21. Recent research studies with college students reveal that _____ thinkers are vulnerable to depression.

22. Being withdrawn, self-focused, and complaining tends to elicit social _____ (empathy/rejection).

Outline the vicious cycle of depression.

Identify two pieces of evidence brought forth by those who do not accept dissociative identity disorder as a genuine disorder.

(Thinking Critically) Dissociation and Multiple Personalities (pp. 554–555)

> If you do not know the meaning of any of the following words, phrases, or expressions in the context in which they appear in the text, refer to page 445 for an explanation: *a ruse; go fishing for it.*

Thinking Critically Preview

Answer guidelines are provided on page 437.

1. Describe the nature and possible causes of dissociative disorders.

Stepping Through Thinking Critically

Answers are provided on page 437.

1. In _____ disorders, a person's _____ _____ becomes separated from painful memories, thoughts, and feelings.

2. A person who develops two or more distinct personalities is suffering from _____ _____ disorder.

3. Nicholas Spanos has argued that such people may merely be playing different _____ .

4. Those who accept this as a genuine disorder point to evidence that differing personalities may be associated with distinct _____ and _____ states.

5. The psychoanalytic and learning perspectives view dissociative disorders as ways of dealing with _____ . Others view them as a protective response to histories of

_____ _____ .

Skeptics claim these disorders are sometimes contrived by _____-_____ people, and sometimes constructed out of the _____-_____ interaction.

Schizophrenia (pp. 556–562)

> If you do not know the meaning of any of the following words, phrases, or expressions in the context in which they appear in the text, refer to page 445 for an explanation: *hodge-podge; flat affect; traffic . . . runs both ways.*

Section Preview

Answer guidelines are provided on page 437.

1. Describe the symptoms and types of schizophrenia.

2. Discuss research on the causes of schizophrenia.

Stepping Through the Section

Answers are provided on page 437.

1. Schizophrenia, or "split mind," refers not to a split personality but rather to a split from _____ .

2. Three manifestations of schizophrenia are disorganized _____ , disturbed _____ , and inappropriate _____ and _____ .

3. The distorted, false beliefs of schizophrenia patients are called _____ .

4. Many psychologists attribute the disorganized thinking of schizophrenia to a breakdown in the capacity for _____ _____ .

5. The disturbed perceptions of people suffering from schizophrenia may take the form of _____ , which usually are _____ (visual/auditory).

6. Some victims of schizophrenia lapse into a zombielike state of apparent apathy, or _____ _____ ; others, who exhibit _____ , may remain motionless for hours.

7. The term *schizophrenia* describes a _____ (single disorder/cluster of disorders).

8. Positive symptoms of schizophrenia include _____ _____ .

   Negative symptoms include _____ _____ _____ .

9. When schizophrenia develops slowly (called _____ schizophrenia), recovery is _____ (more/less) likely than when it develops rapidly in reaction to particular life stresses (called _____ schizophrenia).

10. The brain tissue of schizophrenia patients has been found to have an excess of receptors for the neurotransmitter _____ . Drugs that block these receptors have been found to _____ (increase/decrease) schizophrenia symptoms.

11. Brain scans have shown that many people suffering from schizophrenia have abnormal patterns of brain _____ in the frontal lobes.

12. Enlarged, _____-filled areas and a corresponding _____ of cerebral tissue is also characteristic of schizophrenia. Schizophrenia patients also have a smaller-than-normal _____ , which may account for their difficulty in filtering _____ _____ and focusing _____ .

13. Some scientists contend that the brain abnormalities of schizophrenia may be caused by a prenatal problem, such as a _____ _____ contracted by the mother.

List several pieces of evidence for this theory.

14. Twin and adoptive studies _____ (support/do not support) the contention that heredity plays a role in schizophrenia.

15. The role of the prenatal environment in schizophrenia is demonstrated by the fact that identical twins who share the same _____ , and are therefore more likely to experience the same prenatal _____ , are more likely to share the disorder.

16. Linkage studies have implicated three specific _____ as sites of genes that make some people susceptible to schizophrenia. However, other factors such as prenatal viral infections, deprivation of _____ , or _____ at birth may also be factors in the disease.

17. It appears that for schizophrenia to develop there must be both a _____ predisposition and some _____ trigger. One possible scenario is that abnormalities in the _____ system and in _____ anatomy may make a patient hypersensitive to _____ , which worsens symptoms by increasing the activity of _____ .

List several of the warning signs of schizophrenia in high-risk children.

Personality Disorders (pp. 562–564)

> If you do not know the meaning of any of the following words, phrases, or expressions in the context in which they appear in the text, refer to page 445 for an explanation: *con artist; woven of biological as well as psychological strands.*

Section Preview

Answer guidelines are provided on page 438.

1. Describe the nature and causes of personality disorders and the specific characteristics of the antisocial personality disorder.

Stepping Through the Section

Answers are provided on page 438.

1. Personality disorders exist when an individual has character traits that are enduring and impair _____ _____ .

2. An individual who seems to have no conscience, lies, steals, is generally irresponsible, and may be criminal is said to have an _____ personality. Previously, this person was labeled a _____ .

3. Studies of the children of convicted criminals suggest that there _____ (is/is not) a biological predisposition to such traits.

4. When awaiting electric shocks, antisocial persons show _____ (more/less) arousal of the autonomic nervous system than do control subjects.

5. Some studies have detected early signs of antisocial behavior in children as young as _____ . Antisocial adolescents tended to have been _____ , _____ , unconcerned with _____ _____ , and low in _____ .

6. PET scans of murderers' brains reveal reduced activity in the _____ _____ .

7. As in other disorders, in antisocial personality, genetics _____ (is/is not) the whole story.

Rates of Psychological Disorders (pp. 564–565)

Section Preview

Answer guidelines are provided on page 438.

1. Briefly discuss the prevalence of psychological disorders.

Stepping Through the Section

Answers are provided on page 438.

1. Research reveals that approximately _____ percent of American adults have at some time experienced a psychological disorder and that approximately _____ percent have an active disorder.

2. The incidence of serious psychological disorders is _____ (higher/lower) among those below the poverty line.

3. In terms of age of onset, most psychological disorders appear by _____ (early/middle/late) adulthood. Some, such as the

_____ _____

and _____ , appear during childhood.

Web Sightings

The National Institute of Mental Health (NIMH) (**http://www.nimh.nih.gov/home.htm**) maintains an excellent web site for extending your exploration of psychological disorders. Review the major diagnostic categories and check out the latest research findings regarding our understanding of the causes, prevention, and treatment of specific psychological disorders. Also see the Quicktime videos and animations produced by NIMH's Clinical Brain Disorders Branch. Tour NIMH-funded laboratories around the United States and peek over the shoulders of researchers as they describe their current experiments. And don't stop there! Use Web links at this site as jumping-off points to dozens of other Internet resources that provide information about psychological disorders. To focus your tour, see if you can find the answers to the following questions.

1. What is the *Human Brain Project*?

2. What is the estimated total annual economic impact of mental disorders in the United States? What are some of the hidden costs of mental disorders?

3. What have NIMH researchers recently learned about schizophrenia using state-of-the-art brain-imaging techniques?

4. What are the current (and future) research priorities of NIMH?

5. What is "clozapine treatment"? For whom is it intended? Does it work?

Progress Test 1

Multiple-Choice Questions

Circle your answers to the following questions and check them with the answers on page 438. If your answer is incorrect, read the explanation for why it is incorrect and then consult the appropriate pages of the text (in parentheses following the correct answer).

1. Gender differences in the prevalence of depression may be partly due to the fact that when stressful experiences occur, women tend to _____ while men tend to _____ .
   a. act; think
   b. think; act
   c. distract themselves by drinking; delve into their work
   d. delve into their work; distract themselves by drinking

2. The criteria for classifying behavior as psychologically disordered:
   a. vary from culture to culture.
   b. vary from time to time.
   c. are characterized by both a. and b.
   d. have remained largely unchanged over the course of history.

3. Most mental health workers today take the view that disordered behaviors:
   a. are usually genetically triggered.
   b. are organic diseases.
   c. arise from the interaction of nature and nurture.
   d. are the product of learning.

4. The French reformer who insisted that madness was not demon possession and who called for humane treatment of patients was:
   a. Nadel.
   d. Spanos.
   b. Freud.
   e. Pinel.
   c. Szasz.

5. Which of the following is the most pervasive of the psychological disorders?
   a. depression
   b. schizophrenia
   c. bipolar disorder
   d. generalized anxiety disorder

6. Which of the following is *not* true concerning depression?
   a. Depression is more common in females than in males.
   b. Most depressive episodes appear not to be preceded by any particular factor or event.
   c. Most depressive episodes last less than 3 months.
   d. Most people recover from depression without professional therapy.

7. Which of the following is *not* true regarding schizophrenia?
   a. It occurs more frequently in people born in winter and spring months.
   b. It occurs less frequently as infectious disease rates have declined.
   c. It occurs more frequently in lightly populated areas.
   d. It usually appears during adolescence or early adulthood.

8. Evidence of environmental effects on psychological disorders is seen in the fact that certain disorders, such as _____ , are universal, whereas others, such as _____ , are culture-bound.
   a. schizophrenia; depression
   b. depression; schizophrenia
   c. antisocial personality; neurosis
   d. depression; anorexia nervosa

9. The effect of drugs that block receptors for dopamine is to:
   a. alleviate schizophrenia symptoms.
   b. alleviate depression.
   c. increase schizophrenia symptoms.
   d. increase depression.

10. The diagnostic reliability of DSM-IV:
    a. is unknown.
    b. depends on the age of the patient.
    c. is very low.
    d. is relatively high.

11. The early warning signs of schizophrenia, based on studies of high-risk children, include all but which of the following?
    a. having a severely schizophrenic mother
    b. having been separated from parents
    c. having a short attention span
    d. having matured physically at a very early age

12. (Thinking Critically) The term *insanity* refers to:
    a. legal definitions.
    b. psychotic disorders only.
    c. personality disorders only.
    d. both psychotic disorders and personality disorders.

13. Phobias and obsessive-compulsive behaviors are classified as:
    a. anxiety disorders.
    b. mood disorders.
    c. dissociative disorders.
    d. personality disorders.

14. According to the social-cognitive perspective, a person who experiences unexpected aversive events may develop helplessness and manifest a(n):
    a. obsessive-compulsive disorder.
    b. dissociative disorder.
    c. personality disorder.
    d. mood disorder.

15. Which of the following was presented in the text as evidence of biological influences on anxiety disorders?
    a. Identical twins often develop similar phobias.
    b. PET scans of persons with obsessive-compulsive disorder reveal unusually high activity in an area of the frontal lobes.
    c. Drugs that affect the neurotransmitter serotonin may control obsessive thoughts.
    d. All of the above were presented.
    e. None of the above was presented.

16. Most of the hallucinations of schizophrenia patients involve the sense of:
    a. smell.
    c. hearing.
    b. vision.
    d. touch.

17. When expecting to be electrically shocked, people with an antisocial disorder, as compared to normal people, show:
    a. less fear and greater arousal of the autonomic nervous system.
    b. less fear and less autonomic arousal.
    c. greater fear and greater autonomic arousal.
    d. greater fear and less autonomic arousal.

18. Hearing voices would be a(n) _____ ; believing that you are Napoleon would be a(n) _____ .

    a. obsession; compulsion
    b. compulsion; obsession
    c. delusion; hallucination
    d. hallucination; delusion

19. In treating depression, a psychiatrist would probably prescribe a drug that would:
    a. increase levels of acetylcholine.
    b. decrease levels of dopamine.
    c. increase levels of norepinephrine.
    d. decrease levels of serotonin.

20. When schizophrenia is slow to develop, called _____ schizophrenia, recovery is _____ .
    a. reactive; unlikely   c. process; unlikely
    b. process; likely   d. reactive; likely

Matching Items

Match each term with the appropriate definition or description.

Terms

_____ 1. dissociative disorder
_____ 2. psychotic disorder
_____ 3. mood disorders
_____ 4. social phobia
_____ 5. neurotic disorder
_____ 6. mania
_____ 7. obsessive-compulsive disorder
_____ 8. schizophrenia
_____ 9. hallucination
_____ 10. panic attack

Definitions or Descriptions

a. psychological disorders marked by emotional extremes
b. an extremely elevated mood
c. a false sensory experience
d. any psychological disorder that is severely debilitating and involves bizarre thinking and behavior
e. a sudden escalation of anxiety often accompanied by a sensation of choking or other physical symptoms
f. a disorder in which conscious awareness becomes separated from previous memories, feelings, and thoughts
g. any psychological disorder in which the person continues to think rationally and function socially
h. intense fear of being scrutinized by others
i. a group of disorders marked by disorganized thinking, disturbed perceptions, and inappropriate emotions and actions
j. a disorder characterized by repetitive thoughts and actions

Progress Test 2

Progress Test 2 should be completed during a final chapter review. Answer the following questions after you thoroughly understand the correct answers for the Chapter Review and Progress Test 1.

Multiple-Choice Questions

1. Which of the following is true concerning abnormal behavior?
   a. Definitions of abnormal behavior are culture-dependent.
   b. A behavior cannot be defined as abnormal unless it is considered harmful to society.
   c. Abnormal behavior can be defined as any behavior that is atypical.
   d. Definitions of abnormal behavior are based on physiological factors.

2. The psychoanalytic perspective would most likely view phobias as:
   a. conditioned fears.
   b. displaced responses to incompletely repressed impulses.
   c. biological predispositions.
   d. manifestations of self-defeating thoughts.

3. Many psychologists believe the disorganized thoughts of people with schizophrenia result from a breakdown in:
   a. selective attention.
   b. memory storage.
   c. motivation.
   d. memory retrieval.
   e. memory encoding.

4. Recent evidence links the brain abnormalities of schizophrenia to _____ during prenatal development.
   a. maternal stress
   b. a viral infection contracted
   c. abnormal levels of certain hormones
   d. the weight of the unborn child
   e. alcohol use

5. The fact that disorders such as schizophrenia are universal and influenced by heredity, whereas other disorders such as anorexia nervosa are culture-bound provides evidence for the _____ model of psychological disorders.
   a. medical
   b. bio-psycho-social
   c. social-cultural
   d. psychoanalytic

6. Our early ancestors commonly attributed disordered behavior to:
   a. "bad blood."
   b. evil spirits.
   c. brain injury.
   d. laziness.

7. In general, women are more vulnerable than men to _____ disorders such as _____ .
   a. active; anxiety
   b. passive; depression
   c. active; antisocial conduct
   d. passive; alcohol abuse

8. Which of the following statements concerning the labeling of disordered behaviors is *not* true?
   a. Labels interfere with effective treatment of psychological disorders.
   b. Labels promote research studies of psychological disorders.
   c. Labels may create preconceptions that bias people's perceptions.
   d. Labels may influence behavior by creating self-fulfilling prophecies.

9. (Thinking Critically) Nicholas Spanos considers dissociative identity disorder to be:
   a. a genuine disorder.
   b. merely role playing.
   c. a disorder that cannot be explained according to the learning perspective.
   d. both a. and c.

10. Which neurotransmitter is present in overabundant amounts during the manic phase of bipolar disorder?
    a. dopamine
    b. serotonin
    c. epinephrine
    d. norepinephrine

11. After falling from a ladder, Joseph is afraid of airplanes, although he has never flown. This demonstrates that some fears arise from:
    a. observational learning.
    b. reinforcement.
    c. stimulus generalization.
    d. stimulus discrimination.

12. Which of the following provides evidence that human fears have been subjected to the evolutionary process?
    a. Compulsive acts typically exaggerate behaviors that contributed to our species' survival.
    b. Most phobias focus on objects that our ancestors also feared.
    c. It is easier to condition some fears than others.
    d. All of the above provide evidence.

13. Which of the following is true of the medical model?
    a. In recent years, it has been in large part discredited.
    b. It views psychological disorders as sicknesses that are diagnosable and treatable.

c. It emphasizes the role of psychological factors in disorders over that of physiological factors.

d. It focuses on cognitive factors.

14. (Thinking Critically) Psychoanalytic and learning theorists both agree that dissociative and anxiety disorders are symptoms that represent the person's attempt to deal with:

a. unconscious conflicts.

b. anxiety.

c. unfulfilled wishes.

d. unpleasant responsibilities.

15. Behavior is classified as disordered when it is:

a. atypical.

b. maladaptive.

c. unjustifiable.

d. disturbing.

e. all of the above.

16. Many psychologists dislike using DSM-IV because of its:

a. failure to emphasize observable behaviors in the diagnostic process.

b. learning theory bias.

c. medical model bias.

d. psychoanalytic bias.

e. social-cultural bias.

17. Which of the following is *not* a symptom of schizophrenia?

a. inappropriate emotions

b. disturbed perceptions

c. panic attacks

d. disorganized thinking

18. Social-cognitive theorists contend that depression is linked with:

a. negative moods.

b. maladaptive explanations of failure.

c. self-defeating beliefs.

d. all of the above.

19. According to psychoanalytic theory, memory of losses, especially in combination with internalized anger, is likely to result in:

a. learned helplessness.

b. the self-serving bias.

c. weak ego defense mechanisms.

d. depression.

20. Among the following, which is generally accepted as a possible cause of schizophrenia?

a. an excess of endorphins in the brain

b. being a twin

c. extensive learned helplessness

d. a genetic predisposition

Matching Items

Match each term with the appropriate definition or description.

Terms

_____ 1. dissociative identity disorder
_____ 2. phobia
_____ 3. dopamine
_____ 4. dysthymic disorder
_____ 5. antisocial personality
_____ 6. norepinephrine
_____ 7. serotonin
_____ 8. bipolar disorder
_____ 9. delusions
_____ 10. agoraphobia

Definitions or Descriptions

a. a neurotransmitter for which there are excess receptors in some schizophrenia patients

b. a neurotransmitter that is overabundant during mania and scarce during depression

c. an individual who seems to have no conscience

d. false beliefs that may accompany psychological disorders

e. an anxiety disorder marked by a persistent, irrational fear of a specific object or situation

f. a disorder formerly called multiple personality disorder

g. a neurotransmitter possibly linked to obsessive-compulsive behavior

h. a type of mood disorder

i. a disorder marked by chronic low energy and self-esteem

j. a fear of situations in which help might not be available during a panic attack

Thinking Critically About Chapter 15

Answer these questions the day before an exam as a final check on your understanding of the chapter's terms and concepts.

Multiple-Choice Questions

1. Joe has an intense, irrational fear of snakes. He is suffering from a(n):
   a. generalized anxiety disorder.
   b. obsessive-compulsive disorder.
   c. phobia.
   d. mood disorder.
   e. bipolar disorder.

2. As a child, Monica was criticized severely by her mother for not living up to her expectations. This criticism was always followed by a beating with a whip. As an adult, Monica is generally introverted and extremely shy. Sometimes, however, she acts more like a young child, throwing tantrums if she doesn't get her way. At other times, she is a flirting, happy-go-lucky young lady. Most likely, Monica is suffering from:
   a. phobic disorder.
   b. dissociative schizophrenia.
   c. dissociative identity disorder.
   d. bipolar disorder.

3. Bob has never been able to keep a job. He's been in and out of jail for charges such as theft, sexual assault, and spousal abuse. Bob would most likely be diagnosed as having:
   a. a dissociative identity disorder.
   b. major depressive disorder.
   c. schizophrenia.
   d. an antisocial personality.

4. Julia's psychologist believes that Julia's fear of heights can be traced to a conditioned fear she developed after falling from a ladder. This explanation reflects a _____ perspective.
   a. medical   c. social-cognitive
   b. psychoanalytic   d. learning

5. Before he can study, Rashid must arrange his books, pencils, paper, and other items on his desk so that they are "just so." The campus counselor suggests that Rashid's compulsive behavior may help alleviate his anxiety about failing in school, which reinforces the compulsive actions. This explanation of obsessive-compulsive behavior is most consistent with which perspective?
   a. learning   c. humanistic
   b. psychoanalytic   d. social-cognitive

6. Sharon is continually tense, jittery, and apprehensive for no specific reason. She would probably be diagnosed as suffering a(n):
   a. phobia.
   b. major depressive disorder.
   c. obsessive-compulsive disorder.
   d. generalized anxiety disorder.

7. Jason is so preoccupied with staying clean that he showers as many as ten times each day. Jason would be diagnosed as suffering from a(n):
   a. dissociative disorder.
   b. generalized anxiety disorder.
   c. personality disorder.
   d. obsessive-compulsive disorder.

8. (Close-Up) Although she escaped from war-torn Bosnia two years ago, Zheina still has haunting memories and nightmares. Because she is also severely depressed, her therapist diagnoses her condition as:
   a. dissociative identity disorder.
   b. bipolar disorder.
   c. schizophrenia.
   d. post-traumatic stress disorder.

9. Claiming that she heard a voice commanding her to warn other people that eating is harmful, Sandy attempts to convince others in a restaurant not to eat. The psychiatrist to whom she is referred finds that Sandy's thinking and speech are often fragmented and incoherent. In addition, Sandy has an unreasonable fear that someone is "out to get her" and consequently trusts no one. Her condition is most indicative of:
   a. schizophrenia.
   b. generalized anxiety disorder.
   c. a phobia.
   d. obsessive-compulsive disorder.
   e. personality disorder.

10. Irene occasionally experiences unpredictable episodes of intense dread accompanied by chest pains and a sensation of smothering. Since her symptoms have no apparent cause, they would probably be classified as indicative of:
    a. schizophrenia.
    b. bipolar disorder.
    c. post-traumatic stress disorder.
    d. panic attack.

11. To which of the following is a person *most* likely to acquire a phobia?
    a. heights
    b. being in public
    c. being dirty
    d. All of the above are equally likely.

12. Dr. Jekyll, whose second personality was Mr. Hyde, had a(n) _____ disorder.
    a. anxiety   c. mood
    b. dissociative   d. personality

13. For the past 6 months, a woman has complained of feeling isolated from others, dissatisfied with life, and discouraged about the future. This woman could be diagnosed as suffering from:
    a. bipolar disorder.
    b. major depressive disorder.
    c. generalized anxiety disorder.
    d. dissociative disorder.

14. On Monday, Matt felt optimistic, energetic, and on top of the world. On Tuesday, he felt hopeless and lethargic, and thought that the future looked very grim. Matt would *most* likely be diagnosed as having:
    a. bipolar disorder.
    b. major depressive disorder.
    c. schizophrenia.
    d. panic disorder.

15. Connie's therapist has suggested that her depression stems from unresolved anger toward her parents. Evidently, Connie's therapist is working within the _____ perspective.
    a. learning   c. biological
    b. social-cognitive   d. psychoanalytic

16. Ken's therapist suggested that his depression is a result of his self-defeating thoughts and negative assumptions about himself, his situation, and his future. Evidently, Ken's therapist is working within the _____ perspective.
    a. learning   c. biological
    b. social-cognitive   d. psychoanalytic

17. Alicia's doctor, who thinks that Alicia's depression has a biochemical cause, prescribes a drug that:
    a. reduces norepinephrine.
    b. increases norepinephrine.
    c. reduces serotonin.
    d. increases acetylcholine.

18. Wayne's doctor attempts to help Wayne by prescribing a drug that blocks receptors for dopamine. Wayne has apparently been diagnosed with:
    a. a mood disorder.
    b. an anxiety disorder.
    c. a personality disorder.
    d. schizophrenia.

19. (Close-up) Hussein, who suffers from chronic loneliness, probably attributes his unsatisfactory social relationships to:
    a. an inherited trait.
    b. his own inadequacies.
    c. a cultural norm.
    d. the social incompetence of other people.

20. Janet, whose class presentation is titled "Current Views on the Causes of Schizophrenia," concludes her talk with the statement:
    a. "Schizophrenia is caused by intolerable stress."
    b. "Schizophrenia is inherited."
    c. "Genes may predispose some people to react to particular experiences by developing schizophrenia."
    d. "As of this date, schizophrenia is completely unpredictable and its causes are unknown."

Essay Question

Clinical psychologists label people disordered if their behavior is (1) atypical, (2) disturbing, (3) maladaptive, and (4) unjustifiable. Demonstrate your understanding of the classification process by giving examples of behaviors that might be considered atypical, disturbing, maladaptive, or unjustifiable but, because they do not fit all four criteria, would not necessarily be labeled disordered. (Use the space below to list the points you want to make and organize them. Then write the essay on a separate piece of paper.)

Key Terms

Writing Definitions

Using your own words, on a separate piece of paper write a brief definition or explanation of each of the following terms.

1. psychological disorder
2. medical model
3. bio-psycho-social perspective
4. DSM-IV
5. neurotic disorders
6. psychotic disorders
7. anxiety disorders
8. generalized anxiety disorder
9. panic disorder

10. phobia
11. obsessive-compulsive disorder
12. mood disorders
13. major depressive disorder
14. manic episode
15. bipolar disorder
16. dissociative disorders
17. dissociative identity disorder
18. schizophrenia
19. delusions
20. personality disorders
21. antisocial personality disorder

Cross-Check

As you learned in the Introduction, reviewing and overlearning of material are important to the learning process. After you have written the definitions of the key terms in this chapter, you should complete the crossword puzzle to ensure that you can reverse the process—recognize the term, given the definition.

ACROSS

2. The "common cold" of psychological disorders.
9. Former term for disorders that, while distressing, still allow a person to think normally and function socially.
16. A euphoric, hyperactive state.
17. Category of disorders that includes major depression and bipolar disorder.
18. Mood disorder in which a person alternates between depression and mania.
19. Category of disorders that includes phobias and obsessive-compulsive disorder.

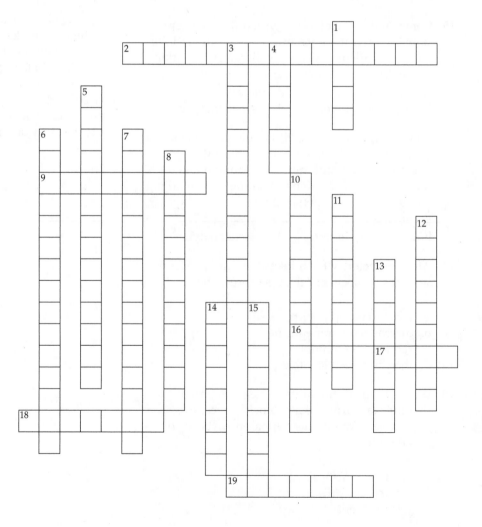

DOWN

1. A widely used system of classifying psychological disorders.
3. Disorders that involve a separation of conscious awareness from one's previous memories, thoughts, and feelings.
4. A persistent, irrational fear of a specific object or situation.
5. False sensory experiences.
6. Biomedical research technique used to determine which genes are involved in a specific psychological disorder.
7. Perspective that assumes that genes, psychological factors, and social and cultural circumstances combine and interact to produce psychological disorders.
8. Subtype of schizophrenia in which emotion is flat or inappropriate.
10. The viewpoint that psychological disorders are illnesses.
11. Subtype of schizophrenia in which there is immobility or excessive, purposeless movement.
12. False beliefs that often are symptoms of schizophrenia.
13. Neurotransmitter for which there are excess receptors in the brains of schizophrenia patients.
14. Category of schizophrenia symptoms that includes having a toneless voice, expressionless face, and a mute or rigid body.
15. Neurotransmitter that is scarce in depression.

Answers

Perspectives on Psychological Disorders

Section Preview

1. Psychological disorders are harmful dysfunctions that are judged to be atypical, disturbing to others, maladaptive, and unjustifiable.
2. According to the medical perspective, psychological disorders are sicknesses that can be diagnosed on the basis of their symptoms and cured through therapy. Psychologists who work from the bio-psycho-social perspective assume that biological, sociocultural, and psychological factors combine and interact to produce psychological disorders.
3. DSM-IV groups some 400 psychological disorders into 17 major categories. Diagnostic classification is intended to describe a disorder, predict its future course, imply its appropriate treatment, and stimulate research into its causes.
4. Most clinicians believe that diagnostic labels help

in describing, treating, and researching the causes of psychological disorders. Critics contend that these labels are arbitrary value judgments that create preconceptions that can bias our perceptions and interpretations. Labels can also affect people's self-images and stigmatize them in others' eyes. Finally, labels can change reality by serving as self-fulfilling prophecies.

Stepping Through the Section

1. harmful dysfunctions; atypical; disturbing; maladaptive; unjustifiable; variable
2. medical; illness; psychopathology
3. Pinel
4. nature; nurture; internal
5. depression; schizophrenia; anorexia nervosa; bulimia; dynamic; anxiety; symptoms
6. bio-psycho-social; genetic predispositions; psychological dynamics; social; cultural
7. DSM-IV; 17
8. psychotic disorders; neurotic disorders; describe; explain
9. show
10. increased; increased
11. a significant

Psychological labels may be arbitrary. They can create preconceptions that bias our perceptions and interpretations and they can affect people's self-images. Moreover, labels can change reality, by serving as self-fulfilling prophecies. Despite these drawbacks, labels are useful in describing, treating, and researching the causes of psychological disorders.

Anxiety Disorders

Section Preview

1. There are four types of anxiety disorder: generalized anxiety disorder, in which a person feels inexplicably tense and apprehensive; phobia, in which a person has an irrational fear of a specific object or situation; obsessive-compulsive disorder, in which a person is troubled by repetitive thoughts or actions, and panic disorder, an extreme form of anxiety in which a person experiences sudden episodes of intense dread.
2. Freud viewed an anxiety disorder as a manifestation of repressed impulses, ideas, and feelings that influence the sufferer's actions and emotions. Learning theorists link anxiety disorders with classical conditioning of fear, which may arise from stimulus generalization. Phobic and compulsive behaviors reduce anxiety by allowing the person to avoid or escape the feared situation;

this reinforces the behavior. According to this perspective, fear may also be learned through observational learning. Biologically oriented researchers see these disorders as evolutionary adaptations or as genetic predispositions to particular fears and high anxiety. The anxiety of persons with obsessive-compulsive disorder, for example, is measurable as unusually high activity in a particular region of the frontal lobes.

Stepping Through the Section

1. generalized anxiety
2. autonomic; panic disorder
3. agoraphobia
4. phobia; specific phobias
5. social phobia
6. obsessive-compulsive; less
7. repressed
8. classical; fears
9. stimulus generalization
10. reinforced; observational
11. are; survival
12. is
13. frontal; serotonin
14. post-traumatic stress; haunting memories, nightmares, social withdrawal, and anxiety or depression; fad

Mood Disorders

Section Preview

1. There are two principal mood disorders: major depressive disorder and the bipolar disorder. Major depressive disorder, the "common cold" of psychological disorders, occurs when signs of depression last 2 weeks or more without any discernible cause. Alternating between depressive episodes and the hyperactive, wildly optimistic state of mania is characteristic of the bipolar disorder.
2. According to the psychoanalytic perspective, depression occurs when significant losses evoke feelings associated with losses experienced in childhood and when unresolved anger is directed inward against the self.

   According to the biological perspective, mood disorders involve genetic predispositions and biochemical imbalances in which norepinephrine is overabundant during mania and scarce during depression. A second neurotransmitter, serotonin, is also scarce during depres-

sion. The brains of depressed people also tend to be less active and even have somewhat smaller frontal lobes.

According to the social-cognitive perspective, depression is a vicious cycle in which stressful experiences trigger self-focused negative thinking and a self-blaming style of explaining events that hamper the way the person thinks and acts. This negative thinking and self-blaming style leads to further negative experiences.

Stepping Through the Section

1. major depressive
2. mania; bipolar
3. phobias; depression
4. dysthymic disorder
5. lethargy, feelings of worthlessness, and loss of interest in family, friends, and activities
6. two weeks
7. can
8. euphoria, hyperactivity, and a wildly optimistic state; 1
9. more; passive; depression, anxiety, and inhibited sexual desire; active; alcohol abuse, antisocial conduct, and lack of impulse control; quite small
10. is
11. increasing; earlier

The psychoanalytic perspective suggests that adulthood depression can be triggered by losses that evoke feelings associated with earlier childhood losses. Alternatively, unresolved anger is turned inward and takes the form of depression.

12. tend; twins; strong
13. linkage analysis; DNA
14. low; norepinephrine; serotonin
15. norepinephrine; norepinephrine; serotonin; reuptake; breakdown
16. less; left frontal; smaller
17. self-defeating; learned helplessness
18. uncontrollable stress

Depressed people are more likely than others to explain failures or bad events in terms that are *stable* (it's going to last forever), *global* (it will affect everything), and *internal* (it's my fault). Such explanations lead to feelings of hopelessness, which in turn feed depression.

19. coincide with
20. self-focused; self-blaming
21. negative
22. rejection

Depression is often brought on by stressful experiences. Depressed people brood over such experiences with maladaptive explanations that produce self-blame and amplify their depression, which in turn triggers other symptoms of depression. In addition, being withdrawn and complaining tends to elicit social rejection and other negative experiences.

(Thinking Critically) Dissociation and Multiple Personalities

Thinking Critically Preview

1. In dissociative disorders, a person's conscious awareness becomes separated from previous memories, thoughts, and feelings. Most mysterious is the dissociative identity disorder, in which people have two or more distinct personalities; however, some skeptics believe that such persons are merely enacting a role for strategic reasons.

   Psychoanalysts view the symptoms of these disorders as defenses against anxiety. Learning theorists see them as behaviors reinforced by anxiety reduction. Some theorists see dissociative behaviors as states that serve as protective escape responses to traumatic childhood experiences. The recent explosion of diagnosis of dissociative disorders in North America has led skeptics to argue that the disorder is a cultural phenomeon, rather than a genuine disorder. However, supporters point to evidence of distinct brain and body states associated with differing personalities

Stepping Through Thinking Critically

1. dissociative; conscious awareness
2. dissociative identity
3. roles
4. brain; body

Skeptics point out that the recent increase in the number of reported cases of dissociative identity disorder indicates that it has become a fad. The fact that the disorder is almost nonexistent outside North America also causes skeptics to doubt the disorder's genuineness.

5. anxiety; childhood trauma; fantasy-prone; therapist-patient

Schizophrenia

Section Preview

1. Schizophrenia is a cluster of disorders in which there is a split from reality that shows itself in disorganized and delusional thinking, disturbed perceptions, and inappropriate emotions and

actions. *Positive symptoms* of schizophrenia include disorganized or deluded thinking and speech as well as inappropriate emotions. *Negative symptoms* include toneless voices, expressionless faces, or mute and rigid bodies. Schizophrenia may develop gradually (chronic, or process, schizophrenia), in which case recovery is doubtful, or rapidly (acute, or reactive, schizophrenia) in response to stress, in which case recovery is much more likely.

2. Some schizophrenia patients have an excess of brain receptors for dopamine. Others have abnormally low brain activity in the frontal lobes or enlarged fluid-filled areas and a corresponding shrinkage of cerebral tissue. Evidence suggests that the brain abnormalities of schizophrenia might be caused by a problem during prenatal development, such as a prenatal viral infection, nutritional deprivation, or oxygen deprivation at birth. In addition, studies of identical twins and adopted children reveal a strong genetic link to schizophrenia. Genes may predispose some people to react to particular experiences by developing a form of schizophrenia. Psychological causes of schizophrenia are difficult to pinpoint due to the variety of forms of the disorder.

Stepping Through the Section

1. reality
2. thinking; perceptions; emotions; actions
3. delusions
4. selective attention
5. hallucinations; auditory
6. flat affect; catatonia
7. cluster of disorders
8. disorganized and deluded thinking, inappropriate emotions; expressionless faces, toneless voices, mute or rigid bodies
9. chronic (or process); less; acute (or reactive)
10. dopamine; decrease
11. activity
12. fluid; shrinkage; thalamus; sensory input; attention
13. viral infection

Risk of schizophrenia increases for those who undergo fetal development during a flu epidemic, or simply during the flu season. People born in densely populated areas and those born during winter and spring months are at increased risk. The months of excess schizophrenia births are reversed in the southern hemisphere, where the seasons are the reverse of the northern hemisphere's. As infectious disease rates have declined, the incidence of schizophrenia has also declined.

14. support

15. placenta; viruses

16. chromosomes; nutrition; oxygen

17. genetic; psychological; dopamine; brain; stress; dopamine

Such signs may include severe, long-lasting schizophrenia in the mother; complications at birth and low birth weight; separation from parents; short attention span and poor muscle coordination; disruptive or withdrawn behavior; emotional unpredictability; and poor peer relations.

Personality Disorders

Section Preview

1. Personality disorders are inflexible and enduring behavior patterns, such as attention-getting emotionality or exaggerated self-importance, that impair a person's social functioning. Those with the antisocial personality disorder display a lack of conscience at an early age, as they begin to lie, steal, fight, or evidence unrestrained sexual behavior. As adults, they exhibit antisocial behavior that may manifest itself in an inability to hold down a job, in marital and parental irresponsibility, or in criminal behavior. Twin and adoption studies suggest that some individuals may possess a genetic vulnerability to the antisocial personality disorder, but the manifestation of the disorder also depends on environmental factors.

Stepping Through the Section

1. social functioning

2. antisocial; psychopath or sociopath

3. is

4. less

5. 3 to 6; impulsive; uninhibited; social rewards; anxiety

6. frontal lobe

7. is not

Rates of Psychological Disorders

Section Preview

1. Research reveals that approximately 32 percent of American adults have experienced a psychological disorder at some time in their lives and that 20 percent have an active disorder. Those who expe-

rience a psychological disorder usually do so by early adulthood. Some disorders, such as the antisocial personality and phobic disorders, often appear earlier, during childhood.

Stepping Through the Section

1. 32; 20

2. higher

3. early; antisocial personality; phobias

Progress Test 1

Multiple-Choice Questions

1. **b.** is the answer. (p. 551)
   c. & d. Men are more likely than women to cope with stress in these ways.

2. **c.** is the answer. (pp. 532–533)

3. **c.** is the answer. Most clinicians agree that psychological disorders may be caused by both psychological (d.) and physical factors (a. and b.) (p. 534)

4. **e.** is the answer. (p. 533)

5. **a.** is the answer. (p. 545)

6. **b.** is the answer. Usually, depression is preceded by a stressful event related to work, marriage, or a close relationship. (p. 551)

7. **c.** is the answer. (p. 559)

8. **d.** is the answer. Although depression is universal, anorexia nervosa and bulimia are rare outside of Western culture. (p. 534)
   a. & b. Schizophrenia and depression are both universal.
   c. The text mentions only schizophrenia and depression as universal disorders. Furthermore, neurosis is no longer utilized as a category of diagnosis.

9. **a.** is the answer. (p. 558)
   b. & d. Thus far, only norepinephrine and serotonin have been implicated in depression and bipolar disorder.
   c. Schizophrenia has been associated with an excess of dopamine receptors. Blocking them alleviates, rather than increases, schizophrenia symptoms.

10. **d.** is the answer. (p. 535)
    b. The text does not mention DSM-IV's reliability in terms of a person's age.

11. **d.** is the answer. There is no evidence that early physical maturation is an early warning sign of schizophrenia. (p. 561)

12. **a.** is the answer. (p. 538)

13. **a.** is the answer. (p. 539)
    b. The mood disorders include major depressive disorder and bipolar disorder.
    c. The dissociative disorders include dissociative amnesia, dissociative fugue, and dissociative identity disorder.
    d. The personality disorders include the antisocial and histrionic personalities.

14. **d.** is the answer. Learned helplessness may lead to self-defeating beliefs, which in turn are linked with depression, a mood disorder. (p. 550)

15. **d.** is the answer. (p. 544)

16. **c.** is the answer. (p. 556)

17. **b.** is the answer. Those with antisocial personality disorders show less autonomic arousal in such situations, and emotions, such as fear, are tied to arousal. (p. 563)

18. **d.** is the answer. Hallucinations are false sensory experiences; delusions are false beliefs. (p. 556)
    a. & b. Obsessions are repetitive and unwanted thoughts. Compulsions are repetitive behaviors.

19. **c.** is the answer. Drugs that relieve depression tend to increase levels of norepinephrine. (p. 549)
    a. Acetylcholine is a neurotransmitter involved in muscle contractions.
    b. It is in certain types of schizophrenia that decreasing dopamine levels is known to be helpful.
    d. On the contrary, it appears that a particular type of depression may be related to *low* levels of serotonin.

20. **c.** is the answer. (p. 557)

Matching Items

1. f (p. 554)	**5.** g (p. 535)	**9.** c (p. 556)
2. d (p. 535)	**6.** b (p. 546)	**10.** e (p. 539)
3. a (p. 545)	**7.** j (p. 539)	
4. h (p. 539)	**8.** i (p. 556)	

Progress Test 2

Multiple-Choice Questions

1. **a.** is the answer. Different cultures have different standards for behaviors that are considered acceptable and normal. (pp. 532–533)
   b. Some abnormal behaviors are simply maladaptive for the individual.
   c. Many individuals who are atypical, such as Olympic gold medalists, are not considered abnormal. There are other criteria that must be met in order for behavior to be considered abnormal.
   d. Although physiological factors play a role in the various disorders, they do not define abnormal behavior. Rather, behavior is said to be abnormal if it is atypical, disturbing, maladaptive, and unjustifiable.

2. **b.** is the answer. (p. 541)
   a. This answer reflects the learning perspective.
   c. Although certain phobias are biologically predisposed, this could not fully explain phobias, nor is it the explanation offered by psychoanalytic theory.
   d. Social-cognitive theorists propose self-defeating thoughts as a cause of depression.

3. **a.** is the answer. Schizophrenia sufferers are easily distracted by irrelevant stimuli, evidently because of a breakdown in the capacity for selective attention. (p. 556)

4. **b.** is the answer. (p. 559)

5. **b.** is the answer. The fact that some disorders are universal and at least partly genetic in origin implicates biological factors in their origin. The fact that other disorders appear only in certain parts of the world implicates sociocultural and psychological factors in their origin. (p. 534)

6. **b.** is the answer. (p. 533)

7. **b.** is the answer. (p. 546)
   a. Anxiety is a passive disorder.
   d. Alcohol abuse is an active disorder.

8. **a.** is the answer. In fact, just the opposite is true. Labels are useful in promoting effective treatment of psychological disorders. (pp. 536–537)

9. **b.** is the answer. (p. 554)
   c. Playing a role is most definitely a learned skill.

10. **d.** is the answer. In bipolar disorder, norepinephrine appears to be overabundant during mania and in short supply during depression. (p. 549)
    a. There is an overabundance of dopamine receptors in some schizophrenia patients.
    b. Serotonin sometimes appears to be scarce during depression.
    c. Epinephrine has not been implicated in psychological disorders.

11. **c.** is the answer. Joseph's fear has generalized from ladders to airplanes. (p. 542)
    a. Had Joseph acquired his fear after seeing someone *else* fall, observational learning would be implicated. This process would not, however, explain how his fear was transferred to airplanes.
    b. There is no indication that Joseph's phobia was acquired through reinforcement.
    d. Through stimulus discrimination, Joseph's fear would *not* have generalized from ladders to airplanes.

12. **d.** is the answer. (pp. 542, 544)

13. **b.** is the answer. (pp. 533–534)
    a. This isn't the case; in fact, the medical model has gained credibility from recent discoveries of genetic and biochemical links to some disorders.
    c. & d. The medical perspective tends to place more emphasis on physiological factors.

14. **b.** is the answer. The psychoanalytic explanation is that these disorders are a manifestation of incompletely repressed impulses over which the person is anxious. According to the learning perspective, the troubled behaviors that result from these disorders have been reinforced by anxiety reduction. (p. 555)
    a. & c. These are true of the psychoanalytic, but not the learning, perspective.

15. **e.** is the answer. (pp. 532–533)

16. **c.** is the answer. DSM-IV was shaped by the medical model. (p. 535)
    a. In fact, just the opposite is true. DSM-IV was revised in order to improve reliability by basing diagnoses on observable behaviors.
    b., d., & e. DSM-IV does not reflect a learning, a psychoanalytic, or a social-cultural bias.

17. **c.** is the answer. Panic attacks are characteristic of certain anxiety disorders, not of schizophrenia. (pp. 556–557)

18. **d.** is the answer. (pp. 550–551)

19. **d.** is the answer. A loss may evoke feelings of anger associated with an earlier loss. Such anger is turned against the self. This internalized anger results in depression. (p. 547)
    a. Learned helplessness would be an explanation offered by the social-cognitive perspective.
    b. The self-serving bias is not discussed in terms of its relationship to depression.
    c. This is the psychoanalytic explanation of anxiety.

20. **d.** is the answer. Risk for schizophrenia increases for individuals who are related to a schizophrenia victim, and the greater the genetic relatedness, the greater the risk. (p. 559)
    a. Schizophrenia victims have an overabundance of the neurotransmitter dopamine, not endorphins.
    b. Being a twin is, in itself, irrelevant to developing schizophrenia.
    c. Although learned helplessness has been suggested by social-cognitive theorists as a cause of self-defeating depressive behaviors, it has not been suggested as a cause of schizophrenia.

Matching Items

1. f (p. 554)   5. c (p. 562)   9. d (p. 556)
2. e (p. 539)   6. b (p. 549)   10. j (p. 540)
3. a (p. 558)   7. g (p. 544)
4. i (p. 545)   8. h (p. 546)

Thinking Critically About Chapter 15

Multiple-Choice Questions

1. **c.** is the answer. An intense fear of a specific object is a phobia. (p. 540)
   a. His fear is focused on a specific object, not generalized.
   b. In this disorder a person is troubled by repetitive thoughts and actions.
   d. & e. Conditioned fears form the basis for anxiety rather than mood disorders.

2. **c.** is the answer. (p. 554)
   a. Phobias focus anxiety on a specific object, activity, or situation
   b. There is no such disorder.
   d. In this mood disorder a person alternates between feelings of hopeless depression and overexcited mania.

3. **d.** is the answer. Repeated wrongdoing and aggressive behavior are part of the pattern associated with the antisocial personality disorder, which may also include marital problems and an inability to keep a job. (p. 562)
   a. Although dissociative identity disorder may involve an aggressive personality, there is nothing in the example to indicate a dissociation.
   b. Nothing in the question indicates that Bob is passive and resigned and having the self-defeating thoughts characteristic of depression.
   c. Bob's behavior does not include the disorganized thinking and disturbed perceptions typical of schizophrenia.

4. **d.** is the answer. In the learning perspective, a phobia, such as Julia's, is seen as a conditioned fear. (pp. 541–542)
   a. Because the fear is focused on a specific stimulus, the medical model does not easily account for the phobia. In any event, it would presumably offer an internal, biological explanation.
   b. The psychoanalytic view of phobias would be that they represent incompletely repressed anxieties that are displaced onto the feared object.
   c. The social-cognitive perspective would emphasize a person's conscious, cognitive processes, not reflexive conditioned responses.

5. a. is the answer. According to the learning view, compulsive behaviors are reinforced because they reduce the anxiety created by obsessive thoughts. Rashid's obsession concerns failing, and his desk-arranging compulsive behaviors apparently help him control these thoughts. (p. 542)

b. The psychoanalytic perspective would view obsessive thoughts as a symbolic representation of forbidden impulses. These thoughts may prompt the person to perform compulsive acts that counter these impulses.

c. & d. The text does not offer explanations of obsessive-compulsive behavior based on the humanistic or social-cognitive perspectives. Presumably, however, these explanations would emphasize growth-blocking difficulties in the person's environment (humanistic perspective) and the reciprocal influences of personality and environment (social-cognitive perspective), rather than symbolic expressions of forbidden impulses.

6. d. is the answer. (p. 539)

a. In phobias, anxiety is focused on a specific object.

b. Major depressive disorder does not manifest these symptoms.

c. The obsessive-compulsive disorder is characterized by repetitive and unwanted thoughts and/or actions.

7. d. is the answer. Jason is obsessed with cleanliness; as a result, he has developed a compulsion to shower. (pp. 540–541)

a. Dissociative disorders involve a separation of conscious awareness from previous memories and thoughts.

b. Generalized anxiety disorder does not have a specific focus.

c. This disorder is characterized by maladaptive character traits.

8. d. is the answer. (p. 543)

a. There is no evidence that Zheina has *lost* either her memory or her identity, as would occur in dissociative disorders.

b. Although she has symptoms of depression, Zheina does not show signs of mania, which occurs in bipolar disorder.

c. Zheina shows no signs of disorganized thinking or disturbed perceptions.

9. a. is the answer. Because Sandy experiences hallucinations (hearing voices), delusions (fearing someone is "out to get her"), and incoherence, she would most likely be diagnosed as suffering from schizophrenia. (pp. 556–557)

b., c., d., & e. These disorders are not characterized by disorganized thoughts and perceptions.

10. d. is the answer. (p. 539)

a. Baseless physical symptoms rarely play a role in schizophrenia.

b. There is no indication that she is exhibiting euphoric behavior.

c. There is no indication that she has suffered a trauma.

11. a. is the answer. Humans seem biologically prepared to develop a fear of heights and other dangers that our ancestors faced. (p. 542)

12. b. is the answer. (p. 554)

13. b. is the answer. The fact that this woman has had these symptoms for more than 2 weeks indicates that she is suffering from major depressive disorder. (p. 545)

14. a. is the answer. Matt's alternating states of the hopelessness and lethargy of depression and the energetic, optimistic state of mania are characteristic of bipolar disorder. (p. 546)

b. Although he was depressed on Tuesday, Matt's manic state on Monday indicates that he is not suffering from major depressive disorder.

c. Matt was depressed, not detached from reality.

d. That Matt is not exhibiting episodes of intense dread indicates that he is not suffering from panic disorder.

15. d. is the answer. Freud believed that the anger once felt toward parents was internalized and would produce depression. (p. 547)

a. & b. The learning and social-cognitive perspectives focus on environmental experiences, conditioning, and self-defeating attitudes in explaining depression.

c. The biological perspective focuses on genetic predispositions and biochemical imbalances in explaining depression.

16. b. is the answer. (pp. 550–552)

17. b. is the answer. Norepinephrine, which increases arousal and boosts mood, is scarce during depression. Drugs that relieve depression tend to increase norepinephrine. (p. 549)

c. Increasing serotonin, which is sometimes scarce during depression, might relieve depression.

d. This neurotransmitter is involved in motor responses but has not been linked to psychological disorders.

18. d. is the answer. Schizophrenia patients sometimes have an excess of receptors for dopamine. Drugs that block these receptors can therefore reduce symptoms of schizophrenia. (p. 558)

a., b., & c. Dopamine receptors have not been implicated in these psychological disorders.

19. b. is the answer. (p. 553)

20. c. is the answer. (p. 559)

Essay Question

There is more to a psychological disorder than being different from other people. Gifted artists, athletes, and scientists have atypical capabilities, yet are not considered psychologically disordered. To be considered disordered, other people must find the atypical behavior disturbing. But what is disturbing in one culture may not be in another, or at another time. Homosexuality, for example, was once classified as a psychological disorder, but it is no longer. Similarly, nudity is common in some cultures and disturbing in others. Atypical and disturbing behaviors are more likely to be considered disordered when judged as maladaptive to the individual. Prolonged feelings of depression or the use of drugs to avoid dealing with problems are examples of maladaptive behaviors that may signal a psychological disorder if they become disabling. Finally, abnormal behavior is most likely to be considered disordered when others find it unjustifiable. A student loudly reciting the Greek alphabet in public, for example, who can justify his or her unusual behavior as being part of a fraternity or sorority ritual, would not be considered psychologically disordered.

Key Terms

Writing Definitions

1. In order to be classified as a **psychological disorder**, behavior must be atypical, disturbing, maladaptive, and unjustifiable. (p. 532)

2. The **medical model** holds that psychological disorders are illnesses that can be diagnosed, treated, and cured, using traditional methods of medicine and psychiatry. (p. 533)

3. The **bio-psycho-social perspective** assumes that *biological*, *psycho*logical, and *socio*cultural factors combine and interact to produce psychological disorders. (p. 534)

4. **DSM-IV** is a short name for the American Psychiatric Association's *Diagnostic and Statistical Manual of Mental Disorders (Fourth Edition)*, which provides a widely used system of classifying psychological disorders. (p. 535)

5. **Neurotic disorders** is a former term for psychological disorders that, while distressing, still allow a person to think normally and function socially. The term is used mainly in contrast to *psychotic disorders*. (p. 535)

6. **Psychotic disorders** is a former term for psychological disorders that are severely debilitating and involve bizarre thoughts and behavior, and a break from reality. (p. 535)

7. **Anxiety disorders** involve distressing, persistent anxiety or maladaptive behaviors that reduce anxiety. (p. 539)

8. In the **generalized anxiety disorder**, the person is continually tense, apprehensive, and in a state of autonomic nervous system arousal for no apparent reason. (p. 539)

9. A **panic disorder** is an episode of intense dread accompanied by chest pain, dizziness, or choking. It is essentially an escalation of the anxiety associated with generalized anxiety disorder. (p. 539)

10. A **phobia** is an anxiety disorder in which a person has a persistent, irrational fear and avoidance of a specific object or situation. (p. 539)

11. The **obsessive-compulsive disorder** is an anxiety disorder in which the person experiences uncontrollable and repetitive thoughts (obsessions) and actions (compulsions). (p. 539)

12. **Mood disorders** are characterized by emotional extremes. (p. 545)

13. **Major depressive disorder** is the mood disorder that occurs when a person exhibits the lethargy, feelings of worthlessness, or loss of interest in family, friends, and activities characteristic of depression for more than a 2-week period and for no discernible reason. Because of its relative frequency, depression has been called the "common cold" of psychological disorders. (p. 545)

14. A **manic episode** is the wildly optimistic, euphoric, hyperactive state that alternates with depression in the bipolar disorder. (p. 546)

15. The **bipolar disorder** is the mood disorder in which a person alternates between depression and the euphoria of a manic state. (p. 546)

Memory aid: Bipolar means having two poles, that is, two opposite qualities. In the **bipolar disorder,** the opposing states are mania and depression.

16. **Dissociative disorders** involve a separation of conscious awareness from one's previous memories, thoughts, and feelings. (p. 554)

Memory aid: To *dissociate* is to separate or pull apart. In the **dissociative disorder** a person becomes dissociated from his or her memories and identity.

17. The **dissociative identity disorder** is a dissociative disorder in which a person exhibits two or more distinct and alternating personalities. (p. 554)

18. **Schizophrenia** refers to the group of severe psychotic disorders whose symptoms may include disorganized and delusional thinking, inappropriate emotions and actions, and disturbed perceptions. (p. 556)

19. **Delusions** are false beliefs that often are symptoms of psychotic disorders. (p. 556)

20. **Personality disorders** are characterized by inflexible and enduring maladaptive character traits that impair social functioning. (p. 562)

21. The **antisocial personality disorder** is a personality disorder in which the person is aggressive, ruthless, and shows no sign of a conscience that would inhibit wrongdoing. (p. 562)

Cross-Check

ACROSS

2. major depressive
9. neurotic
16. mania
17. mood
18. bipolar
19. anxiety

1. DSM-IV
3. dissociative
4. phobia
5. hallucinations
6. linkage analysis
7. bio-psycho-social
8. disorganized
10. medical model
11. catatonia
12. delusions
13. dopamine
14. negative
15. serotonin

FOCUS ON VOCABULARY AND LANGUAGE

Page 531: It's no wonder that studying psychological disorders may therefore at times evoke an *eerie sense* of self-recognition that *illuminates* the dynamics of our own personality dynamics. When reading this chapter, you may sometimes experience the strange, uncanny feeling (*eerie sense*) that Myers is writing about you. On occasion, we all feel, think, and behave in ways similar to disturbed people, and becoming aware of how alike we sometimes are may help shed some light on (*illuminate*) the processes underlying personality.

Perspectives on Psychological Disorders

Page 532: Where should we *draw the line* . . . between normality and abnormality? Myers is addressing the problem of how exactly to define psychological disorders. How do we distinguish (*draw the line*) between someone who is "abnormal" and someone who is not? For psychologists and other mental-health workers a behavior will be labeled psychologically disturbed if it is judged to be atypical, disturbing, maladaptive, and unjustifiable.

Page 533: "*The devil made him do it.*" Our ancestors explained strange and puzzling behavior by appealing to what they knew and believed about the nature of the world (e.g., gods, stars, demons, spirits, etc.). A person, who today would be classified as psychologically disturbed because of his or her bizarre behavior, in the past would have been considered to be possessed by evil spirits or demons (*the devil made him do it*). These types of nonscientific explanations persisted up until the nineteenth century.

Page 535: Thus, *the diagnostic term* provides *a handy shorthand* for describing a complex disorder. Psychology uses a classification system (DSM-IV) to describe and impose order on complicated psychological problems. When a descriptive label (*diagnostic term*) is used to identify a disorder, it does not explain the problem, but it does provide a quick and useful means of communicating a great deal of information in abbreviated form (*a handy shorthand*).

Page 535: Some critics *fault* the manual for *casting too wide a net* and bringing "almost any kind of behavior within the *compass* of psychiatry." . . . The DSM-IV classification system has been received with a less-than-enthusiastic response by some practitioners (*they were not enthralled*). Many criticize (*fault*) the inclusion of a large number of behaviors as psychologically disordered (*it casts too wide a net*) and suggest that just about any behavior is now within the purview (*compass*) of psychiatry. Nevertheless, many other clinicians find DSM-IV a useful and practical tool or device.

Page 537: *Labels* can serve as *self-fulfilling prophecies*. A prophecy is a prediction about the future. When we characterize or classify (*label*) someone as a certain type of person, the very act of labeling may help bring about or create the actions described by the label (*self-fulfilling prophesy*).

Page 538 (Thinking Critically): "Hinckley *Insane*, Public *Mad*." The word *mad* has a number of meanings: (a) angry, (b) insane, (c) foolish and irrational, (d) rash, (e) enthusiastic about something, (f) frantic. John Hinckley, who shot President Reagan, was not sent to prison; instead, he was confined to a mental hospital. The public was angry and upset (*mad*) because Hinckley was judged to be mad (*insane*).

Anxiety Disorders

Page 539: ringing in the ears . . . edgy . . . jittery . . . racing heart, clammy hands, stomach butterflies, sleeplessness . . . furrowed brows . . . twitching eyelids . . . fidgeting. These are all descriptions of the symptoms of generalized anxiety disorder. The person may hear high-pitched sounds (*ringing in the ears*); may be nervous and jumpy (*edgy*); start trembling (*jittery*); have increased heart rate (*racing heart*); have cold, damp, sweaty (*clammy*) hands; and feel as though winged insects are fluttering in the stomach (*stomach butterflies*). The sufferer may worry all the time, be unable to sleep (*insomnia*), and feel apprehensive, which may show in frowning (*furrowed brows*), rapidly blinking eyes (*twitching eyelids*), and restless movements (*fidgeting*).

Page 542: Human behavior was *road tested in the Stone Age*. Myers notes that the development of irrational fears (*phobias*) may have an evolutionary explanation. Just as newly designed vehicles are checked and modified as a result of driving them under normal highway traffic conditions (*they are road tested*), the human mind was changed and modified through adaptations to conditions that existed in a previous era (*road tested in the Stone Age*). We appear to be biologically prepared to develop some fears and not others as a result of our evolutionary heritage.

Page 543 (Close-Up): Years later, images of these events intrude as *flashbacks* and *nightmares*. Many war veterans (*vets*) and others who experienced traumatic stressful events develop post-traumatic stress disorder. Symptoms include terrifying images of the event (*flashbacks*), very frightening dreams (*nightmares*), extreme nervousness, anxiety or depression, and a tendency to become socially isolated.

Page 544: Grooming gone wild becomes hair pulling. The biological perspective explains our tendency to be anxious (*anxiety-prone*) in evolutionary or genetic terms. A normal behavior that once had survival value in our evolutionary past may now be distorted into compulsive action. Thus, compulsive hair pulling may be an exaggerated version of normal grooming behavior (*grooming gone wild*).

Mood Disorders

Page 545: To grind temporarily to a halt and *ruminate*, as depressed people do, is to reassess one's life when feeling threatened. From a biological point of view, depression is a natural reaction to stress and painful events. It is like a warning signal that brings us to a complete stop (*we grind to a halt*) and allows us time to reflect on life and contemplate (*ruminate on*) the meaning of our existence.

Page 545: The difference between a *blue mood* after bad news and a mood disorder is like the difference between gasping for breath for a few minutes after a hard run and being chronically short of breath. We all feel depressed and sad (*we have blue moods*) in response to painful events and sometimes just to life in general. These feelings are points on a continuum; at the extreme end, and very distinct from ordinary depression, are the serious mood disorders (e.g., major depressive disorder) in which the signs of chronic depression (loss of appetite, sleeplessness, tiredness, low self-esteem, and a disinterest in family, friends and social activities) last two weeks or more.

Page 546: If depression is living in *slow motion*, mania is *fast forward*. Bipolar disorder is characterized by mood swings. While depression slows the person down (*like living in slow motion*), the hyperactivity and heightened exuberant state (*mania*) at the other emotional extreme seems to speed the person up, similar to the images you get when you press the fast forward button on the VCR or see a "speeded-up" film.

Page 550: Depressed people *view life through dark glasses*. Social-cognitive theorists point out that biological factors do not operate independently of environmental influences. People who are depressed often have negative beliefs about themselves and about their present and future situations (*they view life through dark glasses*). These self-defeating beliefs can accentuate or amplify a nasty (*vicious*) cycle of interactions between chemistry, cognition, and mood.

Page 551: . . . even small losses can temporarily *sour* our thinking. When loyal basketball fans were depressed by their team's loss, they had a more pessimistic (*bleaker*) assessment of the outcome of future games as well as negative views of their own abilities (*the loss soured their thinking*). Depression can cause self-focused negative thinking.

Page 552: So, there is *two-way traffic* between depressed mood and negative thinking. The latest research shows that there is an interaction (*two-way traffic*) between depression and negative thinking. Depression tends to make people prone to self-blaming and self-focused negative thinking, and in response to painful events this style of thinking puts people at risk for becoming depressed.

Page 552: Misery may love another's company, *but company does not love another's misery.* The old saying "*misery loves company*" means that depressed, sad people like to be with other people. The possible social consequence of being withdrawn, self-focused, self-blaming, and complaining (*depressed*), however, is rejection by others (*company does not love another's misery*).

(Thinking Critically) Dissociation and Multiple Personalities

Page 554: . . . *a ruse* . . . Kenneth Bianchi is a convicted psychopathic murderer who pretended to be a multiple personality in order to avoid jail or the death penalty, and his cunning ploy (*ruse*) fooled many psychologists and psychiatrists. It also raised the question of the reality of dissociative identity as a genuine disorder.

Page 555: Skeptics note how some therapists *go fishing for it.* . . . Those who doubt the existence of dissociative identity disorder (*skeptics*) find it strange that the number of diagnosed cases in North America has increased dramatically (*exploded*) in the last decade. (In the rest of the world it is rare or nonexistent.) In addition, the average number of personalities has multiplied (*mushroomed*) from 3 to 12 per patient. One explanation for the disorder's popularity is that many therapists expect it to be there, so they actively solicit (*go fishing for*) symptoms of dissociative identity disorder from their patients.

Schizophrenia

Page 556: . . . *hodge-podge* . . . The symptoms of schiz-

ophrenia include fragmented and distorted thinking, disturbed perception, and inappropriate feelings and behaviors. Schizophrenia victims, when talking, may move rapidly from topic to topic and idea to idea so that their speech is incomprehensible (*a word salad*). This may be the result of a breakdown in selective attention, whereby an assorted mixture (*hodge-podge*) of stimuli continually distracts the person.

Page 557: Other victims of schizophrenia sometimes lapse into *flat affect*, a zombielike state of apparent apathy. The emotions of schizophrenia are frequently not appropriate for the situation. There may be laughter at a funeral, anger and tears for no apparent reason, or no expression of emotion whatsoever (*flat affect*), which resembles a half-dead, trancelike (*zombielike*) state of indifference (*apathy*).

Page 560: But as the bio-psycho-social perspective emphasizes, the *traffic* between brain biochemistry and psychological experiences *runs both ways.* Neither genetic predispositions nor stressful psychological events alone cause schizophrenia. Rather, there seems to be some interaction (*the traffic runs both ways*) between the two.

Personality Disorders

Page 562: . . . *con artist* . . . A person who has an antisocial personality is usually a male who has no conscience, who lies, steals, cheats, and is unable to keep a job or take on the normal responsibilities of family and society. When combined with high intelligence and no moral sense, the result may be a clever, smooth talking, and deceitful trickster or confidence man (*con artist*).

Page 563: . . . the antisocial personality disorder is *woven* of biological and psychological *strands*. The analogy here is between the antisocial personality and how cloth is made (*woven*). Both psychological and biological factors (*strands*) combine to produce the disorder. If the biological predispositions are fostered (*channeled*) in more positive ways, the result may be a fearless hero; alternatively, the same disposition may produce a killer or a confidence trickster (*con artist*).

16:

Therapy

Chapter Overview

Chapter 16 discusses the major psychotherapies and biomedical therapies for maladaptive behaviors. The various psychotherapies all derive from the perspectives on personality discussed earlier, namely, the psychoanalytic, humanistic, behavioral, and cognitive perspectives. The chapter groups the therapies by perspective but also emphasizes the common threads that run through them. In evaluating the therapies, the chapter points out that, although people who are untreated often improve, those receiving psychotherapy tend to improve somewhat more, regardless of the type of therapy they receive. This section includes a discussion of several popular new alternative therapies.

The biomedical therapies discussed are drug therapies; electroconvulsive therapy; and psychosurgery, which is seldom used. By far the most important of the biomedical therapies, drug therapies are being used in the treatment of psychotic, anxiety, and mood disorders.

Because the origins of problems often lie beyond the individual, the chapter concludes with approaches that aim at preventing psychological disorders by focusing on the family or on the larger social environment as possible contributors to psychological disorders.

NOTE: Answer guidelines for all Chapter 16 questions begin on page 460.

The Psychological Therapies
(pp. 568–581)

> David Myers at times uses idioms that are unfamiliar to some readers. If you do not know the meaning of any of the following words, phrases, or expressions in the context in which they appear in the introduction and this section, refer to pages 469–470 for an explanation: *cracked the genetic code; gawk; common threads; fueled . . . residue; aim to boost; knocks the props out from under you; lore; drinks laced with a drug; aggressive and self-abusive behaviors; colors our feelings; catastrophizing.*

Section Preview

First, skim the section, noting headings and boldface items. Then read the following objectives and, as you read the text, search for the information that will enable you to meet each objective. Answer guidelines are provided on page 460.

1. Briefly explain the current approach to therapy.

2. Discuss the aims and methods of psychoanalysis and psychodynamic therapy, and explain the critics' concerns with these forms of therapy.

3. Identify the basic themes of humanistic therapies and describe Rogers' client-centered (person-centered) approach.

4. Identify the basic assumptions of behavior therapy, and discuss the classical conditioning therapies.

5. Describe the premise behind operant conditioning techniques, and explain the critics' concerns with these techniques.

6. Identify the basic assumptions of the cognitive therapies, and describe group therapy.

Stepping Through the Section

After you have read the section, complete the sentences and answer the questions. As you proceed, evaluate your performance by consulting the answers on page 461. Do not continue with the next section until you understand each answer. If you need to, review or reread the section in the textbook before continuing.

1. Psychological therapy is more commonly called _____ .

2. Therapists who blend several psychotherapy techniques are said to take an _____ approach.

3. The major psychotherapies are based on four perspectives: the _____ , _____ , _____ , and _____ perspectives.

4. Freud's technique in which a patient says whatever comes to mind is called _____ _____ .

5. When, in the course of therapy, a person omits shameful or embarrassing material, _____ is occurring. Insight is facilitated by the analyst's _____ of the meaning of such omissions, of dreams, and of other information revealed during therapy sessions.

6. Freud referred to the hidden meaning of a dream as its _____ _____ .

7. When strong feelings, similar to those experienced in other important relationships, are developed toward the therapist, _____ has occurred.

8. Therapists who are influenced by Freud's psychoanalysis but who talk to the patient face to face are _____ therapists. In addition, they work with patients only _____ (how long?) and for only a few weeks or months.

9. A brief alternative to psychodynamic therapy that has proven effective with _____ patients is _____ _____ . While this approach aims to help people gain _____ into their difficulties, it focuses on _____ _____ rather than on past hurts.

10. Humanistic therapies attempt to help people meet their potential for _____ .

List several ways that humanistic therapy differs from psychoanalysis.

11. The humanistic therapy based on Rogers' theory is called _____-_____ therapy, which is described as _____ therapy because the therapist _____ (interprets/does not interpret) the person's problems.

12. In order to promote growth in clients, Rogerian therapists exhibit _____ , _____ , and _____ .

13. Rogers' technique of restating and clarifying what a person is saying is called

_____ _____ .

Given a nonjudgmental environment that provides _____ _____

_____ , patients are better able to accept themselves as they are and to feel valued and whole.

14. Three tips for listening more actively in your own relationships are to _____ ,

_____ _____ ,

and _____ _____ .

Contrast the assumptions of the behavior therapies with those of psychoanalysis and humanistic therapy.

15. One cluster of behavior therapies is based on the principles of _____

_____ , as developed in Pavlov's experiments. This technique, in which a new, incompatible response is substituted for a maladaptive one, is called _____ .
Two examples of this technique are

_____ _____

and _____ _____ .

16. The technique of systematic desensitization has been most fully developed by the therapist

_____ . The assumption behind this technique is that one cannot simultaneously be _____ and relaxed.

17. The first step in systematic desensitization is the construction of a _____ of anxiety-arousing stimuli. The second step involves training in _____

_____ . In the final step, the person is trained to associate the

_____ state with the

_____ -arousing stimuli.

18. Because it encourages a person to confront a feared situation, desensitization is an example of _____ therapy. In a more aggressive technique called

_____ , a person is forced to confront a feared stimulus until the fear is

_____ . For those who are unable to _____ an anxiety-arousing situation, or too afraid or embarrassed to do so, _____

_____ _____

therapy offers a promising alternative.

19. In helping people to overcome fears of snakes and spiders, for example, therapists sometimes combine systematic desensitization with

_____ _____ .

20. In aversive conditioning, the therapist attempts to substitute a _____ (positive/negative) response for one that is currently _____ (positive/negative).
In this technique, a person's unwanted behaviors become associated with _____ feelings.

21. Therapies that influence behavior by controlling its consequences are based on principles of _____ conditioning. One application of this form of therapy to institutional settings is the _____

_____ , in which desired behaviors are rewarded.

State two criticisms of "behavior modification."

22. Therapists who teach people new, more constructive ways of thinking are using _____ therapy.

23. One variety of cognitive therapy that attempts to reverse the _____ beliefs often associated with _____ by helping clients see their irrationalities. This therapy was developed by _____ .

24. A form of cognitive therapy developed by Adele Rabin builds on the finding that depressed people _____ (do/do not) exhibit the self-serving bias.

25. Treatment that combines an attack on negative thinking with efforts to modify behavior is known as _____-_____ therapy.

26. Training people to restructure their thinking in stressful situations is the goal of _____ _____ training.

List several advantages of group therapy.

27. The most common types of group therapy are _____ and _____ groups for alcoholics, divorced people, and gamblers, for example.

28. The type of group interaction that focuses on the social context in which the individual exists is _____ _____ .

29. In this type of group, therapists focus on improving _____ within the family and helping family members to discover new ways of preventing or resolving _____ .

Evaluating Psychotherapies
(pp. 581–592)

> If you do not know the meaning of any of the following words, phrases, or expressions in the context in which they appear in the text, refer to page 470 for an explanation: *Hang in there; testimonials; ebb and flow of events; clear-cut; fertile soil for pseudotherapies; harness; empathy are hallmarks.*

Section Preview

Answer guidelines are provided on page 462.

1. Discuss the findings regarding the effectiveness of the psychotherapies.

2. (Thinking Critically) Identify two reasons clients' and therapists' perceptions of therapy's effectiveness may be inflated.

3. Discuss the relative effectiveness of different psychotherapies.

4. Evaluate the effectiveness of three popular alternative therapies.

5. Discuss the commonalities among the psychotherapies.

6. Discuss the roles of culture and values in psychotherapy.

Stepping Through the Section

Answers are provided on page 462.

1. In contrast to earlier times, most therapy today _____ (is/is not) provided by psychiatrists.

2. A majority of psychotherapy clients express _____ (satisfaction/dissatisfaction) with their therapy.

3. A long-term study of 500 Massachusetts boys found that those who received intensive counseling _____ (had/did not have) significantly fewer problems than a control group.

4. (Thinking Critically) Clients' and therapists' perceptions of therapy's effectiveness may be inflated by their _____ that a treatment works. This phenomenon is called the _____ _____ .

Another phenomenon that may inflate their perceptions of therapy's effectiveness is the phenomenon called _____

_____ _____

_____ , which is the tendency for _____ emotions to return toward their _____ state.

5. The debate over the effectiveness of psychotherapy began with a study by _____ ; it showed that the rate of improvement for those who received therapy _____ (was/was not) higher than the rate for those who did not.

6. A statistical technique that makes it possible to combine the results of many different psychotherapy outcome studies is called

_____-_____ .

Overall, the results of such analyses indicate that psychotherapy is _____ (somewhat effective/ineffective).

7. As a rule, psychotherapy is most effective with problems that are _____ (specific/nonspecific).

8. Controlled treatment studies have demonstrated that depression may be effectively treated with

_____ , _____ , and _____ therapies. In treating anxiety, _____ and _____ therapies and _____ training have proven effective. Cognitive-behavior therapy has proven effective in treating _____ , and behavior modification in treating _____

_____ .

9. Comparisons of the effectiveness of different forms of therapy reveal _____ (clear/no clear) differences.

10. With phobias, compulsions, and other specific behavior problems, _____ therapies have been the most effective.

11. Today, many forms of _____ _____ are touted as effective treatments for a variety of complaints. Among the

most popular is _____

_____ , in which practitioners move their hands over a patient's body. Empirical support for this form of therapy is _____ (strong/nonexistent).

12. In another popular alternative therapy, a therapist triggers eye movements in patients while they imagine _____

_____ . This therapy, called

_____ _____

_____ _____

_____ has proven

_____ (completely ineffective/somewhat effective) as a treatment for

_____-_____

_____ _____ .

However, skeptics point to evidence that

_____ _____ is

just as effective as triggered eye movements in producing beneficial results.

13. For people who suffer from the winter-time form of depression called _____

_____ _____ ,

timed _____-_____ therapy may be beneficial in shifting secretion of the hormone _____ , which helps regulate _____

_____ .

14. Several studies found that treatment for mild problems offered by paraprofessionals _____ (is/is not) as effective as that offered by professional therapists.

15. Generally speaking, psychotherapists' personal values _____ (do/do not) influence their therapy.

The Biomedical Therapies (pp. 592–598)

> If you do not know the meaning of any of the following words, phrases, or expressions in the context in which they appear in the text, refer to pages 470–471 for an explanation: *cousin drugs; sluggishness, tremors, and twitches; Routinely "popping a Valium"; lift people up; barbaric image; jump-starting the brain.*

Section Preview

Answer guidelines are provided on page 463.

1. Identify the common forms of drug therapy.

2. Describe the use of electroconvulsive therapy and psychosurgery in the treatment of psychological disorders.

Stepping Through the Section

Answers are provided on page 463.

1. The most widely used biomedical treatments are the _____ therapies. Thanks to these therapies, the number of residents in mental hospitals has _____ (increased/decreased) sharply.

2. The field that studies the effects of drugs on the mind and behavior is _____ .

3. When neither the patients nor the staff are aware of which condition a given individual is in, a

_____-_____

study is being conducted.

4. One effect of _____ drugs such as _____ is to help those experiencing _____ (positive/negative) symptoms of schizophrenia by decreasing their responsiveness to irrelevant stimuli; schizophrenia patients who are apathetic and withdrawn may be more effectively treated with the drug _____ . These drugs work by blocking the receptor sites for the neurotransmitter _____ .

5. Valium and Librium are classified as _____ drugs. These drugs depress activity in the _____ _____ _____ .

6. Drugs that are prescribed to alleviate depression are called _____ drugs. These drugs also work by increasing levels of the neurotransmitters _____ and _____ . One example of this type of drug is _____ , which works by blocking the reabsorption of _____ from synapses and is therefore called a _____-_____-_____ drug.

7. Equally effective in calming anxious people and energizing depressed people is _____ _____ , which has positive side effects.

8. Although people with depression often improve after one month on antidepressants, meta-analysis studies demonstrate that a large percentage of the effectiveness is due to a _____ .

9. Current drug therapies work by affecting activity at all the _____ for a given neurotransmitter. A new drug therapy aims to block only those for a brain chemical called _____ _____ , which helps transmit _____ messages.

10. In order to stabilize the mood swings of a bipolar disorder, the drug _____ is often prescribed.

11. The therapeutic technique in which the patient receives an electric shock to the brain is referred to as _____ therapy, abbreviated as _____ .

12. ECT is most often used with patients suffering from severe _____ . Research evidence _____ (confirms/does not confirm) ECT's effectiveness with such patients.

13. One theory of how ECT works suggests that it increases release of the neurotransmitter _____ .

14. A new, gentler procedure called _____ _____ _____ _____ aims to treat depression by presenting pulses through a magnetic coil held close to a person's skull. Unlike ECT, this procedure produces no _____ , _____ loss, or other side effects.

15. The biomedical therapy in which a portion of brain tissue is removed or destroyed is called _____ .

16. In the 1930s, Moniz developed an operation called the _____ . In this procedure, the _____ lobe of the brain is disconnected from the rest of the brain.

17. Today, most psychosurgery has been replaced by the use of _____ or some other form of treatment.

Preventing Psychological Disorders
(pp. 598–599)

> If you do not know the meaning of the following expression in the context in which it appears in the text, refer to page 471 for an explanation: *upstream work.*

Section Preview

Answer guidelines are provided on page 463.

1. Explain the rationale and goals of preventive mental health programs.

Progress Test 1

Multiple-Choice Questions

Circle your answers to the following questions and check them with the answers on page 464. If your answer is incorrect, read the explanation for why it is incorrect and then consult the appropriate pages of the text (in parentheses following the correct answer).

1. Electroconvulsive therapy is most useful in the treatment of:
   a. schizophrenia.
   b. depression.
   c. personality disorders.
   d. anxiety disorders.
   e. bipolar disorder.

2. The technique in which a person is asked to report everything that comes to his or her mind is called _____ _____ ; this technique is favored by _____ therapists.
   a. active listening; cognitive
   b. spontaneous remission; humanistic
   c. free association; psychoanalytic
   d. systematic desensitization; behavior

3. Of the following categories of psychotherapy, which is known for its nondirective nature?
   a. psychoanalysis   c. behavior therapy
   b. humanistic therapy   d. cognitive therapy

4. Which of the following is *not* a common criticism of psychoanalysis?
   a. It emphasizes awareness of past feelings.
   b. It provides interpretations that are hard to disprove.
   c. It is generally a very expensive process.
   d. It gives therapists too much control over patients.

5. Which of the following types of therapy does *not* belong with the others?
   a. cognitive therapy
   b. family therapy
   c. self-help group
   d. support group

6. Which of the following is *not* necessarily an advantage of group therapies over individual therapies?
   a. They tend to take less time for the therapist.
   b. They tend to cost less money for the client.
   c. They are more effective.
   d. They allow the client to test new behaviors in a social context.

7. Which biomedical therapy is *most* likely to be practiced today?
   a. psychosurgery
   b. electroconvulsive therapy
   c. drug therapy
   d. counterconditioning
   e. aversive conditioning

8. The effectiveness of psychotherapy has been assessed both through clients' perspectives and through controlled research studies. What have such assessments found?
   a. Clients' perceptions and controlled studies alike strongly affirm the effectiveness of psychotherapy.
   b. Whereas clients' perceptions strongly affirm the effectiveness of psychotherapy, studies point to more modest results.
   c. Whereas studies strongly affirm the effectiveness of psychotherapy, many clients feel dissatisfied with their progress.
   d. Clients' perceptions and controlled studies alike paint a very mixed picture of the effectiveness of psychotherapy.

9. Which of the following best describes the results of the 30-year follow-up study of 500 Massachusetts boys who had been considered predelinquents?
   a. Predelinquent boys who received counseling had fewer problems as adults than untreated predelinquent boys.
   b. Predelinquent boys who did not receive counseling had slightly fewer problems as adults than boys who received counseling.
   c. Predelinquent boys who underwent behavior therapy had fewer problems as adults than boys who underwent psychoanalysis.
   d. Predelinquent boys who underwent psychoanalysis had fewer problems as adults than boys who underwent behavior therapy.

10. The results of meta-analysis of the effectiveness of different psychotherapies reveals that:
    a. no single type of therapy is consistently superior.
    b. behavior therapies are most effective in treating specific problems, such as phobias.
    c. cognitive therapies are most effective in treating depressed emotions.
    d. all of the above are true.

11. The antipsychotic drugs appear to produce their effects by blocking the receptor sites for:
    a. dopamine.
    c. norepinephrine.
    b. epinephrine.
    d. serotonin.

12. Psychologists who advocate a _____ approach to mental health contend that many psychological disorders could be prevented by changing the disturbed individual's _____ .
    a. biomedical; diet
    b. family; behavior
    c. humanistic; feelings
    d. psychoanalytic; behavior
    e. preventive; environment

13. An eclectic psychotherapist is one who:
    a. takes a nondirective approach in helping clients solve their problems.
    b. views psychological disorders as usually stemming from one cause, such as a biological abnormality.
    c. uses one particular technique, such as psychoanalysis or counterconditioning, in treating disorders.
    d. uses a variety of techniques, depending on the client and the problem.

14. The technique in which a therapist echoes and restates what a person says in a nondirective manner is called:
    a. active listening.
    b. free association.
    c. systematic desensitization.
    d. meta-analysis.
    e. interpretation.

15. Unlike traditional psychoanalytic therapy, interpersonal psychotherapy:
    a. helps people gain insight into the roots of their problems.
    b. offers interpretations of patients' feelings.
    c. focuses on current relationships.
    d. does all of the above.

16. The technique of systematic desensitization is based on the premise that maladaptive symptoms are:
    a. a reflection of irrational thinking.
    b. conditioned responses.
    c. expressions of unfulfilled wishes.
    d. all of the above.

17. The operant conditioning technique in which desired behaviors are rewarded with points or poker chips that can later be exchanged for various rewards is called:
    a. counterconditioning.
    b. systematic desensitization.
    c. a token economy.
    d. exposure therapy.

18. One variety of _____ therapy is based on the finding that depressed people often attribute their failures to _____ .
    a. humanistic; themselves
    b. behavior; external circumstances
    c. cognitive; external circumstances
    d. cognitive; themselves

19. (Thinking Critically and text) A person can derive benefits from psychotherapy simply by believing in it. This illustrates the importance of:
    a. spontaneous remission.
    b. the placebo effect.
    c. the transference effect.
    d. interpretation.

20. Before 1950, the main mental health providers were:
    a. psychologists.
    d. the clergy.
    b. paraprofessionals.
    e. social workers.
    c. psychiatrists.

21. In one research study of therapeutic touch, the experimenter placed a hand over one of the practitioner's unseen hands to see if the practitioner could detect the hovering hand's purported energy field. The results demonstrated that the practitioners were able to do so:
    a. 100 percent of the time.
    b. about 75 percent of the time.
    c. less than 50 percent of the time.
    d. only if the experimenter mentally concentrated on which hand was being "stimulated."

Matching Items

Match each term with the appropriate definition or description.

Terms

_____ **1.** cognitive therapy
_____ **2.** behavior therapy
_____ **3.** systematic desensitization
_____ **4.** cognitive-behavior therapy
_____ **5.** client-centered therapy
_____ **6.** regression toward the mean
_____ **7.** aversive conditioning
_____ **8.** psychoanalysis
_____ **9.** preventive mental health
_____ **10.** biomedical therapy
_____ **11.** counterconditioning

Definitions or Descriptions

a. associates unwanted behavior with unpleasant experiences
b. associates a relaxed state with anxiety-arousing stimuli
c. emphasizes the social context of psychological disorders
d. integrated therapy that focuses on changing self-defeating thinking and unwanted behavior
e. category of therapies that teach people more adaptive ways of thinking and acting
f. the tendency for unusual events to return to their average state
g. therapy developed by Carl Rogers
h. therapy based on Freud's theory of personality
i. treatment with psychosurgery, electroconvulsive therapy, or drugs
j. classical conditioning procedure in which new responses are conditioned to stimuli that trigger unwanted behaviors
k. category of therapies based on learning principles derived from classical and operant conditioning

Progress Test 2

Progress Test 2 should be completed during a final chapter review. Answer the following questions after you thoroughly understand the correct answers for the section reviews and Progress Test 1.

Multiple-Choice Questions

1. Carl Rogers was a _____ therapist who was the creator of _____ .
   a. behavior; systematic desensitization
   b. psychoanalytic; insight therapy
   c. humanistic; client-centered therapy
   d. cognitive; cognitive therapy for depression

2. Using techniques of classical conditioning to develop an association between unwanted behavior and an unpleasant experience is known as:
   a. aversive conditioning.
   b. systematic desensitization.
   c. transference.
   d. electroconvulsive therapy.
   e. a token economy.

3. Which type of psychotherapy emphasizes the individual's inherent potential for self-fulfillment?
   a. behavior therapy   **c.** humanistic therapy
   b. psychoanalysis   **d.** biomedical therapy

4. Light-exposure therapy has proven useful as a form of treatment for people suffering from:
   a. bulimia.
   b. seasonal affective disorder.
   c. schizophrenia.
   d. dissociative identity disorder.

5. Which type of psychotherapy focuses on changing unwanted behaviors rather than on discovering their underlying causes?
   a. behavior therapy
   b. cognitive therapy
   c. humanistic therapy
   d. psychoanalysis

6. The techniques of counterconditioning are based on principles of:
   a. observational learning.
   b. classical conditioning.
   c. operant conditioning.
   d. behavior modification.

7. In which of the following does the client learn to associate a relaxed state with a hierarchy of anxiety-arousing situations?
   a. cognitive therapy
   b. aversive conditioning
   c. counterconditioning
   d. systematic desensitization

8. Principles of operant conditioning underlie which of the following techniques?
   a. counterconditioning
   b. systematic desensitization
   c. flooding
   d. aversive conditioning
   e. the token economy

9. Which of the following is *not* a common criticism of behavior therapy?
   a. Clients may not develop intrinsic motivation for their new behaviors.
   b. Behavior control is unethical.
   c. Although one symptom may be eliminated, another may replace it unless the underlying problem is treated.
   d. All of the above are criticisms of behavior therapy.

10. Which type of therapy focuses on eliminating irrational thinking?
    a. EMDR
    b. client-centered therapy
    c. cognitive therapy
    d. behavior therapy

11. Antidepressant drugs are believed to work by affecting:
    a. dopamine.   c. norepinephrine.
    b. lithium.   d. acetylcholine.

12. The following are some of the conclusions drawn in the text regarding the effectiveness of psychotherapy. For which of these conclusions did the Massachusetts study of predelinquent boys provide evidence?
    a. Clients' perceptions of the effectiveness of therapy usually are very accurate.
    b. Clients' perceptions of the effectiveness of therapy differ somewhat from the objective findings.

   c. Individuals who receive treatment do somewhat better than individuals who do not.
   d. Overall, no one type of therapy is a "winner," but certain therapies are more suited to certain problems.

13. Which of the following is the drug most commonly used to treat bipolar disorder?
    a. Valium   c. Librium
    b. chlorpromazine   d. lithium

14. The most widely prescribed drugs in biomedical therapy are the:
    a. antianxiety drugs.
    b. antipsychotic drugs.
    c. antidepressant drugs.
    d. amphetamines.

15. Which form of therapy is *most* likely to be successful in treating depression?
    a. behavior therapy   c. cognitive therapy
    b. psychoanalysis   d. humanistic therapy

16. Although Moniz won the Nobel prize for developing the lobotomy procedure, the technique is not widely used today because:
    a. it produces a lethargic, immature personality.
    b. it is irreversible.
    c. calming drugs became available in the 1950s.
    d. of all of the above reasons.

17. A meta-analysis of research studies comparing the effectiveness of professional therapists with paraprofessionals found that:
    a. the professionals were much more effective than the paraprofessionals.
    b. the paraprofessionals were much more effective than the professionals.
    c. except in treating depression, the paraprofessionals were about as effective as the professionals.
    d. the paraprofessionals were about as effective as the professionals.

18. Among the common ingredients of the psychotherapies is:
    a. the offer of a therapeutic relationship.
    b. the expectation among clients that the therapy will prove helpful.
    c. the chance to develop a fresh perspective on oneself and the world.
    d. all of the above.

19. Family therapy differs from other forms of psychotherapy because it focuses on:
    a. using a variety of treatment techniques.
    b. conscious rather than unconscious processes.
    c. the present instead of the past.
    d. how family tensions may cause individual problems.

20. One reason that aversive conditioning may only be temporarily effective is that:
    a. for ethical reasons, therapists cannot use sufficiently intense unconditioned stimuli to sustain classical conditioning.
    b. patients are often unable to become sufficiently relaxed for conditioning to take place.
    c. patients know that outside the therapist's office they can engage in the undesirable behavior without fear of aversive consequences.
    d. most conditioned responses are elicited by many nonspecific stimuli and it is impossible to countercondition them all.

21. Cognitive-behavior therapy aims to:
    a. alter the way people act.
    b. Make people more aware of their irrational negative thinking.
    c. Alter the way people think and act.
    d. Countercondition anxiety-provoking stimuli.

Matching Items

Match each term with the appropriate definition or description.

Terms

_____ 1. active listening
_____ 2. token economy
_____ 3. placebo effect
_____ 4. lobotomy
_____ 5. lithium
_____ 6. meta-analysis
_____ 7. psychopharmacology
_____ 8. double-blind technique
_____ 9. Valium
_____ 10. free association
_____ 11. flooding

Definitions or Descriptions

a. type of psychosurgery
b. procedure for statistically combining the results of many experiments
c. mood-stabilizing drug
d. empathic technique used in person-centered therapy
e. the beneficial effect of a person's expecting that treatment will be effective
f. antianxiety drug
g. technique of psychoanalytic therapy
h. an operant conditioning procedure
i. the study of the effects of drugs on the mind and behavior
j. experimental procedure in which both the patient and staff are unaware of a patient's treatment condition
k. an aggressive exposure therapy that forces a person to confront a feared situation

Thinking Critically About Chapter 16

Answer these questions the day before an exam as a final check on your understanding of the chapter's terms and concepts.

Multiple-Choice Questions

1. During a session with his psychoanalyst, Jamal hesitates while describing a highly embarrassing thought. In the psychoanalytic framework, this is an example of:
   a. transference.
   b. insight.
   c. mental repression.
   d. resistance.

2. During psychoanalysis, Jane has developed strong feelings of hatred for her therapist. The analyst interprets Jane's behavior in terms of a _____ of her feelings toward her father.
   a. projection
   b. resistance
   c. regression
   d. transference

3. Given that Jim's therapist attempts to help him by offering genuineness, acceptance, and empathy, she is probably practicing:
   a. psychoanalysis.
   b. behavior therapy.
   c. cognitive therapy.
   d. client-centered therapy.

4. To help Sam quit smoking, his therapist blew a blast of smoke into Sam's face each time Sam inhaled. Which technique is the therapist using?
   a. exposure therapy
   b. behavior modification
   c. systematic desensitization
   d. aversive conditioning

5. After Darnel dropped a pass in an important football game, he became depressed and vowed to quit the team because of his athletic incompetence. The campus psychologist challenged his illogical reasoning and pointed out that Darnel's "incompetence" had earned him an athletic scholarship. The psychologist's response was most typical of a _____ therapist.
   a. behavior
   b. psychoanalytic
   c. client-centered
   d. cognitive

6. Seth enters therapy to talk about some issues that have been upsetting him. The therapist prescribes some medication to help him. The therapist is most likely a:
   a. psychologist.
   b. psychiatrist.
   c. psychiatric social worker.
   d. clinical social worker.

7. In an experiment testing the effects of a new antipsychotic drug, neither Dr. Cunningham nor her patients know whether the patients are in the experimental or the control group. This is an example of the _____ technique.
   a. meta-analysis
   b. within-subjects
   c. double-blind
   d. single-blind

8. A close friend who for years has suffered from wintertime depression is seeking your advice regarding the effectiveness of light-exposure therapy. What should you tell your friend?
   a. "Don't waste your time and money. It doesn't work."
   b. "A more effective treatment for seasonal affective disorder is eye movement desensitization and reprocessing."
   c. "You'd be better off with a prescription for lithium."
   d. "It might be worth a try. There is some evidence that morning light exposure affects the secretion of melatonin, which helps regulate the body's circadian rhythm."

9. A relative wants to know which type of therapy works best. You should tell your relative that:
   a. psychotherapy does not work.
   b. behavior therapy is the most effective.
   c. cognitive therapy is the most effective.
   d. group therapy is best for his problem.
   e. no one type of therapy is consistently the most successful.

10. Leota is startled when her therapist says that she needs to focus on eliminating her problem behavior rather than gaining insight into its underlying cause. Most likely, Leota has consulted a _____ therapist.
    a. behavior
    b. humanistic
    c. cognitive
    d. psychoanalytic

11. In order to help him overcome his fear of flying, Duane's therapist has him construct a hierarchy of anxiety-triggering stimuli and then learn to associate each with a state of deep relaxation. Duane's therapist is using the technique called:
    a. systematic desensitization.
    b. aversive conditioning.
    c. shaping.
    d. free association.

12. A patient in a hospital receives poker chips for making her bed, being punctual at meal times, and maintaining her physical appearance. The poker chips can be exchanged for privileges, such as television viewing, snacks, and magazines. This is an example of the _____ therapy technique called _____ .
    a. psychodynamic; systematic desensitization
    b. behavior; token economy
    c. cognitive; token economy
    d. humanistic; systematic desensitization

13. Ben is a cognitive-behavior therapist. Compared to Rachel, who is a behavior therapist, Ben is more likely to:
    a. base his therapy on principles of operant conditioning.
    b. base his therapy on principles of classical conditioning.
    c. address clients' attitudes as well as behaviors.
    d. focus on clients' unconscious urges.

14. A psychotherapist who believes that the best way to treat psychological disorders is to prevent them from developing would be *most* likely to view disordered behavior as:
    a. maladaptive thoughts and actions.
    b. expressions of unconscious conflicts.
    c. conditioned responses.
    d. an understandable response to stressful social conditions.

15. Linda's doctor prescribes medication that blocks the activity of dopamine in her nervous system. Evidently, Linda is being treated with an _____ drug.
    a. antipsychotic   c. antidepressant
    b. antianxiety   d. anticonvulsive

16. Abraham's doctor prescribes medication that increases the availability of norepinephrine in his nervous system. Evidently, Abraham is being treated with an _____ drug.
    a. antipsychotic
    b. antianxiety
    c. antidepressant
    d. anticonvulsive

17. In concluding her talk entitled "Psychosurgery Today," Ashley states that:
    a. "Psychosurgery is still widely used throughout the world."
    b. "Electroconvulsive therapy is the only remaining psychosurgical technique that is widely practiced."

    c. "With advances in psychopharmacology, psychosurgery has largely been abandoned."
    d. "Although lobotomies remain popular, other psychosurgical techniques have been abandoned."

18. A psychiatrist has diagnosed a patient as having bipolar disorder. It is likely that she will prescribe:
    a. an antipsychotic drug.
    b. lithium.
    c. an antianxiety drug.
    d. a drug that blocks receptor sites for serotonin.

19. Which type(s) of psychotherapy would be most likely to use the interpretation of dreams as a technique for bringing unconscious feelings into awareness?
    a. psychoanalysis
    b. psychodynamic therapy
    c. cognitive therapy
    d. all of the above
    e. both a. and b.

20. Of the following therapists, who would be most likely to interpret a person's psychological problems in terms of repressed impulses?
    a. a behavior therapist
    b. a cognitive therapist
    c. a humanistic therapist
    d. a psychoanalyst

21. Nick survived a car accident in which another passenger died. Feeling anxious and guilty, he sought treatment from an alternative therapist, who used eye movement desensitization and reprocessing to help Nick return to his normally upbeat, optimistic frame of mind. After several months of treatment Nick began feeling better. Although Nick is convinced that the alternative therapy was responsible for his improvement, it is also possible that it was the result of:
    a. regression toward the mean.
    b. a placebo effect.
    c. merely seeking treatment from any practitioner who provided an empathic, trusting environment.
    d. all of the above.

Essay Question

Willie has been diagnosed as suffering from major depressive disorder. Describe the treatment he might receive from a psychoanalyst, a cognitive therapist, and a biomedical therapist. (Use the space below to list points you want to make and organize them. Then write the essay on a separate sheet of paper.)

Key Terms

Using your own words, on a separate piece of paper write a brief definition or explanation of each of the following terms.

1. psychotherapy
2. eclectic approach
3. psychoanalysis
4. resistance
5. interpretation
6. transference
7. client-centered therapy
8. active listening
9. behavior therapy
10. counterconditioning
11. systematic desensitization
12. aversive conditioning
13. token economy
14. cognitive therapy
15. cognitive-behavior therapy
16. family therapy
17. regression toward the mean

18. meta-analysis
19. psychopharmacology
20. lithium
21. electroconvulsive therapy (ECT)
22. psychosurgery
23. lobotomy

Answers

The Psychological Therapies

Section Preview

1. Psychotherapy is "a planned treatment of mental and emotional problems based on an emotionally charged, confiding interaction between a socially sanctioned healer and a sufferer." The various types of psychotherapy derive from psychology's major personality theories: psychoanalytic, humanistic, behavioral, and cognitive. Half of all contemporary psychotherapists take an eclectic approach, using a blend of therapies tailored to meet their clients' particular problems.

2. Psychoanalysis assumes that psychological problems are caused by repressed unconscious impulses and conflicts that develop during childhood, and so its goal is to bring these feelings into conscious awareness and help the person work through them.

   Psychoanalysts may ask their patients to report everything that comes to mind (free association). Blocks in the flow of retrieval (resistance) are believed to indicate the repression of sensitive material. The analyst's interpretations of resistances aim to provide the patients with insight into their underlying meaning. Psychoanalysts interpret dreams for their latent content and the transference of feelings from early relationships in order to expose repressed feelings.

   Psychodynamic therapists also try to understand a patient's symptoms by exploring childhood experiences, but may talk face to face, with therapy lasting for only a few weeks or months. A new form of this therapy, interpersonal psychotherapy, focuses on current relationships (rather than on past hurts) and symptom relief in the here and now.

   Psychoanalysis has been criticized for offering interpretations that are impossible to prove or disprove and for being a lengthy and expensive process that only the relatively well-off can afford.

3. Humanistic therapists aim to boost self-fulfillment by helping people grow in self-awareness and self-acceptance. Unlike psychoanalysis, humanistic therapies focus on conscious thoughts as they occur in the present. Carl Rogers' nondirective client-centered therapy (also called person-centered therapy), which is based on the assumption that most people have within themselves the resources for growth, aims to provide an environment in which therapists exhibit genuineness, acceptance, and empathy. Humanistic therapists often use *active listening* to provide a psychological mirror that helps clients see themselves more clearly.

4. Behavior therapy applies learning principles to eliminate unwanted behavior. Counterconditioning describes classical-conditioning procedures that condition new responses to stimuli that trigger unwanted behaviors. One type of counterconditioning, systematic desensitization, is used to treat phobias, for example, by conditioning people to associate a pleasant, relaxed state with gradually increasing anxiety-provoking stimuli. It is a prime example of exposure therapy. Aversive conditioning is a type of counterconditioning that associates unwanted behavior (such as drinking alcohol) with unpleasant feelings (such as nausea).

5. Operant conditioning procedures are used to treat specific behavioral problems by reinforcing desired behaviors and withholding reinforcement for undesired behaviors. In institutional settings, for example, a token economy is employed to shape desired behaviors. With this procedure, patients earn tokens for exhibiting desired behavior, then exchange the accumulated tokens for various privileges.

   Critics note that because "behavior modification" depends on extrinsic rewards, the appropriate behaviors may disappear when the person leaves the conditioning environment. Second, critics question whether it is ethical for a therapist to exercise so much control over a person's behavior.

6. The cognitive therapies assume that our thinking influences our feelings and that maladaptive thinking patterns can be replaced with new, more constructive ones. Cognitive therapy for depression helps people to discover and reform their habitually negative patterns of thinking. Cognitive-behavior therapy expands upon standard cognitive therapy to include helping people to practice their newly learned positive approach in everyday settings.

Group therapies provide a social context which allows people to discover that others have similar problems and to try out new ways of behaving. Self-help and support groups are examples of the group approach to psychotherapy. Another is family therapy, which treats individuals within their family system.

Stepping Through the Section

1. psychotherapy
2. eclectic
3. psychoanalytic; humanistic; behavioral; cognitive
4. free association
5. resistance; interpretation
6. latent content
7. transference
8. psychodynamic; once a week
9. depressed; interpersonal psychotherapy; insight; current relationships
10. self-fulfillment

Unlike psychoanalysis, humanistic therapy is focused on the present instead of the past, on awareness of feelings as they occur rather than on achieving insights into the childhood origins of the feelings, on conscious rather than unconscious processes, on promoting growth and fulfillment instead of curing illness, and on helping clients take immediate responsibility for their feelings and actions rather than on uncovering the obstacles to doing so.

11. client-centered; nondirective; does not interpret
12. genuineness; acceptance; empathy
13. active listening; unconditional positive regard
14. paraphrase, invite clarification; reflect feelings

Whereas psychoanalysis and humanistic therapies assume that problems diminish as self-awareness grows, behavior therapists doubt that self-awareness is the key. Instead of looking for the inner cause of unwanted behavior, behavior therapy applies learning principles to directly attack the unwanted behavior itself.

15. classical conditioning; counterconditioning; systematic desensitization; aversive conditioning
16. Wolpe; anxious
17. hierarchy; progressive relaxation; relaxed; anxiety
18. exposure; flooding; extinguished; vividly imagine, virtual reality exposure
19. observational learning
20. negative; positive; unpleasant
21. operant; token economy

Behavior modification is criticized because the desired behavior may stop when the rewards are stopped. Also, critics contend that one person should not be allowed to control another.

22. cognitive
23. irrational; depression; Beck
24. do not
25. cognitive-behavior
26. stress inoculation

Group therapy saves therapists time and clients money. The social context of group therapy allows people to discover that others have similar problems and to try out new ways of behaving.

27. self-help; support
28. family therapy
29. communication; conflict

Evaluating Psychotherapies

Section Preview

1. The effectiveness of psychotherapy depends on how it is measured. Although clients' testimonials and clinicians' perceptions strongly affirm the effectiveness of psychotherapy, controlled research studies, such as those originated by Hans Eysenck, report a similar improvement rate among treated and untreated people. More recent research using meta-analysis—combining the results of many different studies—reveals that psychotherapy is somewhat effective and that it is cost-effective compared with the greater costs of physician care for underlying psychological ailments. The same research revealed that although no particular type of therapy proved consistently superior, certain therapies work best with certain disorders. Behavioral conditioning therapies, for example, work best with specific behavior problems. With depression, the cognitive therapies prove most successful.

2. (Thinking Critically) One reason clients' and therapists' perceptions of therapy's effectiveness are vulnerable to inflation is the placebo effect, or the power of belief in a treatment. A second reason is regression toward the mean, or the tendency for unusual events (such as undesirable emotions or other psychological problems) to return toward their average state.

3. Research studies have revealed that although no particular type of therapy proved consistently superior, certain therapies work best with certain disorders. In general, therapy is most effective when problems are clear-cut. Furthermore, cogni-

tive, interpersonal, and behavioral therapies have proven effective in treating depression. For anxiety, cognitive and exposure therapies and stress inoculation training have been successful. Finally, bulimia and bed wetting have been successfully treated with cognitive-behavior therapy and behavior modification, respectively.

4. There have been very few controlled research studies of most forms of alternative therapy. Therapeutic touch is the popular therapy in which practitioners move their hands a few inches over a patient's body, allegedly in order to restore balance to "energy fields." The limited evidence that is available is that therapeutic touch does not work. In eye movement desensitization and reprocessing (EMDR) therapy, a practitioner triggers eye movements in patients, who are imagining traumatic events, by waving a finger in front of their eyes. While EMDR has proven to be beneficial in treating civilian post-traumatic stress disorder, it is probably the combination of exposure therapy and a placebo effect (rather than eye movements) that accounts for this success. Light-exposure therapy may help combat seasonal affective disorder by affecting secretion of melatonin, a hormone which helps regulate circadian rhythms.

5. First, because they enable people to believe that things can and will get better, psychotherapies provide hope for demoralized people. This placebo effect explains why all sorts of treatments may produce cures. Second, therapy offers people a plausible explanation of problems and alternative ways of responding. Third, therapy establishes an empathic, trusting, caring relationship between client and therapist.

6. All therapists have their own values, which may differ radically, as illustrated by Albert Ellis and Allen Bergin's widely divergent views. Because these values influence their therapy, they should be divulged to patients. Value differences may become particularly significant when a therapist from one culture meets a client from another.

Stepping Through the Section

1. is not
2. satisfaction
3. did not have
4. belief; placebo effect; regression toward the mean; unusual; average
5. Eysenck; was not
6. meta-analysis; somewhat effective

7. specific

8. cognitive; interpersonal; behavior; cognitive; exposure; stress inoculation; bulimia; bed wetting

9. no clear

10. behavior

11. alternative therapy; therapeutic touch; nonexistent

12. traumatic events; eye movement desensitization and reprocessing (EMDR); somewhat effective; post-traumatic stress disorder; finger tapping

13. seasonal affective disorder; light-exposure; melatonin; circadian rhythm

14. is

15. do

The Biomedical Therapies

Section Preview

1. Discoveries in psychopharmacology revolutionized the treatment of disordered people and greatly reduced the need for psychosurgery or hospitalization. Antipsychotic drugs such as Thorazine and Clozaril are used to reduce positive and negative symptoms of schizophrenia, respectively. These drugs work by blocking receptor sites for the neurotransmitter dopamine. Antianxiety drugs, such as Valium and Librium, reduce tension and anxiety by depressing central nervous system activity. Antidepressant drugs elevate mood by increasing the availability of the neurotransmitters norepinephrine and serotonin; fluoxetine (Prozac) blocks the reabsorption and removal of serotonin from synapses. The drug lithium is used to stabilize the manic-depressive mood swings of the bipolar disorder.

2. Electroconvulsive therapy (ECT), which is used by psychiatrists to treat severe depression, produces marked improvement in at least 80 percent of patients without discernible brain damage. ECT may work by increasing the release of norepinephrine, or by inducing seizures that calm neural centers in which overactivity produces depression. A new, gentler treatment called repetitive transcranial magnetic stimulation (rTMS) shows promise in reducing depression without the seizures, memory loss, or other side effects associated with ECT.

Because its effects are irreversible, psychosurgery, which removes or destroys brain tissue to change behavior, is the most drastic biomedical intervention. The best-known form, the lobotomy, was developed by Moniz in the 1930s to calm emotional and violent patients. During the 1950s, with advances in psychopharmacology, psychosurgery was largely abandoned.

Stepping Through the Section

1. drug; decreased

2. psychopharmacology

3. double-blind

4. antipsychotic; chlorpromazine (Thorazine); positive; clozapine (Clozaril); dopamine

5. antianxiety; central nervous system

6. antidepressant; norepinephrine; serotonin; fluoxetine (Prozac); serotonin; serotonin-reuptake-inhibitor

7. aerobic exercise

8. placebo effect

9. receptors; substance P; pain

10. lithium

11. electroconvulsive; ECT

12. depression; confirms

13. norepinephrine

14. repetitive transcranial magnetic stimulation (rTMS); seizures; memory

15. psychosurgery

16. lobotomy; frontal

17. drugs

Preventing Psychological Disorders

Section Preview

1. Psychotherapists who view psychological disorders as responses to a disturbed and stressful society contend that the best approach is to prevent problems from developing by treating not only the person but also the person's social context. Accordingly, programs that help alleviate poverty, discrimination, constant criticism, unemployment, sexism, and other demoralizing situations that undermine people's sense of competence, personal control, and self-esteem are thought to be effective in reducing people's risk of psychological disorders.

Progress Test 1

Multiple-Choice Questions

1. **b.** is the answer. Although no one is sure how ECT works, one possible explanation is that it increases release of norepinephrine, the neurotransmitter that elevates mood. (p. 596)

2. **c.** is the answer. (p. 569)
   a. Active listening is a Rogerian technique in which the therapist echoes, restates, and seeks clarification of the client's statements.
   b. Spontaneous remission, which is not mentioned in the text, refers to improvement without treatment.
   d. Systematic desensitization is a process in which a person is conditioned to associate a relaxed state with anxiety-triggering stimuli.

3. **b.** is the answer. (p. 571)

4. **d.** is the answer. This is not among the criticisms commonly made of psychoanalysis. (It would more likely be made of behavior therapies.) (p. 570)

5. **a.** is the answer. (p. 577)
   b., c., & d. Each of these is a type of group therapy.

6. **c.** is the answer. Meta-analysis of the relative effectiveness of different therapies reveals no clear winner; the other factors mentioned are advantages of group therapies. (p. 586)

7. **c.** is the answer. (p. 592)
   a. The fact that its effects are irreversible makes psychosurgery a drastic procedure, and with advances in psychopharmacology, psychosurgery was largely abandoned.
   b. ECT is still widely used as a treatment of major depression, but in general it is not used as frequently as drug therapy.
   d. & e. Counterconditioning and aversive conditioning are not biomedical therapies.

8. **b.** is the answer. Clients' testimonials regarding psychotherapy are generally very positive. The research, in contrast, seems to show that therapy is only *somewhat* effective. (pp. 582, 585–586)

9. **b.** is the answer. Although many of those who received counseling felt it had saved their lives, on a number of measures these men exhibited slightly *more* problems than those who had not received counseling. (p. 583)
   a. Boys who received counseling had slightly *more* problems as adults.

c. & d. This study did not compare the effectiveness of different forms of psychotherapy.

10. **d.** is the answer. (p. 586)

11. **a.** is the answer. By occupying receptor sites for dopamine, these drugs block its activity and reduce its production. (p. 594)

12. **e.** is the answer. (p. 598)

13. **d.** is the answer. Today, half of all psychotherapists describe themselves as eclectic—as using a blend of therapies. (p. 568)
    a. An eclectic therapist may use a nondirective approach with certain behaviors; however, a more directive approach might be chosen for other clients and problems.
    b. In fact, just the opposite is true. Eclectic therapists generally view disorders as stemming from many influences.
    c. Eclectic therapists, in contrast to this example, use a combination of treatments.

14. **a.** is the answer. (p. 572)

15. **c.** is the answer. (p. 571)

16. **b.** is the answer. (p. 573)
    a. This reflects a cognitive perspective.
    c. This reflects a psychoanalytic perspective.

17. **c.** is the answer. (p. 576)
    a. & b. Counterconditioning is the replacement of an undesired response with a desired one by means of aversive conditioning or systematic desensitization.
    d. Exposure therapy exposes a person, in imagination or in actuality, to a feared situation.

18. **d.** is the answer. (p. 577)

19. **b.** is the answer. (pp. 584, 590)
    a. Spontaneous remission refers to improvement without any treatment.
    c. Transference is the psychoanalytic phenomenon in which a client transfers feelings from other relationships onto his or her analyst.
    d. Interpretation is the psychoanalytic procedure through which the analyst helps the client become aware of resistances and understand their meaning.

20. **c.** is the answer. (p. 582)

21. **c.** is the answer. (p. 588)

Matching Items

1. e (p. 577)	5. g (p. 571)	9. c (p. 598)
2. k (p. 573)	6. f (p. 584)	10. i (p. 592)
3. b (p. 573)	7. a (p. 575)	11. j (p. 573)
4. d (p. 579)	8. h (p. 568)	

Progress Test 2

Multiple-Choice Questions

1. **c.** is the answer. (p. 571)
   a. This answer would be a correct description of Joseph Wolpe.
   b. There is no such thing as insight therapy.
   d. This answer would be a correct description of Aaron Beck.

2. **a.** is the answer. (p. 575)
   b. In systematic desensitization, a hierarchy of anxiety-provoking stimuli is gradually associated with a relaxed state.
   c. Transference refers to a patient's transferring of feelings from other relationships onto his or her psychoanalyst.
   d. Electroconvulsive therapy is a biomedical shock treatment.
   e. A token economy is based on operant conditioning techniques.

3. **c.** is the answer. (p. 571)
   a. Behavior therapy focuses on behavior, not self-awareness.
   b. Psychoanalysis focuses on bringing repressed feelings into awareness.
   d. Biomedical therapy focuses on physical treatment through drugs, ECT, or psychosurgery.

4. **b.** is the answer. (p. 589)

5. **a.** is the answer. For behavior therapy, the problem behaviors *are* the problems. (p. 573)
   b. Cognitive therapy teaches people to think and act in more adaptive ways.
   c. Humanistic therapy promotes growth and self-fulfillment by providing an empathic, genuine, and accepting environment.
   d. Psychoanalytic therapy focuses on uncovering and interpreting repressed feelings.
   e. Family therapy focuses on the individual's relation to others.

6. **b.** is the answer. Counterconditioning techniques involve taking an established CS, which triggers an undesirable CR, and pairing it with a new UCS in order to condition a new, and more adaptive, CR. (p. 573)
   a. As indicated by the name, counterconditioning techniques are a form of conditioning; they do not involve learning by observation.
   c. & d. The principles of operant conditioning are the basis of behavior modification, which, in contrast to counterconditioning techniques, involves use of reinforcement.

7. **d.** is the answer. (pp. 573–574)

a. This is a confrontational therapy, which is aimed at teaching people to think and act in more adaptive ways.
b. Aversive conditioning is a form of counterconditioning in which unwanted behavior is associated with unpleasant feelings.
c. Counterconditioning is a general term, including not only systematic desensitization, in which a hierarchy of fears is desensitized, but also other techniques, such as aversive conditioning.

8. **e.** is the answer. (p. 576)
   a., b., & d. These techniques are based on classical conditioning.
   c. This is a type of cognitive therapy.

9. **d.** is the answer. (pp. 576–577)

10. **c.** is the answer. (p. 578)
    a. This is an alternative therapy in which the practitioner triggers eye movements in patients who are imagining traumatic events.
    b. In this humanistic therapy, the therapist facilitates the client's growth by offering a genuine, accepting, and empathic environment.
    d. Behavior therapy concentrates on modifying the actual symptoms of psychological problems.

11. **c.** is the answer. (p. 594)

12. **b.** is the answer. Although many of the treated men offered glowing reports of the effectiveness of their therapy, these testimonials did not accurately reflect the results. (p. 583)
    a. In fact, as this study showed, clients' perceptions of the effectiveness of psychotherapy are often very positive but inaccurate.
    c. On some measures, the treated men exhibited slightly *more* problems than the untreated men.
    d. This study did not compare the effectiveness of different forms of psychotherapy.

13. **d.** is the answer. Lithium works as a mood stabilizer. (p. 596)
    a. & c. Valium and Librium are antianxiety drugs.
    b. Chlorpromazine is an antipsychotic drug.

14. **a.** is the answer. Antianxiety drugs are among the most heavily prescribed of all drugs. (p. 594)

15. **c.** is the answer. (p. 578)
    a. Behavior therapy is most likely to be successful in treating specific behavior problems, such as phobias.
    b. & d. The text does not single out particular disorders for which these therapies tend to be most effective.

16. **d.** is the answer. (p. 597)

17. **d.** is the answer. Even when dealing with seriously depressed adults, the paraprofessionals were as effective as the professionals. (p. 590)

18. **d.** is the answer. (pp. 589–591)

19. **d.** is the answer. (p. 580)

    a. This is true of most forms of psychotherapy.

    b. & c. This is true of humanistic, cognitive, and behavior therapies.

20. **c.** is the answer. Although aversive conditioning may work in the short run, the person's ability to discriminate between the situation in which the aversive conditioning occurs and other situations can limit the treatment's effectiveness. (p. 576)

    a., b., & d. These were not offered in the text as limitations of the effectiveness of aversive conditioning.

21. **c.** is the answer. (p. 579)

Matching Items

1. d (p. 572)
2. h (p. 576)
3. e (p. 590)
4. a (p. 597)
5. c (p. 596)
6. b (p. 585)
7. i (p. 592)
8. j (p. 593)
9. f (p. 594)
10. g (p. 569)
11. k (p. 574)

Thinking Critically About Chapter 16

Multiple-Choice Questions

1. **d.** is the answer. Resistances are blocks in the flow of free association that hint at underlying anxiety. (p. 569)

   a. In transference, a patient redirects feelings from other relationships to his or her analyst.

   b. The goal of psychoanalysis is for patients to gain insight into their feelings.

   c. Although such hesitation may well involve material that has been repressed, the hesitation itself is a resistance.

2. **d.** is the answer. In transference, the patient develops feelings toward the therapist that were experienced in important early relationships but were repressed. (p. 569)

   a. Projection is a defense mechanism in which a person imputes his or her own feelings to someone else.

   b. Resistances are blocks in the flow of free association that indicate repressed material.

   c. Regression is a defense mechanism in which a person retreats to an earlier form of behavior.

3. **d.** is the answer. According to Rogers' client-centered therapy, the therapist must exhibit genuineness, acceptance, and empathy if the client is to move toward self-fulfillment. (p. 571)

   a. Psychoanalysts are much more directive in providing interpretations of clients' problems than are humanistic therapists.

   b. Behavior therapists focus on modifying the behavioral symptoms of psychological problems.

   c. Cognitive therapists teach people to think and act in new, more adaptive ways.

4. **d.** is the answer. Aversive conditioning is the classical conditioning technique in which a positive response is replaced by a negative response. (In this example, the UCS is the blast of smoke, the CS is the taste of the cigarette as it is inhaled, and the intended CR is aversion to cigarettes.) (p. 575)

   a. Exposure therapy exposes someone, in imagination (virtual reality exposure therapy) or actuality, to a feared situation.

   b. Behavior modification applies the principles of operant conditioning and thus, in contrast to the example, uses reinforcement.

   c. Systematic desensitization is used to help people overcome specific anxieties.

5. **d.** is the answer. Because the psychologist is challenging Darnel's illogical, self-defeating attitude, this response is most typical of rational-emotive therapy. (p. 577)

   a. Behavior therapists treat behaviors rather than thoughts.

   b. Psychoanalysts focus on helping patients gain insight into previously repressed feelings.

   c. Client-centered therapists attempt to facilitate clients' growth by offering a genuine, accepting, empathic environment.

6. **b.** is the answer. Psychiatrists are physicians who specialize in treating psychological disorders. As doctors they can prescribe medications. (p. 591)

   a., c., & d. These professionals cannot prescribe drugs.

7. **c.** is the answer. (p. 593)

   a. This is a statistical technique used to combine the results of many different research studies.

   b. In this design, which is not mentioned in the text, there is only a single research group.

   d. This answer would be correct if the experimenter, but not the subjects, knew which condition was in effect.

8. **d.** is the answer. (p. 589)

   a. In fact, there is evidence that light-exposure therapy can be effective in treating SAD.

   b. There is no evidence that EMDR is effective as a treatment for SAD.

   c. Lithium is an antidepressant drug that is often used to treat bipolar disorder.

9. **e.** is the answer. (p. 586)

   a. Psychotherapy has proven "somewhat effective" and more cost-effective than physician care for psychological disorders.

b. & c. Behavior and cognitive therapies are effective in treating specific behavior problems and depression, respectively, but not necessarily in treating other problems.

d. The text does not specify which problems are best treated with group therapy.

10. **a.** is the answer. (p. 573)

b. & c. These types of therapists are more concerned with promoting self-fulfillment (humanistic) and healthy patterns of thinking (cognitive) than with correcting specific problem behaviors.

d. Psychoanalysts see the behavior merely as a symptom and focus their treatment on its presumed underlying cause.

11. **a.** is the answer. (pp. 573–574)

b. Aversive conditioning associates unpleasant states with unwanted behaviors.

c. Shaping is an operant conditioning technique in which successive approximations of a desired behavior are reinforced.

d. Free association is a psychoanalytic technique in which a patient says whatever comes to mind.

12. **b.** is the answer. (p. 576)

13. **c.** is the answer. (p. 579)

a. & b. Behavior therapists make extensive use of techniques based on both operant and classical conditioning.

d. Neither behavior therapists nor cognitive behavior therapists focus on clients' unconscious urges.

14. **d.** is the answer. (p. 598)

a. This would be the perspective of a cognitive behavior therapist.

b. This would be the perspective of a psychoanalyst.

c. This would be the perspective of a behavior therapist.

15. **a.** is the answer. (p. 594)

16. **c.** is the answer. (p. 594)

17. **c.** is the answer. (p. 597)

18. **b.** is the answer. (p. 596)

19. **e.** is the answer. Both psychoanalysis and psychodynamic therapy seek insight into a patient's unconscious feelings. The analysis of dreams, slips of the tongue, and resistances are considered a window into these feelings. (pp. 569, 570)

c. Cognitive therapists avoid reference to unconscious feelings and would therefore be uninterested in interpreting dreams.

20. **d.** is the answer. A key aim of psychoanalysis is to unearth and understand repressed impulses. (p. 569)

a., b., & c. Behavior and cognitive therapists avoid concepts such as "repression" and "unconscious"; behavior and humanistic therapists focus on the present rather than the past.

21. **d.** is the answer. (pp. 584, 589, 590–591)

Essay Question

Psychoanalysts assume that psychological problems such as depression are caused by unresolved, repressed, and unconscious impulses and conflicts from childhood. A psychoanalyst would probably attempt to bring these repressed feelings into Willie's conscious awareness and help him gain insight into them. He or she would likely try to interpret Willie's resistance during free association, the latent content of his dreams, and any emotional feelings he might transfer to the analyst.

Cognitive therapists assume that a person's emotional reactions are influenced by the person's thoughts in response to the event in question. A cognitive therapist would probably try to teach Willie new and more constructive ways of thinking in order to reverse his catastrophizing beliefs about himself, his situation, and his future.

Biomedical therapists attempt to treat disorders by altering the functioning of the patient's brain. A biomedical therapist would probably prescribe an antidepressant drug such as fluoxetine to increase the availability of norepinephrine and serotonin in Willie's nervous system. If Willie's depression is especially severe, a *psychiatrist* might treat it with several sessions of electroconvulsive therapy.

Key Terms

1. **Psychotherapy** is an emotionally charged, confiding interaction between a trained therapist and someone who suffers from psychological difficulties. (p. 568)

2. With an **eclectic approach**, therapists are not locked into one form of psychotherapy, but draw on whatever combination seems best suited to a client's needs. (p. 568)

3. **Psychoanalysis**, the therapy developed by Freud, attempts to give clients self-insight by bringing into awareness and interpreting previously repressed feelings. (p. 568)

Example: The tools of the **psychoanalyst** include free association, the analysis of dreams and transferences, and the interpretation of repressed impulses.

4. **Resistance** is the psychoanalytic term for the blocking from consciousness of anxiety-provoking memories. Hesitation during free association may reflect resistance. (p. 569)

5. **Interpretation** is the psychoanalytic term for the analyst's helping the client to understand resistances and other aspects of behavior, so that the client may gain deeper insights. (p. 569)

6. **Transference** is the psychoanalytic term for a patient's redirecting to the analyst emotions from other relationships. (p. 569)

7. **Client-centered therapy** is a humanistic therapy developed by Rogers, in which growth and self-awareness are facilitated in an environment that offers genuineness, acceptance, and empathy. (p. 571)

8. **Active listening** is a nondirective technique of person-centered therapy, in which the listener echoes, restates, clarifies, but does not interpret, clients' remarks. (p. 572)

9. **Behavior therapy** is therapy that applies principles of operant or classical conditioning to the elimination of problem behaviors. (p. 573)

10. **Counterconditioning** is a category of behavior therapy in which new responses are classically conditioned to stimuli that elicit unwanted behaviors. (p. 573)

11. **Systematic desensitization** is a type of counterconditioning in which a state of relaxation is classically conditioned to a hierarchy of gradually increasing anxiety-provoking stimuli. (p. 573)

    Memory aid: This is a form of counterconditioning in which sensitive, anxiety-triggering stimuli are **desensitized** in a progressive, or **systematic**, fashion.

12. **Aversive conditioning** is a form of counterconditioning in which an unpleasant state becomes associated with an unwanted behavior. (p. 575)

13. A **token economy** is an operant conditioning procedure in which desirable behaviors are promoted in people by rewarding them with tokens, or secondary reinforcers, which can be exchanged for privileges or treats. For the most part, token economies are used in hospitals, schools, and other institutional settings. (p. 576)

14. **Cognitive therapy** focuses on teaching people new and more adaptive ways of thinking and acting. The therapy is based on the idea that our feelings and responses to events are strongly influenced by our thinking, or cognition. (p. 577)

15. **Cognitive-behavior therapy** is an integrated therapy that focuses on changing self-defeating thinking and unwanted behaviors. (p. 579)

16. **Family therapy** views problem behavior as partially engendered by the client's family system and environment. Therapy therefore focuses on relationships and problems among the various members of the family. (p. 580)

17. **Regression toward the mean** is the tendency for unusual events (such as emotions) to return toward their average state. (p. 584)

18. **Meta-analysis** is a procedure for statistically combining the results of many different research studies. (p. 585)

19. **Psychopharmacology** is the study of the effects of drugs on mind and behavior. (p. 592)

    Memory aid: Pharmacology is the science of the uses and effects of drugs. **Psycho**pharmacology is the science that studies the psychological effects of drugs.

20. **Lithium** is an antidepressant drug that is commonly used to stabilize the manic-depressive mood swings of the bipolar disorder. (p. 596)

21. In **electroconvulsive therapy (ECT)**, a biomedical therapy often used to treat major depressive disorder, electric shock is passed through the brain. ECT may work by increasing the availability of norepinephrine, the neurotransmitter that elevates mood. (p. 596)

22. **Psychosurgery** is a biomedical therapy that attempts to change behavior by removing or destroying brain tissue. Since drug therapy became widely available in the 1950s, psychosurgery has been infrequently used. (p. 597)

23. Once used to control violent patients, the **lobotomy** is a form of psychosurgery in which the nerves linking the emotion centers of the brain to the frontal lobes are severed. (p. 597)

FOCUS ON VOCABULARY AND LANGUAGE

Page 567: . . . cracked the genetic code . . . Myers notes the progress we have made in understanding the physical world—mapping (*charting*) the solar system (*heavens*), discovering the structure of DNA (*cracking the genetic code*), finding cures for many diseases, and so on. He contrasts these attainments with the many odd and strange techniques (*bewildering variety of methods*) used to deal with people suffering from psychological disorders, such as cutting holes in the skull, piercing veins or attaching leeches to remove blood from the body (*bleeding*), whipping or striking people in order to force demons out of the body (*"beating the devil out of people"*), and so on.

Page 568 (caption): Visitors paid to *gawk* at the *patients* as if they were viewing zoo animals. In the past, mentally disordered people (*patients*) were confined to hospitals (*insane asylums*) and were often treated badly. For instance, some hospitals raised money by selling tickets to the public who could come and stare (*gawk*) at the inmates (*patients*), much as we do today when we visit the zoo and look at the captive animals.

The Psychological Therapies

Page 568: While each technique is distinctive, there are *common threads*. The most common forms of psychological therapy (**psychotherapy**) are based on the four major perspectives in psychology: psychoanalytic, humanistic, behavioral, and cognitive. While each type of therapy is unique (*distinctive*), the effectiveness of all may derive from similar underlying factors (*common threads*). About fifty percent of psychotherapists claim that they use a combination (*blend*) of techniques (an **eclectic approach**).

Page 568: . . . psychoanalysis assumes that many psychological problems are *fueled* by childhood's *residue* of supposedly *repressed impulses and conflicts*. Freud's psychoanalytic techniques are used by many therapists; their fundamental tenet (*assumption*) is that mental disorders are created and kept in existence (*fueled*) by hidden (*repressed*) childhood urges and opposing psychic forces (*conflicts*). Psychoanalysis attempts to restore the patient to mental health by bringing these submerged (*buried*) feelings into conscious awareness where they can be examined and dealt with (*worked through*). As Myers puts it, psychoanalysis digs up (*unearths*) the past in the hopes of uncovering (*unmasking*) the present.

Page 571: Not surprisingly, then, humanistic therapists *aim to boost* self-fulfillment by helping people grow in self-awareness and self-acceptance. The most popular humanistic technique is Carl Rogers' nondirective person-centered therapy. The goal is to increase (*the aim is to boost*) the client's feelings of accomplishment and achievement (*self-actualization*) by providing nonthreatening opportunities for living in the present, for becoming less critical of one's self, and for becoming more self-aware.

Page 572: "And that just really knocks the props out from under you." In Carl Rogers' therapy sessions, he attempts to be genuine, accepting, and empathic; he also mirrors (*reflects*) back to the client in different words the feelings that were expressed. The client said he had been told that he was no good, and Rogers reflects the feelings he detects by saying that it must seem that the client's self-worth had been undermined (*knocked the props out from under you*).

Page 573: . . . Jones' story of Peter and the rabbit did not immediately become part of psychology's *lore*. Mary Cover Jones was the first to demonstrate **counterconditioning** (replacing a fear response with an incompatible response, such as relaxation through classical conditioning). This technique, however, did not become part of psychology's tradition and store of knowledge (*lore*) until Wolpe developed systematic desensitization more than 30 years later.

Page 575: . . . the therapist offers the client appealing drinks *laced* with a drug that produces *severe nausea*. Behavior therapists, focusing on observable behaviors, use a number of techniques based on well-established learning principles. Two counterconditioning techniques based on classical conditioning are **systematic desensitization** and **aversive conditioning.** In aversive therapy, people who regularly drink too much (*alcoholics*) are given enticing alcoholic beverages which are infused (*laced*) with a substance that induces sickness (*severe nausea*). Alcohol should now be a potent conditioned stimulus that elicits unpleasant feelings; as a result, the alcoholic should want to avoid these drinks. Research shows some limited success with this approach.

Page 576: The combination of positively reinforcing desired behaviors and ignoring or punishing *aggressive and self-abusive* behaviors *worked wonders*. Another type of behavior therapy is based on operant conditioning principles and involves voluntary behavior followed by pleasant or unpleasant consequences. Socially withdrawn autistic children, treated to an intensive 2-year program of positive reinforcement for desired behaviors and punishment for violent and self-injurious (*aggressive and self-abusive*) behaviors, responded extremely well (*it worked wonders for them*).

Page 577: The **cognitive therapies** assume that our thinking *colors* our feelings. . . . The underlying assumption of the cognitive approach to therapy is that thoughts precede and influence (*color*) our feelings. If certain destructive patterns of thinking are learned, then it must be possible to unlearn them and replace them with more constructive ways of viewing what happens to us.

Page 578: . . . *catastrophizing* . . . Aaron Beck, a cognitive therapist, believes that the way to help depressed people feel better is to turn around (*reverse*) their negative, distorted thinking, which tends to transform ordinary events into disasters (*catastrophizing*). The goal is to get them to think about their lives in more positive terms (*get them to take off the dark glasses*).

Evaluating Psychotherapies

Page 578: "*Hang in there* until you find [a psychotherapist] *who fills the bill.*" Each year in the United States about 15 percent of the population seek help for psychological and addictive disorders. Many people, including advice columnist Ann Landers, recommend that troubled people get professional help and that they persevere (*hang in there*) in finding the right therapist to meet their needs (*who fills the bill*).

Page 582: If clients' *testimonials* were the only yardstick, we could strongly affirm the effectiveness of psychotherapy. The question of whether or not psychotherapy is effective is a very complex issue. If the only measure (*yardstick*) was what clients said about their therapy (*testimonials*), then the conclusion would have to be that psychotherapy works. (Three-quarters, or more, of those surveyed were satisfied.) Myers points out that such testimonials can be misleading and invalid.

Page 582: When, with the normal *ebb and flow* of events, the crisis passes, people may attribute their improvement to the therapy. Because of some serious traumatic events (*crises*) in their lives, people may end up seeing a therapist; after many sessions they may feel much better. During the ordinary course (*ebb and flow*) of events, however, the crisis is likely to have passed; thus, their present feelings of well-being may have little to do with the psychotherapy.

Page 586: In general, therapy is most effective when the problem is *clear-cut* (Singer, 1981). Psycho-

therapy tends to work best when the disturbances are well-defined (*clear-cut*) and explicitly stated or understood. For example, those who suffer from irrational fears (*phobias*), are timid or shy (*unassertive*), or have a psychologically caused sexual disorder respond better to therapy than those who suffer from *schizophrenia* or who want a total personality change.

Page 587 (Critical Thinking): The tendency of abnormal states of mind to "regress" to normal, combined with the placebo effect, creates *fertile soil* for *pseudotherapies*. So called alternative therapies may appear to be effective for a couple of reasons: worse than normal mental states tend to diminish and move back to more normal mental states (*regression to the average*) over time, and if people expect that a particular therapy will help them they may get better as a result of their belief alone (*the placebo effect*). These factors provide a basis (*fertile soil*) for the growth and popularity of therapies that have not been empirically validated (*pseudotherapies*).

Page 590: Each therapy, in its individual way, may *harness* the client's own healing powers. Research has shown that actual therapy is better than no treatment, but that placebo-treated people improve significantly. This suggests that therapies work in part because they offer hope; each different type of therapy may be effective to the extent that it capitalizes on and uses (*harnesses*) the clients' ability for self-healing.

Page 590: Indeed, some believe that warmth and *empathy* are *hallmarks* of healers everywhere, whether psychiatrists, witch doctors, or shamans (Torrey, 1986). In general, therapies are approximately the same in effectiveness, but that does not mean that all therapists are equal in this respect. Fundamental qualities (*hallmarks*) of effective therapists are an ability to understand other people's experiences (*empathy*) and a capacity to show genuine concern and care (*warmth*). In addition, good listening skills, a reassuring manner, and concern for gaining (*earning*) the client's respect and trust help in the therapeutic process.

The Biomedical Therapies

Page 593: While researchers continue testing possible *cousin* drugs . . . A relatively new antipsychotic drug, clozapine, is one of the most effective treatments for schizophrenia. It does, however, have a toxic effect on white blood cells in 1 or 2 percent of patients, so scientists are now testing closely related (*cousin*) drugs that are equally effective but appear to be without the poisonous side effects.

Page 594: Antipsychotics such as Thorazine are powerful drugs. These can produce *sluggishness, tremors, and twitches* similar to those of Parkinson's disease, which is marked by too little dopamine (Kaplan & Saddock, 1989). Because of the serious side effects of some antipsychotic drugs—tiredness and apathy (*sluggishness*), shaking limbs (*tremors*), and sudden involuntary spasms (*twitches*)—therapists have to be very careful (*they have to tread a fine line*) in selecting the dose that will relieve the symptoms but will not produce the side effects.

Page 594: Routinely *"popping a Valium"* at the first sign of tension can produce psychological dependence on the drug. The most popular antianxiety drugs (Valium and Librium) are central nervous system depressants, and they reduce tension without causing too much drowsiness. As a consequence, they are prescribed for a variety of problems, including minor emotional stresses. If a person regularly takes an antianxiety drug (*routinely "pops a Valium"*) whenever there is the slightest feeling of anxiety, the result can be psychological dependence on the drug. Withdrawal symptoms for heavy users include increased anxiety and an inability to sleep (insomnia).

Page 594: Just as the antianxiety drugs can calm people down from a state of anxiety, the antidepressants sometimes *lift people up from* a state of depression. Antidepressants work by either increasing the availability of the neurotransmitters norepinephrine or serotonin, blocking their reabsorption, or by inhibiting an enzyme that breaks them down. Thus, they tend to make depressed people feel more alive and aroused (*they lift them up*).

Page 596: ECT therefore gained a *barbaric* image that lingers still. **Electroconvulsive therapy (ECT)** has proven quite effective and is used mainly for chronically depressed people who have not responded to drug therapy. In 1938, when ECT was first introduced, wide-awake patients were strapped to a table to prevent them from hurting themselves during the convulsions and were shocked (*jolted*) with 100 volts of electricity to the brain. Although the procedure is different today, these inhumane (*barbaric*) images tend to remain in people's minds. As Myers notes, ECT is credited with saving many from suicide, but its *Frankensteinlike* image continues. (Dr. Frankenstein is a fictional character who created a monster from the body parts of dead people.)

Page 597: . . . hopes are rising for a gentler alternative for *jump-starting* the brain. (Using power from another car's battery to start a car with a flat or dead battery is called *jump-starting*). Depressed moods appear to improve when a painless procedure called repetitive transcranial magnetic stimulation (rTMS) is used on wide-awake patients. Thus, optimism is increasing (*hopes are rising*) for a better way to activate (*jump-start*) the depressed brain.

Preventing Psychological Disorders

Page 598: Preventive mental health is *upstream work*. Some psychologists believe that prevention is better than cure and they support programs that help relieve and stop poverty, racism, discrimination, and other disempowering or demoralizing situations. The attempt to prevent psychological disorders by getting rid of conditions that may cause them is extremely difficult (*upstream work*).

17:

Stress and Health

Chapter Overview

Behavioral factors play a major role in maintaining health and causing illness. The effort to understand this role more fully has led to the emergence of the interdisciplinary field of behavioral medicine. The subfield of health psychology focuses on questions such as: How do our perceptions of a situation determine the stress we feel? How do our emotions and personality influence our risk of disease? How can psychology contribute to the prevention of illness?

Chapter 17 addresses key topics in health psychology. First and foremost is stress—its nature, its effects on the body, psychological factors that determine how it affects us, and how stress contributes to heart disease, infectious diseases, and cancer. The chapter concludes by looking at physical and psychological factors that promote good health and examining several illness-related behaviors , including smoking, nutrition, and obesity

NOTE: Answer guidelines for all Chapter 17 questions begin on page 487.

Introducing Stress and Health (p. 601)

Introduction Preview

First, skim the introduction. Then read the following objective and, as you read the text, search for the information that will enable you to meet that objective. Answer guidelines are provided on page 487.

1. Identify the major concerns of behavioral medicine and health psychology.

Stepping Through the Introduction

After you have read the section, complete the sentences and answer the questions. As you proceed, evaluate your performance by consulting the answers on page 487. Do not continue with the next section until you understand each answer. If you need to, review or reread the section in the textbook before continuing.

1. The four leading causes of serious illness and death in the United States are _____ _____ , _____ , _____ , and _____ _____ _____ .

2. Today, half the mortality from the 10 leading causes of death can be traced to people's _____ .

3. List several of the behaviors that have been linked to the leading causes of death:

   _____

   _____

4. The new field that integrates behavioral and medical knowledge relevant to health and disease is _____ _____ .

5. The subfield of psychology related to behavioral medicine is called _____ psychology.

Stress and Illness (pp. 602–615)

> David Myers at times uses idioms that are unfamiliar to some readers. If you do not know the meaning of any of the following words, phrases, or expressions in the context in which they appear in the text, refer to pages 494–495 for an explanation: *tense . . . clenched teeth . . . churning stomach; slippery concept; flow through a psychological filter; heart rate zooms; uprooting; a cluster of crises; Daily Hassles; mellow and laid-back; after the honeymoon period; combat ready; headless horseman; Marital spats; bottle up.*

Section Preview

Answer guidelines are provided on page 487.

1. Define *stress* and describe the body's response to stress.

2. Discuss research findings on the health consequences of stressful life events, as well as the impact of perceived control and pessimism on health and our vulnerability to stress.

3. Discuss the role of stress in coronary heart disease, and contrast Type A and Type B personalities.

4. Describe how the immune system defends the body and discuss the effect of stress on the immune system.

Stepping Through the Section

Answers are provided on page 488.

1. Stress is not merely a _____ or a _____ . Rather, it is the _____ by which we perceive and respond to environmental threats and challenges. This definition highlights the fact that stressors can have _____ (only negative/both positive and negative) effects, depending on how they are perceived.

2. In the 1920s, physiologist Walter _____ began studying the effect of stress on the body. He discovered that the hormones _____ and _____ are released into the bloodstream in response to stress. This and other bodily changes due to stress are mediated by the _____ nervous system, thus preparing the body for "_____ _____ ."

3. More recently, physiologists have discovered that in response to stress the cortex triggers the _____ _____ to release the hormone _____ .

4. In studying animals' reactions to stressors, Selye repeatedly found three physiological effects: enlargement of the _____ cortex, shrinkage of the _____ gland, and the formation of bleeding _____ . He referred to this bodily response to stress as the _____ _____ _____ .

5. During the first phase of the GAS—the _____ reaction—the person is in a state of shock due to the sudden arousal of the _____ nervous system.

6. This is followed by the stage of _____ , in which the body's resources are mobilized to cope with the stressor.

7. If stress continues, the person enters the stage of _____ . During this stage, a person is _____ (more/less) vulnerable to disease.

8. In the wake of catastrophic events, such as floods, hurricanes, and fires, there often is an increase in the number of _____ _____ .

9. Research studies have found that people who have recently been widowed, fired, or divorced are _____ (more/no more) vulnerable to illness than other people.

10. For most people, the most significant sources of stress are _____ _____ . The stresses that accompany poverty and unemployment, for example, often compounded by _____ , may account for the higher rates of _____ among residents of urban ghettos.

11. Persistent on-the-job stress can lead to the physical, mental, and emotional exhaustion called _____ .

12. Negative situations are especially stressful when they are appraised as _____ . Control may explain why poorer people are more at risk for premature _____ than those who are more affluent.

13. People at every income level tend to die younger in areas where there is greater income _____ . Among developed countries, for example, life expectancies in the _____ and _____ are _____ (how much?) lower than those in _____ and _____ .

14. People who have an _____ attitude are *less* likely than others to suffer ill health.

15. In animals and humans, sudden lack of control is followed by a drop in immune responses and a rise in the levels of _____ _____ .

16. The leading cause of death in North America is _____ _____ _____ . List several risk factors for developing this condition: _____ _____ _____ .

17. Friedman and Rosenman discovered that tax accountants experience an increase in blood _____ level and blood- _____ speed during tax season. This showed there was a link between coronary warning indicators and _____ .

Friedman and Rosenman, in a subsequent study, grouped people into Type A and Type B personalities. Characterize these types and indicate the difference that emerged between them over the course of this 9-year study.

18. Type A persons tend to engage in certain behaviors that contribute to risk of coronary disease, including _____ _____ .

19. In relaxed situations, Type A persons _____ (differ/do not differ) from Type B persons in measures of physiological reactivity.

20. An experiment by Williams showed that when Type A students were challenged, their output of stress hormones was _____ (greater than/the same as) that of their Type B classmates. These hormones may increase the buildup of _____ in the artery walls. The hardening of the arteries that may result is called _____ .

21. When a person is angered, blood flow is diverted away from the internal organs, including the liver, which is responsible for removing _____ and fat from the blood. This finding may explain why _____ (Type A/Type B) persons have elevated levels of these substances in the blood.

22. The Type A characteristic that is most strongly linked with coronary heart disease is _____ .

23. Depression following a heart attack or the death of a spouse _____ (increases/ has no effect on) one's risk of having a heart

attack or _____ . Negative emotions also explain why a large proportion of hospital patients suffer _____ or _____ disorders.

24. In _____ illnesses, physical symptoms are produced by psychological causes. Examples of such illnesses are certain forms of _____ and _____ . Such illnesses appear to be linked to _____ .

25. The body's system of fighting disease is the _____ system. This system includes two types of white blood cells, called _____ : the _____ _____ , which fight bacterial infections, and the _____ _____ , which form in the _____ and attack viruses, cancer cells, and foreign substances. Another immune agent, called the _____ , pursues and ingests foreign substances.

26. Responding too strongly, the immune system may attack the body's tissues and cause _____ or an _____ reaction. Or it may _____ , allowing a dormant virus to erupt or _____ cells to multiply.

27. _____ (Women/Men) are the immunologically stronger gender. This makes them less susceptible to _____ , but more susceptible to _____ diseases such as _____ and _____ _____ .

28. Stress can suppress the lymphocyte cells, resulting in a(n)_____ (increase/decrease) in disease resistance. Stress diverts energy from the _____ _____ to the _____ and _____ , mobilizing the body for action.

29. Worldwide, the fourth leading cause of death is _____ , caused by the _____ , which is spread primarily through the exchange of _____ and _____ . Stressful life circumstances _____ (have/have not)

been shown to accelerate the progression of this chronic disease.

Characterize the link between stress and cancer.

30. Experiments by Ader and Cohen demonstrate that the functioning of the body's immune system _____ (can/cannot) be affected by conditioning.

Promoting Health (pp. 616–640)

> If you do not know the meaning of any of the following words, phrases, or expressions in the context in which they appear in the text, refer to pages 495–497 for an explanation: *run away from their troubles; "mood boost" . . . couch potatoes!; stepped back . . . overblown and oversold; laughter is the best medicine; heartaches; open heart therapy; cold fact; cool models; slow-motion suicide; gauche rather than cool; role-played; skipping breakfast; win the battle of the bulge; scarfing too many hot fudge sundaes; thinner wallet.*

Section Preview

Answer guidelines are provided on page 488.

1. Identify and discuss different strategies for coping with stress.

2. Describe the relationship between health and social support, and discuss whether there is a "faith factor" in health and longevity.

3. (Thinking Critically) Discuss the growing popularity of complementary and alternative medicine.

4. Explain why people smoke, and discuss ways of preventing and reducing this health hazard.

5. Discuss the relationship between nutrition and physical well-being.

6. Discuss the factors that contribute to obesity.

7. Explain whether genes play no role, some role, or an exclusive role in causing obesity.

Stepping Through the Section

Answers are provided on page 490.

1. Sustained exercise that increases heart and lung fitness is known as _____ exercise. Experiments _____ (have/have not) been able to demonstrate conclusively that such exercise reduces anxiety and depression, and alleviates the effects of stress.

2. Exercise increases the body's production of mood-boosting neurotransmitters such as

   _____ , _____ , and _____ . By one estimate, moderate exercise adds _____ (how many?) years to one's life expectancy.

3. A system for recording a physiological response and providing information concerning it is called _____ . The instruments used in this system _____ (provide/do not provide) the individual with a means of controlling physiological responses.

4. Lowered blood pressure and strengthened immune defenses have been found to be characteristic of people who regularly practice

   _____ .

5. Meyer Friedman found that modifying Type A behavior in a group of heart attack survivors _____ (reduced/did not significantly reduce) the rate of recurrence of heart attacks.

6. Researchers have found that life events may be less stressful for people who have a good sense of

   _____ .

7. Another buffer against the effects of stress is _____ support.

State several possible reasons for the link between health and social support.

8. Until fairly recently in history, the healing traditions of _____ and _____ have worked _____ (together/separately).

9. Polls reveal that most Americans _____ (believe/do not believe) that religion and spirituality are related to health and healing.

10. Several recent studies demonstrate that religious involvement _____ (predicts/does not predict) health and longevity.

State two possible intervening variables that might account for the "faith factor" in health.

11. (Thinking Critically) Acupuncture, masssage therapy, homeopathy, and similar treatments comprise the growing health care market called _____ _____ _____ _____ .

In China, _____ therapies have flourished for centuries, as have acupuncture and acupressure therapies that claim to correct imbalances in the flow of the energy called _____ .

12. (Thinking Critically) Critics of alternative medicine point out that such treatments seem especially effective with _____ diseases such as arthritis and _____ , as well as with diseases that disappear naturally—a phenomenon called _____ _____ .

Critics also argue that the seeming effectiveness of alternative medicine is due to a _____ effect.

13. Advocates of behavioral medicine contend that creating programs to _____ disease by promoting healthy life-styles will result in lower health-care costs than will focusing only on _____ existing diseases.

State several of the physical and psychological problems that are correlated with smoking.

14. Smoking usually begins during _____ and is especially common among those who _____ _____ .

According to _____-_____ theory, those who start smoking have friends who model smoking and pressure them to start.

15. As with other addictions, smokers become _____ on nicotine, develop _____ to its effects, and experience _____ symptoms when attempting to quit.

16. By terminating an aversive state, smoking provides a person with a powerful _____ . In addition, nicotine triggers the release of epinephrine and norepinephrine, which increase _____ , and of neurotransmitters that calm _____ and reduce _____ _____ .

17. Twin studies indicate a _____ (what percent?) heritability of smoking addiction. Smokers and nonsmokers also may differ in a _____ that influences responses to the neurotransmitter _____ .

18. Most programs to help people quit smoking _____ (are/are not) very effective in the long run. The decline in the smoking rate among Americans is most pronounced among _____ (males/females)

and those at _____ (higher/
lower) socioeconomic levels.

19. Worldwide, per-person cigarette consumption is
near an all-time _____
(low/high). Rates of smoking are increasing most
dramatically in _____ countries
where many people are unaware of the dangers
of smoking.

20. A study found that seventh graders who were
taught to cope with peer pressure and advertise-
ments for smoking were _____
(more/less) likely to begin smoking than were
students in a control group.

21. Certain foods may affect mood and behavior by
influencing the formation of specific
_____ .

22. A relaxed state may be facilitated by eating foods
high in _____ , which increase
the amount of tryptophan that the brain receives
and can thus be used for synthesizing the neurotransmitter _____ .
Concentration and alertness, in contrast, may be
improved by meals that have a high
_____ content.

23. Hypertensive people tend to have a higher-than-
normal intake of _____ but a
lower-than-normal intake of
_____ .

24. In developing societies where people face
_____ , obesity is considered a
sign of _____ and
_____ .

25. Eating disorders are rare in countries that do not
have a _____ .

26. Being slightly overweight _____
(poses/does not pose) health risks and is
_____ (more/less) important
than a person's overall fitness.

Cite some of the ways in which obesity is a threat to
physical and psychological health.

27. In one experiment, job applicants were rated as
less worthy of hiring when they were made to
appear _____ .

28. The energy equivalent of a pound of fat is
approximately _____ calories.
The immediate determinant of body fat is the size
and number of _____
_____ one has. This number is,
in turn, determined by several factors, including
_____
_____ .

29. The size of fat cells _____
(can/cannot) be decreased by dieting; the number of fat cells _____ (can/can-
not) be decreased by dieting.

30. Fat tissue has a _____
(higher/lower) metabolic rate than lean tissue.
The result is that fat tissue requires
_____ (more/less) food energy
to be maintained.

31. The body weight "thermostat" of obese people
_____ (is/is not) set to maintain
a higher-than-average weight. When weight
drops below this setting, _____
increases and _____ decreases.

Explain why, metabolically, many obese people find
it so difficult to become and stay thin.

32. Studies of adoptees and twins _____ (do/do not) provide evidence of a genetic influence on obesity.

33. Recent experiments reveal that obese mice have a defective _____ for producing the protein _____ . Increased levels of this protein signal the _____ to curb _____ and increase _____ . When obese mice are given injections of this protein, they become _____ (more/less) active and _____ (gain/lose) weight.

34. Obesity is _____ (more/less) common among lower-class than upper-class women and _____ (does/does not) vary from culture to culture. Throughout the developed world, the percentage of people classified as overweight—defined as a BMI of _____ or over—or as obese—defined as a BMI of _____ or over—is _____ (increasing/decreasing/about the same as it was in 1960).

35. Most obese persons who lose weight _____ (gain/do not gain) it back.

Web Sighting

The World Wide Web is an excellent resource for obtaining late-breaking scientific news, even before it appears in journals and other publications. Many universities and governmental research agencies, for example, maintain public information home pages that issue summaries of research findings that may be of interest to the public. Not only are the summaries "hot off the press," but they generally are written in language that is accessible to the average reader.

The National Institutes of Health (NIH) maintains a web site devoted to its Office of Alternative Medicine (http://altmed.od.nih.gov/) with regular research news updates. Check it out and learn the latest, credible information about various forms of complementary and alternative medicine and a possible genetic basis for obesity. To get started, find a current advertisement for a dietary supplement or other alternative treatment and then use this web resource to answer to following questions:

1. What product or treatment is endorsed in the advertisement? To what group(s) of people is the product or treatment being targeted?

2. What supporting evidence is provided for the product or treatment? Do you consider the evidence presented in the advertisement to be credible and trustworthy? Explain your reasoning.

3. Use NIH's online database to find the scientific community's position regarding the effectiveness of this product or treatment. Has your opinion changed? Why or why not?

Progress Test 1

Circle your answers to the following questions and check them with the answers on page 461. If your answer is incorrect, read the explanation for why it is incorrect and then consult the appropriate pages of the text (in parentheses following the correct answer).

1. Behavioral and medical knowledge about factors influencing health form the basis of the field of:
   a. health psychology.
   b. holistic medicine.
   c. behavioral medicine.
   d. osteopathic medicine.

2. The stress hormones epinephrine and norepinephrine are released by the _____ gland in response to stimulation by the _____ branch of the nervous system.
   a. pituitary; sympathetic
   b. pituitary; parasympathetic
   c. adrenal; sympathetic
   d. adrenal; parasympathetic

3. During which stage of the general adaptation syndrome is a person especially vulnerable to disease?
   a. alarm reaction   c. stage of exhaustion
   b. stage of resistance d. stage of adaptation

4. The leading cause of death in North America is:
   a. lung cancer.
   b. AIDS.
   c. coronary heart disease.
   d. alcohol-related accidents.
   e. accidents.

5. Researchers Friedman and Rosenman refer to individuals who are very time-conscious, super-motivated, verbally aggressive, and easily angered as:
   a. ulcer-prone personalities.
   b. cancer-prone personalities.
   c. Type A.
   d. Type B.

6. One effect of the hormones epinephrine, norepinephrine, and cortisol is to:
   a. lower the level of cholesterol in the blood.
   b. promote the buildup of plaques on the artery walls.
   c. divert blood away from the muscles of the body.
   d. reduce stress.
   e. decrease the amount of fat stored in the body.

7. Genuine illnesses that are caused by stress are called _____ illnesses.
   a. psychophysiological c. psychogenic
   b. hypochondriacal   d. psychotropic

8. Stress has been demonstrated to place a person at increased risk of:
   a. cancer.
   b. progressing from HIV infection to AIDS.
   c. bacterial infections.
   d. viral infections.
   e. all of the above.

9. *Stress* is defined as:
   a. unpleasant or aversive events that cannot be controlled.
   b. situations that threaten health.
   c. the whole process by which we perceive and respond to challenging or threatening events.
   d. anything that decreases immune responses.

10. In one experiment, both "executive" rats and "subordinate" rats received identical electric shocks, the only difference being whether the shocks could be:
    a. predicted.   c. shortened.
    b. weakened.   d. controlled.

11. In recent studies of obese mice, researchers have found that some mice:
    a. had a defective gene for producing leptin, a fat-detecting hormone.
    b. had abnormally high levels of insulin, a hunger-triggering hormone.
    c. could be conditioned to avoid fatty foods.
    d. had fewer-than-normal receptor sites for a fat-detecting hormone.
    e. are immune to changes in hormone levels.

12. Studies have demonstrated that meals that are high in _____ promote relaxation because they raise levels of _____ .
    a. carbohydrates; serotonin
    b. carbohydrates; cortisol
    c. protein; serotonin
    d. protein; cortisol

13. A study in which people were asked to confide troubling feelings to an experimenter found that subjects typically:
    a. did not truthfully report feelings and events.
    b. experienced a sustained increase in blood pressure until the experiment was finished.
    c. became physiologically more relaxed after confiding their problem.
    d. denied having any problems.

14. Research suggests that _____ influences often lead a person to start smoking, whereas _____ influences become important in explaining why people continue to smoke.
    a. biological; social   c. biological; cognitive
    b. social; biological   d. cognitive; biological

15. Some studies demonstrated that mastectomy patients who were determined to conquer their breast cancer:
    a. survived longer than those who were stoic or felt helpless.
    b. had reduced levels of lymphocytes in their bodies.
    c. had elevated levels of cortisol and other "good" stress hormones.
    d. experienced all of the above.

16. Research on genetic influences on obesity reveals that:
    a. the body weight of adoptees correlates with that of their biological parents.
    b. the body weight of adoptees correlates with that of their adoptive parents.
    c. identical twins usually have very different body weights.
    d. the body weights of identical twin women are more similar than those of identical twin men.
    e. none of the above is true.

17. Which of the following was *not* mentioned in the text as a potential health benefit of exercise?
    a. Exercise can increase ability to cope with stress.
    b. Exercise can lower blood pressure.
    c. Exercise can reduce stress, depression, and anxiety.
    d. Exercise improves functioning of the immune system.

18. Research studies demonstrate that after a catastrophe rates of _____ often increase.
    a. psychological disorders
    b. stress-related illnesses
    c. death
    d. all of the above
    e. none of the above

19. In one study, laboratory rats drank sweetened water with a drug that causes immune suppression. After repeated pairings of the taste with the drug:
    a. the animals developed tolerance for the drug and immune responses returned to normal.
    b. sweet water alone triggered immune suppression.
    c. dependency on the drug developed and withdrawal symptoms appeared when the drug was withheld.
    d. many of the animals died.

20. Social support _____ our ability to cope with stressful events.
    a. has no effect on
    b. usually increases
    c. usually decreases
    d. has an unpredictable effect on

21. The AIDS virus is transmitted primarily by:
    a. airborne transmission of HIV.
    b. physical touching.
    c. an exchange of blood or semen.
    d. insect bites.

22. Research has demonstrated that as a predictor of health and longevity, religious involvement:
    a. has a small, insignificant effect.
    b. is more accurate for women than men.
    c. is more accurate for men than women.
    d. rivals nonsmoking and exercise.

Progress Test 2

Progress Test 2 should be completed during a final chapter review. Answer the following questions after you thoroughly understand the correct answers for the section reviews and Progress Test 1.

Multiple-Choice Questions

1. The field of health psychology is concerned with:
   a. the prevention of illness.
   b. the promotion of health.
   c. the treatment of illness.
   d. all of the above.

2. In order, the sequence of stages in the general adaptation syndrome is:
   a. alarm reaction, stage of resistance, stage of exhaustion.
   b. stage of resistance, alarm reaction, stage of exhaustion.
   c. stage of exhaustion, stage of resistance, alarm reaction.
   d. alarm reaction, stage of exhaustion, stage of resistance.

3. AIDS is a disorder that causes a breakdown in the body's:
   a. endocrine system.
   b. circulatory system.
   c. immune system.
   d. respiratory system.

4. "Burnout" refers to the:
   a. physical, emotional, and mental exhaustion brought on by persistent job-related stress.
   b. formation of plaques in the coronary arteries.
   c. tendency to respond to stress with anger.
   d. suppression of immune responses.

5. Which of the following statements concerning Type A and B persons is true?
   a. Even when relaxed, Type A persons have higher blood pressure than Type B persons.
   b. When stressed, Type A persons show greater output of epinephrine, norepinephrine, and cortisol than Type B persons.
   c. Type B persons tend to suppress anger more than Type A persons.
   d. Type A persons tend to sleep more than Type B persons.
   e. Type A persons tend to drink fewer caffeinated drinks than Type B persons.

6. According to the text, one-half of all deaths from the 10 leading causes of death in the United States can be attributed to:
   a. stress.
   b. obesity.
   c. nutrition.
   d. behavior.

7. The disease- and infection-fighting cells of the immune system are:
   a. B lymphocytes.
   b. T lymphocytes.
   c. both a. and b.
   d. antigens.

8. One effect of stress on the body is to:
   a. suppress the immune system.
   b. facilitate the immune system response.
   c. increase disease resistance.
   d. increase the growth of B and T lymphocytes.

9. Compared to men, women:
   a. have stronger immune systems.
   b. are less susceptible to infections.
   c. are more susceptible to self-attacking diseases such as multiple sclerosis.
   d. have none of the above characteristics.
   e. have all the characteristics described in a., b., and c.

10. In response to uncontrollable shock, levels of stress hormones _____ and immune responses are _____ .
    a. decrease; suppressed
    b. increase; suppressed
    c. decrease; increased
    d. increase; increased

11. Allergic reactions and arthritis are caused by:
    a. an overreactive immune system.
    b. an underreactive immune system.
    c. the presence of B lymphocytes.
    d. the presence of T lymphocytes.

12. Research on cancer patients reveals that:
    a. those who bottle up their emotions are less likely to survive than those who express them.
    b. patients' attitudes can influence their rate of recovery.
    c. cancer occurs slightly more often than usual among those widowed, divorced, or separated.
    d. all of the above are true.

13. The component of Type A behavior that is the most predictive of coronary disease is:
    a. time urgency.
    b. competitiveness.
    c. high motivation.
    d. impatience.
    e. anger.

14. Which of the following is true concerning smoking treatment programs?
    a. Most are effective in the long run.
    b. Hypnosis is more effective than behavior modification.
    c. Treatment programs are more effective with women than with men.
    d. Most participants eventually resume smoking.

15. During biofeedback training:
    a. a subject is given sensory feedback for a subtle body response.
    b. biological functions controlled by the autonomic nervous system may come under conscious control.
    c. the accompanying relaxation is much the same as that produced by other, simpler methods of relaxation.
    d. all of the above occur.

16. Research on obesity indicates that:
    a. pound for pound, fat tissue requires more calories to maintain than lean tissue.
    b. once fat cells are acquired they are never lost, no matter how rigorously one diets.
    c. one pound of weight is lost for every 3500-calorie reduction in diet.
    d. when weight drops below the set point, hunger and metabolism also decrease.

17. The number of fat cells a person has is influenced by:
    a. genetic predisposition.
    b. childhood eating patterns.
    c. adulthood eating patterns.
    d. all of the above.

18. Relaxation is the most effective technique for preventing:
    a. alcoholism.
    b. a stressful environment.
    c. smoking.
    d. a repeat heart attack.

19. Which of the following was offered in the text as a reason people continue to smoke?
    a. Social pressure from peers is strong.
    b. Cigarettes serve as powerful reinforcers.
    c. Regular use of nicotine impairs the brain's ability to produce neurotransmitters such as serotonin.
    d. Most adults who smoke don't really want to quit.

20. The tendency to overeat when food is plentiful:
    a. is a recent phenomenon that is associated with the luxury of having ample food.
    b. emerged in our prehistoric ancestors as an adaptive response to alternating periods of feast and famine.
    c. is greater in developed, than in developing, societies.
    d. is stronger in women than in men.

21. Which of the following was not suggested as a possible explanation of the "faith factor" in health?
    a. Having a coherent worldview is a buffer against stress.
    b. Religious people tend to have healthier lifestyles.
    c. Those who are religious have stronger networks of social support.
    d. Because they are more affluent, religiously active people receive better health care.

22. (Thinking Critically) Acupuncture, aromatherapy, and homeopathy are forms of:
    a. psychophysiological medicine.
    b. complementary and alternative medicine.
    c. Chi therapy.
    d. psychosomatic medicine.

True–False Items

Indicate whether each statement is true or false by placing *T* or *F* in the blank next to the item.

_____ 1. Most obese people who lose weight eventually gain it back.

_____ 2. Stressors tend to increase activity in the immune system and in this way make people more vulnerable to illness.

_____ 3. Events are most stressful when perceived as both negative and controllable.

_____ 4. Worldwide, per-person cigarette consumption is at an all-time low.

_____ 5. The single most important factor in causing obesity is heredity.

_____ 6. Obesity is often a sign of status and affluence in developing countries.

_____ 7. Optimists cope more successfully with stressful events than do pessimists.

_____ 8. Type A persons are more physiologically reactive to stress than are Type B persons.

_____ 9. Chronic stress can lead to headaches and hypertension.

_____ 10. People with few social and community ties are more likely to die prematurely than are those who have many social ties.

_____ 11. People tend to die younger in areas where there is greater income inequality.

Thinking Critically About Chapter 17

Answer these questions the day before an exam as a final check on your understanding of the chapter's terms and concepts.

Multiple-Choice Questions

1. Which of the following is *not* necessarily a reason that obese people have trouble losing weight?
   a. Fat tissue has a lower metabolic rate than lean tissue.
   b. Once a person has lost weight, it takes fewer calories to maintain his or her current weight.
   c. The tendency toward obesity may be genetically based.
   d. Obese people tend to lack willpower.

2. After an initial rapid weight loss, a person on a diet loses weight much more slowly. This slowdown occurs because:
   a. most of the initial weight loss is simply water.
   b. when a person diets, metabolism decreases.
   c. people begin to "cheat" on their diets.
   d. insulin levels tend to increase with reduced food intake.

3. Concluding her presentation on spirituality and health, Maja notes that:

   a. historically, religion and medicine joined hands in caring for the sick.

   b. most Americans believe that spirituality and religion are related to health.

   c. people who attend religious services weekly have healthier life-styles.

   d. all of the above are true.

4. Malcolm's report on the effects of nicotine mentions each of the following *except*:

   a. increased heart rate.

   b. appetite suppression.

   c. increased circulation to extremities.

   d. release of endorphins triggered by nicotine.

5. Ricardo has an important psychology exam in the afternoon. In an effort to improve his concentration and alertness, he orders a lunch that is high in _____ and low in _____ .

   a. carbohydrates; protein

   b. carbohydrates; fat

   c. protein; carbohydrates

   d. protein; fat

6. (Close-Up) Which of the following would be the *worst* piece of advice to offer to someone trying to lose weight?

   a. "In order to treat yourself to one 'normal' meal each day, eat very little until the evening meal."

   b. "Reduce your consumption of saturated fats."

   c. "Boost your metabolism by exercising regularly."

   d. "Without increasing total caloric intake, increase the relative proportion of carbohydrates in your diet."

7. Each semester, Bob does not start studying until just before midterms. Then he is forced to work around the clock until after final exams, which makes him sick, probably because he is in the _____ phase of the _____ .

   a. alarm; post-traumatic stress syndrome

   b. resistance; general adaptation syndrome

   c. exhaustion; general adaptation syndrome

   d. depletion; post-traumatic stress syndrome

8. Connie complains to the campus psychologist that she has too much stress in her life. The psychologist tells her that the level of stress people experience depends primarily on:

   a. how many activities they are trying to do at the same time.

   b. how they appraise the events of life.

   c. their physical hardiness.

   d. how predictable stressful events are.

9. Calvin was a social worker who counseled troubled families. After several years of breaking up fights and removing abused children from their homes for their own protection, Calvin became so depressed and cynical about his job that he began finding it difficult to go to work. Calvin was probably suffering from:

   a. a Type A response.

   b. the exhaustion phase of the GAS.

   c. the alarm reaction of the GAS.

   d. burnout.

10. Karen and Kyumi are taking the same course with different instructors. Karen's instructor schedules quizzes every Friday, while Kyumi's instructor gives the same number of quizzes on an unpredictable schedule. Assuming that their instructors are equally difficult, which student is probably under more stress?

    a. Karen

    b. Kyumi

    c. There should be no difference in their levels of stress.

    d. It is impossible to predict stress levels in this situation.

11. Jill is an easygoing, noncompetitive person who is happy in her job and enjoys her leisure time. She would *probably* be classified as:

    a. Type A.   c. Type C.

    b. Type B.   d. atherosclerotic.

12. A white blood cell that is formed in the thymus and that attacks cancer cells is:

    a. a macrophage.   c. a T lymphocyte.

    b. a B lymphocyte.   d. any of the above.

13. When would you expect that your immune responses would be *weakest*?

    a. during summer vacation

    b. during exam weeks

    c. just after receiving good news

    d. Immune activity would probably remain constant during these times.

14. Which of the following would be the *best* piece of advice to offer a person who is trying to minimize the adverse effects of stress on his or her health?
    a. "Avoid challenging situations that may prove stressful."
    b. "Learn to play as hard as you work."
    c. "Maintain a sense of control and a positive approach to life."
    d. "Keep your emotional responses in check by keeping your feelings to yourself."

15. I am a widely abused drug that has a calming effect by stimulating the release of dopamine in the central nervous system. What am I?
    a. caffeine   c. nicotine
    b. alcohol   d. cocaine

16. Kenny and his brother have nearly identical eating and exercise habits, yet Kenny is obese and his brother is very thin. The most likely explanation for the difference in their body weights is that they differ in:
    a. their set points.
    b. their metabolic rates.
    c. both a. and b.
    d. none of the above.

17. Dr. Williams, who conducts smoking cessation clinics, explains to his clients that smoking is best understood as an interaction of psychological, biological, and social influences. Dr. Williams is working within the _____ perspective.
    a. behavioral medicine
    b. behavioral
    c. general adaptation syndrome
    d. psychophysiological

18. Philip's physician prescribes a stress management program to help Philip control his headaches. The physician has apparently diagnosed Philip's condition as a _____ illness, rather than a physical disorder.
    a. psychogenic   c. psychophysiological
    b. hypochondriac   d. biofeedback

19. Camelia is worried that her 12-year-old son might begin smoking because many of his classmates do. According to the text, Camelia can most effectively help her son not begin smoking by:
    a. telling him about the dangers of smoking.
    b. telling him that if he begins smoking she will withhold his allowance.

    c. using role-playing to teach him refusal techniques to counteract peer pressure to smoke.
    d. insisting that he not associate with anyone who smokes.

20. You have just transferred to a new campus and find yourself in a potentially stressful environment. According to the text, which of the following would help you cope with the stress?
    a. believing that you have some control over your environment
    b. being able to predict when stressful events will occur
    c. feeling optimistic that you will eventually adjust to your new surroundings
    d. All of the above would help.

21. (Thinking Critically) Andrew, who is convinced that an expensive herbal remedy "cured" his arthritis, has decided to turn to homeopathy and herbal medicine for all of his health care. You caution him by pointing out that:
    a. arthritis is a cyclical disease that often improves on its own.
    b. botanical herbs have never been proven effective in controlled experiments.
    c. alternative medicine is a recent fad in this country that has few proponents in other parts of the world.
    d. all of the above are true.

22. In one study of grave markers in Scotland, researchers found that those with the largest markers tended to live the longest. What possible explanation was offered for this link between economic status and longevity?
    a. People who buy large grave stones are above average in religious activity.
    b. Because those who purchase large grave stones tend to be more affluent, they likely perceived greater control in their lives.
    c. Having a small grave stone may indicate that the person was unhappy, and had low self-esteem .
    d. All of the above explanations were offered in the text.

Essay Question

Discuss several factors that enhance a person's ability to cope with stress. (Use the space below to list the points you want to make and organize them. Then write the essay on a separate sheet of paper.)

Key Terms

Writing Definitions

Using your own words, on a separate piece of paper write a brief definition or explanation of each of the following terms.

1. behavioral medicine
2. health psychology
3. stress
4. general adaptation syndrome (GAS)
5. burnout
6. coronary heart disease
7. Type A
8. Type B
9. psychophysiological illness
10. lymphocytes
11. aerobic exercise
12. biofeedback
13. complementary and alternative medicine

Cross-Check

As you learned in the Introduction, reviewing and overlearning of material are important to the learning process. After you have written the definitions of the key terms in this chapter, you should complete the crossword puzzle to ensure that you can reverse the process—recognize the term, given the definition.

ACROSS

2. "Hardening" of the arteries that leads to heart disease.
7. Fat-detecting hormone.
10. State of exhaustion brought on by unrelenting stress.

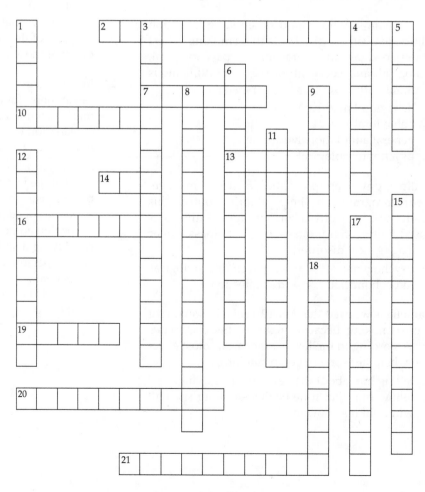

13. Coronary-prone behavior pattern.
14. The three-stage bodily reaction to stress.
16. Type of exercise that may help alleviate anxiety.
18. During the _____ stage of the stress reaction, the body's sympathetic nervous system is suddenly activated.
19. Psychologist who first described the general adaptation syndrome.
20. During the _____ stage of the stress reaction, the body's reserves are depleted.
21. The "big eater" of the immune system.

DOWN

1. Friedman and Rosenman's term for easygoing, relaxed people.
3. Subfield of psychology that contributes to behavioral medicine.
4. The body's weight thermostat.
5. The processes by which people appraise and react to events they perceive as threatening.
6. Phrase coined by Cannon to describe the response of the sympathetic nervous system to a stressor.
8. Our reaction to a potential stressor is determined in part by whether we feel we have _____ _____ over an event.
9. Interdisciplinary health field that treats disease and promotes health.
11. Another name for the stress hormone adrenaline.
12. When our body weight drops below its set point, _____ decreases.
15. White blood cells that form in the bone marrow and release antibodies that fight bacterial infections.
17. The leading cause of death in the United States.

Answers

Introducing Stress and Health

Introduction Preview

1. Because half the mortality from the 10 leading causes of death can be traced to people's behavior, the interdisciplinary field of behavioral medicine emerged with the goal of identifying and modifying these behavioral sources of illness. Health psychology's major concerns include the following: how our emotions and responses to stress influence our risk of disease, how people decide they are sick and whether they will seek and follow treatment, what attitudes and behaviors help prevent illness and promote health and well-being, and how we can reduce or control stress.

Stepping Through the Introduction

1. heart disease; cancer; stroke; chronic lung disease
2. behavior
3. cigarette smoking, alcohol abuse, unprotected sex, ignoring doctors' orders, insufficient exercise, use of illicit drugs, poor nutrition
4. behavioral medicine
5. health

Stress and Illness

Section Preview

1. Stress is the whole process by which we appraise and respond to events that threaten or challenge us. Stress triggers an outpouring of epinephrine, norepinephrine, and cortisol from nerve endings in the adrenal glands of the sympathetic nervous system. These stress hormones increase heart rate and respiration, divert blood to skeletal muscles, and release fat from the body's stores to prepare the body for "fight or flight." Hans Selye saw the body's reaction to stress as having three phases (general adaptation syndrome): the alarm reaction, in which the body's resources are mobilized; resistance, in which stress hormones flow freely to help cope with the stressor; and exhaustion, when reserves are depleted and illness is more likely.

2. Some studies have shown that stressful events, such as catastrophes, are closely followed by an increase in psychological disorders and even deaths. The level of stress we experience depends on how we appraise such events. Catastrophes, significant life changes, and daily hassles are especially stressful when they are appraised as uncontrollable and negative, and when we have a pessimistic outlook. Pessimism and a perceived loss of control, for example, trigger an outpouring of stress hormones. In such circumstances, the mental, physical, and emotional exhaustion of burnout can occur and vulnerability to disease may increase. Lack of control may help explain the fact that poor people are at increased risk for poor health and premature death. Regardless of their income, people also tend to die younger in areas where there is greater income inequality.

3. Friedman and Rosenman discovered that stress triggers a variety of physical changes, such as increased cholesterol and blood-clotting speed, that may promote coronary heart disease. According to their designation, Type A people are competitive, hard-driving, impatient, verbally

aggressive, and easily angered, and thus more prone to coronary disease. The most significant factor is the tendency toward the negative emotions of anger and depression. In contrast, Type B people are more relaxed and easygoing.

4. The immune system includes two types of white blood cells (lymphocytes) that defend the body by destroying foreign substances. The B lymphocytes form in the bone marrow and release antibodies that combat bacterial infections. The T lymphocytes form in the thymus and other lymphatic tissue and attack cancer cells, viruses, and foreign substances. Another immune agent, the macrophage, identifies and ingests harmful invaders.

Stress lowers the body's resistance to disease by suppressing the disease-fighting lymphocytes of the immune system. This may explain the link between stress and AIDS, and between stress and cancer. Stress and negative emotions are positively correlated with the progression from HIV infection to AIDS and a more rapid decline in the health of those who are already infected. Animal research has shown that when the immune system is weakened by stress, tumor cells develop sooner and grow larger. Research has also shown that immune suppression can be classically conditioned. Conversely, studies of cancer patients demonstrate that reducing stress and creating a hopeful, relaxed state may improve chances of survival.

Stepping Through the Section

1. stimulus; response; process; both positive and negative

2. Cannon; epinephrine, or adrenaline; norepinephrine, or noradrenaline; sympathetic; fight or flight

3. adrenal glands; cortisol

4. adrenal; thymus; ulcers; general adaptation syndrome

5. alarm; sympathetic

6. resistance

7. exhaustion; more

8. psychological disorders and stress-related health complaints

9. more

10. daily hassles; racism; hypertension

11. burnout

12. uncontrollable; death

13. inequality; United States; Britain; two to four years; Japan; Sweden

14. optimistic

15. stress hormones (cortisol)

16. coronary heart disease; smoking, obesity, high-fat diet, physical inactivity, elevated blood pressure and cholesterol levels

17. cholesterol; clotting; stress

Type A people were competitive, hard-driving, super-motivated, impatient, verbally aggressive, and easily angered. Type B people were more relaxed and easygoing. Heart attack victims over the course of the study came overwhelmingly from the Type A group.

18. smoking, sleeping less, and drinking more caffeinated beverages

19. do not differ

20. greater than; plaques; atherosclerosis

21. cholesterol; Type A

22. the negative emotions, especially the anger associated with an aggressively reactive temperament

23. increases; stroke; mood; anxiety

24. psychophysiological; hypertension; headaches; stress

25. immune; lymphocytes; B lymphocytes; T lymphocytes; thymus; macrophage

26. arthritis; allergic; underreact; cancer

27. Women; infections; self-attacking; lupus; multiple sclerosis

28. decrease; immune system; brain; muscles

29. AIDS; human immunodeficiency virus (HIV); blood; semen; have

Stress can affect the spread of cancer by weakening the body's defenses against malignant cells. When rodents were inoculated with tumor cells, tumors developed sooner in those that were also exposed to uncontrollable stress. Stress does not cause cancer, however; nor can relaxation prevent it. Cancer patients who remain hopeful and who share their negative emotions with others survive longer than those who keep their feelings bottled up.

30. can

Promoting Health

Section Preview

1. Stress management includes aerobic exercise, biofeedback, relaxation, social support, and spirituality. Aerobic exercise can reduce stress, depression, and anxiety. Research has also shown that those who exercise regularly tend to live longer and suffer from fewer illnesses than those who don't. Exercise may produce its benefits by

increasing the production of mood-boosting neurotransmitters, by strengthening the heart, and by lowering both blood pressure and the blood pressure reaction to stress.

Biofeedback systems allow people to monitor their subtle physiological responses and enjoy a calm, tranquil experience. Simple relaxation produces the same effects, however, including lowered blood pressure and strengthened immune defenses.

2. People with strong social support systems eat better, exercise more, smoke and drink less, and have more opportunities to confide painful feelings. Research shows that such people report fewer illnesses and are less likely to die prematurely than people who lack close supportive relationships. Until fairly recently in history, the healing traditions of religion and medicine worked together. As medicine matured, however, the two traditions separated. There is mounting evidence, however, of a "faith factor" in health and healing. The correlation between religious involvement and health may be due to the fact that religiously active people tend to have healthier life-styles, have stronger networks of social support, and be married.

3. The growing popularity of acupuncture, massage therapy, homeopathy, spiritual healing, and other forms of complementary and alternative medicine in the United States indicates that many people believe such therapies are effective. However, critics point out that alternative medicine seems most effective with cyclical diseases that improve anyway, and with conditions that naturally disappear (spontaneous remission). They also suggest that much of the apparent effectiveness of such treatments is due to a placebo effect. Unfortunately, controlled research studies simply haven't been conducted for many alternative therapies.

4. Smoking usually begins during early adolescence among those who earn low grades, who feel less in control of their futures, and whose friends, parents, and siblings are smokers. Because adolescent smokers tend to be perceived by other teenagers as socially adept, self-conscious adolescents may begin to emulate these models in order to receive the social rewards of peer acceptance. People continue smoking because they develop dependence and tolerance and experience withdrawal symptoms when nicotine is not present, and because smoking serves as a reinforcer that terminates the aversive states that accompany nicotine withdrawal. Nicotine also triggers the release of epinephrine, norepinephrine, and other neurotransmitters, which boost alertness and calm anxiety. Twin studies also point to a large heritability component in smoking; studies have also shown differences between smokers and nonsmokers in a gene that influences responses to dopamine.

Smoking prevention programs that "inoculate" adolescents against peer pressure to smoke by teaching refusal skills have proven effective in reducing the rate of smoking. Programs for adults —counseling, drug treatments, hypnosis, and aversive conditioning, for example—are less effective because all but one-fifth of the participants eventually return to smoking.

5. High-carbohydrate foods increase the amount of the amino acid tryptophan reaching the brain, which raises the level of the relaxation-promoting neurotransmitter serotonin. Low-carbohydrate, high-protein foods improve alertness and concentration. Well-nourished children are happier and more active than children who are malnourished, who may even suffer enduring cognitive deficits when their intake of protein is insufficient. Diets that are based on too many empty sugar calories increase risk of cancer, diabetes, osteoporosis, and other chronic diseases, while those that are higher than normal in salt and lower than normal in calcium may promote hypertension. Finally, diets that are rich in certain "good" fats may reduce depression and support mental health.

6. Obesity is a threat to both physical and psychological well-being. The number of fat cells in our bodies is determined by genetic predisposition, early eating patterns, and adult overeating. Fat cells may shrink in size with dieting, but they will never decrease in number. Because fat tissue has a low metabolic rate, it takes less food energy to maintain, and it is therefore difficult for dieters to lose weight. Because obese persons probably have a higher-than-average set-point weight, when they diet their hunger increases and metabolism decreases, making it even more difficult for them to lose weight.

7. Adoption and twin studies both provide evidence for a genetic influence on body weight. Recent animal studies reveal that obese mice may have a defective gene for producing the fat-signaling protein, leptin. When obese mice are treated with leptin, they eat less, become more active, and lose weight. In obese humans, leptin receptors are insensitive to leptin. In spite of these studies, genes cannot explain why the percentage of overweight and obese people is increasing worldwide

or why obesity is much more common in lower-class than in upper-class women and more common among Americans than Europeans.

Stepping Through the Chapter

1. aerobic; have
2. norepinephrine; serotonin; endorphins; 2
3. biofeedback; do not provide
4. relaxation
5. reduced
6. humor
7. social

People with strong social ties may be healthier because they eat better, exercise more, and smoke and drink less. Close relationships also provide the opportunity to bolster self-esteem and to confide painful feelings, which may mitigate physical reactions to stressful events.

8. religion; medicine; together
9. believe
10. predicts

Religiously active people have healthier life-styles. They also tend to have stronger networks of social support and are more likely to be married.

11. complementary and alternative medicine; herbal; Qi or Chi
12. cyclical; allergic reactions; spontaneous remission; placebo
13. prevent; treating

Smoking is associated with lung cancer, respiratory ailments, heart disease, higher rates of depression, chronic disabilities, and divorce.

14. early adolescence; earn low grades, feel less competent and in control of their future, and have friends, parents, and siblings who smoke; social-cognitive
15. dependent; tolerance; withdrawal
16. reinforcer; alertness; anxiety; pain sensitivity
17. 60 percent; gene; dopamine
18. are not; males; higher
19. high; developing
20. less
21. neurotransmitters
22. carbohydrates; serotonin; protein
23. salt; calcium
24. famine; affluence; status
25. thin-ideal for women
26. does not; less

Obesity increases one's risk of diabetes, high blood pressure and heart disease, gallstones, arthritis, and certain types of cancer. It negatively affects self-image and the perceptions of others, particularly if the excess weight is seen as the fault of the individual.

27. obese
28. 3500; fat cells; genetic predisposition, early childhood eating patterns, adult overeating
29. can; cannot
30. lower; less
31. is; hunger; metabolism

Obese persons have higher set-point weights than nonobese persons. During a diet, metabolic rate drops to defend the set-point weight. The dieter therefore finds it hard to progress beyond an initial weight loss. When the diet is concluded, the lowered metabolic rate continues, so that relatively small amounts of food may prove fattening. Also, some people have lower metabolic rates than others.

32. do
33. gene; leptin; brain; eating; activity; more; lose
34. more; does; 25; 30; increasing
35. gain

Progress Test 1

1. c. is the answer. (p. 601)
   a. Health psychology is a subfield within behavioral medicine.
   b. Holistic medicine is an older term that refers to medical practitioners who take more of an interdisciplinary approach to treating disorders.
   d. Osteopathy is a medical therapy that emphasizes manipulative techniques for correcting physical problems.

2. c. is the answer. (p. 603)
   a., b., & d. The pituitary does not produce stress hormones nor is the parasympathetic division involved in arousal.

3. c. is the answer. (p. 604)
   a. & b. During these stages the body's defensive mechanisms are at peak function.
   d. This is not a stage of the GAS.

4. c. is the answer. Coronary heart disease is followed by cancer, stroke, and chronic lung disease. AIDS has not yet become one of the four leading causes of death in North America among the general population. (p. 609)

5. c. is the answer. (p. 609)
   a. & b. Researchers have not identified such personality types.

d. Individuals who are more easygoing are labeled Type B.

6. **b.** is the answer. These stress hormones accelerate the buildup of plaques, or masses formed by cholesterol deposits, on the artery walls. This likely occurs because during arousal blood is diverted from internal organs such as the liver, which removes cholesterol from the blood, to the muscles of the body. These hormones are released in response to stress; they do not reduce stress. (p. 610)

7. **a.** is the answer. (p. 611)
   b. Hypochondriacs think something is wrong with them, but nothing physical can be detected.
   c. *Psychogenic* means "originating in the mind." One's reaction to stress is partially psychological, but this term is not used to refer to stress-related illness.
   d. There is no such term.

8. **e.** is the answer. Because stress depresses the immune system, stressed individuals are prone to all of these conditions. (pp. 607, 612–613)

9. **c.** is the answer. (p. 602)
   a., b., & d. Whether an event is stressful or not depends on how it is appraised.

10. **d.** is the answer. (p. 607)

11. **a.** is the answer. (p. 635)

12. **a.** is the answer. Certain high-carbohydrate foods raise the levels of serotonin, which facilitates relaxation by increasing the amount of tryptophan reaching the brain. (p. 631)
    b. Cortisol is a stress hormone and hence not related either to carbohydrates or to relaxation.
    c. & d. Meals that are high in protein promote alertness.

13. **c.** is the answer. The finding that talking about grief leads to better health makes a lot of sense in light of this physiological finding. (p. 621)
    a., b., & d. The study by Pennebaker did not find these to be true.

14. **b.** is the answer. People generally *start* smoking in adolescence in order to gain peer acceptance; they continue smoking primarily because they have become addicted to nicotine. Thus, the factors that motivate people to start smoking are best described as social, whereas the factors that explain continued smoking are mainly biological. (pp. 536–537)

15. **a.** is the answer. (pp. 627–628)

16. **a.** is the answer. (p. 635)

17. **d.** is the answer. Regular aerobic exercise has been shown to increase ability to cope with stress, lower blood pressure, and reduce depression and anxiety. The text does not cite evidence that exercise enhances immune function. (pp. 616–617)

18. **d.** is the answer. (pp. 605–606)

19. **b.** is the answer. (p. 614)

20. **b.** is the answer. (p. 620)

21. **c.** is the answer. (p. 612)

22. **d.** is the answer. (p. 623)
    b. & c. The text does not indicate that a gender difference exists in the "faith factor" in health.

Progress Test 2

Multiple-Choice Questions

1. **d.** is the answer. This chapter deals with the topics of health psychology, namely, preventing illness, as by developing better ways to cope with stress; treating illness, as by improving the ways in which people notice and explain symptoms; and promoting health, for example, through nutrition and weight control. (p. 601)

2. **a.** is the answer. (p. 604)

3. **c.** is the answer. (p. 612)

4. **a.** is the answer. (p. 607)
   b. This defines atherosclerosis.
   c. This defines the Type A personality.

5. **b.** is the answer. The greater reactivity of Type A people includes much higher levels of stress hormones in stress situations. (p. 610)
   a. Under relaxed situations, there is no difference in blood pressure.
   c. Anger, both expressed and suppressed, is more characteristic of Type A people.
   d. & e. Type A persons tend to sleep less and drink more caffeinated drinks.

6. **d.** is the answer. Behaviors that contribute to the leading causes of mortality include smoking, excessive alcohol consumption, maladaptive responses to stress, insufficient exercise, use of illicit drugs, and poor nutrition. (p. 601)

7. **c.** is the answer. B lymphocytes fight bacterial infections; T lymphocytes attack cancer cells, viruses, and foreign substances. (p. 611)
   d. Antigens cause the production of antibodies when they are introduced into the body.

8. **a.** is the answer. A variety of studies have shown that stress depresses the immune system, increasing the risk and potential severity of many diseases. (pp. 611–612)

9. **e.** is the answer. (p. 611)

10. **b.** is the answer. Both human and animal studies indicate that uncontrollable negative events trigger an outpouring of stress hormones and a drop in immune responses. (p. 609)

11. **a.** is the answer. (p. 611)
    b. An *under*reactive immune system would make an individual more susceptible to infectious diseases or the proliferation of cancer cells.
    c. & d. Lymphocytes are the disease- and infection-fighting white blood cells of the immune system.

12. **d.** is the answer. (p. 613)

13. **e.** is the answer. The crucial characteristic of Type A behavior seems to be a tendency to react with negative emotions, especially anger; other aspects of Type A behavior appear not to predict heart disease, and some appear to be helpful to the individual. (p. 610)

14. **d.** is the answer. No particular treatment seemed to stand out in terms of effectiveness. All but one-fifth of the people who quit smoking in such programs eventually return to the habit. (p. 629)

15. **d.** is the answer. In biofeedback training, subjects are given sensory feedback about autonomic responses. Although biofeedback may promote relaxation, its benefits may be no greater than those produced by simpler, and less expensive, methods. (pp. 617–618)

16. **b.** is the answer. Fat cells may change in size as a person gains or loses weight, but their number never decreases. (p. 634)
    a. In fact, because of its lower metabolic rate, fat tissue can be maintained on *fewer* calories.
    c. Because metabolism slows as food intake is restricted, a 3500-calorie reduction may not reduce weight by one pound.
    d. In fact, just the opposite is true.

17. **d.** is the answer. (p. 634)

18. **d.** is the answer. Friedman's subjects who received counseling on relaxation experienced half as many repeat heart attacks as did a control group. (p. 619)

19. **b.** is the answer. By alleviating the aversive physiological state of nicotine withdrawal, cigarettes act as negative reinforcers. (p. 628)
    a. This is one explanation of why adolescents *start* smoking.
    c. There is no evidence that this occurs.
    d. Most smokers would like to quit smoking.

20. **b.** is the answer. (p. 632)
    c. If anything, just the opposite is true.
    d. Men and women do not differ in the tendency to overeat.

21. **d.** is the answer. As a group, religiously active people are no more affluent than other people. (pp. 623–625)

22. **b.** is the answer. (p. 624)
    a. There is no such subfield of medicine.
    b. Chi is an alleged form of energy, imbalances of which Chinese herbal therapies and acupuncture are intended to treat.
    d. The term psychosomatic was once used to describe psychologically caused symptoms. Many forms of alternative medicine, including acupuncture, are intended to treat a full range of symptoms and diseases.

True-False Items

1. T (p. 637)   6. T (p. 632)   11. T (p. 608)
2. F (p. 611)   7. T (p. 608)
3. F (p. 607)   8. T (p. 610)
4. F (p. 630)   9. T (p. 611)
5. F (p. 636)   10. T (p. 620)

Thinking Critically About Chapter 17

Multiple-Choice Questions

1. **d.** is the answer. Most researchers today discount the idea that people are obese because they lack willpower. (p. 634)

2. **b.** is the answer. Following the initial weight loss, metabolism drops as the body attempts to defend its set-point weight. This drop in metabolism means that eating an amount that once produced a loss in weight may now actually result in weight gain. (p. 634)

3. **d.** is the answer. (pp. 622–625)

4. **c.** is the answer. Nicotine *reduces* circulation to the extremities of the body. (p. 628)

5. **c.** is the answer. High-protein foods seem to improve alertness, whereas high-carbohydrate foods seem to promote relaxation. (pp. 631–632)

6. **a.** is the answer. Dieting, including fasting, lowers the body's metabolic rate and reduces the amount of food energy needed to maintain body weight. (p. 638)
    b., c., & d. Each of these strategies would be a good piece of advice to a dieter.

7. **c.** is the answer. According to Selye's general adaptation syndrome, diseases are most likely to occur in this final stage. (p. 604)
    a. & b. Resistance to disease is greater during the alarm and resistance phases because the body's mobilized resources are not yet depleted.

d. There is no such thing as the "depletion phase." Moreover, the post-traumatic stress syndrome refers to the haunting nightmares and anxiety of those who have suffered extreme stress, such as that associated with combat.

8. **b.** is the answer. (p. 603)

a., c., & d. Each of these is a factor in coping with stress, but it is how an event is *perceived* that determines whether it is stressful or not.

9. **d.** is the answer. Burnout refers to the physical, mental, and emotional exhaustion that may emerge from unrelenting job-related stress. (p. 607)

a. A Type A personality is one who responds to stress with anger.

b. & c. The alarm reaction and exhaustion are the first and third phases of the general adaptation syndrome.

10. **b.** is the answer. Unpredictable events are more stressful than predictable events. (p. 607)

11. **b.** is the answer. (p. 609)

a. Type A persons are hard-driving and competitive.

c. There is no such thing as a "Type C" person.

d. Atherosclerosis refers to the blockage of the arteries that leads to coronary heart disease. Type A persons are more susceptible to atherosclerosis than Type B persons.

12. **c.** is the answer. (p. 611)

a. Macrophages are immune agents that search for and ingest harmful invaders.

b. B lymphocytes form in the bone marrow and release antibodies that fight bacterial infections.

13. **b.** is the answer. Stressful situations, such as exam weeks, decrease immune responses. (p. 612)

14. **c.** is the answer. (pp. 607–608)

a. This is not realistic.

b. & d. These might actually *increase* the health consequences of potential stressors.

15. **c.** is the answer. (p. 628)

a. Caffeine has a stimulating rather than a calming effect.

b. Alcohol *depresses* activity in the central nervous system.

c. Cocaine increases dopamine by blocking its reuptake from synapses.

16. **c.** is the answer. Individual differences in metabolism and set point explain why it is possible for two people to have very different weights despite similar patterns of eating and exercise. (p. 635)

17. **a.** is the answer. (p. 601)

b. The behavioral perspective would emphasize only learned factors in smoking.

c. The general adaptation syndrome is a sequence of bodily responses to stress.

d. Psychophysiological illnesses are illnesses not caused by any known physical disorder.

18. **c.** is the answer. (p. 611)

a. The text does not discuss any such thing as a "psychogenic" illness.

b. Hypochondriasis is the misinterpreting of normal physical sensations as symptoms of a disease.

d. Biofeedback is a system for recording information regarding a subtle physiological state, such as blood pressure.

19. **c.** is the answer. (p. 630)

20. **d.** is the answer. (pp. 607–608)

21. **a.** is the answer. (p. 625)

b. In fact, botanical herbs have given us many widely used drugs, including morphine and penicillin, each of which was proven to be useful in controlled research studies.

c. Herbal remedies and acupuncture—to name two forms of complementary and alternative medicine—have a long tradition in other parts of the world, and remain enormously popular today.

22. **b.** is the answer. (p. 608)

Essay Question

When potentially stressful events occur, a person's appraisal is a major determinant of their impact. Catastrophes, significant life events, and daily hassles are especially stressful when appraised as negative, unpredictable, and uncontrollable, and when the person has a pessimistic outlook on life. Under these circumstances, stressful events may suppress immune responses and make the person more vulnerable to disease. If stressors cannot be eliminated, aerobic exercise, biofeedback, relaxation, and social support can help the person cope. Aerobic exercise can reduce stress, depression, and anxiety, perhaps by increasing production of mood-boosting neurotransmitters. During biofeedback training, people enjoy a calm, relaxing experience that can be helpful in reducing stress. Research demonstrates that people who regularly practice relaxation techniques enjoy a greater sense of tranquility and have lower blood pressure and stronger immune responses. People with strong social ties eat better, exercise more, and smoke and drink less. Social support may also help people evaluate and overcome stressful events. In addition, confiding painful feelings to others has been demonstrated to reduce the physiological responses linked to stress.

Key Terms

1. **Behavioral medicine** is the interdisciplinary field that applies behavioral and medical knowledge to the treatment of disease and the promotion of health. (p. 601)

2. **Health psychology** is a subfield of psychology that studies how health and illness are influenced by emotions, stress, personality, life-style, and other psychological factors. (p. 601)

3. **Stress** refers to the process by which people perceive and react to stressors, or to events they perceive as threatening or challenging. (p. 602)

4. The **general adaptation syndrome (GAS)** is the three-stage sequence of bodily reaction to stress outlined by Hans Selye. (p. 604)

5. **Burnout** refers to a state of physical, mental, and emotional exhaustion brought on by unrelenting job-related stress. (p. 607)

6. The leading cause of death in the United States today, **coronary heart disease** results from the clogging of the coronary arteries and the subsequent reduction in blood and oxygen supply to the heart muscle. (p. 609)

7. **Type A** personality is Friedman and Rosenman's term for the coronary-prone behavior pattern of competitive, hard-driving, impatient, verbally aggressive, and anger-prone people. (p. 609)

8. **Type B** personality is Friedman and Rosenman's term for the coronary-resistant behavior pattern of easygoing people. (p. 609)

9. A **psychophysiological illness** is any genuine illness such as hypertension and headaches that is apparently linked to stress rather than caused by a physical disorder. (p. 611)

Memory aid: Psycho- refers to mind; *physio-* refers to body; a **psychophysiological illness** is a mind-body disorder.

10. **Lymphocytes** are the two types of white blood cells of the immune system that fight bacterial infections (B lymphocytes) and viruses, cancer cells, and foreign substances in the body (T lymphocytes). (p. 611)

11. **Aerobic exercise** is any sustained activity such as running, swimming, or cycling that promotes heart and lung fitness and may help alleviate depression and anxiety. (p. 616)

12. **Biofeedback** refers to a system for electronically recording, amplifying, and feeding back information regarding a subtle physiological state. (p. 617)

Memory aid: A **biofeedback** device, such as a brain-wave trainer, provides auditory or visual feedback about biological responses.

13. **Complementary and alternative medicine** is a collection of health care remedies and treatments that have not been accepted by medical science nor verified by controlled research trials. (p. 624)

Cross-Check

ACROSS

2. atherosclerosis	
7. leptin	
10. burnout	
13. Type A	
14. GAS	
16. aerobic	
18. alarm	
19. Selye	
20. exhaustion	
21. macrophage	

1. Type B	
3. health psychology	
4. set point	
5. stress	
6. fight or flight	
8. perceived control	
9. behavioral medicine	
11. epinephrine	
12. metabolism	
15. B lymphocytes	
17. heart disease	

FOCUS ON VOCABULARY AND LANGUAGE

Stress and Illness

Page 602: Afterward, she notices her *tense* muscles, *clenched teeth*, and *churning stomach*. Our response to stress can be beneficial (e.g., Karl's escape from the snake) or destructive (e.g., Karen's reaction to relatively minor routine problems or *daily hassles*). Following a number of stressful events (missing her train, rush-hour pedestrian traffic, late for an appointment, etc.), she becomes aware of her physiological reaction. Her muscles feel strained and taut (*tense*), her jaws are clamped shut (*clenched teeth*), and her stomach feels upset (*churning stomach*).

Page 602: Stress is a *slippery concept.* The term *stress* is often used to describe a stimulus (a threatening or challenging event) or a response (fear or anxiety). Most psychologists refer to the former as a *stressor,* the latter as a *stress reaction,* and use the word *stress* to refer to the entire process of evaluating and dealing with threatening events. Thus, stress is not a simple or easily grasped (understood) construct (*it is a slippery concept*).

Pages 602–603: The events of our lives *flow through a psychological filter.* Myers makes the important point that it is not so much the actual events that happen to us, but rather, it is our evaluation and appraisal of these events that determine their effect on us. Thus, it is not just your experiences, but what you think about them (*they flow through a psychological filter*) that affects your well-being.

Page 604: Your heart rate *zooms.* According to Selye's general adaptation syndrome (GAS), there are three phases in our response to stress: *alarm reaction, resistance,* and *exhaustion.* During the first phase, the sympathetic nervous system responds rapidly; your heart rate quickly increases (*zooms*), blood is directed to the muscles, and you experience the weakness associated with being startled. You are now ready to fight or cope with the stressor (*resistance phase*); if the situation is not resolved soon, you will experience *exhaustion* (the third phase).

Page 606: . . . *uprooting* . . . Refugees and others who are forcibly made to leave their homes (*they are uprooted*) have increased rates of depression, anxiety, psychological disorders, and other stress symptoms. In most instances, the health impairments come from long-term exposure to stress.

Page 606: Experiencing *a cluster of crises* puts one even more at risk. Important and significant changes in our lives are other types of life-event stressors that increase the probability of health problems. If a number of these events occur close together (*a cluster of crises*), people become more vulnerable to disease.

Page 606: Daily Hassles Small, routine, annoying events and the little things that go wrong day by day (*daily hassles*) can have an accumulative effect on health and well-being. Some people can handle these daily hassles (*they shrug them off*) while others are severely distressed (*"driven up the wall"*) by these inconveniences. Continual work-related hassles can lead to mental, physical, and emotional exhaustion (**burnout**).

Page 610: Moreover, not one of the *"pure"* Type Bs —the most *mellow* and *laid-back* of their group—had suffered a *heart attack.* Researchers have identified two personality types: Type As are reactive (*easily angered*), competitive, verbally aggressive, highly motivated, always rushed, and lacking in patience; Type Bs are less easily angered (*mellow*), are easy-going (*laid-back*), patient, understanding, and non-competitive. The most prototypical (*"pure"*) Type Bs were the least likely to be afflicted by coronary heart disease (*heart attacks*).

Page 610: But *after the honeymoon period,* in which the finding seemed definitive and revolutionary, other researchers began asking, Is the finding reliable? The discovery of the relationship between personality type (A or B) and health and well-being aroused much interest. However, once the initial excitement abated (*after the honeymoon period*), other investigators started more detailed research and asked questions about the specific mechanisms involved in personality type and risk of disease.

Page 610: These findings suggest that reactive Type A individuals are more often *"combat ready."* Research has shown that Type As are physiologically more reactive and ready to fight (*combat ready*) than Type Bs. When stressed, their sympathetic nervous systems operate to increase the levels of cholesterol and fat in the blood; in addition, their negative (*toxic*) emotions, especially anger and depression, make them more coronary-prone.

Page 611: Your immune system is not *a headless horseman.* The immune system does not operate as an autonomous system independent of other systems (*a headless horseman*). Instead, it works in close harmony with various brain systems and with the endocrine system, which secretes hormones. All these interact and affect each other in a very complex way.

Page 612: Marital spats are not good for health. Research has shown that when couples argue or fight (have *marital spats*), their negative emotions increase, and they are more likely to suffer suppression of their immune systems.

Page 613: What is more, cancer patients who *bottle up* their negative emotions have less chance of survival than do those who verbalized their feelings. . . . Patients' attitudes can have an effect on the outcome of their disease. Those who are always trying to please others (*ever-nice*) or are constantly looking for approval and afraid to express their true feelings (*bottled-up emotions*) are more likely to die sooner compared to those who openly and honestly talk about how they feel.

Promoting Health

Page 616: Many of them had, quite literally, *run away from their troubles.* Many research studies have shown the beneficial effect of aerobic exercise on depression and anxiety. In one study, women who took up jogging (*running*) showed a substantial reduction in depression. As Myers humorously puts it, they had, in reality, *run away from their problems.*

Page 617: The *"mood boost"* is reaping health dividends as well. So off your *duffs, couch potatoes!* Regular exercise increases longevity and cardiovascular fitness, reduces depression and anxiety, and enhances positive emotional states (*boosts our moods*). So the popular trend toward being more physically active has many benefits (*is reaping dividends*). Myers admonishes those of us who sit around, watch TV, and eat junk food (*couch potatoes*) to get off our back-sides (*duffs*) and get active.

Page 618: After a decade of study, researchers *stepped back* to assess the results and decided the initial claims for biofeedback were *overblown and oversold* (Miller, 1985). Biofeedback became very popular in the 1970s, and the reports of its effectiveness for all kinds of problems led to much excitement. By the mid-1980s, however, when researchers took the time (*stepped back*) to evaluate the research findings objectively, it became clear that these assertions were exaggerated (*overblown*) and falsely promoted (*oversold*). Simple relaxation without the use of costly equipment is just as beneficial.

Page 619: Although it would probably be an over-statement to suggest that *"laughter is the best medicine,"* there is reason to suspect that those who laugh, last. Research has shown the beneficial health effects of laughter, which appears to act as a block or *buffer* against stress-induced problems (*"laughter is the best medicine"*). Those who have a good sense of humor and can find something funny in stressful life events tend to be healthier and may live longer (*those who laugh, last*). (This final phrase is a twist on the saying *"Those who laugh last, laugh longest"* or *"Getting the last laugh."*)

Page 620: . . . *heartaches* . . . *Heartaches* is a term that refers to persistent mental anguish or suffering, usually resulting from the loss of a loved one or from disappointment in love. Myers points out that while close relationships and family tend to contribute to our well-being and contentment, they also can be the cause of much misery, strain, and strife (*heartaches*).

Page 621: Talking about our troubles can be *"open heart therapy."* Research has shown that those with close, supportive friends and family tend to have fewer health problems and live longer. One reason for this may be that trusting relationships provide the opportunity to talk about our problems and feelings and, just as "open-heart surgery" can save lives, having someone to talk to can be a form of *"open-heart therapy."*

Page 628: . . . *cool models* . . . People usually begin to smoke during early adolescence; those who don't start during the teen years are much less likely to become habitual smokers as adults. Smoking starts much like many other behaviors, through imitating others (*through modeling*); teenage smokers are often viewed by their peers as self-possessed, mature, strong, outgoing, and friendly (*cool models*).

Page 628: . . . *slow-motion suicide.* Smoking is continued because, among other reasons, it offers a pleasant feeling (*pleasurable lift*) and it escapes or avoids the unpleasant persistent desire (*craving*) of deprivation or withdrawal. The negative aspect of smoking, however, is the increased health risk which over time may result in the death of the smoker (*slow-motion suicide*).

Page 629: But among college students and graduates, smoking has become *gauche* rather than *cool.* . . . High school dropouts and those of lower socioeconomic status are more likely to smoke than college or university students and graduates. For this population, smoking is seen as undesirable, unpopular, and socially unacceptable (*gauche*) instead of being fashionably trendy (*cool*).

Page 630: They also *role-played* calling someone a *"chicken"* for not trying a cigarette and responding with statements like, "I'd be a real *chicken* if I smoked just to impress you." As part of an effort to stop youngsters from trying cigarettes in the first place, researchers set up a smoking *"inoculation"* program. Students were trained to be mentally prepared (*inoculated*) to resist arguments about the desirability of cigarette smoking by acting the part of (*role-playing*) a person who is being called a coward (*a chicken*) for refusing to smoke. These and other smoking prevention programs have met with some success.

Page 632: Does *skipping* breakfast matter? Researchers have found that what we eat (*nutrition*) affects the way we feel, think, and act. Children who have a well-balanced diet of nourishing foods are more energetic and happy at play, and people who eat breakfast are more attentive and awake and less tired later in the day than those who miss (*skip*) the first meal of the day.

Page 632: And why do so few overweight people *win the battle of the bulge*? Most overweight people who diet do not manage to permanently lose the many pounds of fat they want to (*they do not win the battle of the bulge*). Myers discusses a number of factors: (a) the number of fat cells in the body does not decrease when you diet; (b) the tissue in fat is easier to maintain and uses less energy than other tissue; and (c) when body weight drops below the set point, your overall metabolic rate slows down. For those wanting to diet, Myers lists some useful tips (see p. 638).

Page 635: Being overweight is therefore *not* simply a matter of *scarfing* too many *hot fudge sundaes.* And losing weight is not simply a matter of *mind over platter*. Research has shown that being obese (*over-weight*) is not a function of hungrily devouring (*scarfing*) an excessive number of desserts made from ice cream covered with chocolate sauce, fruit, whipped cream, etc. (*hot fudge sundaes*), nor is it a matter of willpower (*mind over matter*) or the ability to be able to resist the food on your plate (*mind over platter*).

Page 637: For most people, however, the only long-term result is a *thinner wallet*. Most commercial weight-loss programs cost a great deal of money but, at best, only help people lose weight temporarily. For those who lose and then regain weight over and over again (*yo-yo dieting*), the end result is usually a greater weight gain each time and ultimately having less money (*thinner wallets*).

CHAPTER 18:

Social Psychology

Chapter Overview

Chapter 18 demonstrates the powerful influences of social situations on the behavior of individuals. Central to this topic are research studies on attitudes and actions, conformity, compliance, and group and cultural influences. The social principles that emerge help us to understand how individuals are influenced by advertising, political candidates, and the various groups to which they belong. Although social influences are powerful, it is important to remember the significant role of individuals in choosing and creating the social situations that influence them.

The chapter also discusses how people relate to one another, from the negative—developing prejudice, behaving aggressively, and provoking conflict—to the positive—being attracted to people who are nearby and/or similar and behaving altruistically.

The chapter concludes with a discussion of techniques that have been shown to promote conflict resolution.

Although there is some terminology for you to learn in this chapter, your primary task is to absorb the findings of the many research studies discussed. The chapter headings, which organize the findings, should prove especially useful to you here. In addition, you might, for each main topic (conformity, group influence, aggression, etc.), ask yourself the question, "What situational factors promote this phenomenon?" The research findings can then form the basis for your answers.

NOTE: Answer guidelines for all Chapter 18 questions begin on page 514.

Social Thinking (pp. 643–649)

David Myers at times uses idioms that are unfamiliar to some readers. If you do not know the meaning of any of the following words, phrases, or expressions in the context in which they appear in the text, refer to page 525 for an explanation: *typecast; tart-tongued remark; free-loaders; people often talk and act a different game; brainwashed; chicken-and-egg spiral; heartening implications.*

Section Preview

First, skim the section, noting headings and boldface items. Then read the following objectives and, as you read the text, search for the information that will enable you to meet each objective. Answer guidelines are provided on page 514.

1. Discuss attribution theory, focusing on the fundamental attribution error, and describe some possible effects of attribution.

2. Define *attitude* and identify the conditions under which attitudes predict behavior.

3. Describe how actions influence attitudes, and explain how cognitive dissonance theory accounts for this phenomenon.

Stepping Through the Section

After you have read the section, complete the sentences and answer the questions. As you proceed, evaluate your performance by consulting the answers on page 515. Do not continue with the next section until you understand each answer. If you need to, review or reread the section in the textbook before continuing.

1. Psychologists who study how we think about, influence, and relate to one another are called

_____ _____ .

2. Heider's theory of how we explain others' behavior is the _____ theory. According to this theory, we attribute behavior either to an internal cause, which is called a

_____ _____ ,

or to an external cause, which is called a

_____ _____ .

3. Most people tend to_____ (overestimate/underestimate) the extent to which people's actions are influenced by social situations because their _____ is focused on the person. This tendency is called the

_____

_____ . When a person is explaining his or her *own* behavior, this tendency is _____ (stronger/weaker). When observers view the world from others' perspectives, attributions are _____ (the same/reversed).

Give an example of the practical consequences of attributions.

4. Beliefs and feelings that predispose our responses are called _____ .

5. The many research studies on attitudes and actions conducted during the 1960s

_____ (challenged/supported) the common assumption that our actions are guided by our attitudes.

List three conditions under which our attitudes do predict our actions. Give examples.

6. Many research studies demonstrate that our attitudes are strongly influenced by our

_____ . One example of this is the tendency for people who agree to a small request to comply later with a larger one. This is the _____ - _____ -

_____ - _____

phenomenon.

7. When you follow the social prescriptions for how you should act as, say, a college student, you are adopting a _____ .

8. Taking on a set of behaviors, or acting in a certain way, generally _____ (changes/does not change) people's attitudes.

9. According to _____

_____ theory, thoughts and feelings change because people are motivated to justify actions that would otherwise seem hypocritical. This theory was proposed by

_____ .

10. Dissonance theory predicts that people induced (without coercion) to behave contrary to their true attitudes will be motivated to reduce the resulting _____ by changing their _____ .

Social Influence (pp. 649–661)

> If you do not know the meaning of any of the following words, phrases, or expressions in the context in which they appear in the text, refer to pages 525–526 for an explanation: *canned laughter; open-minded; draw slips from a hat; draw back; kindness and obedience on a collision course; zap; devilish villains; tug-of-war; one-way flight to annihilation; waffles.*

Section Preview

Answer guidelines are provided on page 515.

1. Describe the results of Asch's experiments on conformity, and distinguish between normative and informational social influence.

2. Summarize the findings from Milgram's obedience studies.

3. Discuss how the presence of others may produce social facilitation, social loafing, or deindividuation.

4. Describe group polarization and show how it can be a source of groupthink.

5. Discuss how personal control and social control interact in guiding behavior, and explain how a minority can influence the majority.

Stepping Through the Section

Answers are provided on page 516.

1. The "chameleon effect" refers to our natural tendency to unconsciously _____ others' expressions, postures, and voice tones.

2. Copycat violence is a serious example of the effects of _____ on behavior.

3. The term that refers to the tendency to adjust one's behavior to coincide with an assumed group standard is _____ .

4. The psychologist who first studied the effects of group pressure on conformity is _____ .

5. In this study, when the opinion of other group members was contradicted by objective evidence, subjects _____ (were/were not) willing to conform to the group opinion.

6. One reason that people comply with social pressure is to gain approval or avoid rejection; this is called _____ _____ .

Understood rules for accepted and expected behavior are called social _____ .

7. Another reason people comply is that they have genuinely been influenced by what they have learned from others; this type of influence is called _____ _____ .

8. In one experiment, Robert Baron found that subjects were more likely to conform to the group's judgments when the task was construed as _____ (important/unimportant) and when it was _____ (easy/difficult).

9. Conformity rates tend to be lower in _____ (individualistic/collectivistic) cultures.

10. The classic social psychology studies of obedience were conducted by _____ .
When ordered by the experimenter to electrically shock the "learner," the majority of subjects (the "teachers") in these studies _____ (complied/refused). Recent studies have found that women's compliance rates in similar situations were _____ (higher than/lower than/similar to) men's.

List the conditions under which obedience was highest in Milgram's studies.

11. In getting people to administer increasingly larger shocks, Milgram was in effect applying the _____-_____-_____-_____ technique.

12. The tendency to perform a task better when other people are present is called _____ _____ . In general, people become aroused in the presence of others, and arousal enhances the correct response on a(n) _____ (easy/difficult) task. Later research revealed that arousal strengthens the response that is most _____ in a given situation.

13. Researchers have found that the reactions of people in crowded situations are often _____ (lessened/amplified).

14. Ingham found that people worked _____ (harder/less hard) in a team tug-of-war than they had in an individual contest. This phenomenon has been called _____ _____ .

15. The feeling of anonymity and loss of restraint that an individual may develop when in a group is called _____ .

16. Over time, the initial differences between groups usually _____ (increase/decrease). The enhancement of each group's prevailing tendency is called _____ _____ .

Future research studies will reveal whether electronic discussions on the _____ also demonstrate this tendency.

17. When the desire for group harmony overrides realistic thinking in individuals, the phenomenon known as _____ has occurred.

18. In considering the power of social influence, we cannot overlook the interaction of

_____ _____ (the power of the situation) and

_____ _____ (the power of the individual).

19. When our expectations of how people will behave cause us to treat them in ways that elicit such behaviors, our expectations become

_____ _____ .

20. A minority opinion will have the most success in swaying the majority if it takes a stance that is _____ (unswerving/flexible).

Social Relations (pp. 661–688)

> If you do not know the meaning of any of the following words, phrases, or expressions in the context in which they appear in the text, refer to pages 526–528 for an explanation: *"horsing around"; with the toss of a coin; boost ingroup members' self-esteem; Ferdinand; skyrocketed; she melts; an outlet for bottled-up impulses; diabolical images; familiarity breeds fondness; "beauty is only skin deep"; E.T. was uglier than Darth Vader; opposites retract; revved up; bystanders turns people away from the path that leads to helping; blasé; "sneaky," "smart-alecky stinkers"; down the tension ladder to a safer rung.*

Section Preview

Answer guidelines are provided on page 516.

1. Describe the roles of social inequalities, ingroup bias, and scapegoating in prejudice.

2. Discuss the cognitive roots of prejudice.

3. Describe the impact of biology, aversive events, and learning experiences on aggressive behavior.

4. Discuss the effects of television violence and pornographic films on viewers.

5. Identify factors that fuel conflict, and discuss effective ways of resolving such conflict.

6. Identify the determinants of social attraction and distinguish between passionate and companionate love.

7. Describe and explain the bystander effect.

8. Discuss how social exchange theory and social norms explain altruism.

Stepping Through the Section

Answers are provided on page 517.

1. Prejudice is an _____ and usually _____ attitude toward a group that involves overgeneralized beliefs known as _____ .

2. Americans today express _____ (less/the same/more) racial and gender prejudice than they did fifty years ago.

3. Blatant forms of prejudice _____ (have/have not) diminished. However, even people who deny holding prejudiced attitudes may carry negative _____ about race or gender.

4. Worldwide, _____ (women/men) are more likely to live in poverty, and two-thirds of children without basic schooling are _____ (girls/boys). However, people tend to perceive women as being more _____ and _____ , and less _____ than men.

5. For those with money, power, and prestige, prejudice often serves as a means of _____ social inequalities.

6. In the phenomenon called the _____ prophecy, discrimination increases prejudice through the reactions it provokes in its _____ . Equally damaging is the tendency of people to _____ victims for their plight.

7. Through our _____ _____ , we associated ourselves with certain groups.

8. Prejudice is also fostered by the _____ _____ , a tendency to favor groups to which one belongs— called the _____ —while excluding others, or the _____ .

9. That prejudice derives from attempts to blame others for one's frustration is proposed by the _____ theory.

10. Research suggests that prejudice may also derive from _____ , the process by which we attempt to simplify our world by classifying people into groups. One by-product of this process is that people tend to _____ the similarity of those within a group.

11. Another factor that fosters the formation of group stereotypes and prejudice is the tendency to _____ from vivid or memorable cases.

12. The belief that people get what they deserve— that the good are rewarded and the bad punished—is expressed in the _____ - _____ phenomenon. This phenomenon is based in part on _____ _____ , the tendency to believe that one would have foreseen how something turned out.

13. Aggressive behavior is defined by the text as _____ _____ .

14. Freud believed that people have a self-destructive _____ _____ that is manifested as aggression when it is _____ toward others. Today, most psychologists _____ (do/do not) consider human aggression to be instinctive.

15. In humans, aggressiveness _____ (varies/does not vary) greatly from culture to culture and person to person.

16. That there are genetic influences on aggression can be shown by the fact that many species of animals have been _____ for aggressiveness.

17. Twin studies suggest that genes _____ (do/do not) influence human aggression.

18. In humans and animals, aggression is activated and inhibited by _____ systems, such as those in the _____ _____ , which are in turn influenced by _____ and other substances in the blood.

19. The aggressive behavior of animals can be manipulated by altering the levels of the hormone _____ . When this level is _____ (increased/decreased), aggressive tendencies are reduced.

20. High levels of testosterone correlate with _____ , low tolerance for _____ , and _____ . Among teenage boys and adult men, high testosterone also correlates with _____ , hard _____ _____ , and aggressive responses to _____ . With age, testosterone levels—and aggressiveness— _____ (increase/decrease).

21. One drug that unleashes aggressive responses to provocation is _____ .

22. According to the _____- _____ principle, inability to achieve a goal leads to anger, which may generate aggression.

23. Aggressive behavior can be learned through _____ , as shown by the fact that people use aggression where they've found it pays, and through _____ of others.

24. Crime rates are higher in countries in which there is a large disparity between those who are _____ and those who are _____ . High violence rates also are typical of cultures and families in which there is minimal _____ _____ .

25. Violence on television appears to promote aggressive behavior as a result of four factors: the excitement of television causes _____ ; seeing violence triggers _____ related to violence; TV violence erodes viewers' _____ ; and viewers tend to _____ behaviors they have seen.

26. A woman's risk of rape is generally _____ (greater/less) today than it was half a century ago. Most rapes _____ (are/are not) reported.

27. Studies of pornography and aggression _____ (generally/do not generally) show a relationship between availability of pornography and the incidence of sexual aggression.

Comment on the impression of women that pornography frequently conveys and the effects this impression has on attitudes and behavior.

Summarize the findings of the Zillmann and Bryant study on the effects of pornography on attitudes toward rape.

28. Experiments have shown that it is not eroticism but depictions of _____ _____ that most directly affect men's acceptance and performance of aggression against women. Such depictions may create _____ _____ to which people respond when they are in new situations, or are uncertain how to act.

29. A perceived incompatibility of actions, goals, or ideas is called _____ . This perception can take place between individuals, _____ , or _____ .

30. Two destructive social processes that contribute to conflict are _____ _____ and _____ perceptions.

31. When the "non-zero-sum game" is played, most people fall into the social trap by mistrusting the other player and pursuing their own _____ .

32. The diabolical images people in conflict form of each other are called _____-_____ perceptions.

33. Several psychological tendencies foster biased perceptions. First, leaders, like other people, tend to accept credit for good deeds but not blame for bad deeds, a phenomenon called the

_____ _____ .

Second, conflicting parties tend to attribute the other's actions to a negative disposition, an example of the _____

_____ _____ .

Preconceived attitudes, or _____ , also contribute to the problem, as does the _____ that often emerges within a group as the members' attitudes become _____ .

34. A prerequisite for, and perhaps the most powerful predictor of, attraction is _____ .

35. When people are repeatedly exposed to unfamiliar stimuli, their liking of the stimuli _____ (increases/decreases). This phenomenon is the _____ _____ effect. Robert Zajonc contends that this phenomenon was _____ for our ancestors, for whom the unfamiliar was often dangerous. One implication of this is that _____ against those who are culturally different may be an _____ emotional response.

36. Our first impression of another person is most influenced by the person's _____ .

37. In a sentence, list several of the characteristics that physically attractive people are judged to possess: _____ _____ .

38. A person's attractiveness _____ (is/is not) strongly related to his or her self-esteem or happiness. Since 1970, the number of women unhappy with their appearance has _____ (increased/decreased/remained stable).

39. Cross-cultural research reveals that men judge women as more attractive if they have a _____ appearance, whereas

women judge men who appear

_____ , _____ , and _____ as more attractive.

40. People also seem to prefer physical features that are neither unusually _____ or _____ .

41. Relationships in which the partners are very similar are _____ (more/less) likely to last.

42. Compared with strangers, friends and couples are more likely to be similar in terms of

_____

_____ .

Explain what a reward theory of attraction is and how it can account for the three predictors of liking—proximity, attractiveness, and similarity.

43. Hatfield has distinguished two types of love: _____ love and _____ love.

44. According to the two-factor theory, emotions have two components: physical _____ and a _____ label.

45. When college men were placed in an aroused state, their feelings toward an attractive woman _____ (were/were not) more positive than those of men who had not been aroused.

46. Companionate love is promoted by _____—mutual sharing and giving by both partners. Another key ingredient of loving relationships is the revealing of intimate aspects of ourselves through _____ .

47. An unselfish regard for the welfare of others is called _____ .

48. According to Darley and Latané, people will help only if a three-stage decision-making process is completed: Bystanders must first _____ the incident, then _____ it as an emergency, and finally _____ _____ for helping.

49. When people who overheard a seizure victim calling for help thought others were hearing the same plea, they were _____ (more/less) likely to go to his aid than when they thought no one else was aware of the emergency.

50. In a series of staged accidents, Latané and Darley found that a bystander was _____ (more/less) likely to help if other bystanders were present. This phenomenon has been called the _____ _____ .

Identify the circumstances in which a person is most likely to offer help during an emergency.

51. The idea that social behavior aims to maximize rewards and minimize costs is proposed by _____ _____ theory.

52. One rule of social behavior tells us to return help to those who have helped us; this is the _____ norm. Another tells us to help those who need our help; this is the _____ _____ norm.

53. Conflict resolution is most likely in situations characterized by _____ , _____ , and _____ .

54. In most situations, establishing contact between two conflicting groups _____ (is/is not) sufficient to resolve conflict.

55. In Sherif's study, two conflicting groups of campers were able to resolve their conflicts by working together on projects in which they shared _____ goals.

56. When conflicts arise, a third-party _____ may facilitate communication and promote understanding.

57. Osgood has advanced a strategy of conciliation called GRIT, which stands for _____ and _____ _____ in _____ - _____ . The key to this method is each side's offering of a small _____ gesture in order to increase mutual trust and cooperation.

Progress Test 1

Multiple-Choice Questions

Circle your answers to the following questions and check them with the answers on page 518. If your answer is incorrect, read the explanation for why it is incorrect and then consult the appropriate pages of the text (in parentheses following the correct answer).

1. In his study of obedience, Stanley Milgram found that the majority of subjects:
   a. refused to shock the learner even once.
   b. complied with the experiment until the "learner" first indicated pain.
   c. complied with the experiment until the "learner" began screaming in agony.
   d. complied with all the demands of the experiment.

2. According to cognitive dissonance theory, dissonance is most likely to occur when:
   a. a person's behavior is not based on strongly held attitudes.
   b. two people have conflicting attitudes and find themselves in disagreement.
   c. an individual does something that is personally disagreeable.
   d. an individual is coerced into doing something that he or she does not want to do.

3. Which of the following statements is true?
   a. Groups are almost never swayed by minority opinions.
   b. Group polarization is most likely to occur when group members frequently disagree with one another.
   c. Groupthink provides the consensus needed for effective decision making.
   d. A group that is like-minded will probably not change its opinions through discussion.

4. Conformity increased under which of the following conditions in Asch's studies of conformity?
   a. The group had three or more people.
   b. The group had high status.
   c. Individuals were made to feel insecure.
   d. The group was unanimous.
   e. All of the above increased conformity.

5. Social traps are situations in which:
   a. conflicting parties realize that they have shared goals, the attainment of which requires their mutual cooperation.
   b. conflicting parties have similar, and generally negative, views of one another.
   c. conflicting parties each pursue their self-interests and become caught in mutually destructive behavior.
   d. two conflicting groups meet face-to-face in an effort to resolve their differences.

6. The phenomenon in which individuals lose their identity and relinquish normal restraints when they are part of a group is called:
   a. groupthink.   c. empathy.
   b. cognitive dissonance.   d. deindividuation.

7. Subjects in Asch's line-judgment experiment conformed to the group standard when their judgments were observed by others but not when they were made in private. This tendency to conform in public demonstrates:
   a. social facilitation.
   b. overjustification.
   c. informational social influence.
   d. normative social influence.

8. In Milgram's obedience studies, subjects were *less* likely to follow the experimenter's orders when:
   a. they heard the "learner" cry out in pain.
   b. they merely administered the test while someone else delivered the shocks.
   c. the "learner" was an older person or mentioned having some physical problem.
   d. they saw another subject disobey instructions.

9. *Aggression* is defined as behavior that:
   a. hurts another person.
   b. is intended to hurt another person.
   c. is hostile, passionate, and produces physical injury.
   d. has all of the above characteristics.

10. Which of the following is true about aggression?
    a. It varies too much to be instinctive in humans.
    b. It is just one instinct among many.
    c. It is instinctive but shaped by learning.
    d. It is the most important human instinct.

11. Research studies have found a positive correlation between aggressive tendencies in animals and levels of the hormone:
    a. estrogen.   d. testosterone.
    b. adrenaline.   e. epinephrine.
    c. noradrenaline.

12. Research studies have indicated that the tendency of viewers to misperceive normal sexuality, devalue their partners, and trivialize rape is:
    a. increased by exposure to pornography.
    b. not changed after exposure to pornography.
    c. decreased in men by exposure to pornography.
    d. decreased in both men and women by exposure to pornography.

13. Increasing the number of people that are present during an emergency tends to:
    a. increase the likelihood that people will cooperate in rendering assistance.
    b. decrease the empathy that people feel for the victim.
    c. increase the role that social norms governing helping will play.
    d. decrease the likelihood that anyone will help.

14. Which of the following was *not* mentioned in the text discussion of the roots of prejudice?
    a. people's tendency to overestimate the similarity of people within groups
    b. people's tendency to assume that exceptional, or especially memorable, individuals are unlike the majority of members of a group
    c. people's tendency to assume that the world is just and that people get what they deserve
    d. people's tendency to discriminate against those they view as "outsiders"

15. The mere exposure effect demonstrates that:
    a. familiarity breeds contempt.
    b. opposites attract.
    c. birds of a feather flock together.
    d. familiarity breeds fondness.

16. In one experiment, college men were physically aroused and then introduced to an attractive woman. Compared to men who had not been aroused, these men:
    a. reported more positive feelings toward the woman.
    b. reported more negative feelings toward the woman.
    c. were ambiguous about their feelings toward the woman.
    d. were more likely to feel that the woman was "out of their league" in terms of attractiveness.
    e. focused more on the woman's attractiveness and less on her intelligence and personality.

17. The deep affection that is felt in long-lasting relationships is called _____ love; this feeling is fostered in relationships in which _____ .
    a. passionate; there is equity between the partners
    b. passionate; traditional roles are maintained
    c. companionate; there is equity between the partners
    d. companionate; traditional roles are maintained

18. Which of the following is associated with an increased tendency on the part of a bystander to offer help in an emergency situation?
    a. being in a good mood
    b. having recently needed help and not received it
    c. observing someone as he or she refuses to offer help
    d. being a female

19. The belief that those who suffer deserve their fate is expressed in the:
    a. just-world phenomenon.
    b. phenomenon of ingroup bias.
    c. fundamental attribution error.
    d. mirror-image perception principle.

20. According to social exchange theory, a person's tendency toward altruistic behavior is based on:
    a. a determination of the relatedness of those who will be affected.
    b. a cost-benefit analysis of any action.
    c. social norms.
    d. all of the above.

Matching Items

Match each term with the appropriate definition or description.

Terms

_____ 1. social facilitation
_____ 2. social loafing
_____ 3. bystander effect
_____ 4. conformity
_____ 5. ingroup bias
_____ 6. normative social influence
_____ 7. informational social influence
_____ 8. group polarization
_____ 9. stereotype
_____ 10. attribution
_____ 11. altruism
_____ 12. mere exposure effect

Definitions or Descriptions

a. a causal explanation for someone's behavior
b. a generalized belief about a group of people
c. people work less hard in a group
d. performance is improved by an audience
e. the tendency to favor one's own group
f. the effect of social approval or disapproval
g. adjusting one's behavior to coincide with a group standard
h. group discussion enhances prevailing tendencies
i. the effect of accepting others' opinions about something
j. unselfish regard for others
k. the tendency that a person is less likely to help someone in need when others are present
l. the increased liking of a stimulus that results from repeated exposure to it

Progress Test 2

Progress Test 2 should be completed during a final chapter review. Answer the following questions after you thoroughly understand the correct answers for the section reviews and Progress Test 1.

Multiple-Choice Questions

1. Which theorist argued that aggression was a manifestation of a person's "death instinct" redirected toward another person?
   a. Milgram
   b. Freud
   c. Lorenz
   d. Janis
   e. Asch

2. We tend to perceive the members of an ingroup as _____ and the members of an outgroup as _____ .
   a. similar to one another; different from one another
   b. different from one another; similar to one another
   c. above average in ability; below average in ability
   d. below average in ability; above average in ability

3. Regarding the influence of alcohol and testosterone on aggressive behavior, which of the following is true?
   a. Consumption of alcohol increases aggressive behavior; injections of testosterone reduce aggressive behavior.
   b. Consumption of alcohol reduces aggressive behavior; injections of testosterone increase aggressive behavior.
   c. Consumption of alcohol and injections of testosterone both promote aggressive behavior.
   d. Consumption of alcohol and injections of testosterone both reduce aggressive behavior.

4. Most people prefer mirror-image photographs of their faces. This is best explained by:
   a. the principle of equity.
   b. the principle of self-disclosure.
   c. the mere exposure effect.
   d. mirror-image perceptions.
   e. deindividuation.

5. Research studies have shown that frequent exposure to sexually explicit films:
   a. may promote increased acceptance of promiscuity.
   b. diminishes the attitude that rape is a serious crime.
   c. may lead individuals to devalue their partners.
   d. may produce all of the above effects.

6. Research studies indicate that in an emergency situation the presence of others often:
   a. prevents people from even noticing the situation.
   b. prevents people from interpreting an unusual event as an emergency.
   c. prevents people from assuming responsibility for assisting.
   d. leads to all of the above.

7. Two neighboring nations are each stockpiling weapons. Each sees its neighbor's actions as an act of aggression and its own actions as self-defense. Evidently, these nations are victims of:
   a. the self-fulfilling prophecy.
   b. groupthink.
   c. the self-serving bias.
   d. the fundamental attribution error.

8. Which of the following factors is the *most* powerful predictor of friendship?
   a. similarity in age
   b. common racial and religious background
   c. similarity in physical attractiveness
   d. physical proximity

9. Most researchers agree that:
   a. television violence leads to aggressive behavior.
   b. although there is a correlation between television watching and aggressiveness, it's impossible to establish causation.
   c. paradoxically, watching excessive television violence ultimately diminishes an individual's aggressive tendencies.
   d. television violence is too unreal to promote aggression in viewers.

10. When subjects in an experiment were told that a woman to whom they would be speaking had been instructed to act in a friendly or unfriendly way, most of them subsequently attributed her behavior to:
    a. the situation.
    b. the situation *and* her personal disposition.
    c. her personal disposition.
    d. their own skill or lack of skill in a social situation.

11. Which of the following is true?
    a. Attitudes and actions rarely correspond.
    b. Attitudes predict behavior about half the time.
    c. Attitudes are excellent predictors of behavior.
    d. Attitudes predict behavior under certain conditions.

12. People with power and status may become prejudiced because:
    a. they tend to justify the social inequalities between themselves and others.
    b. those with less status and power tend to resent them.
    c. those with less status and power appear less capable.
    d. they feel proud and are boastful of their achievements.

13. Which of the following most accurately states the effects of crowding on behavior?
    a. Crowding makes people irritable.
    b. Crowding sometimes intensifies people's reactions.
    c. Crowding promotes altruistic behavior.
    d. Crowding usually weakens the intensity of people's reactions.

14. Research has found that for a minority to succeed in swaying a majority, the minority must:
    a. make up a sizable portion of the group.
    b. express its position as consistently as possible.
    c. express its position in the most extreme terms possible.
    d. be able to convince a key leader of the majority.

15. Which of the following conclusions did Milgram derive from his studies of obedience?
    a. Even ordinary people, without any particular hostility, can become agents in a destructive process.
    b. Most people are able, under the proper circumstances, to suppress their natural aggressiveness.
    c. The need to be accepted by others is a powerful motivating force.
    d. All of the above conclusions were reached.

16. Which of the following best summarizes the relative importance of personal control and social control of our behavior?
    a. Situational influences on behavior generally are much greater than personal influences.
    b. Situational influences on behavior generally are slightly greater than personal influences.
    c. Personal influences on behavior generally are much greater than situational influences.
    d. Situational and personal influences interact in determining our behavior.

17. Which of the following best describes how GRIT works?
    a. The fact that two sides in a conflict have great respect for the other's strengths prevents further escalation of the problem.
    b. The two sides engage in a series of reciprocated conciliatory acts.
    c. The two sides agree to have their differences settled by a neutral, third-party mediator.
    d. The two sides engage in cooperation in those areas in which shared goals are possible.

18. Which of the following is important in promoting conformity in individuals?
    a. whether an individual's behavior will be observed by others in the group
    b. whether the individual is male or female
    c. the size of the room in which a group is meeting
    d. the age of the members in a group
    e. whether the individual is of a higher status than other group members

19. Which theory describes how we explain others' behavior as being due to internal dispositions or external situations?
    a. social exchange theory
    b. reward theory
    c. two-factor theory
    d. attribution theory

20. Which of the following is most likely to promote groupthink?
    a. The group's leader fails to take a firm stance on an issue.
    b. A minority faction holds to its position.
    c. The group consults with various experts.
    d. Group polarization is evident.

True–False Items

Indicate whether each statement is true or false by placing *T* or *F* in the blank next to the item.

_____   1. When explaining another's behavior, we tend to underestimate situational influences.
_____   2. When explaining our own behavior, we tend to underestimate situational influences.

_____ 3. An individual is more likely to conform when the rest of the group is unanimous.

_____ 4. The tendency of people to conform is influenced by the culture in which they were socialized.

_____ 5. A bystander is more likely to offer help in an emergency if other bystanders are present.

_____ 6. Counter-attitudinal behavior (acting contrary to our beliefs) often leads to attitude change.

_____ 7. Human aggression is instinctual.

_____ 8. Group polarization tends to prevent groupthink from occurring.

_____ 9. Crowded conditions usually subdue people's reactions.

_____ 10. When individuals lose their sense of identity in a group, they often become more uninhibited.

Thinking Critically About Chapter 18

Answer these questions the day before an exam as a final check on your understanding of the chapter's terms and concepts.

Multiple-Choice Questions

1. After waiting in line for an hour to buy concert tickets, Teresa is told that the concert is sold out. In her anger she pounds her fist on the ticket counter, frightening the clerk. Teresa's behavior is best explained by:
   a. evolutionary psychology.
   b. the reciprocity norm.
   c. social exchange theory.
   d. the frustration-aggression principle.

2. Before she gave a class presentation favoring gun control legislation, Wanda opposed it. Her present attitude favoring such legislation can best be explained by:
   a. attribution theory.
   b. cognitive dissonance theory.
   c. social exchange theory.
   d. evolutionary psychology.
   e. two-factor theory.

3. Which of the following would most likely be subject to social facilitation?
   a. proofreading a page for spelling errors
   b. typing a letter with accuracy
   c. playing a difficult piece on a musical instrument

   d. giving a speech
   e. running quickly around a track

4. Jane and Sandy were best friends as freshmen. Jane joined a sorority; Sandy didn't. By the end of their senior year, they found that they had less in common with each other than with the other members of their respective circles of friends. Which of the following phenomena most likely explains their feelings?
   a. group polarization
   b. groupthink
   c. deindividuation
   d. social facilitation

5. Which of the following strategies would be *most* likely to foster positive feelings between two conflicting groups?
   a. Take steps to reduce the likelihood of social traps.
   b. Separate the groups so that tensions diminish.
   c. Have one representative from each group visit the other and field questions.
   d. Increase the amount of contact between the two conflicting groups.
   e. Have the groups work on a superordinate goal.

6. José is the one student member on the college board of trustees. At the board's first meeting, José wants to disagree with the others on several issues but in each case decides to say nothing. Studies on conformity suggest all except one of the following are factors in José's not speaking up. Which one is *not* a factor?
   a. The board is a large group.
   b. The board is prestigious and most of its members are well known.
   c. The board members are already aware that José and the student body disagree with them on these issues.
   d. Because this is the first meeting José has attended, he feels insecure and not fully competent.

7. Given the tendency of people to categorize information according to preformed schemas, which of the following stereotypes would Juan, a 65-year-old political liberal and fitness enthusiast, be most likely to have?
   a. "People who exercise regularly are very extraverted."
   b. "All political liberals are advocates of a reduced defense budget."
   c. "Young people today have no sense of responsibility."
   d. "Older people are lazy."

8. Ever since their cabin lost the camp softball competition, the campers have become increasingly hostile toward one camper in their cabin, blaming her for every problem in the cabin. This behavior is best explained in terms of:
   a. the ingroup bias.
   b. prejudice.
   c. the scapegoat theory.
   d. the reciprocity norm.
   e. mirror-image perceptions.

9. Maria recently heard a speech calling for a ban on aerosol sprays that endanger the earth's ozone layer. Maria's subsequent decision to stop using aerosol sprays is an example of:
   a. informational social influence.
   b. normative social influence.
   c. deindividuation.
   d. social facilitation.

10. Mr. and Mrs. Samuels are constantly fighting, and each perceives the other as hard-headed and insensitive. Their conflict is being fueled by:
    a. self-disclosure.
    b. stereotypes.
    c. a social trap.
    d. mirror-image perceptions.

11. Which of the following situations should produce the *greatest* cognitive dissonance?
    a. A soldier is forced to carry out orders he finds disagreeable.
    b. A student who loves animals has to dissect a cat in order to pass biology.
    c. As part of an experiment, a subject is directed to deliver electric shocks to another person.
    d. A student volunteers to debate an issue, taking the side he personally disagrees with.

12. Professor Washington's students did very poorly on the last exam. The tendency to make the fundamental attribution error might lead her to conclude that the class did poorly because:
    a. the test was unfair.
    b. not enough time was given for students to complete the test.
    c. students were distracted by some social function on campus.
    d. students were unmotivated.

13. Students at State University are convinced that their school is better than any other; this most directly illustrates:
    a. an ingroup bias.
    b. prejudice and discrimination.

   c. the scapegoat effect.
   d. the just-world phenomenon.
   e. mirror-image perceptions.

14. After Sandy helped Jack move into his new apartment, Jack felt obligated to help Sandy when she moved. Jack's sense of responsibility can best be explained by:
    a. evolutionary psychology.
    b. two-factor theory.
    c. the social responsibility norm.
    d. the reciprocity norm.

15. Ahmed and Monique are on a blind date. Which of the following will probably be *most* influential in determining whether they like each other?
    a. their personalities
    b. their beliefs
    c. their social skills
    d. their physical attractiveness

16. Opening her mail, Joan discovers a romantic greeting card from her boyfriend. According to the two-factor theory, she is likely to feel the most intense romantic feelings if, prior to reading the card, she has just:
    a. completed her daily run.
    b. finished reading a chapter in her psychology textbook.
    c. awakened from a nap.
    d. finished eating lunch.
    e. been listening to a tape of love songs.

17. Driving home from work, Althea saw a car run off the road and burst into flames. Althea stopped her car, ran to the burning vehicle, and managed to pull the elderly driver to safety before the car exploded. Althea's behavior can best be explained by:
    a. the social responsibility norm.
    b. the reciprocity norm.
    c. two-factor theory.
    d. reward theory.

18. Having read the chapter, which of the following is best borne out by research on attraction?
    a. Birds of a feather flock together.
    b. Opposites attract.
    c. Familiarity breeds contempt.
    d. Absence makes the heart grow fonder.

19. George's discriminatory behavior toward minorities often provokes anger in his victims, which only serves to increase George's prejudice. George's behavior is an example of the:

   a. blame-the-victim dynamic.

   b. self-fulfilling prophecy.

   c. just-world phenomenon.

   d. scapegoat phenomenon.

20. Which of the following is an example of the foot-in-the-door phenomenon?

   a. To persuade a customer to buy a product a store owner offers a small gift.

   b. After agreeing to wear a small "Enforce Recycling" lapel pin, a woman agrees to collect signatures on a petition to make recycling required by law.

   c. After offering to sell a car at a ridiculously low price, a car salesperson is forced to tell the customer the car will cost $1000 more.

   d. All of the above are examples.

Essay Question

The Panhellenic Council on your campus has asked you to make a presentation on the topic "Social Psychology" to all freshmen who have signed up to "rush" a fraternity or sorority. In a fit of cynicism following your rejection last year by a prestigious fraternity or sorority, you decide to speak on the negative influences of groups on the behavior of individuals. What will you discuss? (Use the space below to list the points you want to make and organize them. Then write the essay on a separate sheet of paper.)

Key Terms

Writing Definitions

Using your own words, on a separate piece of paper write a brief definition or explanation of each of the following terms.

1. social psychology
2. attribution theory
3. fundamental attribution error
4. attitudes
5. foot-in-the-door phenomenon
6. cognitive dissonance theory
7. conformity
8. normative social influence
9. informational social influence
10. social facilitation
11. social loafing
12. deindividuation
13. group polarization
14. groupthink
15. self-fulfilling prophecy
16. prejudice
17. stereotype
18. ingroup
19. outgroup
20. ingroup bias
21. scapegoat theory
22. just-world phenomenon
23. aggression
24. frustration-aggression principle
25. conflict
26. social trap
27. mere exposure effect
28. passionate love
29. companionate love
30. equity
31. self-disclosure
32. altruism
33. bystander effect
34. social exchange theory
35. superordinate goals
36. GRIT

Cross-Check

As you learned in the Introduction, reviewing and overlearning of material are important to the learning process. After you have written the definitions of the key terms in this chapter, you should complete the crossword puzzle to ensure that you can reverse the process—recognize the term, given the definition.

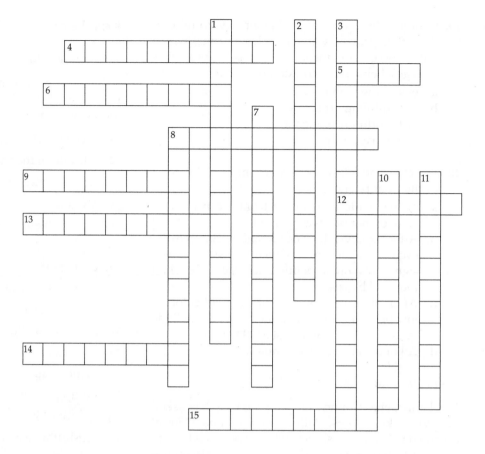

ACROSS

4. A generalized belief about a group of people.
5. A strategy of conflict resolution in which both groups make conciliatory gestures. (abbrev.)
6. Theory that proposes that prejudice provides an outlet for anger by finding someone to blame.
8. The tendency to change one's attitudes to coincide with those held by a group.
9. An unselfish regard for the welfare of others.
12. Mutual giving and receiving in a relationship.
13. Type of love that refers to an aroused state of intense positive absorption in another person.
14. Perceived incompatibility between individuals or groups.
15. Personal beliefs and feelings that influence our behavior.

DOWN

1. A person's tendency not to offer help to someone if others are present.
2. Type of social influence that results when one goes along with a group when one is unsure of what to do.
3. Psychological discomfort we experience when two of our thoughts conflict.
7. Phenomenon whereby people who agree to a small request are more likely to comply later with a larger request.
8. Type of love in which there is a deep, enduring attachment.
10. Our tendency to underestimate situational influences and overestimate dispositional influences upon the behavior of others is the _____ attribution error.
11. A causal explanation of a given behavior.

Answers

Social Thinking

Section Preview

1. According to attribution theory, people explain others' behavior as being due either to their dispositions or to their situations. Because people have enduring personality traits, we tend to overestimate the influence of personality and underestimate the impact of situational influences, particularly when explaining others' behavior. This is called the *fundamental attribution error*. When explaining our own behavior, or when we take another's perspective, we are less likely to make this type of error. Our attributions, of course, have important practical consequences. For example, there are political implications to the question of whether people's behavior is attributed to social conditions or to their own choices, abilities, and shortcomings.

2. An attitude is a belief and feeling that predisposes our reactions to objects, people, and events. Our attitudes are most likely to guide our actions when outside influences on what we say and do are minimal, when the attitude is specifically relevant to the behavior, and when we are aware of our attitudes.

3. Studies of the foot-in-the-door phenomenon and role playing demonstrate that our actions can influence our attitudes. The foot-in-the-door phenomenon is the tendency for people who agree to a small request to comply later with a larger one. Similarly, people who play a role tend to adjust their attitudes to coincide with behavior enacted while playing the role. The theory of cognitive dissonance maintains that when our thoughts and behaviors don't coincide, we experience tension. To relieve this tension, we bring our attitudes into line with our actions.

Stepping Through the Section

1. social psychologists

2. attribution; dispositional attribution; situational attribution

3. underestimate; attention; fundamental attribution error; weaker; reversed

Our attributions—to individuals' dispositions or to situations—have important practical consequences. A hurtful remark from an acquaintance, for example, is more likely to be forgiven if it is attributed to a temporary situation than to a mean disposition.

4. attitudes

5. challenged

Attitudes predict actions when other influences on the attitudes and actions are minimized, when the attitude is specifically relevant to the behavior, and when we are especially aware of our attitudes. Thus, our attitudes are more likely to predict behavior when we are not attempting to adjust our behavior to please others, when we are in familiar situations in which we don't have to stop and think about our attitudes, and when the attitude pertains to a specific behavior, such as purchasing a product or casting a vote.

6. actions or behavior; foot-in-the-door

7. role

8. changes

9. cognitive dissonance; Festinger

10. dissonance; attitudes

Social Influence

Section Preview

1. Suggestibility studies conducted by Solomon Asch demonstrate that a unanimous group makes us unsure about our behavior or thinking, and so we are more likely to conform to the group standard, even if it is incorrect. Conformity is promoted when people feel incompetent or insecure, when they are in groups of three or more, when the group is unanimous and of high status and attractiveness, when no prior commitment has been made, when behavior will be observed, and when people have been socialized in a culture that encourages respect for social standards. We conform to gain social approval (normative social influence) or because the group provides valuable information (informational social influence).

2. Subjects in Milgram's experiments were ordered to teach a list of word pairs to another person by punishing the learner's wrong answers with electric shocks. Obedience was highest when the experimenter was nearby and was perceived as a legitimate authority supported by a prestigious institution, when the victim was depersonalized or at a distance, and when there was no role model for defiance.

3. Social facilitation occurs when tasks are simple or well-learned but not when they are difficult or unfamiliar. When observed by others, people become aroused. Arousal *facilitates* the most likely response—the correct one on an easy task, an incorrect one on a difficult task. Social loafing occurs when people who work anonymously as part of a group exert less effort than those individually accountable for performance. Deindividuation occurs when group participation makes individuals feel aroused, anonymous, and less self-conscious. The uninhibited and impulsive behavior of mobs may occur as a result of this phenomenon.

4. Group polarization refers to the enhancement of a group's prevailing tendencies that occurs when like-minded members discuss issues and attitudes. The unrealistic group decision making called groupthink occurs when the desire for group harmony outweighs the desire for realistic thinking. It is fed by overconfidence, conformity, self-justification, and group polarization. Groupthink can be prevented when the leader welcomes dissenting opinions and invites criticism.

5. The power of the situation (social control) and of the individual (personal control) interact in two significant ways. First, when feeling pressured, people may react by doing the opposite. Second, people often choose or help create the situations that influence their behavior. Their expectations may cause them to act in ways that trigger the expected results. In this way, expectations may be self-fulfilling.

The impact of a minority in swaying the majority opinion illustrates the power of personal control. Research reveals that a minority that unswervingly holds to its position is more likely to be successful in swaying the majority than a minority that waffles.

Stepping Through the Section

1. mimic
2. suggestibility
3. conformity
4. Asch
5. were
6. normative social influence; norms
7. informational social influence
8. important; difficult
9. individualistic
10. Milgram; complied; similar to

Obedience was highest when the person giving the orders was close at hand and perceived to be a legitimate authority figure, the authority figure was supported by a prestigious institution, the victim was depersonalized, and when there were no role models for defiance.

11. foot-in-the-door
12. social facilitation; easy; likely
13. amplified
14. less hard; social loafing
15. deindividuation
16. increase; group polarization; Internet
17. groupthink
18. social control; personal control
19. self-fulfilling
20. unswerving

Social Relations

Section Preview

1. Prejudice is an unjustifiable and usually negative attitude toward a group. People who have money, power, and prestige may become prejudiced toward those less fortunate in order to rationalize social inequalities. The reactions provoked in victims of discrimination may further increase prejudice. The tendencies to favor one's own group (ingroup bias) and to blame victims for their plight may also lead to prejudice. According to the scapegoat theory of prejudice, when people are frustrated or angry, blaming another individual or group may provide an outlet for their anger.

2. Stereotyped beliefs emerge as a result of our tendency to cognitively simplify the world. One way to do this is by categorizing people into groups and then overestimating the similarity of people within groups other than our own. Group stereotypes are also influenced by vivid but exceptional cases involving individuals from other groups, because they are more readily available to memory. Another cognitive root of prejudice is the just-world phenomenon, or the idea that good is rewarded and evil is punished, so those who are successful are good and those who suffer are bad. Hindsight bias also fosters prejudice, as people blame victims after the fact for "getting what they deserved."

3. Biology influences aggression at three levels—the genetic, the neural, and the biochemical. Studies of human twins and selective breeding in animals reveal that genes influence aggression. Electrical stimulation and injuries to certain regions of the limbic system, such as the amygdala, suggest that animal and human brains have neural systems that control aggressive behavior (although no one spot in the brain actually controls aggression). Studies of animal aggression and violent criminals demonstrate that aggressive tendencies increase with blood levels of the hormone testosterone (although the reverse is also true).

   A variety of psychological factors influence aggression. The frustration-aggression principle indicates that pain, insults, excessive heat, and other aversive stimuli can evoke hostility. Learning also plays a role in aggression. Aggressive reactions are more likely in situations in which experience has taught the individual that aggression will be rewarded. Furthermore, children who observe aggressive models often imitate their behavior.

4. Correlational and experimental studies reveal a link between children's viewing of violent television programs and their later aggressiveness as teenagers and young adults. Experts maintain that the effects of viewing violent programs stem from a combination of factors, including arousal by the violent excitement, the strengthening of violence-related ideas, the erosion of inhibitions, and imitation.

   Research indicates that depictions of sexual violence portray women as enjoying being the victims of sexual aggression, and this perception increases the acceptance of coercion in sexual relationships. Repeated viewing of pornographic films can also lead viewers to trivialize rape and devalue their partners.

5. Conflict is a seeming incompatibility of actions, goals, or ideas among individuals, groups, or nations. Conflict is fostered by social traps in which conflicting parties get caught up in mutually destructive behavior by pursuing their own self-interests. Another factor that fuels conflict is the tendency for those in conflict to form diabolical images of each other (mirror-image perceptions). The psychological roots of distorted perceptions include the self-serving bias, the fundamental attribution error, stereotyping, group polarization, and groupthink.

Conflict resolution is most likely in situations characterized by cooperation, communication, and conciliation. Studies by Sherif and others demonstrate that cooperation between groups in the pursuit of superordinate goals is more effective than mere contact between conflicting groups in reducing differences. Communication between conflicting groups can be facilitated by a third-party mediator when conflicts are so intense that civil discussion between the groups is not possible. When cooperation and communication are impossible between conflicting groups, Osgood's "Graduated and Reciprocated Initiatives in Tension-Reduction" (GRIT) may help reduce hostilities. GRIT promotes trust and cooperation between groups by having each group initiate one or more small, conciliatory acts.

6. Studies of attraction indicate that proximity is the most powerful predictor of friendship, in part because being repeatedly exposed to any person or thing tends to increase our liking for it (mere exposure effect). Experiments also reveal that physical appearance is the most powerful factor in the first impression a person triggers. Although many aspects of attractiveness vary with place and time, some may be universal. Once relationships are formed, similarity of attitudes, beliefs, interests, and other characteristics increases attraction between people.

Passionate love is an intense state of physical arousal triggered by another person, usually at the beginning of a relationship, that is cognitively labeled as love. Companionate love is the steadier, deeply felt attachment that emerges as love matures. Companionate love is fostered by feelings of equity between the partners in a relationship, and the acceptability of self-disclosures.

7. The bystander effect states that a bystander is less likely to give aid if other bystanders are present. Darley and Latané maintain that bystanders will help only if they notice the incident, interpret it as an emergency, and assume responsibility for helping. At each step in this decision-making process the presence of other bystanders makes it less likely a helping decision will be made. Further research reveals that bystanders are most likely to help when they have seen someone else being helpful, when they are not in a hurry, when the victim appears similar to them and deserving of assistance, when they are in a small town or rural area, when they feel guilty, when they are focused on others and not preoccupied, and when they are in a good mood.

8. The social exchange theory maintains that self-interest underlies all human interactions, including altruism, so that our constant goal is to maximize rewards and minimize costs. This theory helps explain why people often help those whose approval they seek or who can reciprocate favors in the future.

People are also sensitive to social norms that promote helping. The reciprocity norm, for example, dictates that we should help those who have helped us. The social responsibility norm is the expectation that we should help those who need our help.

Stepping Through the Section

1. unjustifiable; negative; stereotypes

2. less

3. have; associations

4. women; girls; nurturant; sensitive; aggressive

5. justifying

6. self-fulfilling; victims; blame

7. social identities

8. ingroup bias; ingroup; outgroup

9. scapegoat

10. categorization; overestimate

11. overgeneralize

12. just-world; hindsight bias

13. any physical or verbal behavior intended to hurt or destroy

14. death instinct; displaced; do not

15. varies

16. bred

17. do

18. neural; limbic system (or the amygdala); hormones

19. testosterone; decreased

20. irritability; frustration; impulsiveness; delinquency; drug use; frustration; decrease

21. alcohol

22. frustration-aggression

23. rewards; observation (or imitation)

24. rich; poor; father care

25. arousal; ideas; inhibitions; imitate

26. greater; are not

27. generally

Pornography tends to portray women as enjoying being the victims of sexual aggression, and this perception increases the acceptance of coercion in sexual relationships.

The Zillmann and Bryant study found that after viewing sexually explicit films for several weeks, undergraduates were more likely to recommend a lighter prison sentence for a convicted rapist than were subjects who viewed nonerotic films.

28. sexual violence; social scripts

29. conflict; groups; nations

30. social traps; distorted

31. self-interests

32. mirror-image

33. self-serving bias; fundamental attribution error; stereotypes; groupthink; polarized

34. proximity

35. increases; mere exposure; adaptive; prejudice; automatic

36. appearance

37. Attractive people are perceived as happier, more sensitive, more successful, and more socially skilled.

38. is not; increased

39. youthful; mature; dominant; affluent

40. large; small

41. more

42. attitudes, beliefs, interests, religion, race, education, intelligence, smoking behavior, economic status, age

Reward theories of attraction say that we are attracted to, and continue relationships with, those people whose behavior provides us with more benefits than costs. Proximity makes it easy to enjoy the benefits of friendship at little cost, attractiveness is pleasing, and similarity is reinforcing to us.

43. passionate; companionate

44. arousal; cognitive

45. were

46. equity; self-disclosure

47. altruism

48. notice; interpret; assume responsibility

49. less

50. less; bystander effect

People are most likely to help someone when they have just observed someone else being helpful; when they are not in a hurry; when the victim appears to need and deserve help; when they are in some way similar to the victim; when in a small town; when feeling guilty; when not preoccupied; and when in a good mood.

51. social exchange

52. reciprocity; social responsibility

53. cooperation; communication; conciliation

54. is not

55. superordinate

56. mediator

57. Graduated; Reciprocated Initiatives; Tension-Reduction; conciliatory

Progress Test 1

Multiple-Choice Questions

1. **d.** is the answer. In Milgram's initial experiments, 63 percent of the subjects fully complied with the experiment. (p. 653)

2. **c.** is the answer. Cognitive dissonance is the tension we feel when we are aware of a discrepancy between our thoughts and actions, as would occur when we do something we find distasteful. (p. 648)
   a. Dissonance requires strongly held attitudes, which must be perceived as not fitting behavior.
   b. Dissonance is a personal cognitive process.
   d. In such a situation the person is less likely to experience dissonance, since the action can be attributed to "having no choice."

3. **d.** is the answer. In such groups, discussion usually strengthens prevailing opinion; this phenomenon is known as group polarization. (p. 658)
   a. Minority opinions, especially if consistently and firmly stated, can sway the majority in a group.
   b. Group polarization, or the strengthening of a group's prevailing tendencies, is most likely in groups where members agree.
   c. When groupthink occurs, there is so much consensus that decision making becomes less effective.

4. **e.** is the answer. (p. 652)

5. **c.** is the answer. Social traps foster conflict in that two parties, by pursuing their self-interests, create a result that neither group wants. (p. 675)
a. As Sherif's studies demonstrated, the possession of shared or superordinate goals tends to reduce conflict between groups.
b. This is an example of mirror-image perceptions, which, along with social traps, foster conflict.
d. Face-to-face confrontations between conflicting parties generally do not reduce conflict, nor are they social traps.

6. **d.** is the answer. (p. 658)
a. Groupthink refers to the mode of thinking that occurs when the desire for group harmony overrides realistic and critical thinking.
b. Cognitive dissonance refers to the discomfort we feel when two thoughts (which include the knowledge of our *behavior*) are inconsistent.
c. Empathy is feeling what another person feels.

7. **d.** is the answer. Normative social influence refers to influence on behavior that comes from a desire to look good to others. Subjects who were observed conformed because they didn't want to look like oddballs. (p. 652)
a. Social facilitation involves performing tasks better or faster in the presence of others.
b. Overjustification occurs when a person is rewarded for doing something that is already enjoyable.
c. Informational social influence is the tendency of individuals to accept the opinions of others, especially in situations where they themselves are unsure.

8. **d.** is the answer. Role models for defiance reduce levels of obedience. (p. 654)
a. & c. These did not result in diminished obedience.
b. This "depersonalization" of the victim resulted in increased obedience.

9. **b.** is the answer. Aggression is any behavior, physical or verbal, that is intended to hurt or destroy. (p. 666)
a. A person may accidentally be hurt in a nonaggressive incident; aggression does not necessarily prove hurtful.
c. Verbal behavior, which does not result in physical injury, may also be aggressive. Moreover, acts of aggression may be cool and calculated, rather than hostile and passionate.

10. **a.** is the answer. The very wide variations in aggressiveness from culture to culture indicate that aggression cannot be considered an instinct, or unlearned, universal characteristic of the species. (p. 666)

11. **d.** is the answer. (p. 667)

12. **a.** is the answer. (pp. 673–674)

13. **d.** is the answer. This phenomenon is known as the bystander effect. (p. 683)
a. This answer is incorrect because individuals are less likely to render assistance at all if others are present.
b. Although people are less likely to assume responsibility for helping, this does not mean that they are less empathic.
c. This answer is incorrect because norms such as the social responsibility norm encourage helping others, yet people are less likely to help with others around.

14. **b.** is the answer. In fact, people tend to overgeneralize from vivid cases, rather than assume that they are unusual. (pp. 665–666)
a., c., & d. Each of these is an example of a cognitive (a. & c.) or a social (d.) root of prejudice.

15. **d.** is the answer. Being repeatedly exposed to novel stimuli increases our liking for them. (p. 677)
a. For the most part, the opposite is true.
b. & c. The mere exposure effect concerns our tendency to develop likings on the basis, not of similarities or differences, but simply of familiarity, or repeated exposure.

16. **a.** is the answer. This result supports the two-factor theory of emotion and passionate attraction, according to which arousal from any source can facilitate an emotion, depending on how we label the arousal. (p. 681)

17. **c.** is the answer. Deep affection is typical of companionate love, rather than passionate love, and is promoted by equity, whereas traditional roles may be characterized by the dominance of one sex. (pp. 681–682)

18. **a.** is the answer. (p. 684)
b. & c. These factors would most likely decrease a person's altruistic tendencies.
d. There is no evidence that one sex is more altruistic than the other.

19. **a.** is the answer. (p. 666)
b. Ingroup bias is the tendency of people to favor their own group.
c. The fundamental attribution error is the tendency of people to underestimate situational influences when observing the behavior of other people.

d. The mirror-image perception principle is the tendency of conflicting parties to form similar, diabolical images of each other.

20. b. is the answer. (pp. 684)
a. This is a tenet of evolutionary psychology.
c. Social exchange theory focuses on costs and benefits, rather than on norms.

Matching Items

1. d (p. 657)   5. e (p. 664)   9. b (p. 662)
2. c (p. 657)   6. f (p. 652)   10. a (p. 643)
3. k (p. 684)   7. i (p. 652)   11. j (p. 683)
4. g (p. 651)   8. h (p. 658)   12. l (p. 677)

Progress Test 2

Multiple-Choice Questions

1. **b.** is the answer. (p. 666)
   a. Milgram conducted studies of obedience.
   c. Lorenz, too, was an instinct theorist, but only Freud argued the existence of a "death instinct."
   d. Janis studied the process that led to group-think.
   e. Asch studied conformity.

2. **b.** is the answer. (p. 665)
   a. We are keenly sensitive to differences within our group, less so to differences within other groups.
   c. & d. Although we tend to look more favorably on members of the ingroup, the text does not suggest that ingroup bias extends to evaluations of abilities.

3. **c.** is the answer. (p. 667)

4. **c.** is the answer. The mere exposure effect refers to our tendency to like what we're used to, and we're used to seeing mirror images of ourselves. (p. 677)
   a. Equity refers to equality in giving and taking between the partners in a relationship.
   b. Self-disclosure is the sharing of intimate feelings with a partner in a loving relationship.
   d. Although people prefer mirror images of their faces, mirror-image perceptions are often held by parties in conflict. Each party views itself favorably and the other negatively.
   e. Deindividuation involves a loss of self-awareness.

5. **d.** is the answer. (pp. 673–674)

6. **d.** is the answer. (p. 683)

7. **d.** is the answer. In this case, each nation has mistakenly attributed the other's action to a *dispositional* trait, whereas its own action is viewed as a *situational* response. (p. 643)

8. **d.** is the answer. Because it provides people with an opportunity to meet, proximity is the most powerful predictor of friendship, even though, once a friendship is established, the other factors mentioned become more important. (p. 677)

9. **a.** is the answer. (pp. 670–671)
   b. Although some researchers take this view, the consensus, as expressed by the National Institute of Mental Health, is that violence on television does lead to aggressive behavior.
   c. & d. Most viewers would maintain the opposite.

10. **c.** is the answer. In this example of the fundamental attribution error, even when given the situational explanation for the woman's behavior, students ignored it and attributed her behavior to her personal disposition. (p. 643–644)

11. **d.** is the answer. Our attitudes are more likely to guide our actions when other influences are minimal, when there's a specific connection between the two, and when we're keenly aware of our beliefs. The presence of other people would more likely be an outside factor that would lessen the likelihood of actions being guided by attitude. (p. 646)

12. **a.** is the answer. Such justifications arise as a way to preserve inequalities. The just-world phenomenon presumes that people get what they deserve. According to this view, someone who has less must deserve less. (p. 666)

13. **b.** is the answer. (p. 657)
   a. & c. Crowding may amplify irritability or altruistic tendencies that are already present. Crowding does not, however, produce these reactions as a general effect.
   d. In fact, just the opposite is true. Crowding often intensifies people's reactions.

14. **b.** is the answer. (p. 660)
   a. Even if they made up a sizable portion of the group, although still a minority, their numbers would not be as important as their consistency.
   c. & d. These aspects of minority influence were not discussed in the text; however, they are not likely to help a minority sway a majority.

15. **a.** is the answer. (p. 655)

16. **d.** is the answer. The text emphasizes the ways in which personal and social controls interact in influencing behavior. It does not suggest that one factor is more influential than the other. (p. 660)

17. b. is the answer. (p. 687)
a. GRIT is a technique for reducing conflict through a series of conciliatory gestures, not for maintaining the status quo.
c. & d. These measures may help reduce conflict but they are not aspects of GRIT.

18. a. is the answer. As Solomon Asch's experiments demonstrated, individuals are more likely to conform when they are being observed by others in the group. The other factors were not discussed in the text and probably would not promote conformity. (p. 652)

19. d. is the answer. (p. 643)

20. d. is the answer. Group polarization, or the enhancement of a group's prevailing attitudes, promotes groupthink, which leads to the disintegration of critical thinking. (p. 659)
a. Groupthink is more likely when a leader highly favors an idea, which may make members reluctant to disagree.
b. A strong minority faction would probably have the opposite effect: It would diminish group harmony while promoting critical thinking.
c. Consulting experts would discourage groupthink by exposing the group to other opinions.

True-False Items

1. T (p. 643)	**6.** T (p. 648)
2. F (p. 643)	**7.** F (p. 666)
3. T (p. 652)	**8.** F (pp. 658–659)
4. T (p. 653)	**9.** F (p. 657)
5. F (pp. 683–684)	**10.** T (p. 658)

Thinking Critically About Chapter 18

1. d. is the answer. According to the frustration-aggression principle, the blocking of an attempt to achieve some goal—in Teresa's case, buying concert tickets—creates anger and can generate aggression. (p. 668)
a. Evolutionary psychology maintains that aggressive behavior is a genetically based drive. Teresa's behavior clearly was a reaction to a specific situation.
b. The reciprocity norm—that we should return help to those who have helped us—would not engender Teresa's angry reaction.
c. Social exchange theory views behavior as an exchange process in which people try to maximize the benefits of their behavior by minimizing the costs. Teresa's behavior likely brought her few benefits while exacting some costs, including

potential injury, embarrassment, and retaliation by the clerk.

2. b. is the answer. Dissonance theory focuses on what happens when our actions contradict our attitudes. (p. 648)
a. Attribution theory holds that we give causal explanations for others' behavior, often by crediting either the situation or people's dispositions.
c. Social exchange theory maintains that social behaviors maximize benefits and minimize costs. It is not clear in this example whether Wanda perceives such costs and benefits.
d. & e. These are not theories of social influence.

3. e. is the answer. Social facilitation, or better performance in the presence of others, occurs for easy tasks but not for more difficult ones. For tasks such as proofreading, typing, playing an instrument, or giving a speech, the arousal resulting from the presence of others can lead to mistakes. (p. 657)

4. a. is the answer. Group polarization means that the tendencies within a group—and therefore the differences among groups—grow stronger over time. Thus, because the differences between the sorority and nonsorority students have increased, Jane and Sandy are likely to have little in common. (p. 658)
b. Groupthink is the tendency for realistic decision making to disintegrate when the desire for group harmony is strong.
c. Deindividuation is the loss of self-consciousness and restraint that sometimes occurs when one is part of a group.
d. Social facilitation refers to improved performance of a task in the presence of others.

5. e. is the answer. Sherif found that hostility between two groups could be dispelled by giving the groups superordinate, or shared, goals. (p. 685)
a. Although reducing the likelihood of social traps might reduce mutually destructive behavior, it would not lead to positive feelings between the groups.
b. Such segregation would likely increase ingroup bias and group polarization, resulting in further group conflict.
c. This might help, or it might increase hostilities; it would not be as helpful a strategy as communication through an outside mediator or, as in e., cooperation toward a superordinate goal.
d. Contact by itself is not likely to reduce conflict.

6. **c.** is the answer. Prior commitment to an opposing view generally tends to work against conformity. In contrast, large group size, prestigiousness of a group, and an individual's feelings of incompetence and insecurity all strengthen the tendency to conform. (p. 652)

7. **c.** is the answer. People tend to overestimate the similarity of people within groups other than their own. Thus, Juan is not likely to form stereotypes of fitness enthusiasts (a.), political liberals (b.), or older adults (d.), because these are groups to which he belongs. (p. 665)

8. **c.** is the answer. According to the scapegoat theory, when things go wrong, people look for someone on whom to take out their anger and frustration. (pp. 664–665)
   a. These campers are venting their frustration on a member of their *own* cabin group (although this is not always the case with scapegoats).
   b. Prejudice refers to an unjustifiable and usually negative attitude toward another group.
   d. The reciprocity norm, which refers to our tendency to help those who have helped us, was not discussed as a root of prejudice.
   e. Mirror-image perceptions involve our perceptions of groups other than our own, not of members of our ingroup.

9. **a.** is the answer. As illustrated by Maria's decision to stop buying aerosol products, informational social influence occurs when people have genuinely been influenced by what they have learned from others. (p. 652)
   b. Had Maria's behavior been motivated by the desire to avoid rejection or to gain social approval (which we have no reason to suspect is the case), it would have been an example of normative social influence.
   c. Deindividuation refers to the sense of anonymity a person may feel as part of a group.
   d. Social facilitation is the improvement in performance of well-learned tasks that may result when one is observed by others.

10. **d.** is the answer. The couple's similar, and presumably distorted, feelings toward each other fuel their conflict. (p. 676)
    a. Self-disclosure, or the sharing of intimate feelings, fosters love.
    b. Stereotypes are overgeneralized ideas about groups.
    c. Social traps are situations in which conflicting parties engage in mutually destructive behavior while pursuing their own self-interests.

11. **d.** is the answer. In this situation, the counter-attitudinal behavior is performed voluntarily and cannot be attributed to the demands of the situation. (p. 648)
    a., b., & c. In all of these situations, the counter-attitudinal behaviors should not arouse much dissonance because they can be attributed to the demands of the situation.

12. **d.** is the answer. The fundamental attribution error refers to the tendency to underestimate situational influences in favor of this type of dispositional attribution when explaining the behavior of other people. (p. 643)
    a., b., & c. These are situational attributions.

13. **a.** is the answer. (p. 664)
    b. Prejudices are unjustifiable and usually negative attitudes toward other groups. They may result from an ingroup bias, but they are probably not why students favor their own university.
    c. Scapegoats are individuals or groups toward which prejudice is directed as an outlet for the anger of frustrated individuals or groups.
    d. The just-world phenomenon is the tendency for people to believe others "get what they deserve."
    e. Mirror-image perception refers to the tendency of conflicting parties to form similar, diabolical images of each other.

14. **d.** is the answer. (p. 685)
    a. Evolutionary psychology is not discussed in terms of altruism, but it would maintain that altruistic actions are predisposed by our genes.
    b. The two-factor theory holds that emotions consist of physical arousal and an appropriate cognitive label.
    c. The social responsibility norm refers to the social attitude that we should help those who need our help.

15. **d.** is the answer. Hundreds of experiments indicate that first impressions are most influenced by physical appearance. (p. 678)

16. **a.** is the answer. According to the two-factor theory, physical arousal can intensify whatever emotion is currently felt. Only in the situation described in a. is Joan likely to be physically aroused. (p. 681)

17. **a.** is the answer. (p. 685)
    b. The reciprocity norm mandates that we help those who have helped us.
    c. The two-factor theory of emotion, which assumes that emotions are based on physical arousal and a cognitive label, makes no predictions regarding altruism.
    d. The reward theory, which states that social

behavior is maintained by rewards, would explain Althea's altruism as being due to her having previously been rewarded for similar altruistic actions.

18. **a.** is the answer. Friends and couples are much more likely than randomly paired people to be similar in views, interests, and a range of other factors. (p. 680)

    b. The opposite is true.

    c. The mere exposure effect demonstrates that familiarity tends to breed fondness.

    d. This is unlikely, given the positive effects of proximity and intimacy.

19. **b.** is the answer. By eliciting reactions in others that fuel his prejudice, George is fulfilling his expectation, or "prophecy," regarding members of a particular minority. (p. 660)

20. **b.** is the answer. In the foot-in-the-door phenomenon, compliance with a small initial request, such as wearing a lapel pin, later is followed by compliance with a much larger request, such as collecting petition signatures. (p. 646)

Essay Question

Your discussion might focus on some of the following topics: normative social influence; conformity, which includes suggestibility; obedience; group polarization; and groupthink.

As a member of any group with established social norms, individuals will often act in ways that enable them to avoid rejection or gain social approval. Thus, a fraternity or sorority pledge would probably be very suggestible and likely to eventually conform to the attitudes and norms projected by the group—or be rejected socially. In extreme cases of pledge hazing, acute social pressures may lead to atypical and antisocial individual behaviors—for example, on the part of pledges complying with the demands of senior members of the fraternity or sorority. Over time, meetings and discussions will probably enhance the group's prevailing attitudes (group polarization). This may lead to the unrealistic and irrational decision making that is groupthink. The potentially negative consequences of groupthink depend on the issues being discussed, but may include a variety of socially destructive behaviors.

Key Terms

Writing Definitions

1. **Social psychology** is the scientific study of how we think about, influence, and relate to one another. (p. 643)

2. **Attribution theory** deals with our causal explanations of behavior. We attribute behavior to the individual's disposition or to the situation. (p. 643)

3. The **fundamental attribution error** is our tendency to underestimate the impact of situations and to overestimate the impact of personal dispositions upon the behavior of others. (p. 643)

4. **Attitudes** are personal beliefs and feelings that may predispose a person to respond in particular ways to objects, people, and events. (p. 645)

5. The **foot-in-the-door phenomenon** is the tendency for people who agree to a small request to comply later with a larger request. (p. 646)

6. **Cognitive dissonance theory** refers to the theory that we act to reduce the psychological discomfort we experience when our behavior conflicts with what we think and feel, or more generally, when two of our thoughts conflict. This is frequently accomplished by changing our attitude rather than our behavior. (p. 648)

   Memory aid: *Dissonance* means "lack of harmony." **Cognitive dissonance** occurs when two thoughts, or cognitions, are at variance with one another.

7. **Conformity** is the tendency to change one's thinking or behavior to coincide with a group standard. (p. 651)

8. **Normative social influence** refers to the pressure on individuals to conform in order to avoid rejection or gain social approval. (p. 652)

   Memory aid: *Normative* means "based on a norm, or pattern, regarded as typical for a specific group." **Normative social influence** is the pressure groups exert on the individual to behave in ways acceptable to the group standard.

9. **Informational social influence** results when one goes along with a group when one is unsure or lacks information. (p. 652)

10. **Social facilitation** is the improvement in performance of simple or well-learned tasks that occurs when other people are present. (p. 657)

11. **Social loafing** is the tendency for individual effort to be diminished when one is part of a group working toward a common goal. (p. 657)

12. **Deindividuation** refers to the loss of self-awareness and self-restraint that sometimes occurs in group situations that foster arousal and anonymity. (p. 658)

    Memory aid: As a prefix, *de-* indicates reversal or undoing. To **deindividuate** is to undo one's individuality.

13. **Group polarization** refers to the enhancement of a group's prevailing tendencies through discussion, which often has the effect of accentuating the group's differences from other groups. (p. 658)

    Memory aid: To *polarize* is to "cause thinking to concentrate about two poles, or contrasting positions."

14. **Groupthink** refers to the unrealistic thought processes and decision making that occur within groups when the desire for group harmony becomes paramount. (p. 659)

    Example: The psychological tendencies of self-justification, conformity, and group polarization foster the development of the "team spirit" mentality known as **groupthink**.

15. A **self-fulfilling prophecy** occurs when our expectations of how people will behave cause us to treat them in ways that elicit such behaviors. (p. 660)

16. **Prejudice** is an unjustifiable and usually negative attitude toward a group and its members. (p. 662)

17. A **stereotype** is a generalized (often overgeneralized) belief about a group of people. (p. 662)

18. The **ingroup** refers to the people and groups with whom we share a common identity. (p. 664)

19. The **outgroup** refers to the people and groups that are excluded from our ingroup. (p. 664)

20. The **ingroup bias** is the tendency to favor one's own group. (p. 664)

21. The **scapegoat theory** proposes that prejudice provides an outlet for anger by finding someone to blame. (p. 569)

22. The **just-world phenomenon** is a manifestation of the commonly held belief that good is rewarded and evil is punished. The logic is indisputable: "If I am rewarded, I must be good." (p. 666)

23. **Aggression** is any physical or verbal behavior intended to hurt or destroy. (p. 666)

24. The **frustration-aggression principle** states that aggression is triggered when people become angry because their efforts to achieve a goal have been blocked. (p. 668)

25. **Conflict** is a perceived incompatibility of actions, goals, or ideas between individuals or groups. (p. 675)

26. A **social trap** is a situation in which conflicting parties become caught up in mutually harmful behavior as they pursue their perceived best interests. (p. 675)

27. The **mere exposure effect** refers to the fact that repeated exposure to an unfamiliar stimulus increases our liking of it. (p. 677)

28. **Passionate love** refers to an aroused state of intense positive absorption in another person, especially at the beginning of a relationship. (p. 681)

29. **Companionate love** refers to a deep, enduring, affectionate attachment. (p. 681)

30. **Equity** refers to the condition in which there is mutual giving and receiving between the partners in a relationship. (p. 682)

31. **Self-disclosure** refers to a person's sharing intimate feelings with another. (p. 682)

32. **Altruism** is unselfish regard for the welfare of others. (p. 683)

33. The **bystander effect** is the tendency of a person to be less likely to offer help to someone if there are other people present. (p. 684)

34. **Social exchange theory** states that our social behavior revolves around exchanges, in which we try to minimize our costs and maximize our benefits. (p. 684)

35. **Superordinate goals** are mutual goals that require the cooperation of individuals or groups otherwise in conflict. (p. 685)

36. **GRIT** (Graduated and Reciprocated Initiatives in Tension-Reduction) is a strategy of conflict resolution based on the defusing effect that conciliatory gestures can have on parties in conflict. (p. 687)

Cross-Check

ACROSS	DOWN
4. stereotype	1. bystander effect
5. GRIT	2. informational
6. scapegoat	3. cognitive dissonance
8. conformity	7. foot-in-the-door
9. altruism	8. companionate
12. equity	10. fundamental
13. passionate	11. attribution
14. conflict	
15. attitudes	

FOCUS ON VOCABULARY AND LANGUAGE

Social Thinking

Page 644: . . . I still assumed that the young actress was *typecast* because she was well-suited for the part. David Myers tells us about seeing a young girl play the part of a miserable old woman in a high school play and his mistaken belief that she got the part because she had the same qualities as the character she was portraying (*she was typecast*). Although he knew she was acting the part (a situational factor), he still believed that her behavior reflected her personal disposition or personality. This type of mistake is called the **fundamental attribution error.**

Page 644: Happily married couples attribute *their spouse's tart-tongued remark* to a temporary situation ("She must have had a bad day at work"). How we make attributions can have serious consequences. Couples who think that their partner's sarcastic or unkind comment (*tart-tongued remark*) was due to a cruel personality (*mean disposition*) are more likely to be dissatisfied with their marriages than couples who believe that the same remark was simply a result of some situational influence, such as a stressful day at work.

Page 645: . . . *freeloaders.* This refers to people who voluntarily live off other people. Those who believe that people are poor and/or unemployed because of personal dispositions tend to underestimate the influence of situational variables. Thus, they might call someone on welfare a *freeloader* rather than simply a victim of circumstances.

Page 645: Moreover, studies of people's attitudes and behaviors regarding cheating, religion, and racial minorities revealed that *people often talk and act a different game.* Social psychologists were surprised to find that what people think, feel, or believe (*attitudes*) is not always reflected in their behaviors (*people often talk and act a different game*). This apparent inconsistency led to further studies which showed that attitudes correlate with behavior (a) when the influence of others is negligible, (b) when the behavior and the attitude are specific rather than general, and (c) when we are made conscious or mindful of our beliefs and feelings.

Page 646: . . . *"brainwashed"* . . . This refers to a person's beliefs, values, and attitudes being changed by relentless indoctrination and mental torture. One component of this mind-changing process (*"thought-control"*) involves use of the **foot-in-the-door phenomenon,** whereby a person is first coerced into agreeing to a small request, then to complying with much greater requests. Frequently, people's attitudes change to be consistent with their new behavior.

Page 647: This *chicken-and-egg spiral* of actions feeding attitudes feeding actions enables behavior to escalate. Whether used for good or for bad, the foot-in-the-door strategy involves starting with small requests (*trifling demands*), then slowly increasing the level of demand. The new behavior will be followed by a change in attitude which, in turn, will make the behavior more likely and that will then lead to more change in belief, etc. (*the chicken-and-egg spiral*).

Page 649: The attitudes-follow-behavior principle has some *heartening implications.* When our attitudes and behaviors are inconsistent, we feel a certain amount of tension (**cognitive dissonance**), which makes us want to do something to reduce this uncomfortable state. Thus, if we are feeling depressed (*down in the dumps*) and we behave in a more outgoing manner, talk in a more positive way, and *act* as though we are happy, we may, in fact, start feeling much better. As Myers notes, the feelings-follow-actions notion has positive ramifications (*heartening implications*).

Social Influence

Page 650: Laughter, even *canned laughter,* can be *infectious.* Many TV and radio comedy shows do not have live audiences. Instead, they play recorded soundtracks of people laughing (*canned laughter*) at the appropriate moments; the laughter can be very contagious (*infectious*) for listeners, making them laugh heartily, too. This is a form of suggestibility.

Page 653: When influence supports what we approve, we applaud those who are *"open-minded"* and *"sensitive"* enough to be *"responsive."* We can be influenced by others because they provide useful knowledge (**informational influence**) or because we want them to view us favorably and not ignore us (**normative influence**). Conformity that is consistent with what we believe is true will be seen in a positive light (the conformists are *"open-minded,"* etc.), and conformity that is not will be viewed negatively (*"submissive conformity"*).

Page 653 You and another person *draw slips from a hat* to see who will be the "teacher" (which your slip says) and who will be the "learner." In Milgram's famous obedience experiments participants were deceived into believing they were randomly assigned to one of two conditions ("teacher" or "learner") by picking a piece of paper out of a container (*drawing slips from a hat*). All the subjects were actually "teachers" and were asked to "shock" the "learners" whenever they made mistakes on a memory task. A majority of the participants complied with the experimenter's request.

Page 653: When you hear these pleas, you *draw back. But the experimenter prods you:* "Please continue—the experiment requires that you continue." If you were a participant ("teacher") in Milgram's experiment, you would be pressured (*prodded*) by the research assistant to carry on with the experiment even though you may show great reluctance (*you draw back*) after hearing the "learner's" cries of distress at being "shocked."

Page 655: With *kindness and obedience on a collision course,* obedience usually won. Milgram's research on obedience showed that social factors that foster conformity are powerful enough to make almost any one of us behave in ways inconsistent with our beliefs. When subjects were in a conflict over (*torn between*) whether to refuse to harm an individual or to follow orders (*kindness and obedience were on a collision course*), they usually did what they were asked to do.

Page 655: Milgram entrapped his subjects not by asking them first to *zap* "learners" with enough electricity to make their hair stand on end. Milgram used the foot-in-the-door tactic to get his subjects to comply with his requests to shock (*zap*) the "learners" with larger and larger voltages. He started with a small amount (*a little tickle*) of electricity; after obtaining compliance (*obedience*), he asked them to increase the level, and so on. Subjects tended to rationalize their behavior; for some, their attitudes became consistent with their behavior over the course of the experiment.

Page 655: Contrary to our images of *devilish villains,* evil doesn't require *monstrous characters;* all it takes is ordinary people corrupted by an evil situation.... We tend to think that pain and suffering (*evil*) are always caused by inhumane and cruel people (*devilish villains* or *monstrous characters*), but the research in social psychology shows that almost anyone can be led to behave badly given the right (or wrong) circumstances.

Page 657: In a team *tug-of-war,* for example, do you suppose the effort that a person puts forth would be more than, less than, or the same as the effort he or she would exert in a *one-on-one tug-of-war*? In a game in which opponents pull on each end of a rope (*tug-of-war*), when two individuals compete (*one-on-one*), they work much harder (*exert more effort*) than if they were members of a group competing on the same

task. This lowering of individual effort when part of a team is called **social loafing**. (Note: The term *to loaf* means *to work less hard, to slack off, to take it easy,* or *to free ride.*)

Page 659: Assuming—wrongly—that support was unanimous, he launched the *Challenger* on its *one-way flight to annihilation.* Irving Janis investigated the variables that led to bad decisions and their consequent fiascoes and tragedies. The space shuttle *Challenger* disaster was the result of **groupthink**: People were overly optimistic of success, there was a desire by some to be nonobstructionist team players, group pressure to go ahead was very strong, and important information was withheld from the ultimate decision maker. Believing that everyone was in agreement, the NASA executive gave permission to dispatch the shuttle, which exploded within minutes (*one-way flight to annihilation*).

Page 660: They repeatedly found that a minority that unswervingly holds to its position is far more successful in swaying the majority than is a minority that *waffles.* Committed individuals and small groups of individuals can convince (*sway*) the majority to their point of view if they adhere strictly to their agenda and do not appear to be uncertain or unsure (*to waffle*).

Social Relations

Page 662: In one study, most whites perceived a white man shoving a black as *"horsing around."* Prejudices involve beliefs, emotions, and tendencies to behave in certain ways. They are a form of pre-judgment that influences (*colors*) how we interpret what we see. Thus, in an experiment in which white people saw a white man pushing a black person, most interpreted the behavior as playful activity (*horsing around*); when the roles were reversed, the behavior was more likely to be described as aggressive or hostile (*violent*).

Page 664: Even arbitrarily creating an us-them distinction—created by grouping people *with the toss of a coin*—leads people to show favoritism to their own group when dividing rewards (Tajfel, 1982; Wilder, 1981). One of the factors affecting prejudice is our propensity to define ourselves through identification with a particular group (**ingroup bias**); this in turn creates an outgroup consisting of those who do not belong to our group. Even if the groups are artificially created by random assignment (*with the toss of a coin*), we will tend to see our own group as more deserving, superior, and so on.

Page 665: In addition to providing a convenient emotional outlet for anger, despised outgroups can also *boost ingroup members' self-esteem.* When we have a problem, we frequently look for someone, who is usually innocent, to blame (*scapegoating*); these target people or groups are then a convenient source for venting our anger and frustration. In addition, having someone else to disparage can increase our own status and sense of self-worth (*boost our self-esteem*).

Page 667: A raging bull will become a gentle *Ferdinand* when its testosterone level is reduced by castration. Biological explanations of aggression examine the influences of genes, clusters of neurons in the brain, and biochemical agents in the blood, such as hormones and alcohol. Levels of the male sex hormone can be reduced by castration; thus, an aggressive, ferocious bull can be reduced to a playful, friendly animal similar to the fictional character (*Ferdinand*) of children's stories.

Page 670: In Beijing, for example, the percentage of homes with television *skyrocketed* from 32 percent in 1980 to 95 percent by the end of the decade (Lull, 1988). Researchers have studied the correlation between watching violent acts on TV and crime and aggression in society and have concluded that there is a positive correlation. Thus, in countries where TV-watching has risen dramatically (*skyrocketed*), there is likely to be an increase in violence.

Page 673: In less graphic form, the same unrealistic script—she resists, he persists, *she melts*—is commonplace on TV and in romance novels. A common theme in certain types of films and books is the idea that if the main male character overcomes the lovely female's reluctance to be romantically or sexually involved, then she will be totally devoted to him (*she melts*). This depiction of male-female relationships, in both pornographic and non-pornographic media, has little to do with reality and may, in fact, promote sexual aggression.

Page 674: Contrary to much popular opinion, viewing such *depictions* does not provide *an outlet* for *bottled-up impulses.* Laboratory studies have demonstrated that watching media that show sexual violence against women does not decrease the acceptance and performance of aggression against females. In contrast to what many believe, such portrayals (*depictions*) do not allow vicarious expression (*an outlet*) for pent-up hostile urges (*bottled-up impulses*) and may have the opposite effect.

Page 676: Psychologists have noted that those in conflict have a curious tendency to form *diabolical images* of one another. We have a propensity to perceive our enemies in a very distorted manner, often categorizing them as evil, cruel, untrustworthy, and devilish (*diabolical*). They, of course, view us in the same way; the biased pictures we form of each other are called *mirror-image perceptions.*

Page 677: Within certain limits . . . *familiarity breeds fondness.* Under some circumstances, the more often we see (*become familiar with*) someone, the more likely it is that we will grow to like (*become fond of*) that person. This is called the **mere exposure effect.**

Page 678: . . . "beauty is only skin deep" . . . This saying suggests that physical attractiveness (*beauty*) is only a superficial quality (*skin deep*). Research, however, has shown that how we look influences social interactions, how frequently we date, our popularity, how we are perceived by others, etc.

Page 680: Until you got to know him, *E.T. was uglier than Darth Vader.* E.T. was a small, unattractive, extraterrestrial creature (and just as repulsive looking as Darth Vader, another movie character), but as we came to know and like his cute little personality, he no longer appeared so ugly. Studies have shown that with increased exposure to people, we come to like them and are less likely to notice their physical blemishes (*imperfections*) and more likely to become aware of their endearing characteristics.

Page 680: In real life, *opposites retract.* The old saying "*opposites attract*" has not been supported by research in social psychology. In fact, we tend to dislike those we do not perceive as similar to ourselves (*opposites retract*). Rather than fostering *contempt,* Myers humorously suggests that similarity breeds *content.*

Page 681: To be *revved up* and to associate some of that arousal with a desirable person is to feel the pull of passion. Research has shown that one component of romantic or passionate love is physiological arousal; a second aspect is some cognitive interpretation and labeling of that feeling. So, if a person is in an aroused state (*revved up*) and this is easily linked to the presence of an attractive person, then attributions of romantic love may be made. As Myers cheerfully notes, rather than *absence, adrenaline makes the heart grow fonder* (intensifies love).

Page 683: At each step, the presence of other *bystanders turns people away from the path that leads to helping.* Darley and Latané displayed their findings in a flow diagram (See Figure 18.16, p. 683). At each decision point (i.e., noticing the event, interpreting it as an emergency, and assuming responsibility), the presence of others who appear to have observed the event (*bystanders*) causes people to be less likely to give assistance to someone in need (*they are turned away from the path that leads to helping*).

Page 683: . . . *blasé* . . . This means to be indifferent or uncaring. We arrive at the decision (especially in ambiguous situations) to help or not to help by watching the reactions of others. If they appear to be unconcerned (*blasé*), we may conclude that there is no emergency and thus may not intervene or help. This **bystander effect** means that the presence of others decreases the probability that any particular observer will provide help.

Page 685: Before long, each group became intensely proud of itself and hostile to the other group's "sneaky," "smart-alecky stinkers." In Sherif's experiment, competitive conditions were created in order to foster the formation of two antagonistic groups. Each group soon saw itself as superior to the other group's "dishonest and sly" (*sneaky*) "rotten know-it-alls" (*smart-alecky stinkers*). Sherif then used shared objectives and common problems (**superordinate goals**) to create reconciliation and cooperation.

Page 687: Conciliations allow both parties to begin edging *down the tension ladder to a safer rung* where communication and mutual understanding can begin. Social psychologist Charles Osgood has developed a tactic called **GRIT** (Graduated and Reciprocated Initiatives in Tension-Reduction) for increasing cooperation and trust between parties in conflict. When one side makes a small gesture or offer of goodwill (*a conciliatory act*), the other side has an opportunity to reciprocate and thus move the conflict toward some resolution (*down the tension ladder to a safer rung*) and start the process of mutual respect and understanding.